Programming Applications for Microsoft® Office Outlook® 2007

Randy Byrne

Ryan Gregg

PUBLISHED BY
Microsoft Press
A Division of Microsoft Corporation
One Microsoft Way
Redmond, Washington 98052-6399

Library of Congress Control Number: 2006940673

Printed and bound in the United States of America.

1 2 3 4 5 6 7 8 9   QWT   2 1 0 9 8 7

Distributed in Canada by H.B. Fenn and Company Ltd.

A CIP catalogue record for this book is available from the British Library.

Microsoft Press books are available through booksellers and distributors worldwide. For further information about international editions, contact your local Microsoft Corporation office or contact Microsoft Press International directly at fax (425) 936-7329. Visit our Web site at www.microsoft.com/mspress. Send comments to mspinput@microsoft.com.

Acquisitions Editor: Ben Ryan
Developmental Editor: Devon Musgrave
Project Editor: Melissa von Tschudi-Sutton
Production: nSight, Inc.

Body Part No. X13-24186

To Marie Byrne, Louis D. Cohen, and Harriet Grossman Cohen.

You set the example and always provided love and inspiration.

— Randy Byrne

To my parents, Randall and Cheri Gregg.

— Ryan Gregg

Contents at a Glance

Table of Contents

What do you think of this book? We want to hear from you!

Microsoft is interested in hearing your feedback so we can continually improve our books and learning resources for you. To participate in a brief online survey, please visit:

www.microsoft.com/learning/booksurvey/

Part III   Working with Outlook Data

5   Built-in Item Types 115

What do you think of this book? We want to hear from you!

Microsoft is interested in hearing your feedback so we can continually improve our books and learning resources for you. To participate in a brief online survey, please visit:

www.microsoft.com/learning/booksurvey/

Foreword

Hello, my name is Brian, and I'm a developer. Now, you may wonder, is that a problem? Actually, it is. You see, if an application provides an object model, I will code it. Ever since I started programming on Windows, I've been attracted to applications that expose their features via a programmatic application programming interface (API), allowing me to make them my own. Each release of Microsoft Outlook—from the first release in 1996 to the newest release in 2007—has provided ways for me and you to customize and extend, to make it our own.

While early releases of Outlook provided extensibility via VBScript, C++ extensions, and automation, it was Outlook 2000 that sparked a hot and heavy relationship that I've maintained to this day. Outlook 2000 let me write in-process add-ins using my component technology and programming language of choice: COM and Visual Basic. Reading the documentation on how to write an add-in brought joy to my heart. All I had to do was implement a COM interface, *IDTExtensibility2,* and I could bring the power of component-based solutions to Outlook. I had the power to do just about anything I wanted. With the ability to bind my code to Outlook via its rich set of events or via user interface (UI) elements such as command bars, I could create compelling applications on top of Outlook for myself and customers. I was excited.

I proceeded to write articles, speak at conferences, and tinker. I got involved with creating *digital dashboards* where I was able to mix COM, Visual Basic, VBScript, DHTML, and the Outlook View Control to provide information displays consolidating local and remote information for quick and efficient review. It was at one of these conferences—in either the desert of Arizona or the sweltering heat of an Atlanta summer—that I met Randy Byrne. I had picked up Randy's first edition of the book you hold in your hands, and I was looking forward to meeting him. I found his writing style pleasant, and the golden nuggets of insight in how to build applications on top of Outlook always made my solutions better. What was great about meeting Randy was that he was just as friendly as his writing made him out to be—something a bit unusual for a technical subject like programming. Talking with Randy about Outlook was always pleasant, and it never seemed to bother him when I asked what was either a simple question or something I had missed on page 562 of his book.

Randy updated the book for Outlook 2002, and I got my copy. Updated with essential information, such as how to deal with the new object model guard released in the wake of viruses like *Melissa,* I once again was indebted to Randy for taking the time to make the long journey that is writing a book. And, as in the past, whenever I'd run into Randy at shows, like Microsoft's annual technical show Tech Ed, we'd exchange pleasantries, chat, and of course have the occasional discussion about Outlook.

As Outlook matured, programming options changed. Microsoft released the Common Language Runtime and the .NET Framework, Visual Basic .NET, and Visual C#. This new generation of development technologies sparked a new revolution and interest in programming the Windows platform. The increases in productivity that the new languages brought and the deep richness of the Framework's class libraries made it easy to leave the world of COM behind for the managed world. However, applications built upon COM can't be rewritten overnight. Thus, if you wanted to work with Outlook, you still needed to deal with COM. From the managed world, that means knowing COM and .NET. You need to understand the impact of two different memory models and the cost of marshaling between two call stacks.

Outlook 2003 proved a less significant update than previous versions for developers. This led Randy and other authors to forgo writing updated and new versions of their books. But Randy wasn't just relaxing. He founded Micro Eye, Inc., to provide Outlook consulting services as well as popular add-ins like ZipOut. But something wonderful happened. Randy joined Microsoft as a Program Manager on the Outlook team. My heart filled with joy. With "one of us" on the inside, Outlook could only get better for developers like me (after all, it's always about me). And get better it has.

Outlook 2007 is the most significant release of the product to date. While many will cite features such as the Ribbon, application task panes, and form regions as great new features, I'm most happy with the unification of the programming model and a better Outlook object model guard. Since early betas, I've poked and prodded at Outlook 2007 to see what I could do. No longer do I need to drop down to CDO or use third-party libraries to get around issues in the object model or runtime. It's a great way to work. However, don't get me wrong—I'm a sucker for shiny and new. The new Ribbon, I have to say, is just darn pretty and, once you get used to it, very functional. Naturally, I want to get my solutions using the Ribbon. In addition, form regions remove issues I've had for years when working with the built-in Outlook forms. Issues in the past that often had me eschew them completely and instead rely upon other form technologies such as Windows Forms.

Yet, I have to admit, I have stumbled. Some of the new features of Outlook 2007 have forced me to think a bit harder than normal. And that is why I was elated to find out that Randy was updating "the book" for Outlook 2007. Better yet, he enlisted a cohort on the Outlook team to be his coauthor. I had read Ryan Gregg's blog and MSDN articles, and I knew Randy had made a great decision. As I read my draft copy of their book, I didn't want to put it down. For one thing, Randy and Ryan have written this book for me. Okay—not just for me, but for you and me, the managed developer. Providing examples in both C# and Visual Basic for download, they take you on a journey, exploring what Outlook 2007 has to offer you. More importantly, they provide insight into why you should do things for performance and safety. In addition, because both of them are on the team, you know they write with firsthand knowledge and authority. This book is for those of you who want to write the best Outlook 2007 solutions.

On a trip to Redmond this fall, they asked me to write the foreword. I was not only honored but eager. After all, I knew without a doubt that this would be the book I would immediately acquire once published. I knew it would be the book I would recommend without hesitation. And here you have it. You hold *the* book on programming Outlook 2007 for managed developers. I'm sure I might have something to say about Outlook 2007 at a conference or in an article, but I know I won't be writing a book. There's no need. Now close the cover and get to the register. You've got solutions to build.

Brian A. Randell

Upland, California

January 2007

Acknowledgments

A very large cast was required to produce Microsoft Office Outlook 2007. As Program Managers on the product team, we first want to thank all the Outlook team members who worked constantly to define, create, and test their individual features. For many of these improvements in Outlook 2007, the platform team was able to provide an object model to expose the feature to the developer community. Without the hard work of the feature teams, the platform would be diminished.

Beyond the product team as a whole, Randy Byrne wants to thank two individuals who were willing to take a risk by bringing him into the Outlook product team: Will Kennedy, General Manager of Outlook, and Marc Olson, the Group Program Manager of Outlook when he was recruited by Microsoft. Will's challenge to the platform team to provide better documentation is, in part, responsible for this book. Without adequate documentation, developing for Outlook can be a painful experience. For the platform team, two individuals stand out for praise. The first is Peter Allenspach, Group Program Manager, whose enthusiasm, knowledge, and dedication helped to make the Outlook platform what it is today. Peter actually wrote the draft of Chapter 2, "Outlook as a Platform," but modestly declined to be listed as a coauthor. The second is Ryan Gregg, Program Manager and coauthor, who brought fantastic managed coding skills to the team. There isn't an Outlook add-in project that Ryan couldn't complete in a matter of hours or, at most, days. We also want to offer special thanks to Program Managers Rainer Schiller and Rajesh Ramanathan for their work in helping the platform effort.

Drew Carlson, Development Manager, brought his vast historical knowledge of the Outlook platform to our team. His sense of humor was always invaluable when we struggled with difficult decisions. Matt Hainje, Development Lead, managed the developers for the platform team and was our platform architect. Talking over problems with Matt always provided food for thought, and he always challenged us on the Program Manager side to think clearly about our design decisions. The following individual Outlook developers deserve thanks for their great platform contributions: Michael J. Smith, Julia Cai, Andrew Coates, Rock Hymas, Brian Hill, and Wes Haggard.

Jim Reynolds, Test Lead, put together a great test team for our platform effort and helped us prepare a Microsoft Exchange server environment for this book. On Jim's team, we want to thank Scott Mitten, Garett Sakamoto, Olga Gerasimova, Raja Iqbal, Kumiko Yada, Sid Patel, Shu Zhang, and Anh Phan for all their hard work. Garett deserves special mention for doing the late-night testing to ensure that we met performance goals for the new *Table* object. John Guin, also a Test Lead, pitched in to provide extraordinary testing for form regions.

Of course, there are others who deserve acknowledgment even though they were not directly part of the platform effort in Outlook 2007. Angela Wong, Programmer Writer for Office User Assistance, was an invaluable contributor to the content of this book. Angela authored the Outlook 2007 Developer's Reference and made sure that the pyramids (the metaphor we adopted for the Developer's Reference and this book) were built on time and without calamity.

Thanks so much, Angela, for all your hard work. Bill Jacob, a Support Engineer in Messaging Developer Support, took on the task of reviewing many of the chapters in this book. Bill's knowledge of Outlook developer issues is encyclopedic, and we both owe him an enormous debt of gratitude for taking on the reviewing chore. When you're next in Redmond, the beers are on us! Also on the product support side, we offer special thanks to Stephen Griffin, whose knowledge of all things MAPI is legendary. We'd also like to thank the following individuals at Microsoft who contributed to this book in one way or another: Ronna Pinkerton, Jean Philippe Bagel, Carlos Brito, Kendall Keil, Chris Antos, GT Herbert, Alon Brown, Bob Novitskey, and all our friends at Business Contact Manager including Jeff Keyes, Chris Heydemann, Nick Thomson, and Dmitri Davydok. For their help in making Outlook a less challenging environment for managed code developers, we offer praise and special appreciation for KD Hallman, Eric Carter, Andrew Whitechapel, Misha Shneerson, and John Durant.

Finally, several individuals who have been awarded Microsoft Most Valuable Professional (MVP) status have acted as a sounding board for ideas. Sue Mosher, Outlook MVP extraordinaire and owner of OutlookCode.com, provided excellent feedback about how we could improve Outlook platform documentation. Her object model bug reports during the beta were also greatly appreciated. Yes, we do enjoy finding bugs before we ship! David Kane, Outlook MVP, offered valuable pragmatic advice on how we could improve the Outlook developer experience. Finally, Dmitry Streblechenko, still a wizard of Extended MAPI, provided encouragement for the changes we made to improve object model guard security.

Because a book of this type is by its very nature a group effort, I want to thank the Microsoft Press team behind this book. Our acquisitions editor, Ben Ryan, put this book on the schedule and gave us guidance about how to write a book and do our Program Manager jobs at the same time. Melissa von Tschudi-Sutton, our project editor, deserves a big cheer for keeping us on track and on schedule. Melissa, it's been great to work with you. The team at our production vendor, nSight, also deserves kudos. Cindy Gierhart acted as project manager. Jay Harlow, also an Outlook MVP, served as technical editor, and Teresa Horton was the copy editor. Again, I thank the nSight team for their professionalism and enthusiasm.

Randy Byrne   I want to thank my wonderful wife, Susan Cohen Byrne, for her patience and understanding while I completed yet another book. When immersed in writing a book for developers, it helps to come up from the depths and have a great partner to talk to and share some laughs. My beautiful daughters, Lily and Zoe, fill me with pride and joy, and those feelings help start the day and get the job done. Additional thanks go to my dear friends Susan Brown, Steve Ekstrom, Steve Cohen, Fern Friedman, and Davide Atenoux for their support and encouragement.

Ryan Gregg   I'd like to thank my parents, Randall Gregg and Cheri Gregg, for their constant love and encouragement to reach for and obtain my dreams. Even from 1,800 miles away, there isn't a day that goes by that I don't feel their impact on my life, and I'm grateful for all they have done to help me along the way. I'd also like to thank my close friends Jessica, Zack, Garett, Jared, and Melissa for helping me stay grounded and always pushing me to do the best.

Introduction

Microsoft Office Outlook 2007 offers compelling new product features including Instant Search, task flagging, the To-Do Bar, Calendar overlays, sharing with friends and coworkers, Really Simple Syndication (RSS) feeds, Electronic Business Cards, Microsoft Office SharePoint Server integration, and plenty of other features that make Outlook 2007 the most exciting release in the history of the product. As a developer, you can benefit from the innovation built into Outlook 2007. The Outlook 2007 object model has been expanded with more than double the number of objects compared to previous versions. New form region technology allows you to create custom forms that have the same look and feel as Outlook's.

If you are a seasoned Microsoft .NET developer, why should you care about these platform improvements in Outlook 2007? In the past, .NET development against Outlook could be compared with finding your way through a maze. You never knew when you were going to hit an insurmountable obstacle or retrace your steps. If you wanted to do anything at a lower level or do advanced but commonplace tasks such as display the Address Book or access named properties, you were out of luck. You had to write Extended Messaging Application Programming Interface (MAPI) code, but you hit a catch-22 because Extended MAPI code is not supported for .NET development. Time to pull down those C++ books from the shelf. For many developers, writing C++ native code is a barrier to entry and contradicts your commitment to writing managed code.

Hopefully, the platform improvements in Outlook 2007 solve both the barrier to entry and the requirement to learn C++ and Extended MAPI for advanced solutions. One of the primary goals for Outlook 2007 extensibility is to unify existing programming models so that the Outlook object model is sufficient for an Outlook developer. The Outlook 2007 platform removes the roadblocks that developers experienced in previous versions of Outlook. Outlook 2007 allows you to write managed solutions that are fully supported because they use only the Outlook object model. For the vast majority of scenarios, you write code with application programming interfaces (APIs) that are supported for .NET development.

Why We Wrote This Book

We wrote this book because, quite frankly, there has been a lack of guidance from the product team about best coding and design practices for an Outlook solution. This book attempts to remedy this deficiency by providing top-level suggestions about when and how to integrate with Outlook. We've also done our best to deliver reusable .NET code samples that you can adapt for your application. As platform program managers for Outlook, we are passionate about improving and expanding Outlook extensibility to accommodate a wide range of solutions. Although each release of Outlook aims to accommodate the most relevant and requested new features for the Outlook user community, not every need will be addressed by a product release. As a developer, the Outlook platform lets you address the gaps in Outlook's feature set. Use your ingenuity and the Outlook platform to fill these needs. The Outlook solution landscape is vast, and your contribution is welcomed and encouraged.

Who This Book Is For

This book is aimed at beginning to intermediate-level developers who want to write managed solutions for Outlook using Microsoft Visual Studio 2005. Other developers who are writing native solutions, whether in C++ or Microsoft Visual Basic 6.0, will also benefit from the discussion of the new programmability features in Outlook 2007. A basic knowledge of Microsoft Visual Basic .NET or Microsoft Visual C# is required to understand the code samples provided with this book. Component Object Model (COM) add-ins are the primary customization technology for extending Outlook. Of course, this means that there are interop issues to be considered when writing managed code against a COM-based type library such as the Outlook object model. We've tried to address these interop issues when they are relevant to writing managed code for Outlook. It's important to note, however, that the focus of this book is writing applications for Outlook rather than writing managed code per se.

There are several other extensibility technologies that are not covered in this book, except to note their usage in Outlook 2007 or previous versions. This book is not for developers who are looking for a deep dive into Extended MAPI, Exchange Client Extensions (ECEs), or Collaboration Data Objects (CDO) version 1.21.

How This Book Is Organized

This book is organized into five major parts, which can be read as a whole or used in part as your needs dictate. Although we both share responsibility for all the content of this book, Randy wrote Chapters 1, 3 through 8, 10, 11, 15, 17, 18, and the Introduction. Ryan authored Chapters 9, 12 through 14, 16, and 19. Peter Allenspach created the initial draft of Chapter 2, and Randy provided additional content for the version delivered in this book.

Part I: Introducing Microsoft Office Outlook 2007

Chapter 1, "What's New in Microsoft Office Outlook 2007," provides an overview of the major new programmability features in Outlook 2007. Use this chapter to familiarize yourself with the new capabilities of the Outlook object model and Outlook form regions. Form regions provide an improved model for adding user interface (UI) elements to Outlook 2007. Chapter 2, "Outlook as a Platform," covers the program team's rationale behind the new extensibility areas in Outlook 2007. This chapter also provides prescriptive guidance about how to build solutions that are deeply integrated with Outlook. It covers the internal MAPI architecture used to build Outlook and discusses the architectural pillars of the product.

Part II: Quick Guide to Building Solutions

This section is for the developer who has a stack of projects to complete but insufficient time to get them coded and tested. Chapter 3, "Writing Your First Outlook Add-in Using Visual Basic .NET," walks you through the process of creating an add-in, writing code for a custom context menu item, and adding a COM shim and setup project to the solution. Chapter 4, "Writing Your First Outlook Add-in Using C#," does the same for C# developers. Use these chapters as a learning tool or to jumpstart your own solution.

Part III: Working with Outlook Data

These chapters familiarize you with the objects used to represent and contain data. Chapter 5, "Built-in Item Types," focuses on the core item types in the Outlook object model. You'll see plenty of code samples that illustrate how to work with these objects. Chapter 6, "Accessing Outlook Data," discusses the objects such as the *Store* and *Folder* objects that act as containers for items. In Chapter 6, you discover how to use the *Items* collection and *Table* object to access items. Because Outlook is a messaging client, you need to send items to recipients or understand the identity of the message sender. Chapter 7, "Address Books and Recipients," introduces you to the objects that represent recipients and address books. Later in the section, you learn how to write event handlers in Chapter 8, "Responding to Events." Events are the crux of any add-in that seeks to understand user actions or enforce its own business logic. Chapter 9, "Sharing Information with Other Users," shows you how to share Outlook items with other users. Finally, the chapters that conclude this section concentrate on organizing and searching Outlook data. Chapter 10, "Organizing Outlook Data," discusses the use of task flagging, color categories, rules, search folders, and views to organize data for a user. Chapter 11, "Searching Outlook Data," provides in-depth coverage of Outlook query syntax and offers plenty of code samples to solve common search problems.

Part IV: Providing a User Interface for Your Solution

If your application requires a UI, this section is for you. Chapter 12, "Introducing the Outlook User Interface," introduces you to the UI objects in Outlook. In Chapter 13, "Creating Form Regions," you learn how to create a simple form region in a step-by-step fashion. Of course, a UI that lacks appropriate controls is not very practical. Consequently, Chapter 14, "Form Region Controls," covers all the new Outlook controls that you can use on a form region. The Microsoft Office Fluent user interface is the term used to describe the new UI for the 2007 Microsoft Office system. The Ribbon is a component of the Microsoft Office Fluent user interface and the term used throughout this book to refer to the Ribbon component. Chapter 15, "Extending the Ribbon," discusses how Ribbon extensibility works in Outlook. This chapter addresses very specific Ribbon extensibility issues that you need to be aware of when you customize the Ribbon for Outlook. Chapter 16, "Completing Your User Interface," covers specialized topics such as Outlook property pages and custom task panes.

Part V: Advanced Topics

This section covers advanced topics that might be relevant for your solution. Chapter 17, "Using the *PropertyAccessor* Object," discusses how to use the *PropertyAccessor* object to access low-level properties on numerous objects. Chapter 18, "Add-in Setup and Deployment," covers what you need to know to deploy your solution to a target computer. Finally, Chapter 19, "Trust and Security," discusses the significant changes that have been made to object model security in Outlook 2007.

Sample Code on the Web

The code samples provided in this book are primarily Visual C#, but equivalent Visual Basic .NET samples are available from this book's companion Web site. All of the code samples discussed in this book can be downloaded from the book's companion Web site at the following address:

http://www.microsoft.com/mspress/companion/978-0-7356-2249-3/

Before you can run the sample code, you must download the sample code installation package available on the book's companion Web site. Once you have downloaded the sample code installation package to your hard disk, double-click SampleCode_978-0-7356-2249-4.msi to begin the setup process. Follow the steps in the setup wizard to complete the installation.

The sample code installation package will install SampleCodeCS and SampleCodeVB to the following folder:

My Documents\Visual Studio 2005\Projects

The CS suffix denotes C# sample code and snippets. The VB suffix denotes Visual Basic sample code and snippets. Additionally, links to Outlook add-in templates and to other sample Outlook add-ins discussed in this book are provided on the book's companion Web site.

 Note   The name of your personal documents folder depends on the operating system installed on your computer. On Microsoft Windows Vista, your personal documents folder is named Documents. On Microsoft Windows XP, your personal documents folder is named My Documents. You should adjust path specifications for your personal documents folder according to your installed operating system.

If you install the sample add-ins on Windows Vista, you must run Visual Studio 2005 as Administrator to build the Sample Code solutions. To run Visual Studio 2005 as Administrator, follow these steps:

1. Click the Start menu, and locate Microsoft Visual Studio 2005.

2. Right-click Microsoft Visual Studio 2005.

3. Select the Run As Administrator command.

To run the C# sample code add-in, follow these steps:

1. Close Outlook 2007.

2. In the My Documents\Visual Studio 2005\Projects\SampleCodeCS folder, open the SampleCodeCS solution.

3. In Solution Explorer, select SampleCodeCSSetup.

4. From the Build menu, select Rebuild SampleCodeCSSetup.

5. [Optional] After the build process has completed, from the Project menu, select Install to install the solution.

6. Start Outlook to start the add-in in Run mode or press F5 to start the add-in in Debug mode.

If Outlook does not launch in Debug mode, perform the following steps:

1. In Solution Explorer, select SampleCodeAddinCS.

2. On the Project menu, click SampleCodeAddinCS Properties, and then click the Debug tab.

3. Under Start Action, select the Start External Program check box, and then click Browse.

4. In the [Drive:]\Program Files\Microsoft Office\Office12 folder, select Outlook.exe.

To run the Visual Basic sample code add-in, follow these steps:

1. Close Outlook 2007.

2. In the My Documents\Visual Studio 2005\Projects\SampleCodeVB folder, open the SampleCodeVB solution.

3. In Solution Explorer, select SampleCodeVBSetup.

4. From the Build menu, select Rebuild SampleCodeVBSetup.

5. [Optional] After the build process has completed, from the Project menu, select Install to install the solution.

6. Start Outlook to start the add-in in Run mode or press F5 to start the add-in in Debug mode.

If Outlook does not launch in Debug mode, perform the following steps:

1. In Solution Explorer, select SampleCodeAddinVB.

2. From the Project menu, click SampleCodeAddinVB Properties, and then click the Debug tab.

3. Under Start Action, select the Start External Program check box, and then click Browse.

4. In the [Drive:]\Program Files\Microsoft Office\Office12 folder, select Outlook.exe.

Once you have installed the sample code add-in, you can run individual methods by selecting the chapter number and name in the Outlook 2007 Sample Code dialog box, shown in the following figure.

To run a method in the Sample Add-in, follow these steps:

1. Follow earlier instructions to launch the Sample Add-in in Debug mode.

2. Click the Sample Code command button (shown in the following figure) on the Standard command bar in the Outlook Explorer window. The Explorer window represents the main Outlook application window in which the contents of a folder are displayed.

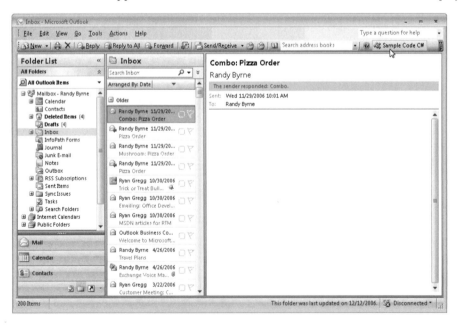

3. The Outlook 2007 Sample Code dialog box displays.

4. Select a chapter from the Chapter drop-down list.

5. From the Methods list box, select a method from the Methods list box.

6. Click the Run Selected Method command button to run the method.

Because methods in the sample code add-in often write to the trace listeners in the *Listeners* collection, consider running the sample code add-in in Debug mode. The sample code is organized by chapter in the sample code add-in project. In the sample code add-in project, simply navigate to the correct chapter in the Solution Explorer to examine the sample code for a given chapter. You can set breakpoints in the sample code and step the code to facilitate your learning process.

Code Snippets

When you download and install the sample code, you also install the code snippets that accompany this book. Code samples that are available as a snippet are identified throughout this book by the graphic shown in the page margin. Use these snippets in your own code as required. The installation package will install Outlook code snippets to the Programming Applications for Microsoft Office Outlook 2007 folder under the My Code Snippets folder. Depending on the language used by the snippet, the My Code Snippets folder is under either the Visual C# or the Visual Basic folder. Typically personal snippet folders are located here:

My Documents\Visual Studio 2005\Code Snippets\Visual C#\My Code Snippets

or

My Documents\Visual Studio 2005\Code Snippets\Visual Basic\My Code Snippets

Before you can use the code snippets, you must install them through the Code Snippets Manager:

1. Select Code Snippets Manager on the Tools menu in Visual Studio 2005.

2. Select the snippet language in the Language drop-down.

3. Click the Add button, and then open the Programming Applications for Microsoft Office Outlook 2007 folder in the appropriate location.

4. Click OK to close the Code Snippets Manager dialog box.

To insert a code snippet by browsing in the code editor, follow these steps:

1. Right-click the Code Editor where you want to insert the code.

2. On the shortcut menu, click Insert Snippet. The IntelliSense code snippet picker appears.

3. Navigate to the task of your choice and click it. The snippet code is inserted into your code.

4. Once you have added the snippet to your code, there might be parts of it that need customization, such as replacing variable names with more appropriate names or adding *using* (C#) or *Imports* (Visual Basic) directives. The code editor helps you with the process of correcting your code.

Building the Sample Add-Ins

Several sample add-ins in addition to the code sample add-in are available on this book's companion Web site. Some of the chapters discuss these sample add-ins, so you will want to download and build these sample add-ins as well as the sample code add-in. The Outlook 2007 sample add-ins run only on Visual Studio 2005 Standard Edition, Visual Studio 2005 Professional Edition, or Visual Studio 2005 Team System. If you are using Microsoft Visual C# Express Edition or Microsoft Visual Basic Express Edition to open the sample add-ins, you will not be able to build the setup and deployment project and install the sample add-ins.

The following procedures assume that you have downloaded and installed the sample add-ins from the book's companion Web site.

To run a sample add-in, follow these steps:

1. Close Outlook 2007.

2. In the My Documents\Visual Studio 2005\Projects*SolutionName* folder, open the *SolutionName* solution.

3. In Solution Explorer, select AddinNameSetup.

4. From the Build menu, select Rebuild AddinNameSetup.

5. [Optional] After the build process has completed, from the Project menu, select Install to install the solution.

6. Start Outlook to start the add-in in Run mode or press F5 to start the add-in in Debug mode.

If Outlook does not launch in Debug mode, perform the following steps:

1. In Solution Explorer, select AddinName.

2. From the Project menu, select AddinName Properties, and then click the Debug tab.

3. Under Start Action, select the Start External Program check box and click Browse.

4. In the Drive:\Program Files\Microsoft Office\Office12 folder, select Outlook.exe.

Note   If you install the sample add-ins on Windows Vista, an update to Visual Studio 2005 might be required. To build add-ins such as the Prepare Me sample, you need to start Visual Studio with elevated privilege.

System Requirements

The following table lists the components required to run the code samples for this book.

Table I-1   **System Requirements**

Component	Requirement
Software	Microsoft Office Outlook 2007
	Microsoft Visual Studio 2005
	Microsoft Visual Studio 2005 Tools for the 2007 Microsoft Office System (optional)
Computer and processor	500 megahertz (MHz) processor or higher
Memory	256 megabyte (MB) of RAM or higher
Hard disk	1.5 gigabyte (GB) for Outlook 2007; a portion of this disk space will be freed after installation if the original download package is removed from the hard drive. Sample code that accompanies this book requires 5 MB.
Drive	CD-ROM or DVD drive
Display	1024 × 768 or higher resolution monitor
Operating system	Windows XP with Service Pack (SP) 2, Windows Server 2003 with SP1, Windows Vista, or later operating system
Other	Connectivity to Microsoft Exchange Server 2000 or later is required for certain advanced functionality in Outlook 2007. Instant Search requires Microsoft Windows Desktop Search 3.0. Dynamic Calendars require server connectivity. Connectivity to Microsoft Windows Server 2003 with SP1 or later running Microsoft Windows SharePoint Services is required for certain advanced collaboration functionality. Connectivity to Microsoft Office SharePoint Server 2007 is required for certain advanced functionality. Microsoft Internet Explorer 6.0 or later, 32-bit browser only. Internet functionality requires Internet access (fees might apply).

Support for This Book

Every effort has been made to the accuracy of this book and companion CD content. Microsoft Press provides corrections to this book through the Web at the following location:

http://www.microsoft.com/learning/support

To connect directly to the Microsoft Knowledge Base and enter a query regarding a question or issue that you may have, go to the following address:

http://www.microsoft.com/learning/support/search.asp

If you have comments, questions, or ideas regarding the book or companion Web content, or if you have questions that are not answered by querying the Knowledge Base, please send them to Microsoft Press using either of the following methods:

E-Mail: mspinput@microsoft.com

Postal Mail:

Microsoft Press
Attn: Programming Applications for Microsoft Office Outlook 2007, Editor
One Microsoft Way
Redmond, WA 98052–6399

Please note that product support is not offered through the preceding mail addresses. For support information, please visit the Microsoft Product Support Web site at the following address:

http://support.microsoft.com

Part I
Introducing Microsoft Office Outlook 2007

Chapter 1
What's New in Microsoft Office Outlook 2007

This chapter provides a top-level view of the enhancements and additions for developers in Microsoft Office Outlook 2007. Subsequent chapters provide in-depth discussions about how to extend Outlook 2007.

Outlook 2007 introduces significant new improvements in its object model and forms technology to accommodate developer wants and provide a more comprehensive platform for Outlook-based solutions. The following are the pillars of the Office Outlook 2007 extensibility vision:

- Unification, so that developers no longer require Collaboration Data Objects 1.21 (CDO), Exchange Client Extensions, or other third-party libraries to complete their solutions. Application programming interfaces (APIs) such as CDO and Messaging Application Programming Interface (MAPI) are unsupported for managed solutions. The Outlook object model is fully supported for Microsoft .NET development.

- Performance, so that developers do not have to resort to other APIs when enumerating the contents of a folder or performing search operations.

- Trust and security, so that the Outlook object model cannot be used as a means to propagate e-mail–based worms and viruses.

- Forms, so that your application can support a richer and more contemporary user interface.

- Innovation, so that developers can access the new features of Outlook such as search, task flagging, category coloring, side-by-side calendars, and sharing through the Outlook object model.

The remainder of this chapter introduces you to the major new platform features of Outlook 2007. These improvements will make your life as an Outlook developer more productive so that you can concentrate on creating a first-class solution rather than searching the Web for workarounds. Previous versions of Outlook have made it difficult, especially for .NET developers, to complete an Outlook development project without resorting to unsupported APIs or third-party libraries. Outlook 2007 remedies this situation from an object model perspective, and provides some great new user interface technologies that will appeal to end users.

Managed Code and Outlook 2007

Outlook 2007 extensibility is still COM-based. If you program against the Outlook object model using Microsoft Visual Studio 2005, you still use Primary Interop Assemblies (PIAs) to provide the interop layer between your managed assembly and the Outlook object model. You can benefit from the app domain isolation provided by the Visual Studio 2005 COM Shim Wizard or Microsoft Visual Studio 2005 Tools for the 2007 Microsoft Office System (VSTO) system to improve the resiliency of your solution. The focus of this book is managed add-in development for Outlook 2007. The code examples provided are primarily Visual C#, but equivalent Visual Basic .NET samples are available on the Web site that accompanies this book. I'll focus on how you complete Outlook development tasks using managed code. Along the way, you'll learn about specific issues such as object lifetime and instance variable scope that affect managed code developers using the Outlook 2007 PIAs.

Form Regions

Form regions allow you to customize both built-in and custom items in ways that were impossible in previous versions of Outlook. For example, previous versions of Outlook only allowed customization of the first page of a Contact item. In Outlook 2007, you can use form regions to customize the first page of any built-in Outlook item. You can add controls bound to custom fields for your solution or work with the Outlook controls that bind to Outlook data such as subject or start time. From a user interface perspective, form regions are the most important and exciting new addition to the Outlook extensibility platform. Here is a quick guide to what you can accomplish with form regions:

- You can add a new user interface as an adjoining form region to the default page of any standard Outlook form. A standard form represents a built-in Outlook item type such as a Contact item.

- If you are using adjoining or separate form regions only to add a user interface to a standard form, you can choose to specify the message class of the form regions as the same message class as that of the standard form (for example, *IPM.Contact*), or as a custom message class derived from the standard message class (for example, *IPM.Contact.Sales*).

- You can use separate form regions to replace the default page of a standard form, or replace the entire standard form. In this case, you must specify a derived message class (for example, *IPM.Contact.Sales*) for these form regions and register the form regions for that message class.

- Multiple add-ins can add form regions to the same form.

- Use the Outlook controls that ship with Outlook 2007 to create your form region. All controls on a form region are correctly themed. Outlook controls also support a full range of control events such as MouseUp, MouseDown, Keypress, and others. In-the-box controls for Outlook 2007 include the following:

- ❑ Microsoft Office Outlook Body Control
- ❑ Microsoft Office Outlook Business Card Control
- ❑ Microsoft Office Outlook Category Control
- ❑ Microsoft Office Outlook Check Box Control
- ❑ Microsoft Office Outlook Combo Box Control
- ❑ Microsoft Office Outlook Command Button Control
- ❑ Microsoft Office Outlook Contact Photo Control
- ❑ Microsoft Office Outlook Date Control
- ❑ Microsoft Office Outlook Frame Header Control
- ❑ Microsoft Office Outlook InfoBar Control
- ❑ Microsoft Office Outlook Label Control
- ❑ Microsoft Office Outlook List Box Control
- ❑ Microsoft Office Outlook Option Button Control
- ❑ Microsoft Office Outlook Page Control
- ❑ Microsoft Office Outlook Recipient Control
- ❑ Microsoft Office Outlook Sender Photo Control
- ❑ Microsoft Office Outlook Text Box Control
- ❑ Microsoft Office Outlook Time Control
- ❑ Microsoft Office Outlook Time Zone Control

Chapters 12 through 14 discuss how to design and deploy form regions in your solution. If you are wondering when to use form regions as opposed to other form technologies such as InfoPath forms, the simplest answer is that Outlook form regions are the best choice for extending Outlook forms and data. For example, you might want to add catering information to an Outlook appointment item, and a form region is a great place to expose information such as caterer, menu selections, and delivery time to the users of your solution. InfoPath forms are also exposed in Outlook 2007, but are best used for data that is not integrated directly with Outlook. For example, a survey such as a hardware inventory survey is more appropriate for an InfoPath form.

In the 2007 Microsoft Office system, other Microsoft applications make use of form regions to integrate their user interface into Outlook. Figure 1-1 shows a Microsoft Business Contact Manager form region for a Business Contact item. Notice that by using the new Outlook controls such as the Electronic Business Card Control and Contact Photo Control, this custom form is tightly integrated with the look and feel of a built-in Outlook Contact Inspector. An Inspector designates the window in which an Outlook item is displayed. At the same time, the developers of Business Contact Manager can display their own custom data on the first page of their form.

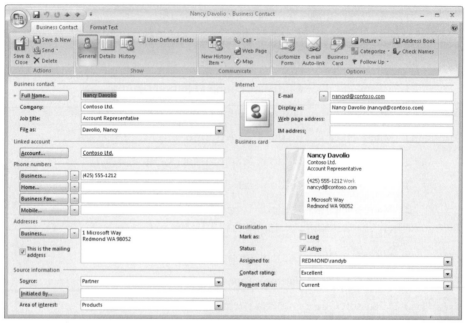

Figure 1-1   Microsoft Business Contact Manager uses form region technology in a Business Contact item.

Security

Thanks to the Outlook object model guard, Outlook 2007 continues to remain secure from the threat of e-mail worms or viruses. The Outlook object model guard prevents e-mail worms and viruses from accessing e-mail addresses or other confidential information stored in Outlook. However, developers should understand that Outlook 2007 has introduced an important change in the way that the Outlook object model guard operates. Although the behavior of the object model guard has not changed significantly for Outlook add-ins, Outlook 2007 allows external applications to run without object model guard prompts provided that the machine on which your code is running has functional antivirus software installed and all antivirus definitions are current.

This change represents a major departure from the way the object model guard worked in previous versions for external out-of-process COM callers. Before Outlook 2007, external COM callers were always untrusted from the perspective of the object model guard. This means that external applications had to resort to Extended Messaging Application Programming Interface (also known as Extended MAPI) or third-party libraries to prevent display of Outlook 2007 object model guard warning dialog boxes such as the one shown in Figure 1-2.

Figure 1-2   Address warning dialog box appears when untrusted code accesses a protected property or method.

The object model guard was originally introduced for Microsoft Outlook 98 and Microsoft Outlook 2000 product versions. Since the introduction of the object model guard, developers have struggled with it because it often confused end users and frustrated legitimate developers. Moreover, if you needed to use CDO 1.21 for property operations or improved performance, you faced a different security model that did not integrate with the Outlook add-in trust model. Because the Outlook 2007 object model has removed the need for CDO, Outlook 2007 offers a new and improved security story for developers. The overall goal is to remove development roadblocks for legitimate Outlook developers.

Table Object

One of the most frequent complaints from developers is lack of performance when using the Outlook object model. The *Table* and related objects address these complaints. The *Table* object lets you enumerate items in a folder. It also provides you with the ability to specify table columns and to filter and sort rows in the table. Unlike Outlook item-level objects, the rows in the table represent light items rather than hydrated full items. For this reason, the new *Table* object offers a significant performance improvement over the legacy *Items* collection. For very large collections (greater than 1,000 items), the *Table* performs in approximately 10 to 20 percent of the time required for enumeration of the *Items* collection object without the use of *Items.SetColumns*. Unlike the *Items* collection, the *Table* object encourages developers to write performant code and does not have the pitfalls of the *Items* collection, where a developer could retrieve the *Body* property or the *Attachments* collection on each *MailItem* and in turn see performance suffer dramatically.

You'll learn about the *Table* object in detail in Chapter 11, "Searching Outlook Data." From the standpoint of usability, programming the *Table* object is very straightforward. You call the *GetTable* method on a *Folder* object, and then iterate over the rows in the *Table* object using the *GetNextRow* method. Depending on the folder type, there is a default set of columns that you can access using the indexer on the *Row* object. If the default column set does not contain the property you need, you can add or remove columns from the table. It's as simple as that. To give you an idea, here is a C# code sample that enumerates all the items in the Inbox that contain the word "Office" in the subject:

```
private void DemoTable()
{
    string filter = "@SQL=" + "\""+ "urn:schemas:httpmail:subject"
        + "\"" + " ci_startswith 'Office'";
    Outlook.Table table =
        Application.Session.GetDefaultFolder(
        Outlook.OlDefaultFolders.olFolderInbox).GetTable(
        filter, Outlook.OlTableContents.olUserItems);
    while (!table.EndOfTable)
    {
        Outlook.Row nextRow = table.GetNextRow();
        Debug.WriteLine (nextRow["Subject"]);
    }
}
```

Improved Search

Instant Search with word wheeling and hit highlighting delivers a vastly improved search experience for users of Outlook 2007. As a developer, you might be wondering if you can exploit this feature and drive Outlook's search engine programmatically. The answer is yes; you can leverage Instant Search both in the *Table* object and in the Outlook Explorer window. An Explorer designates the main Outlook window in which the contents of a folder is displayed. From the developer's standpoint, you can create queries that cause Outlook to use the same search engine that delivers instant results in the Outlook user interface.

For programmatic search, the Outlook restriction language supports two new keywords: *ci_startswith* and *ci_phrasematch*. If Windows Desktop Search (WDS) is installed and operational on a given *Store*, you can search the contents of a folder in that *Store* using these keywords. The *ci_* keywords are designed to return results on string properties such as body or subject. Full details are provided in Chapter 11. You can also use the *ci_* keywords when you create a search folder programmatically. The use of these keywords forces Outlook to construct the search folder using the Instant Search engine. Because search folders can also include subfolders, you can create search folders that span multiple folders. The *Search* object also supports the *Table* object, so it's best practice to use *Search.GetTable* to return rows in a search folder. If you persist the search folder by calling *Save* on the *Search* object, that search folder will continue to use the WDS engine to populate the search folder in a performant manner.

If you need to control Outlook Instant Search in the Outlook Explorer window, you should consider the new *Search* method on the *Explorer* object. The *Search* method lets you programmatically specify a query string for Instant Search just as if the user had typed the criteria in the Instant Search pane. Some solution developers might want to develop a custom task pane that only is visible when the user navigates to his or her application folder. A custom task pane is a new user interface element that you create programmatically for an Outlook Explorer or

Inspector window. This custom task pane would enable the user to search the application folder or all related folders using controls in the custom task pane. The Instant Search query would be built using the controls in the task pane and makes your custom search very discoverable for the user.

Enhanced Events

Events are the oxygen of add-in development. Although Outlook has a considerable number of events compared to other Microsoft Office applications, most of these events are repeated across different item types. In an effort to improve your ability to listen to events in Outlook 2007, the events have been enhanced to support common developer scenarios. For example, one of the biggest gaps in Outlook's previous event model was the *ItemRemove* event on the *Items* collection object. The *ItemRemove* event fires when an item has been removed from a folder, but it does not tell the user which item has been removed. There were a number of published hacks to work around this limitation. You can now remove those hacks from your code. Outlook 2007 introduces *BeforeItemMove* and *BeforeFolderMove* events on the *Folder* object. These events provide reliable event handling when an item or subfolder is removed from a folder. The item or folder that is being removed is passed as a parameter to the event, and the event is cancelable when you must prevent removal of certain items or folders to maintain data integrity for your solution.

Another important change in the Outlook events model is that you have the ability to customize context menus based on events that fire on the *Application* object. The following *Application*-level events let you customize the context menu by adding, removing, or repurposing controls:

- *AttachmentContextMenuDisplay*
- *FolderContextMenuDisplay*
- *ItemContextMenuDisplay*
- *ShortcutContextMenuDisplay*
- *StoreContextMenuDisplay*
- *ViewContextMenuDisplay*

If you've used the Office object model to customize command bars, then writing code for command bar events is straightforward. The event passes a *CommandBar* object that represents the context menu that is about to be displayed. You then write code to modify the controls on that *CommandBar* object. Figure 1-3 displays a custom Instant Search context menu added to the item context menu. This context menu provides quick access to searches for other messages from the sender of the item.

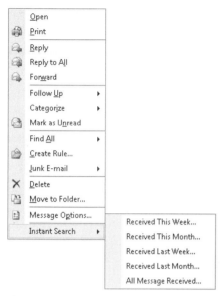

Figure 1-3   Custom context menu for Instant Search is created in the *ItemContextMenuDisplay* event.

Another area where events have been improved is in the area of attachment events for items. The number of attachment events has been expanded to include the following:

- *AttachmentRemove*

- *BeforeAttachmentAdd*

- *BeforeAttachmentPreview*

- *BeforeAttachmentRead*

- *BeforeAttachmentWriteToTempFile*

These events let you know when an attachment is being added, read, previewed in the Reading Pane, or written to a temporary file. The goal for providing these new attachment events is to achieve parity with attachment events in Microsoft Exchange Client Extensions (ECEs). ECEs, an API that predates Microsoft Outlook 97, requires C++ coding skills, and is not supported for .NET development. In the interest of providing full support for .NET developers, we've identified the lacking events in the Outlook object model when compared with ECEs. The *ItemLoad* event on the *Application* object is another ECE parity event that fires whenever an item is loaded into memory, whether as a result of creating an item, viewing an item in the Reading Pane, or opening the item in an Inspector window. In previous versions of Outlook, you had only the *NewInspector* event to tell you that an item is about to be displayed in an Inspector window. The *ItemLoad* event makes the following scenario possible:

1. A user edits an item using in-cell editing in a View.

2. You need to enforce business logic to prevent changing a custom field to a value that is invalid.

3. You use the *ItemLoad* event to hook up an event handler for the *CustomPropertyChange* event for the item.

4. The *CustomPropertyChange* event handles your solution business logic and prevents invalid values during the in-cell editing process.

Other events added to the Outlook 2007 object model provide support for new Outlook features or fill in gaps from previous versions. For example, an item now offers a *BeforeAutoSave* event that lets you write custom business logic before an auto save occurs. In Outlook 2007, auto save occurs for all item types rather than just mail items. If the item does not have all appropriate fields completed, you can cancel the auto save or display an alert to the user.

AddressEntry Enhancements

Previous versions of the object model had several coverage gaps regarding address books and recipients. To remedy this problem, the Outlook 2007 object model provides parity with the ability of CDO 1.21 to display the Address Book programmatically and return detailed information about *AddressEntry* objects. The *SelectNamesDialog* object lets you display the Outlook Address Book dialog box and set options such as the number of buttons, button captions, and initial address list displayed.

SelectNamesDialog Object

For example, let's assume that you need to display an Address Book dialog box that prompts the user for recipients in his or her Contacts folder. In previous versions of Outlook, you had to resort to CDO 1.21 or third-party libraries to achieve this functionality. In Outlook 2007, you can display the Address Book by obtaining an instance of the *SelectNamesDialog* object. Here is a brief description of what you can do with the *SelectNamesDialog* object (see Figure 1-4):

- Set the dialog box caption.
- Control the number of recipient selectors and change the caption for a given selector.
- Set or get the initial address list shown in the dialog box, and determine if the initial address list is the only address list available in the dialog box.
- Determine if multiple recipients can be selected.
- Display the Outlook Address Book dialog box.
- Obtain a *Recipients* collection object that contains all the recipients selected in the dialog box.

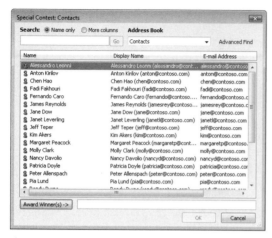

Figure 1-4   Customize the Outlook Address Book using the *SelectNamesDialog* object.

ExchangeUser and *ExchangeDistributionList* Objects

Now that you can display the Outlook Address Book programatically, you might wonder how you can discover additional information about the selected recipients. If the recipient is a Simple Mail Transfer Protocol (SMTP) address, there isn't much you can do beyond the recipient's display name and SMTP address. However, if the recipient is a Microsoft Exchange recipient, the Outlook 2007 object model makes the process much easier. You can use two new objects that derive from the legacy *AddressEntry* object:

- *ExchangeUser*

- *ExchangeDistributionList*

These objects derive from the *AddressEntry* object. Unlike the legacy *AddressEntry* object, they provide full programmatic details on an *AddressEntry* that represents an Exchange user or an Exchange distribution list. You can obtain properties on these objects such as *PrimarySMTPAddress*, *LastName*, *FirstName*, *OfficeLocation*, *Department*, and so forth. You can also determine the manager or the *ExchangeUser* object or obtain an *AddressEntries* collection that represents all the direct reports for the given *ExchangeUser* object.

Sharing Objects

Outlook 2007 makes sharing information with others easier than it has been in previous versions. There are a variety of sharing mechanisms such as Exchange public folders or Microsoft SharePoint sites. Sharing objects are discussed in detail in Chapter 9, "Sharing Information with Other Users." Let's focus briefly on sharing personal information such as contacts or calendars. You can create solutions that share personal information with coworkers or with friends and family. Add-ins that enable users to share information will provide a great opportunity for developers in Outlook 2007. You can use sharing objects to extend Outlook and provide more complex sharing scenarios for your customers.

Here is a quick look at several sharing objects that you can use in your solutions:

- The *SharingItem* object, which lets you programmatically send sharing messages in an Exchange environment

- The *CalenderSharing* object, which lets you export a calendar date range to an *ICal* attachment

- The *OpenSharedFolder* method on the *Namespace* object, which lets you open several sharing resources, including a WebCal Uniform Resource Locator (URL), RSS URL, or SharePoint URL

- The *OpenSharedItem* method on the *Namespace* object, which lets you open an item in Outlook's .msg format, vCard format, or iCal format

Rules Objects

Rules are one of the most powerful features of Outlook for staying organized and responding to the continuous flow of messages into your Inbox. In previous versions of Outlook, developers were not able to create rules programmatically. In Outlook 2007, you can programmatically create rules, determine conditions or exceptions that determine whether the rule will run, and set actions to occur. Typical rule actions include moving or copying an item to a folder, setting one or more categories on the item, or marking the item as a task. Items flagged for follow-up appear in your To-Do list, which represents an important new feature in Outlook 2007. You can also establish rule conditions or exceptions that determine whether the rule executes. Typical rule conditions are whether the message is from or to a recipient, whether you are on the To or Cc line of a message, whether the message contains specific words in the body or subject, or whether the item is from a specified RSS feed.

The rule objects are simple to use and can be used to create rules programmatically for your solution. For more information on rule objects, see Chapter 10, "Organizing Outlook Data." Here is a quick guide to new rule objects in Outlook 2007:

- All *Rules* defined for the logged-on session are contained in the *Rules* collection object. Obtain the *Rules* collection object by calling *GetRules* on the *DefaultStore* property of the *Namespace* object.

- You can enumerate the *Rule* objects in the *Rules* collection. When you enumerate *Rules*, you can enable or disable a rule programmatically.

- To create a new *Rule*, call *Rules.Create*. When you call the *Create* method, you must specify an *OlRuleType* argument. A *Rule* can be an *OlRuleType.olRuleReceive* or an *OlRuleType.olRuleSend* rule. These enum values correspond to Send or Receive Rules in the Outlook Rules Wizard.

- Once you have an instance of a new *Rule* object, you can programmatically enable *Rule.Actions*, *Rule.Conditions*, and *Rule.Exceptions*. Each of these objects represents static collection objects. You cannot programmatically add your own *Rule* actions, for example, to the *RuleActions* collection object.

- Some rule actions or conditions can only be enabled or disabled. For example, you can only enable or disable the *OnlyToMe* rule condition. Other rule conditions require that you set additional properties on the rule condition.

- Once you have finished setting rule actions, conditions, and exceptions, you should call *Rules.Save* to persist the newly created *Rule* object.

- You can also call *Rule.Execute* to run the *Rule* object programmatically. You don't have to save the rule to call *Rule.Execute*.

PropertyAccessor Object

Like the *Table* object, the *PropertyAccessor* object offers a momentous change in what you can accomplish using the Outlook object model. *PropertyAccessor* provides access to Outlook object properties that are not available through the Outlook object model. For readers familiar with CDO 1.21, *PropertyAccessor* is a replacement for the *CDO Fields* and *Field* objects. Unlike CDO, *PropertyAccessor* uses a readable string value instead of an integer tag value to access both built-in and custom properties on Outlook objects. The following objects support *PropertyAccessor*:

AddressEntry	AddressList
AppointmentItem	Attachment
ContactItem	DistListItem
DocumentItem	ExchangeDistributionList
ExchangeUser	Folder
JournalItem	MailItem
MeetingItem	NoteItem
PostItem	Recipient
RemoteItem	ReportItem
SharingItem	Store
TaskItem	TaskRequestAcceptItem
TaskRequestDeclineItem	TaskRequestItem
TaskRequestUpdateItem	

PropertyAccessor Sample Code

Let's take a look at how you would write code to use the *PropertyAccessor* object. When a message is delivered via SMTP, the message is stamped with a Transport Header that contains information about the routing used to deliver the message to its destination. In previous versions of

Outlook, developers would have to resort to CDO, Extended MAPI, or third-party libraries to read this property. In Outlook 2007, you can use the *PropertyAccessor* object to read the value of the Transport Header (*PR_TRANSPORT_MESSAGE_HEADERS*). The following code example shows you how to restrict the *Table* object for messages where the *Transport Header* property is not null. Use *Namespace.GetItemFromID* to open a *Row* object, and then use the *GetProperty* method of the *PropertyAccessor* object to display the Transport Header in a message box.

```
void DemoPropertyAccessorGetProperty()
{
    string EntryID = "";
    //Proptag for PR_TRANSPORT_MESSAGE_HEADERS
    string PR_TRANSPORT_MESSAGE_HEADERS =
        @"http://schemas.microsoft.com/mapi/proptag/0x007D001E";
    string filter = "@SQL=" + "Not("
        + "\"" + PR_TRANSPORT_MESSAGE_HEADERS + "\"" + " Is Null)";
    Outlook.Table table = Application.Session.GetDefaultFolder(
        Outlook.OlDefaultFolders.olFolderInbox).GetTable(
        filter, Outlook.OlTableContents.olUserItems);
    if (table.GetRowCount() > 0)
    {
        Outlook.Row nextRow = table.GetNextRow();
        EntryID = nextRow["EntryID"].ToString();
    }
    else
    {
        return;
    }
    //Get MailItem using GetItemFromID
    Outlook.MailItem mail =
        (Outlook.MailItem)
        Application.Session.GetItemFromID(EntryID, Type.Missing);
    //Obtain an instance of PropertyAccessor class
    Outlook.PropertyAccessor PA = mail.PropertyAccessor;
    string Transport = (string)PA.GetProperty(
        PR_TRANSPORT_MESSAGE_HEADERS);
    //Call GetProperty
    MessageBox.Show(this, Transport,
        "Transport Header: " + mail.Subject);
}
```

Chapter 17, "Using the *PropertyAccessor* Object," provides you with all the technical details of using the *PropertyAccessor* object in your solution. The key point to remember is that *PropertyAccessor* should be used only for properties that are not exposed directly in the Outlook object model. You can also use *PropertyAccessor* to create named properties on items that are hidden from views and do not display in an Outlook Inspector.

Developer Reference

Although the Outlook Developer Reference is not a new object model feature, it does represent a significant improvement in the developer experience when programming Outlook 2007. The entry point for the Developer Reference is no longer available in the main Outlook Help viewer. To display the Developer Reference, follow these simple steps:

1. Press Alt + F11 to open the Outlook VBA editor.

2. Press F1 to display the Outlook Developer Reference shown in Figure 1-5.

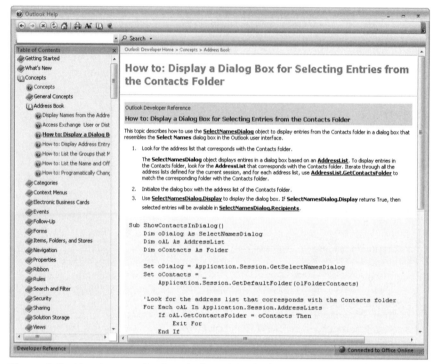

Figure 1-5   Use the completely redesigned Outlook 2007 Developer Reference as your primary help source.

What's new about the Outlook 2007 Developer Reference? Here are the key points that should make this the first place you look for help in programming Outlook 2007:

- A Visual Studio look and feel. The Help viewer and the Help content itself has been changed so that the VBA documentation resembles the help for Visual Studio 2005.

- Organization by objects and then members that belong to that object. Previous versions of Outlook developer help were organized by properties, methods, and events. The older organizational scheme made it difficult to understand how a member related to a given object. For example, there was only one topic for the *Add* method, whether it applied to the *Items*, *Folders*, or *Attachments* collection objects. Now each member topic is specific to its parent object.

■ Task-based topics are available in the "How Do I..." book. Many developers know what they want to accomplish, but they don't necessarily know which objects and members will let them complete the task. Task-based topics address this need. If you have a task-based sample that you'd like to add to the "How Do I..." book, please see that Help topic for instructions on submitting your own task-based solution. If your code is used in the Outlook Developer Reference, a link will be provided to your Web site along with the code sample.

■ Expanded What's New topics document the changes between versions of the object model. This section lists all new objects, collections, and enumerations in Outlook 2007. It also provides you with information about changes that could potentially break existing solutions.

Summary

Outlook 2007 has more than doubled the number of objects available when you program Outlook. The improvements to the Outlook object model are more than quantitative, however. After many versions in which extensibility was an afterthought, Outlook 2007 has specifically targeted platform improvements as an overall product goal. Form regions are the most visible sign of these platform investments. Unification is part of an ongoing effort across this and future versions to ensure that the Outlook object model is all that you need to complete a professional solution.

Managed code developers are the target audience for this book. If you are a managed code developer, you should be happy with these changes because writing code using other APIs such as CDO, ECEs, or Extended MAPI was unsupported for .NET development. Developer nirvana isn't guaranteed in this release, but Microsoft has made great strides in enabling your work as an Outlook developer. The remainder of this book will get you started on the journey. It's then up to you to create some great solutions for Outlook 2007.

Chapter 2
Outlook as a Platform

The platform is an essential cornerstone that contributes to the success of Microsoft Office Outlook 2007. Outlook won't ever have every single feature that customers ask for. The platform allows independent software vendors (ISVs) to leverage this business opportunity by complementing Outlook functionality not available in the shipped Outlook product. The platform also allows organizations to tailor Outlook to meet their specific needs and implement custom business logic or requirements within Outlook.

The goal of this chapter is to provide an overview of the Outlook platform capabilities with high-level guidance of when to integrate with Outlook and how to accomplish this integration. This chapter contains no code samples and focuses on a top-level view of the Outlook platform. If you are not familiar with the Outlook platform, consider reading this chapter to gain a sense of the Outlook development landscape. If you are familiar with the Outlook platform and want to dive directly into the Outlook object model, add-in construction, and Microsoft Visual Basic .NET or C# sample code, you can skip this chapter and proceed directly to Chapter 3, "Writing Your First Outlook Add-In Using Visual Basic .NET," or Chapter 4, "Writing Your First Outlook Add-In Using C#."

Why Integrate with Outlook?

For users around the globe, Outlook is the information hub they depend on for messaging, time, contact, and information management. Outlook allows the user to prioritize, organize, and search information. Users especially value Outlook's offline capabilities, which allow them to remain connected with work when they're on the go. They often spend many hours daily in Outlook. From an application perspective, Outlook is where users live. The Outlook platform provides ISVs and organizations with the opportunity to extend, enrich, and customize the Outlook experience for these users.

The Outlook platform allows the introduction of entirely new features or adjustment of Outlook's built-in functionality to meet specific needs. Outlook's solution landscape is vast, and here is a quick, although incomplete, glance at solutions that target Outlook:

- Device synchronization applications
- Antivirus, phishing, and spam solutions
- Integration of customer relationship management (CRM) systems, line of business (LOB) applications, workflow, archiving, and document management

- Mail utilities that include attachment compression, content encryption, thread compression, and productivity solutions

- Unified messaging and other forms of communications (fax, voice messaging, video)

One interesting characteristic of a seamlessly integrated Outlook solution is that the customer perceives it as being a native Outlook feature. This user perception is desirable because it helps make Outlook predictable, consistent, and easy to use. Deep integration can be accomplished by adopting Outlook's user experience metaphors and paying attention to customer expectations. For example, it's important for a solution to support offline capabilities, meaning the customer can get work done even when there's no network or limited connectivity. If the solution introduces form customizations, they show up in the Reading Pane and also when the form is opened in a separate window. The associated functionality for these custom forms is exposed in context menus, Ribbon, and command bars. Users can search, sort, filter, categorize, drag, or create rules for the data that the solution introduces in the same way they would if they were working with Outlook's built-in data. The solution offers a consistent experience across different computers by roaming preferences (just like Outlook roams views), categories, and rules in Microsoft Exchange mailboxes.

A successful Outlook solution accomplishes more than just introducing a new feature; it actually solves a customer problem in a holistic manner by guiding the user end-to-end to get his or her job done. Many such Outlook solutions leverage the user's familiarity with Outlook by building on Outlook's extensive usability experience, therefore reducing or eliminating the need for additional user training.

The contrast to a seamless Outlook solution is a superficial integration that takes advantage of users living in Outlook. Outlook is not designed to be a generic shell. Such integrations often cause user confusion because they don't work like the rest of Outlook and introduce functionality that does not really belong to Outlook. These inconsistencies can have an impact beyond the solution on all of Outlook because the user does not know what constitutes the boundary between Outlook and the solution.

The prime goal of the Outlook platform is to facilitate integration of your solution into Outlook. The Outlook platform is not about offering a palette of reusable controls that can be used outside the context of Outlook or supporting server scenarios like running the Outlook object model in Microsoft ASP.NET applications, automating mailboxes of an organization, or installing the Outlook implementation of the Messaging Application Programming Interface (MAPI) on a server.

Customers expect Outlook solutions to build on Outlook strengths such as cached Exchange mode. Outlook offers rich functionality that is also available when the customer works offline or without network connectivity. Critical information is stored in a user's mailbox and is easily accessible thanks to integrated Instant Search, a new feature in Outlook 2007. Outlook's cached Exchange capability means that customers also expect data associated with Outlook solutions such as a CRM integration to work offline and be easily searchable. Customers also expect that basic Outlook functionality like categories, rules, flagging for follow-up, or responding to mail works consistently for all data showing up in Outlook.

Outlook's core functionality revolves around Mail, Calendaring, Contacts, and Tasks. These types are prominently exposed in the Navigation Pane and have dedicated forms, views, and appropriate actions such as Send, Reply, Reply to All, and Forward. For example, media types (pictures, music, or videos) are not native Outlook types and are less deeply integrated into Outlook; they show up as attachments in the Reading Pane and on an Inspector. Outlook 2007 offers a richer preview experience for attachments, but otherwise Outlook is not optimized for these types. If the solution you're about to write is not about extending Outlook's core types, then integrating into Outlook might not be the right answer for your customers. In this case, you should investigate delivering the functionality of your solution as part of a separate standalone application.

For those solutions that follow the guidelines established in this chapter and deeply integrate with Outlook, the Outlook 2007 platform enhancements enable your solution in the following ways:

- The consolidated Outlook 2007 object model is sufficient for most solutions and replaces deprecated application programming interfaces (APIs) such as Collaboration Data Objects (CDO) 1.21. The Outlook object model is fully supported for Microsoft .NET Framework development.

- Form regions allow you to integrate your user interface with Outlook's built-in forms and provide a rich palette of controls to ensure that you can clone existing Outlook forms.

- Ribbon extensibility (referred to as RibbonX) and custom task panes ensure that your solution is integrated with the discoverability and usability improvements in the 2007 Microsoft Office system.

These enhancements are not only geared toward external developers; many Outlook integrations developed within Microsoft rely heavily on these Outlook 2007 platform enhancements: Microsoft Business Contact Manager, Microsoft Exchange Unified Messenger Add-in, and Microsoft Outlook Mobile Service as well as other Microsoft add-ins that ship with Office 2007. This internal Microsoft usage helps to ensure that the platform is stable, performant, and offers a comprehensive set of functionality.

Different Types of Outlook Integration

There are two different categories of Outlook integration from a platform perspective: data integration and functional integration. Many real-world Outlook solutions utilize both types of integration. The following discussion introduces the two types of Outlook integration, cites specific implementations that ship with Outlook 2007, and then proposes guidelines for achieving data and functional integration with your solution and Outlook.

Data Integration

This model is used by solutions that want to either simply access Outlook data or bring their data into Outlook and let Outlook manage the data from that point on.

Examples of Data Integration

The following list provides some general categories of data integration and also focuses on specific data integration solutions:

- **Synchronization of Contacts, Calendar, and Mail**   These solutions enable two-way synchronization of Outlook folders with miscellaneous portable devices and mobile phones.

- **Connector/provider applications**   These applications bring data into Outlook from other sources like messaging and collaboration back ends or CRM systems.

- **Online Meeting integration**   Adds Online Meeting to the Outlook Calendar and introduces additional information for a meeting like dial-in number, access code, and URLs to resources. Shows these fields on meeting requests.

- **Calendar Gadget for Microsoft Windows SideShow**   This add-in shipping with Office 2007 obtains one week of appointments and meetings from the default Outlook Calendar and passes this data to Windows SideShow gadgets.

How Did Microsoft Office Outlook 2007 Calendar Gadget for Windows SideShow Do It?

The Microsoft Office Outlook 2007 Calendar Gadget for Windows SideShow is an in-process Component Object Model (COM) add-in for Outlook. It relies primarily on the Outlook object model. The add-in allows users to view their calendar on Windows SideShow-compatible devices. Windows SideShow, shown in Figure 2-1, is new for Microsoft Windows Vista and enables developers to write gadgets or mini-applications to send data from the computer to devices connected to the computer. A Windows SideShow-compatible device can take several forms, such as a display attached to the lid of a laptop, a front-panel display on a desktop or server, or a small display in a keyboard. It can also be part of an existing device such as a cell phone, portable media player, or digital picture frame.

Figure 2-1   Windows SideShow uses the Outlook object model to gather its data.

SideShow Implementation   Windows SideShow is implemented as an Outlook add-in. The add-in enumerates calendar items on the user's default calendar, and sends about a week's worth of calendar data to the Windows SideShow platform. The add-in only reads calendar data; there is no integration into the Outlook user experience. Writing this functionality as a trusted COM add-in ensures that the code by default won't trigger any Outlook security prompts. The default date range is 2 days previous and 5 days ahead. The information is updated every day, as well as when calendar changes are detected. The primary data format used is *iCalendar*. The add-in generates its own *iCalendar* representations of the appointments on a background thread for performance reasons, and sends those directly down to the devices. For Windows SideShow-compatible devices that do not support *iCalendar*, the add-in provides a simple text-only version of the content that shows the user's next five appointments within the next 24 hours. This is very useful information on small text displays, such as those embedded in keyboards, as it gives the user at-a-glance access to his or her important upcoming appointments. This data is refreshed at a regular interval. When there are no Windows SideShow–compatible devices connected to the computer, the add-in does nothing except wait for devices to be connected to minimize the performance impact for Outlook.

Paying Attention to Performance   The first performance goal is to ensure that the add-in is only retrieving calendar data when there's actually a SideShow device present and active. Only doing work when required is an important guideline applying to all add-ins. The second goal is to ensure that users won't notice when the SideShow add-in accesses Outlook data. Any operation has to be less than 250 milliseconds in duration for users to not perceive the operation as a hang. This requirement is especially important because the user did not initiate the sync to the SideShow device, so the user would not understand why Outlook suddenly appears to hang.

Minimizing the performance impact to Outlook represents the main design challenge when utilizing the Outlook object model for add-ins without a user interface (UI). All calls into the object model occur on Outlook's main UI thread; thus they have the ability to negatively affect the user experience by causing sporadic hangs, stutters, and feelings of sluggishness. To address these issues, the Calendar Gadget performs as little work as necessary on the Outlook UI thread, reserving the bulk of the heavy lifting for a background thread. To minimize the cross-thread marshaling, all calls into the object model occur on the main thread. When processing the calendar, the add-in handles one appointment at a time, and then sets a timer before processing the next item to allow the message pump to process other messages. For each calendar appointment, it extracts the important properties, stores them in a temporary object, and queues it for the worker thread. Generating the *iCal* items on the worker thread is more efficient than utilizing Outlook's save as *iCalendar* functionality for single appointments. Bulk exporting *iCalendar* items through the *CalendarSharing* object is not an option because SideShow gadgets don't support *iCal* recurrence.

Functional Integration

Functional integration is the model that's followed by solutions that want to introduce new functionality into the Outlook user experience through customizing command bars for Outlook's main Explorer window, introducing custom forms with RibbonX, or providing custom task panes for Outlook Explorer or Inspector windows.

Examples of Functional Integration

There are many ways to categorize functional integration. The following list provides some examples of functional integration.

- **Mail applications**   Compression of attachments, archiving mail, adding disclaimers to mail messages, encryption, and content security

- **Corporate compliance**   Restricting Reply All, ensuring that messages are addressed to correct recipients

- **E-mail protection**   Spam blocking and antivirus

- **Utilities**   Printing of Calendars or Contacts

- **Productivity tools**   Helping a user become more productive with Outlook by enhancing search, prioritization, and organizational schemes

- **Unified messaging**   Directing voice mails and other communications to a user's Inbox

How Did Unified Messaging Add-In for Outlook 2007 Do It?

The Unified Messaging add-in for Exchange provides integrated support for listening to voice mails within Outlook. Voice mails can be viewed using a form region that includes an inline Media Player and a private field for taking notes (see Figure 2-2). A form region is a new technology in Outlook 2007 that allows you to replace or integrate with Outlook's built-in forms. The Unified Messaging add-in also provides the ability to have the Exchange server make an outbound phone call to a specified number and play the voice mail. This feature is useful when privacy is a concern, or when the computer does not have speakers. The add-in introduces an additional Tools Options page for viewing and editing Unified Messaging preferences. A user can reset his or her PIN, update his or her voice mail greetings, and define the default folder when accessing the Exchange mailbox with a phone.

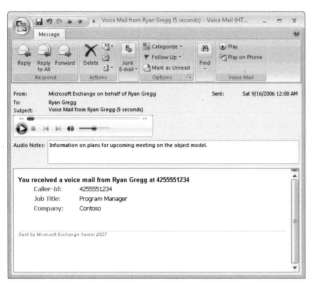

Figure 2-2   The Unified Messaging add-in uses Outlook 2007 form regions.

Unified Messaging Implementation   The Unified Messaging add-in relies on the Outlook object model, form regions, and RibbonX. The add-in introduces a custom form region with its own custom message class for Exchange voice messages. The form region renders in the Reading Pane and in a separate Inspector window. It hosts a Windows Media Player control and extends the default Ribbon by adding controls for playing the voice mail and initiating Play on Phone. A custom string property is used to store the voice mail annotations. The add-in uses property pages to add a new tab to Outlook's Tools Options dialog box. It also utilizes two Exchange Web services. The Auto-Discover Web service is used to locate the appropriate Exchange Server that provides Unified Messaging support, and the Unified Messaging Web service provides advanced features specific to Unified Messenger for voice mails, such as Play on Phone.

Paying Attention to Discovering Unified Messenger Availability   The add-in is scoped to voice messages with a certain message class and offers its functionality once it discovers that Exchange Unified Messaging is available. This implementation decision has been made to minimize the performance impact for users without Unified Messenger capabilities and to limit the attack surface. This is not at all to say that the Unified Messenger add-in is insecure; it actually went through an in-depth security analysis. It's simply following a good security practice, which is to only enable functionality when required. The add-in attempts to locate the Exchange Unified Messaging Server over different network connections using corporate local area network (LAN), Internet, virtual private network (VPN), or remote procedure call

(RPC) over Secure Hypertext Transfer Protocol (HTTPS). If it fails to find the server, it will disable the Tools Options tab and *Play on Phone* command.

Integration Guidelines

The goal for the Outlook 2007 platform enhancements is to enable developers to build rich solutions by relying on only the Outlook object model, form regions, RibbonX, custom task panes, and also, in some cases, Extended MAPI.

Data Integration

There's a wide range of data integration scenarios and there are many options available to accomplish those scenarios. This breadth of options makes it important to define clear goals first so that the appropriate data integration path can be identified. The purpose of the following discussion is to identify the data integration scenarios. After the scenarios have been identified, the focus will be on how the data integration can be accomplished.

Integrating with Data That Is Already in Outlook

Many customers have one single Outlook MAPI profile that often contains only one store containing all Outlook data (mail, contacts, calendar, and tasks). Examples are customers with an Exchange account or multiple Post Office Protocol (POP) accounts. If there's more than one store associated with the Outlook profile, then it's likely to be either one or more proxy Personal Folders File (.pst) stores used for Hotmail and Internet Message Access Protocol (IMAP) e-mail replication or an archive .pst file.

One example of such a data integration scenario would be synchronizing calendar and contact data from Outlook to a device. When configured to run against Exchange, Outlook would replicate these appointment and contact items to the default folders for these items while this Outlook sync integration would then sync the data from and to the device. Because the Outlook platform does not offer a sync API, it's up to this sync integration to keep track of replication state and perform conflict resolution. For example, an item might have changed both in Outlook and on the device. The sync integration code has to detect that the items have changed and attempt a conflict resolution. Ideally, conflict resolution does not involve the user and is silent. If a user has added a contact phone number on the device and changed the mailing address in Outlook, the sync code can silently merge these two changes.

The two APIs that accomplish data integration are the Outlook object model and Extended MAPI.

Bringing Data into Outlook

Since the introduction of cached Exchange mode in Microsoft Office Outlook 2003, customers expect data to be available locally when they're on the go without network connectivity or connected over a high-latency/low-bandwidth network connection. This means that customers also expect that the data associated with solutions is available offline. Often the back-end data repository contains much more data than what's suitable to cache locally, asking for a model allowing to cache only the critical subset and offering online access to the rest.

The data can be locally cached in a dedicated Outlook .pst-based store, meaning that there's a separate store offering its own folder hierarchy exposed in the Outlook Navigation Pane. There are two options to accomplish the replication: the solution can replicate the data into the .pst either by writing its own replication algorithm using a combination of MAPI and the Outlook object model, or by relying on the Replication API. The Replication API provides the functionality for a MAPI Transport provider to synchronize Outlook items between a server and a private, .pst-based local store created for that provider.

Another option is to introduce either a custom MAPI store provider that offers online-only access to the back end or a store provider that locally caches the data. One more alternative is a hybrid architecture, which locally caches the most critical data and offers online access to the rest.

Customizing Outlook Items

Besides identifying in what store the data should be persisted, a solution also needs to determine if the data can be stored in the properties already defined by Outlook or if new custom properties have to be introduced. MAPI provides the foundation for Outlook data storage. MAPI predates Extensible Markup Language (XML), which means that there's no schema associated with MAPI items. Outlook items represent simple property bags that are preserved when items are moved or copied within and across stores. If an Outlook item requires additional properties and these properties need to be visible within Outlook, then the custom properties must be created through the Outlook object model's *UserProperties* object. In this case, the properties would appear in the Outlook Field Chooser so they can be added or removed from Views or displayed in an Outlook Inspector window. Creating properties directly through MAPI won't do the job, but once the property is created through the object model it can be accessed with MAPI.

Another question that you must ask is whether or not a custom item type identified by a custom message class is required. A custom message class is typically introduced if the item is rendered by a custom form, which is covered later in the section "User Interface Integration and Data Presentation."

Data Integration with Outlook Object Model

The Outlook object model is by far the most comprehensive and powerful API for programming Outlook, but performance considerations have to be factored in. The Outlook object model runs on Outlook's foreground thread, meaning performance is critical especially if your application requires that you synchronize a significant amount of data. Performance will be likely the most demanding aspect for data integration. Performance considerations include the following:

- Using appropriate object model members, including the new *Table* object and Instant Search queries.

- Data throttling, where you fetch data when the machine is in an idle state.

- Data granularity, so that you read and write data in small chunks.

It's recommended to couple the solution lifetime to Outlook and only run when Outlook does, including running against the same MAPI profile that Outlook is logged into.

Data Integration with Extended MAPI

Extended MAPI allows data access and runs on a separate thread. The tricky part is that MAPI sits below Outlook's business logic, which means that writing data is complex and opaque for certain scenarios. If the data access scenario involves mail or contact items, then using MAPI is acceptable. If the scenario involves appointment or task items, MAPI is problematic. The business logic of Outlook's Calendar is complicated, and many properties such as the recurrence pattern are stored as an opaque binary blob. In addition, all meeting actions have many side effects, including meeting deletion, sending a meeting cancellation, or changing properties such as location or time and then sending a meeting update. Task assignments and recurrence are opaque in a manner similar to that of appointment items. If possible, it's recommended that the MAPI integration only be executed when Outlook is running and against the same Outlook profile the user is logged into.

Data Integration with MAPI Store or Address Book Providers

Although MAPI providers offer a rich model for creating a store or Address Book provider, you should be aware that writing such a provider, especially a MAPI store provider, is a complex task requiring developers with extensive unmanaged C++ and MAPI coding skills. If you are writing a custom MAPI store provider, your store will not be indexed by the Instant Search engine. If you rely on folder home pages for your custom store, those pages are disabled by default in a nondefault store as a security mitigation. Keep these limitations in mind before you decide to invest your resources in writing a MAPI store or Address Book provider.

Data Integration with Replication API

The Replication API, documented as part of the Outlook 2007 Integration API Reference, offers another option for replicating items from a back-end data repository into an Outlook .pst-based store. The Replication API is used for replicating the data into a dedicated .pst-based store and keeping track of the synchronization state. Because the business logic for appointment, contact, and task items is only exposed in the Outlook object model, this API is not ideal for these types. The positive aspect of this approach is that it does not require the introduction of a custom MAPI store provider, which is complex to write and maintain. Critical Outlook 2007 functionality such as Instant Search will work without modifications on your part provided that Windows Desktop Search is installed and enabled for your store.

Business Logic

Outlook implements business logic for both built-in and custom items. Events in the Outlook object model allow you to write code that overrides or modifies that business logic.

Business Logic for Built-In Items

Integrating into Outlook through the Outlook object model ensures that the Outlook solution also benefits from Outlook's rich business logic for different Outlook item types. When an item is accessed through MAPI, the Outlook business logic is bypassed.

Outlook's business logic is invoked whenever an item of a certain type is loaded. For example, if an item is programmatically opened without a UI or a user opens a contact item (*MessageClass* is *IPM.Contact*) or a customized contact rendered with a form region (*MessageClass* is *IPM.Contact.OwnVersion*), then Outlook's contact business logic is invoked. For a discussion of how *MessageClass* relates to built-in and custom types, see Chapter 5, "Built-In Item Types." Calendaring involves considerable business logic, and the following examples provide you with an overview:

- Appointment items ensure that the start time of the meeting is before the end time.

- Appointments also support recurrence, including exceptions; for example, a weekly meeting on Wednesday at 5 P.M. except for this week, when the meeting is on Thursday at 2 P.M.

- The recurrence also accommodates non-Gregorian calendars, like birthdays based on lunar calendars.

- A cancellation is sent when the meeting is deleted from the calendar or an attendee is removed.

- Meeting requests are processed when they arrive in the mailbox and get tentatively added to the calendar.

- When the user accepts or declines a meeting, the user is asked to send a response to the organizer.

- Meeting responses from meeting attendees are automatically added to the meeting's Tracking tab in the organizer's calendar.

For contact items, the business logic primarily revolves around keeping related fields in sync, for example the *FullName* property with *FirstName*, *MiddleName*, *LastName*, *Suffix*, and *Prefix* or *FileAs* with *CompanyName* or the name fields. Addresses (Home, Business, Other) are also stored as both individual fields (city, country, postal code, state, street) and as free-form multiline fields with custom formatting.

Custom Business Logic

Outlook does not allow turning off or overwriting the built-in business logic for the different item types. In other words, if a solution introduces an item with a *MessageClass* of *IPM.Contact.OwnVersion*, Outlook's business logic for contacts will kick in, and if the *FirstName* field changes it will also update the *FullName* field. Although the Outlook business logic cannot be overwritten, Outlook's rich event model provides developers with a way to customize and refine Outlook's built-in behavior. This customization can be accomplished by writing an Outlook add-in with an event handler that gets called when Outlook saves an item, a built-in or custom property is changed, a file gets attached, or an e-mail is sent. This rich event model allows Outlook solutions to extend built-in actions and perform additional data validation.

Another option is to customize built-in actions or introduce new custom actions as part of introducing a form region to render a custom item type. If the solution intends to introduce its own item type and control the business logic associated with the item, you should consider basing the custom item on a Post item. The Post item is the closest item type to a "start-from-scratch" item, as this is the item type with the least built-in Outlook business logic. Custom properties can be added to this custom Post item using the *UserProperties* object, and your add-in can control custom property business logic by implementing event handlers hooked up to item or form control change events.

User Interface Integration and Data Presentation

This section enumerates the different Outlook UI extensibility mechanisms and provides guidelines for how to integrate your UI with Outlook. The goal of UI integration is that customers don't perceive your UI as different from the Outlook UI. The entry points of your UI should be parallel with entry points for the Outlook UI.

Outlook Explorer Window

The Outlook Explorer window shown in Figure 2-3 is the main Outlook application window and displays folder contents. A word of caution is in order before discussing the Explorer window. Although Outlook offers the ability to extend its UI, you should consider that the surface area for customization is limited in the Explorer window. This constraint means that it's often desirable to integrate with the existing UI rather than layering your custom UI on top of the Outlook UI. It's quite common for a user to have a number of add-ins installed. If each one of them introduces a new top-level menu and toolbar for the Outlook Explorer, the UI will become busy to a point that Outlook usability as a whole suffers.

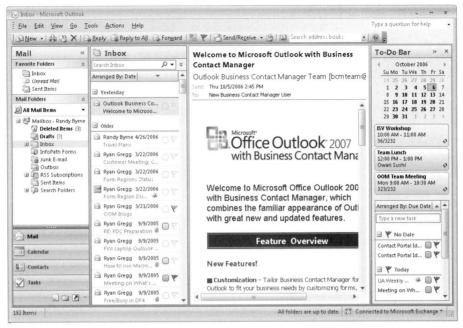

Figure 2-3   The Outlook Explorer window.

Instead of introducing a new menu or toolbar, consider merging custom commands with existing menus. Add-in preferences can be exposed under an additional tab in the Outlook Tools Options dialog box. Another solution is to make the functionality available only when the user actually needs it. In short, your UI should be context-sensitive. If an Outlook solution has its own store, then a custom UI can be available when the user works in this store and be hidden otherwise.

Introducing a custom task pane for Outlook Explorer is challenging because Outlook 2007 also introduces the To-Do Bar, meaning that many users will run Outlook with four panes (the Navigation Pane, the View Pane, the Reading Pane, and the To-Do Bar). Introducing a fifth vertical pane is not desirable unless you locate a custom task pane in a horizontal location at the bottom of the Explorer window. To avoid user confusion, add-ins should not automatically hide or collapse panes without user interaction.

Command Bars

The menu bar, standard, and advanced toolbars that appear at the top of the Outlook Explorer window are built using Office command bars. Add-ins can introduce a custom toolbar or add, remove, or hide commands in built-in menu bars and toolbars. Command bars are an Office extensibility mechanism shared by different Office applications. With Office 2007, Microsoft Word, Excel, and PowerPoint use the Ribbon exclusively, whereas Outlook 2007 is a hybrid, relying on command bars for Outlook Explorer windows and the Ribbon for Outlook Inspector windows.

Navigation Pane

The Navigation Pane shown in Figure 2-4 appears on the left side of the Explorer window and allows the user to select different Outlook modules, such as Mail or Calendar. Additionally, the Navigation Pane displays a list of folders for each module. The object model includes support for switching modules, controlling which modules are displayed, and modifying the grouping of folders in modules that have folder groups. The Outlook platform does not allow you to add a new module to the Navigation Pane.

Figure 2-4   Outlook Navigation Pane.

View Pane

The View Pane shown in Figure 2-5 typically renders the contents of a folder with a view optimized for the item types stored in the folder. For example, mail items are displayed in a table view, meetings and appointments in a calendar view, and contacts as business cards. The Outlook 2007 object model allows fully dynamic view customization in the View Pane. You can add or modify folder views programmatically. View fields can be added or removed, Group By fields can be added or removed, a filter can be applied, and almost all aspects of the view can be customized programmatically.

Figure 2-5   Outlook View Pane.

Reading Pane

The Reading Pane shown in Figure 2-6 displays the currently selected item or attachment. Outlook 2007 provides the ability to customize the look of the Reading Pane for both items and attachments. Form regions can be used to extend or replace how an item is rendered in the Reading Pane. A custom preview handler also can be registered to control the way an attachment is previewed in the Reading Pane.

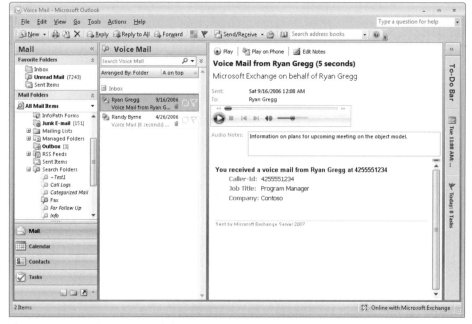

Figure 2-6   Reading Pane with form region customization.

To-Do Bar

The To-Do Bar displayed in Figure 2-7 provides a quick summary of upcoming appointments and tasks. Items are added to the To-Do Bar by creating a new task item or by flagging mail or contact items for follow-up.

Figure 2-7   Outlook To-Do Bar.

Context Menus

The Explorer window contains a number of context menus that can be customized. The Navigation Pane offers the store and folder context menus, the View Pane offers the items and views context menus, the Reading Pane offers the attachment context menu, and the To-Do Bar also supports the item context menu.

Property Pages

Configuration options for your solution can be integrated into the Outlook Tools Options dialog box by using a property page similar to the one shown in Figure 2-8. Property pages can also be used to extend the Folder Properties dialog box.

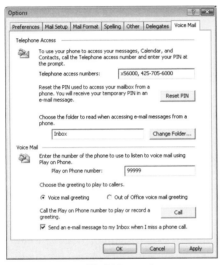

Figure 2-8   Unified Messaging property page in the Tools Options dialog box.

Outlook Inspector Window

New to Outlook 2007, form regions are the centerpiece for customizing the Inspector window and the Reading Pane. Form regions allow for an additive UI by introducing an adjoining form region that shows up on the bottom of the first tab of a custom or built-in Outlook Inspector window. Figure 2-9 illustrates an adjoining form region on an Outlook Inspector window. Separate regions provide more control. They can be either added to or replace one or all of the tabs of an existing form. If, for example, a Contact form needs to be completely customized, the add-in can introduce a new form region that is used whenever an *IPM.Contact.MyCustomer* item is displayed. The add-in can also register *IPM.Contact.MyCustomer* as the default form used when a user creates a new Contact in the MyCustomer folder. Outlook's built-in Inspectors can essentially be cloned due to the introduction of a number of additional controls for use in form regions. Controls that ship with Outlook 2007 include simple label, edit, list box, and combo box controls, as well as more complex controls to duplicate Outlook's date/time picker, category strip, and scheduling controls. All controls support data binding to built-in or custom properties. Unlike controls in previous versions of Outlook, both the control hosting surface and the controls placed on that surface use Windows themes.

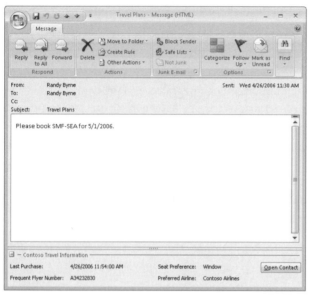

Figure 2-9   The Outlook Inspector Window with adjoining form region.

Although not an immediate component of the Outlook platform, Ribbon extensibility (known as RibbonX) allows you to add custom groups and commands to the Ribbon for a given Inspector type. Figure 2-10 illustrates a custom group added to the Ribbon on the Inspector for an appointment item. You can also repurpose built-in commands, hide built-in groups and commands, and insert your custom commands into built-in groups. RibbonX offers a superior control palette to Office command bars. You can leverage new picture galleries in your solution or utilize a host of controls that had no equivalent in the Office command bars object model.

Figure 2-10   Prepare for Meeting sample add-in customizes the Ribbon for an Outlook appointment item.

Custom task panes provide another customization option for the Outlook Inspector window. Whereas form regions target the extension and customization of the Outlook Inspector itself by typically displaying new user properties, custom task panes facilitate bringing related data into Outlook just like a built-in task pane such as the Research Pane. Figure 2-11 shows the Prepare for Meeting custom task pane in an Appointment Inspector window.

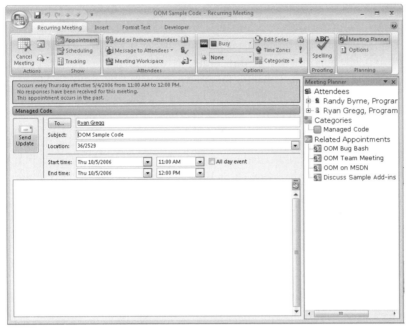

Figure 2-11   Custom task pane in an Appointment Inspector window.

Use Interface Integration Example

Let's look at an add-in with the goal of customizing Outlook Contacts as customers of a shoe store. Shoe Size and Customer ID are two additional properties that need to be tracked for each customer. The add-in would introduce an adjoining form region for Contacts containing these two properties and store the data as user properties in the backing Contact item. The add-in would rely on the Outlook built-in Contact Inspector to render the rest of the form. RibbonX would be used to add a new verb to the Ribbon, allowing the user to check store inventory for shoes in a corresponding size and then show the results in a custom task pane docked to the Outlook Contact Inspector. This "Check for shoes" verb could also be added to the item context menu so the clerk could enumerate the available shoes in a custom task pane docked to the Outlook Explorer window. The Views object model would be used to create a new custom List View for the Customer Contact folder including these two new properties. The add-in could also introduce a custom toolbar that shows up when this Customer Contact folder is selected and allows the store clerk to restrict the Customer list and only display customers with a specified shoe size.

InfoPath Forms

The following discussion concentrates on the use of InfoPath forms. Although not strictly a component of the Outlook platform, InfoPath e-mail forms do provide a compelling way to collect survey data from messaging recipients. This section helps you understand the purpose and design of InfoPath forms. You'll learn when InfoPath forms are appropriate in comparison to Outlook forms. Although there is no direct link between the Outlook object model and the InfoPath development environment, an InfoPath e-mail form uses aspects of the platform such as MessageClass and form-based rules that will help you understand the platform as a whole.

Microsoft Office InfoPath 2007 is a forms application that provides users with a way to gather structured information. Because InfoPath uses XML standards, data collected in InfoPath forms can be integrated directly into existing business processes such as databases, Web services, or workflows. Alternatively, collected data can be saved as individual files on collaborative sites such as a Microsoft Office SharePoint Server document library. Integration with other Office applications, such as Outlook 2007 and Microsoft Office Excel 2007, allows the forms experience to reach more users and provide easier data analysis. Use of InfoPath Forms Services even allows users to fill out InfoPath forms in the browser.

When to Use InfoPath Forms

InfoPath forms are best suited to collecting data by integrating into the e-mail functionality of Outlook. These forms can target data collection in an ad hoc manner, such as status reports and surveys, or be designed to integrate tightly with existing business processes and LOB applications using databases, Web services, and workflows. Forms designed to target people, calendar, or task information are better suited to using Outlook forms. Such forms can add new capabilities on top of Outlook, such as a customer relations form, or can extend certain information on existing Outlook forms, such as adding an employee number to a contact item.

An example of a common InfoPath form scenario is a weekly status report. Although certain information in the form could be derived from Outlook, the majority of the information pertains to business processes. In this case, an InfoPath status report form can be published to all team members as an InfoPath e-mail form. Each team member completes and submits the form, which is submitted back to the manager. Individual reports can be merged together to form a single report, which can be again submitted to the manager's manager, and so on.

Alternatively, the status report could be part of an LOB application. For example, if the status report tracks sales numbers, then data could be submitted directly to the back-end CRM system using InfoPath's built-in support for XML Web services. Subsequent workflow operations could send updated sales numbers, reports, and tasks to other members of the sales team.

Creating and Deploying InfoPath Forms

InfoPath forms are created using the design environment inside InfoPath 2007. The InfoPath design environment allows form designers to drag and drop controls to quickly build the form.

When a form designer creates a new InfoPath form, he or she actually creates what is known as a form template. A form template defines the data structure, appearance, and behavior of the forms that users fill out. Think of a form template as a blueprint—the starting point that enables users to create new forms that use and store data in the same way. Because a form template must be available before you can fill out a form, form templates must be deployed to a location where users can access them. Form templates are commonly deployed to locations on a company network, such as shared folders, Web servers, or libraries on Microsoft Windows SharePoint Services version 3 sites. Forms can also be deployed via installable packages (.msi or .js).

If a user has permission to access the location where a form template is stored, he or she can fill out a form based on that template by using InfoPath, a Web browser, a mobile device, or Outlook 2007. Whether a form is filled out by using InfoPath or one of the other methods depends on several factors, including how a form template is designed and the technology available when the form is deployed. For example, to fill out a form in Outlook 2007, the form must be published to a list of e-mail recipients.

Using InfoPath E-Mail Forms in Outlook 2007

You can use InfoPath forms in Outlook 2007 to help streamline the processes you use to collaborate and share data. That's because you can open, fill out, and submit InfoPath e-mail forms with Outlook 2007. If you receive an InfoPath e-mail form, you can reply to it, forward it, and store it just as you would with other items in Outlook 2007.

InfoPath e-mail forms also allow added analysis features. By storing collections of related e-mail forms in InfoPath Forms folders in Outlook 2007, you can organize and review data easily. For example, if you collect status report forms from your team, you can store the completed forms in an InfoPath Forms folder. Besides keeping all related forms in one place, you can also choose to show data from each form in columns in a custom view for that folder thanks to Outlook 2007 read-only promotion of a subset of XML properties for InfoPath forms. This allows for quickly grouping, filtering, and sorting data from multiple forms. The InfoPath form is stored as an XML attachment of an item with message class set to *IPM.InfoPath.FormID*, meaning the XML payload (data, schema) is opaque to Outlook. Outlook defers rendering, editing, and actions (for example, responding to these forms) to InfoPath. Because InfoPath is built on XML standards, information can be quickly merged into a single InfoPath form or exported for more detailed analysis in Excel.

APIs

The following section discusses the architecture and APIs that serve as the foundation for Outlook and any third-party address book, store, or transport provider used to extend Outlook.

Architecture

To understand the role of the different APIs, it's best to take a quick look at the overall Outlook architecture illustrated in Figure 2-12. Significant parts of Outlook are built on top of its own implementation of MAPI.

The three MAPI pillars used by Outlook are as follows:

- MAPI Address Book providers
- MAPI store providers
- Outlook Transport is partially built as a MAPI Transport infrastructure

Figure 2-12 provides a simplified perspective of the Outlook architecture. MAPI is the common foundation for both Outlook and CDO 1.2.1, which implement their own separate business logic. One goal for the Outlook 2007 platform enhancements was to unify these APIs all under the Outlook object model. This unification means that now all applications built on top of the Outlook object model will go through the very same business logic that Outlook relies on internally for its Personal Information Management (PIM) data types.

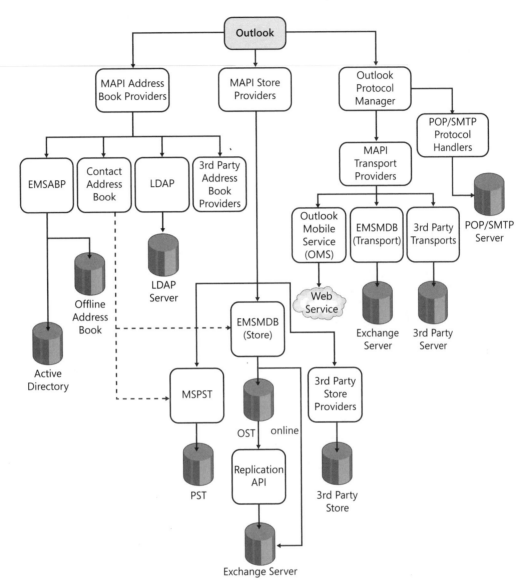

Figure 2-12   Outlook 2007 architecture.

Outlook Object Model

The object model constitutes the heart of the Outlook platform. The goal for the Outlook 2007 platform enhancements is to enable developers to build rich solutions by relying on the Outlook object model. The following areas provide the pillars of the Outlook 2007 platform.

Unification

The Outlook object model is the central piece of the Outlook platform. One of the prime goals of the Outlook 2007 platform enhancements was to unify existing APIs such as CDO, Exchange Client Extensions (ECEs), and a subset of Extended MAPI into the Outlook object model. As part of the unification, many events were added to the Outlook object model to accomplish parity with ECEs. The Outlook object model now provides equivalent objects for CDO's *AddressBook*, *InfoStores*, *Fields*, and *HiddenMessages* objects. The new *PropertyAccessor* and *Table* objects offer alternatives to the *IMAPIProp* and *IMAPITable* interfaces in Extended MAPI.

Unification means that the Outlook object model will be the sole API developers will rely on when writing a tightly integrated Outlook solution. Solution developers are no longer shut out by entry barriers caused by fragmented APIs. Unification reduces the cost of writing Outlook solutions because developers have to familiarize themselves with only one API. If possible, you should avoid relying on CDO and ECE when writing new Outlook solutions. These APIs are primarily supported to ensure compatibility with existing solutions. Application compatibility represents another important goal. The Outlook 2007 object model is compatible with previous Outlook versions; newly added functionality enhances the object model without removing or altering existing objects or methods. Unlike CDO, ECE, and MAPI, the Outlook object model is fully supported for managed code development.

Performance

Performance is another critical attribute for writing successful Outlook integrations. Our customers spend much time in Outlook and expect it to remain responsive at all times. The new *Table* object provides lightweight read-only row items for performant enumeration, sort, and search of Outlook data. Enumerating items with the *Table* object is approximately an order of magnitude faster than the enumeration of the *Items* collection without calling the *SetColumns* method. Making the Outlook object model performant is also essential to ensure that developers won't have to fall back to Extended MAPI or CDO when writing their solutions. The Outlook object model also allows developers to leverage the Outlook 2007 integrated Instant Search infrastructure by using the content indexer for prefix and substring matching for searching Outlook items and attachments.

Security and Trustworthiness

Outlook 2007 has improved the object model guard that warns the user when a program attempts to send e-mail messages or get address book information, making it easier for Outlook developers to write solutions that do not trigger Outlook security warnings. At the same time, Outlook remains secure and trustworthy out of the box and allows administrators control over which solutions should run in the enterprise. By default, all installed add-ins have trusted access to the Outlook object model, meaning they won't trigger any security prompts. If antivirus software is installed, these prompts also don't show up when an external application accesses the object model from a different process. IT administrators can define security preferences through the existing Outlook security form stored in Exchange Public Folders or using Windows Group Policies. Group Policy administration of Outlook security settings is new to Outlook 2007.

Innovation

Outlook 2007 introduces a wide range of new features that can be controlled programmatically:

- Sharing protocols (webcal://, feed://, stssync://)
- Calendar improvements (side-by-side, overlay, *ICal* sharing)
- Electronic business cards
- Task flagging
- Color categories
- Time zones for appointments
- Navigation groups and folder in the Navigation Pane

Besides providing the object model for these new features, Outlook 2007 programmatically exposes rules and views. The chapters in this book provide detailed information and sample code on using the objects that represent these features in your solution.

Form Regions

Outlook solutions can rely on Outlook custom forms with form pages or the new Outlook 2007 form regions to customize the forms associated with Outlook. The new separate and adjoining form regions in Outlook 2007 provide an additive or replacement UI to custom and built-in forms. Outlook 2007 form regions are the preferred form of customization technology because they have the following advantages over Outlook custom forms with form pagess:

- Form regions are supported in the Reading Pane.
- An additive UI can be provided through adjoining form regions. One item type can support multiple adjoining form regions from different add-ins.
- Outlook 2007 also introduces a full palette of Outlook form controls for form regions, allowing developers to clone the look and functionality of Outlook built-in forms:
  - Category Strip and Button
  - Contact Photo
  - Electronic Business Card Preview
  - Scheduling Free/Busy
  - InfoBar

❑   Date Picker, Time Picker, and TimeZone

❑   Sender Contact Photo

- Form regions and controls support Windows themes, meaning they have the same appearance as Outlook built-in forms.

- Form regions are installed locally as part of the Outlook solution and no longer rely on the Outlook forms cache. Form regions are no longer deployed through the Exchange Public Folder organizational forms library.

- The business logic for a form region is implemented in an add-in and no longer in VBScript behind an Outlook form. The form and add-in make up an Outlook solution that is installed and updated at the same time.

- Form region controls support additional events besides the *Click* event.

- Compared to forms in earlier versions of Outlook, form regions are easily localized without creating a separate form definition for each language supported for your solution.

- Form regions support auto-layout, allowing the developer to define placement and resizing rules at design time that Outlook obeys at run time when drawing the forms.

Form regions are based on earlier Outlook forms technology. You design form regions in the Outlook Forms Designer shown in Figure 2-13.

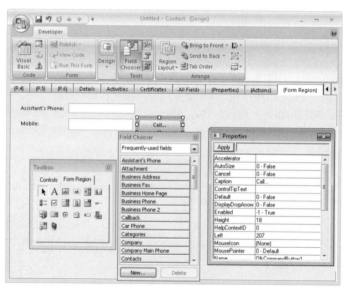

Figure 2-13   Designing form regions in the Outlook Forms Designer.

Form regions can provide an additional UI to built-in forms or completely customize the forms area, which involves the introduction of a custom item type with a customized message class such as *IPM.Contact.MyItem*.

The following list describes the available types of form regions for built-in or custom forms:

- **Adjoining**   An adjoining form region allows showing an additive UI on the bottom of the main tab of a built-in or custom form. Many custom form scenarios involve adding a small number of fields and don't require a change to the rest of the form. An adjoining form region addresses this scenario. More than one adjoining form region is supported per form and each form region is expandable and collapsible. They enable lightweight extension of forms without having to redesign the entire form and also facilitate more than one solution extending the Outlook form.

- **Separate**   A separate form region allows adding an additional tab to a built-in or custom form.

MAPI as a Platform Component

MAPI was introduced in the early 1990s as a specification for a messaging subsystem and all the components that interact with it. MAPI was created to provide a standardized application-level interface that allowed messaging components to communicate with widely incompatible messaging systems. The interfaces between components are not APIs, but rather COM interfaces. MAPI is not a library, meaning there are different implementations of MAPI developed by Microsoft and other ISVs.

In the context of this chapter, MAPI refers to the Outlook implementation of MAPI that gets installed as part of Outlook. The Outlook implementation of MAPI is a cornerstone of Outlook's own architecture and enables ISVs to tightly integrate into Outlook. MAPI differentiates between consumers (client applications) and producers (access providers) of messaging services. Outlook does both; it is a rich application offering a consistent user experience across different back ends and also ships a number of MAPI providers enabling connectivity to a wide range of back-end servers. The MAPI solution landscape for Outlook also covers both aspects: from MAPI clients such as antivirus software accessing e-mail messages to MAPI providers adding additional address book, store, and transport capabilities to Outlook. From a MAPI perspective, Outlook is a MAPI client with its own MAPI subsystem implementation and a number of MAPI service providers.

The main programming interface for MAPI is an object-based interface known as the MAPI programming interface. Based on COM, the MAPI programming interface is used by the MAPI subsystem and by messaging-based client applications and service providers written in unmanaged C or C++. Writing managed MAPI code is not supported.

What happened in the last decade since MAPI was introduced? The Exchange Client with separate Personal Address Book (PAB) and Calendaring (Schedule+) components became Outlook with tightly integrated Calendaring, Contacts, Tasks, Notes, and Journaling. Outlook as a PIM is implemented on top of the MAPI 1.0 specifications.

In other words, the additional functionality is not directly exposed through MAPI but through other APIs sitting on top of the MAPI infrastructure (Outlook object model, Outlook integration APIs, CDO). MAPI itself knows about e-mail items and address book entries but is agnostic to other PIM types like Contact, Appointment, Task, and Journal items. For MAPI these items are simply mail items with extra properties. MAPI does not know the meaning of these properties, nor is it aware of the business logic. Recurrence for an appointment item is a binary blob, and start time and end time are two individual properties not coupled with each other. This means MAPI APIs are great for mail and address book functionality and to some degree for also reading other PIM items, but MAPI is largely not suitable to create or update them, as it would be up to the caller to be intimately familiar with item properties and business logic.

The recommendation is to use higher-level APIs like the Outlook object model to create or modify Outlook items. Using the object model ensures that the items are created in a consistent manner so that the proper side effects are triggered. For example, when a meeting organizer changes the meeting time, an update needs to be sent to all attendees; simply changing the property would leave the meeting in an inconsistent state.

One significant difference between MAPI and the Outlook object model is that MAPI runs in the caller's process, whereas the Outlook object model runs on Outlook's foreground thread, making it very critical to write performant code. MAPI does not specify the protocol used between client and server. This architecture allowed Outlook to add support for the popular Internet protocols (POP, Simple Mail Transfer Protocol [SMTP], IMAP, Lightweight Directory Access Protocol [LDAP]) and formats (Multipurpose Internet Mail Extensions [MIME], iCal, vCard) that emerged in the mid-1990s on top of its MAPI-based infrastructure. This enabled ISVs to either rely on these standards to integrate with Outlook or use MAPI to implement a custom solution. Outlook has positioned itself as the premier offline client. One significant enhancement is cached Exchange built on top of a refined synchronization protocol when running against Exchange. ISVs can benefit from these capabilities by also making their solutions work seamlessly whether the user is online or offline.

Over time, the MAPI spooler was replaced in Outlook by the MAPI protocol handler, and the MAPI form servers infrastructure by Outlook forms and form regions in Outlook 2007. For additional information on development tasks using MAPI, please search for the MAPI Software Development Kit on MSDN.

MAPI Profiles

MAPI profiles allow storing different configurations for a specific user. A profile defines what stores, address books, and accounts, including preferences associated with them, should be loaded when Outlook is booted into this profile. MAPI profiles are stored in the registry under HKEY_CURRENT_USER (HKCU). For example, the user can have a profile configured with a business Exchange account and another profile with private POP and Hotmail accounts. MAPI profiles predate Windows user profiles. One scenario for which they were introduced was multiple users sharing the same computer, but with Windows supporting fast user switching this is no longer a driving factor. When multiple profiles are set up, Outlook is typically configured to prompt at boot to allow the user to select which profile Outlook should load. Currently most users have only one single profile and add all the services they need to this single profile. A large percentage of Outlook users keep Outlook running throughout the entire day; closing Outlook and restarting the application is often too cumbersome to get to the mail sent to a different account. Solutions integrating with Outlook should be able to handle multiple profiles, but the majority of users run with only one profile.

MAPI Service Providers

MAPI service providers come in three varieties: transport providers, message store providers, and Address Book providers. Providers are dynamic-link libararies (DLLs) that implement a specific pseudo-COM API, such as IMessageStore, and the underlying required interfaces, such as IMAPIProp. MAPI providers are registered in Mapisvc.inf so the Outlook implementation of MAPI can discover these new services and make them available under Account Settings on the Tools menu. The user can configure these services for each Outlook profile. Administrators can also preconfigure Outlook profiles by creating and deploying Outlook profile file (PRF) files.

 Note   Outlook 2007 no longer relies on Mapisvc.inf to discover its own built-in MAPI providers.

The Outlook 2007 Integration API Reference available on MSDN includes updated sample code for different MAPI providers.

MAPI Message Store Provider   A message store provider supports creating, submitting, and storing messages. Outlook relies on these MAPI messages to store Mail, Contacts, Appointments, and Tasks. Additionally, other Outlook components such as views or rules are stored in hidden messages. The stores associated with MAPI store providers show up in the Outlook folder list and in Outlook's Navigation Pane, shown in Figure 2-14.

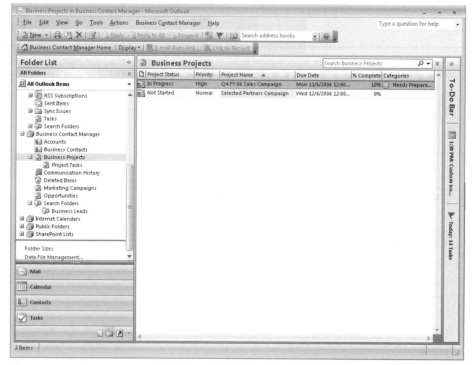

Figure 2-14   Business Contact Manager folder hierarchy implemented as MAPI store provider.

Outlook's Message Store Provider   Outlook 2007 ships with the following MAPI message store providers:

- Mspst32.dll contains the MAPI provider for Outlook Personal Folders files (.pst). Offline Folder files (.ost) are also .pst-based and therefore also rely on this provider.

- Emsmdb32.dll is the Electronic Messaging System Microsoft Database provider. EMSMDB implements both a transport and a message store, and as such is a dual provider. The transport provides the ability to submit messages to Exchange Server. This provider also enables reading and writing messages to an Exchange store.

- Bcmms32.dll implements the MAPI store provider for the Business Contact Manager functionality of Outlook 2007. This storage is SQL Express and contains Contact-based items (Account and Business Contacts), Task-based items (Opportunity, Business Projects, Project Task, Marketing Campaign) and Journal-based items (Business Notes and Phone logs) but no Mail, Calendar, and Notes items or folders.

Custom Message Store Provider   Writing a MAPI store provider allows a solution to integrate data from another source like a local database, server back end for messaging, CRM, or LOB application into Outlook. Writing a message store provider is complex and requires unmanaged C++ and MAPI development proficiency. Before you consider writing a custom message store provider, it's recommended that you also evaluate other alternatives. An alternative to a MAPI custom store provider is to cache the data in a .pst-based store by using the Outlook Replication API documented in the Outlook 2007 Integration API Reference.

MAPI Transport Providers   The purpose of a MAPI transport provider is to facilitate the transmission of messages over different protocols. An example would be sending e-mail messages over a Web service or using a separate transport to communicate with a back-end service. Microsoft LiveMeeting uses a separate transport provider to communicate with LiveMeeting server.

Outlook's MAPI Transport Providers   Outlook 2007 ships with the following MAPI transport providers:

- Omsxp.dll implements the Outlook Mobile Service (OMS) transport provider for sending Short Message Service (SMS) and Multimedia Messaging Service (MMS) text and multimedia messages through the Outlook Mobile Service Web service to a cellular carrier that routes these messages to mobile phones. The OMS provider delivers to recipients with e-mail type MOBILE. The OMS provider also converts the MAPI message to an XML payload as part of submitting the message.

- Emsmdb32.dll is the Electronic Messaging System Microsoft Database provider. As mentioned earlier, EMSMDB implements both a transport and a message store, and as such is a dual tightly-coupled provider.

> **Note**   Outlook does not internally rely on a physical MAPI transport provider for submitting messages through SMTP (POP or IMAP configurations), HTTP (Hotmail), or Exchange (cached Exchange mode).

Custom MAPI Transport Providers   Outlook Mobile Service offers the canonical example of such a provider. New to Outlook 2007, Outlook Mobile Service enables delivery to recipients with a custom e-mail type such as MYADRTYPE. When the user sends a message to such a recipient, MAPI will ask each registered transport if it knows how to deliver to recipients with type MYADRTYPE. Only the custom MAPI transport provider knows how to transport this item and therefore gets to deliver the message. The transport provider can serialize the MAPI message into another format such as XML or MIME during the submission process.

MAPI Address Book Provider   An Address Book provider enables recipient e-mail lookup and directory browsing. Recipients can be either single users or distribution lists. An Address Book provider introduces a new list of entries into the Address Book. As shown in Figure 2-15, the OMS address list shows up in the Address List drop-down box along with Global Address List and Outlook Address Book in the Outlook Address Book. This address list will also be searched during name resolution when a user clicks the Check Names button on the Ribbon or during automatic background name resolution.

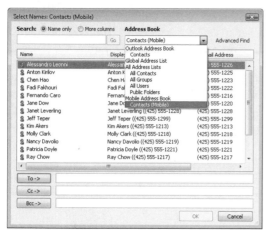

Figure 2-15   Outlook Mobile Service Address Book provider.

Outlook's MAPI Address Book Provider   Outlook 2007 ships four different MAPI Address Book providers:

- Emsabp32.Dll (Electronic Messaging System Address Book provider) implements the Address Book provider used when Exchange accounts are configured. It implements *IAddrBook* and supports both online mode against Microsoft Active Directory directory service via Name Service Provider Interface (NSPI) and offline mode against Offline Address Book (OAB), which is either downloaded from an Exchange Public Folder or with Background Intelligent Transfer Service (BITS) from a Web server.

- Contab32.dll contains the Outlook Address Book, also known as the Contact Address Book provider. This provider exposes Personal Contacts Personal Distribution Lists stored in Contacts folders in the Address Book.

- Emablt32.dll is the Outlook LDAP provider enabling Outlook to connect to a variety of different LDAP servers.

- Omsxp.dll implements the Outlook Mobile Service Address Book provider, which allows addressing of SMS messages. It's a sibling of the Outlook Address Book. It shows the mobile number instead of the e-mail address for Outlook Contacts. When the user picks a user from this provider, a recipient with type MOBILE is created. This provider is configured once the user adds an Outlook Mobile Service account to an Outlook profile.

Custom MAPI Address Book Provider   An Address Book provider allows integrating another source of contact information into Outlook, typically for addressing e-mail messages. Writing such a provider is difficult, so alternatives should be considered. If possible, rely on the built-in LDAP provider or, if the data set is relatively small, replicate data into an Outlook Contacts folder and rely on the Outlook Address Book provider.

Outlook 2007 Integration API Reference

The Microsoft Office Outlook 2007 Integration API Reference provides a set of complimentary APIs that allow developers to create a tight integration with Outlook. The Replication API is worth looking at especially for data integration scenarios. These APIs are version specific; they were introduced for Outlook 2003 (meaning they're not supported for versions before Outlook 2003) and were enhanced and slightly modified for Outlook 2007. Although it's a platform goal to maintain compatibility for these APIs, it should be assumed that solutions relying on these APIs need to be revised for every major version of Office. Because these APIs offer deep Outlook integration, they have to be adjusted when the internal Outlook architecture evolves. Fortunately, the transition from Outlook 2003 to Outlook 2007 involves very little work.

The components of the Outlook 2007 Integration API Reference are as follows:

- The Account Management API provides access to user account information and notifications of account changes.

- The Offline State API supports Outlook callbacks, notifying clients of changes in a user's connection state in Outlook—for example, from being online to being offline in Outlook.

- The Data Degradation Layer API enables data access to stores, items, and folders in either Unicode/Wide or ANSI (Windows System Codepage) for both Unicode and ANSI stores. For ANSI stores the data is downgraded (degraded) from Unicode to ANSI.

- The Free/Busy API provides free/busy status information about specific user accounts within a specific time range.

- The MAPI–MIME Conversion API supports conversion between MIME objects and MAPI messages.

- The Replication API supports synchronizing Outlook folders and Outlook items between a local store and a server. The most powerful API documented in this reference, it allows .ost-based offline storage and replication. A CRM solution can, for example, use these APIs to replicate data from the CRM database back end.

- The Store API provides miscellaneous store functionality.

Simple MAPI

Simple MAPI is a very limited library of only 12 functions. Originally, Simple MAPI was developed to enable the Microsoft Mail client to communicate with Microsoft Mail post offices. Extended MAPI completely supersedes the older version. These simple APIs continue to offer applications an easy way to offer e-mail capabilities by integrating into the default e-mail program. For example, Office applications or the Windows Shell use Simple MAPI for Send To functionality. This API is not recommended for further use.

Deemphasized and Phased-Out Components

Outlook solutions should no longer rely on the following technologies and APIs. Although most of these components continue to be supported in Outlook 2007, you should consider updating your code to use the new technologies introduced in this version of Outlook. If you are creating a new solution that only targets Outlook 2007, use of these deprecated technologies is not recommended.

Collaboration Data Objects 1.2.1

CDO 1.2.1 is an API that sits on top of MAPI for creating, sending, and receiving e-mail as well as calendaring and public folder applications. Thanks to the unification effort for Outlook 2007, all critical CDO functionality is now incorporated in the Outlook 2007 object model. If you use CDO, you should consider removing your solution's dependency on CDO. CDO used to be an optionally installed component, but with Office 2007 it's only available as a Web download. Existing versions of CDO will be removed by Office 2007 Setup.

Exchange Client Extensions

As the name indicates, this extensibility technology was introduced for the Microsoft Exchange 4.0 client to customize menus and toolbars, preprocess outgoing and incoming messages, add property sheets, and provide MAPI forms integration. Outlook, the successor of the Exchange client, later added support for ECEs. Outlook 2007 added a large number of new events to the Outlook object model, enabling developers to phase out their code relying on ECEs. ECEs also enable the customization of command bars for Outlook items; these customizations manifest themselves on the Add-ins tab of the Ribbon.

Outlook Custom Forms with Form Pages

Outlook 2007 continues to support Outlook custom forms with form pages, except for one-off form definitions, which were deprecated for security and reliability reasons. In one-off forms, the form is embedded in the message and contains definitions for custom properties and VBScript. One-off forms no longer run script and do not propagate custom properties to a recipient. A one-off form will render in a built-in form instead of the custom form definition stored in the form. Although Outlook custom forms with form pages continue to be supported in Outlook 2007, solutions that target Outlook 2007 should use form regions in place of these legacy forms.

MAPI Form Server (IMAPIForm)

MAPI Form Server is a pluggable forms infrastructure introduced with MAPI 1.0. Outlook 2007 continues to support this technology, but it's expected to be deprecated in a future Office release.

Exchange Forms Designer Forms

Exchange Forms Designer forms were included with Exchange 4.0 and 5.0 and were designed for the pre-Outlook Exchange client. Outlook 97 also included the Exchange Forms Designer. This form development package has its own design environment based on 16-bit Microsoft Visual Basic 4.0. Outlook has supported using these forms, but since Outlook 2002 you must download the necessary runtime files for these forms to work. Although they are considered obsolete, Outlook 2007 continues to support these forms if you have the runtime installed.

Electronic Forms Designer (Microsoft Mail 3.0) Forms

Electronic Forms Designer forms are based on 16-bit Microsoft Mail 3.0 technology. These forms work in Outlook 97 through Outlook 2002 and have a dependency on the Microsoft Mail 3.0 client extension. Outlook 2003 and Outlook 2007 do not include this extension and therefore Electronic Forms Designer forms are not supported in Outlook 2003 and later versions.

Development Tools

The following section discusses development tools that you can use to create an Outlook solution. The development tool that you select to create your solution depends in part on your scenario and also on the resources within your company. If you have a large number of developers who have moved from Microsoft Visual Basic 6.0 to Microsoft Visual Basic .NET, then Visual Basic will be a natural choice for your development tool. If you have trained C# developers, then C# would be your preference. Although the sample code in this book has been written using C#, the code is also provided online in Visual Basic versions. The Microsoft Visual Basic .NET version of the sample code is not listed directly in the book because of space considerations rather than as a matter of preference. Visual Basic .NET sample code is available on the Web site for this book.

Visual Basic for Applications

Microsoft Visual Basic for Applications (VBA) is the development environment that ships with Outlook 2007. However, unlike other Office applications like Word and Excel, Outlook VBA is a prototyping tool only. Although Outlook VBA can be used to create personal productivity macros, it is not suitable for the development and deployment of a professional solution. The limitations of Outlook VBA are as follows:

- The Outlook VBA project is contained in a single file named VBAProject.otm. Only one Outlook VBA project can be deployed in a given user profile on a machine. This architecture means that only one VBAProject.otm can be deployed for a user. If another solution overwrites the VBAProject.otm file, the customizations in the original file are lost.

- Unlike other Office applications, Outlook VBA cannot be attached to a document so that customization travels with the document or template.

- Custom task panes are not supported in Outlook VBA.

- You cannot customize the Ribbon using Outlook VBA. Only command bars can be customized in Outlook VBA.

- You cannot record macros in Outlook VBA.

Visual Studio Tools for Office

Microsoft Visual Studio 2005 Tools for the 2007 Microsoft Office System (VSTO) is a recommended development environment for Outlook add-ins. As shown in Figure 2-16, VSTO provides an abundance of benefits to the Outlook developer. Due to scheduling considerations, VSTO is not used for the sample add-ins in this book. The sample add-ins use a COM shim architecture and do not utilize VSTO features. Both MSDN and third-party publications will provide you with plenty of information to get you started using VSTO. A short list of VSTO benefits includes the following:

- Use of the Common Language Runtime (CLR) 2.0. The CLR offers type safety, memory management and garbage collection, and a host of useful classes and features that are well documented in the extensive literature available on MSDN.

- A professional development environment with integrated debugger.

- Templates that provide the framework for creating a managed Outlook add-in using either C# or Visual Basic .NET.

- AppDomain isolation. For an Outlook developer, AppDomain isolation prevents an add-in from crashing due to an unhandled exception in another add-in. It also prevents an add-in from crashing other add-ins in a shared AppDomain.

- Support for new 2007 Office system extensibility features, including:
    - ❑ Outlook form regions
    - ❑ RibbonX
    - ❑ Custom task panes

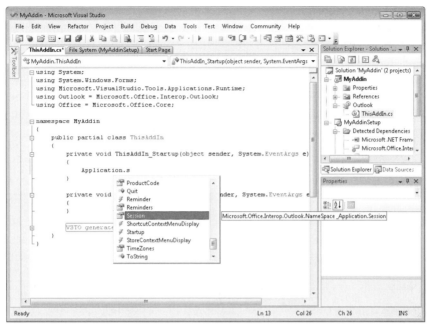

Figure 2-16   Using VSTO to develop an add-in for Outlook 2007.

Managed Versus Native Code

Microsoft Visual Studio represents the strategic development platform for Microsoft, and the recommendation of Visual Studio 2005 or VSTO for Outlook add-in development follows that strategic direction. If your team is trained in either Visual Basic .NET or C#, they will be able to develop professional Outlook solutions using the guidance provided in this book. However, you might wonder if managed code is suitable for all Outlook solutions. The answer, of course, depends on your scenario. If your solution requires development of any of the following platform components, you should consider using a native code development environment such as Microsoft C++:

- Transport, Address Book, or custom store providers

- Synchronization using Replication API

- Extended MAPI functionality not available in the Outlook 2007 object model

Another indication that you should consider native code rather than managed code is performance. Although Outlook 2007 has targeted performance improvements over previous versions, you should understand that managed code requires the Outlook Primary Interop Assemblies (PIAs) to provide the Interop layer between .NET Framework assemblies and the COM-based Outlook object model. This Interop layer does add a performance consideration to using managed code. Although this performance layer is not an obstacle for the vast majority of Outlook solutions, it is a gating factor if your solution repeatedly enumerates large numbers of Outlook items, for example. Remember that the Outlook object model operates on the foreground thread, so operations that poll the Outlook data store using the object model and the foreground thread can degrade the performance of Outlook as a whole. When you have to satisfy stringent performance requirements, you should consider a native development environment such as C++. If you must write native code, you should also weigh the additional cost in time and resources required by C++ development against going with a solution built using C# or Visual Basic .NET. The final decision is yours, and the choice of development tool is dictated first by your scenario, and second by your resources and budget.

Add-In Model

The primary customization technology for the Outlook 2007 platform is a COM add-in. Of course, you can create a managed add-in using VSTO or Visual Studio 2005. Managed add-ins use an Interop layer to connect to the Outlook host application, but they still use the basic COM add-in technology. In Outlook 2007, add-ins have achieved new prominence because an add-in is the only way that you can create Outlook 2007 form regions, Ribbon customizations for an Outlook Inspector, and Office custom task panes. Add-ins are also the preferred method for creating event listeners that implement the business logic of your solution. Your add-in can leverage the improved event model in Outlook 2007 to determine when an item is being saved or sent, an attachment is being added or removed from an item, an item is being deleted from a folder, or a custom or built-in item property is being changed. And those are just a few of the event listeners that are possible in Outlook.

Outlook has supported COM add-ins since Microsoft Office 2000, which is when the COM add-in architecture was first introduced in Office. The core architecture involved in creating a COM add-in has not changed in terms of how the Office application communicates with COM add-ins. Office 2007 continues to use the same architecture that was first implemented in Office 2000.

Overall, unless there is a specific reason that dictates otherwise, COM add-ins are the recommended way for developers to create a custom solution that integrates with Outlook. Of course, there are many factors to take into account when designing a custom solution, but key benefits of using a COM add-in in Outlook include the following:

- COM add-ins are the supported way to create an Outlook-based solution that can be deployed (as opposed to Outlook VBA). Deployment can occur through a standard Windows installer (.msi) or through a push technology such as Microsoft Systems Management Server.

- COM add-ins allow a solution to be trusted so that Object Model Guard security prompts are not generated when the object model is used to access the address book or recipient information, or to programmatically send e-mail. In Outlook 2007, all add-ins are trusted by default from the perspective of the Outlook object model guard. In locked-down environments, IT administrators can use the Outlook security form in Exchange public folders or use group policy objects to control a list of trusted add-ins.

■ Even if you are developing a standalone application, you could also develop a proxy add-in and have the standalone program interact with the COM add-in by using public methods and properties exposed by the add-in. In this way, any functionality that would typically generate a security prompt can be done from within the add-in. Outlook 2007 also provides the ability to turn off security prompts when antivirus software is installed and current. This ability can also be controlled via group policy.

■ COM add-ins are the replacement technology for ECEs. Previous versions of the Outlook object model did not provide some key functionality that you could achieve in a client extension, so many developers still developed extensions in C++ because they provided more options. However, due to the many object model improvements in Outlook 2007, the COM add-in architecture is even more viable for many developers.

There are some scenarios where an add-in is not recommended for an Outlook solution. It's worthwhile to point these out so that you don't attempt to create a solution with the wrong technology. Add-ins and the Outlook object model are not recommended if you need to create any of the following components:-

■ **Windows service application**   Because the Outlook object model can display UI elements and operates on Outlook's foreground thread, the Outlook object model and add-in technology are not suitable for use in a Windows service application. For a service application, you can use CDO or Extended MAPI. Because CDO is being deprecated in this release, it is suggested that you use Extended MAPI for a Windows service application.

■ **Web application**   The Outlook object model is not suitable for use in a Web application. Exchange 2007 offers Web services for use in a Web application. Previous versions of Exchange offer the Web Distributed Authoring and Versioning (WebDAV) protocol or the Exchange OLE DB (ExOLEDB) provider for use in Web applications.

Summary

This chapter has taken you on a tour of the Outlook platform. Along the way, you've learned how some solutions that ship with the 2007 Office system have taken advantage of the Outlook 2007 object model and form regions. In brief, this chapter has described the pillars of the Outlook 2007 platform enhancements. You've also been exposed to how Outlook relies on MAPI as the cornerstone of its internal architecture. During this discussion, prescriptive guidance has been provided to offer suggestions about how to build solutions on top of Outlook. Although prescriptive guidance must always be tied to practical scenarios, it's hoped that you will follow these guidelines to make your solution integrate seamlessly with Outlook 2007.

Part II
Quick Guide to Building Solutions

Chapter 3
Writing Your First Outlook Add-in Using Visual Basic .NET

The goal of this chapter is to walk you through the process of creating a Microsoft Visual Basic add-in for Microsoft Office Outlook 2007. Once you've created and built the project, you will be able to use the add-in in your everyday activities. Unlike the C# sample code in the rest of this book, this code focuses on Visual Basic development experience. Although the steps you need to follow in Visual Basic are not that different from the steps required for Visual C#, it will be helpful to the Visual Basic developer to cover all the steps in detail necessary to create, build, and deploy an Outlook 2007 add-in. If you are interested in obtaining practical results in a very short time, this chapter is for you.

When you have finished this chapter, you will have:

- Used the Outlook add-in templates supplied with this book.

- Created a new Outlook add-in project for Visual Basic.

- Written code to add a custom pop-up menu to the context menu for a mail item.

- Built a Component Object Model (COM) shim project so that the add-in runs in a separate application domain.

- Built a setup project so that you can deploy the Instant Search add-in.

Microsoft Visual Studio 2005 continues to provide built-in support for developing Office add-ins through the Shared add-in template, but this template is missing some key blocks of code that are useful for writing Outlook 2007 COM add-ins in managed code. Although using Microsoft Visual Studio 2005 Tools for the 2007 Microsoft Office System (VSTO) offers another preferred development approach, it is not covered in this chapter. You can easily adapt the code in this chapter to work with VSTO. For this example, you'll learn how to write an add-in based on the Outlook add-in template for Visual Basic supplied on the Web site that contains sample code for this book.

Introducing the Instant Search Add-In

The Instant Search add-in places an Instant Search command at the bottom of an item's context menu, as shown in Figure 3-1. Instant Search is a pop-up command bar control that lets the user take advantage of Outlook's Instant Search feature and display messages from the sender sent last week, this week, last month, this month, or all messages. The search results are displayed in a separate Explorer window, shown in Figure 3-2.

Figure 3-1   Instant Search pop-up menu.

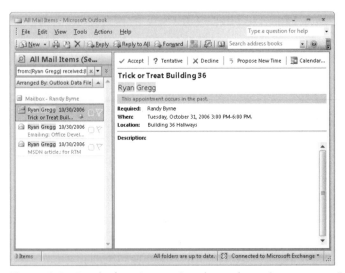

Figure 3-2   Results from Instant Search are shown in a separate Explorer window.

Install the Outlook Add-in Templates

To get you started writing Outlook add-ins, templates for both Visual Basic and Visual C# are provided on the Web site that contains the sample code for this book. Before you can create the Instant Search add-in, you must install the Outlook Add-in Templates.

To install the Outlook Add-in Templates, follow these steps:

1. Download the Outlook Add-in Template's installation package from this book's companion Web site.

2. Double-click OutlookAddinTemplates.msi to begin the installation process.

3. In the Microsoft Office Outlook 2007 Add-in Templates Setup dialog box, click Next.

4. After reviewing the End-User License Agreement, select I Agree to accept the agreement, and then click Next.

5. Click Next to confirm that you wish to start the installation.

6. If you are installing the templates on Microsoft Windows Vista, you will see the User Account Control dialog box after installation begins. Click Allow to indicate that you trust the setup package for the Outlook Add-in templates.

7. After the installation has completed, click Close to dismiss the Setup Wizard dialog box.

Creating the Instant Search Add-In

To create a Visual Studio solution for the Instant Search add-in, follow these steps:

1. Open Visual Studio 2005, and press Ctrl+Shift+N to display the New Project dialog box.

2. In the Project Types list, click the Other Project Types node.

3. Under Visual Studio Installed Templates, click Blank Solution.

4. In the Name text box, type **InstantSearchVB** (as shown in Figure 3-3), and then click OK to create the solution.

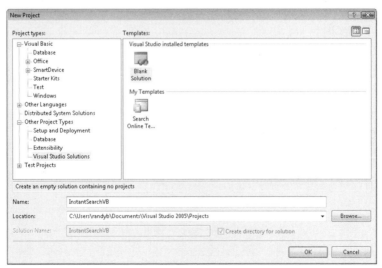

Figure 3-3   Visual Studio 2005 New Project dialog box for InstantSearchVB solution.

Now that the custom templates are installed and you've created a Visual Studio solution to contain your add-in, shim, and setup projects, proceed by creating an add-in project using the template.

To create a Visual Studio add-in project using the add-in template, follow these steps:

1. From the File menu, select the Add pop-up menu, and then select New Project to add a new project to the InstantSearchVB solution.

2. In the Project Types list, click the Visual Basic node.

3. In the Templates list, from the My Templates group, select Office Outlook 2007 Visual Basic Add-In.

4. In the Name text box, type **InstantSearchAddinVB**, as shown in Figure 3-4, and then click OK.

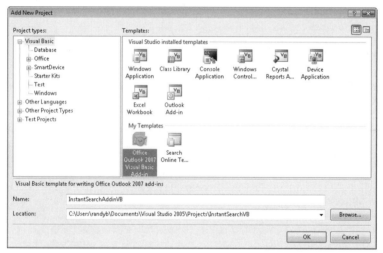

Figure 3-4   Visual Studio 2005 New Project dialog box for InstantSearchAddinVB project.

5. You will then see the InstantSearchAddinVB project in the Visual Studio editor, shown in Figure 3-5.

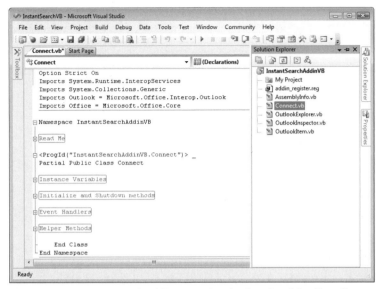

Figure 3-5   InstantSearchAddinVB project in the Visual Studio editor.

Writing Code

The next step in completing the Instant Search add-in is to write code in the project. Before you start to write code, you should understand that the template is a generic project aimed at typical Outlook add-in scenarios. The template creates code that allows you to track multiple instances of Inspector or Explorer windows. For the Instant Search add-in, you don't need to track Inspector or Explorer windows, so you will comment out the existing code in the *InitializeAddin* and *ShutdownAddin* methods. At this point, you should follow this procedure to remove the code in these methods:

1. Locate the *InitializeAddin* and *ShutdownAddin* methods, shown in Figure 3-6, in the *Connect* class. You might need to expand the "Initialize and Shutdown methods" region before you can see the *InitializeAddin* and *ShutdownAddin* methods.

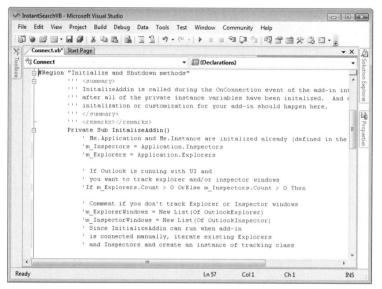

Figure 3-6   The Initialize and Shutdown methods region in the *Connect* class.

2. Comment out all the code in the *InitializeAddin* method.

3. Comment out all the code in the *ShutdownAddin* method.

The *InitializeAddin* Method

The *InitializeAddin* method runs when your add-in is loaded by the host application, which in this case is Outlook 2007. If you were to examine the *Connect.Designer.vb* class, *InitializeAddin* gets called in the *OnConnection* method of the add-in. *OnConnection* is a method called by Office add-ins that must implement the *IDTExtensibility2* interface. *Connect.Designer.vb* abstracts the details of the *IDTExtensiblity2* interface and provides you with two methods, *InitializeAddin* and *ShutdownAddin*, which correspond to Startup and Shutdown events. Without getting into too many details about the *IDTExtensibility2* interface, *InitializeAddin* is called when the add-in is loaded by the host application at boot time or when the add-in is loaded through a user action such as connecting the add-in manually via the COM Add-Ins dialog box. You use *InitializeAddin* and *ShutdownAddin* to create and destroy class-level instance variables that are required for your add-in and to wire up event handlers required by your solution. In the case of the InstantSearchAddinVB project, no code is required in the *InitializeAddin* or *ShutdownAddin* methods.

Note   To examine *Connect.Designer.vb* in the Solution Explorer, you need to show all files in the project. To display the Solution Explorer, press Ctrl+R. To show all files, select the Project menu in Visual Studio, and then select Show All Files.

Turn *Option Strict* On

The *Option Strict* directive is not turned on by default in the Outlook Visual Basic template. However, it is strongly recommended that you navigate to the top of the *Connect* class and type **Option Strict On**. *Option Strict On* involves more work on your part because you must cast Outlook members that return a type of *Object* to the correct type. Because *Option Strict On* provides strong typing, prevents unintended type conversions with data loss, disallows late binding, and improves performance, you should add this directive to the *Connect* class.

Adding Instance Variables

The next step is to create class-level instance variables in the *Connect* class to represent command bar controls on the context menu for an item. Context menus in Outlook use the familiar Office command bars object model that has been present in several versions of Office. Context menu commands do not use the new Ribbon extensibility model.

To add instance variables to the *Connect* class, follow these steps:

1. Display the Solution Explorer by pressing Ctrl+R.

2. Double-click Connect.vb in the Solution Explorer to display the Code Editor for the *Connect* class.

3. Locate the instance variables region shown in Figure 3-7 in Connect.vb. You might need to expand the "Instance Variables" region before you can see the *InitializeAddin* method.

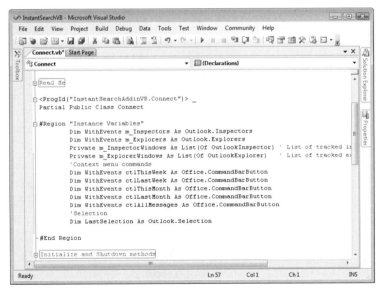

Figure 3-7 Class-level instance variables in the *Connect* class.

4. Type the following code in the instance variables region in the *Connect* class:

```
'Context menu commands
Dim WithEvents ctlThisWeek As Office.CommandBarButton
Dim WithEvents ctlLastWeek As Office.CommandBarButton
Dim WithEvents ctlThisMonth As Office.CommandBarButton
Dim WithEvents ctlLastMonth As Office.CommandBarButton
Dim WithEvents ctlAllMessages As Office.CommandBarButton
'Selection
Dim LastSelection As Outlook.Selection
```

Hooking Up Events in Visual Basic

If you use the *WithEvents* keyword when you declare an event-aware instance variable, Visual Studio does all the work for you to hook up the event. Because the *Application* instance variable that represents the *Outlook.Application* object has been declared *WithEvents* in *Connect.Designer.vb*, all the application-level events are available in the right drop-down list in the Visual Studio Code Editor. All you have to do is select the event and then write code in the event handler. The relevant events for item context menus are the *ItemContextMenuDisplay* and *ContextMenuClose* events on the *Application* object.

ItemContextMenuDisplay Event

The *ItemContextMenuDisplay* event occurs before a context menu for either a single high-lighted Outlook item or for one or more selected Outlook items is to be displayed, allowing the *CommandBar* object representing the context menu to be customized by an add-in. For the Instant Search add-in, the Instant Search pop-up on the context menu is displayed only when a single mail item is selected. When more than one mail item is selected or when the single selected item is not a mail item, the Instant Search pop-up on the context menu does not appear. Because the *Application* instance variable that represents the *Outlook.Application* object in the *Connect* class is declared using *WithEvents*, the *Application* variable appears in the left drop-down list of the Code Editor for the *Connect* class. When you select the *Application* object in the left drop-down list and then select the correct event name in the right drop-down list, the event procedure is stubbed out for you.

To write code for the *ItemContextMenuDisplay* event, follow these steps:

1. In the *Connect* class Code Editor, select the *Application* object in the left drop-down list.

2. Select the *ItemContextMenuDisplay* event in the right drop-down list.

3. Write the following code in the *ItemContextMenuDisplay* event handler:

```
Private Sub Application_ItemContextMenuDisplay( _
ByVal CommandBar As Microsoft.Office.Core.CommandBar, _
ByVal Selection As Microsoft.Office.Interop.Outlook.Selection) _
Handles Application.ItemContextMenuDisplay
    Dim ctlInstantSearch As Office.CommandBarPopup
    Try
```

```vb
        If Selection.Count = 0 Then
            Exit Sub
        End If
        'Determine selection and only modify context menu
        'for MailItem and Selection.Count = 1
        'IsInstantSearchEnabled must also return True
        Dim oItem As New OutlookItem(Selection.Item(1))
        If oItem.Class = Outlook.OlObjectClass.olMail _
        AndAlso Selection.Count = 1 _
        AndAlso oItem.Parent.Store.IsInstantSearchEnabled Then
            ctlInstantSearch = CType(CommandBar.FindControl( _
            Tag:="InstantSearchAddinVB.ctlInstantSearch"), _
            Office.CommandBarPopup)
            If ctlInstantSearch Is Nothing Then
                ctlInstantSearch = CType(CommandBar.Controls.Add _
                (Type:=Office.MsoControlType.msoControlPopup, _
                Parameter:="InstantSearchAddinVB.ctlInstantSearch"), _
                Office.CommandBarPopup)
                With ctlInstantSearch
                    .Caption = "Instant Search"
                    .Tag = "InstantSearchAddinVB.ctlInstantSearch"
                    .BeginGroup = True
                End With
                LastSelection = Selection
                'Add controls to popup
                ctlThisWeek = CType(ctlInstantSearch.CommandBar.Controls _
                .Add(Office.MsoControlType.msoControlButton), _
                Office.CommandBarButton)
                ctlThisWeek.Caption = "Received This Week..."
                ctlThisMonth = CType(ctlInstantSearch.CommandBar.Controls _
                .Add(Office.MsoControlType.msoControlButton), _
                Office.CommandBarButton)
                ctlThisMonth.Caption = "Received This Month..."
                ctlLastWeek = CType(ctlInstantSearch.CommandBar.Controls _
                .Add(Office.MsoControlType.msoControlButton), _
                Office.CommandBarButton)
                ctlLastWeek.Caption = "Received Last Week..."
                ctlLastMonth = CType(ctlInstantSearch.CommandBar.Controls _
                .Add(Office.MsoControlType.msoControlButton), _
                Office.CommandBarButton)
                ctlLastMonth.Caption = "Received Last Month..."
                ctlAllMessages = CType(ctlInstantSearch.CommandBar.Controls _
                .Add(Office.MsoControlType.msoControlButton), _
                Office.CommandBarButton)
                ctlAllMessages.Caption = "All Messages Received..."
            End If
        End If
    Catch ex As Exception
        Debug.WriteLine(ex.Message)
    End Try
End Sub
```

This event procedure looks at the *Selection* object passed in the event. If *Selection.Count* is zero, then the code exits from the event procedure and no command bar pop-up is created. The *Selection* collection, like other collection objects in the Outlook object model, is one-based and the indexer for the *Selection* object returns a type *Object*. The *OutlookItem* class uses reflection to determine the common properties of an Outlook item and allows you to determine the underlying type of the item *Object*. For complete details on the *OutlookItem* class, see the section "The *OutlookItem* Helper Class" in Chapter 6, "Accessing Outlook Data."

If *Selection.Count* is one and the item returned by the indexer of the *Selection* object represents a *MailItem* and the *IsInstantSearchEnabled* property returns *True* on the *Store* object that contains the item, then the Office *CommandBar* object model is used to create a pop-up menu represented by the instance variable *ctlInstantSearch. ctlInstantSearch* represents an *Office.CommandBarPopup* object. To add the pop-up menu to the item context menu, you call the *Add* method on the *CommandBar* object passed in the *ItemContextMenuDisplay* event. Once the pop-up menu has been added, you then set the *Caption* and *Tag* properties for *ctlInstantSearch*. The *Caption* property is set to "Instant Search" and the *Tag* property is set to the *ProgID* of the Instant Search add-in, "InstantSearchAddinVB.Connect."

Once you have instantiated the *CommandBarPopup* object that represents the Instant Search pop-up menu, you then add additional *CommandBarControl* objects that represent additional menu items on the pop-up menu. Each of the menu items corresponds to the following time intervals for messages received:

- This Week
- Last Week
- This Month
- Last Month
- All Messages

Note that the instance variables *ctlThisWeek, ctlLastWeek, ctlThisMonth, ctlLastMonth*, and *ctlAllMessages* are also declared using *WithEvents*. You'll write code for the *Click* event for these instance variables later in the chapter.

ContextMenuClose Event

The *ContextMenuClose* event occurs just after a context menu is closed so that add-ins can dispose of any object references that have been obtained from other context menu events such as *ItemContextMenuDisplay*. In the case of the Instant Search add-in, the *LastSelection* object is set to *Nothing*.

To write code for the *ContextMenuClose* event, follow these steps:

1. In the *Connect* class Code Editor, select the *Application* object in the left drop-down list.

2. Select the *ContextMenuClose* event in the right drop-down list.

3. Write the following code in the *ContextMenuClose* event handler:

```
Private Sub Application_ContextMenuClose( _
ByVal ContextMenu As Microsoft.Office.Interop.Outlook.OlContextMenu) _
    Handles Application.ContextMenuClose
    LastSelection = Nothing
End Sub
```

The *DisplayInstantSearchExplorer* Method

To reduce the amount of code you need to write, the *DisplayInstantSearchExplorer* method is called from the *Click* event procedures for the submenu controls on the Instant Search pop-up menu. The *DisplayInstantSearchExplorer* method displays the results of an Instant Search query in a new Explorer window by calling the *Search* method on the *Explorer* object. The *Search* method is new to Outlook 2007 and allows you to use the Advanced Query Syntax of Microsoft Windows Desktop Search to return results. For additional details on Advanced Query Syntax, see Chapter 11, "Searching Outlook Data." This method takes three arguments, shown in Table 3-1.

Table 3-1   Parameters for the *DisplayInstantSearchExplorer* Method

Parameter	Required	Type	Description
Folder	Yes	Outlook.Folder	Represents the *Folder* object that contains the item on which the context menu is being displayed.
InstantSearch	Yes	String	A *String* that contains a valid Advanced Query Syntax query.
ShowToDoBar	Yes	Boolean	If *ShowToDoBar* equals *True*, displays the To-Do Bar in the new Explorer window. If *False*, hides the To-Do Bar.

To write code for the *DisplayInstantSearchExplorer* method, follow these steps:

1. In the *Connect* class Code Editor, click at the bottom of the *Connect* class before the *End Class* statement.

2. Write the following code in the *DisplayInstantSearchExplorer* method:

```
Private Sub DisplayInstantSearchExplorer( _
    ByVal Folder As Outlook.Folder, _
    ByVal InstantSearch As String, _
    ByVal ShowToDoBar As Boolean)
    Dim exp As Outlook.Explorer = _
    Application.Explorers.Add(Folder, _
    Outlook.OlFolderDisplayMode.olFolderDisplayNoNavigation)
    'Call Explorer.Search to automate Instant Search
    exp.Search(InstantSearch, _
    Outlook.OlSearchScope.olSearchScopeAllFolders)
    exp.Display()
    exp.ShowPane(Outlook.OlPane.olToDoBar, ShowToDoBar)
End Sub
```

Writing Code for Submenu *Click* Events

Next you write code for the submenu *Click* events on the five menu items that exist on the Instant Search pop-up menu. When the user clicks any one of the submenu items, the *Click* event for the *Office.CommandBarButton* is called. The code in the *Click* event simply calls the *DisplayInstantSearchFolder* method with the correct parameters to display an Explorer window that shows the results of the search. Once you've completed this task, you'll be ready to build the Instant Search add-in.

To write code for submenu *Click* events, follow these steps:

1. In the *Connect* class Code Editor, select the *ctlThisWeek* object in the left drop-down list.

2. Select the *Click* event in the right drop-down list.

3. Write the code shown in the *ctlThisWeek_Click* event handler.

4. Repeat the preceding sequence for *ctlLastWeek, ctlThisMonth, ctlLastMonth,* and *ctlAllMessages* objects.

```
Private Sub ctlThisWeek_Click( _
ByVal Ctrl As Microsoft.Office.Core.CommandBarButton, _
ByRef CancelDefault As Boolean) Handles ctlThisWeek.Click
    If LastSelection.Count = 1 Then
        Dim oMail As Outlook.MailItem = _
        CType(LastSelection.Item(1), Outlook.MailItem)
        Dim fromAddress As String = oMail.SenderName
        Dim currentFolder As Outlook.Folder _
        = CType(oMail.Parent, Outlook.Folder)
        Dim SearchQuery As String = "from:(" & fromAddress & ")" _
        & " received:(this week)"
        DisplayInstantSearchExplorer(currentFolder, SearchQuery, False)
    End If
End Sub


Private Sub ctlThisMonth_Click( _
ByVal Ctrl As Microsoft.Office.Core.CommandBarButton, _
ByRef CancelDefault As Boolean) Handles ctlThisMonth.Click
    If LastSelection.Count = 1 Then
        If LastSelection.Count = 1 Then
            Dim oMail As Outlook.MailItem = _
            CType(LastSelection.Item(1), Outlook.MailItem)
            Dim fromAddress As String = oMail.SenderName
            Dim currentFolder As Outlook.Folder _
            = CType(oMail.Parent, Outlook.Folder)
            Dim SearchQuery As String = "from:(" & fromAddress & ")" _
            & " received:(this month)"
            DisplayInstantSearchExplorer(currentFolder, SearchQuery, False)
        End If
    End If
End Sub


Private Sub ctlLastWeek_Click( _
ByVal Ctrl As Microsoft.Office.Core.CommandBarButton, _
```

```vb
ByRef CancelDefault As Boolean) Handles ctlLastWeek.Click
    If LastSelection.Count = 1 Then
        Dim oMail As Outlook.MailItem = _
        CType(LastSelection.Item(1), Outlook.MailItem)
        Dim fromAddress As String = oMail.SenderName
        Dim currentFolder As Outlook.Folder _
        = CType(oMail.Parent, Outlook.Folder)
        Dim SearchQuery As String = "from:(" & fromAddress & ")" _
        & " received:(last week)"
        DisplayInstantSearchExplorer(currentFolder, SearchQuery, False)
    End If
End Sub

Private Sub ctlLastMonth_Click( _
ByVal Ctrl As Microsoft.Office.Core.CommandBarButton, _
ByRef CancelDefault As Boolean) Handles ctlLastMonth.Click
    If LastSelection.Count = 1 Then
        Dim oMail As Outlook.MailItem = _
        CType(LastSelection.Item(1), Outlook.MailItem)
        Dim fromAddress As String = oMail.SenderName
        Dim currentFolder As Outlook.Folder _
        = CType(oMail.Parent, Outlook.Folder)
        Dim SearchQuery As String = "from:(" & fromAddress & ")" _
        & " received:(last month)"
        DisplayInstantSearchExplorer(currentFolder, SearchQuery, False)
    End If
End Sub

Private Sub ctlAllMessages_Click( _
ByVal Ctrl As Microsoft.Office.Core.CommandBarButton, _
ByRef CancelDefault As Boolean) Handles ctlAllMessages.Click
    If LastSelection.Count = 1 Then
        Dim oMail As Outlook.MailItem = _
        CType(LastSelection.Item(1), Outlook.MailItem)
        Dim fromAddress As String = oMail.SenderName
        Dim currentFolder As Outlook.Folder _
        = CType(oMail.Parent, Outlook.Folder)
        Dim SearchQuery As String = "from:(" & fromAddress & ")"
        DisplayInstantSearchExplorer(currentFolder, SearchQuery, False)
    End If
End Sub
```

Building the Add-in Project

You're now ready to build the Instant Search add-in project. Before you build the project, you should check the Error window to ensure that you don't have an error in your code.

To build the Instant Search add-in project, follow these steps:

1. Press Ctrl+W, and then press Ctrl+E to display the Error list window.

2. Ensure that there are no errors in your code. If there are errors, Visual Studio will suggest how you should correct them.

3. From the Build menu, select Build InstantSearchAddinVB.

4. In the status bar, you should see "Build Succeeded" if the build completed successfully.

5. Save the Instant Search add-in project from the File menu by selecting Save All or by pressing Ctrl+Shift+S. Click OK to save the project to the InstantSearchAddinVB folder.

Creating a Shim Project

Now that you've successfully created the InstantSearchAddinVB project, the next step is to create a COM shim for the add-in. If you don't use VSTO to create your add-in for Outlook 2007, you should shim your managed extension to provide application domain isolation. For details on the concept of an application domain, represented by the *AppDomain* object, search for "AppDomain" in the Visual Studio 2005 Developer's Reference. Application domain isolation means that an exception in another add-in will not cause your add-in to crash or operate in an unexpected manner. Similarly, if your add-in encounters an unhandled exception, it will not cause all other managed add-ins running in the Outlook process to crash. Provided by either the COM shim or VSTO, application domain isolation offers several advantages.

When Outlook loads add-ins, an add-in that causes an error during boot can be placed on a disabled add-in list. Because Outlook cannot distinguish between one shared add-in and another, Outlook places Mscoree.dll on its disabled list and consequently all shared managed add-ins are disabled. With application domain isolation, disabling one add-in does not disable all other managed add-ins.

Application domain isolation prevents an unhandled exception in one add-in from crashing all other add-ins in the same application domain. Unexpected behavior can occur when add-ins share the same application domain. For example, if add-in A calls *ReleaseCOMObject* and *FinalReleaseCOMObject* on an object that it shares with add-in B and both add-ins are in the same application domain, add-in B encounters an access violation when it attempts to access the shared object.

If an Exchange administrator uses the Outlook security form in an Exchange public folder or group policy to maintain a list of trusted add-ins, trusting a shared add-in means trusting Mscoree.dll, which in effect trusts all shared add-ins and negates the intended action, which is to trust a single add-in. For additional information on Outlook security and the concept of a trusted add-in, see Chapter 19, "Trust and Security." For VSTO add-ins, the administrator trusts the manifest of the managed add-in assembly. For COM shim add-ins, the administrator trusts the COM shim that acts as a proxy for the managed add-in.

A COM shim acts as a native proxy for your managed add-in. COM shims must be written in C++. However, thanks to the COM Shim Wizard that is available on MSDN or on the Web site that accompanies this book, knowledge of C++ is completely optional. Basically, you only need to click through the COM Shim Wizard, and all the C++ code will be written for you automatically.

To install the Visual Studio COM Shim Wizard, follow these steps:

1. Download the file by clicking the Download link on the Web site that accompanies this book and saving the file to your hard disk. You can also download the COM Shim Wizard from MSDN. Search for "COM Shim Wizard" at *http://msdn.microsoft.com*.

2. Double-click the COMShimWizardSetup.msi program file on your hard disk to start the setup program and accept the defaults to complete the installation unless you are installing the wizard on Windows Vista.

3. If you are installing the COM Shim Wizard on Windows Vista, you might have to turn User Account Control off temporarily to get the installation to complete successfully. To turn off User Account Control, launch User Accounts in Windows Control Panel. When you start the installation for the COM Shim Wizard under Windows Vista, you should install the program for Everyone instead of Just Me.

To create a Visual Studio shim project using the COM Shim Wizard, follow these steps:

1. From the File menu, select the Add pop-up menu, and then select New Project to add a new project to the InstantSearchVB solution.

2. Expand the Other Languages node in the Project Types list.

3. Under Other Languages, expand the Visual C++ node.

4. Under Visual C++, click the COMShims node, and then in the Visual Studio Installed Templates group, click Addin Shim.

5. In the Name text box, type **InstantSearchShimVB** as shown in Figure 3-8, and then click OK.

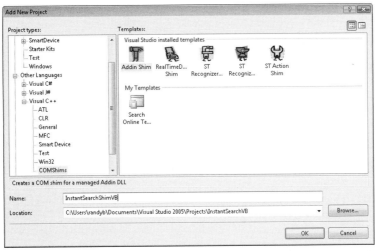

Figure 3-8   Visual Studio 2005 New Project dialog box for InstantSearchShimVB project.

6. The COM Shim Wizard page shown in Figure 3-9 will appear. Click the ellipsis (...) to specify the location of the managed assembly for your add-in.

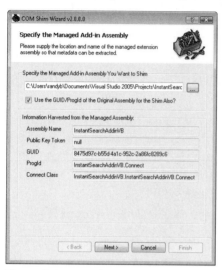

Figure 3-9   Specify The Managed Add-in Assembly page of the COM Shim Wizard.

7. Locate the managed assembly named InstantSearchAddinVB.dll in this folder under your Documents folder:

    Visual Studio 2005\Projects\InstantSearchVB\InstantSearchAddinVB\bin\Release

8. In the Release folder, select InstantSearchAddinVB.dll and click Open.

9. A Security Warning dialog box appears to indicate that you should strong-name your add-in dynamic link library (DLL). In this case, you do not provide a strong-name key for the add-in. In the Security Warning dialog box, click Yes.

10. Click Next to move to the next page of the COM Shim Wizard.

11. In the Description text box, clear the suggested description and type **Instant Search Add-in (VB)**.

12. In the Friendly Name text box, clear the suggested friendly name and type **Microsoft Outlook Sample Instant Search Add-in (VB)**.

13. In the Which Host Applications Is This Add-In Used For list, select the Microsoft Outlook check box, as shown in Figure 3-10.

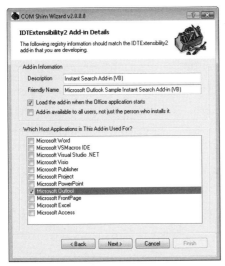

Figure 3-10 IDTExtensibility2 Add-In Details page of the COM Shim Wizard.

14. Click Next to display the Summary wizard page shown in Figure 3-11.

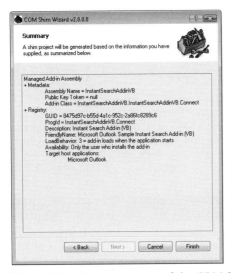

Figure 3-11 Summary page of the COM Shim Wizard.

15. Click Finish to add the InstantSearchShimVB project to the InstantSearchVB solution.

For the InstantSearchShimVB.dll to work correctly with the managed component InstantSearchAddinVB.dll, both DLLs must be in the same folder. To accommodate this requirement, you should change the Output Directory for the shim DLL to be the same as the folder for the managed add-in DLL.

To set the Output Directory for the COM shim project, follow these steps:

1. In the Solution Explorer window, click InstantSearchShimVB.

2. From the Project menu, select Properties.

3. In the InstantSearchShimVB Property Pages dialog box shown in Figure 3-12, expand the Configuration Properties node and click the General node.

4. In the Output Directory combo box, type **..\InstantSearchAddinVB\bin\Release**, and then click OK.

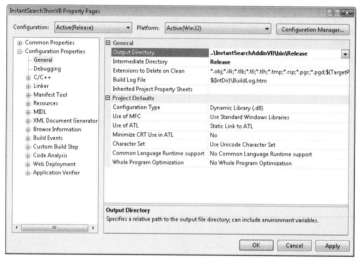

Figure 3-12   Property Pages dialog box for the InstantSearchShimVB project.

Creating a Setup Project

The next step is to add a setup project to your solution. Once you have a setup project, you will be able to deploy the add-in to other users. Of course, you can modify this add-in to suit your own requirements.

To create a Visual Studio setup project, follow these steps:

1. From the File menu, select the Add pop-up menu, and then select New Project to add a new project to the InstantSearchVB solution.

2. In the Project Types list, expand the Other Project Types node.

3. Under Other Project Types, click the Setup and Deployment node.

4. In the Visual Studio Installed Templates group, click Setup Project.

5. In the Name text box, type **InstantSearchSetupVB** as shown in Figure 3-13 and then click OK.

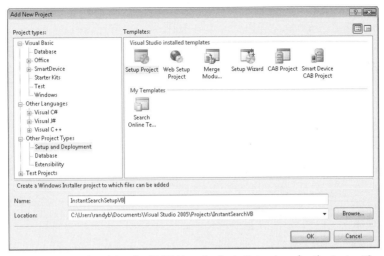

Figure 3-13   Visual Studio 2005 New Project dialog box for the InstantSearchSetupVB project.

Next you'll set properties on the InstantSearchSetupVB project so that the user installing the project sees the correct title for the solution during setup.

To set properties on the InstantSearchSetupVB project, follow these steps:

1.   In the Solution Explorer window, click InstantSearchSetupVB.

2.   Press F4 to open the Properties dialog box shown in Figure 3-14.

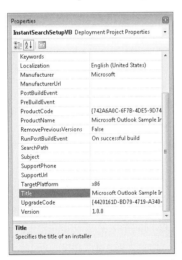

Figure 3-14   Properties dialog box for the InstantSearchSetupVB project.

3.   For the Title and ProductName properties of the Setup project, type **Microsoft Outlook Sample Instant Search Add-in (VB)**.

Finally, you need to add project outputs to the setup project. In this case, you'll add project outputs for both the managed add-in DLL and the shim DLL. Adding a project output to the setup project installs these DLLs to the Application folder created by the setup project.

To add primary outputs to the setup project, follow these steps:

1. In the Solution Explorer window, click InstantSearchSetupVB.

2. From the Project menu, select the Add pop-up menu, and then select Project Output to add new project outputs to the InstantSearchSetupVB solution.

3. In the Add Project Output Group dialog box shown in Figure 3-15, in the Project drop-down list box, select InstantSearchAddinVB, and then click OK.

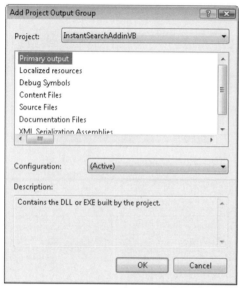

Figure 3-15   Add Project Output Group dialog box.

4. Repeat the step to display the Add Project Output Group dialog box, but this time in the Project drop-down list box, select InstantSearchShimVB, and then click OK.

5. In the Solution Explorer, under the InstantSearchSetupVB project, click Primary Output from InstantSearchShimVB and press F4 to display the Properties dialog box.

6. In the Properties window shown in Figure 3-16, click the Register property and select vsdrpCOMSelfReg in the drop-down list box.

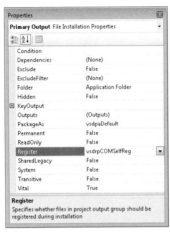

Figure 3-16   Properties window for primary output from InstantSearchShimVB.

At this point, both InstantSearchAddinVB and InstantSearchShimVB should be listed as project outputs for the InstantSearchSetupVB project.

Building the Setup Project

You're almost at the finish line. In just a few more steps, you'll have an add-in that you can install on your own machine or that of a colleague.

To build the setup project, follow these steps:

1. In the Solution Explorer window, click InstantSearchSetupVB.

2. From the Build menu, select Build Solution to build the entire InstantSearchVB solution.

Installing the Instant Search Add-In

Assuming that the solution built successfully, you can now install the Instant Search add-in using the built setup project.

To install the setup project, follow these steps:

1. In the Solution Explorer window, right-click InstantSearchSetupVB and select Install on the context menu.

2. Click through the Setup dialog boxes to install Microsoft Outlook Sample Instant Search Add-in (VB).

3. Click Close when the setup process is complete.

> **Note**   If you are installing the add-in on Windows Vista, you will see the User Account Control dialog box after installation begins. Click Allow to indicate that you trust the setup package for the Microsoft Outlook Sample Instant Search Add-in (VB).

Testing the Instant Search Add-in Solution

Now that you've built the complete InstantSearchVB solution, you can proceed to test the add-in to ensure that all the steps were followed correctly and that you don't see unexpected results.

What to Expect

When you launch Outlook after setup of the add-in and you right-click a mail message in your Inbox, you should see the Instant Search pop-up menu shown in Figure 3-1 at the bottom of the item's context menu. When you select a command on the Instant Search pop-up menu such as Received This Week, you should see a new Explorer window that displays all messages received from the sender during this week.

When you close Outlook, the Instant Search add-in should not cause Outlook to remain in memory. See the "Debug Mode" section later in this chapter for suggestions about how to determine whether Outlook remains in memory after you shut down Outlook.

Troubleshooting

If you do not see the Instant Search pop-up menu, check to ensure that the Instant Search add-in is installed. If the add-in is not installed, then you need to re-examine the steps to ensure that you did not miss a critical step.

To determine if the Instant Search add-in is installed correctly, follow these steps:

1. From the Tools menu in the Outlook Explorer window, select Trust Center.

2. In the left pane of the Trust Center dialog box, click Add-Ins. At the bottom of the dialog box, in the Manage drop-down list box, ensure that COM Add-Ins is selected, and click Go to display the COM Add-Ins dialog box.

3. The COM Add-Ins dialog box should indicate that the add-in is installed and connected as shown in Figure 13-17.

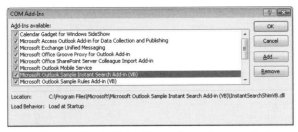

Figure 3-17   The COM Add-Ins dialog box can help you troubleshoot your add-in.

Debug Mode

So far you've stepped through creating an add-in, and the endpoint was to use the add-in in Run mode in Outlook. What should you do when confronted with the real-world experience of writing your add-in from scratch? Although you should follow the same steps overall that are described in this chapter, when you are coding the add-in project you will run the add-in project in Debug mode. To run the add-in in Debug mode, you must set the start action for your add-in in the add-in project.

To set the start action for your add-in, follow these steps:

1. In the Solution Explorer window, click InstantSearchAddinVB.

2. From the Project menu, select InstantSearchAddinVB Properties.

3. In the Properties dialog box, click the Debug tab.

4. Under Start Action, select the Start External Program check box.

5. Click the ellipsis (...) to open the Select File dialog box.

6. In the Office12 folder, select Outlook.exe as shown in Figure 3-18. The Office12 folder is typically located here:

   C:\Program Files\Microsoft Office\Office12\Outlook.exe

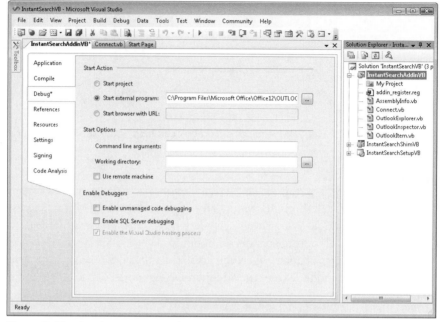

Figure 3-18   Set the start action for your add-in on the Debug tab.

Debugging Code

Before you attempt to debug your add-in, you should shut down Outlook. If Outlook is running, your debug session might not yield the expected results. Use the Windows Task Manager to ensure that Outlook is not running before you start in Debug mode. If Outlook is not running, you will not see Outlook.exe in the process list in the Task Manager.

To ensure that Outlook is not running before you start debugging, follow these steps:

1. Press Ctrl+Alt+Delete to launch the Windows Task Manager.

2. In the Windows Security dialog box, click Task Manager.

3. In the Windows Task Manager dialog box, click the Processes tab.

4. Ensure that Outlook.exe is not in the list of running processes.

One interesting way to ensure that Outlook has shut down cleanly is to use the Mail application in Control Panel to force Outlook to boot with a profile prompt. If the profile prompt appears when you start Outlook in Debug mode, you can be assured that no previous instance of Outlook was running when you started your debug session. When you have completed debugging, you can remove the profile prompt by using the Mail application again.

Once you have your add-in project set up to perform debugging, you can use the great debugging features of Visual Studio 2005. These features include debugging tools such as setting breakpoints, using watch and locals windows, and using edit and continue. Be aware that when you hit a breakpoint in your code, you might cause Outlook to become unresponsive until you continue execution.

To debug your add-in, follow these steps:

1. Ensure that Outlook is shut down.

2. Set your breakpoints before you begin the debugging process.

3. Press F5 to launch Outlook and begin the debugging process.

4. From the Visual Studio Debug menu, select Stop Debugging to stop debugging. Outlook closes when you stop the debugging process.

Summary

This chapter has provided you with end-to-end instructions on how to build an Outlook add-in using Visual Studio 2005. The add-in you have created leverages the new Instant Search feature of Outlook 2007. To ensure add-in stability, the Instant Search add-in is provided with its own application domain by way of a COM shim. Finally, you also created a setup project so that you can deploy the add-in to other users. You should be able to use the understanding you've gained in this chapter to move on to create an add-in with your own unique design and features. Happy coding!

Chapter 4

Writing Your First Outlook Add-in Using C#

The goal of this chapter is to walk you through the process of creating a Visual C# add-in for Microsoft Office Outlook 2007. Once you've created and built the project, you will be able to use the add-in in your everyday activities. If you are interested in obtaining practical results in a very short time, this chapter is for you.

In this chapter, you'll learn how to:

- Use the Outlook add-in templates supplied with this book.

- Create a new Outlook add-in project for Visual C#.

- Write code to add a custom pop-up menu to the context menu for a mail item.

- Build a Component Object Model (COM) shim project so that the add-in runs in a separate application domain.

- Build a setup project so that you can deploy the Instant Search add-in.

Microsoft Visual Studio 2005 continues to provide built-in support for developing Office add-ins through the Shared add-in template, but this template is missing some key blocks of code that are useful for writing Outlook 2007 COM add-ins in managed code. Although using Microsoft Visual Studio 2005 Tools for the 2007 Microsoft Office System (VSTO) offers another preferred development approach, it is not covered in this chapter. You can easily adapt the code in this chapter to work with VSTO. For this example, you'll learn how to write an add-in based on the Outlook Add-in Template for Visual C# supplied on the Web site that contains sample code for this book.

Introducing the Instant Search Add-In

The Instant Search add-in places an Instant Search command at the bottom of an item's context menu, as shown in Figure 4-1. Instant Search is a pop-up command bar control that lets the user take advantage of Outlook's Instant Search feature and display messages from the sender sent last week, this week, last month, this month, or all messages. The search results are displayed in a separate Explorer window, shown in Figure 4-2.

Figure 4-1   Instant Search pop-up menu.

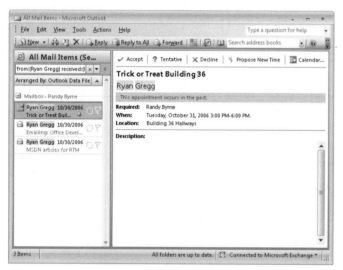

Figure 4-2   Results from Instant Search are shown in a separate Explorer window.

Install the Outlook Add-in Templates

To get you started writing Outlook add-ins, templates for both Visual Basic and Visual C# are provided on the Web site that contains the sample code for this book. Before you can create the Instant Search add-in, you must install the Outlook Add-in Templates.

To install the Outlook Add-in Templates, follow these steps:

1. Download the Outlook Add-in Templates installation package from this book's companion Web site.

2. Double-click OutlookAddinTemplates.msi to begin the installation process.

3. In the Microsoft Office Outlook 2007 Add-in Templates Setup dialog box, click Next.

4. After reviewing the End-User License Agreement, select I Agree to accept the agreement, and then click Next.

5. Click Next to confirm that you wish to start the installation.

6. If you are installing the templates on Microsoft Windows Vista, you will see the User Account Control dialog box after installation begins. Click Allow to indicate that you trust the setup package for the Outlook Add-in Templates.

7. After installation has completed, click Close to dismiss the Setup Wizard dialog box.

Creating the Instant Search Add-In

To create a Visual Studio solution for the Instant Search add-in, follow these steps:

1. Open Visual Studio 2005, and press Ctrl+Shift+N to display the New Project dialog box.

2. In the Project Types list, click the Other Project Types node.

3. Under Visual Studio Installed Templates, click Blank Solution.

4. In the Name text box, type **InstantSearchCS**, as shown in Figure 4-3, and click OK to create the solution.

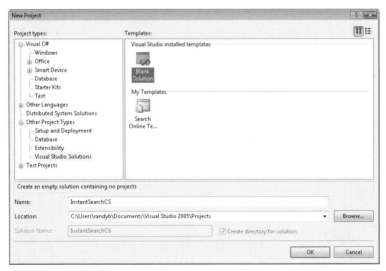

Figure 4-3 Visual Studio 2005 New Project dialog box for the InstantSearchCS solution.

Now that the custom templates are installed and you've created a Visual Studio solution to contain your add-in, shim, and setup projects, proceed by creating an add-in project using the template.

To create a Visual Studio add-in project using the add-in template, follow these steps:

1. From the File menu, select the Add pop-up menu, then select New Project to add a new project to the InstantSearchCS solution.

2. In the Project Types list, click the Visual C# node.

3. In the Templates list, from the My Templates group, select Office Outlook 2007 Visual C# Add-in.

4. In the Name text box, type **InstantSearchAddinCS**, as shown in Figure 4-4, and click OK.

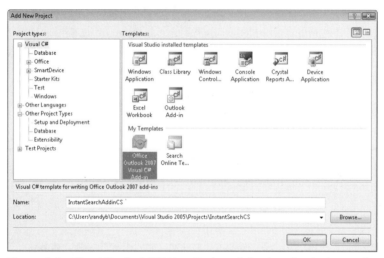

Figure 4-4   Visual Studio 2005 New Project dialog box for the InstantSearchAddinCS project.

You will then see the InstantSearchAddinCS project in the Visual Studio editor, shown in Figure 4-5.

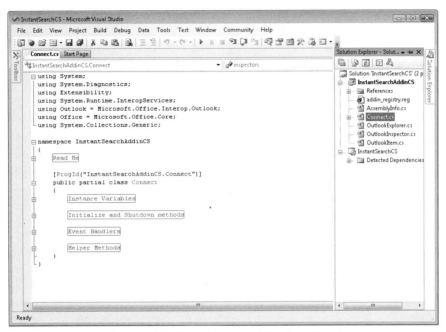

Figure 4-5   InstantSearchAddinCS project in the Visual Studio editor.

Writing Code

The next step in completing the Instant Search add-in is to write code in the project. Before you start to write code, you should understand that the template is a generic project aimed at typical Outlook add-in scenarios. The template creates code that allows you to track multiple instances of Inspector or Explorer windows. For the Instant Search add-in, you don't need to track Inspector or Explorer windows so you will comment out the existing code in the *InitializeAddin* and *ShutdownAddin* methods. At this point, you should follow the next procedure to remove the code in these methods.

To remove the code in the *InitializeAddin* and *ShutdownAddin* methods, follow these steps:

1. Locate the *InitializeAddin* and *ShutdownAddin* methods shown in Figure 4-6 in the *Connect* class. You might need to expand the "Initialize and Shutdown methods" region before you can see the *InitializeAddin* and *ShutdownAddin* methods.

2. Comment out all the code in the *InitializeAddin* method.

3. Comment out all the code in the *ShutdownAddin* method.

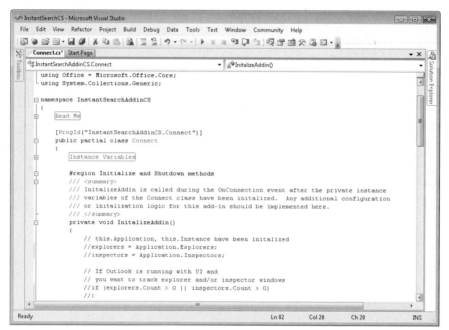

Figure 4-6   The Initialize and Shutdown methods region in the *Connect* class.

InitializeAddin Method

The *InitializeAddin* method runs when your add-in is loaded by the host application, which in this case is Outlook 2007. If you were to examine the *Connect.Designer.cs* class, *InitializeAddin* gets called in the *OnConnection* method of the add-in. *OnConnection* is a method called by Office add-ins that must implement the *IDTExtensibility2* interface. *Connect.Designer.cs* abstracts the details of the *IDTExtensibility2* interface and provides you with two methods, *InitializeAddin* and *ShutdownAddin,* which correspond to Startup and Shutdown events. Without getting into too many details about the *IDTExtensibility2* interface, *InitializeAddin* is called when the add-in is loaded by the host application at boot time or when the add-in is loaded through a user action such as connecting the add-in manually via the COM Add-Ins dialog box. You use *InitializeAddin* and *ShutdownAddin* to create and destroy class-level instance variables that are required for your add-in, and to wire up event handlers required by your solution. In the case of the InstantSearchAddinCS project, you need to wire up event handlers for the *ItemContextMenuDisplay* and *ContextMenuClose* events for the *Application* object in the *InitializeAddin* event. You remove those event handlers in the *ShutdownAddin* event.

Note   To examine *Connect.Designer.cs* in the Solution Explorer, you need to show all files in the project. To display the Solution Explorer, press Ctrl+R. To show all files, in Visual Studio, select the Project menu, and then select Show All Files.

Adding Instance Variables

The next step is to create class-level instance variables in the *Connect* class to represent command bar controls on the context menu for an item. Context menus in Outlook use the familiar Office command bars object model that has been included in several versions of Office. Context menu commands do not use the new Ribbon extensibility model.

To add instance variables to the *Connect* class, follow these steps:

1. Display the Solution Explorer by pressing Ctrl+R.

2. In the Solution Explorer, double-click *Connect.cs* to display the Code Editor for the *Connect* class.

3. Locate the instance variables region shown in Figure 4-7 in *Connect.cs*. You might need to expand the "Instance Variables" region before you can see the *InitializeAddin* method.

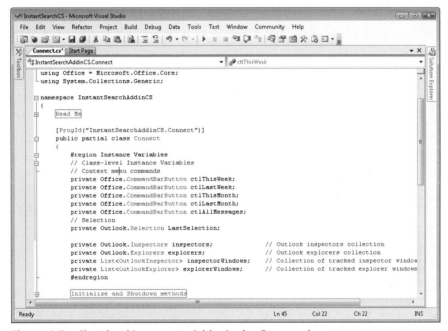

Figure 4-7   Class-level instance variables in the *Connect* class.

4. Type the following code in the instance variables region in the *Connect* class:

```
// Context menu commands
private Office.CommandBarButton ctlThisWeek;
private Office.CommandBarButton ctlLastWeek;
private Office.CommandBarButton ctlThisMonth;
private Office.CommandBarButton ctlLastMonth;
private Office.CommandBarButton ctlAllMessages;
// Selection
private Outlook.Selection LastSelection;
```

Hooking Up Events in Visual C#

Hooking up Outlook events is somewhat more complicated in Visual C# than it is in Visual Basic, but once you get the basic concept, it is a straightforward process and Visual C# will handle most of the work for you. Each event has a corresponding event handler method that is called when the event fires. To hook up the event handler method, you select the event member from the parent object and then use the += operator to create an event delegate that handles the event. The relevant events for item context menus are the *ItemContextMenuDisplay* and *ContextMenuClose* events on the *Application* object.

ItemContextMenuDisplay Event

The *ItemContextMenuDisplay* event occurs before a context menu is to be displayed for either a single highlighted Outlook item or for one or more selected Outlook items, allowing the *CommandBar* object representing the context menu to be customized by an add-in. For the Instant Search add-in, the Instant Search pop-up on the context menu is displayed only when a single mail item is selected. When more than one mail item is selected or when the single selected item is not a mail item, the Instant Search pop-up on the context menu does not appear.

To hook up the event handlers for the *ItemContextMenuDisplay* and *ContextMenuClose* events, follow these steps:

1. In the *Connect* class Code Editor, click inside the *InitializeAddin* method. Remember that you just commented out the existing code in this method.

2. Type **Application** and then press the period key (.).

3. In the Intellisense window, use your mouse or the keyboard to scroll to the *ItemContextMenuDisplay* event.

4. Press the Enter key to select the *ItemContextMenuDisplay* event.

5. Type +=. Visual C# will offer to hook up the event for you. At this point, press the Tab key.

6. Press the Tab key again to insert the event delegate.

7. Type **Application** and then press the period key (.).

8. In the Intellisense window, use your mouse or the keyboard to scroll to the *ContextMenuClose* event.

9. Press the Enter key to select the *ContextMenuClose* event.

10. Type +=. Visual C# will offer to hook up the event for you. At this point, press the Tab key.

11. Press the Tab key again to insert the event delegate. At this point, you should see the following lines of code to hook up the event handlers:

```
Application.ItemContextMenuDisplay +=
    new Outlook.ApplicationEvents_11_ItemContextMenuDisplayEventHandler(
    Application_ItemContextMenuDisplay);
Application.ContextMenuClose +=
    new Outlook.ApplicationEvents_11_ContextMenuCloseEventHandler(
    Application_ContextMenuClose);
```

To write code for the *ItemContextMenuDisplay* event, follow these steps:

1. In the *Connect* class Code Editor, find the *Application_ItemContextMenuDisplay* event handler that was created when you hooked up the *ItemContextMenuDisplay* event.

2. Remove the line that Visual Studio inserted into the event handler:

```
throw new Exception("The method or operation is not implemented.");
```

3. Write the following code in the *Application_ItemContextMenuDisplay* event handler:

```
private void Application_ItemContextMenuDisplay(
    Microsoft.Office.Core.CommandBar CommandBar,
    Microsoft.Office.Interop.Outlook.Selection Selection)
{
    Office.CommandBarPopup ctlInstantSearch;
    try
    {
        if (Selection.Count == 0)
            return;

        OutlookItem oItem = new OutlookItem(Selection[1]);

        if ((Selection.Count == 1) &&
            (oItem.Class == Outlook.OlObjectClass.olMail) &&
            (oItem.Parent.Store.IsInstantSearchEnabled))
        {
            ctlInstantSearch = (Office.CommandBarPopup)
                CommandBar.FindControl(
                Type.Missing, Type.Missing,
                "InstantSearchAddinCS.ctlInstantSearch",
                Type.Missing, Type.Missing);
            if (ctlInstantSearch == null)
            {
                ctlInstantSearch = (Office.CommandBarPopup)
                    CommandBar.Controls.Add(
                    Office.MsoControlType.msoControlPopup, Type.Missing,
                    "InstantSearchAddinCS.ctlInstantSearch",
                    Type.Missing, Type.Missing);
                ctlInstantSearch.Caption = "Instant Search";
                ctlInstantSearch.Tag = "InstantSearchAddinCS.ctlInstantSearch";
                ctlInstantSearch.BeginGroup = true;
                LastSelection = Selection;
                //Add controls to popup
                ctlThisWeek =
                    (Office.CommandBarButton)
                    ctlInstantSearch.CommandBar.Controls.Add(
                    Office.MsoControlType.msoControlButton,
                    Type.Missing, Type.Missing, Type.Missing, Type.Missing);
```

```csharp
            ctlThisWeek.Caption = "Received This Week...";
            ctlThisMonth =
                (Office.CommandBarButton)
                ctlInstantSearch.CommandBar.Controls.Add(
                Office.MsoControlType.msoControlButton,
                Type.Missing, Type.Missing, Type.Missing, Type.Missing);
            ctlThisMonth.Caption = "Received This Month...";
            ctlLastWeek =
                (Office.CommandBarButton)
                ctlInstantSearch.CommandBar.Controls.Add(
                Office.MsoControlType.msoControlButton,
                Type.Missing, Type.Missing, Type.Missing, Type.Missing);
            ctlLastWeek.Caption = "Received Last Week...";
            ctlLastMonth =
                (Office.CommandBarButton)
                ctlInstantSearch.CommandBar.Controls.Add(
                Office.MsoControlType.msoControlButton,
                Type.Missing, Type.Missing, Type.Missing, Type.Missing);
            ctlLastMonth.Caption = "Received Last Month...";
            ctlAllMessages =
                (Office.CommandBarButton)
                ctlInstantSearch.CommandBar.Controls.Add(
                Office.MsoControlType.msoControlButton,
                Type.Missing, Type.Missing, Type.Missing, Type.Missing);
            ctlAllMessages.Caption = "All Message Received...";
            // Hook up event listeners for the buttons
            ctlThisWeek.Click +=
                new Microsoft.Office.Core.
                _CommandBarButtonEvents_ClickEventHandler(
                ctlThisWeek_Click);
            ctlLastWeek.Click +=
                new Microsoft.Office.Core.
                _CommandBarButtonEvents_ClickEventHandler(
                ctlLastWeek_Click);
            ctlThisMonth.Click +=
                new Microsoft.Office.Core.
                _CommandBarButtonEvents_ClickEventHandler(
                ctlThisMonth_Click);
            ctlLastMonth.Click +=
                new Microsoft.Office.Core.
                _CommandBarButtonEvents_ClickEventHandler(
                ctlLastMonth_Click);
            ctlAllMessages.Click +=
                new Microsoft.Office.Core.
                _CommandBarButtonEvents_ClickEventHandler(
                ctlAllMessages_Click);
            }
        }
    }
    catch (Exception ex)
    {
        Debug.WriteLine(ex.Message);
    }
}
```

This event procedure looks at the *Selection* object passed in the event. If *Selection.Count* is zero, then the code exits from the event procedure and no command bar pop-up is created. The *Selection* collection, like other collection objects in the Outlook object model, is one-based and the indexer for the *Selection* object returns a type *Object*. The *OutlookItem* class uses reflection to determine the common properties of an Outlook item and allows you to determine the underlying type of the item *Object*. For complete details on the *OutlookItem* class, see the section "*OutlookItem* Helper Class" in Chapter 6, "Accessing Outlook Data."

If *Selection.Count* is one and the item returned by the indexer of the *Selection* object represents a *MailItem* and the *IsInstantSearchEnabled* property returns *True* on the *Store* object that contains the item, then the Office *CommandBar* object model is used to create a pop-up menu represented by the instance variable *ctlInstantSearch*. *ctlInstantSearch* represents an *Office.CommandBarPopup* object. To add the pop-up menu to the item context menu, you call the *Add* method on the *CommandBar* object passed in the *ItemContextMenuDisplay* event. Once the pop-up menu has been added, you then set the *Caption* and *Tag* properties for *ctlInstantSearch*. The *Caption* property is set to "Instant Search" and the *Tag* property is set to the *ProgID* of the Instant Search add-in, "InstantSearchAddinCS.Connect."

Once you have instantiated the *CommandBarPopup* object that represents the Instant Search pop-up menu, you then add additional *CommandBarControl* objects that represent additional menu items on the pop-up menu. Each of the menu items corresponds to the following time intervals for messages received:

- This Week
- Last Week
- This Month
- Last Month
- All Messages

Note that the instance variables *ctlThisWeek*, *ctlLastWeek*, *ctlThisMonth*, *ctlLastMonth*, and *ctlAllMessages* also require event handlers. You'll write code for the *Click* event for these instance variables later in the chapter.

ContextMenuClose Event

The *ContextMenuClose* event occurs just after a context menu is closed so that add-ins can dispose of any object references that have been obtained from other context menu events such as *ItemContextMenuDisplay*. In the case of the Instant Search add-in, the *LastSelection* object is set to *null*.

To write code for the *ContextMenuClose* event, follow these steps:

1. In the *Connect* class Code Editor, find the *Application_ContextMenuClose* event handler that was created when you hooked up the *ContextMenuClose* event.

2. Remove the line that Visual Studio inserted into the event handler:

    ```
    throw new Exception("The method or operation is not implemented.");
    ```

3. Write the following code in the *Application_ContextMenuClose* event handler:

    ```
    private void Application_ContextMenuClose(
        Microsoft.Office.Interop.Outlook.OlContextMenu ContextMenu)
    {
        // Use this method to clean up any state for the context menu
        LastSelection = null;
    }
    ```

Cleaning Up Event Handlers

In the *ShutdownAddin* method, you need to clean up any existing event handlers for Outlook to shut down efficiently and correctly. For the Instant Search add-in, you remove the event delegates for both the *ItemContextMenuDisplay* and *ContextMenuClose* events.

To remove event delegates for *ItemContextMenuDisplay* and *ContextMenuClose* events, follow these steps:

1. In the *Connect* class Code Editor, click inside the *ShutdownAddin* method. Remember that you previously commented out the existing code in this method.

2. Type the following code into the *ShutdownAddin* method:

    ```
    Application.ItemContextMenuDisplay -=
        new Outlook.ApplicationEvents_11_ItemContextMenuDisplayEventHandler(
        Application_ItemContextMenuDisplay);
    Application.ContextMenuClose -=
        new Outlook.ApplicationEvents_11_ContextMenuCloseEventHandler(
        Application_ContextMenuClose);
    ```

DisplayInstantSearchExplorer Method

To reduce the amount of code you need to write, the *DisplayInstantSearchExplorer* method is called from the *Click* event procedures for the submenu controls on the Instant Search pop-up menu. The *DisplayInstantSearchExplorer* method displays the results of an Instant Search query in a new Explorer window by calling the *Search* method on the *Explorer* object. The *Search* method is new to Outlook 2007 and allows you to use the Advanced Query Syntax of Windows Desktop Search to return results. For additional details on Advanced Query Syntax, see Chapter 11, "Searching Outlook Data." This method takes three arguments, shown in Table 4-1.

Table 4-1   Parameters for the *DisplayInstantSearchExplorer* Method

Parameter	Required	Type	Description
Folder	Yes	Outlook.Folder	Represents the *Folder* object that contains the item on which the context menu is being displayed.

Table 4-1 Parameters for the *DisplayInstantSearchExplorer* Method

Parameter	Required	Type	Description
InstantSearch	Yes	string	A *string* object that contains a valid Advanced Query Syntax query.
ShowToDoBar	Yes	bool	If *ShowToDoBar* equals *true*, displays the To-Do Bar in the new Explorer window. If *false*, hides the To-Do Bar.

To write code for the *DisplayInstantSearchExplorer* method, follow these steps:

1. In the *Connect* class Code Editor, click at the bottom of the *Connect* class before the closing bracket (}).

2. Write the following code in the *DisplayInstantSearchExplorer* method:

```
private void DisplayInstantSearchExplorer(
    Outlook.Folder Folder,
    string InstantSearch,
    bool ShowToDoBar)
{
    Outlook.Explorer exp =
        this.Application.Explorers.Add(
        Folder,
        Outlook.OlFolderDisplayMode.olFolderDisplayNoNavigation);
    //Call Explorer.Search to automate Instant Search
    exp.Search(InstantSearch ,
        Outlook.OlSearchScope.olSearchScopeAllFolders);
    exp.Display();
    exp.ShowPane(Outlook.OlPane.olToDoBar, ShowToDoBar);
}
```

Writing Code for Submenu *Click* Events

Next you write code for the submenu *Click* events on the five menu items that exist on the Instant Search pop-up menu. When the user clicks any one of the submenu items, the *Click* event for the *Office.CommandBarButton* is called. The code in the *Click* event simply calls the *DisplayInstantSearchFolder* method with the correct parameters to display an Explorer window that shows the results of the search. Once you've completed this task, you'll be ready to build the Instant Search add-in.

To write code for submenu *Click* events, follow these steps.

1. In the *Connect* class Code Editor, find the *ctlThisWeek_Click*, *ctlLastWeek_Click*, *ctlThisMonth_Click*, *ctlLastMonth_Click*, and *ctlAllMessages_Click* event handlers that were created when you hooked up the relevant events.

2. Write the following code in the event handlers for each control:

```
private void ctlThisWeek_Click(
    Microsoft.Office.Core.CommandBarButton Ctrl, ref bool CancelDefault)
    {
```

```csharp
        if (LastSelection.Count == 1)
        {
            Outlook.MailItem oMail = (Outlook.MailItem)LastSelection[1];
            string fromAddress = oMail.SenderName;
            Outlook.Folder currentFolder = (Outlook.Folder)oMail.Parent;
            string SearchQuery = "from:(" + fromAddress + ")" +
                " received:(this week)";
            DisplayInstantSearchExplorer(currentFolder, SearchQuery, false);
        }
    }

    private void ctlLastWeek_Click(
        Microsoft.Office.Core.CommandBarButton Ctrl, ref bool CancelDefault)
    {
        if (LastSelection.Count == 1)
        {
            Outlook.MailItem oMail = (Outlook.MailItem)LastSelection[1];
            string fromAddress = oMail.SenderName;
            Outlook.Folder currentFolder = (Outlook.Folder)oMail.Parent;
            string SearchQuery = "from:(" + fromAddress + ")" +
                " received:(last week)";
            DisplayInstantSearchExplorer(currentFolder, SearchQuery, false);
        }
    }

    private void ctlThisMonth_Click(
        Microsoft.Office.Core.CommandBarButton Ctrl, ref bool CancelDefault)
    {
        if (LastSelection.Count == 1)
        {
            Outlook.MailItem oMail = (Outlook.MailItem)LastSelection[1];
            string fromAddress = oMail.SenderName;
            Outlook.Folder currentFolder = (Outlook.Folder)oMail.Parent;
            string SearchQuery = "from:(" + fromAddress + ")" +
                " received:(this month)";
            DisplayInstantSearchExplorer(currentFolder, SearchQuery, false);
        }
    }

    private void ctlLastMonth_Click(
        Microsoft.Office.Core.CommandBarButton Ctrl, ref bool CancelDefault)
    {
        if (LastSelection.Count == 1)
        {
            Outlook.MailItem oMail = (Outlook.MailItem)LastSelection[1];
            string fromAddress = oMail.SenderName;
            Outlook.Folder currentFolder = (Outlook.Folder)oMail.Parent;
            string SearchQuery = "from:(" + fromAddress + ")" +
                " received:(last month)";
            DisplayInstantSearchExplorer(currentFolder, SearchQuery, false);
        }
    }

    private void ctlAllMessages_Click(
        Microsoft.Office.Core.CommandBarButton Ctrl, ref bool CancelDefault)
```

```
    {
        if (LastSelection.Count == 1)
        {
            Outlook.MailItem oMail = (Outlook.MailItem)LastSelection[1];
            string fromAddress = oMail.SenderName;
            Outlook.Folder currentFolder = (Outlook.Folder)oMail.Parent;
            string SearchQuery = "from:(" + fromAddress + ")";
            DisplayInstantSearchExplorer(currentFolder, SearchQuery, false);
        }
    }
}
```

Building the Add-in Project

You're now ready to build the Instant Search add-in project. Before you build the project, you should check the Error window to ensure that you don't have an error in your code.

To build the Instant Search add-in project, follow these steps:

1. Press Ctrl+W and then press Ctrl+E to display the Error list window.

2. Ensure that there are no errors in your code. If there are errors, Visual Studio will suggest how you should correct the errors.

3. From the Build menu, select Build InstantSearchAddinCS.

4. In the status bar, you should see "Build Succeeded" if the build completed successfully.

5. Save the Instant Search add-in project from the File menu by selecting Save All or by pressing Ctrl+Shift+S. Click OK to save the project to the InstantSearchAddinCS folder.

Creating a Shim Project

Now that you've successfully created the InstantSearchAddinCS project, the next step is to create a COM shim for the add-in. If you don't use VSTO to create your add-in for Outlook 2007, you should shim your managed extension to provide application domain isolation. For details on the concept of an application domain, represented by the *AppDomain* object, search for AppDomain in the Visual Studio 2005 Developer's Reference. Application domain isolation means that an exception in another add-in will not cause your add-in to crash or operate in an unexpected manner. Similarly, if your add-in encounters an unhandled exception, it will not cause all other managed add-ins running in the Outlook process to crash. Provided by either the COM shim or VSTO, application domain isolation offers several advantages.

When Outlook loads add-ins, an add-in that causes an error during boot can be placed on a disabled add-in list. Because Outlook cannot distinguish between one shared add-in and another, Outlook places Mscoree.dll on its disabled list, and consequently all shared managed add-ins are disabled. With application domain isolation, disabling one add-in does not disable all other managed add-ins.

Application domain isolation prevents an unhandled exception in one add-in from crashing all other add-ins in the same application domain. Unexpected behavior can occur when add-ins share the same application domain. For example, if add-in A calls *ReleaseCOMObject* or *FinalReleaseCOMObject* on an object that it shares with add-in B and both add-ins are in the same application domain, add-in B encounters an access violation when it attempts to access the shared object.

If an Exchange administrator uses the Outlook security form in an Exchange public folder or group policy to maintain a list of trusted add-ins, trusting a shared add-in means trusting Mscoree.dll, which in effect trusts all shared add-ins and negates the intended action, which is to trust a single add-in. For additional information on Outlook security and the concept of a trusted add-in, see Chapter 19, "Trust and Security." For VSTO add-ins, the administrator trusts the manifest of the managed add-in assembly. For COM shim add-ins, the administrator trusts the COM shim that acts as a proxy for the managed add-in.

A COM shim acts as a native proxy for your managed add-in. COM shims must be written in C++. However, thanks to the COM Shim Wizard that is available on MSDN or on the Web site that accompanies this book, knowledge of C++ is completely optional. Basically you only need to click through the COM Shim Wizard and all the C++ code will be written for you automatically.

To install the Visual Studio COM Shim Wizard, follow these steps:

1. Download the file by clicking the Download link on the Web site that accompanies this book and saving the file to your hard disk. You can also download the COM Shim Wizard from MSDN. Search for "COM Shim Wizard" at *http://msdn.microsoft.com*.

2. Double-click the COMShimWizardSetup.msi program file on your hard disk to start the setup program and accept the defaults to complete the installation unless you are installing the wizard on Windows Vista.

3. If you are installing the COM Shim Wizard on Windows Vista, you might have to turn User Account Control off temporarily to get the installation to complete successfully. To turn off User Account Control, launch User Accounts in Windows Control Panel. When you start the installation for the COM Shim Wizard under Windows Vista, you should install the program for *Everyone* instead of *Just Me*.

To create a Visual Studio shim project using the COM Shim Wizard, follow these steps:

1. From the File menu, select the Add pop-up menu, then select New Project to add a new project to the InstantSearchCS solution.

2. In the Project Types list, expand the Other Languages node.

3. Under Other Languages, expand the Visual C++ node.

4. Under Visual C++, click the COMShims node, then from the Visual Studio Installed Templates group, click Addin Shim.

5. In the Name text box, type **InstantSearchShimCS** as shown in Figure 4-8, and click OK.

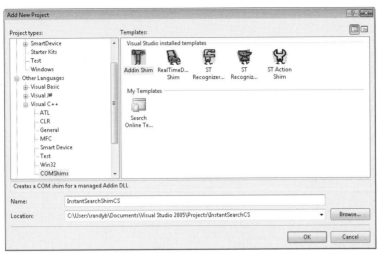

Figure 4-8 Visual Studio 2005 New Project dialog box for InstantSearchShimCS project.

6. The COM Shim Wizard page shown in Figure 4-9 will appear. Click the ellipsis (…) to specify the location of the managed assembly for your add-in.

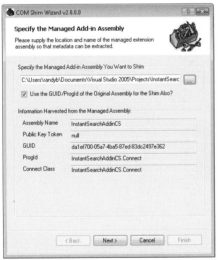

Figure 4-9 Specify the Managed Add-in Assembly dialog box in the COM Shim Wizard.

7. Locate the managed assembly named InstantSearchAddinCS.dll in this folder under your Documents folder:

    Visual Studio 2005\Projects\InstantSearchCS\InstantSearchAddinCS\bin\Release

8. Select InstantSearchAddinCS.dll in the Release folder and click Open.

9. A Security Warning dialog box appears to indicate that you should strong-name your add-in dynamic-link library (DLL). In this case, you do not provide a strong-name key for the add-in. In the Security Warning dialog box, click Yes.

10. Click Next to move to the next page of the COM Shim Wizard.

11. In the Description text box, clear the suggested description and type **Instant Search Add-in (CS)**.

12. In the Friendly Name text box, clear the suggested friendly name and type **Microsoft Outlook Sample Instant Search Add-in (CS)**.

13. In the Which Host Applications Is This Add-in User For list, select the Microsoft Outlook check box as shown in Figure 4-10.

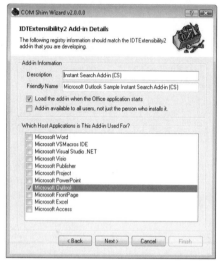

Figure 4-10 IDTExtensibility2 Add-in Details page in the COM Shim Wizard.

14. Click Next to display the Summary wizard page shown in Figure 4-11.

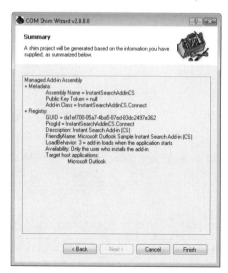

Figure 4-11 Summary wizard page in the COM Shim Wizard.

15. Click Finish to add the InstantSearchShimCS project to the InstantSearchCS solution.

For the InstantSearchShimCS.dll to work correctly with the managed component InstantSearchAddinCS.dll, both DLLs must be in the same folder. To accommodate this requirement, you should change the Output Directory for the Shim DLL to be the same as the folder for the managed add-in DLL.

To set the Output Directory for the COM shim project, follow these steps:

1. In the Solution Explorer window, click InstantSearchShimCS.

2. From the Project menu, select Properties.

3. In the InstantSearchShimCS Property Pages dialog box shown in Figure 4-12, expand the Configuration Properties node and click the General node.

4. In the Output Directory combo box, type **..\InstantSearchAddinCS\bin\Release** and then click OK.

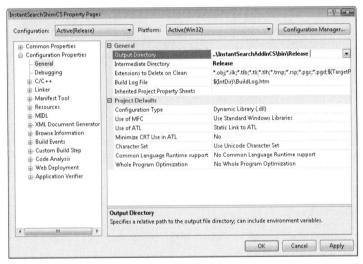

Figure 4-12   Property Pages dialog box for the InstantSearchShimCS project.

Creating a Setup Project

The next step is to add a setup project to your solution. Once you have a setup project, you will be able to deploy the add-in to other users. Of course, you can modify this add-in to suit your own requirements.

To create a Visual Studio setup project, follow these steps:

1. From the File menu, select the Add pop-up menu, and then select New Project to add a new project to the InstantSearchCS solution.

2. In the Project Types list, expand the Other Project Types node.

3. Under Other Project Types, click the Setup and Deployment node.

4. In the Visual Studio Installed Templates group, click Setup Project.

5. In the Name text box, type **InstantSearchSetupCS** as shown in Figure 4-13, and then click OK.

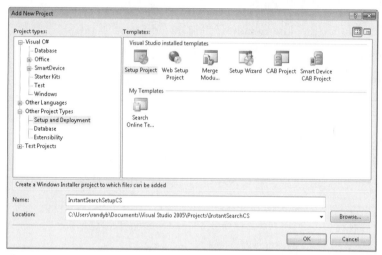

Figure 4-13   Visual Studio 2005 New Project dialog box for InstantSearchSetupCS project.

Next you'll set properties on the InstantSearchSetupCS project so that the user installing the project sees the correct title for the solution during setup.

To set properties on the InstantSearchSetupCS project, follow these steps:

1. In the Solution Explorer window, click InstantSearchSetupCS.

2. Press F4 to open the Properties dialog box, shown in Figure 4-14.

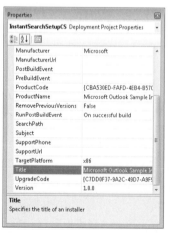

Figure 4-14   Properties dialog box for the InstantSearchSetupCS project.

3. For the *Title* and *ProductName* properties of the setup project, type **Microsoft Outlook Sample Instant Search Add-in (CS)**.

Finally, you need to add project outputs to the setup project. In this case, you'll add project outputs for both the managed add-in DLL and the shim DLL. Adding a project output to the setup project installs these DLLs to the Application folder created by the setup project.

To add primary outputs to the setup project, follow these steps:

1. In the Solution Explorer window, click InstantSearchSetupCS.

2. From the Project menu, select the Add pop-up menu, then select Project Output to add new project outputs to the InstantSearchSetupCS solution.

3. In the Add Project Output dialog box shown in Figure 4-15, in the Project drop-down list, select InstantSearchAddinCS, and then click OK.

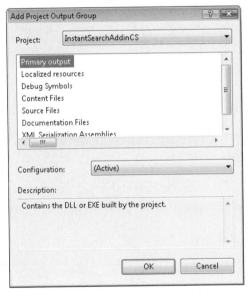

Figure 4-15   Add Project Output dialog box.

4. Repeat the step to display the Add Project Output dialog box, but this time, in the Project drop-down list box, select InstantSearchShimCS, and then click OK.

5. In the Solution Explorer, under the InstantSearchSetupCS project, click Primary Output From InstantSearchShimCS and press F4 to display the Properties dialog box.

6. In the Properties dialog box shown in Figure 4-16, click the *Register* property and select vsdrpCOMSelfReg in the drop-down list box.

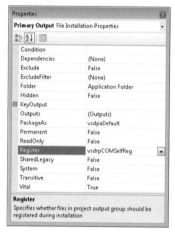

Figure 4-16   Properties dialog box for primary output from InstantSearchShimCS.

At this point, both InstantSearchAddinCS and InstantSearchShimCS should be listed as project outputs for the InstantSearchSetupCS project.

Building the Setup Project

You're almost at the finish line. In just a few more steps, you'll have an add-in that you can install on your machine or that of a colleague.

To build the setup project, follow these steps:

1. In the Solution Explorer window, click InstantSearchSetupCS.

2. From the Build menu, select Build Solution to build the entire InstantSearchCS solution.

Installing the Instant Search Add-In

Assuming that the solution built successfully, you can now install the Instant Search add-in using the built setup project.

To install the setup project, follow these steps:

1. In the Solution Explorer window, right-click InstantSearchSetupCS, and from the context menu, select Install.

2. Click through the Setup dialog boxes to install Microsoft Outlook Sample Instant Search Add-in (CS).

3. When the setup process is complete, click Close.

> **Note**   If you are installing the add-in on Windows Vista, you will see the User Account Control dialog box after installation begins. Click Allow to indicate that you trust the setup package for the Microsoft Outlook Sample Instant Search Add-in (CS).

Testing the Instant Search Add-in Solution

Now that you've built the complete InstantSearchCS solution, you can proceed to test the add-in to ensure that all the steps were followed correctly and that you don't see unexpected results.

What to Expect

When you launch Outlook after setup of the add-in and you right-click a mail message in your Inbox, you should see the Instant Search pop-up menu shown in Figure 4-1 at the bottom of the item's context menu. When you select a command on the Instant Search pop-up menu such as Received This Week, you should see a new Explorer window that displays all messages received from the sender during this week.

When you close Outlook, the Instant Search add-in should not cause Outlook to remain in memory. See the section "Debug Mode" later in this chapter for suggestions about how to determine whether Outlook remains in memory after you shut it down.

Troubleshooting

If you do not see the Instant Search pop-up menu, check to ensure that the Instant Search add-in is installed. If the add-in is not installed, you need to re-examine the steps to ensure that you did not miss a critical step.

To determine if the Instant Search add-in is installed correctly, follow these steps:

1. In the Outlook Explorer window, from the Tools menu, select Trust Center.

2. In the left pane of the Trust Center dialog box, click Add-ins. At the bottom of the dialog box, in the Manage drop-down list box, ensure that COM Add-ins is selected, then click Go to display the COM Add-ins dialog box.

3. The COM Add-ins dialog box should indicate that the add-in is installed and connected as shown in Figure 4-17.

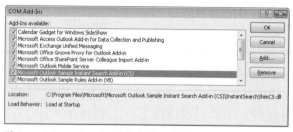

Figure 4-17   The COM Add-ins dialog box can help you troubleshoot your add-in.

Debug Mode

So far you've stepped through creating an add-in, and the endpoint was to use the add-in in Run mode in Outlook. What should you do when confronted with the real-world experience of writing your add-in from scratch? Although you should follow the same steps overall that are described in this chapter, when you are coding the add-in project you will run the add-in project in Debug mode. To run the add-in in Debug mode, you must set the start action for your add-in in the add-in project.

To set the start action for your add-in, follow these steps:

1. In the Solution Explorer window, click InstantSearchAddinCS.

2. From the Project menu, select InstantSearchAddinCS Properties.

3. In the Properties dialog box, click the Debug tab.

4. Under Start Action, select the Start External Program check box.

5. Click the ellipsis (…) to open the Select File dialog box.

6. In the Office12 folder, select Outlook.exe, as shown in Figure 4-18. The Office 12 folder is typically located here:

    C:\Program Files\Microsoft Office\Office12\outlook.exe

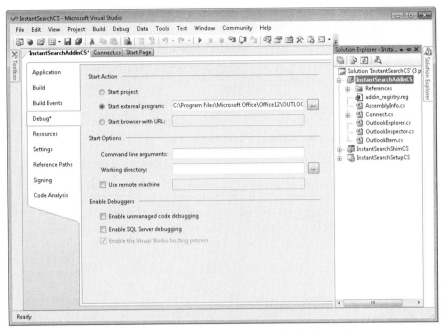

Figure 4-18   Set the start action for your add-in on the Debug tab.

Debugging Code

Before you attempt to debug your add-in, you should shut down Outlook before you proceed. If Outlook is running, your debug session might not yield the expected results. Use the Windows Task Manager to ensure that Outlook is not running before you start in Debug mode. If Outlook is not running, you will not see Outlook.exe in the process list in the Task Manager.

To ensure that Outlook is not running before you start debugging, follow these steps:

1. Press Ctrl+Alt+Delete to launch the Windows Task Manager.

2. In the Windows Security dialog box, click Task Manager.

3. In the Windows Task Manager dialog box, click the Processes tab.

4. Ensure that Outlook.exe is not in the list of running processes.

One interesting way to ensure that Outlook has shut down cleanly is to use the Mail application in Control Panel to force Outlook to boot with a profile prompt. If the profile prompt appears when you start Outlook in Debug mode, you can be assured that no previous instance of Outlook was running when you started your debug session. When you have completed debugging, you can remove the profile prompt by using the Mail application again.

Once you have your add-in project set up to perform debugging, you can use the great debugging features of Visual Studio 2005. These features include debugging tools such as setting breakpoints, using watch and locals windows, and using edit and continue. Be aware that when you hit a breakpoint in your code, you might cause Outlook to become unresponsive until you continue execution.

To debug your add-in, follow these steps:

1. Ensure that Outlook is shut down.
2. Set your breakpoints before you begin the debugging process.
3. Press F5 to launch Outlook and begin the debugging process.
4. From the Visual Studio Debug menu, select Stop Debugging to stop debugging. Outlook closes when you stop the debugging process.

Summary

This chapter has provided you with end-to-end instructions on how to build an Outlook add-in using Visual Studio 2005. The add-in you have created leverages the new Instant Search feature of Outlook 2007. To ensure add-in stability, the Instant Search add-in is provided with its own application domain by way of a COM shim. Finally, you also have created a setup project so that you can deploy the add-in to other users. You should be able to use the understanding you've gained in this chapter to move on to create an add-in with your own unique design and features. Happy coding!

Part III
Working with Outlook Data

Chapter 5
Built-in Item Types

This chapter introduces you to the built-in item types in Microsoft Office Outlook 2007. We'll cover the basic types used in the Outlook object model to represent e-mail messages, appointments, contacts, and tasks.

- **Introduction to built-in and custom types**   Explains the difference between Outlook's built-in and custom types. The *MessageClass* property on an item provides the distinction between a built-in and custom type.

- **Creating an item**   You'll learn how to create a built-in item type programmatically and how to write code that uses the properties and methods of that type.

- **Properties and methods of built-in types**   Code samples for using the important properties and methods of built-in types such as *MailItem*, *AppointmentItem*, *ContactItem*, and *TaskItem*. This chapter concentrates especially on the properties and methods that are new to Outlook 2007.

Introduction to Built-in and Custom Item Types

Outlook features built-in types that are appropriate to modules such as Mail, Calendar, Contacts, and Tasks. Modules provide a way of conceptualizing the type of work that an Outlook user needs to perform. For example, you navigate to the Mail module to send and respond to e-mail messages. If you need to work with contacts, you navigate to the Contacts module to display your contacts in views such as the Card or Electronic Business Card view. The trend in Outlook 2007 is to break down some of the fences between individual modules. For example, you can now view tasks on the Calendar or on the To-Do Bar in the Mail module. You can also view upcoming appointments on the To-Do Bar, so the notion of item type being tied to module no longer applies in all cases.

Built-in item types are specialized for the functionality particular to each module. These built-in types also provide you with business logic that pertains to the specific type. For example, appointment items have a start and end time, and start time must always precede end time. Recurring appointments follow defined patterns of recurrence, but recurrence exceptions allow variations in the recurrence patterns. Meetings (appointments with attendees) also have business logic that relates to how meeting updates and cancellations are handled, and how the meeting is represented on the attendees' calendar. In this chapter, you learn how you can use built-in item types that lend themselves to the functionality that you want to expose in your solution.

Before a discussion of how these types can be used in your code, you should understand all the built-in types available in Outlook 2007. Table 5-1 lists all the objects that represent built-in and custom items in Outlook and the corresponding base message class. Note that an asterisk after the base message class (for example, IPM.Sharing.*) indicates that multiple message classes are used for a given built-in type. The IPM prefix in the message class stands for "interpersonal message" and applies to the visible item types in Outlook. Custom items cannot be derived from the base class representing the built-in item. From an object model perspective, a custom item is still represented by the base class for a particular item type. However, as explained later in this chapter, custom items use a custom message class by appending an identifier to the base message class.

Table 5-1   Built-in Outlook Item Types

Object	Base message class	OlObjectClass	Description
AppointmentItem	IPM.Appointment	olAppointment	Represents an appointment item in a Calendar folder.
ContactItem	IPM.Contact	olContact	Represents a contact item in a Contacts folder.
DistListItem	IPM.DistList	olDistributionList	Represents an Outlook distribution list in a Contacts folder.
DocumentItem	IPM.Document.*	olDocument	Represents an Office document that has been dragged into an Outlook folder. The type of document is appended to the message class so that Word documents have a message class of *IPM.Document.Word.Document.8*.
JournalItem	IPM.Journal	olJournal	Represents a journal item in a Journal folder.
MailItem	IPM.Note	olNote	Represents a mail message in an Outlook folder such as Drafts, Inbox, or Sent Items.
MeetingItem	IPM.Schedule.Meeting.Response IPM.Schedule.Meeting.Resp.Pos IPM.Schedule.Meeting.Resp.Neg IPM.Schedule.Meeting.Resp.Tent IPM.Schedule.Meeting.Resp.Canceled	olMeetingRequest	Represents a meeting request, cancellation, accept, decline, or tentative message in an Outlook folder.

Table 5-1   **Built-in Outlook Item Types**

Object	Base message class	OlObjectClass	Description
NoteItem	IPM.StickyNote	olNote	Represents a note in the Notes folder.
PostItem	IPM.Post	olPost	Represents a post in an Outlook folder. The new Outlook 2007 RSS item is also typed as a *PostItem* object. Unlike a normal post item, an RSS item has some special properties and a message class of *IPM.Post.Rss*.
RemoteItem	IPM.Remote	olRemote	Represents a mail message that has not been fully downloaded from the server. Typically a remote item only provides message subject, date received, sender, and the first 255 characters of the message body.
ReportItem	REPORT.IPM.Note.*	olReport	Represents a mail delivery report such as a nondelivery report that appears in the Inbox when delivery fails.
SharingItem	IPM.Sharing.*	olSharing	Represents a sharing invitation to view another user's folder in the Inbox.
StorageItem	Any valid message class, defaults to IPM.Storage	olStorageItem	Represents a hidden message in a folder.
TaskItem	IPM.Task	olTask	Represents a task in a Tasks folder.
TaskRequestAccept-Item	IPM.TaskRequest.Accept	olTaskRequest-Accept	Represents an accept response to a task request in the Inbox.
TaskRequest-DeclineItem	IPM.TaskRequest.Decline	olTaskRequest-Decline	Represents a decline response to a task request in the Inbox.
TaskRequestItem	IPM.TaskRequest	olTaskRequest	Represents a task request in the Inbox.
TaskRequestUp-dateItem	IPM.TaskRequest.Update	olTaskRequest-Update	Represents an update to a task request in the Inbox.

Understanding *MessageClass*

The distinguishing factor for a built-in item versus a custom item is the item's message class. *MessageClass* is a string property on all Outlook item types, and each item type is identified with a unique message class. *MessageClass* corresponds to *PR_MESSAGE_CLASS* on the underlying *IMessage* exposed by the Messaging Application Programming Interface (MAPI). Outlook uses *MessageClass* to determine how to display the item in an Outlook Inspector window. It also uses *MessageClass* to type the item as *MailItem*, *ContactItem*, and so forth. For example, all built-in contact items have a message class equal to *IPM.Contact*. Custom item types append a custom identifier to the built-in item's message class. For example, if you create a custom form named *Shoe Store*, the message class for that custom item would be *IPM.Contact.Shoe Store*. In addition to a unique message class, custom types support both custom properties and custom actions.

Built-in vs. Custom Types

If you are new to the Outlook object model, this profusion of types might confuse or intimidate you. Think of an Outlook item as a property bag that also has some item-specific verbs such as *Send* or common verbs such as *Save* or *Display*. Although all Outlook items have properties in common, other item types wrap Outlook's internal business logic and expose a specific set of properties based on a specific item type. For example, an *AppointmentItem* exposes both *StartTime* and *EndTime*. *EndTime* must occur after *StartTime*, or Outlook will raise an error when you attempt to save the item.

To make matters more perplexing, the Outlook object model distinguishes between items that are displayed in a window and the data storage for that item. An *Inspector* object is a generic object that represents any Outlook item displayed in a window. If you need to know which type of item is displayed in a given Inspector window, you examine the *Inspector.CurrentItem* property, which returns an object that represents the underlying item type. For the best Microsoft .NET Framework coding experience, you should cast that *object* to the appropriate type such as *MailItem*.

Creating an Item

There are several ways that you can create an item in Outlook. Unfortunately, you cannot create an Outlook item using a New clause. You must use one of the following methods to create an item:

- *Application.CreateItem*
- *Application.CreateItemFromTemplate*
- *Items.Add*
- *Namespace.OpenSharedItem*

Once you have created the item, you should call the *Save* method to persist the item to a folder or the *Send* method if you want to send the item to one or more recipients.

To create a built-in Outlook item in a default folder, you must use the *CreateItem* method of the Outlook *Application* object. If you want to create a custom item (such as *IPM.Contact.Sample*) or a built-in item in a nondefault folder, use the *Items.Add* method described later in this chapter.

Application.CreateItem Method

Here are general guidelines for creating items with the *CreateItem* method:

- Use *CreateItem* to create a built-in item such as a contact or appointment item in the default folder for that item.

- *CreateItem* returns an *object,* and you should cast the returned *object* to the appropriate type.

- You must call *Item.Save* to persist the item. When you save a nonsendable item created with *CreateItem,* the item is saved into the default folder for the item in the default store.

> **Note**   If a *MailItem* is saved but not sent, the item is saved in the Drafts folder rather than the Inbox.

- If you need to create a custom item, you should use the *Add* method of the *Items* collection on the *Folder* object.

- If you need to create a built-in item in a nondefault folder, you should use the *Add* method of the *Items* collection on the *Folder* object.

The following code sample creates a *ContactItem* object in the default Contacts folder:

```
private void CreateContact()
{
    Outlook.ContactItem contact = Application.CreateItem(
        Outlook.OlItemType.olContactItem) as Outlook.ContactItem;
    contact.FirstName = "Nancy";
    contact.LastName = "Freehafer";
    contact.CompanyName = "Contoso Ltd.";
    contact.EmailAddress = "nancyf@contoso.com";
    contact.Save();
}
```

If you want to use a helper method for creating items, take a look at the *OutlookHelper* class in the sample code on this book's companion Web site. The static *OutlookHelper* class allows you to use several overrides for each item type. You can also use these helper procedures as code snippets to simplify item creation. Here are three overrides for *MailItemCreate*:

```
internal static Outlook.MailItem MailItemCreate()
{
    return Application.CreateItem(
        Outlook.OlItemType.olMailItem) as Outlook.MailItem;
}
```

```
internal static Outlook.MailItem MailItemCreate(
    string subject)
{
    Outlook.MailItem mail = Application.CreateItem(
        Outlook.OlItemType.olMailItem) as Outlook.MailItem;
    mail.Subject = subject;
    return mail;
}

internal static Outlook.MailItem MailItemCreate
    (string subject, string body)
{
    Outlook.MailItem mail = Application.CreateItem(
        Outlook.OlItemType.olMailItem) as Outlook.MailItem;
    mail.Subject = subject;
    mail.Body = body;
    return mail;
}
```

For example, the following code example creates a mail message and assigns subject and body in one call. When the *Display* method is called, the programmatically created message is displayed to the user.

```
private void CreateMail()
{
    Outlook.MailItem mail =
        OutlookHelper.MailItemCreate("Test Message", "Body text");
    mail.Display(false);
}
```

Application.CreateItemFromTemplate Method

You can also create an item by using the *CreateItemFromTemplate* method. This method is useful if you have an Outlook form template file (.oft) stored on disk that you want to use as a message template. Template files can contain preformatted text, stationery, or images that you want to include in the message. If the template file contains code behind the form, the form code will not run. The *CreateItemFromTemplate* method takes two arguments: the path to the template file and the optional folder where the item will be created when saved. The following code example opens Ivy.oft, assigns a subject, and then saves the message to the Drafts folder:

```
private void CreateItemFromTemplate()
{
    Outlook.Folder folder =
        Application.Session.GetDefaultFolder(
        Outlook.OlDefaultFolders.olFolderDrafts) as Outlook.Folder;
    Outlook.MailItem mail =
        Application.CreateItemFromTemplate(
        @"c:\ivy.oft", folder) as Outlook.MailItem;
    mail.Subject = "Congratulations";
    mail.Save();
}
```

Items.Add() Method

Items.Add provides another way to add items programmatically. The *Items* collection is available on a *Folder* object. The *Items.Add* method should be used in the following situations:

- Use *Items.Add* to create a built-in item or custom item in any folder that is appropriate for the item that you wish to create. For example, you should use `Items.Add("IPM.Contact.Shoe Store")` in a Contacts folder.

- The optional *Type* argument can specify a built-in item by passing an *OlItemType* enum value. To create a custom item, provide a string representing a valid message class. If you do not specify *Type*, the item returned defaults to the type of the *Folder* or to *MailItem* if the parent folder is not typed.

- *Items.Add* returns an *object*, and you should cast the returned *object* to the appropriate type.

- You must call *Item.Save* to persist the item.

> **Note**   *Type* can be one of the following *OlItemType* constants: *olAppointmentItem, olContactItem, olJournalItem, olMailItem, olNoteItem, olPostItem,* or *olTaskItem,* or any valid message class.

The following code sample adds a custom contact item named Shoe Store to the Shoe Store folder, which is a subfolder of the default Contacts folder:

```
private void CreateCustomItem()
{
    Outlook.Folder folder =
        Application.Session.GetDefaultFolder(
        Outlook.OlDefaultFolders.olFolderContacts).Folders[
        "Shoe Store"] as Outlook.Folder;
    Outlook.ContactItem contact =
        folder.Items.Add(
        "IPM.Contact.Shoe Store") as Outlook.ContactItem;
    contact.FirstName = "Michael";
    contact.LastName = "Sullivan";
    contact.UserProperties["Shoe Size"].Value  = "9";
    contact.Save();
}
```

Namespace.OpenSharedItem() Method

The *OpenSharedItem* method on the *Namespace* object is new to Outlook 2007. It allows you to create an item from a file. Use the *OpenSharedItem* method to open messages stored as Outlook message format (.msg) files, iCalendar appointment (.ics) files, or vCard (.vcf) files. Be sure to cast the *object* returned by this method to the appropriate item type and call the *Save* method to persist the item. The item returned by *OpenSharedItem* will be saved in the default folder for the specific item type. If you need to move the item to a nondefault folder, use the *Move* method for the item.

The *ImportContacts* procedure imports all the vCard files in a file system folder and saves the contacts into the folder specified by the *targetFolder* parameter.

```
private void ImportContacts(string path, Outlook.Folder targetFolder)
{
    Outlook.ContactItem contact;
    Outlook.ContactItem moveContact;
    if (Directory.Exists(path))
    {
        string[] files = Directory.GetFiles(path, "*.vcf");
        foreach (string file in files)
        {
            contact = Application.Session.OpenSharedItem(file)
                as Outlook.ContactItem;
            if (targetFolder ==
                Application.Session.GetDefaultFolder(
                Outlook.OlDefaultFolders.olFolderContacts)
                as Outlook.Folder)
            {
                contact.Save();
            }
            else
            {
                moveContact = contact.Move(targetFolder)
                    as Outlook.ContactItem;
                moveContact.Save();
            }
        }

    }
}
```

MailItem, PostItem, and *SharingItem* Objects

The *MailItem* object represents a received message in a mail folder or a sent message in a folder such as the Sent Items folder. *MailItem* is one of the most important Outlook item types. This section also covers some of the methods and properties of the *PostItem* and *SharingItem* objects, close relatives of *MailItem*. The properties of the *PostItem* object are similar to the properties of the *MailItem* object, so they are discussed together in this section. The *SharingItem* object is new to Outlook 2007. For a detailed discussion of the *SharingItem* object, see Chapter 9, "Sharing Information with Other Users."

Appropriate Uses of *MailItem* and *PostItem*

From a developer's perspective, a *MailItem* object is used to compose or read a message that is transmitted to one or more recipients. For compose messages, you can also set the body text, subject, and recipients of the message. For read messages, you can get body text, subject, recipients, and take actions such as Reply, Reply All, and Forward. The uses of *MailItem* are extensive. At the simplest level, you might want to enforce certain organizational mail rules such as ensuring that Reply All is limited to a maximum number of recipients. Another simple scenario is preventing attachments greater than the maximum attachment size from being attached to a message. Intermediate scenarios that apply to *MailItem* revolve around disclaimers and inspection of the body text for keywords or inappropriate language. Finally, more complex scenarios can be built around organizing incoming messages in a folder hierarchy, associating received messages with a specific customer record, or creating an approval workflow. Some of these scenarios can be accomplished using the new *Rules* object in Outlook 2007. However, the *Rules* object does not cover every scenario. In some cases, your solution requires that you write code that utilizes the *MailItem* object.

The *PostItem* object is typically used for folder-based conversations in a shared folder such as a Microsoft Exchange public folder. Custom post items can be used for specific scenarios that require additional custom properties that are not available on the built-in *PostItem* object. For example, a Product Ideas folder might contain posts that allow the user to mark the posts by product category and product technology. Another use of *PostItem* is as a type of blank item that allows you to build from scratch. In this case, *PostItem* serves as a base class that you decorate with custom properties and actions.

Compose *MailItem*

To create a compose *MailItem*, use the *CreateItem* method of the *Application* object. Once you have a *MailItem* object, you can set properties on the item. Once you have set properties such as *Subject* or added recipients to the *Recipients* collection, you can send the message programmatically by calling the *Send* method.

Adding Recipients

Recipient and *AddressEntry* objects are discussed in detail in Chapter 7, "Address Books and Recipients." The example code that follows creates a new *MailItem*, sets the Subject to "Quarterly Sales Report FY06 Q4," addresses the message to the user's manager, attaches C:\Sales reports\fy06q4.xlsx, and then sends the message.

> **Note**   The sample code will run correctly only against a Microsoft Exchange Server account. The code assumes that a manager relationship has been established for users in Microsoft Active Directory directory service. The code uses the new *ExchangeUser* object to determine the current user's manager by calling the *GetExchangeUserManager* method.

```
private void SendSalesReport()
{
    Outlook.MailItem mail = Application.CreateItem(
        Outlook.OlItemType.olMailItem) as Outlook.MailItem;
    mail.Subject = "Quarterly Sales Report FY06 Q4";
    Outlook.AddressEntry currentUser =
        Application.Session.CurrentUser.AddressEntry;
    if (currentUser.Type == "EX")
    {
        Outlook.ExchangeUser manager =
            currentUser.GetExchangeUser().GetExchangeUserManager();
        //Add recipient using display name, alias, or smtp address
        mail.Recipients.Add(manager.PrimarySmtpAddress);
        mail.Recipients.ResolveAll();
        mail.Attachments.Add(@"c:\sales reports\fy06q4.xlsx",
            Outlook.OlAttachmentType.olByValue , Type.Missing, Type.Missing);
        mail.Send();
    }
}
```

Set the Clear-Text Body

For all item types, you can set the clear-text body for the message by using the *Item.Body* property. For example, the following line sets the message body to "This is the message body."

```
mail.Body = "This is the message body.";
```

Set the HTML Body

If you want to format the message body, then you should consider using the *HTMLBody* property. Note that the *HTMLBody* property is only available on *MailItem*, *PostItem*, and *SharingItem* objects. The following procedure creates a compose note (shown in Figure 5-1) that displays "**This** is the *message* body."

```
private void CreateHTMLMail()
{
    Outlook.MailItem mail = Application.CreateItem(
        Outlook.OlItemType.olMailItem) as Outlook.MailItem;
    mail.HTMLBody = "<body>" +
        "<B>This</B> is the <I>message</I> body.</body>";
    mail.Display(false);
}
```

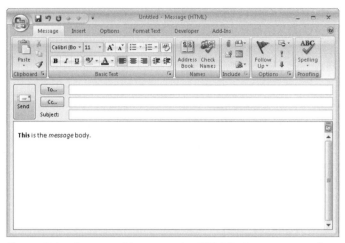

Figure 5-1   Compose Note uses the *HTMLBody* property to format the message body.

Formatting the Body Using *WordEditor*

If you need to format the message body for item types other than *MailItem*, *PostItem*, or *SharingItem*, you must use the *Item.GetInspector().WordEditor* property. The *WordEditor* property returns a Word *Document* object. By using the Word *Selection* object, you can use the Word object model to format the text in the body of the item. To use the Word object model in your solution, you must add a reference to the Microsoft Word 12.0 Object Model. To add a reference to the Word object model, follow these steps:

1. On the Project menu, select Add Reference.

2. Click the COM tab.

3. Select Microsoft Word 12.0 Object Model, and then click OK.

> **Note**   You can use the *WordEditor* object only when an *Inspector* is displayed in the Outlook user interface. If you attempt to access the *Inspector.WordEditor* object before the item is displayed, Outlook will raise an error. The *Word.Selection* object provides methods and properties that allow you to add and format text in an Outlook item. The best practice for using the *Word.Selection* object is to write code in the Inspector's *Activate* event. If you attempt to use the *NewInspector* event of the *Inspectors* object or the *Open* event for the item to access the *Word.Selection* object, Outlook will raise runtime error 4605, "This method or property is not available because the document is locked for editing."

The following code sample uses the *WordEditor* to create a message body for a *ContactItem*. The sample code utilizes several events, namely the *Inspectors_NewInspector* event and the *Inspector_Activate* event. For a complete discussion of Outlook events, see Chapter 8, "Responding to Events." Like the example for the *HTMLBody* property, the message body displays "**This** is the *message* body."

```
// Instance variables with class-level scope
Outlook.Inspectors m_Inspectors;
Outlook.Inspector m_Inspector;

// Startup procedure
private void ThisApplication_Startup()
{
    m_Inspectors = ThisApplication.Inspectors;
    m_Inspectors.NewInspector +=
        new Outlook.InspectorsEvents_NewInspectorEventHandler(
        Inspectors_NewInspector);
}

private void Inspectors_NewInspector(Outlook.Inspector Inspector)
{
    try
    {
        OutlookItem olItem = new OutlookItem(Inspector.CurrentItem);
        // Make sure this is a new contact item
        if (olItem.Class == Outlook.OlObjectClass.olContact &
            olItem.Size = 0)
        {
            m_Inspector = Inspector;
            m_Inspector.Activate +=
                new Outlook.InspectorEvents_ActivateEventHandler(
                Inspector_Activate);
        }
        else
        {
            m_Inspector.Activate -=
                new Outlook.InspectorEvents_ActivateEventHandler(
                Inspector_Activate);
            m_Inspector = null;
        }
    }
    catch (Exception ex)
    {
        Debug.WriteLine(ex.Message);
    }
}

private void Inspector_Activate()
{
    try
    {
        //Word objects
        Word.Application wordApplication;
        Word.Document doc;
        Word.Selection sel;
        //Test for null since Outlook
        //can be installed in standalone mode
        if (m_Inspector != null)
        {
            doc = m_Inspector.WordEditor;
            wordApplication = doc.Parent as Word.Application;
```

```
                sel = wordApplication.Selection;
                sel.BoldRun();
                sel.TypeText("This");
                sel.BoldRun;
                sel.TypeText(" is the ");
                sel.ItalicRun();
                sel.TypeText("message");
                sel.ItalicRun();
                sel.TypeText(" body.");
            }
        }
        catch (Exception ex)
        {
            Debug.WriteLine(ex.Message);
        }
    }
}
```

Important   You should always test for *null* (*Nothing* in Microsoft Visual Basic) when you access the *WordEditor* property of the *Inspector* object. It is possible for Outlook to be installed in standalone mode. In this case, Word is not installed and the Word object model is not available.

Body Formats

When you set the *HTMLBody* property, Outlook automatically sets the *BodyFormat* property of the *MailItem* to *OlBodyFormat.olFormatHTML*. You can control the message format of a *MessageItem*, *PostItem*, or *SharingItem* by setting the *BodyFormat* property. The *BodyFormat* property overrides the user's default mail format setting.

Note   If you change the *BodyFormat* property from Rich Text Format (RTF) to Hypertext Markup Language (HTML) or from HTML to RTF, the formatting of the message will be lost. The *BodyFormat* property is available only for *MailItem*, *PostItem*, and *SharingItem* objects.

The following procedure checks the *BodyFormat* property for a new *MailItem*. If the *BodyFormat* is not RTF, then the *BodyFormat* property is set to RTF. Note that Outlook does not provide a method for obtaining the raw RTF stream through the Outlook object model.

```
private void SendMessageUsingRTF()
{
    Outlook.MailItem mail = Application.CreateItem(
        Outlook.OlItemType.olMailItem) as Outlook.MailItem;
    //Test default format
    if (mail.BodyFormat != Outlook.OlBodyFormat.olFormatRichText)
    {
        mail.BodyFormat = Outlook.OlBodyFormat.olFormatRichText;
    }
    //Cannot set RTF stream directly
    mail.Subject = "RTF Message";
```

```
    mail.Body = "RTF Body";
    mail.Display(false);
}
```

Adding Attachments

To add attachments to any item type, use the *Add* method of the *Attachments* collection. The *Add* method requires several parameters that are explained in Table 5-2.

Table 5-2 *Add* **Method Parameters**

Name	Required/ Optional	Type	Description
Source	Required	Object	The source of the attachment. Source can be a file represented by a full file system path or an Outlook item that constitutes an embedded message.
Type	Optional	Long	The type of the attachment, which can be one of the *OlAttachmentType* constants: *olByValue*, *olByReference*, *olEmbeddedItem*, *olOLE*.
Position	Optional	Long	This parameter applies only to e-mail messages using Microsoft Outlook Rich Text Format; it is the position where the attachment should be placed within the body text of the message. A value of 1 for the *Position* parameter specifies that the attachment should be positioned at the beginning of the message body. A value *n* greater than the number of characters in the body of the e-mail item specifies that the attachment should be placed at the end. A value of 0 makes the attachment hidden.
DisplayName	Optional	String	This parameter applies only if the mail item is in RTF and *Type* is set to *olByValue*; the name is displayed in an *Inspector* object for the attachment or when viewing the properties of the attachment. If the mail item is in Plain Text or HTML format, then the attachment is displayed using the file name in the *Source* parameter.

For most attachments, you will use the *OlAttachmentType.olByValue* constant and pass a path to the file you wish to attach in the *Add* method. If you want to attach an Outlook message file format file (.msg), pass both the path to the .msg file and *OlAttachmentType.olEmbeddedItem* in the *Add* method. The following line from the earlier Sales Report example adds a Microsoft Excel workbook to the message:

```
mail.Attachments.Add(@"c:\sales reports\fy06q4.xlsx",
    Outlook.OlAttachmentType.olByValue,
    System.Type.Missing, System.Type.Missing);
```

Attachment Security

Outlook protects users from malicious code that is transported via e-mail. By default, attachments with certain file extensions such as .exe and .bat are blocked whether the attachment is added by the user or programmatically. These attachments are known as Level 1 attachments, and a blocked attachment cannot be opened by the user or programmatically. Level 1 attachments are not available in the *Attachments* collection so they cannot be saved or enumerated programmatically. Level 2 attachments provide a lesser degree of threat to the user, but Level 2 attachments must be saved to the file system before they can be opened. Outlook 2007 introduces the new *BlockLevel* property on the *Attachment* object that lets you determine the security status of the attachment. *Attachment.BlockLevel* returns an *OlBlockLevelStatus* value. Valid *OlBlockLevelStatus* values are as shown in Table 5-3.

Table 5-3 *OlBlockLevelStatus* **Enumeration**

Name	Description
olAttachmentBlockLevelNone	There is no restriction on the type of the attachment based on its file extension.
olAttachmentBlockLevelOpen	There is a restriction on the type of the attachment based on its file extension such that users must first save the attachment to disk before opening it.

> **More Info**   Attachment security is covered in detail in Chapter 19, "Trust and Security."

Saving Attachments

The *SaveAsFile* method on the *Attachment* object allows you to save attachments to the file system. The *RemoveAttachmentsAndSaveToDisk* procedure provides a useful utility that removes all attachments greater than a specified size from mail items in a folder. Attachments where *Attachment.Type = OlAttachmentType.olByValue* are removed from the message. This procedure illustrates some important concepts in Outlook development:

- Using a restriction clause to provide a subset of items in a folder. For additional details, see Chapter 11, "Searching Outlook Data."

- Outlook collections such as the *Attachments* collection are one-based. If you use the *Index [n]* operator for an Outlook collection, you can reference *Attachments[1]* to *Attachments[n]* where n represents *Attachments.Count*. In Visual Basic, you reference *Attachments(1)* to *Attachments(n)*.

- To remove items from a collection, you cannot use a *foreach* (C#) or *For...Each* (Visual Basic) construct. If you do so, you will fail to iterate over the correct number of items in the collection. Instead, use the *Index* operator to obtain the first item in the collection and then delete the first item in the collection. Use a *while* construct to determine when you have deleted the appropriate number of items in the collection.

```csharp
private void RemoveAttachmentsAndSaveToDisk(string path,
    Outlook.Folder folder, int size)
{
    Outlook.Items attachItems;
    Outlook.Attachment attachment;
    Outlook.Attachments attachments;
    int byValueCount;
    int removeCount;
    bool saveMessage;
    try
    {
        //The restriction will find all items that
        //have attachments and MessageClass = IPM.Note
        string filter = "@SQL=" + "\""
            + "urn:schemas:httpmail:hasattachment"
            + "\"" + " = True" + " AND " + "\""
            + "http://schemas.microsoft.com/mapi/proptag/0x001A001E"
            + "\"" + " = 'IPM.Note'";
        attachItems = folder.Items.Restrict(filter);
        foreach (Outlook.MailItem mail in attachItems)
        {
            saveMessage = false;
            byValueCount = 0;
            attachments = mail.Attachments;
            //Obtain the count of ByValue attachments
            foreach(Outlook.Attachment attach in attachments)
            {
                if (attach.Size > size
                    & attach.Type ==
                    Outlook.OlAttachmentType.olByValue)
                {
                    byValueCount = byValueCount + 1;
                }
            }
            if (byValueCount > 0)
            {
                //removeCount is number of attachments to remove
                removeCount = attachments.Count - byValueCount;
                while (mail.Attachments.Count != removeCount)
                {
                    //Use indexer to obtain
                    //first attachment in collection
                    attachment = mail.Attachments[1];
                    //You can refine this code to save
                    //separate copies of attachments
                    //with the same name
                    attachment.SaveAsFile(path + @"\"
                        + attachment.FileName);
                    attachment.Delete();
                    if (saveMessage != true)
                    {
                        saveMessage = true;
```

```
                    }
                }
                if (saveMessage)
                {
                    mail.Save();
                }
            }
        }
    }
    catch (Exception ex)
    {
        Debug.WriteLine(ex.Message);
    }
}
```

Sending the Message

To send a message, you call the *Send* method. On a *PostItem*, the *Post* method is analogous to the *Send* method. The *Send* method is available on the following objects:

- *AppointmentItem*
- *MailItem*
- *MeetingItem*
- *SharingItem*
- *TaskItem*

> **Note**   Calling the *Send* method does not guarantee that the message will be submitted to the Outbox and transported to message recipients. For example, if the user is connected to an Exchange server, he or she can establish delayed delivery options. Calling the *Send* method will always place the item in the Outbox. Other factors including network connectivity, online versus offline state, and delayed delivery options will determine when the message is delivered to recipients.

Send Using a Specific Account

New to Outlook 2007, the *SendUsingAccount* property allows you to send an item using a specific e-mail account. Before discussing sending using an account, a review of Outlook profiles and accounts is helpful. A profile is a collection of e-mail accounts such as an Exchange Server, Post Office Protocol 3 (POP3), Internet Message Access Protocol (IMAP), or Hypertext Transfer Protocol (HTTP) account. A profile can contain one or more accounts. A new profile is created automatically when you run Outlook for the first time, and after that the profile runs each time you start Outlook. Most users need only one profile. However, sometimes it is useful to have more than one profile. For example, you might want one profile for work and another profile for home. The Outlook object model does not allow you to create or modify profiles and accounts programmatically. However, the new *Namespace.CurrentProfileName* and *Application.DefaultProfileName* properties provide the name of the current profile and default profile, respectively.

If you want to send an item using a specific e-mail account, you must first obtain an *Account* object that represents the e-mail account that you want to use to send the item. Once you have obtained that *Account* object, simply set the *SendUsingAccount* property to that *Account* object and then call the *Send* method. The following example creates a message with an attached itinerary document and sends the message using the MSN Hotmail account:

```
private void SendUsingAccountExample()
{
    Outlook.MailItem mail = Application.CreateItem(
        Outlook.OlItemType.olMailItem) as Outlook.MailItem;
    mail.Subject = "Our itinerary";
    mail.Attachments.Add(@"c:\travel\itinerary.doc",
        Outlook.OlAttachmentType.olByValue,
        Type.Missing, Type.Missing);
    Outlook.Account account =
        Application.Session.Accounts["MSN Hotmail"];
    mail.SendUsingAccount = account;
    mail.Send();
}
```

Read *MailItem*

From an object model perspective, a read message is no different than a compose message. To clarify, a read message refers to a received message rather than a message that has been read or has not been read (unread) by the user. Your Inbox and its subfolders are populated by read messages. A read message is a *MailItem* where the *MailItem.Size* is greater than zero and the *MailItem.Sent* is *true*. A read *MailItem* also has properties that are empty on a compose *MailItem*. For example, properties such as *SenderName* or *SenderEmailAddress* will always return an empty string for a compose note.

Distinguishing a Read Note from a Compose Note

The easiest and most effective way to determine whether an item is a compose note or a read note is to examine the *Size* and *Sent* properties of the item. For example, the following *IsReadNote* method determines whether the *mail* instance variable is a read note or a compose note:

```
private bool IsReadNote(Outlook.MailItem mail)
{
    if (mail != null)
    {
        if (mail.Size > 0 && mail.Sent)
        {
            return true;
        }
        else
        {
```

```
            return false;
        }
    }
    else
        throw new ArgumentNullException();
}
```

Determining the Sender Display Name and SMTP Address

Let's assume that you want to determine the sender display name and Simple Mail Transfer Protocol (SMTP) address for a received mail item. The simplest option is to examine the *MailItem.SenderName* or the *MailItem.SenderEmailAddress* properties. This technique works without a problem if the sender is external to your organization. Without diving too far into Exchange addresses, *SenderEmailAddress* does not return an SMTP address if the sender of the message is internal to your organization. In this case, you need to use the new *PropertyAccessor* object to return the sender's SMTP address.

The following *GetSenderSMTPAddress* procedure illustrates the use of the new *PropertyAccessor* object to obtain values that are not exposed directly in the Outlook object model. For complete details regarding the *PropertyAccessor* object, see Chapter 17, "Using the *PropertyAccessor* Object." The code example examines the *SenderEMailType* property of the received *MailItem* object. If *SenderEMailType* equals EX, then the sender of the message resides on an Exchange server in your organization. You can then use the *PropertyAccessor* to obtain the *EntryID* property of the sender, use the *GetAddressEntryFromID* method on the *Namespace* object, and then obtain an *AddressEntry* object for the sender. Once you have an *AddressEntry* object for the sender, you examine the *AddressEntryType* property of the *AddressEntry* object. You can then cast the *AddressEntry* object to a new *ExchangeUser* object that exposes the *PrimarySMTPAddress* property as a first-class member of the *ExchangeUser* object. If the *AddressEntry* object for the sender does not represent an *ExchangeUser* object, you can examine the *PR_SMTP_ADDRESS* property of the *AddressEntry* object by using the *PropertyAccessor* object. Use this procedure in your own code whenever you want to determine the SMTP address for the sender of a *MailItem* object.

```
private string GetSenderSMTPAddress(Outlook.MailItem mail)
{
    string PR_SENT_REPRESENTING_ENTRYID =
        @"http://schemas.microsoft.com/mapi/proptag/0x00410102";
    string PR_SMTP_ADDRESS =
        @"http://schemas.microsoft.com/mapi/proptag/0x39FE001E";
    if (mail.SenderEmailType == "EX")
    {
        string senderEntryID =
            mail.PropertyAccessor.BinaryToString(
            mail.PropertyAccessor.GetProperty(
            PR_SENT_REPRESENTING_ENTRYID));
        Outlook.AddressEntry sender =
            Application.Session.
            GetAddressEntryFromID(senderEntryID);
```

```
            if (sender != null)
            {
                //Now we have an AddressEntry representing the Sender
                if (sender.AddressEntryUserType ==
                    Outlook.OlAddressEntryUserType.
                    olExchangeUserAddressEntry
                    || sender.AddressEntryUserType ==
                    Outlook.OlAddressEntryUserType.
                    olExchangeRemoteUserAddressEntry)
                {
                    //Use the ExchangeUser object PrimarySMTPAddress
                    Outlook.ExchangeUser exchUser =
                        sender.GetExchangeUser();
                    if (exchUser != null)
                    {
                        return exchUser.PrimarySmtpAddress;
                    }
                    else
                    {
                        return null;
                    }
                }
                else
                {
                    return sender.PropertyAccessor.GetProperty(
                        PR_SMTP_ADDRESS) as string;
                }
            }
            else
            {
                return null;
            }
        }
        else
        {
            return mail.SenderEmailAddress;
        }
    }
```

Creating a Response

You create a response to a *MailItem* by calling the *Forward*, *Reply*, or *ReplyAll* methods on the item. Each of these methods returns a *MailItem* object. When you call the *Forward*, *Reply*, or *ReplyAll* methods, you create a response using the default response style for the appropriate response type. The default response style is controlled by the the user's response style settings in the E-Mail Options dialog box shown in Figure 5-2. To display the E-Mail Options dialog box, follow these steps:

1. In the Outlook Explorer window, from the Tools menu, select Options.

2. Click the Preferences tab.

3. Click E-Mail Options.

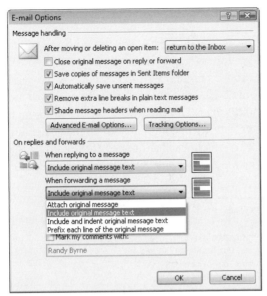

Figure 5-2   The E-Mail Options dialog box allows the user to set reply and forward styles.

Responding Using an *Action* Object

If you want to create a response using a nondefault response style, you can use the *Actions* collection on the item; obtain an *Action* object representing the type of response such as *Reply*, *ReplyAll*, or *Forward*; set the *Action.ReplyStyle*; and then call the *Execute* method of the *Action* object to obtain a *MailItem* object that uses the specified reply style. For example, the following example displays two reply messages to the user. Both messages are replies to an item in the Inbox. The first message, represented by the *mail1* instance variable, uses the user's default reply style. The second message, represented by the *mail2* instance variable, uses the *OlReplyStyle.olReplyTickOriginalText* reply style.

```
private void SetReplyStyleExample()
{
    Outlook.MailItem mail = Application.Session.
        GetDefaultFolder(
        Outlook.OlDefaultFolders.olFolderInbox).Items.Find(
        "[MessageClass]='IPM.Note'") as Outlook.MailItem;
    //Default reply action
    Outlook.MailItem mail1 = mail.Reply() as Outlook.MailItem;
    mail1.Display(false);
    //Reply using Action object
    Outlook.Action action = mail.Actions["Reply"];
    action.ReplyStyle =
        Outlook.OlActionReplyStyle.olReplyTickOriginalText;
    Outlook.MailItem mail2 = action.Execute() as Outlook.MailItem;
    mail2.Display(false);
}
```

Adding an Electronic Business Card

Electronic Business Cards in Outlook 2007 provide a great new way to share your contact information with others. Fortunately, developers can leverage this functionality. To send a message with an Electronic Business Card (see Figure 5-3), you call the *AddBusinessCard* method on the *MailItem* object. Electronic Business Cards can only be added to messages where the mail format is HTML. The *AddBusinessCard* procedure takes a string representing an e-mail address and attempts to find a *ContactItem* with that address in the default Contacts folder. A *ContactItem* can have up to three distinct e-mail addresses. If the contact is found, the *AddBusinessCard* method is called on the *MailItem* represented by the *mail* instance variable. Finally, the message is displayed to the user.

```csharp
private void AddBusinessCard(string eMailAddress)
{
    Outlook.MailItem mail = Application.CreateItem(
        Outlook.OlItemType.olMailItem) as Outlook.MailItem;
    mail.BodyFormat = Outlook.OlBodyFormat.olFormatHTML;
    Outlook.ContactItem contact = Application.Session.
        GetDefaultFolder(
        Outlook.OlDefaultFolders.olFolderContacts).Items.Find(
        "[Email1Address]='" + eMailAddress + "'" + " OR " +
        "[Email2Address]='" + eMailAddress + "'" + " OR " +
        "[Email3Address]='" + eMailAddress + "'")
        as Outlook.ContactItem;
    if (contact == null)
    {
        return;
    }
    mail.AddBusinessCard(contact);
    mail.Display(false);
}
```

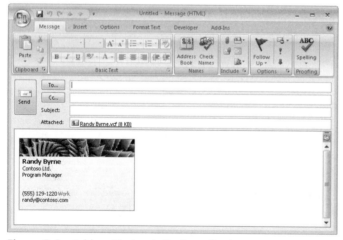

Figure 5-3   Add an Electronic Business Card to a message programmatically.

Create a To-Do Item

To-do items are also new to Outlook 2007. A to-do item is any Outlook item—such as a task, an e-mail message, or a contact—that has been flagged for follow-up. To-do items appear in the To-Do Bar. The To-Do Bar occupies a separate pane in the Outlook Explorer window and provides a convenient location for the user to see upcoming appointments and to-do items. The following item types can be marked programmatically as to-do items:

- *MailItem*
- *PostItem*
- *SharingItem*
- *ContactItem*
- *DistListItem*

By default, a *TaskItem* is always a to-do item and will appear in the To-Do Bar. To create a to-do item using code, you call the *MarkAsTask* method on the item and provide an *OlMarkInterval* constant. The *OlMarkInterval* constant controls where the to-do item appears on the To-Do Bar. Valid *OlMarkInterval* constants are listed in Table 5-4.

Table 5-4   *OlMarkInterval* Enumeration

Name	Description
olMarkLater	Mark the task due with no date.
olMarkNextWeek	Mark the task due next week.
olMarkThisWeek	Mark the task due this week.
olMarkToday	Mark the task due today.
olMarkTomorrow	Mark the task due tomorrow.

When you call *MarkAsTask*, several other properties such as *TaskStartDate*, *TaskDueDate*, *TaskCompletedDate*, and *TaskSubject* can be set on the item. Depending on the value of *OlMarkInterval*, the properties listed in Table 5-5 are set to the specified default values.

Table 5-5   Default Properties Depend on *OlMarkInterval* Value

Enumeration value	Property values
olMarkLater	*IsMarkedAsTask* is set to *true*.
	TaskSubject is set to the value of the *Subject* property for the Outlook item.
	TaskStartDate, *TaskDueDate*, and *TaskCompletedDate* are set to *null* (*Nothing* in Visual Basic).
	ToDoTaskOrdinal is set to the current date and time.

Table 5-5   Default Properties Depend on *OlMarkInterval* Value

Enumeration value	Property values
olMarkNextWeek	*IsMarkedAsTask* is set to *true*.
	TaskSubject is set to the value of the *Subject* property for the Outlook item.
	TaskStartDate is set to the first working day of next week.
	TaskDueDate is set to the last working day of next week.
	TaskCompletedDate is set to *null* (*Nothing* in Visual Basic).
	ToDoTaskOrdinal is set to the current date and time.
olMarkThisWeek	*IsMarkedAsTask* is set to *true*.
	TaskSubject is set to the value of the *Subject* property for the Outlook item.
	TaskStartDate is set to a date two working days ahead of the current date. If that value would exceed the value of *TaskDueDate*, then *TaskStartDate* is set to the value of *TaskDueDate*.
	TaskDueDate is set to the last working day of the current week.
	TaskCompletedDate is set to *null* (*Nothing* in Visual Basic).
	ToDoTaskOrdinal is set to the current date and time.
olMarkToday	*IsMarkedAsTask* is set to *true*.
	TaskSubject is set to the value of the *Subject* property for the Outlook item.
	TaskStartDate and *TaskDueDate* are set to the current date.
	TaskCompletedDate is set to *null* (*Nothing* in Visual Basic).
	ToDoTaskOrdinal is set to the current date and time.
olMarkTomorrow	*IsMarkedAsTask* is set to *true*.
	TaskSubject is set to the value of the *Subject* property for the Outlook item.
	TaskStartDate and *TaskDueDate* are set to one day after the current date.
	TaskCompletedDate is set to *null* (*Nothing* in Visual Basic).
	ToDoTaskOrdinal is set to the current date and time.

Creating a to-do item is simple. Just call the *MarkAsTask* method on the item and then save the item. If you want to create a reminder, you'll need a few additional lines of code. The following procedure creates a to-do item marked for follow-up tomorrow and sets a reminder for tomorrow at 10:00 A.M.

```
private void CreateToDoItemExample()
{
    //Date operations
    DateTime today = DateTime.Parse("10:00 AM");
    TimeSpan duration = TimeSpan.FromDays(1);
    DateTime tomorrow = today.Add(duration);
    Outlook.MailItem mail = Application.Session.
        GetDefaultFolder(
        Outlook.OlDefaultFolders.olFolderInbox).Items.Find(
        "[MessageClass]='IPM.Note'") as Outlook.MailItem;
```

```
      mail.MarkAsTask(Outlook.OlMarkInterval.olMarkTomorrow);
      mail.TaskStartDate = today;
      mail.ReminderSet = true;
      mail.ReminderTime = tomorrow;
      mail.Save();
}
```

If you want to mark an item as a to-do item programmatically, you should be aware of the following behaviors:

- You must explicitly call the *Save* method on the item after you call *MarkAsTask*.

- To set a reminder on the to-do item, set the *ReminderSet* property to *true* and use the standard *Reminder* properties such as *ReminderTime* to set the time of the reminder. In Outlook 2007, you can now use *Reminder* properties to set a reminder on a *ContactItem*.

- Set nondefault values for *TaskStartDate* and *TaskDueDate* after you call the *MarkAsTask* method.

- To clear the to-do item, call the *ClearTaskFlag* method on the item.

- To mark the to-do item as complete, set the *TaskCompletedDate* on the item. If the *TaskCompletedDate* is set, the item will not appear in the To-Do Bar. Marking the to-do item as complete does not clear the to-do item.

- The *TaskSubject* of the item controls how the to-do item is displayed in the To-Do Bar. By default, the *TaskSubject* of the item is set to the *Item.Subject*. Set the *TaskSubject* property to create a different subject for the to-do item.

- To change the position of the to-do item within its To-Do Bar group such as Today or Tomorrow, set a different value for the *ToDoTaskOrdinal* property. *ToDoTaskOrdinal* returns or sets a *Date* value that represents the ordinal value of the task for the item in its To-Do Bar group.

- If an item is marked as a to-do item, the item's *IsMarkedAsTask* property returns *true*. *IsMarkedAsTask* is a computed property. See Chapter 11 for information on how to search for to-do items in Outlook queries.

PostItem Object

The *PostItem* object represents a message posted in a folder. Unlike a *MailItem* object, a *PostItem* object is not sent to a recipient. From a user perspective, posts are typically used for threaded discussions in a folder. For a developer, a *PostItem* object can also serve as an empty canvas that you decorate with user interface, properties, and actions that are appropriate to your solution. Think of a *PostItem* object as a "blank" item that you can customize when Outlook's built-in types are too overloaded with properties or business logic for your requirements.

Creating a *PostItem*

You create a *PostItem* object by using the *CreateItem* or *Items.Add* methods discussed earlier. If you do create a *PostItem* object using *CreateItem*, the post will be saved in the user's Inbox. Because *PostItem* objects are used in application folders rather than the Inbox, you will generally use the *Items.Add* method to create the *PostItem* object. To persist a *PostItem* object, you call the *Post* method rather than the *Save* method.

Responding to a *PostItem*

To respond to a *PostItem* object, you can call the *Reply* or *Forward* methods on the *PostItem* or execute the Reply to Folder *Action* object obtained from the *Actions* collection object. The *Reply* and *Forward* methods return a *MailItem* object. The Reply to Folder *Action* returns a *PostItem* object. The following code sample creates a *PostItem* object and posts the item in the current folder. It then uses the Reply to Folder *Action* object to create a reply to the original *PostItem* object.

```
private void CreateDiscussionExample()
{
    Outlook.PostItem post = Application.
        ActiveExplorer().CurrentFolder.Items.Add("IPM.Post")
        as Outlook.PostItem;
    post.Subject = "My Subject";
    post.Post();
    Outlook.PostItem replyPost =
        post.Actions["Reply to Folder"].Execute()
        as Outlook.PostItem;
    replyPost.Subject = "RE: " + post.Subject;
    replyPost.Post();
}
```

AppointmentItem Object

An *AppointmentItem* object represents an appointment in the Calendar folder. An *AppointmentItem* object can represent a one-time appointment, an event, a meeting, or recurring events, appointments, and meetings. A meeting usually involves more than one person and is created when an *AppointmentItem* object is sent to other users, who then receive it in the form of a *MeetingItem* object in their respective Inbox folders.

An appointment or meeting can be recurring—that is, set to occur more than once on a regular or repetitive basis. When this occurs, a *RecurrencePattern* object is created for the *AppointmentItem* object. An instance of a recurring appointment can be changed or deleted. This creates an exception to the recurrence pattern, and this exception is represented by an *Exception* object. All *Exception* objects associated with a given *AppointmentItem* object are contained in an *Exceptions* collection associated with the *AppointmentItem*.

Appropriate Uses of *AppointmentItem*

Use the *AppointmentItem* object if you need to create standard appointments programmatically. If your solution focuses on adding value to Outlook's built-in calendaring functionality, you should consider using a form region to add a custom user interface to Outlook's built-in appointment item. For a complete discussion of form regions, see Chapter 13, "Creating Form Regions."

One-Time Appointments

One-time appointments are the simplest items to work with from a developer's point of view. You'll learn about one-time appointments first, and then move on to more complex topics on meeting requests and recurring appointments.

Setting Start and End Time

Outlook enforces its internal business logic for the start and end times of an appointment. The end time must always follow the start time. If the end time does not follow the start time, Outlook raises an error when you attempt to save the appointment. When you set the start and end times of an appointment, the time is set in local time according to the current time zone.

Using the *TimeZone* Object

The *TimeZone* object is new to Outlook 2007. You obtain a *TimeZone* object from the *TimeZones* collection, which represents all the time zones known to Microsoft Windows. You can use the *TimeZone* object to set or get the new *StartTimeZone* and *EndTimeZone* properties on the *AppointmentItem* object. If you need to know the user's current time zone, you should obtain the *CurrentTimeZone* property of the *TimeZones* object. The *TimeZones* object has a helper method, *ConvertTime*, that allows you to convert a given date and time value in a source time zone to a date and time value in a destination time zone.

Before using the *TimeZone* object in your code, you should understand how Outlook stores and displays dates on items. In the Outlook user interface, all dates are displayed in local time. Local time is expressed in the user's current time zone, controlled by the user's settings in the Windows Control Panel. The object model also sets or gets properties such as *Appointment.Start* and *Appointment.End* in local time. However, Outlook stores date and time values internally as Coordinated Universal Time (UTC) rather than local time. If you were to examine the internal value of *Appointment.Start* using the *PropertyAccessor* object, you would find that the internal date and time value actually is equal to the local date and time value converted to the equivalent UTC date and time value.

The time zone information is used to map the appointment to the correct UTC time when the appointment is saved, and into the correct local time when the item is displayed in the calendar. To examine the UTC time values for an appointment based on the *StartTimeZone* or *EndTimeZone* properties, you should use the *StartUTC* and *EndUTC* properties on the *AppointmentItem* object.

Changing *StartTimeZone* affects the value of *AppointmentItem.Start,* which is always represented in the local time zone, *Application.TimeZones.CurrentTimeZone*. Changing *EndTimeZone* also changes the value of *AppointmentItem.End*, which is always represented in the local time zone, *Application.TimeZones.CurrentTimeZone*.

Depending on the circumstances, changing the *StartTimeZone* or *EndTimeZone* might or might not cause Outlook to recalculate and update the *AppointmentItem.StartInStartTimeZone* and *AppointmentItem.EndInEndTimeZone* properties. *StartInStartTimeZone* and *EndInEndTimeZone* set or get values that are *DateTime* values rather than *TimeZone* objects.

As an example, in the appointment Inspector, if you are the organizer of an appointment with a start time at 1 P.M. Eastern Standard Time (EST) and end time at 3 P.M. EST, changing the appointment to have an *EndTimeZone* of Pacific Standard Time (PST) will result in an appointment lasting from 1 P.M. EST to 3 P.M. PST, with the *EndInEndTimeZone* remaining as 3 P.M. However, if you are not the organizer, changing the *EndTimeZone* from EST to PST will cause Outlook to recalculate and update the *EndInEndTimeZone*, and the appointment will last from 1 P.M. EST to 12 P.M PST.

Another example is changing the *EndTimeZone* property, resulting in an appointment end time that occurs before a previously set appointment start time, in which case Outlook recalculates and updates the *EndInEndTimeZone*. For example, an appointment with a start time at 1 P.M. PST and end time at 3 P.M. PST has its *EndTimeZone* changed to EST. In this case, changing the *EndTimeZone* would result in Outlook recalculating and updating the *EndInEndTimeZone* to 6 P.M. (in EST).

The following code sample creates an appointment that starts in the Pacific time zone (GMT–8:00) and ends in the Eastern time zone (GMT–5:30):

```
private void TimeZoneExample()
{
    Outlook.AppointmentItem appt = Application.CreateItem(
        Outlook.OlItemType.olAppointmentItem)
        as Outlook.AppointmentItem;
    Outlook.TimeZones tzs = Application.TimeZones;
    //Obtain timezone using indexer and locale-independent key
    Outlook.TimeZone tzEastern = tzs["Eastern Standard Time"];
    Outlook.TimeZone tzPacific = tzs["Pacific Standard Time"];
    appt.Subject = "SEA - JFK Flight";
    appt.Start = DateTime.Parse("8/9/2006 8:00 AM");
    appt.StartTimeZone = tzPacific;
    appt.End = DateTime.Parse("8/9/2006 5:30 PM");
    appt.Display(false);
}
```

Note   You should retrieve a specific *TimeZone* from the *TimeZones* object by using the locale-independent key for the *TimeZone* in the Windows registry. Locale-independent *TimeZone* keys are listed under the following key: HKEY_LOCAL_MACHINE\SOFTWARE \Microsoft\Windows NT\CurrentVersion\Time Zones.

Creating a Reminder

To create a reminder on an *AppointmentItem* object, you set the *ReminderSet* property to *true*. To remove a reminder, set the *ReminderSet* property to *false*. The following sample creates a reminder on a private appointment for wine tasting in Napa, California. If you want to change the time when the reminder will fire from the user's default value, use the *ReminderMinutesBeforeStart* property to set the number of minutes that the reminder will appear before the start of the appointment. The following example creates an appointment for wine tasting, sets the *Sensitivity* property for the item to *Outlook.OlSensitivity.olPrivate*, and then creates a reminder for the appointment that fires 2 hours (120 minutes) before the appointment starts:

```
private void ReminderExample()
{
    Outlook.AppointmentItem appt = Application.CreateItem(
        Outlook.OlItemType.olAppointmentItem)
        as Outlook.AppointmentItem;
    appt.Subject = "Wine Tasting";
    appt.Location = "Napa CA";
    appt.Sensitivity = Outlook.OlSensitivity.olPrivate;
    appt.Start = DateTime.Parse("10/21/2006 10:00 AM");
    appt.End = DateTime.Parse("10/21/2006 3:00 PM");
    appt.ReminderSet = true;
    appt.ReminderMinutesBeforeStart = 120;
    appt.Save();
}
```

All-Day Events

An event is an activity that lasts 24 hours or longer. Examples of events include trade shows, seminars, or vacations. To create an all-day event programmatically, set the *AllDayEvent* property to *true*. Events and annual events do not occupy blocks of time in the user's calendar; instead, they appear as banners. A banner appears at the top of a calendar day or week view. An all-day appointment displays the user's time as busy when viewed by other people, but an event or annual event displays the user's time as free.

If you create an *AppointmentItem* object, set the *AllDayEvent* property to *true*, and do not set the *Start* and *End* properties, the event will occur today. If you want the event to occur on a future date, you must set the *AllDayEvent* property to *true* and set the *Start* property to 12:00 A.M.(midnight) on the day you want the event to begin. If the event has a duration of only one day, set the *End* property to 12:00 A.M. on the day following the day on which the event begins. Otherwise you should set the *End* property to 12:00 A.M. on a date that is more than one day after the start date. If you set the *Start* or *End* time to a date and time value that does not occur at 12:00 A.M., the appointment will become a multiday appointment rather than an all-day event.

For example, the following code sample creates an all-day event that begins on June 11, 2007 and ends on June 15, 2007. Note that the *End* property for the appointment is set to 12:00 A.M. on June 16, 2007:

```
private void AllDayEventExample()
{
    Outlook.AppointmentItem appt = Application.CreateItem(
        Outlook.OlItemType.olAppointmentItem)
        as Outlook.AppointmentItem;
    appt.Subject = "Developer's Conference";
    appt.AllDayEvent = true;
    appt.Start = DateTime.Parse("6/11/2007 12:00 AM");
    appt.End = DateTime.Parse("6/16/2007 12:00 AM");
    appt.Display(false);
}
```

Appointment Attendees

It's worthwhile to spend a brief amount of time discussing appointments versus meetings. A simple appointment or simple event does not have attendees. A meeting is an appointment that has one or more attendees. An appointment that represents a meeting exists on the organizer's calendar and also on an attendee's calendar if the attendee replies with accept or tentative to the meeting request from the organizer. All three types of appointments (simple appointment, appointment where current user is organizer, appointment where current user is attendee) are represented by an *AppointmentItem* object. To invite attendees, add recipients to the *Recipients* object for the *AppointmentItem* object. To send a meeting request for the *Appointment* item, call the *Send* method of the *AppointmentItem* object.

Using the *Recipients* Collection to Add Attendees

Meeting attendees can be one of the types shown in Table 5-6.

Table 5-6 Types of Meeting Attendees

Attendee type	Description
Required	The attendee represents an attendee for whom meeting attendance is required.
Optional	The attendee represents an attendee for whom meeting attendance is optional.
Resource	The attendee represents a resource such as a conference room or equipment for a meeting.

To set the attendee type for a meeting attendee, you add a recipient to the *Recipients* collection for the *AppointmentItem* object that represents the meeting. Only the organizer of the meeting can add attendees. If an attendee wants to invite others to the meeting, he or she forwards the appointment from his or her calendar to additional invitees. You can obtain the programmatic equivalent of a forwarded appointment by calling the *Forward* method on the *AppointmentItem* object in the attendee's calendar.

The *MeetingAttendeesExample* provides you with sample code for adding attendees to a meeting. Notice that the *Type* property of the *Recipient* object is typed as an *int* (*Integer* in Visual Basic) rather than *OlMeetingRecipientType*. You must cast the appropriate *OlMeetingRecipientType* constant to an *int* before you can assign the value to the *Type* property of the *Recipient* object. This code also calls the *ResolveAll* method of the *Recipients* collection. If *ResolveAll* returns *true*, the *Send* method on the *AppointmentItem* object sends the meeting request to attendees. If *ResolveAll* returns *false*, the appointment is displayed to the user.

```
private void MeetingAttendeesExample()
{
    Outlook.Recipient recip;
    Outlook.AppointmentItem appt = Application.CreateItem(
        Outlook.OlItemType.olAppointmentItem)
        as Outlook.AppointmentItem;
    appt.MeetingStatus = Outlook.OlMeetingStatus.olMeeting;
    appt.Subject = "Sales Strategy FY2007";
    appt.Start = DateTime.Parse("5/17/2007 10:00 AM");
    appt.End = DateTime.Parse("5/17/2007 11:00 AM");
    recip = appt.Recipients.Add("someone@example.com");
    recip.Type = (int)Outlook.OlMeetingRecipientType.olOptional;
    recip = appt.Recipients.Add("teamdistributionlistalias");
    recip.Type = (int)Outlook.OlMeetingRecipientType.olRequired;
    recip = appt.Recipients.Add("Conf Room 36/2731");
    recip.Type = (int)Outlook.OlMeetingRecipientType.olResource;
    if (appt.Recipients.ResolveAll() == true)
    {
        appt.Send();
    }
    else
    {
        appt.Display(false);
    }
}
```

Checking Attendee Availability

To check attendee availability for an existing meeting on an appointment organizer's calendar, you enumerate the *Recipients* collection for the *AppointmentItem* object and examine the *MeetingResponseStatus* property of the *Recipient* object. For example, the following code looks for the Sales Strategy FY2007 meeting created in the previous code sample. If the appointment is found, the code enumerates the *MeetingResponseStatus* property for each *Recipient* in the *Recipients* collection for the *AppointmentItem* object.

```csharp
private void CheckAttendeeStatus()
{
    Outlook.AppointmentItem appt = Application.Session.
        GetDefaultFolder(Outlook.OlDefaultFolders.olFolderCalendar).
        Items.Find("[Subject]='Sales Strategy FY2007'")
        as Outlook.AppointmentItem;
    if (appt != null)
    {
        foreach (Outlook.Recipient recip in appt.Recipients)
        {
            switch (recip.MeetingResponseStatus)
            {
                case Outlook.OlResponseStatus.olResponseAccepted:
                    Debug.WriteLine("Accepted: " + recip.Name);
                    break;
                case Outlook.OlResponseStatus.olResponseTentative:
                    Debug.WriteLine("Tentative: " + recip.Name);
                    break;
                case Outlook.OlResponseStatus.olResponseDeclined:
                    Debug.WriteLine("Declined: " + recip.Name);
                    break;
                case Outlook.OlResponseStatus.olResponseOrganized:
                    Debug.WriteLine("Organizer: " + recip.Name);
                    break;
                case Outlook.OlResponseStatus.olResponseNone:
                    Debug.WriteLine("None: " + recip.Name);
                    break;
                case Outlook.OlResponseStatus.olResponseNotResponded:
                    Debug.WriteLine("Not responded: " + recip.Name);
                    break;
            }
        }
    }
}
```

Recurring Appointments

The *RecurrencePattern* object provides the ability to create recurring appointments at predictable intervals—daily, weekly, monthly, or yearly. Of course, recurring appointments are shifted or canceled to accommodate the flexible schedules of end users. To that end, the Outlook object model offers the *Exception* object, which allows you to create exceptions to a standard recurrence pattern.

Creating a Recurring Appointment

A recurring appointment is represented by an *AppointmentItem* object with the *IsRecurring* property set to *true*. However, you cannot set this property directly. Instead, you create a recurring appointment by calling the *GetRecurrencePattern* method of the *AppointmentItem* object and then saving the item. The following example illustrates how to create an appointment named Test Appointment and then call the *GetRecurrencePattern* method to make it a recurring appointment:

```
private void CreateRecurringAppointment()
{
    Outlook.AppointmentItem appt = Application.CreateItem(
        Outlook.OlItemType.olAppointmentItem)
        as Outlook.AppointmentItem;
    appt.Subject = "Weekly Extensibility Team Meeting";
    Outlook.RecurrencePattern pattern = appt.GetRecurrencePattern();
    appt.Save();
}
```

The *GetRecurrencePattern* method returns a *RecurrencePattern* object. You can change the recurrence pattern of the appointment by setting properties of the appointment's *RecurrencePattern* object.

> **Note**   If you call *GetRecurrencePattern* without setting the properties of the *RecurrencePattern* object, Outlook uses the default *RecurrencePattern* object. The default *RecurrencePattern* object occurs weekly on the weekday on which the appointment is created and has no end date.

Setting the Recurrence Pattern of an Appointment

When a new recurring appointment is created, it inherits a default recurrence pattern based on the time at which the appointment was created. To change the recurrence pattern of an appointment, set the appropriate properties of the appointment's *RecurrencePattern* object.

To set a nondefault *RecurrencePattern* object for a recurring appointment, you must set the *RecurrenceType* property before you set other *RecurrencePattern* properties. Valid *RecurrencePattern* properties for a given *RecurrenceType* are shown in Table 5-7.

Table 5-7   Valid *RecurrencePattern* Properties by RecurrenceType

OlRecurrence type	Valid *RecurrencePattern* properties
olRecursDaily	Duration, EndTime, Interval, NoEndDate, Occurrences, PatternStartDate, PatternEndDate, StartTime
olRecursWeekly	DayOfWeekMask, Duration, EndTime, Interval, NoEndDate, Occurrences, PatternStartDate, PatternEndDate, StartTime
olRecursMonthly	DayOfMonth, Duration, EndTime, Interval, NoEndDate, Occurrences, PatternStartDate, PatternEndDate, StartTime
olRecursMonthNth	DayOfWeekMask, Duration, EndTime, Interval, Instance, NoEndDate, Occurrences, PatternStartDate, PatternEndDate, StartTime

Table 5-7 Valid *RecurrencePattern* Properties by RecurrenceType

OlRecurrence type	Valid *RecurrencePattern* properties
olRecursYearly	DayOfMonth, Duration, EndTime, Interval, MonthOfYear, NoEndDate, Occurrences, PatternStartDate, PatternEndDate, StartTime
olRecursYearNth	DayOfWeekMask, Duration, EndTime, Interval, Instance, NoEndDate, Occurrences, PatternStartDate, PatternEndDate, StartTime

Creating a Recurring Appointment Using *DayOfWeekMask*

The following example uses *GetRecurrencePattern* to obtain the *RecurrencePattern* object for a newly created *AppointmentItem*. The properties *RecurrenceType, DayOfWeekMask, PatternStartDate, PatternEndDate, Duration, StartTime, EndTime,* and *Subject* are set, and the appointment is saved and then displayed with the pattern: "Occurs every Monday, Wednesday, and Friday effective 7/10/2006 until 8/25/2006 from 2:00 PM to 3:00 PM."

```
private void RecurringAppointmentEveryMondayWednesdayFriday()
{
    Outlook.AppointmentItem appt = Application.CreateItem(
        Outlook.OlItemType.olAppointmentItem)
        as Outlook.AppointmentItem;
    appt.Subject = "Recurring Appointment DaysOfWeekMask Example";
    Outlook.RecurrencePattern pattern = appt.GetRecurrencePattern();
    pattern.RecurrenceType = Outlook.OlRecurrenceType.olRecursWeekly;
    // Logical OR for DayOfWeekMask creates pattern
    pattern.DayOfWeekMask = Outlook.OlDaysOfWeek.olMonday |
        Outlook.OlDaysOfWeek.olWednesday |
        Outlook.OlDaysOfWeek.olFriday;
    pattern.PatternStartDate = DateTime.Parse("7/10/2006");
    pattern.PatternEndDate = DateTime.Parse("8/25/2006");
    pattern.Duration = 60;
    pattern.StartTime = DateTime.Parse("2:00:00 PM");
    pattern.EndTime = DateTime.Parse("3:00:00 PM");
    appt.Save();
    appt.Display(false);
}
```

Creating a Recurring Event

The next recurrence example uses *GetRecurrencePattern* to obtain the *RecurrencePattern* object for a multiday event rather than an appointment. To create a recurring event instead of an appointment, you must set the *Duration* property to 1440, which is the number of minutes in a day (60 * 24). You must also set the *StartTime* and *EndTime* properties for the *RecurrencePattern* object to 12:00 A.M. The properties *RecurrenceType, DayOfWeekMask, PatternStartDate, PatternEndDate, Duration, StartTime, EndTime,* and *Subject* are set, the appointment is saved, and then it is displayed with the pattern: "Occurs every Monday, Tuesday, Wednesday, Thursday, and Friday effective 7/10/2006 until 8/4/2006."

```
private void RecurringEventEveryWeekday()
{
    Outlook.AppointmentItem appt = Application.CreateItem(
        Outlook.OlItemType.olAppointmentItem)
        as Outlook.AppointmentItem;
    appt.Subject = "Recurring Event Every Weekday Example";
    Outlook.RecurrencePattern pattern = appt.GetRecurrencePattern();
    pattern.RecurrenceType = Outlook.OlRecurrenceType.olRecursWeekly;
    // Logical OR for DayOfWeekMask creates pattern
    pattern.DayOfWeekMask = Outlook.OlDaysOfWeek.olMonday |
        Outlook.OlDaysOfWeek.olTuesday |
        Outlook.OlDaysOfWeek.olWednesday |
        Outlook.OlDaysOfWeek.olThursday |
        Outlook.OlDaysOfWeek.olFriday;
    pattern.PatternStartDate = DateTime.Parse("7/10/2006");
    pattern.PatternEndDate = DateTime.Parse("8/4/2006");
    //Duration for all-day event = 60 * 24 = 1440
    pattern.Duration = 1440;
    //All-day event starts and ends at 12:00 AM
    pattern.StartTime = DateTime.Parse("12:00:00 AM");
    pattern.EndTime = DateTime.Parse("12:00:00 AM");
    appt.Save();
    appt.Display(false);
}
```

Creating a MonthNth or YearNth Recurrence

MonthNth and YearNth recurrences are similar in that they occur on the Nth day of every month or year. To set a MonthNth or YearNth recurrence, you must set the *RecurrenceType* property to the correct *OlRecurrenceType* value and also set the *DayOfWeekMask* and *Interval* properties. The *Interval* property indicates the Nth day of pattern (monthly or yearly) on which the recurrence occurs. This recurrence example creates a recurrence that occurs on the Nth day of every year. For a YearNth recurrence, you must also set the *MonthOfYear* property to indicate the month of the recurrence. The properties *RecurrenceType*, *DayOfWeekMask*, *MonthOfYear*, *Instance*, *Occurrences*, *StartTime*, *EndTime*, and *Subject* are set, the appointment is saved, and it is then displayed with the pattern: "Occurs the first Monday of June effective 6/1/2007 until 6/6/2016 from 2:00 PM to 5:00 PM."

```
private void RecurringYearNthAppointment()
{
    Outlook.AppointmentItem appt = Application.CreateItem(
        Outlook.OlItemType.olAppointmentItem)
        as Outlook.AppointmentItem;
    appt.Subject = "Recurring YearNth Appointment";
    Outlook.RecurrencePattern pattern = appt.GetRecurrencePattern();
    pattern.RecurrenceType = Outlook.OlRecurrenceType.olRecursYearNth;
    pattern.DayOfWeekMask = Outlook.OlDaysOfWeek.olMonday;
    pattern.MonthOfYear = 6;
    pattern.Instance = 1;
    pattern.Occurrences = 10;
    pattern.Duration = 180;
```

```
        pattern.PatternStartDate = DateTime.Parse("6/1/2007");
        pattern.StartTime = DateTime.Parse("2:00:00 PM");
        pattern.EndTime = DateTime.Parse("5:00:00 PM");
        appt.Save();
        appt.Display(false);
    }
```

Working with a Single Appointment in a Series

To determine whether an instance of a recurring appointment occurs at a particular time, use the *GetOccurrence* method of the *RecurrencePattern* object. This method returns an *AppointmentItem* object representing the instance of the recurring appointment.

> **Important**   The *GetOccurrence* method will produce an error if an instance of the recurring appointment does not start at the date and time you provide. If it is possible that your code supplies a date and time that does not match an instance of a recurring appointment (because of user input, for example), you should be able to handle the error appropriately.

The following example illustrates how to use the *GetOccurrence* method to determine whether a recurring appointment (created by the code in the previous example) starts on a date and time provided by the user. The *try...catch* block ensures that the procedure will continue if the user enters anything that does not match the start date and time of an instance of the recurring appointment. After calling the *GetOccurrence* method, you should test the *singleAppt* variable to determine whether it is set to *null*, indicating that the method failed and did not return an *AppointmentItem* object.

```
private void CheckOccurrenceExample()
{
    Outlook.AppointmentItem appt = Application.Session.
        GetDefaultFolder(Outlook.OlDefaultFolders.olFolderCalendar).
        Items.Find(
        "[Subject]='Recurring Appointment DaysOfWeekMask Example'")
        as Outlook.AppointmentItem;
    if (appt != null)
    {
        try
        {
            Outlook.RecurrencePattern pattern =
                appt.GetRecurrencePattern();
            Outlook.AppointmentItem singleAppt =
                pattern.GetOccurrence(DateTime.Parse(
                "7/21/2006 2:00 PM"))
                as Outlook.AppointmentItem;
            if (singleAppt != null)
            {
                Debug.WriteLine("7/21/2006 2:00 PM occurrence found.");
            }
        }
```

```
        catch (Exception ex)
        {
            Debug.WriteLine(ex.Message);
        }
    }
}
```

Once you retrieve the *AppointmentItem* object representing an instance of a recurring appointment, you can delete or change the appointment instance. When this happens, Outlook creates an *Exception* object. The properties of this object describe the changes that were made to the instance. All of the *Exception* objects for a recurring appointment are contained in an *Exceptions* collection associated with the appointment's *RecurrencePattern* object.

The *AppointmentItem* property of the *Exception* object returns the *AppointmentItem* object that constitutes the exception to the original recurrence pattern of the recurring appointment. You can use the methods and properties of the *AppointmentItem* object to work with the appointment exception. The following example changes the subject of an instance of the recurring appointment created by the code in the previous section. It then uses the *AppointmentItem* property of the resulting *Exception* object to change the start time of the appointment exception.

```
private void CreateExceptionExample()
{
    Outlook.AppointmentItem appt = Application.Session.
        GetDefaultFolder(Outlook.OlDefaultFolders.olFolderCalendar).
        Items.Find(
        "[Subject]='Recurring Appointment DaysOfWeekMask Example'")
        as Outlook.AppointmentItem;
    if (appt != null)
    {
        try
        {
            Outlook.RecurrencePattern pattern =
                appt.GetRecurrencePattern();
            Outlook.AppointmentItem myInstance =
                pattern.GetOccurrence(DateTime.Parse(
                "7/21/2006 2:00 PM"))
                as Outlook.AppointmentItem;
            if (myInstance != null)
            {
                myInstance.Subject = "My Exception";
                myInstance.Save();
                Outlook.RecurrencePattern newPattern =
                    appt.GetRecurrencePattern();
                Outlook.Exception myException =
                    newPattern.Exceptions[1];
                if (myException != null)
                {
                    Outlook.AppointmentItem myNewInstance =
                        myException.AppointmentItem;
                    myNewInstance.Start =
```

```
                            DateTime.Parse("7/21/2006 1:00 PM");
                    myNewInstance.End =
                            DateTime.Parse("7/21/2006 2:00 PM");
                    myNewInstance.Save();
                }
            }
        }
        catch (Exception ex)
        {
            Debug.WriteLine(ex.Message);
        }
    }
}
```

The following two sections describe how to use the *Exception* object to work with changed or deleted instances of a recurring appointment.

Determining the Original Date of an *Exception*

The *OriginalDate* property of the *Exception* object returns the start date and time of the changed appointment before it was changed. The following example uses the *OriginalDate* property to retrieve the original start date of the appointment exception created in the previous section. In addition, it uses the *Start* property of the *AppointmentItem* associated with the *Exception* object to provide the new start date of the appointment.

```
private void ShowOriginalDateExample()
{
    Outlook.AppointmentItem appt = Application.Session.
        GetDefaultFolder(Outlook.OlDefaultFolders.olFolderCalendar).
        Items.Find(
        "[Subject]='Recurring Appointment DaysOfWeekMask Example'")
        as Outlook.AppointmentItem;
    if (appt != null)
    {
        try
        {
            Outlook.RecurrencePattern pattern =
                appt.GetRecurrencePattern();
            Outlook.Exception myException =
                pattern.Exceptions[1];
            if (myException != null)
            {
                string msg =
                    "The occurrence originally occurred on "
                    + myException.OriginalDate
                    + ". The exception now occurs on "
                    + myException.AppointmentItem.Start;
                Debug.WriteLine(msg);
            }
        }
        catch (Exception ex)
        {
```

```
        Debug.WriteLine(ex.Message);
        }
    }
}
```

Determining Whether an Appointment Instance Was Deleted

When an appointment in a recurring series is deleted, an *Exception* object representing the deleted appointment is created, and the *Deleted* property of the *Exception* object is set to *true*. The following example uses the *Delete* method of the *AppointmentItem* object to delete the appointment instance changed in the previous section. It then tests the value of the *Deleted* property of the *Exception* object representing the deleted appointment to determine whether the appointment was actually deleted.

```
private void CheckDeletedExceptionExample()
{
    Outlook.AppointmentItem appt = Application.Session.
        GetDefaultFolder(Outlook.OlDefaultFolders.olFolderCalendar).
        Items.Find(
        "[Subject]='Recurring Appointment DaysOfWeekMask Example'")
        as Outlook.AppointmentItem;
    if (appt != null)
    {
        try
        {
            Outlook.RecurrencePattern pattern =
                appt.GetRecurrencePattern();
            Outlook.AppointmentItem singleAppt =
                pattern.GetOccurrence(DateTime.Parse(
                "7/21/2006 1:00:00 PM"));
            singleAppt.Delete();
            Outlook.Exception myException =
                pattern.Exceptions[1];
            if (myException.Deleted)
            {
                Debug.WriteLine("7/21/2006 1:00 PM deleted.");
            }
        }
        catch (Exception ex)
        {
            Debug.WriteLine(ex.Message);
        }
    }
}
```

Using *GlobalAppointmentID*

In Outlook 2007, there are situations where the *EntryID* property of *AppointmentItem* objects might change, such as when an item is moved to a different folder or to a different store. The *EntryID* property can also change when a user performs certain functions in Outlook, such as exporting and then reimporting data.

Therefore, each Outlook appointment item is assigned a Global Object ID, a unique global identifier that does not change during those situations. The Global Object ID is a MAPI property that Outlook uses to correlate meeting updates and responses with a particular meeting on the calendar. The Global Object ID is the same across all copies of the item. In the object model, the Global Object ID is represented by the *GlobalAppointmentID* property.

If you need to ensure that you are working with the correct instance of an *AppointmentItem* object, you can examine the item's *GlobalAppointmentID* property. *GlobalAppointmentID* is a string that does not change even if the *AppointmentItem* is moved or the organizer makes changes to the meeting. The *GlobalAppointmentID* property is especially useful in scenarios where your code is using the Outlook object model to synchronize appointments with a mobile device.

MeetingItem Object

A *MeetingItem* object represents a request for a meeting received in a user's Inbox mail folder. You cannot create a *MeetingItem* object directly. Instead, Outlook creates a *MeetingItem* object in each recipient's Inbox folder when a user sends an *AppointmentItem* object with its *MeetingStatus* property set to *OlMeetingStatus.olMeeting*. The following example shows how to create an appointment and then send the appointment as a meeting request to a required attendee, an optional attendee, and a conference room (known as a resource).

Working with Meeting Requests

Most often, you do not work directly with a *MeetingItem* object. For example, you do not use the *MeetingItem* object to accept or decline the meeting. Instead, you use the appointment associated with the meeting request.

The *GetAssociatedAppointment* method of the *MeetingItem* object returns an *AppointmentItem* object that you can use to accept or refuse the meeting request or to directly add the meeting (as an appointment) to the Calendar folder.

You can also directly access an *AppointmentItem* object that has its *MeetingStatus* property set to *OlMeetingStatus.olMeeting* to determine which recipients have accepted or declined the meeting request. The following sections illustrate how to work with a meeting request through the appointment associated with the meeting.

Retrieving the Appointment Associated with a Meeting

The *MeetingItem* object is a message containing a request to add an appointment to the recipient's calendar; it is not the appointment itself. To access the appointment associated with the meeting request, you use the *GetAssociatedAppointment* method of the *MeetingItem* object. This method requires a *bool* (*Boolean* in Visual Basic) argument that specifies whether the appointment is added to the user's Calendar.

The following example calls the *GetAssociatedAppointment* method of each *MeetingItem* in the user's Inbox and then uses the returned *AppointmentItem* object to write the subject of the appointment to the trace listeners in the *Listeners* collection. Note that the argument of *GetAssociatedAppointment* is set to *false* so that the appointment is not added to the user's Calendar.

```
private void MeetingRequestsExample()
{
    Outlook.Folder folder = Application.Session.
        GetDefaultFolder(Outlook.OlDefaultFolders.olFolderInbox)
        as Outlook.Folder;
    string filter = "[MessageClass] = " +
        "'IPM.Schedule.Meeting.Request'";
    Outlook.Items items = folder.Items.Restrict(filter);
    foreach(Outlook.MeetingItem request in items)
    {
        Outlook.AppointmentItem appt =
            request.GetAssociatedAppointment(false);
        if(appt != null)
        {
            Debug.WriteLine(appt.Subject);
        }
    }
}
```

Responding to a Meeting Request

To respond to a meeting request, you use the *GetAssociatedAppointment* method of the *MeetingItem* object to obtain the *AppointmentItem* object associated with the meeting request. You then use the *Respond* method of the *AppointmentItem* object to notify the meeting organizer whether the meeting has been accepted, declined, or tentatively added to the receiving user's Calendar.

The *Respond* method allows you to send the notification without user intervention, or it can allow the user to edit the response before sending it. The *Respond* method accepts three parameters: the first specifies the actual response (accept, decline, or tentative), and the second two are *bool* (*Boolean* in Visual Basic) values that determine whether the user will be given the opportunity to edit the response.

To send the notification without requiring action by the user, you call the *Respond* method with the second parameter set to *true* and then send the *AppointmentItem* as shown in the following example:

```
private void AutoAcceptMeetingRequests()
{
    Outlook.Folder folder = Application.Session.
        GetDefaultFolder(Outlook.OlDefaultFolders.olFolderInbox)
        as Outlook.Folder;
    string filter = "[MessageClass] = " +
        "'IPM.Schedule.Meeting.Request'";
```

```csharp
Outlook.Items items = folder.Items.Restrict(filter);
foreach (Outlook.MeetingItem request in items)
{
    Outlook.AppointmentItem appt =
        request.GetAssociatedAppointment(true);
    if (appt != null)
    {
        appt.Respond(
            Outlook.OlMeetingResponse.olMeetingAccepted,
            true, Type.Missing);
    }
}
}
```

If you want to allow the user to choose how to respond (that is, whether to send a response and whether to edit the body of the response before sending), call the *Respond* method with the second parameter set to *false* and the third parameter set to *true*, as shown here:

```csharp
private void PromptUserMeetingRequest()
{
    Outlook.Folder folder = Application.Session.
        GetDefaultFolder(Outlook.OlDefaultFolders.olFolderInbox)
        as Outlook.Folder;
    string filter = "[MessageClass] = " +
        "'IPM.Schedule.Meeting.Request'";
    Outlook.Items items = folder.Items.Restrict(filter);
    foreach (Outlook.MeetingItem request in items)
    {
        Outlook.AppointmentItem appt =
            request.GetAssociatedAppointment(true);
        if (appt != null)
        {
            appt.Respond(
                Outlook.OlMeetingResponse.olMeetingAccepted,
                false, true);
        }
    }
}
```

You can use the *Respond* method to display a dialog box that gives the user three choices:

- Edit The Response Before Sending
- Send The Response Now
- Don't Send A Response

Outlook immediately sends the *AppointmentItem* to the meeting organizer if the user selects Send The Response Now. If the user selects Edit The Response Before Sending, Outlook opens the item to allow the user to change recipients, the subject, or the body text before sending the response. Instead of giving the user the choice of how to respond, you can call the *Respond* method with the second and third parameters both set to *false*. The result is the same as when the user selects Edit The Response Before Sending.

Determining the Status of a Recipient of a Meeting Request

An *AppointmentItem* object created from a *MeetingItem* object has an associated *Recipients* collection object. You can use the *MeetingResponseStatus* property of the *Recipient* objects in this collection to determine whether a given recipient has accepted or declined the requested meeting.

The following example returns the *MeetingResponseStatus* property for the user's manager. If the user's manager is not found in the *Recipients* collection, *CheckManagerResponseStatus* returns *null*. This example requires an Exchange Server account to run correctly. To check that the *Recipient* object is the same as the *ExchangeUser* object that represents the user's manager, the code calls the new *CompareEntryIDs* method of the *Namespace* object. If the two objects are equivalent, *CompareEntryIDs* returns *true*. If the entry identifiers are not equivalent, *CompareEntryIDs* returns *false*. Entry identifiers cannot be compared directly because one object can be represented by two different binary values. Use *CompareEntryIDs* to determine whether two entry identifiers represent the same object.

```csharp
private object CheckManagerResponseStatus(
    Outlook.AppointmentItem appt)
{
    try
    {
        Outlook.AddressEntry user =
            Application.Session.CurrentUser.AddressEntry;
        Outlook.ExchangeUser userEx = user.GetExchangeUser();
        if (userEx == null)
        {
            return null;
        }
        Outlook.ExchangeUser manager =
            userEx.GetExchangeUserManager();
        if (manager == null)
        {
            return null;
        }
        foreach (Outlook.Recipient recip in appt.Recipients)
        {
            if (Application.Session.CompareEntryIDs(
                recip.AddressEntry.ID, manager.ID))
            {
                return recip.MeetingResponseStatus;
            }
        }
        return null;
    }
    catch (Exception ex)
    {
        Debug.WriteLine(ex.Message);
    }
}
```

ContactItem Object

A *ContactItem* object represents a contact in a Contacts folder. A Contacts folder can serve as an address list so that you send messages to contacts that have an e-mail address. A *ContactItem* object can represent a unique person or an entity such as a business or organization. Because an important component of the Outlook experience is about people and communications, the *ContactItem* object is one of the favorite Outlook items for developer customization.

Appropriate Uses of *ContactItem*

ContactItem scenarios are extensive. One of the most frequent uses of the *ContactItem* object is in customer relationship applications. For small business applications, a solution like Microsoft Business Contact Manager creates a rich user experience and several custom types based on the *ContactItem*. For medium-sized businesses, a solution like Microsoft Customer Relations Manager creates a different set of custom contact types to represent customers, vendors, opportunities, and so forth. Other custom solutions extend Outlook's built-in contact behavior. For example, you could create a form region that displays driving directions from the user's home location to the contact's business address. Still other contact solutions revolve around shared contacts in a non-Exchange environment.

Working with Contact Properties

Think of an Outlook *ContactItem* object as a very large property bag. It has more than 100 properties such as *Department*; *OfficeLocation*; *IMAddress*; mailing addresses for home, office, and other locations; three e-mail addresses; and multiple phone numbers for office, home, mobile, and pager. If the built-in properties are not sufficient, you can add custom properties using the *UserProperties* collection.

Setting the Contact Name and Company

When you create a *ContactItem* object, you can set its *FirstName*, *MiddleName*, and *LastName* properties. If the contact represents an entity rather than a person, you would set the *CompanyName* property. The following simple code example creates a *ContactItem* object and sets commonly used properties for the contact. If you run this code sample, you'll notice that a dialog box appears to resolve the contact's business telephone number. This dialog box appears when you call the *ShowCheckPhoneDialog* method on the *ContactItem* object. This dialog box allows the user to resolve a phone number based on local dialing conventions.

```
private void CreateContactExample()
{
    Outlook.ContactItem contact = Application.CreateItem(
        Outlook.OlItemType.olContactItem) as Outlook.ContactItem;
    contact.FirstName = "Nancy";
    contact.LastName = "Freehafer";
    contact.JobTitle= "Account Representative";
    contact.CompanyName = "Contoso Ltd.";
```

```
    contact.OfficeLocation = "36/2529";
    contact.BusinessTelephoneNumber = "4255551212 x432";
    contact.WebPage = "http://www.contoso.com";
    contact.BusinessAddressStreet = "1 Microsoft Way";
    contact.BusinessAddressCity = "Redmond";
    contact.BusinessAddressState = "WA";
    contact.BusinessAddressPostalCode = "98052";
    contact.BusinessAddressCountry =
        "United States of America";
    contact.Email1Address = "nancyf@contoso.com";
    contact.Email1AddressType = "SMTP";
    contact.Email1DisplayName =
        "Nancy Freehafer (nancyf@contoso.com)";
    contact.Display(false);
    contact.ShowCheckPhoneDialog(
        Outlook.OlContactPhoneNumber.
        olContactPhoneBusiness);
}
```

Adding Items to the *Links* Collection Object

You can link an Outlook item to a contact by using the *Links* collection. You can add *Link* items to any Item type except for *StorageItem* and *SharingItem* objects. Linked items appear on the Activities page of the contact item. The following example shows you how to use the *Add* method of the *Links* collection to add the contact created in the previous example to a task. Only *ContactItem* objects can be added as members of the *Links* collection for an item. You cannot add a *DistListItem* object to the *Links* collection.

```
private void LinkedContactExample()
{
    Outlook.ContactItem contact =
        Application.Session.GetDefaultFolder(
        Outlook.OlDefaultFolders.olFolderContacts).Items.Find(
        "[Subject] = 'Nancy Freehafer'")
        as Outlook.ContactItem;
    if (contact != null)
    {
        Outlook.TaskItem task = Application.CreateItem(
            Outlook.OlItemType.olTaskItem) as Outlook.TaskItem;
        task.Links.Add(contact);
        task.Subject = "Linked Contact Example";
        DateTime startDate = DateTime.Now;
        task.StartDate = startDate;
        task.DueDate = startDate.AddDays(7);
        task.ReminderSet = true;
        task.Display(false);
    }
}
```

> **Note**   The Contacts button that allows a user to link an item to a contact is hidden by default in Outlook 2007. To make the Contacts button visible in the Inspector window for an item, follow these steps:
>
> 1. In the Outlook Explorer window, from the Options menu, select Tools.
> 2. Click the Preferences tab.
> 3. On the Preferences tab, click Contact Options.
> 4. Select the Show Contact Linking On All Forms check box.
> 5. Click OK twice.

Electronic Business Cards

Electronic Business Cards are new to Outlook 2007. An Electronic Business Card is another view of a contact that captures specific information from that contact and allows you to share that information with other people in a highly recognizable form. You can send an Electronic Business Card programmatically as shown in the earlier section "Adding an Electronic Business Card." The Outlook 2007 object model fully supports Electronic Business Cards. Table 5-8 lists the members of the *ContactItem* object that pertain to Electronic Business Cards.

Table 5-8   *ContactItem* Members for Electronic Business Cards

ContactItem member	Description
BusinessCardLayoutXML	Returns or sets a String representing the Extensible Markup Language (XML) for the business card on the parent *ContactItem* object. For more information on the format of the XML, see the Office 2007 XML Schema reference.
BusinessCardType	Returns an *OlBusinessCardType* constant that determines the type of Electronic Business Card. *OlBusinessCardType* can be either an Inter-Connect business card (which cannot be modifed through the Outlook object model), or an Outlook business card.
AddBusinessCardLogo	Adds a logo picture to the business card on the parent *ContactItem* object by specifying the path of a picture to load. A business card can only have one logo picture, so any existing business card logo will be replaced. Standard graphic formats are supported (.bmp, .jpg, .png, and .gif).
ForwardAsBusinessCard	Forwards the *ContactItem* object as an Electronic Business Card and returns a *MailItem* object.
ResetBusinessCard	Resets the business card on the contact item to the default value, deleting any custom layout and business card logo. For contacts with an InterConnect card type, this resets the contact to using an Outlook business card.

Table 5-8 *ContactItem* Members for Electronic Business Cards

ContactItem member	Description
SaveBusinessCardImage	Saves an image of the business card generated from the parent *ContactItem* object; saves the business card image in the specified path. Depending on the extension specified, this outputs the image in Portable Network Graphics (.png) format or *Joint Photographic Experts Group (.jpg)* format.
ShowBusinessCardEditor	Displays the Edit Business Card dialog box to the user. Calling this method retrieves the data for the specified *ContactItem* object and then modally displays that data in the Edit Business Card dialog box. An error occurs if the data cannot be retrieved.

Let's take a quick look at how you can modify an Electronic Business Card in your code. The following example uses the XML document class to obtain the *layout* attribute in the string returned for *BusinessCardLayoutXML* for the *ContactItem* object created in the earlier *CreateContactItem* example. The sample changes the card layout from left-aligned to right-aligned. Although this sample is a simple one, it shows you a basic technique that you can extend in a powerful way to modify card layouts.

```
private void BusinessCardLayoutExample()
{
    Outlook.ContactItem contact =
        Application.Session.GetDefaultFolder(
        Outlook.OlDefaultFolders.olFolderContacts).Items.Find(
        "[Subject] = 'Nancy Freehafer'")
        as Outlook.ContactItem;
    if (contact != null)
    {
        XmlDocument doc = new XmlDocument();
        doc.LoadXml(contact.BusinessCardLayoutXml);
        XmlElement root = doc.DocumentElement;
        string layoutValue = root.GetAttribute("layout");
        if (layoutValue == "left")
        {
            root.SetAttribute("layout", "right");
            contact.BusinessCardLayoutXml = doc.OuterXml;
            contact.Save();
        }
    }
}
```

Note   For complete documentation of the schema for Electronic Business Cards, see the Electronic Business Card layout book in the 2007 Microsoft Office System XML Schema Reference. The Schema Reference is available in the 2007 Microsoft Office System Resource Kit.

TaskItem Object

The *TaskItem* object represents a single item in a Tasks folder. A task is similar to an appointment in that it can be sent to others (much like a meeting request) and can be a recurring task. Unlike an appointment, however, an uncompleted recurring task has only a single instance. When an instance of a recurring task is marked as complete, Outlook creates a second instance of the task for the next time period in the task's recurrence pattern.

Appropriate Uses of *TaskItem*

Solutions that focus on tasks are typically built around the concept of a project that contains many tasks and subtasks. A custom task item could represent a subtask of a parent task. Tasks that have not been completed appear on the To-Do Bar. Also new to Outlook 2007, tasks can appear in the daily task list on a Calendar view. Tasks in the daily task list can be arranged by task due or start date. In general, built-in and custom task items help users organize their time and meet important deadlines.

Creating a Recurring Task

You can use the *GetRecurrencePattern* method of the *TaskItem* object to create a recurring task, in much the same manner as you would create a recurring appointment. (For more information, see the section "Creating a Recurring Appointment" earlier in this chapter.) The following example shows how to create a task and then call the *GetRecurrencePattern* method to make the task a recurring task:

```
private void CreateRecurringTask()
{
    Outlook.TaskItem task = Application.CreateItem(
        Outlook.OlItemType.olTaskItem) as Outlook.TaskItem;
    task.Subject = "Tax Preparation";
    task.StartDate = DateTime.Parse("4/1/2007 8:00 AM");
    task.DueDate = DateTime.Parse("4/15/2007 8:00 AM");
    Outlook.RecurrencePattern pattern =
        task.GetRecurrencePattern();
    pattern.RecurrenceType = Outlook.OlRecurrenceType.olRecursYearly;
    pattern.PatternStartDate = DateTime.Parse("4/1/2007");
    pattern.NoEndDate = true;
    task.ReminderSet = true;
    task.ReminderTime = DateTime.Parse("4/1/2007 8:00 AM");
    task.Save();
}
```

As with a recurring meeting, you use the *RecurrencePattern* object associated with the task to specify how often and when the task will recur. Unlike a recurring appointment, however, a recurring task does not have multiple occurrences. Instead, when a recurring task is marked as completed, Outlook creates a copy of the task for the next date in the recurrence pattern.

Consequently, the *RecurrencePattern* object of a task does not support the *GetOccurrence* method or the *Exceptions* property.

> **Note**   The *Regenerate* property of the *RecurrencePattern* object is used to control the regeneration of the task as each occurrence of a recurring task is completed.
>
> To create a recurrence pattern, you must first set the *RecurrenceType* property to set the frequency, then set the *Regenerate* property to *true* to regenerate the task. After setting *Regenerate* to *true*, do not set it to *false*. If you subsequently set *Regenerate* to *false*, you should set up the recurrence pattern again by getting a new *RecurrencePattern* object.
>
> The *Regenerate* property has no effect for a *RecurrencePattern* object where the *Parent* object of the *RecurrencePattern* object is an *AppointmentItem* object.

Delegating a Task

In much the same way as you can invite others to a meeting by sending them an *AppointmentItem* object, you can delegate a task to others by sending them a *TaskItem* object. Before sending the object, however, you must first use the *Assign* method to create an assigned task. The following example shows how to create and delegate a task using the *Assign* and *Send* methods:

```
private void AssignTaskExample()
{
    Outlook.TaskItem task = Application.CreateItem(
        Outlook.OlItemType.olTaskItem) as Outlook.TaskItem;
    task.Subject = "Tax Preparation";
    task.StartDate = DateTime.Parse("4/1/2007 8:00 AM");
    task.DueDate = DateTime.Parse("4/15/2007 8:00 AM");
    Outlook.RecurrencePattern pattern =
        task.GetRecurrencePattern();
    pattern.RecurrenceType = Outlook.OlRecurrenceType.olRecursYearly;
    pattern.PatternStartDate = DateTime.Parse("4/1/2007");
    pattern.NoEndDate = true;
    task.ReminderSet = true;
    task.ReminderTime = DateTime.Parse("4/1/2007 8:00 AM");
    task.Assign();
    task.Recipients.Add("accountant@example.com");
    task.Recipients.ResolveAll();
    task.Send();
}
```

When a task is assigned and sent to another user, the user receives a *TaskRequestItem* object. You can use this object to access the task associated with the request and to respond to the task request.

TaskRequestItem Object

A *TaskRequestItem* object represents a request to assign a task in the Inbox of the user to whom the task is being assigned. The *TaskRequestItem* object is similar to several related task objects (the *TaskRequestAcceptItem*, *TaskRequestDeclineItem*, and *TaskRequestUpdateItem* objects) that are associated with task accept, decline, or update messages.

The following example filters the new *Table* object so that it contains only rows where the *MessageClass* value equals *IPM.TaskRequest* and writes the subject of each task request in the user's Inbox folder to the trace listeners in the *Listeners* collection:

```
private void ShowTaskRequests()
{
    string filter = "[MessageClass] = 'IPM.TaskRequest'";
    Outlook.Table table =
        Application.Session.GetDefaultFolder
        (Outlook.OlDefaultFolders.olFolderInbox).GetTable
        (filter, Outlook.OlTableContents.olUserItems);
    while (!table.EndOfTable)
    {
        Outlook.Row nextRow = table.GetNextRow();
        Debug.WriteLine(nextRow["Subject"]);
    }
}
```

Working with Task Requests

As with a *MeetingItem* object, usually you will not work directly with a *TaskRequestItem* object. For example, you do not use the *TaskRequestItem* object to accept or decline the task. Instead, you use the task associated with the task request.

The *GetAssociatedTask* method of the *TaskRequestItem* object returns a *TaskItem* object that you can use to accept or refuse the task.

Retrieving the Associated Task of a Task Request

Using the *GetAssociatedTask* method, you can access the task associated with a *TaskRequestItem* object. Properties of the *TaskItem* object returned by this method contain additional information about the assigned task, such as its due date.

> **Important**   Before you call the *GetAssociatedTask* method for a *TaskRequestItem* object, you must first process the *TaskRequestItem* object. By default, this is done automatically (unless the user has cleared the Process Requests And Responses On Arrival check box in the Tracking Options dialog box, which is available through the E-Mail Preferences dialog box on the Preferences tab of the Tools Options dialog box). You can also process a *TaskRequestItem* object by calling its *Display* method. Note that when a *TaskRequestItem* object is processed, its associated task is added to the user's Tasks folder.

The following code example writes the subject and due date of every task request in the user's Inbox to the trace listeners in the *Listeners* collection. This example is similar to the one in the previous section, but it uses the *GetAssociatedTask* method to access the *DueDate* property of the task associated with the task request. Unlike the previous example, the restriction is applied to the *Items* collection for the Inbox folder, and *GetAssociatedTask* is used in a *foreach* loop to access the associated task for each task request. Note that this example assumes that the *TaskRequestItem* objects have already been processed.

```
private void ShowAssociatedTasks()
{
    string filter = "[MessageClass] = 'IPM.TaskRequest'";
    Outlook.Items items =
        Application.Session.GetDefaultFolder
        (Outlook.OlDefaultFolders.olFolderInbox).
        Items.Restrict(filter);
    foreach (Outlook.TaskRequestItem taskRequest in items)
    {
        Outlook.TaskItem task = taskRequest.GetAssociatedTask(false);
        Debug.WriteLine(String.Format("Subject: " + task.Subject
            + "\n"+ "Due: " + task.DueDate + "\n"));
    }
}
```

Responding to a Task Request

To accept, decline, or modify a task request, use the *Respond* method of the *TaskItem* object returned by the *GetAssociatedTask* method of a *TaskRequestItem* object. The following example retrieves the first *TaskRequestItem* object in the user's Inbox and accepts it:

```
private void AcceptTaskRequest()
{
    string filter = "[MessageClass] = 'IPM.TaskRequest'";
    Outlook.Items items =
        Application.Session.GetDefaultFolder
        (Outlook.OlDefaultFolders.olFolderInbox).
        Items.Restrict(filter);
    if (items.Count > 0)
    {
        Outlook.TaskRequestItem taskRequest =
            (Outlook.TaskRequestItem)items[1];
        Outlook.TaskItem task =
            taskRequest.GetAssociatedTask(false);
        task.Respond(
            Outlook.OlTaskResponse.olTaskAccept, true, false);
        task.Send();
    }
}
```

Note that if you set the second parameter of the *Respond* method to *true*, you must call the *Send* method of the *TaskItem* object.

When the *Respond* method is used to respond to a task request, the initiating user receives a *TaskRequestAcceptItem*, *TaskRequestDeclineItem*, or *TaskRequestUpdateItem* object, depending on the type of response. You work with these objects in much the same way as a *TaskRequestItem* object in that you use the object's *GetAssociatedTask* method to retrieve the *TaskItem* object associated with the request and then call the methods and access the properties of the *TaskItem* object.

Other Item Types

This section contains a description of additional built-in Outlook item types. Except for *StorageItem*, which corresponds to a hidden item, each item type represents an item that can be created in the Outlook user interface.

DistListItem Object

The *DistListItem* object represents an Outlook distribution list in an Outlook Contacts folder. A distribution list can contain multiple recipients and is used to send messages to everyone in the list. Don't confuse an Outlook distribution list with an Exchange distribution list. To learn more about how an Exchange distribution list is represented in the Outlook object model, see "The *ExchangeDistributionList* Object" in Chapter 7.

The following code sample uses the *Table* object to find all contacts in the default Contact folder where the contact is categorized as a Top Customer and where the *Email1Address* property is not empty. The *Email1Address* name is then added as a column in the *Table* object. A *Recipient* object is created using the *CreateRecipient* method on the *Namespace* object. When you call the *AddMember* method of the *DistListItem* object, you must pass a resolved *Recipient* object as a parameter to the *AddMember* method. Finally, the Top Customers distribution list is displayed to the user.

```
private void CreateDistributionList()
{
    Outlook.DistListItem distList = Application.CreateItem(
        Outlook.OlItemType.olDistributionListItem)
        as Outlook.DistListItem;
    distList.Subject = "Top Customers";
    //Find top customer category in Contacts folder
    string filter = "[Categories] = 'Top Customer'"
        + " AND [Email1Address] <> ''";
    Outlook.Table table =
        Application.Session.GetDefaultFolder
        (Outlook.OlDefaultFolders.olFolderContacts).
        GetTable(filter, Outlook.OlTableContents.olUserItems);
    table.Columns.Add("Email1Address");
    while (!table.EndOfTable)
    {
        Outlook.Row nextRow = table.GetNextRow();
        Outlook.Recipient recip =
            Application.Session.CreateRecipient(
            nextRow["Email1Address"].ToString());
        //Resolve the Recipient before calling AddMember
        recip.Resolve();
```

```
            distList.AddMember(recip);
        }
        distList.Display(false);
    }
```

JournalItem Object

The *JournalItem* object represents a journal item in a Journal folder. Journal items provide a convenient way to record activity in relationship to any Outlook item. A journal entry can be as simple as the record of a phone call or as complex as the composite of several interactions with customers.

Because the *JournalItem* object records activities in time, the two most important methods of the *JournalItem* object are the *StartTimer* and *StopTimer* methods. The following example finds the contact created in the *CreateContactExample* procedure in the earlier section "Setting the Contact Name and Company," creates a journal item, adds a link to the contact for the journal item, and then starts the journal's timer with the *StartTimer* method:

```
private void LinkJournalItemToContact()
{
    Outlook.ContactItem contact =
        Application.Session.GetDefaultFolder(
        Outlook.OlDefaultFolders.olFolderContacts).Items.Find(
        "[Subject] = 'Nancy Freehafer'")
        as Outlook.ContactItem;
    if (contact != null)
    {
        Outlook.JournalItem journal =
            Application.CreateItem(
            Outlook.OlItemType.olJournalItem)
            as Outlook.JournalItem;
        journal.Subject = contact.Subject;
        journal.Companies = contact.CompanyName;
        journal.Links.Add(contact);
        journal.Display(false);
        journal.StartTimer();
    }
}
```

NoteItem Object

The *NoteItem* object represents a note in a Notes folder. Don't confuse the *NoteItem* object with a *MailItem* object. Because the message class of a *MailItem* object is *IPM.Note*, the objects can sometimes be confused. The *NoteItem* object is not customizable. You cannot create a custom note in the Outlook Forms Designer.

The *Subject* property of a *NoteItem* object is read-only because it is calculated from the body text of the note. The *Subject* property is not available until you have saved the note. To set the body of the note, use the *Body* property. If you obtain the *Inspector* for the *NoteItem* object, certain *Inspector* properties such as *WordEditor* will always return *null* (*Nothing* in Visual Basic). To assign a color to a *NoteItem* object, set the *Categories* property of the *NoteItem* object. The color assigned to the category will act as the color of the *NoteItem* object.

The following simple code example creates a note that acts as a visual reminder to order pizza for the team meeting:

```
private void OrderPizzaNote()
{
    Outlook.NoteItem note =
        Application.CreateItem(
        Outlook.OlItemType.olNoteItem)
        as Outlook.NoteItem;
    note.Body = "Order Pizza for Team Meeting";
    note.Categories = "Urgent";
    note.Save();
}
```

StorageItem Object

A *StorageItem* object represents an item that is always saved as a hidden item in the parent folder and stores private data for Outlook solutions. A *StorageItem* object is stored at the folder level, allowing it to roam with the account and be available online or offline.

The Outlook object model does not provide any collection object for *StorageItem* objects. However, you can use *Folder.GetTable* to obtain a *Table* object with all the hidden items in a *Folder* object, when you set the *TableContents* parameter to *OlTableContents.olHiddenItems*. If ensuring that data stored with the *StorageItem* object is a primary concern, then you should encrypt the data before storing it with the *StorageItem* object. Although *StorageItem* objects cannot be opened by the end user, there are tools that that allow a user to inspect the hidden messages in a folder.

Once you have obtained a *StorageItem* object, you can do the following to store solution data:

- Add attachments to the item for storage.
- Use explicit built-in properties of the item such as *Body* to store custom data.
- Add custom properties to the item using the *UserProperties.Add* method. Note that, in this case, the optional *AddToFolderFields* and *DisplayFormat* arguments of the *UserProperties.Add* method will be ignored.
- Use the *PropertyAccessor* object to get or set custom properties.

The default message class for a new *StorageItem* is *IPM.Storage*. If the *StorageItem* object existed as a hidden message in a version of Outlook prior to Outlook 2007, the message class will remain unchanged. To prevent modification of the message class, *StorageItem* does not expose an explicit *MessageClass* property.

The following code sample is from the PrepareMe sample add-in that is available on this book's companion Web site. The add-in uses a *StorageItem* object to store application-specific data that roams and is available online and offline. You create or retrieve a *StorageItem* object by calling the *GetStorage* method on the folder that contains the item. If the *StorageItem* object does not exist, *GetStorage* will create the hidden item for you. It is a recommended practice to set the subject of the *StorageItem* object to the *ProgID* for your add-in.

```
Outlook.StorageItem storage =
    this.Application.Session.GetDefaultFolder(
    Outlook.OlDefaultFolders.olFolderInbox).GetStorage(
    "IPM.Note.PrepareMeAddinCS",
    Outlook.OlStorageIdentifierType.olIdentifyByMessageClass);
Outlook.UserProperty userProp =
    (Outlook.UserProperty)storage.
    UserProperties["MessagesFromAttendee"];
if (userProp == null)
{
    //First run, so add default values
    storage.Subject = "PrepareMeAddinCS.UserSettings";
    storage.UserProperties.Add("MessagesFromAttendee",
        Outlook.OlUserPropertyType.olInteger,
        Type.Missing, Type.Missing);
    storage.UserProperties["MessagesFromAttendee"].Value = 4;
    storage.UserProperties.Add("RelatedAppointments",
        Outlook.OlUserPropertyType.olInteger,
        Type.Missing, Type.Missing);
    storage.UserProperties["RelatedAppointments"].Value = 4;
    storage.UserProperties.Add("ExpandDistributionLists",
        Outlook.OlUserPropertyType.olYesNo,
        Type.Missing, Type.Missing);
    storage.UserProperties["ExpandDistributionLists"].Value = 0;
    storage.Save();
}
//Read values from StorageItem
m_MessagesFromAttendee = (int)storage.
    UserProperties["MessagesFromAttendee"].Value;
m_RelatedAppointments = (int)storage.
    UserProperties["RelatedAppointments"].Value;
m_ExpandDistributionLists = (bool)storage.
    UserProperties["ExpandDistributionLists"].Value;
```

To create and retrieve a *StorageItem* object, you need to understand how the *GetStorage* method works on a *Folder* object. The *GetStorage* method obtains a *StorageItem* object on a *Folder* object using the identifier specified by *StorageIdentifier* and has the identifier type specified by *StorageIdentifierType*.

If you specify the *EntryID* property for the *StorageItem* object by using the *olIdentifyByEntryID* value for *StorageIdentifierType*, then the *GetStorage* method returns the *StorageItem* with the specified *EntryID* property. If no *StorageItem* object can be found using that *EntryID* property or if the *StorageItem* object does not exist, the *GetStorage* method raises an error.

If you specify the message class for the *StorageItem* object by using the *olIdentifyByMessageClass* value for *StorageIdentifierType*, the *GetStorage* method returns the *StorageItem* object with the specified message class. If there are multiple items with the same message class, the *GetStorage* method returns the item with the most recent *PR_LAST_MODIFICATION_TIME*. If no *StorageItem* exists with the specified message class, the *GetStorage* method creates a new *StorageItem* object with the message class specified by *StorageIdentifier*.

If you specify the *Subject* value of the *StorageItem* object, the *GetStorage* method returns the *StorageItem* with the *Subject* specified in the *GetStorage* call. If there are multiple items with the same subject, the *GetStorage* method will return the item with the most recent *PR_LAST_MODIFICATION_TIME*. If no *StorageItem* object exists with the specified subject, the *GetStorage* method creates a new *StorageItem* object with the subject specified by *StorageIdentifier*.

GetStorage returns an error if the store provider does not support hidden items, if the parent *Folder* object is read-only, or if the parent *Folder* object does not support the creation of hidden items, such as a Hotmail, IMAP, SharePoint, or public folder.

Summary

This chapter provided you with an overview of the built-in Outlook item types. You should now have an understanding of how to create these built-in items programmatically. Although the chapter didn't cover every property and method of the built-in item types, you should also know how to use the important properties and methods of each item type. For a comprehensive listing of the properties and methods that pertain to each object, see the Outlook 2007 Developer Reference.

Chapter 6
Accessing Outlook Data

This chapter provides an overview of the ways you can work with Microsoft Office Outlook 2007 data. You'll learn about *Stores* and *Folders* objects as the containers for Outlook items, and you'll also get an introduction to the *Items* and *Table* objects that allow you to enumerate the items in a folder.

This chapter covers the following topics:

- An overview of Outlook Data Storage

- Using the *Stores* collection and *Store* object

- Working with the *Folders* collection and *Folder* object

- Coding strategies for accessing items in a folder

- When to use the *Items* collection and the new *Table* object

- The new features of the *Table* object and how to manipulate *Row* and *Column* objects

An Overview of Outlook Data Storage

Outlook stores its data in different containers depending on account type and configuration. Examples of different mail account types are Microsoft Exchange, Post Office Protocol 3 (POP3), Internet Message Access Protocol (IMAP), and Hypertext Transfer Protocol (HTTP). For example, an Exchange account allows users to store their data in an Offline Folder File (.ost), which provides both online and offline access to items without depending on the availability of the Exchange server for the user's mailbox. It's also possible to configure an Exchange account for online use, meaning that Outlook items are only accessible if the user is connected to an Exchange server. A robust solution must be able to handle the different types of data storage available depending on account and account configuration.

Exchange Server

The following sections describe data storage on an Exchange server. If an Exchange server is configured for the current profile, only one *Account* object in the *Accounts* collection will have *Account.AccountType* equal to *OlAccountType.olExchange*.

Online Mode

To determine whether the user's Exchange account is configured in online mode, you need to examine the *ExchangeConnectionMode* property of the *Namespace* object. As previously described, online mode refers to a configuration where Outlook is connected directly to the user's Exchange mailbox server. The value returned by the *ExchangeConnectionMode* property only applies to the user's primary mailbox. It does not apply to a delegate or public folder Exchange store. If *ExchangeConnection Mode* returns *OlExchangeConnectionMode.olOnline*, then the user's Exchange account is configured in online mode. As a developer, you should be aware of the following issues of an Exchange account configured for online mode:

- The behavior of search queries can change if the user is running in online mode. *Store.IsInstantSearchEnabled* will always return *false* when running against an Exchange account configured for online mode. If you are running in online mode against Microsoft Exchange Server 2007, Instant Search results can be returned provided that content indexing is enabled on the server. However, there is no way to determine whether content indexing is enabled on Exchange Server if Outlook is running in online mode.

- You should exercise caution when enumerating items in a folder using the *Items* collection. Depending on the configuration of the Exchange server by the server administrator and whether you are running in a separate *AppDomain*, your code could raise an exception after you enumerate 255 items in a folder. To avoid this exception, you should consider calling *Marshal.ReleaseComObject* within the scope of a *foreach* construct.

Cached Mode

Cached mode provides performance and reliability benefits by caching data from the user's Exchange server in an Offline Folder File (.ost). Use the *ExchangeConnectionMode* property to determine if Outlook is operating in cached mode. The *ExchangeConnectionMode* property also determines how cached mode is operating, which includes information about how headers, bodies, and attachments are downloaded to the .ost file from the Exchange server. Table 6-1 lists the possible values for the *OlExchangeConnectionMode* enumeration.

Table 6-1   *OlExchangeConnectionMode* Values

Value	Description
olCachedConnectedDrizzle	The account is using cached Exchange mode such that headers are downloaded first, followed by the bodies and attachments of full items.
olCachedConnectedFull	The account is using cached Exchange mode on a local area network or a fast connection with the Exchange server. The user can also select this state manually, disabling auto-detect logic and always downloading full items regardless of connection speed.
olCachedConnectedHeaders	The account is using cached Exchange mode on a dial-up or slow connection with the Exchange server, such that only headers are downloaded. Full item bodies and attachments remain on the server. The user can also select this state manually, regardless of connection speed.
olCachedDisconnected	The account is using cached Exchange mode with a disconnected connection to the Exchange server.
olCachedOffline	The account is using cached Exchange mode, and the user has selected Work Offline from the File menu.

Table 6-1   *OlExchangeConnectionMode* Values

Value	Description
olDisconnected	The account has a disconnected connection to the Exchange server.
olNoExchange	The account does not use an Exchange server.
olOffline	The account is not connected to an Exchange server and is in the classic offline mode. This also occurs when the user selects Work Offline from the File menu.
olOnline	The account is connected to an Exchange server and is in the classic online mode.

Personal Folder Files (.pst)

Personal Folder Files (.pst) are the most common data storage container for Outlook. If users have a POP3 account and do not have an Exchange account, they will always store their data in a .pst file. Typically, IMAP and HTTP accounts also store their data in a .pst file. If you want to add content to the user's .pst file, then the Outlook object model is the preferred method of adding items. You cannot write directly to .pst files. The first type of .pst file is the Outlook 97–2002 Personal Folders File, which is compatible with all versions of Outlook including Outlook 2007. The second type of .pst file is the Office Outlook Personal Folders File, which is compatible with Microsoft Outlook 2003 and Outlook 2007. This .pst file format provides much greater storage capacity for items and folders than the original .pst file format. It also supports multilingual Unicode data.

Custom Store Providers

Advanced Messaging Application Programming Interface (MAPI) developers can write custom store providers to create additional sets of folders that can be used in Outlook. One of the common types of custom store provider is known as a wrapped .pst, and it builds on the architecture of Outlook's native .pst file. Programming a custom store provider is not discussed in this book. For a general discussion of MAPI store providers, see Chapter 2, "Outlook as a Platform." For more information on custom store providers, see the "Microsoft Office Outlook 2007 Integration API Reference" published on MSDN. In most cases, you can use the Outlook object model to add items to folders in a custom store provider and to write events that respond to changes in folder content.

Accounts Collection and *Account* Object

The *Accounts* collection and the *Account* object provide you with a method of enumerating accounts for the current profile. You obtain the *Accounts* collection from the *Namespace* object. The *Account* object offers some basic properties such as *DisplayName*, *AccountType*, *UserName*, and *SmtpAddress* to help you understand the identity of the account. The *Accounts* collection and *Account* objects do not allow you to establish or modify an account programmatically. Accounts for profiles other than the current profile are not supported. Certain account types such as RSS Feeds, SharePoint Lists, Internet Calendars, and Published Calendars are not available in the *Accounts* collection. Only e-mail accounts are represented in the *Accounts* collection. The following procedure enumerates all the *Account* objects in the current profile and writes the account *DisplayName*, *UserName*, and *SmtpAddress* properties to the trace listeners in the *Listeners* collection:

```
private void EnumerateAccounts()
{
    Outlook.Accounts accounts =
        Application.Session.Accounts;
    foreach(Outlook.Account account in accounts)
    {
        try
        {
            Debug.WriteLine(String.Format("Account: "
            + account.DisplayName
            + "\n" + "UserName: "
            + account.UserName
            + "\n" + "SmtpAddress: "
            + account.SmtpAddress + "\n"));
        }
        catch(Exception ex)
        {
            Debug.WriteLine(ex.Message);
        }
    }
}
```

Stores Collection and *Store* Object

Both the *Stores* collection and the *Store* object are new to Outlook 2007. These objects provide information about the stores in a given profile and also let you determine the characteristics of a given *Store* object.

Stores Collection

The *Stores* collection lets you enumerate the stores in a given profile. It also provides events that tell you when a *Store* object has been added to the current profile or when a *Store* object is about to be removed. You can use the *BeforeStoreRemove* event to prevent removal of a *Store* object that is required for your solution. You obtain the *Stores* collection from the *Namespace* object. The following code sample enumerates the stores in the current profile. If the *IsDataFileStore* property of the *Store* object returns *true* to indicate it is a .pst or .ost store, then the *DisplayName* and *FilePath* properties of the *Store* object are written to the trace listeners in the *Listeners* collection.

```
private void EnumerateStores()
{
    Outlook.Stores stores = Application.Session.Stores;
    foreach(Outlook.Store store in stores)
    {
        if (store.IsDataFileStore == true)
```

```
        {
            Debug.WriteLine(String.Format("Store: "
            + store.DisplayName
            + "\n" + "File Path: "
            + store.FilePath + "\n"));
        }
    }
}
```

Adding or Removing a *Store* Programmatically

To add a *Store* object, you call the *AddStoreEx* method on the *Namespace* object. The only *Store* object that you can add or remove programmatically is a .pst store. To remove a *Store* object, use the *RemoveStore* method of the *Namespace* object. The following code sample adds a Unicode store by specifying *OlStoreType.olUnicode* as the *Type* parameter for the *AddStoreEx* method. It also places the .pst in the default location for user .pst files, Documents and Settings*UserName*\\Local Settings\\Application Data\\Microsoft\\Outlook. Note that *Environment.SpecialFolder.LocalApplicationData* is used to retrieve the path to the Application Data folder under the Local Settings folder. Once the .pst store has been added, the sample code removes the *Store* object by calling the *RemoveStore* method on the *Namespace* object. *RemoveStore* requires a *Folder* object to remove the *Store* object. In this case, the code enumerates the *Stores* collection to find the *Store* object that has just been added based on the *FilePath* property of the *Store* object. If the *FilePath* property of the *Store* object is the same as the path to MyUnicodeStore.pst, the *GetRootFolder* method of the *Store* object returns a reference to the root folder of the .pst file. This *Folder* object is passed to the *RemoveStore* method to remove the *Store* object. Note that *RemoveStore* only removes the store from the current profile. It does not delete the .pst file from the file system.

```
private void CreateUnicodePST()
{
    string path = Environment.GetFolderPath(
        Environment.SpecialFolder.LocalApplicationData)
        + @"\Microsoft\Outlook\MyUnicodeStore.pst";
    try
    {
        Application.Session.AddStoreEx(
            path, Outlook.OlStoreType.olStoreUnicode);
        Outlook.Stores stores = Application.Session.Stores;
        foreach (Outlook.Store store in stores)
        {
            if (store.FilePath == path)
            {
                Outlook.Folder folder =
                    store.GetRootFolder() as Outlook.Folder;
                //Remove the store
                Application.Session.RemoveStore(folder);
            }
        }
    }
    catch (Exception ex)
```

```
        {
            Debug.WriteLine(ex.Message);
        }
    }
```

Working with the *Store* Object

The *Store* object has several useful properties, methods, and events. The following sections discuss how you can use these members in your code.

ExchangeStoreType Property

The *ExchangeStoreType* property distinguishes among different Exchange store types, such as primary Exchange mailbox, Exchange mailbox, Public Folder store, or non-Exchange store. If the *Store* object is not an Exchange store, *ExchangeStoreType* will return *OlExchangeStoreType.olNotExchange*. *ExchangeStoreType* will return *OlExchangeStoreType.olExchangeMailbox* for a *Store* object that represents a mailbox for which the current user is a delegate. For the *Store* object that represents the user's primary mailbox, *ExchangeStoreType* will return *OlExchangeStoreType.olExchangePrimaryMailbox*. This property does not distinguish among every type of store including Hotmail, HTTP, IMAP, and so forth. Use *Account.AccountType* for the type of server associated with an e-mail account, such as Exchange, HTTP, IMAP, or POP3.

FilePath and *IsDataFileStore* Properties

You can use the *FilePath* property in conjunction with the the *IsDataFileStore* property. The *FilePath* property returns the file path of a Personal Folders File (.pst) store or an Offline Folder File (.ost) store. If the store is not a .pst or .ost store, *FilePath* returns an empty string.

IsDataFileStore supports both Exchange stores and POP3 stores and will return *false* for HTTP-type stores such as Hotmail and MSN and for IMAP stores. For Exchange stores, *IsDataFileStore* will return *false* if the user profile is not using cached Exchange mode. *IsDataFileStore* will also return *false* when the store is an Exchange Public Folder store (*Store.ExchangeStoreType* equals *olExchangePublicFolder*).

IsDataFileStore does not indicate whether the store is located on a local hard drive. For example, a .pst file could be located on a mapped network drive and *IsDataFileStore* would still return *true*.

The return value of *IsDataFileStore* can change if the user is configured for classic Exchange offline mode. When the user is offline and using classic Exchange offline mode, *IsDataFileStore* returns *true*. When the user is online and using classic Exchange online mode, *IsDataFileStore* returns *false*.

GetRootFolder Method

To return the root folder for a given *Store* object, use the *GetRootFolder* method. The *GetRootFolder* method returns a *Folder* object that represents the root folder in the *Store* object. You can use the *GetRootFolder* method to enumerate the subfolders of the root folder of the *Store* object. Unlike *NameSpace.Folders*, which contains all folders for all stores in the current profile, *Store.GetRootFolder.Folders* allows you to enumerate all folders for a given *Store* object in the current profile. To determine the name of the current profile, examine the *CurrentProfileName* property of the *Namespace* object. If the store provider does not support root folders, *GetRootFolder* will raise an error. Your code should be able to handle this possibility.

GetSearchFolders Method

To return all the search folders for a given *Store* object, use the *GetSearchFolders* method. A search folder is a virtual folder that provides a view of all e-mail items that match specific search criteria. The *GetSearchFolders* method returns a *Folders* object. *GetSearchFolders* returns all the visible active search folders for the *Store* object. It does not return uninitialized or aged-out search folders. *GetSearchFolders* returns a *Folders* collection object with *Folders.Count* equal to zero (0) if no search folders have been defined for the *Store* object. The following code sample enumerates the search folders for the default store and writes the folder path for the search folder to the trace listeners in the *Listeners* collection:

```
private void EnumerateSearchFolders()
{
    Outlook.Store store =
        Application.Session.DefaultStore;
    Outlook.Folders folders = store.GetSearchFolders();
    foreach (Outlook.Folder folder in folders)
    {
        Debug.WriteLine(folder.FolderPath);
    }
}
```

GetSpecialFolder Method

A special folder exists in a store and represents a special type of search folder that is not available in the collection of visible search folders. *GetSpecialFolder* returns a *Folder* object. For example, a store can support an All Tasks special folder that contains all of the items marked for follow-up for the given store. Why would you use *GetSpecialFolder* instead of *GetDefaultFolder* to return items marked for follow-up? *GetDefaultFolder* only returns the items marked for follow-up for the default store. If you need to enumerate items marked for follow-up in all stores in the current profile, you should use *GetSpecialFolder* to return the folder that contains items marked for follow-up in each store in the profile. The following *EnumerateAllTasksFolder* procedure enumerates all stores in the profile and then uses *GetSpecialFolder(OlSpecialFolder.olSpecialFolderAllTasks)* to return a *Folder* object for the parent *Store* object. If the *Folder* object is not *null*, then you use the *Table* object to obtain the *Subject* property for each item marked for follow-up.

```
private void EnumerateAllTasksFolders()
{
    Outlook.Stores stores =
        Application.Session.Stores;
```

```
foreach (Outlook.Store store in stores)
{
    Outlook.Folder folder =
        store.GetSpecialFolder(
        Outlook.OlSpecialFolders.olSpecialFolderAllTasks)
        as Outlook.Folder;
    if (folder != null)
    {
        Outlook.Table table = folder.GetTable(
            "", Outlook.OlTableContents.olUserItems);
        while (!table.EndOfTable)
        {
            Outlook.Row nextRow = table.GetNextRow();
            Debug.WriteLine(nextRow["Subject"]);
        }
    }
}
```

Folders Collection and *Folder* Objects

The *Folders* collection and *Folder* objects represent the folder hierarchy where Outlook items are stored. Each *Folder* object has a *Folders* property that returns a *Folders* collection object. The *Folder* object supports two means of obtaining items in a folder. The *Items* collection object lets you enumerate, restrict, and find items in a folder. New to Outlook 2007, the *Table* object provides a performant read-only row set that also lets you enumerate, restrict, or find items in a folder. Each item is represented by a *Row* object with a default number of columns. If you need additional columns beyond the default, you can use the *Add* method of the table's *Columns* collection to add columns to the *Table* object. From the perspective of a managed code developer, you should think of the *Table* object as Outlook's Component Object Model (COM) equivalent to the Microsoft .NET Framework *System.Data.IDataReader* interface. The following discussion covers the *Folders* collection and *Folder* objects. At the end of this chapter, you learn how to use either the *Items* collection or the *Table* object to access the data in a folder.

An Overview of Folder Types

Before you learn about the *Folders* collection and *Folder* objects, it's a good idea to step back and consider how folders are typed and how your specific scenario might dictate the type of folder you use in your solution. In Outlook, folders are typed according to the type of item that they contain. For example, a Calendar folder always contains appointment items. A Contacts folder can contain contact items and private distribution lists. Mail folders generally contain mail or post items. However, there are notable exceptions to this rule. For example, the Deleted Items folder is typed as a Mail folder, but it can contain items of any item type.

Some solutions do not require special content folders to hold solution-specific items. In this case, you only need to understand the folder type (for example, Calendar folder for appointment items) and how that folder type contains items that are appropriate to your solution. Other solutions require content folders in addition to the default folders in your mailbox that contain custom items that have custom properties and enforce the business logic of your solution. The following discussion provides a scenario-based overview of folder types.

Placeholder Folders

Placeholder folders provide a logical hierarchy for your application folders. Public folder and mailbox folder applications sometimes include placeholder folders that provide a logical means of organizing the application folders that actually hold the items manipulated by a user. If you are creating an Exchange placeholder folder, you can assign permissions to a placeholder folder, which prevents users from adding, editing, or deleting items in the folder. One example of a placeholder folder is the RSS Subscriptions folder under the root mailbox folder. The actual RSS feed folders that contain RSS items are subfolders of the RSS Subscriptions placeholder folder. Another example of a placeholder folder would be a top-level placeholder folder named Sales with regional placeholder folders for East, West, South, and Midwest. Under the regional folders you could add application folders named Current Customers and Prospective Customers that contain items holding the data for your application.

Content Folders

Content folders provide a place to store and organize information. Default folders such as Inbox, Calendar, Contacts, and Tasks are good examples of content folders. Microsoft SharePoint folders that contain Microsoft Word documents, Microsoft Excel workbooks, or Microsoft PowerPoint presentations are also examples of content folders. Another example of a content folder would be a folder that holds items that are essential to your application. For example, Microsoft Business Contact Manager creates content folders that contain business contacts, opportunities, and so forth.

Search Folders

Search folders are virtual folders that can aggregate information from multiple physical folders. You can create search folders programmatically depending on the requirements of your solution. For example, you might want to create one or more search folders that use a categories scheme to organize mail from customer contacts.

Discussion Folders

Discussion folders provide a public forum for users to submit, share, and respond to ideas and information. For example, you can create a discussion folder for posting job openings, job candidate information, and interview responses for a candidate. You can create a Technical Users Group folder where writers and designers can post, read, and share information and solutions to problems. Typically, a discussion folder contains post items that can be used for posts and replies.

Planning the Folder Design of Your Solution

To create folders that meet the needs of your users, it is essential to plan them first. If you dive headfirst into creating a folder hierarchy and its contents, you might have to redesign both your folder structure and the custom forms contained in those folders if business rules change or design requirements are overlooked. Careful planning avoids expensive, time-consuming redesigns. Your motto when you approach folder design should be to plan, plan, and plan again. Although planning processes differ with each organization and application, these are general steps you should follow when planning the folder design of your solution:

- Determine who will plan, design, and implement the folder.

- Decide whether the folder is stored in Exchange public folders, an individual mailbox, or perhaps a shared or delegated mailbox.

- When you identify folder users and their needs, evaluate their requirements in terms of folder roles and permissions. Folder roles and permissions can only be created for Exchange server folders, whether those folders are public folders or folders in a mailbox. For example, what is the default permission on the application folder? Can your users modify the folder items created by other users? Create a list of user groups that will have access to your folder and determine whether they have permission to create, edit, or delete folder items.

- You also need to consider which forms will be available in your folders and which users can modify those forms.

- Be aware that folder users do not have to correspond to individual mailbox accounts. Exchange distribution lists provide a convenient way for you to manage the users who have been assigned to a public folder permissions role such as editor or author.

- Consider whether data should be consolidated in a single location, typically for backup and reporting purposes.

- Consider whether data should be accessible in a user's default folders so that it will synchronize with mobile devices.

- Create a design plan that identifies the problems to be solved and how the folder will solve them. The design plan should include preliminary graphics of form windows or views to be created.

Folders Collection

The *Folders* collection contains a set of *Folder* objects that represent all the available Outlook folders in a specific subset at one level of the folder tree. The parent object of a *Folders* collection object is always a *Folder* object. You can use the *Add* method of the *Folders* collection to add one or more folders to the parent *Folder* object. To enumerate folders, use the index operator to reference each folder in the collection. If you want to enumerate all folders in a given *Store* object, use the *GetRootFolder* method (discussed earlier) to obtain the root folder of the store. You can then use the *Folders* property on the *Folder* object that represents the root folder to walk the folder list for a given *Store* object.

Adding a *Folder* Object to the Folder List

You can use the *Add* method of the *Folders* collection to add a *Folder* object to the Outlook folder list. The following example uses the *Add* method of the *Folders* collection to add a folder called My New Folder as a subfolder of the Inbox folder. The folder is then displayed to the user.

```
private void AddMyNewFolder()
{
    Outlook.Folder folder =
        Application.Session.GetDefaultFolder(
        Outlook.OlDefaultFolders.olFolderInbox)
        as Outlook.Folder;
    Outlook.Folders folders = folder.Folders;
    try
    {
        Outlook.Folder newFolder = folders.Add(
            "My New Folder", Type.Missing)
            as Outlook.Folder;
        newFolder.Display();
    }
    catch (Exception ex)
    {
        MessageBox.Show(
            "Could not add 'My New Folder'",
            "Add Folder",
            MessageBoxButtons.OK,
            MessageBoxIcon.Error);
    }
}
```

Note   The *Add* method of the *Folders* collection takes two arguments: *Name*, a *string* that represents the folder name, and *Type*, an *object* that represents the folder type.

The first argument specifies the folder name for the new folder. The folder name must be unique. If the folder name already exists in the *Folders* collection, Outlook raises an error.

The second argument specifies the folder type. *Type* is an *object* type that represents the Outlook folder type for the new folder. If the folder type is not specified, the new folder will default to the same type as the folder in which it is created.

Type can be one of the following *OlDefaultFolders* constants: *olFolderCalendar*, *olFolderContacts*, *olFolderDrafts*, *olFolderInbox*, *olFolderJournal*, *olFolderNotes*, or *olFolderTasks*. (The constants *olFolderDeletedItems*, *olFolderOutbox*, *olFolderJunk*, *olFolderConflicts*, *olFolderLocalFailures*, *olFolderServerFailures*, *olFolderSyncIssues*, *olPublicFoldersAllPublicFolders*, *olFolderRssFeeds*, *olFolderToDo*, *olFolderManagedEmail*, and *olFolderSentMail* cannot be specified for this argument.)

Iterating Through a Collection of Folders

To iterate through a collection of folders, you should use the *Folders* property to obtain the subfolders of the parent *Folder* object. The following *EnumerateFoldersInDefaultStore* procedure walks through the folders in the user's default store by obtaining the root folder for the default store. Once you have the root folder, you call the *EnumerateFolders* procedure on the root folder. *EnumerateFolders* is a generic procedure that you can adapt to your own code requirements. *EnumerateFolders* is called recursively to enumerate all the folders in a hierarchy. Both *EnumerateFoldersInDefaultStore* and *EnumerateFolders* are listed here. The *EnumerateFolders* procedure simply writes the *FolderPath* property of the *Folder* to the trace listeners in the *Listeners* collection.

```
private void EnumerateFoldersInDefaultStore()
{
    Outlook.Folder root =
        Application.Session.
        DefaultStore.GetRootFolder() as Outlook.Folder;
    EnumerateFolders(root);
}

private void EnumerateFolders(Outlook.Folder folder)
{
    Outlook.Folders childFolders =
        folder.Folders;
    if (childFolders.Count > 0)
    {
        foreach(Outlook.Folder childFolder in childFolders)
        {
            //Write the folder path
            Debug.WriteLine(childFolder.FolderPath);
            //Call EnumerateFolders using childFolder
            EnumerateFolders(childFolder);
        }
    }
}
```

Folder Object

The *Folder* object represents a folder in the Outlook folder list. The *Folder* object serves as the gateway to the *Items* collection or the *Table* object that lets you access each item in the folder.

MAPIFolder Object vs. *Folder* Object

Previous versions of Outlook supported the *MAPIFolder* object. This object has been deprecated in Outlook 2007. Although existing solutions that access this object will still run, you should use the *Folder* object for Outlook 2007 or later versions. The *Folder* object has almost the same members of *MAPIFolder*, plus some new ones, including *BeforeFolderMove*, *BeforeItemMove*, *GetCalendarExporter*, *GetStorage*, *GetTable*, *PropertyAccessor*, *Store*, and *UserDefinedProperties*.

Properties and methods that returned a *MAPIFolder* object in previous versions of the Outlook object model will continue to do so in Outlook 2007. To use the *Folder* object instead of the *MAPIFolder* object, you must cast the *MAPIFolder* object returned by legacy properties and methods to a *Folder* object.

Working with the *Folder* Object

To add a new folder programmatically, use the *Add* method of the *Folders* collection discussed earlier. To work with an existing folder, the Outlook object model offers several different methods to access a specific folder.

GetDefaultFolder Method

The *GetDefaultFolder* method of the *Namespace* object returns a default folder in the user's default store. For example, the following example uses *GetDefaultFolder* to return the user's RSS Feeds root folder and displays a message box containing the folder names for all RSS feeds under the RSS Feeds folder:

```
private void GetRSSFeeds()
{
    Outlook.Folder folder =
        Application.Session.GetDefaultFolder(
        Outlook.OlDefaultFolders.olFolderRssFeeds)
        as Outlook.Folder;
    if (folder != null)
    {
        if (folder.Folders.Count > 0)
        {
            StringBuilder sb = new StringBuilder();
            foreach (Outlook.Folder subfolder
                in folder.Folders)
            {
                sb.AppendLine(subfolder.Name);
            }
            MessageBox.Show(sb.ToString(),
                "RSS Feeds",
                MessageBoxButtons.OK,
                MessageBoxIcon.Information);
        }
    }
}
```

Note   *GetDefaultFolder* takes an *OlDefaultFolders* value to return the correct default folder. Don't assume that *GetDefaultFolder* will always return a *Folder* object for all possible values of *OlDefaultFolders*. For example, if you specify *olFolderManagedEmail* as *FolderType* but the Managed Folders group has not been deployed, then *GetDefaultFolder* will return *null* (*Nothing* in Microsoft Visual Basic).

Parent Property and *Folders* Property

You can also reference folders by navigation from a specific folder. Each item and folder exposes a *Parent* property that returns the parent folder for that object. Each folder also exposes a *Folders* property that returns a *Folders* collection that contains the subfolders of the parent folder. If you need to access a specific subfolder of the *Folders* collection, you obtain the *Folder* object that represents the subfolder by using the indexer on the *Folders* collection. The indexer requires that you supply the name of the subfolder or the one-based integer index within the collection.

GetFolderFromID Method

The *GetFolderFromID* method of the *Namespace* object returns a *Folder* object based on the *EntryID* and *StoreID* parameters that are passed to the method. The *EntryID* and *StoreID* properties of the *Folder* object can be used to identify a folder in Outlook. The *EntryID* property corresponds to the MAPI property *PR_ENTRYID* and the *StoreID* property corresponds to the MAPI property *PR_STORE_ENTRYID*. The *EntryID* and *StoreID* properties, which are analogous to primary keys in a database table, let you identify both *Folder* and *Item* objects in the Outlook folder hierarchy. Once you have these values, you can use the *GetFolderFromID* method to return a *Folder* object. You can also use the *GetFolderFromID* method to return both default and nondefault folders in any *Store* object provided that the current user has access rights to that folder.

 Important   Although *EntryID* values are guaranteed to be unique within a store, it's important to realize that the *EntryID* property of an item might not stay consistent depending on how the user interacts with the data. For example, if an item is moved from one store to another and then moved back to the original store, the *EntryID* property of the item will change. Also, if a user exports the data in a folder and then imports it back again, the *EntryID* property for each item will change because new items are actually being created by this process. Any custom solution should take into account the possibility that the *EntryID* property for a given item might change.

The following example shows how you can cause the user to select a folder from the folder list. The *PickFolder* method of the *Namespace* object displays the Select Folder dialog box to the user. You cannot customize the folder list displayed in this dialog box. Once the user selects a folder, the code displays the *EntryID*, *StoreID* *UnReadItemCount*, *DefaultMessageClass*, *CurrentView.Name*, and *FolderPath* properties for the selected folder, and then uses the *GetFolderFromID* method to reinstantiate the *Folder* object and display the folder.

```
private void ShowFolderInfo()
{
    Outlook.Folder folder =
        Application.Session.PickFolder()
        as Outlook.Folder;
    if (folder != null)
    {
```

```
        StringBuilder sb = new StringBuilder();
        sb.AppendLine("Folder EntryID:");
        sb.AppendLine(folder.EntryID);
        sb.AppendLine();
        sb.AppendLine("Folder StoreID:");
        sb.AppendLine(folder.StoreID);
        sb.AppendLine();
        sb.AppendLine("Unread Item Count: "
            + folder.UnReadItemCount);
        sb.AppendLine("Default MessageClass: "
            + folder.DefaultMessageClass);
        sb.AppendLine("Current View: "
            + folder.CurrentView.Name);
        sb.AppendLine("Folder Path: "
            + folder.FolderPath);
        MessageBox.Show(sb.ToString(),
            "Folder Information",
            MessageBoxButtons.OK,
            MessageBoxIcon.Information);
        Outlook.Folder folderFromID =
            Application.Session.GetFolderFromID(
            folder.EntryID, folder.StoreID)
            as Outlook.Folder ;
        folderFromID.Display();
    }
}
```

GetFolder(folderPath) Procedure

So far you've seen how to retrieve a default folder using the *GetDefaultFolder* method or retrieve a default or nondefault folder using the folder's *EntryID* and *StoreID* properties. What happens if you don't know the *EntryID* and *StoreID* properties and the folder is a nondefault folder? If you know the path to the folder, you can use the *GetFolder* procedure shown next to obtain the correct *Folder* object. The *GetFolder* procedure splits the *FolderPath* property into a *string* array and then uses the array to find the correct *Folder* object starting from the top of the *FolderPath* property. *GetFolder* returns a *Folder* object. If *GetFolder* does not find the specified folder, it returns *null* (*Nothing* in Visual Basic). The *FolderPath* property supplied to the *GetFolder* procedure is specified as follows:

*RootFolder**Folder**Subfolder*

where RootFolder represents the root folder of the store, Folder is a subfolder of the root, and the Subfolder represents a subfolder of Folder. Of course, there can be additional subfolders below the Subfolder. If you are specifying the *FolderPath* property in C#, be sure to escape the *FolderPath* property with the @ character. Typical *FolderPath* specifications are as follows:

- \\Mailbox – UserName\Inbox\Sales Reports
- \\Public Folders\All Public Folders\Human Resources\Documents\Training Material
- \\Archive 2007\Calendar

If you need to determine the root folder for a user's default store, obtain the root folder by calling the *GetRootFolder* method on the *DefaultStore* object as demonstrated in the *GetKeyContacts* example next. Once you have the *FolderPath* property for the folder that you want to reference, supply the *FolderPath* argument to the *GetFolder* procedure.

```
private void GetKeyContacts()
{
    string folderPath =
        Application.Session.
        DefaultStore.GetRootFolder().FolderPath
        + @"\Contacts\Key Contacts";
    Outlook.Folder folder = GetFolder(folderPath);
    if (folder != null)
    {
        //Work with folder here
        Debug.WriteLine("Found Key Contacts");
    }
}
```

The complete listing for the *GetFolder* procedure is shown here.

```
//folderPath is a string
//that indicates path to folder
//Usage: myFolder =
//GetFolder(@"\\Mailbox - UserName\Inbox\Subfolder");
public Outlook.Folder GetFolder(string folderPath)
{
    Outlook.Folder folder;
    string backslash = @"\";
    try
    {
        if (folderPath.StartsWith(@"\\"))
        {
            folderPath = folderPath.Remove(0, 2);
        }
        String[] folders =
            folderPath.Split(backslash.ToCharArray());
        folder =
            Application.Session.Folders[folders[0]]
            as Outlook.Folder;
        if (folder != null)
        {
            for (int i = 1; i <= folders.GetUpperBound(0); i++)
            {
                Outlook.Folders subFolders = folder.Folders;
                folder = subFolders[folders[i]]
                    as Outlook.Folder;
                if (folder == null)
                {
                    return null;
                }
            }
        }
    }
```

```
            return folder;
    }
    catch { return null; }
}
```

Folder Properties and Methods

There are several properties on the *Folder* object that determine the type of folder that you are working with and the default message class for that folder. If you need more information about the capabilities of the folder represented by the *Folder* object, you can examine the *UserDefinedProperties* collection or use the *PropertyAccessor* object to retrieve additional folder properties. The following discussion will help you to understand how to use those properties in your code.

DefaultItemType Property

The *DefaultItemType* property indicates the default item type supported for the folder. Table 6-2 lists the folder type and the corresponding *OlDefaultItemType* value returned by *Folder.DefaultItemType*.

Table 6-2   Possible *Folder.DefaultItemType* Values

Folder type	*DefaultItemType* returns
Mail	OlItemType.olMailItem
Calendar	OlItemType.olAppointmentItem
Contacts	OlItemType.olContactItem
Tasks	OlItemType.olTaskItem
Journal	OlItemType.olJournalItem
Notes	OlItemType.olNoteItem

DefaultMessageClass Property

The *DefaultMessageClass* property indicates the default message class for the folder. For example, if the *Folder* object represents a Contacts folder, the *DefaultMessageClass* property is *IPM.Contact*. If a custom form or a replacement or replace-all form region has been established as the default form for the folder, you must use the *PropertyAccessor* object to determine the message class of the default form. The *DefaultMessageClass* property will not tell you the message class of the default form for the folder. The following *GetDefaultMessageClass* procedure uses the *PropertyAccessor* object to determine the default form a folder. For additional information on using the *PropertyAccessor* object, see Chapter 17, "Using the *PropertyAccessor* Object." Use the *GetDefaultMessageClass* procedure in your code to determine the correct default message class for a folder. If the folder property *PR_DEF_POST_MSGCLASS* is not found and Outlook raises an error, then the *catch* block returns the *DefaultMessageClass* property for the *Folder* object.

```
private string GetDefaultMessageClass(Outlook.Folder folder)
{
    if (folder == null)
        throw new ArgumentNullException();
    try
    {
        const string PR_DEF_POST_MSGCLASS =
            @"http://schemas.microsoft.com/mapi/proptag/0x36E5001E";
        string messageClass =
            folder.PropertyAccessor.GetProperty(
            PR_DEF_POST_MSGCLASS).ToString();
        return messageClass;
    }
    catch
    {
        return folder.DefaultMessageClass;
    }
}
```

GetCalendarExporter Method

The *GetCalendarExporter* method returns a *CalendarSharing* object for the parent *Folder* object. If the parent *Folder* object does not represent a Calendar folder, Outlook raises an error. The following example uses the *GetCalendarExporter* method to return a *CalendarSharing* object from the default Calendar folder with one week of free, busy, and subject details. It then calls the *ForwardAsICal* method on the *CalendarSharing* object and displays the message with an ICalendar payload to the user.

```
private void DemoCalendarSharing()
{
    //Get instance of CalendarSharing object
    Outlook.CalendarSharing calShare =
        Application.Session.GetDefaultFolder
        (Outlook.OlDefaultFolders.olFolderCalendar).
        GetCalendarExporter();
    //Free busy and subject details
    calShare.CalendarDetail =
        Outlook.OlCalendarDetail.olFreeBusyAndSubject;
    //Set start and end dates
    calShare.StartDate = DateTime.Today;
    calShare.EndDate = calShare.StartDate.AddDays(1);
    //Call ForwardAsICal method
    Outlook.MailItem mail =
        calShare.ForwardAsICal(Outlook.OlCalendarMailFormat
        .olCalendarMailFormatDailySchedule);
    //Add recipient
    mail.Recipients.Add("someone@example.com");
    mail.Recipients.ResolveAll();
    //Set subject
    string CalName =
        Application.Session.GetDefaultFolder
    (Outlook.OlDefaultFolders.olFolderCalendar).Name;
    mail.Subject =
        Application.Session.CurrentUser.Name +
```

```
        CalName.PadLeft(CalName.Length + 1);
    //Display calendar sharing item
    mail.Display(false);
}
```

GetStorage Method

The *GetStorage* method creates or retrieves a *StorageItem* object in a folder. A *StorageItem* object is hidden from the user and cannot be displayed programmatically. In an Exchange environment, a *StorageItem* object is typically used to roam solution settings and ensure that those settings are available online and offline. For example, you might want to store an order number value that is available on all machines where a given user might log in to Outlook. Rather than store that value in the Windows registry, you persist the order number in a custom Order Number *UserProperty* property on a *StorageItem* object in the user's Inbox folder. You can assign a custom message class to the storage item or identify it by subject. If you provide a subject, it's a good idea to use the Programmatic Identifier (ProgID) for your add-in. Outlook also stores settings in hidden messages. A few examples of Outlook settings stored in hidden messages are calendar working hours, autoarchive settings, and categories.

The following code sample retrieves the Extensible Markup Language (XML) stored in the hidden message in the Calendar folder with the message class equal to *IPM.Configuration.WorkHours*. Notice that the *PropertyAccessor* object returns the XML as an object. This object contains a byte stream rather than a string representation of the XML. To convert the XML to a string, use *System.Text.Encoding.Ascii.GetText* to convert *byte* to a *string*. Once you have the XML, you can use a variety of methods to determine the working hours start and end time as well as workdays. For additional information on the *GetStorage* method, see the Outlook 2007 Developer Reference and the section on *StorageItem* in Chapter 5, "Built-in Item Types."

```
private string GetWorkHoursXML()
{
    try
    {
        Outlook.StorageItem storage =
            Application.Session.GetDefaultFolder(
            Outlook.OlDefaultFolders.olFolderCalendar).GetStorage(
            "IPM.Configuration.WorkHours",
            Outlook.OlStorageIdentifierType.olIdentifyByMessageClass);
        Outlook.PropertyAccessor pa = storage.PropertyAccessor;
        //PropertyAccessor will return a byte array for this property
        byte[] rawXmlBytes = (byte[])pa.GetProperty(
            "http://schemas.microsoft.com/mapi/proptag/0x7C080102");
        //Use Encoding to convert the array to a string
        return System.Text.Encoding.ASCII.GetString(rawXmlBytes);
    }
    catch
    {
        return string.Empty;
    }
}
```

UserDefinedProperties Collection

The *UserDefinedProperties* collection represents the user-defined custom properties for the *Folder* object. This object addresses a common complaint of Outlook developers. If you define custom properties on the items in your solution, those properties must be defined at the folder as well as the item level. The *UserProperties* collection on an item such as a *ContactItem* object allows you to define user properties on an item and assign values to a specific *UserProperty* object. The *Add* method on the *UserProperties* collection contains an optional *bool* (*Boolean* in Visual Basic) parameter *AddToFolderFields* that ensures that the *UserProperty* object is added to the folder as well as the item. The custom *UserProperty* object must be added to both the folder and the item. When you write your code, you add the custom property to both the item and the folder. So far, all is well. If the custom property is not added to the folder through developer error or user action (an end user can delete the custom property in the Outlook Field Chooser or move the item to a different folder), *Find* and *Restrict* operations that use that property will fail.

The *UserDefinedProperties* collection allows you to add, access, and remove *UserDefinedProperty* objects at the folder level. The *UserDefinedProperties* collection is new to Outlook 2007. Each *Folder* object exposes a *UserDefinedProperties* collection that represents the user-defined properties for that folder. Your application logic can test whether your custom properties exist in the folder and add them if they do not or if they have been removed. The point to remember is that if your custom properties are not defined at the folder level, you won't be able to use Outlook queries to find or restrict items with those custom properties. *Find* and *Restrict* operations are discussed in Chapter 11, "Searching Outlook Data."

> **Note** To actually persist a custom property represented by a *UserDefinedProperty* object in a folder, you must save the custom property with the same name in the item itself. Storing a value in a *UserDefinedProperty* object for the folder has no effect. You should use the item's *UserProperties* collection to access the *UserProperty* object that you want to set, and then set the *Value* property on the *UserProperty* object. Be sure to call the *Save* method on the item to persist your changes.

```
private void DemoUserDefinedProperty()
{
    Outlook.Folder folder =
        Application.ActiveExplorer().CurrentFolder
        as Outlook.Folder;
    Outlook.PostItem post = folder.Items.Add("IPM.Post")
        as Outlook.PostItem;
    //Add UserProperty to PostItem
    post.UserProperties.Add("ColorID",
        Outlook.OlUserPropertyType.olText,
        false, Type.Missing);
    post.UserProperties["ColorID"].Value = "Green";
    post.Subject = "UserProperty Example";
    post.Save();
    Outlook.PostItem findPost;
```

```
        try
        {
            //Items.Find will fail unless custom property
            //is defined in the folder
            findPost =
                folder.Items.Find("[ColorID] = 'Green'")
                as Outlook.PostItem;
        }
        catch(Exception ex)
        {
            Debug.WriteLine(ex.Message);
        }
        //Add ColorID field to the folder
        folder.UserDefinedProperties.Add("ColorID",
            Outlook.OlUserPropertyType.olText,
            Type.Missing, Type.Missing);
        //Now the find works ok
        Outlook.PostItem findPostOK;
        try
        {
            findPostOK =
                folder.Items.Find("[ColorID] = 'Green'")
                as Outlook.PostItem;
            if (findPostOK != null)
            {
                Debug.WriteLine("Found PostItem");
            }
            //Clean up by deleting PostItem and ColorID
            findPostOK.Delete();
            Outlook.UserDefinedProperty userProperty =
                folder.UserDefinedProperties["ColorID"];
            userProperty.Delete();
        }
        catch(Exception ex)
        {
            Debug.WriteLine(ex.Message);
        }
    }
```

Folder Permissions

One additional consideration for accessing data in folders is folder permissions. For folders hosted on an Exchange server (online mode or cached Exchange mode), folders have permissions that control whether the logged-on user can add, edit, or delete items in folders. Folders in a Personal Folders File (.pst) do not support folder permissions. If your solution operates within the context of the user's mailbox, then permissions are less of an issue because the logged-on user typically has Owner permissions on his or her mailbox folders. The following section describes how you assign folder permissions through the Outlook user interface. The *Folder* object does not expose a member that lets you programmatically get or set folder permissions. However, you can use the *SharingItem* object in an Exchange environment to grant permissions to other users.

Assigning Folder Permissions

You assign permissions to users to define the functions they can perform in the folder. You determine who can view and use the folder in the folder's Properties dialog box on the Permissions tab by adding user or distribution list names in the Name list box. After the names are added to the Name list box, you can assign roles to define the permissions for each user or distribution list, as shown in Figure 6-1.

Figure 6-1   Permissions for a Calendar folder.

To display the Permissions tab, follow these steps:

1. In the Folder List, right-click the folder where you want to set permissions.

2. On the context menu, click Change Sharing Permissions.

The names in the Name list box determine who can view and use the folder. If you create the folder, you are automatically given owner permissions for the folder. With owner permissions, you can add users to and remove users from the Name list box. You can also change permissions for selected users.

One name in the Name list box is Default. The permissions defined for Default are granted to all users who have access to the folder. If you want to give a particular user permissions other than Default, add the user's name to the Name list box, and then set permissions for that user.

You can remove any name from the Name list box except Default and, if you are the sole owner of the folder, your name. If you remove Default or your name, they will reappear the next time you view the Permissions tab.

Assigning Roles

When you set permissions for a user, you define the functions that the user can perform within the folder. You can set permissions by using predefined roles or by using custom roles:

- **Predefined roles**   Predefined groups of permissions that are available from the Roles drop-down list box.

- **Custom roles**   Permissions you set for the user that do not match any of the predefined roles.

To assign roles to users, follow these steps:

1. On the Permissions tab in the Name list box, select the user name for which you want to set permissions.

2. In the Roles drop-down list box, select a role for the user.

Table 6-3 lists the roles and the predefined permissions that are assigned to each one.

Table 6-3   Roles and Folder Permissions

Role	Description
Owner	Create, read, modify, and delete all items and files and create subfolders. As the folder owner, you can change permissions others have for the folder.
Publishing Editor	Create, read, modify, and delete all items and files and create subfolders.
Editor	Create, read, modify, and delete all items and files.
Nonediting Author	Create and read items. This person or group cannot edit but can delete items and files you create.
Publishing Author	Create and read items and files, create subfolders, and modify and delete items and files you create.
Author	Create and read items and files, and modify and delete items and files you create.
Reviewer	Read items and files only.
Contributor	Create items and files only. The user cannot open the folder.
None	The user cannot open the folder.
Custom	Perform activities defined by the folder owner from options selected on the Permissions tab.

To assign a custom role, follow these steps:

1. In the Name list box, select the user name for which you want to set permissions.

2. In the Roles drop-down list box, select the role that most closely resembles the permissions you want to grant to the user.

3. Under Permissions, select the options you want. If the permissions do not match a role, Custom will display in the Roles drop-down list box. If the permissions match a role, that role will display in the Roles drop-down list box.

Using the *SharingItem* Object to Assign Folder Permissions

Outlook 2007 does not directly support setting permissions on the *Folder* object. If you need to programmatically set folder permissions across multiple mailboxes, the suggested approach is to use an Exchange Server application programming interface (API) such as the Web Distributed Authoring and Versioning (WebDAV) protocol or the Exchange OLE DB Provider (ExOLEDB). Only WebDAV is suitable for use in client-side code. For additional information on these APIs, see the appropriate version of the Microsoft Exchange Server Software Development Kit on MSDN. However, if you cannot gain programmatic access to Exchange servers in your organization, Outlook 2007 does offer an indirect mechanism for setting folder permissions. You can use a *SharingItem* object to assign a limited subset of folder permissions. For complete details, including code samples, see the section "Using the *SharingItem* Object" in Chapter 9, "Sharing Information with Other Users."

Accessing Items in a Folder

At this point, you should have a good understanding of how to navigate the Outlook folder hierarchy using the Outlook object model. Once you have instantiated the appropriate folder, the next consideration is accessing the items in the folder. This section discusses ways that you can enumerate items in the folder. Restricting and searching for items is covered in detail in Chapter 11.

Performance Considerations

Performance is always an important factor when accessing items in a folder, especially when the folder contains a large number of items. For this discussion, more than 1,000 items in a folder is considered a large number of items. Although performance is dependent on other factors such as disk I/O, CPU speed, and available memory, you don't want your code to be responsible for a performance bottleneck. Generally, you want to keep all operations that enumerate folders and items to less than one second in duration, if possible. The Outlook object model operates on Outlook's main foreground thread, so you will block Outlook responsiveness if your code execution goes into a loop that does not perform adequately. Performance was one of the reasons that developers turned to other APIs such as Collaboration Data Objects (CDO) or Extended MAPI in past versions of Outlook, but Outlook 2007 offers some important innovations that seek to address performance concerns.

The primary performance improvement in Outlook 2007 is the *Table* object. The *Table* object provides a read-only row set that lets you enumerate, filter, and sort the rows in the table. You navigate the rows returned by the *Table* object in a forward-only manner. Each row represents an item in the parent *Folder* object. Unlike the *Items* collection, the *Table* object encourages developers to write efficient code and does not have the disadvantages of the *Items* collection, where a developer could retrieve the *Body* property or the *Attachments* collection on the item and in turn see performance degrade dramatically. Although performance results are dependent on a variety of factors, in general the *Table* object lets you enumerate results in approximately 10 percent to 20 percent of the time required by the *Items* collection without the use of the *SetColumns* method.

Should you use the *Table* object or the *Items* collection to achieve the best performance when enumerating items? The general recommendation would be to use the *Table* object because it is inherently faster than the *Items* collection. However, there are occasions when you should use the *Items* collection rather than the *Table* object. The clear recommendation for the *Items* collection is when you need to enumerate recurrences in a Calendar folder. The *Table* object in Outlook 2007 only returns the master series for recurring appointments; it does not return individual appointment occurrences or exceptions.

However, there are other scenarios where you should consider the *Items* collection. Deciding which approach to take depends on a variety of factors. For example, if you want to delete many items in a folder you should probably use the *Items* collection because you will need to access these items in a read/write manner. For scenarios where you only need to change or delete one or a few items, using the *Table* object should be more efficient. Although the *Row* object that represents an item is read-only, in this scenario it should be more efficient as there are only a limited number of items to change or delete. If you need to perform write operations on the item or delete the item, you can instantiate a full item by obtaining the *EntryID* column from the *Row* object and then using the *GetItemFromID* method of the *Namespace* object.

OutlookItem Helper Class

The *OutlookItem* helper class is available in C# and Visual Basic versions with the code that accompanies this book. Because upcoming code samples implement this class, you need to understand the rationale behind the *OutlookItem* class.

The *OutlookItem* class uses reflection to expose properties and methods that are common to all items. It also provides IntelliSense for these common members. Unfortunately, the COM-based Outlook object model returns *object* for many members such as *Namespace.GetItemFromID*, *Inspector.CurrentItem*, *Items[]*, and so forth. To use *object* in a strongly typed code environment such as C# or Visual Basic (with *Option Strict On*), you always need to cast the *object* representing the item to an Outlook type such as *MailItem*. The *OutlookItem* class helps you to cast *object* to the correct Outlook type and also allows you to use common members directly on the *OutlookItem* object.

For example, the following code displays all the selected items in the active Explorer window. Because the *Display* method is common to all items, it appears as a method on the *OutlookItem* class. The variable *myItem* is an instance of *OutlookItem*, and you can simply write *myItem.Display()* to display each item in the *Selection* object.

```
private void DisplaySelectedItems()
{
    Outlook.Selection selection =
        Application.ActiveExplorer().Selection;
    for (int i = 1; i <= selection.Count; i++)
```

```
    {
        OutlookItem myItem = new OutlookItem(selection[i]);
        myItem.Display();
    }
}
```

> **Important**   The use of reflection in the *OutlookItem* class can slow the performance of your
> code. Avoid the use of the *OutlookItem* class in a *foreach* construct on the *Items* collection
> where you are looping over hundreds or thousands of items. When you need to enumerate
> a large number of items, consider using the *Restrict* method to reduce the number of items or
> use the *Table* object to return read-only *Row* objects. You can use the *EntryID* column
> returned in the *Table* object to open the item with the *GetItemFromID* method of the
> *Namespace* object and then cast the returned *object* to the appropriate type.

Items Collection

The *Items* collection is the old standby for enumerating items through the object model. It has
been a feature of the object model for many versions of Outlook. In general, you should prefer
the *Table* object in Outlook 2007 when you enumerate or restrict items in a folder. However,
there are some circumstances when you might want to use the *Items* collection instead of the
Table object. The following sections cover those areas where the *Items* collection is preferred to
the *Table* object. The *Restrict* and *Sort* methods of the *Items* object are covered only briefly in
this chapter. For a detailed discussion of searching for items using either the *Table* object or
the *Items* collection, see Chapter 11.

Deleting Items in a Collection

For example, let's assume that you want to delete meeting responses from the user's Sent
Items folder. You could use the *Table* object to return rows representing the meeting responses
and then open each item by using the *GetItemFromID* method on the *Namespace* object and
then casting the item to a *MeetingItem* object. At this point, you would call the *Delete* method
on the *MeetingItem* object. You can write simpler code by restricting the *Items* collection and
then deleting each object in the restricted *Items* collection. Note that when you delete items
from the *Items* collection, you cannot use a *foreach* construct or an incrementing *for(int i=1;
i<=items.Count; i++)* loop. You should use a decrementing *for(int i=items.Count; i>0; i–)* loop to
delete the items in the collection. The following code sample restricts the items in the Deleted
Items folder and then deletes each item. This method is much more efficient than looping
over all the items in the folder and only deleting items with the appropriate *MessageClass*
property.

```
private void DeleteMeetingRequestsAndResponses()
{
    //Obtain Sent Items folder
    Outlook.Folder folder =
        Application.Session.GetDefaultFolder(
```

```
        Outlook.OlDefaultFolders.olFolderSentMail)
        as Outlook.Folder;
    //Create filter string
    string filter = "[MessageClass] = 'IPM.Schedule.Meeting.Request'"
        + " OR "
        + "[MessageClass] = 'IPM.Schedule.Meeting.Resp.Pos'"
        + " OR "
        + "[MessageClass] = 'IPM.Schedule.Meeting.Resp.Neg'"
        + " OR "
        + "[MessageClass] = 'IPM.Schedule.Meeting.Resp.Tent'"
        + " OR "
        + "[MessageClass] = 'IPM.Schedule.Meeting.Resp.Canceled'"
        + " OR "
        + "[MessageClass] = 'IPM.Schedule.Meeting.Canceled'";
    Outlook.Items meetingItems = folder.Items.Restrict(filter);
    try
    {
        for (int i = meetingItems.Count; i > 0; i--)
        {
            try
            {
                //Get the first item in the collection
                Outlook.MeetingItem meeting = meetingItems[i]
                    as Outlook.MeetingItem;
                meeting.Delete();
            }
            catch { }
        }
    }
    catch(Exception ex)
    {
        Debug.WriteLine(ex.Message);
    }
}
```

Using *SetColumns* and *ResetColumns* to Improve Performance

You can enhance the performance of the *Items* collection by caching the properties that you want to use on each item in the *Items* collection. To cache properties on the *Items* collection, call the *SetColumns* method before you enumerate the items in the collection. The *SetColumns* method takes one argument, a comma-delimited string of property names. Once you have completed enumerating the items in the collection, you should call the *ResetColumns* method to clear the property cache. The following code sample uses *SetColumns* to cache the *FileAs*, *CompanyName*, and *JobTitle* properties for a subset of items in the Contacts folder. Notice that the restriction for the *Items* collection specifies that *CompanyName* and *JobTitle* are not *null*. If you don't test for *null* or empty strings in the restriction, you should do so if you attempt to use the property in string concatenation.

```
private void EnumerateContactsWithSetColumns()
{
    //Obtain Contacts folder
```

```
Outlook.Folder folder =
    Application.Session.GetDefaultFolder(
    Outlook.OlDefaultFolders.olFolderContacts)
    as Outlook.Folder;
string filter = "Not([CompanyName] Is Null)" +
    " AND Not([JobTitle] Is Null)";
Outlook.Items items = folder.Items.Restrict(filter);
items.SetColumns("FileAs, CompanyName, JobTitle");
for (int i = 1; i <= items.Count; i++)
{
    //Create an instance of OutlookItem
    OutlookItem myItem = new OutlookItem(items[i]);
    if (myItem.Class == Outlook.OlObjectClass.olContact)
    {
        //Use InnerObject to return ContactItem
        Outlook.ContactItem contact =
            myItem.InnerObject as Outlook.ContactItem;
        StringBuilder sb = new StringBuilder();
        sb.AppendLine(contact.FileAs);
        sb.AppendLine(contact.CompanyName);
        sb.AppendLine(contact.JobTitle);
        sb.AppendLine();
        Debug.WriteLine(sb.ToString());
    }
}
items.ResetColumns();
}
```

 Note   You cannot specify custom properties in the *UserDefinedProperties* collection for the *Folder* object in the *SetColumns* method. You also cannot specify computed properties or property objects such as *IsMarkedAsTask* or *Attachments*. If the specified property is not available on items in the folder (such as *FirstName* in the Inbox folder), Outlook raises an error.

Use *IncludeRecurrences* to Expand Recurring Appointments

If you need to expand recurring appointments in a Calendar folder, you must use the *Items* collection and set the *IncludeRecurrences* property to *true*. The *Table* object does not support recurrences in Outlook 2007. The *IncludeRecurrences* property only has an effect if the *Items* collection contains appointments and is sorted by the *Start* property in ascending order. The default value of *IncludeRecurrences* is *false*. Use this property when you want to retrieve all appointments for a given date range, where recurring appointments would not normally appear because they are not actual items in a folder. If you need to sort and filter appointment items that contain recurring appointments, you must do so in this order:

- Create a filter and call the *Restrict* method on the *Items* collection for the Calendar folder based on *Start* and *End* properties. In the following code sample, this *Items* collection is named *calendarItems*. If you don't create this filter, you will have an *Items* collection for all recurrences in the Calendar folder and performance will suffer.

- Call the *Sort* method to sort the items in ascending order.

- Set *IncludeRecurrences* to *true*.

- Create another filter, and call the *Restrict* method again on the previously restricted *Items* collection. In the following code sample, the second *Items* collection is named *restrictedItems*. At this point, you can enumerate the items in *restrictedItems*.

```csharp
private void FilterRecurringAppointments()
{
    Outlook.Folder folder =
        Application.Session.GetDefaultFolder(
        Outlook.OlDefaultFolders.olFolderCalendar)
        as Outlook.Folder;
    //Set end value
    DateTime end = DateTime.Now;
    //Set start value
    DateTime start = end.AddDays(-7);
    //Initial restriction is Jet query for date range
    string filter1 = "[Start] >= '" +
        start.ToString("g")
        + "' AND [End] <= '" +
        end.ToString("g") + "'";
    Outlook.Items calendarItems = folder.Items.Restrict(filter1);
    calendarItems.Sort("[Start]", Type.Missing);
    calendarItems.IncludeRecurrences = true;
    //Create DASL query for second restriction
    string filter2;
    if (Application.Session.DefaultStore.IsInstantSearchEnabled)
    {
        filter2 = "@SQL="
            + "\"" + "urn:schemas:httpmail:subject" + "\""
            + " ci_startswith 'Office'";
    }
    else
    {
        filter2 = "@SQL="
            + "\"" + "urn:schemas:httpmail:subject" + "\""
            + " like '%Office%'";
    }
    Outlook.Items restrictedItems =
        calendarItems.Restrict(filter2);
    foreach (Outlook.AppointmentItem appt in restrictedItems)
    {
        StringBuilder sb = new StringBuilder();
        sb.AppendLine(appt.Subject);
        sb.AppendLine("Start: " + appt.Start);
        sb.AppendLine("End: " + appt.End);
        sb.AppendLine();
        Debug.WriteLine(sb.ToString());
    }
}
```

If the collection includes recurring appointments with no end date, setting the *IncludeRecurrences* property to *true* might cause the collection to be of infinite count. Be sure to include a test for this in any loop. You should not use the *Count* property of the *Items* collection when iterating the *Items* collection with the *IncludeRecurrences* property set to *true*. The value of *Count* will be an undefined value. Instead, use a *foreach* construct to iterate the items in the filtered collection.

Obtaining Recurring Appointments in a Date Range

To obtain recurring appointments in a date range, use the *Items* collection and apply a restriction for *Start* and *End* properties. After you apply the filter, you must call the *Sort* method and set the *IncludeRecurrences* property to *true*. For best performance, keep the date range as small as possible. The following *DemoApptsInRange* procedure calls the *GetRecurringAppointments* routine, which returns an *Items* collection that contains *AppointmentItem* objects that fall within the range specified by the *startTime* and *endTime* parameters passed to the method.

> **Note** When you create a filter for the *Restrict* method that specifies *Start* and *End* times, you must format the *DateTime* string without seconds in the time portion. If you use seconds, the query will fail. In the *GetAppointmentsInRange* procedure, the *g* format specifier in the *DateTime.ToString()* method ensures that a string containing a short date and short time are used in the filter.

```csharp
private void DemoApptsInRange()
{
    Outlook.Folder calFolder =
        Application.Session.GetDefaultFolder(
        Outlook.OlDefaultFolders.olFolderCalendar)
        as Outlook.Folder;
    DateTime start = DateTime.Now;
    DateTime end = start.AddDays(7);
    Outlook.Items rangeAppts = GetAppointmentsInRange(
        calFolder, start, end);
    if (rangeAppts != null)
    {
        foreach(Outlook.AppointmentItem appt in rangeAppts)
        {
            Debug.WriteLine(appt.Subject);
        }
    }
}

private Outlook.Items GetAppointmentsInRange(
    Outlook.Folder folder, DateTime startTime, DateTime endTime)
{
    string filter = "[Start] >= '"
    + startTime.ToString("g")
    + "' AND [End] <= '"
    + endTime.ToString("g") + "'";
    try
    {
        Outlook.Items calItems = folder.Items.Restrict(filter);
        calItems.Sort("[Start]", Type.Missing);
```

```
        calItems.IncludeRecurrences = true;
        if (calItems.Count > 0)
        {
            return calItems;
        }
        else
        {
            return null;
        }
    }
    catch { return null; }
}
```

Table Object

The *Table* object represents a set of items from a *Folder* or *Search* object, with items as rows of the table and properties as columns of the table. New to Outlook 2007, the *Table* object has been added to the Outlook object model to address performance concerns with the *Items* collection. It makes it easier for developers to write performant code and supports new query operators that let you take advantage of the new Instant Search feature in Outlook 2007.

Using the *GetTable* Method

To obtain an instance of the *Table* object, you call the *GetTable* method on a *Folder* object or a *Search* object. The *GetTable* method takes two optional parameters when called against a *Folder* object: *Filter* (a string that contains a valid Outlook query) and *TableContents* (an *OlTableContents* value). The *Filter* parameter allows you to restrict the *Table* object and return a subset of items in the folder. If you specify an empty string for the filter or pass *Type.Missing*, all items in the folder will be returned in the table. The *TableContents* parameter determines whether the *Row* objects in the parent *Table* object represent hidden items in the folder or user items, meaning items that can be viewed and opened by the logged-on user. If you specify *Type.Missing* for the *TableContents* parameter, user items will be returned in the table.

The *GetTable* method does not take parameters when called against a *Search* object (which represents an Outlook search folder). You cannot view hidden items in a search folder, and the restriction for the *Search* object is specified in the *Filter* parameter of the *AdvancedSearch* method that creates the *Search* object. *AdvancedSearch* is a method on the *Application* object that returns a *Search* object. For additional information on the *Search* object and search folders, see Chapter 10, "Organizing Outlook Data."

By default, each item in the returned *Table* object contains only a default subset of the item's properties. You can regard each *Row* object of a table as an item in the folder, each *Column* object as a property of the item, and the *Table* object as an in-memory lightweight row set that allows fast enumeration and filtering of items in the folder. Although additions and deletions of the underlying folder are reflected by the rows in the table, the *Table* object does not support any events for adding, changing, and removing of rows. If you require a writable object, call *Row["EntryID"]* to obtain the item's *EntryID* property, then call the *GetItemFromID* method of the *Namespace* object to obtain a full item object that supports read and write operations.

Once you have an instance of a *Table* object, enumerating the items in the table is simple. Test if the *EndOfTable* property returns *true*. If it returns *false*, call the *GetNextRow* method to return a *Row* object. The *Table* object contains a default number of *Column* objects available in the *Columns* collection. You can add or remove columns from the default *Columns* collection. Each *Column* object represents a property of the underlying item represented by the *Row* object. Using the Indexer, the *Row* object can return a *Column* property by the name of the *Column* object or a one-based integer index. You iterate in a forward-only manner through the *Table* object by calling *GetNextRow* until the *EndOfTable* property returns *true*. If you need to return to the start of the table, call the *MoveToStart* method. The *Table* object does not support a move previous or move last operation. Additionally, the *Table* object supports a *Sort* method to perform a single-column sort on the rows.

The following code sample obtains a *Table* object for the Inbox folder. The *Table* object is sorted by the *LastModificationTime* property, and the subject of each item is written to the trace listeners in the *Listeners* collection.

```
private void DemoTableForInbox()
{
    //Obtain Inbox
    Outlook.Folder folder =
        Application.Session.GetDefaultFolder(
        Outlook.OlDefaultFolders.olFolderInbox)
        as Outlook.Folder;
    //Obtain Table using defaults
    Outlook.Table table =
        folder.GetTable(Type.Missing, Type.Missing);
    table.Sort("LastModificationTime",
        Outlook.OlSortOrder.olDescending);
    while (!table.EndOfTable)
    {
        Outlook.Row nextRow = table.GetNextRow();
        Debug.WriteLine(nextRow["Subject"]);
    }
}

private void DemoTableForInbox()
{
    //Obtain Inbox
    Outlook.Folder folder =
        Application.Session.GetDefaultFolder(
        Outlook.OlDefaultFolders.olFolderInbox)
        as Outlook.Folder;
    //Obtain Table using defaults
    Outlook.Table table =
        folder.GetTable(Type.Missing, Type.Missing);
    table.Sort("LastModificationTime",
        Outlook.OlSortOrder.olDescending);
    while (!table.EndOfTable)
```

```
    {
        Outlook.Row nextRow = table.GetNextRow();
        Debug.WriteLine(nextRow["Subject"]);
    }
}
```

GetArray Method

You can squeeze additional performance from the *Table* object by using the *GetArray* method. This method takes an optional integer *MaxRows* parameter that determines how many rows will be returned in the array. *GetArray* returns a two-dimensional array representing a set of row and column values from the *Table* object. The array is zero-based; an array index (i, j) indexes into the ith column and jth row in the array. Columns in the array correspond to columns in the table, and rows in the array correspond to rows in the table. If *MaxRows* is greater than the total number of rows in the table, Outlook returns a "Could not complete the operation. One or more parameter values are not valid" error.

The *DemoGetArrayForTable* procedure uses *GetArray* to return an *Array* object that contains elements for every row in the table. Note that the array elements are zero-based rather than one-based as is the case with Outlook collections. The first dimension of the *Array* object contains the elements that represent the rows of the table. The second dimension of the *Array* object contains the elements that represent the columns of a given row.

```
private void DemoGetArrayForTable()
{
    //Obtain Inbox
    Outlook.Folder folder =
        Application.Session.GetDefaultFolder(
        Outlook.OlDefaultFolders.olFolderInbox)
        as Outlook.Folder;
    Outlook.Table table =
        folder.GetTable("", Outlook.OlTableContents.olUserItems);
    Array tableArray = table.GetArray(table.GetRowCount()) as Array;
    for(int i = 0; i < tableArray.GetUpperBound(0); i++)
    {
        for (int j = 0; j < tableArray.GetUpperBound(1); j++)
        {
            Debug.WriteLine(tableArray.GetValue(i, j));
        }
    }
}
```

Default *Columns* Set

Based on data access models that are familiar to most developers, the *Table* object supports a *Columns* collection. The default *Columns* collection depends on the *DefaultItemType* property of the *Table* object's parent *Folder* object. The default columns for different folder types are shown in Table 6-4 through Table 6-7. See the earlier section on the *DefaultItemType* property for a discussion of how *DefaultItemType* relates to the *Folder* object type.

Table 6-4 Default Columns Returned for All Folder Types Including Inbox, SentItems, DeletedItems, and Search Folders

Column	Description
1	EntryID
2	Subject
3	CreationTime
4	LastModificationTime
5	MessageClass

Table 6-5 Calendar Folder Default Columns

Column	Description
1	EntryID
2	Subject
3	CreationTime
4	LastModificationTime
5	MessageClass
6	Start
7	End
8	IsRecurring

Table 6-6 Contacts Folder Default Columns

Column	Description
1	EntryID
2	Subject
3	CreationTime
4	LastModificationTime
5	MessageClass
6	FirstName
7	LastName
8	CompanyName

Table 6-7 Tasks Folder Default Columns

Column	Description
1	EntryID
2	Subject
3	CreationTime
4	LastModificationTime
5	MessageClass
6	DueDate
7	PercentComplete
8	IsRecurring

You can specify the *Column* object within a *Row* object by specifying the index of the column. Index can be either a string representing the name of the *Column* object or a one-based integer value. The property value might return null. If *Row[Index]* can return null, be sure that your code tests for null values.

Adding Columns to the Table

To add columns to the table, you call the *Add* method of the *Columns* collection. This method adds the *Column* object specified by *Name* property to the *Columns* collection and resets the table. If *Columns.Add* returns an error, it will not change the current row in the table.

Name can be an explicit built-in or custom property name, or a property name referenced by namespace. For more information on referencing properties by namespace, see Chapter 17.

Valid *Name* Values   If you are adding a property that is an explicit built-in property in the object model, for example, the *JobTitle* property of the *ContactItem* object, you must specify *Name* as the explicit built-in property name in English. Localized property names are not supported. For certain types of properties, the format used when adding these properties as columns affects how their values are expressed in the *Table* object. For more information on property value representation in a *Table* object, see the section "Factors That Determine Property Value Representation" later in this chapter. Table 6-8 summarizes valid values for the *Name* argument of *Columns.Add*.

Table 6-8   Valid *Name* Values for *Columns.Add*

Name	Remarks
Valid Built-in Property Name such as *ReceivedTime, JobTitle, AssistantName,* or *AssistantTelephoneNumber*. or Valid Custom Property Name that has been added to the folder's *UserDefinedProperties* collection such as [Shoe Size].	You must supply the English name of the property. Localized names for built-in properties are not supported. Date and time values are returned as local time. Property names are case-insensitive. Custom property names that contain space characters must be enclosed in brackets ([ ]) and can represent localized names.
MAPI Proptag namespace such as http://schemas.microsoft.com/mapi/proptag/0x0037001E	Date and time values returned as Coordinated Universal Time (UTC) time. Namespace names are case-sensitive.
MAPI ID namespace such as http://schemas.microsoft.com/mapi/id/{GUID}/HHHHHHHH	Date and time values returned as UTC time. Namespace names are case-sensitive.
MAPI String namespace such as http://schemas.microsoft.com/mapi/string/{GUID}/myprop	Must append type specifier to the end of the property name. Date and time values are returned as UTC time. Namespace names are case-sensitive.
Content-class specific namespace such as urn:schemas:contacts:givenName	Date and time values are returned as UTC time. Namespace names are case-sensitive.

Appending Type Information   If you are adding a custom property to a *Table* object, referencing the property by the MAPI string namespace, you will have to explicitly append the type of the property to the end of the property reference. For example, to add the custom property *MyCustomProperty*, which has the type Unicode *string*, you will have to explicitly append the MAPI property type *001F* to the reference, resulting in *http://schemas.microsoft.com/mapi /string/{HHHHHHHH-HHHH-HHHH-HHHH-HHHHHHHHHHHH}/MyCustomProperty /0000001F*, where *{HHHHHHHH-HHHH-HHHH-HHHH-HHHHHHHHHHHH}* represents the namespace GUID, *MyCustomProperty* represents the named property name, and *0000001F* represents the *PT_UNICODE MAPI* property type (0x001F) plus a Hex prefix (0x0000).

The correlation of commonly used MAPI property types to COM variant types and .NET Framework types is shown in Table 6-9. Use the Hex value plus the leading 0000 characters when you specify the MAPI property type for any MAPI string namespace properties that you specify in *Columns.Add*.

Table 6-9   MAPI Property Types

MAPI property type	Hex value	COM variant type	.NET Framework type in system namespace	Description
PT_BINARY	0102	VT_BLOB	Byte [ ]	Binary (unknown format)
PT_BOOL	000B	VT_BOOL	Boolean	Boolean
PT_CURRENCY	0006	VT_CY	Double	8-byte integer (scaled by 10,000)
PT_DOUBLE	0005	VT_R8	Double	8-byte real (floating point)
PT_ERROR	000A	VT_ERROR	UInt32	SCODE value; 32-bit unsigned integer
PT_FLOAT	0004	VT_R4	Single	4-byte real (floating point)
PT_LONG	0003	VT_I4	Int64	4-byte integer
PT_MV_STRING8	101E or 101F	VT_ARRAY	String[ ]	Multivalued string (keywords)
PT_NULL	0001	VT_NULL	Null (Nothing in Visual Basic)	Null (no valid data)
PT_SHORT	0002	VT_I2	Int32	2-byte integer
PT_SYSTIME	0040	VT_DATE	DateTime	8-byte real (date in integer, time in fraction)
PT_STRING8	001E	VT_BSTR	String	String
PT_UNICODE	001F	VT_BSTR	String	Unicode string

When to Use *Columns.Add*   Certain properties cannot be added to a *Table* object using *Columns.Add*, including binary properties, computed properties, and Hypertext Markup Language (HTML) or Rich Text Format (RTF) body content. For more information, see the section titled "Invalid Properties" later in this chapter.

Although the *SetColumns* method of the *Items* collection can be used to facilitate caching certain properties for extremely fast access to those properties of an *Items* collection, some properties are not allowed for *SetColumns*. Because these limitations do not apply to *Columns.Add*, the *Table* object is a less restrictive alternative than the *Items* collection.

To see how *Columns.Add* works in practice, consider the following code sample. Before adjusting the column set, the code creates a filter that will only return items in the Inbox that have one or more attachments. The *PR_HASATTACH* property is used to create the initial table restriction. Following the restriction, the sample code uses the *RemoveAll* method to remove all columns from the *Table* object. It then adds the *EntryID, Subject*, and *ReceivedTime* properties using the built-in property names. The *ReceivedTime* property is also added as a MAPI namespace name so that the value returned in the table is a UTC Date/Time value. Finally, the code walks the table and writes *Subject* and *ReceivedTime* (Local and UTC) to the trace listeners in the *Listeners* collection.

```
private void DemoTableColumns()
{
    const string PR_HASATTACH =
        "http://schemas.microsoft.com/mapi/proptag/0x0E1B000B";
    //Obtain Inbox
    Outlook.Folder folder =
        Application.Session.GetDefaultFolder(
        Outlook.OlDefaultFolders.olFolderInbox)
        as Outlook.Folder;
    //Create filter
    string filter = "@SQL=" + "\""
        + PR_HASATTACH + "\"" + " = 1";
    Outlook.Table table =
        folder.GetTable(filter,
        Outlook.OlTableContents.olUserItems);
    //Remove default columns
    table.Columns.RemoveAll();
    //Add using built-in name
    table.Columns.Add("EntryID");
    table.Columns.Add("Subject");
    table.Columns.Add("ReceivedTime");
    table.Sort("ReceivedTime", Outlook.OlSortOrder.olDescending);
    //Add using namespace
    //Date received
    table.Columns.Add(
        "urn:schemas:httpmail:datereceived");
    while (!table.EndOfTable)
    {
        Outlook.Row nextRow = table.GetNextRow();
        StringBuilder sb = new StringBuilder();
        sb.AppendLine(nextRow["Subject"].ToString());
        //Reference column by name
        sb.AppendLine("Received (Local): "
            + nextRow["ReceivedTime"]);
        //Reference column by index
        sb.AppendLine("Received (UTC): " + nextRow[4]);
        sb.AppendLine();
        Debug.WriteLine(sb.ToString());
    }
}
```

Factors That Determine Property Value Representation

There are several factors that affect the type and format of a property in a *Table* object. String properties are affected by the store provider, and binary, date, and multivalued properties are affected by the way the property is referenced when it is first added to *Table* with the *Add* method of the *Columns* collection.

String Properties Affected by Store Providers   The length of the value of a string property depends on the store provider. For Exchange and .ost and .pst stores, the length of the string value will not exceed 255 bytes. This means that string values longer than 255 bytes will be truncated after the first 255 characters.

For example, if you use *Columns.Add* to add the *PR_INTERNET_TRANSPORT_HEADERS* property (referenced by namespace as *http://schemas.microsoft.com/mapi/proptag /0x007d001e*) to a *Table* object, the *Table* object will only store the first 255 characters of the full content of the property. If you need to determine the full content of the property, you must use the *EntryID* property in the *GetItemFromID* method of the *Namespace* object to obtain a full item. Once you have the item, you can use the *PropertyAccessor* object to obtain the complete property value.

> **Note**   You should be aware that the size of the property value that can be returned by the *PropertyAccessor* object is store-dependent. For .ost and .pst stores, the *PropertyAccessor* object can get *PT_STRING8* and *PT_BINARY* properties that are less than or equal to 4088 bytes. If the property size exceeds 4088 bytes, Outlook will raise an error.

Date, Binary, and Multivalued Properties Affected by Property Reference   The type and format of a binary, date, or multivalued property are affected by how the property is referenced when it is first added to a *Table* object. You should determine if the property is referenced by its explicit built-in name (if it has one) or by namespace (regardless of the existence of an explicit built-in name). Built-in name references sometimes return a different column value than a namespace reference. Table 6-10 summarizes the difference in the property value representation (in terms of type and format) per original property type.

Table 6-10   Values Returned in *Table* Object Depend on Property Specifier

Type	Return type if property specified using built-in name	Return type if property specified using namespace
Binary (PT_BINARY)	String	Byte array
Date (PT_SYSTIME)	Local DateTime	UTC DateTime
Multivalued, also known as keywords type such as *Categories* property (PT_MV_STRING8)	String containing comma-separated values	One-dimensional array containing one element for each keyword

To better understand how to add a MAPI string namespace property to the *Table* object and how multivalued properties affect the values returned in a *Column* object, another code sample is in order. The *TableMultiValuedProperties* procedure restricts the *Table* object to return rows where the *Categories* property is not *null*. The property that represents the *Categories* property uses the MAPI string namespace. A Distributed Authoring and Versioning (DAV) Searching and Locating (DASL) filter is constructed for items that have categories (the actual filter restricts on categories that are not *null*). The type specifier *0000001f* is concatenated with the *categoriesProperty* constant to add a *Categories* column to the *Table* object. Finally, the *Column* object that represents the *Categories* property contains a one-dimensional string array where each element of the array represents a category assigned to the item. Both the item *Subject* property and the *Categories* property are written to the trace listeners of the *Listeners* collection.

```
void TableMultiValuedProperties()
{
    const string categoriesProperty =
        "http://schemas.microsoft.com/mapi/string/"
        + "{00020329-0000-0000-C000-000000000046}/Keywords";
    //Inbox
    Outlook.Folder folder =
        Application.Session.GetDefaultFolder(
        Outlook.OlDefaultFolders.olFolderInbox)
        as Outlook.Folder;
    //Call GetTable with filter for categories
    string filter = "@SQL="
        + "Not(" + "\"" + categoriesProperty
        + "\"" + " Is Null)";
    Outlook.Table table =
        folder.GetTable(filter,
        Outlook.OlTableContents.olUserItems);
    //Add categories column and append type specifier
    table.Columns.Add(categoriesProperty + "/0000001F");
    while (!table.EndOfTable)
    {
        Outlook.Row nextRow = table.GetNextRow();
        string[] categories =
            (string[])nextRow[categoriesProperty + "/0000001F"];
        Debug.WriteLine("Subject: " + nextRow["Subject"]);
        Debug.Write("Categories: ");
        foreach(string category in categories)
        {
            Debug.Write("\t" + category);
        }
        Debug.WriteLine("\n");
    }
}
```

Invalid Properties

Some properties cannot be added to the *Table* object using *Columns.Add*. Other properties cannot be used in a filter for the *Restrict* method of the *Table* object. If you attempt to add an invalid property in *Columns.Add*, Outlook raises a "The property *Name* does not support this operation" error where *Name* is the property that you are attempting to add. Table 6-11 lists properties that are invalid for use in the *Table* object.

Table 6-11   Invalid Properties for the *Table* Object

Property	For *Columns.Add*	For table filter
Binary properties such as *EntryID*	Supported via built-in or namespace property representation.	Not supported. Outlook will raise an error.
Body properties including *Body* and *HTMLBody* and namespace representation of those properties including *PR_RTF_COMPRESSED*	The *Body* property is supported with a condition that only the first 255 bytes of the value are stored in a *Table* object. Other properties representing the body content in HTML or RTF are not supported. Because only the first 255 bytes of *Body* are returned, if you want to obtain the full body content of an item in text or HTML, use the item's *EntryID* in *GetItemFromID* to obtain the item object. Then retrieve the full value of *Body* through the item object.	Only the *Body* property represented in text is supported in a filter. This means that the property must be referenced in a DASL filter as *urn:schemas:http-mail:textdescription*, and you cannot filter on any HTML tags in the body. To improve performance, use context indexer keywords in the filter to match strings in the body.
Computed properties, such as *AutoResolvedWinner* and *BodyFormat* (see the complete list of computed properties later in this section)	Not supported.	Not supported.
Multivalued properties, such as *Categories*, *Children*, *Companies*, and *VotingOptions*	Supported.	Supported, provided that you can create a DASL query using the namespace representation.
Properties returning an object, such as *Attachments*, *Parent*, *Recipients*, *RecurrencePattern*, and *UserProperties*	Not supported.	Not supported.

The following list is a list of known invalid properties that cannot be added to the *Table* object using *Columns.Add*. Outlook raises an error if you attempt to add a property in this list. Many of these properties are available on the full item. If you need to examine these properties, you should consider using the *Items* collection in place of the *Table* object.

- *AutoResolvedWinner*
- *BodyFormat*
- *Class*

- *Companies*
- *ContactNames*
- *DLName*
- *DownloadState*
- *FlagIcon*
- *HtmlBody*
- *InternetCodePage*
- *IsConflict*
- *IsMarkedAsTask*
- *MeetingWorkspaceURL*
- *MemberCount*
- *Permission*
- *PermissionService*
- *RecurrenceState*
- *ResponseState*
- *Saved*
- *Sent*
- *Submitted*
- *TaskSubject*
- *Unread*
- *VotingOptions*

Although these computed properties cannot be added to the column set for the table, you can work around this limitation by using a DASL query to restrict the items that appear in the *Table* object. If a namespace representation of the computed property exists, you can use the namespace property to create a DASL query that restricts the *Table* object to return rows for a specified value of the computed property. For example, the following code sample returns all Inbox items where *IsMarkedAsTask* equals *true*. It then writes certain to-do properties such as *TaskSubject, TaskDueDate, TaskStartDate,* and *TaskCompletedDate* to the trace listeners of the *Listeners* collection.

```
private void GetToDoItems()
{
    //Obtain Inbox
    Outlook.Folder folder =
        Application.Session.GetDefaultFolder(
        Outlook.OlDefaultFolders.olFolderInbox)
```

```
        as Outlook.Folder;
    //DASL filter for IsMarkedAsTask
    string filter = "@SQL=" + "\"" +
        "http://schemas.microsoft.com/mapi/proptag/0x0E2B0003"
        + "\"" + " = 1";
    Outlook.Table table =
        folder.GetTable(filter,
        Outlook.OlTableContents.olUserItems);
        table.Columns.Add ("TaskStartDate");
        table.Columns.Add ("TaskDueDate");
        table.Columns.Add ("TaskCompletedDate");
        //Use GUID/ID to represent TaskSubject
        table.Columns.Add(
            "http://schemas.microsoft.com/mapi/id/" +
            "{00062008-0000-0000-C000-000000000046}/85A4001E");
    while (!table.EndOfTable)
    {
        Outlook.Row nextRow = table.GetNextRow();
        StringBuilder sb = new StringBuilder();
        sb.AppendLine("Task Subject: " + nextRow[9]);
        sb.AppendLine("Start Date: "
            + nextRow["TaskStartDate"]);
        sb.AppendLine("Due Date: "
            + nextRow["TaskDueDate"]);
        sb.AppendLine("Completed Date: "
            + nextRow["TaskCompletedDate"]);
        sb.AppendLine();
        Debug.WriteLine(sb.ToString());
    }
}
```

Row Helper Methods

The *Table* object supports the helper methods shown in Table 6-12 to support conversion of binary and date/time property values. The *GetArray* method is also included in this list even though it doesn't serve as a conversion function. *GetArray* returns columns in a *Row* object as a one-dimensional array.

Table 6-12   Row Helper Methods

Method	Description
BinaryToString	Converts a binary value to its string representation
GetArray	Returns columns in a *Row* object as a one-dimensional array
LocalTimeToUTC	Converts a local date/time value to UTC
StringToBinary	Converts a string value to its binary representation
UTCToLocalTime	Converts a UTC date/time to local time

A quick code sample should help you to understand how to use these methods. Let's assume that you want to return the *PR_SENT_REPRESENTING_ENTRYID* property for the first item in the Inbox. This property can be used to open an *AddressEntry* object representing the sender of the message. If you convert the binary value of this property to a string, you can use the string representation to return an *AddressEntry* object from the *GetAddressEntryFromID* method of the *Namespace* object. After the *PR_SENT_REPRESENTING_ENTRYID* property is added to the *Table* object, the code uses the *BinaryToString* method to obtain the string representation of *PR_SENT_REPRESENTING_ENTRYID*. This string is passed to the *GetAddressEntryFromID* method. Once you have an *AddressEntry* object, you can call the *Details* method of the *AddressEntry* object to display a modal dialog box that contains detailed information about the sender.

```
private void DemoRowHelperMethods()
{
    const string PR_SENT_REPRESENTING_ENTRYID =
        "http://schemas.microsoft.com/mapi/proptag/0x00410102";
    //Obtain Inbox
    Outlook.Folder folder =
        Application.Session.GetDefaultFolder(
        Outlook.OlDefaultFolders.olFolderInbox)
        as Outlook.Folder;
    Outlook.Table table =
        folder.GetTable("",
        Outlook.OlTableContents.olUserItems);
    table.Sort("ReceivedTime",
        Outlook.OlSortOrder.olDescending);
    table.Columns.Add(PR_SENT_REPRESENTING_ENTRYID);
    if (!table.EndOfTable)
    {
        //First row in Table
        Outlook.Row nextRow = table.GetNextRow();
        //EntryID of sender
        string senderID = nextRow.BinaryToString(6);
        Outlook.AddressEntry addrEntry =
            Application.Session.GetAddressEntryFromID(
            senderID);
        //Display modal dialog
        addrEntry.Details(0);
    }
}
```

Returning Hidden Items

The *Table* object has one more important feature that you should be aware of. You can use the *Table* object to return hidden items in the folder by setting the *TableContents* parameter in the *GetFolder* method to *OlTableContents.olHiddenItems*. You can also pass a filter restriction in the *GetTable* method to return a subset of hidden items in a folder. Returning hidden items in the *Table* object differs from the *GetStorage* method discussed in Chapter 5. *GetStorage* returns only one single hidden item. The *Table* object can return all or a subset of hidden items in a folder. The following code sample uses the *Table* object to write the *Subject* and *MessageClass* for each hidden item in the Inbox to the trace listeners of the *Listeners* collection.

```csharp
private void TableForInboxHiddenItems()
{
    //Inbox
    Outlook.Folder folder =
        Application.Session.GetDefaultFolder(
        Outlook.OlDefaultFolders.olFolderInbox)
        as Outlook.Folder;
    //Call GetTable with OlTableContents.olHiddenItems
    Outlook.Table table =
        folder.GetTable("",
        Outlook.OlTableContents.olHiddenItems);
    while (!table.EndOfTable)
    {
        Outlook.Row nextRow = table.GetNextRow();
        //Test for null subject
        if (nextRow["Subject"]==null)
        {
            Debug.WriteLine(nextRow["MessageClass"]);
        }
        else
        {
            Debug.WriteLine(nextRow["Subject"] + " "
                + nextRow["MessageClass"]);
        }
    }
}
```

Summary

This chapter focuses on the *Folders* collection and *Folder* objects as containers for Outlook items. You've learned how to access and enumerate folders to work with the items that are contained within the folder. The *Items* collection has some targeted usage scenarios that revolve around recurring appointments in Calendar folders and obtaining items for write operations. If you want to optimize performance, the new *Table* object is the best way to retrieve items in a *Folder* or *Search* object. The *Table* object also provides the maximum amount of flexibility, as you can easily obtain item properties that are not available on the built-in item types.

Chapter 7

Address Books and Recipients

To communicate electronically, you need an addressing system. This chapter first provides an overview of common address books in Outlook including the Exchange Global Address List, the Outlook Address Book, and custom address books. Once you have the overview, you will dive into the *Recipients* collection and the *Recipient* object. These objects provide the foundation for related objects such as the *AddressEntry* object. Derived from the *AddressEntry* object, the *ExchangeUser* object exposes detailed information about a user on Microsoft Exchange. This information includes manager and direct reports relationships. The *ExchangeDistributionList* object lets you enumerate Exchange distribution list owners and membership. There are plenty of code samples to help you get started. Finally, you display the Outlook Address Book programmatically using the *SelectNamesDialog* object.

In this chapter, you will:

- Use the *Recipient* object to determine *PrimarySmtpAddress*.

- Learn how to use the new *ExchangeUser* and *ExchangeDistributionList* objects.

- Learn about *AddressList* and *AddressEntry* objects.

- Display the Outlook 2007 Address Book dialog box programmatically, modify dialog labels and recipient selectors, and return a *Recipients* collection.

An Overview of Outlook Address Books

This chapter focuses on the objects that allow you to send items to a collection of recipients or, conversely, allow you to understand which recipient sent an item or the recipients to whom the item was addressed. Before we discuss how to use address-related objects, here's a quick overview of the address book providers that ship with Outlook.

Exchange Global Address List

If the user is configured with an Exchange account, his or her mailbox sits on an Exchange server, and the Exchange Address Book provider provides services that allow the Outlook client to render addresses in the Address Book dialog box and resolve recipients to a unique Exchange address. Chapter 2, "Outlook as a Platform," provides an extensive discussion of address book providers and the Exchange Address Book provider in particular.

The Exchange Global Address List (GAL) contains an aggregated list of all messaging recipients for an organization. All data in the GAL comes from Microsoft Windows Active Directory directory service by way of global catalog servers. The GAL contains entries for individual mailbox users, remote users (known as Exchange contacts, which you should not confuse with an Outlook contact) who do not belong to the corporate domain, e-mail distribution lists, and resources such as conference rooms. In an Exchange environment, there will always be a GAL in the *AddressLists* collection. You should be aware that it is possible for a given mailbox or address entity (such as an Exchange public folder) to be hidden from the GAL.

> **Note**   Because Microsoft Office Outlook 2007 requires Microsoft Exchange Server 2000 or later, technologies such as Microsoft Exchange 5.5 directory services are no longer used. Exchange 2000 and later versions always integrate directly with Windows Active Directory. Due to this integration, services such as distribution lists and address lists are delivered through Active Directory.

A new feature of Outlook 2007 when running against a Microsoft Exchange 2007 server is the hierarchical address book. When the hierarchical address book is turned on by an Exchange administrator, members of an organization are displayed in a tree view control and they are grouped by department. The Outlook 2007 object model does not provide programmatic access to the nodes of the hierarchical address book.

Exchange Containers

Exchange 2000 and later versions support the concept of an address list container, which allows the user to select a subset of addresses in the GAL for display in the Outlook Address Book dialog box. An Exchange administrator can create a build rule for an Exchange container by using the Exchange System Manager console. These build rules use the lightweight directory access protocol (LDAP) search filter syntax to create an Exchange container. For example, you could create an address list of all full-time employees in the engineering department of your organization. Similarly, you can create a container for all conference rooms across the entire company. From an Outlook object model perspective, you cannot create an Exchange container programmatically. You can enumerate the containers within the *AddressLists* collection and then enumerate all the *AddressEntry* objects within the individual container.

Offline Address Book

Cached mode allows an Exchange user to work when disconnected from the Exchange server. The offline address book (OAB) provides similar functionality for the address book in a disconnected state. The OAB contains user properties that Outlook utilizes to send an e-mail message or display information about a user. By using an OAB, Outlook does not have to connect to the Exchange server to resolve names or open the information for each user. This design reduces network traffic and improves performance.

The OAB is a snapshot of information from the GAL. Consequently, not all the information in the GAL is available in the OAB. The following information in the GAL is not available in the OAB:

- Custom properties added by a server administrator, such as the employee ID of each employee

- Information about the organizational hierarchy, such as manager and direct reports lists
- Distribution list memberships

Using the Offline Address Book dialog box available through the Send/Receive Setting dialog box, the user or an IT administrator can elect to download full OAB details or no details. Your code should examine the *ExchangeConnectionMode* property of the *Namespace* object to determine if the user is in a disconnected state. If the user is disconnected, your code should handle the possibility that you won't be able to obtain custom properties, information about the user's position in the organizational hierarchy, or distribution list membership. For complete details on the *ExchangeConnectionMode* property, see Chapter 6, "Accessing Outlook Data."

Outlook Address Book

The Outlook Address Book (also known as the Contacts Address Book, or CAB) provider allows Outlook to display addresses for all items that contain at least one e-mail address or fax number entry in a Contacts folder. By default, the Outlook Address Book for your default Contacts folder is shown as an address list in the Outlook Address Book. If the user is configured for only a Post Office Protocol 3 (POP3) or Internet Message Access Protocol (IMAP) account, the Outlook Address Book is the only address book that will appear by default. The user can control whether nondefault Contacts folders will appear in the address book. You can also programmatically control whether a Contacts folder appears in the Outlook Address Book by setting the *ShowAsOutlookAB* property on the *Folder* object. Typically, all Outlook users will have a CAB in their list of address books. Outlook 2007 provides new methods that let you obtain the corresponding Contacts folder for a given Contacts address list.

Other Address Book Providers

Although there are other address book providers that can be installed with Outlook 2007, these address book providers represent the exception rather than the rule. Internet directory services are used to find e-mail addresses that are not in a local Outlook Address Book or a corporate-wide directory such as the GAL. LDAP provides access to Internet directories. To communicate with an LDAP server, Outlook requires network connectivity to connect to the LDAP server. Depending on the capabilities of the LDAP server, an address entry for an Internet directory might only return the distinguished name and display name for the address entry.

You can also install custom address book providers that appear in the *AddressLists* collection. Custom address book providers return an *AddressList.AddressListType* equal to *OlAddressList.olCustomAddressList*. An example of a custom address book provider is the Microsoft Office Outlook Messaging Service (OMS) provider that ships with Outlook 2007. If OMS is configured as an address book, then OMS provides an address list for all items in the default Contacts folder that have a mobile phone number. Unlike the Outlook Address Book that returns address entries that have an e-mail address or fax number, OMS only returns address entries that have a mobile phone number.

The *Recipients* Collection and *Recipient* Objects

Before discussing Outlook address books and address entries, it's helpful to understand the *Recipients* collection and *Recipient* objects. Think of a *Recipient* object as a virtual *AddressEntry* object. Unlike an *AddressEntry* object, a *Recipient* object has no corresponding address book container per se. *AddressEntry* objects can be stored in a variety of locations, including an Outlook Contacts folder or the Exchange GAL. Once a *Recipient* object is resolved to a physical *AddressEntry* object, you can use the *AddressEntry* property of the *Recipient* object to return the actual *AddressEntry* object for the *Recipient* object. A *Recipient* object is said to be resolved when its *Resolved* property equals *true*.

You add *Recipient* objects to the *Recipients* collection to create recipients for an outbound e-mail message, sharing request, or meeting request. You can examine the *Recipients* collection to enforce certain mail rules, such as controlling Reply All behavior to prevent corporate spam. When an inbound item arrives in your mailbox, it also has a *Recipients* collection that lets you understand the destination recipients of the message. Outlook also stamps inbound messages with certain properties that you can use to determine the sender of a message or the organizer of an appointment.

Outlook Object Model Guard Considerations

You should be aware that when you attempt to access a *Recipient*, *Recipients*, *SelectNamesDialog*, *AddressEntry*, *AddressEntries*, *AddressList*, or *AddressLists* object, Outlook will display an Address Book warning dialog box unless your code is trusted from the perspective of the object model guard. The Outlook object model guard is discussed in detail in Chapter 19, "Trust and Security." See the discussion in Chapter 19 about how to ensure that your code is trusted and does not display security prompts when you access objects that contain e-mail addresses.

The *CreateRecipient* Method

Typically, *Recipient* objects are associated with sendable items such as a *MailItem* object. Sendable items always expose a *Recipients* property that lets you access the *Recipients* collection for the item. However, it is possible to create a free-standing *Recipient* object that is not bound to the *Recipients* collection of an item. To create a *Recipient* object, you use the *CreateRecipient* method of the *Namespace* object. This unbound *Recipient* object can be passed to a method such as *GetSharedDefaultFolder* that allows you to open a shared Exchange folder and display that folder in an Explorer window. *GetSharedDefaultFolder* is used in Exchange delegate scenarios where the delegate has permission to access the folder of the delegator. You must resolve the *Recipient* object before you pass it to the *GetSharedDefaultFolder* method. To resolve a *Recipient* object, you call its *Resolve* method.

When you create a *Recipient* object using the *CreateRecipient* method of the *Namespace* object or the *Add* method of the *Recipients* collection, you must provide a recipient name.

The *Recipient* object is then resolved against this name. A recipient name can take any of the following formats:

■ **Display name**   The display name of the recipient as it appears in an address list. Display names are not necessarily unique, and you should not assume that a given name will resolve.

■ **Alias**   An Exchange alias is a unique identifier that corresponds to the Messaging Application Programming Interface (MAPI) property *PR_ACCOUNT*. An Exchange alias is unique, but does not guarantee that the recipient will resolve.

■ **Simple Mail Transfer Protocol (SMTP) address**   An SMTP address takes the form *username@domain*. For example, *someone@example.com* is a valid SMTP address.

The following code sample opens the Calendar folder of the current user's manager. If the user does not have permission to open the manager's Calendar folder or an error occurs, an alert dialog box is displayed to the user.

```
private void DisplayManagerCalendar()
{
    Outlook.AddressEntry addrEntry =
        Application.Session.CurrentUser.AddressEntry;
    if (addrEntry.Type  == "EX")
    {
        Outlook.ExchangeUser manager =
            Application.Session.CurrentUser.
            AddressEntry.GetExchangeUser().GetExchangeUserManager();
        if (manager != null)
        {
            Outlook.Recipient recip =
                Application.Session.CreateRecipient(manager.Name);
            if (recip.Resolve())
            {
                try
                {
                    Outlook.Folder folder =
                        Application.Session.GetSharedDefaultFolder(
                        recip, Outlook.OlDefaultFolders.olFolderCalendar)
                        as Outlook.Folder;
                    folder.Display();
                }
                catch
                {
                    MessageBox.Show("Could not open manager's calendar.",
                        "GetSharedDefaultFolder Example",
                        MessageBoxButtons.OK,
                        MessageBoxIcon.Error);
                }
            }

        }
    }
}
```

Working with the *Recipients* Collection Object

The *Recipients* collection implements typical collection object methods such as *Add*, *Remove*, and *Item* (the Index operator). It also supports a *ResolveAll* method that resolves all the *Recipient* objects in the collection. If all *Recipient* objects in the collection are resolved, then *ResolveAll* returns *true*. If one or more of the *Recipient* objects fail to resolve, then *ResolveAll* returns *false*.

Adding Recipients to a *MailItem* Object

When you add a *Recipient* object to the *Recipients* collection of a *MailItem* object, you can control whether the recipient is a To, Cc, or Bcc recipient by setting the *Type* property of the *Recipient* object. Unfortunately, the *Type* property of the *Recipient* object is typed as an *int* (*Integer* in Microsoft Visual Basic) and does not correlate to a specific recipient type enumeration. You can, however, determine the type of a message *Recipient* object by setting the *Type* property to a value from the *OlMailRecipientType* enumeration. The following code sample sets To, Cc, and Bcc recipients for a message by setting the *Recipient.Type* property to the correct value of *OlMailRecipientType*:

```
private void SetRecipientTypeForMail()
{
    Outlook.MailItem mail = Application.CreateItem(
        Outlook.OlItemType.olMailItem) as Outlook.MailItem;
    mail.Subject = "Sample Message";
    Outlook.Recipient recipTo =
        mail.Recipients.Add("someone@example.com");
    recipTo.Type = (int)Outlook.OlMailRecipientType.olTo;
    Outlook.Recipient recipCc =
        mail.Recipients.Add("someonecc@example.com");
    recipCc.Type = (int)Outlook.OlMailRecipientType.olCC;
    Outlook.Recipient recipBcc =
        mail.Recipients.Add("someonebcc@example.com");
    recipBcc.Type = (int)Outlook.OlMailRecipientType.olBCC;
    mail.Recipients.ResolveAll();
    mail.Display(false);
}
```

Adding Recipients to an *AppointmentItem* Object

Adding recipients to an *AppointmentItem* object that represents a meeting request is very similar to adding recipients to a message. In the case of an *AppointmentItem* object, you use the *OlMeetingRecipientType* enumeration to specify whether the recipient of the message is a required, optional, or resource attendee. The following code sample creates an appointment and adds required and optional attendees. It also adds a conference room for the meeting. Notice that you must set the *MeetingStatus* property to *OlMeetingStatus.olMeeting* to change the appointment into a meeting request.

```
private void SetRecipientTypeForAppt()
{
    Outlook.AppointmentItem appt =
        Application.CreateItem(
        Outlook.OlItemType.olAppointmentItem)
        as Outlook.AppointmentItem;
    appt.Subject = "Customer Review";
    appt.MeetingStatus = Outlook.OlMeetingStatus.olMeeting;
    appt.Location = "36/2021";
    appt.Start = DateTime.Parse("10/20/2006 10:00 AM");
    appt.End = DateTime.Parse("10/20/2006 11:00 AM");
    Outlook.Recipient recipRequired =
        appt.Recipients.Add("Ryan Gregg");
    recipRequired.Type =
        (int)Outlook.OlMeetingRecipientType.olRequired;
    Outlook.Recipient recipOptional =
        appt.Recipients.Add("Peter Allenspach");
    recipOptional.Type =
        (int)Outlook.OlMeetingRecipientType.olOptional;
    Outlook.Recipient recipConf =
        appt.Recipients.Add("Conf Room 36/2021 (14) AV");
    recipConf.Type =
        (int)Outlook.OlMeetingRecipientType.olResource;
    appt.Recipients.ResolveAll();
    appt.Display(false);
}
```

Resolving Recipients

To resolve a recipient, you can call the *ResolveAll* method of the *Recipients* collection or the *Resolve* method of the *Recipient* object. Both of these methods return a *bool* (*Boolean* in Visual Basic) that indicates whether the recipient has been resolved. To determine the resolution status, you can examine the *Resolved* property of the *Recipient* object. When the *Resolved* property is *false*, the *EntryID* property of the *Recipient* object is *null* (*Nothing* in Visual Basic). When a *Recipient* object is resolved, it is resolved against address lists in the user's profile according to the *ResolutionOrder* property of the *AddressList* objects in the *AddressLists* collection. For more information about resolution order, see the section "Determining Resolution Order of Address Lists" later in this chapter.

It is possible for an address not to be resolved due to an ambiguous or invalid name. For example, let's assume that you want to resolve a recipient where the recipient name equals "Jane." Because there could be more than one individual named Jane in an organization, Outlook displays the Check Names dialog box (also known as the Ambiguous Name Resolution dialog box) shown in Figure 7-1 to allow the user to resolve an ambiguous name.

Figure 7-1   The Check Names dialog box.

You can write code that will display the Check Names dialog box programmatically if the recipient cannot be resolved. The following *ResolveRecipient* method displays the Check Names dialog box if the name cannot be resolved. If the user cancels the Check Names dialog box, the code presents the Select Names dialog box to the user. The Select Names dialog box is the Outlook Address Book. If the user selects a name from the Select Names dialog box and the name is resolved, then *ResolveRecipient* returns the *AddressEntry* property of the resolved *Recipient* object. If the user cancels the Select Names dialog box, *ResolveRecipient* returns *null*.

```
private void ResolveRecipients(Outlook.Recipients recips)
{
    if (recips == null)
    {
        throw new ArgumentNullException();
    }
    if (recips.ResolveAll())
    {
        return;
    }
    else
    {
        for(int i = recips.Count; i > 0; i--)
        {
            if (!recips[i].Resolve())
            {
                Outlook.SelectNamesDialog snd =
                    Application.Session.
                    GetSelectNamesDialog();
                snd.Recipients.Add(recips[i].Name);
                snd.NumberOfRecipientSelectors =
                    Outlook.OlRecipientSelectors.olShowTo;
                snd.AllowMultipleSelection = false;
                snd.Display();
                if (!snd.Recipients.ResolveAll())
                {
                    recips.Remove(i);
```

```
            }
            else
            {
                recips.Remove(i);
                recips.Add(snd.Recipients[1].Address);
            }
            snd = null;
        }
    }
}
}
```

> **Note**   The Check Names dialog box and the Select Names dialog box are parented to the main Outlook window. The Check Names dialog box is modal to the Select Names dialog box. The Select Names dialog box is modeless. You cannot parent these dialog boxes to your own custom dialog box.

Obtaining the SMTP Address of a Recipient

The *Recipient* object does not directly expose the SMTP address of a resolved recipient. However, you can use the *PropertyAccessor* object to obtain the MAPI property *PR_SMTP_ADDRESS*. The following *GetSMTPAddress* method returns the SMTP address of a resolved recipient:

```
private string GetSMTPAddress(Outlook.Recipient recip)
{
    const string PR_SMTP_ADDRESS =
        "http://schemas.microsoft.com/mapi/proptag/0x39FE001E";
    if (recip != null)
    {
        if (!recip.Resolved)
        {
            return null;
        }
        else
        {
            Outlook.PropertyAccessor pa = recip.PropertyAccessor;
            try
            {
                string smtpAddress =
                    pa.GetProperty(PR_SMTP_ADDRESS).ToString();
                return smtpAddress;
            }
            catch { return null; }
        }
    }
    else
    {
        throw new ArgumentNullException();
    }
}
```

The *AddressLists* Collection and *AddressList* Objects

The *AddressLists* collection represents all address lists available in the current profile. You obtain an instance of the *AddressLists* collection from the *AddressLists* property of the *Namespace* object.

Enumerating *AddressList* Objects

To enumerate the *AddressList* objects in the *AddressLists* collection, use a *foreach* construct as shown in the following example. This example creates a string that contains the *Name*, *ResolutionOrder*, *IsReadOnly*, and *IsInitialAddressList* properties of the *AddressList* object and writes the string to the trace listeners of the *Listeners* collection.

```
private void EnumerateAddressLists()
{
    Outlook.AddressLists addrLists =
        Application.Session.AddressLists;
    foreach (Outlook.AddressList addrList in addrLists)
    {
        StringBuilder sb = new StringBuilder();
        sb.AppendLine("Display Name: " + addrList.Name);
        sb.AppendLine("Resolution Order: "
            + addrList.ResolutionOrder.ToString());
        sb.AppendLine("Read-only : "
            + addrList.IsReadOnly.ToString());
        sb.AppendLine("Initial Address List: "
            + addrList.IsInitialAddressList.ToString());
        sb.AppendLine("");
        Debug.WriteLine(sb.ToString());
    }
}
```

The *AddressListType* Property

To determine the type of *AddressList* object, you should use the new *AddressListType* property. This property returns an *OlAddressListType* constant. Valid *OlAddressListType* values are shown in Table 7-1.

Table 7-1   *OlAddressListType* Values

Value	Description
OlCustomAddressList	A custom address book provider
OlExchangeContainer	A container for address lists on an Exchange server
olExchangeGlobalAddressList	An Exchange GAL
olOutlookAddressList	An address list that corresponds to the Outlook Contacts Address Book
olOutlookLdapAddressList	An address list that uses LDAP

Determining Resolution Order of Address Lists

New to Outlook 2007, the *ResolutionOrder* property lets you determine the resolution order for a specific *AddressList* object. The *ResolutionOrder* property indicates the order that Outlook uses to resolve recipient addresses.

> **Note**   The order of resolution for the *ResolutionOrder* property is one-based. The first *AddressList* object to be used for resolving recipient names has a *ResolutionOrder* value equal to 1. If an *AddressList* object is not used to resolve addresses, then its *ResolutionOrder* property has a value of −1.

The *ResolutionOrder* property corresponds to the position of the address list in the When Sending Mail, Check Names Using These Address Lists In The Following Order list box in the Addressing dialog box shown in Figure 7-2. To access the Addressing dialog box, click Tools. In the Address Book dialog box, click Options.

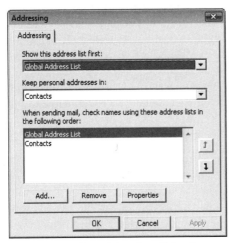

Figure 7-2   The Addressing dialog box controls resolution order.

The *ResolutionOrder* property is read-only. You cannot change the resolution order of an address list through the Outlook object model.

Finding a Specific *AddressList* Object

The *AddressLists* collection does not support an explicit method to find an address list. Because the *AddressLists* collection is generally a small collection, you can simply iterate over the collection and find the specific *AddressList* object by performing a name comparison. There are some helper methods that have been introduced in Outlook 2007 to return the GAL in particular. Because the name of the GAL is dependent on the locale, Outlook 2007 introduces the *GetGlobalAddressList* method on the *Namespace* object. The following code sample displays a message with the number of address entries in the GAL.

```
private void DemoGetGlobalAddressList()
{
    Outlook.AddressList gal =
        Application.Session.GetGlobalAddressList();
    string message = "There are " + gal.AddressEntries.Count
        + " entries in the GAL.";
    MessageBox.Show(message, "Global Address List",
        MessageBoxButtons.OK, MessageBoxIcon.Information);
}
```

Determining the Contacts Folder for a Contacts Address Book

One of the problems that troubled developers in past versions of Outlook was the inability to obtain a reference to the Contacts folder that corresponded to a given CAB. Because multiple CABs can have the same name, resolving the address book name to a Contact folder name was not productive. In Outlook 2007, the *GetContactsFolder* method on the *AddressList* object solves this problem for you. If the *AddressList* object represents a *Contacts* folder, then *GetContactsFolder* will return a *Folder* object that represents the Contacts folder. If the *AddressList* object does not represent a Contacts folder or the Contacts folder cannot be found (in the case of a Contacts folder in the Public Folders store), then *GetContacts Folder* returns *null* (*Nothing* in Visual Basic).

To demonstrate how this works in practice, take a look at the following code sample. This sample uses the *GetDefaultFolder* method to return the default Contacts folder. Once you've obtained a *Folder* object representing the default Contacts folder, you enumerate the *AddressLists* collection and use *GetContactsFolder* to find the *AddressList* object that represents the default Contacts folder (see Figure 7-3). You compare the *EntryID* values of these two folder objects using the new *CompareEntryIDs* method of the *Namespace* object. Once you have a match, you set the *InitialAddressList* property of the *SelectNamesDialog* object to the *AddressList* object that represents the default Contacts folder. When you set this property of the *SelectNamesDialog* object, you cause the specified *AddressList* object to be displayed first in the Outlook Address Book no matter what the default settings are for the initial address list. Finally, the Outlook Address Book is displayed by calling the *Display* method of the *SelectNamesDialog* object.

```
private void ShowContactsFolderAsInitialAddressList()
{
    Outlook.AddressLists addrLists;
    Outlook.Folder contactsFolder =
        Application.Session.GetDefaultFolder(
        Outlook.OlDefaultFolders.olFolderContacts)
        as Outlook.Folder;
    addrLists = Application.Session.AddressLists;
    foreach(Outlook.AddressList addrList in addrLists)
    {
        Outlook.Folder testFolder =
            addrList.GetContactsFolder() as Outlook.Folder;
        if (testFolder != null)
        {
            //Test to determine if Folder returned
```

```
                  //by GetContactsFolder has same EntryID
                  //as default Contacts folder.
                  if (Application.Session.CompareEntryIDs(
                      contactsFolder.EntryID, testFolder.EntryID))
                  {
                      Outlook.SelectNamesDialog snd =
                          Application.
                          Session.GetSelectNamesDialog();
                      snd.InitialAddressList = addrList;
                      snd.Display();
                  }
              }
          }
      }
```

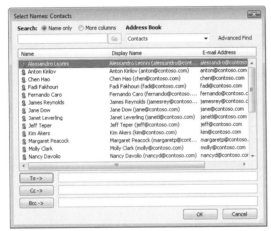

Figure 7-3   Use the *GetContactsFolder* method to display the Contacts address list.

The *AddressEntries* Collection and *AddressEntry* Object

The *AddressEntries* collection and *AddressEntry* object let you access the contents of an individual *AddressList* object. The *AddressEntries* object represents the collection of *AddressEntry* objects in the parent *AddressList* object. The *AddressEntry* object represents an individual address entry in an address list. The *AddressEntry* object has been enhanced in Outlook 2007 so that you can accurately determine the type of the *AddressEntry* object. For users connected to an Exchange server, Outlook 2007 introduces two objects that derive from the base *AddressEntry* object, the *ExchangeUser* and *ExchangeDistributionList* objects. Later in this chapter you'll see how these new objects make your development work easier when discovering information about an Exchange user. If your organization has implemented an organizational hierarchy in Active Directory, you can use the *ExchangeUser* object to build an organizational chart or traverse the hierarchy by understanding manager and direct reports relationships.

To enumerate addresses in an address list, you obtain the *AddressEntries* collection from the *AddressEntries* property of the *AddressList* object. The following code sample enumerates the first

100 primary SMTP addresses in the GAL. To obtain the SMTP address for an *AddressEntry* object, you must cast it to an *ExchangeUser* or *ExchangeDistributionList* object using the *GetExchangeUser* or *GetExchangeDistributionList* methods on the *AddressEntry* object. In the case of an *AddressEntry* object that represents an Exchange user, this method returns an *ExchangeUser* object that exposes properties of the *AddressEntry* object in a first-class manner. Instead of using property tags as required by Collaboration Data Objects 1.21, you simply use the correct *ExchangeUser* property such as *JobTitle*, *Department*, *Alias*, *PhoneNumber*, or *PrimarySMTPAddress*.

```
private void EnumerateGAL()
{
    Outlook.AddressList gal =
        Application.Session.GetGlobalAddressList();
    if (gal != null)
    {
        for (int i = 1;
            i <= Math.Min(100,gal.AddressEntries.Count -1); i++)
        {
            Outlook.AddressEntry addrEntry =
                gal.AddressEntries[i];
            if(addrEntry.AddressEntryUserType ==
                Outlook.OlAddressEntryUserType.
                olExchangeUserAddressEntry
                || addrEntry.AddressEntryUserType ==
                Outlook.OlAddressEntryUserType.
                olExchangeRemoteUserAddressEntry)
            {
                Outlook.ExchangeUser exchUser =
                    addrEntry.GetExchangeUser();
                Debug.WriteLine(exchUser.Name + " "
                    + exchUser.PrimarySmtpAddress);
            }
            if (addrEntry.AddressEntryUserType ==
                Outlook.OlAddressEntryUserType.
                olExchangeDistributionListAddressEntry)
            {
                Outlook.ExchangeDistributionList exchDL =
                    addrEntry.GetExchangeDistributionList();
                Debug.WriteLine(exchDL.Name + " "
                    + exchDL.PrimarySmtpAddress);
            }
        }
    }
}
```

The *AddressEntryUserType* Property

To determine the type of *AddressEntry* object, you should use the new *AddressEntryUserType* property. This property returns an *OlAddressEntryUserType* constant. Valid *OlAddressEntryUserType* values are shown in Table 7-2.

Table 7-2 *OlAddressEntryUserType* **Values**

Value	Description
olExchangeAgentAddressEntry	An address entry that is an Exchange agent
olExchangeDistributionListAddressEntry	An address entry that is an Exchange distribution list
olExchangeOrganizationAddressEntry	An address entry that is an Exchange organization
olExchangePublicFolderAddressEntry	An address entry that is an Exchange public folder
olExchangeRemoteUserAddressEntry	An Exchange user that belongs to a different Exchange forest
olExchangeUserAddressEntry	An Exchange user that belongs to the same Exchange forest
olLdapAddressEntry	An address entry that uses LDAP
olOtherAddressEntry	A custom or some other type of address entry such as FAX or MOBILE
olOutlookContactAddressEntry	An address entry in an Outlook Contacts folder
olOutlookDistributionListAddressEntry	An address entry that is an Outlook distribution list
olSmtpAddressEntry	An address entry that uses SMTP

Finding a Specific *AddressEntry* Object

The Outlook object model does not provide a method to find a specific *AddressEntry* object in the *AddressEntries* collection. You also cannot restrict the *AddressEntries* collection to return a subset of *AddressEntry* objects. If you need to find a specific *AddressEntry* object in an *AddressList* object, you must enumerate the list to find a match. However, you can use recipient resolution to perform a function similar to finding a specific address entry. See the section "Resolving Recipients" earlier in this chapter.

The *GetAddressEntryFromID* Method

If you have the *EntryID* value of an *AddressEntry* object, you can use the *GetAddressEntryFromID* method of the *Namespace* object to return the *AddressEntry* object represented by the *EntryID* value. *GetAddressEntryFromID* is new to Outlook 2007. The *GetSenderSMTPAddress* procedure uses the *GetAddressEntryFromID* method to return an *AddressEntry* object that represents the sender of a message.

Although the Outlook object model provides you with the ability to return the *SenderName* and *SenderEmailAddress* properties for a *MailItem* object, these properties don't correlate to a unique SMTP address. To obtain the *EntryID* value of the sender's *AddressEntry*, the code uses the *PropertyAccessor* object to return the MAPI property *PR_SENT_REPRESENTING_ENTRYID*. This property always represents the sender of the message rather than the delegate in a delegate scenario. In the case of a delegate scenario, the *PR_SENDER_ENTRYID* would represent the delegate rather than the delegator.

```csharp
private string GetSenderSMTPAddress(Outlook.MailItem mail)
{
    if (mail == null)
    {
        throw new ArgumentNullException();
    }
    string PR_SENT_REPRESENTING_ENTRYID =
        @"http://schemas.microsoft.com/mapi/proptag/0x00410102";
    string PR_SMTP_ADDRESS =
        @"http://schemas.microsoft.com/mapi/proptag/0x39FE001E";
    if (mail.SenderEmailType == "EX")
    {
        string senderEntryID =
            mail.PropertyAccessor.BinaryToString(
            mail.PropertyAccessor.GetProperty(
            PR_SENT_REPRESENTING_ENTRYID));
        Outlook.AddressEntry sender =
            Application.Session.
            GetAddressEntryFromID(senderEntryID);
        if (sender != null)
        {
            //Now we have an AddressEntry representing the Sender
            if (sender.AddressEntryUserType ==
                Outlook.OlAddressEntryUserType.
                olExchangeUserAddressEntry
                || sender.AddressEntryUserType ==
                Outlook.OlAddressEntryUserType.
                olExchangeRemoteUserAddressEntry)
            {
                //Use the ExchangeUser object PrimarySMTPAddress
                Outlook.ExchangeUser exchUser =
                    sender.GetExchangeUser();
                if (exchUser != null)
                {
                    return exchUser.PrimarySmtpAddress;
                }
                else
                {
                    return null;
                }
            }
            else
            {
                return sender.PropertyAccessor.GetProperty(
                    PR_SMTP_ADDRESS) as string;
            }
        }
        else
        {
            return null;
        }
    }
    else
    {
        return mail.SenderEmailAddress;
    }
}
```

Displaying *AddressEntry* Details

To display the Details dialog box for an address entry, you call the *Details* method of the *AddressEntry* object. The dialog box displayed depends on the type of address entry. If the *AddressEntry* object represents an Exchange user, then a dialog box similar to Figure 7-4 is displayed. If the *AddressEntry* object represents an Exchange distribution list, then a dialog box similar to Figure 7-5 is displayed.

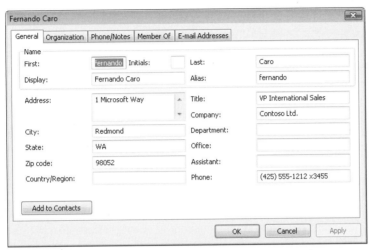

Figure 7-4   Details dialog box for an *AddressEntry* object that represents an Exchange user.

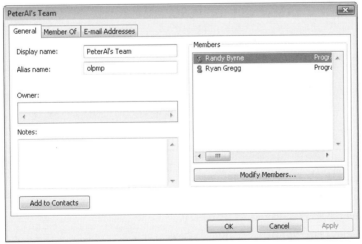

Figure 7-5   Details dialog box for an *AddressEntry* object that represents an Exchange distribution list.

If the *AddressEntry* object represents an Outlook contact, then a Contact Inspector will be displayed. If the *AddressEntry* object represents an Outlook personal distribution list, an Outlook distribution list Inspector will appear. If the *AddressEntry* object represents an SMTP address, then a dialog box similar to Figure 7-6 will be displayed.

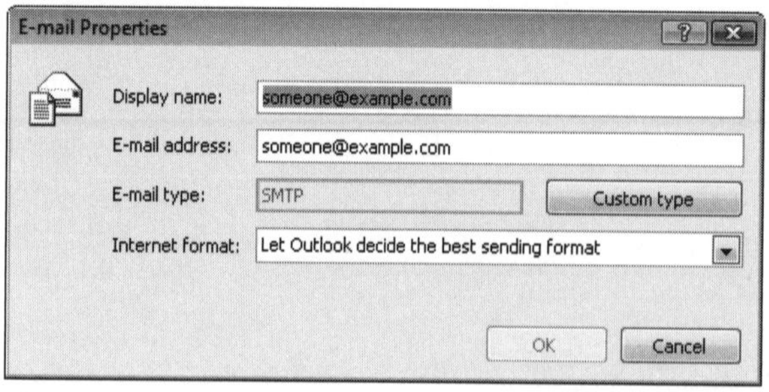

Figure 7-6   Details dialog box for an SMTP *AddressEntry* object.

Getting Availability Information for a User

You can determine whether someone is available at a given time using the *GetFreeBusy* method of the *AddressEntry* object. This method returns a string representing 30 days of availability (also known as free/busy) information starting at midnight on a specified date. Each character in the string indicates whether the person is available during a specified time period. The *CompleteFormat* parameter of the *GetFreeBusy* method allows you to specify the granularity of availability details.

If *CompleteFormat* is set to *false*, the default value, the string returned by the *GetFreeBusy* method contains one of the characters shown in Table 7-3 for each time slot in the availability string.

Table 7-3   *CompleteFormat* Equals *false*

Character	Description
0	The time slot represents a free period.
1	The time slot represents a tentative, out of office, or busy period.

If *CompleteFormat* is set to *true*, the string returned by the *GetFreeBusy* method contains one of the characters shown in Table 7-4 for each time slot in the availability string.

Table 7-4   *CompleteFormat* Equals *true*

Character	Description
0	The time slot represents a free period.
1	The time slot represents a tentative period.
2	The time slot represents a busy period.
3	The time slot represents an out of office period.

For example, the following statement returns a string 1,440 characters long (48 half-hour periods over 30 days) containing 0 for each half-hour period the person is free, 1 for each period the person has a busy time marked tentative, 3 for each period the person has a busy time marked out of office, and 2 for other busy periods:

```
string status = myAddressEntry.GetFreeBusy("7/1/07", 30, true);
```

The following statement returns a string 720 characters long (24 one-hour periods over 30 days) containing 0 for each hour the person is free and 1 for each hour the person is busy, regardless of how the busy periods are designated:

```
string status = myAddressEntry.GetFreeBusy("7/1/07", 60, false);
```

The following code sample displays the next time that the user's manager has an open time slot with a duration of 60 minutes. Note that this code sample makes assumptions about the manager's working hours and compares the free/busy string character representing a time slot to default working hours. If you want to expand this sample to use actual working hours, take a look at the *GetWorkHoursXML* sample in the section "*GetStorage* Method" in Chapter 6. If you have sufficient permission on another user's calendar, you can obtain working hours from that user's Calendar folder.

```
private void GetManagerOpenInterval()
{
    const int slotLength = 60;
    Outlook.AddressEntry addrEntry =
        Application.Session.CurrentUser.AddressEntry;
    if (addrEntry.Type == "EX")
    {
        Outlook.ExchangeUser manager =
            Application.Session.CurrentUser.
            AddressEntry.GetExchangeUser().GetExchangeUserManager();
        if (manager != null)
        {
            string freeBusy = manager.GetFreeBusy(
                DateTime.Now, slotLength, true);
            for (int i = 1; i < freeBusy.Length; i++)
            {
                if (freeBusy.Substring(i, 1) == "0")
                {
                    //Get number of minutes into
                    //the day for free interval
                    double busySlot = (i - 1) * slotLength;
                    //Get an actual date/time
                    DateTime dateBusySlot =
                        DateTime.Now.Date.AddMinutes(busySlot);
                    //dateBusySlot.AddMinutes(busySlot);
                    if (dateBusySlot.TimeOfDay >=
                        DateTime.Parse("8:00 AM").TimeOfDay &
                        dateBusySlot.TimeOfDay <=
                        DateTime.Parse("5:00 PM").TimeOfDay &
                        !(dateBusySlot.DayOfWeek == DayOfWeek.Saturday |
                        dateBusySlot.DayOfWeek == DayOfWeek.Sunday))
                    {
                        StringBuilder sb = new StringBuilder();
                        sb.AppendLine(manager.Name
                            + " first open interval:");
                        sb.AppendLine(dateBusySlot.ToString("f"));
```

```
                          Debug.WriteLine(sb.ToString());
                    }
                }
            }
        }
    }
}
```

> **Note**   You cannot obtain availability information for an *AddressEntry* object that represents an Exchange distribution list. If you need to determine availability information for members of a distribution list, you should obtain the members of the list by using the *GetExchangeDistributionListMembers* method. Once you have an *AddressEntries* collection that represents the members of the list, determine if the *AddressEntry* object in the collection represents an *ExchangeUser* object. If the *AddressEntry* object represents an *ExchangeUser* object, then call the *GetFreeBusy* method on each individual *ExchangeUser* object in the distribution list.

The *ExchangeUser* Object

The *ExchangeUser* object provides detailed information about an *AddressEntry* object that represents an Exchange mailbox user. The *ExchangeUser* object is derived from the *AddressEntry* object, and is returned instead of an *AddressEntry* object when the caller performs a query interface on the *AddressEntry* object. To perform the cast, just call the *GetExchangeUser* method on the *AddressEntry* object.

Working with *ExchangeUser* Properties

The *ExchangeUser* object provides first-class access to properties applicable to Exchange users such as *FirstName*, *LastName*, *JobTitle*, and *OfficeLocation*. This object also implements properties for Japanese phonetic rendering (yomigana) of the following properties:

- *YomiCompanyName*
- *YomiDepartment*
- *YomiDisplayName*
- *YomiFirstName*
- *YomiLastName*

If these properties are not supported on the version of Exchange Server on which the user's mailbox is located, they will return an empty string.

You can also access other custom properties specific to the Exchange user that are not exposed in the object model through the *PropertyAccessor* object. An example of an Exchange custom property would be a property that represents the EmployeeID of the mailbox user (defined as an extension to the Active Directory schema) or a legacy Exchange custom attribute property.

> **Note** Some of the explicit built-in properties on the *ExchangeUser* object are read/write properties. Setting these properties requires the code to be running under an appropriate Exchange administrator account. Without sufficient permissions, calling the *ExchangeUser.Update* method will result in a Permission Denied error. Outlook raises the error when you attempt to save the underlying *AddressEntry* object rather than when you set the property.

Obtaining an *ExchangeUser* Object from an *AddressEntry* Object

To obtain an *ExchangeUser* object from an *AddressEntry* object, you call the *GetExchangeUser* method on an *AddressEntry* object. The following procedure obtains the *AddressEntry* property for the *Recipient* object returned by *Namespace.CurrentUser*. If the *AddressEntry* object represents an Exchange mailbox user, then the *GetExchangeUser* method is called to return an *ExchangeUser* object. The *Name, PrimarySMTPAddress, JobTitle, Department, OfficeLocation, BusinessTelephoneNumber*, and *MobileTelephoneNumber* properties are written to the trace listeners of the *Listeners* collection.

```
private void GetCurrentUserInfo()
{
    Outlook.AddressEntry addrEntry =
        Application.Session.CurrentUser.AddressEntry;
    if (addrEntry.Type == "EX")
    {
        Outlook.ExchangeUser currentUser =
            Application.Session.CurrentUser.
            AddressEntry.GetExchangeUser();
        if (currentUser != null)
        {
            StringBuilder sb = new StringBuilder();
            sb.AppendLine("Name: "
                + currentUser.Name);
            sb.AppendLine("STMP address: "
                + currentUser.PrimarySmtpAddress);
            sb.AppendLine("Title: "
                + currentUser.JobTitle);
            sb.AppendLine("Department: "
                + currentUser.Department);
            sb.AppendLine("Location: "
                + currentUser.OfficeLocation);
            sb.AppendLine("Business phone: "
                + currentUser.BusinessTelephoneNumber);
            sb.AppendLine("Mobile phone: "
                + currentUser.MobileTelephoneNumber);
            Debug.WriteLine(sb.ToString());
        }
    }
}
```

The *GetExchangeUserManager* Method

The *GetExchangeUserManager* method returns an *ExchangeUser* object that represents the manager of an *ExchangeUser* object in the organizational hierarchy. The logged-on user must be online for this method to return an *ExchangeUser* object. If the user is not online, then *GetExchangeUserManager* will return *null* (*Nothing* in Visual Basic). Your code should test for this possibility. Similar to the *GetCurrentUser* procedure earlier, this routine writes manager information to the trace listeners of the *Listeners* collection.

```
private void GetManagerInfo()
{
    Outlook.AddressEntry currentUser =
        Application.Session.CurrentUser.AddressEntry;
    if (currentUser.Type == "EX")
    {
        Outlook.ExchangeUser manager =
            currentUser.GetExchangeUser().GetExchangeUserManager();
        if (manager != null)
        {
            StringBuilder sb = new StringBuilder();
            sb.AppendLine("Name: "
                + manager.Name);
            sb.AppendLine("STMP address: "
                + manager.PrimarySmtpAddress);
            sb.AppendLine("Title: "
                + manager.JobTitle);
            sb.AppendLine("Department: "
                + manager.Department);
            sb.AppendLine("Location: "
                + manager.OfficeLocation);
            sb.AppendLine("Business phone: "
                + manager.BusinessTelephoneNumber);
            sb.AppendLine("Mobile phone: "
                + manager.MobileTelephoneNumber);
            Debug.WriteLine(sb.ToString());
        }
    }
}
```

The *GetDirectReports* Method

The *GetDirectReports* method returns an *AddressEntries* collection that represents the address entries for all the direct reports of a given Exchange user. If the user has no direct reports, then *GetDirectReports().Count* will equal zero (0). The logged-on user must be online for this method to return an *AddressEntries* collection. If the user is not online, *GetDirectReports* will return *null* (*Nothing* in Visual Basic). Your code should test for this possibility. The following procedure obtains a reference to the current user's manager and then writes information about each of the manager's direct reports to the trace listeners of the *Listeners* collection:

```
private void GetManagerDirectReports()
{
    Outlook.AddressEntry currentUser =
        Application.Session.CurrentUser.AddressEntry;
    if (currentUser.Type == "EX")
    {
        Outlook.ExchangeUser manager =
            currentUser.GetExchangeUser().GetExchangeUserManager();
        if (manager != null)
        {
            Outlook.AddressEntries addrEntries =
                manager.GetDirectReports();
            if (addrEntries != null)
            {
                foreach (Outlook.AddressEntry addrEntry
                    in addrEntries)
                {
                    Outlook.ExchangeUser exchUser =
                        addrEntry.GetExchangeUser();
                    StringBuilder sb = new StringBuilder();
                    sb.AppendLine("Name: "
                        + exchUser.Name);
                    sb.AppendLine("Title: "
                        + exchUser.JobTitle);
                    sb.AppendLine("Department: "
                        + exchUser.Department);
                    sb.AppendLine("Location: "
                        + exchUser.OfficeLocation);
                    Debug.WriteLine(sb.ToString());
                }
            }
        }
    }
}
```

The *GetMemberOfList* Method

The *GetMemberOfList* method returns an *AddressEntries* collection that represents the address entries for all distribution lists where the Exchange user is a member. If the user is not a member of any distribution lists, then *GetMemberOfList().Count* will equal zero (0). The logged-on user must be online for this method to return an *AddressEntries* collection. If the user is not online, *GetMemberOfList* will return *null* (*Nothing* in Visual Basic). Your code should test for this possibility. The following procedure obtains a reference to the current user and then writes information about each of the user's distribution lists to the trace listeners of the *Listeners* collection:

```
private void GetCurrentUserMembership()
{
    Outlook.AddressEntry currentUser =
        Application.Session.CurrentUser.AddressEntry;
    if (currentUser.Type == "EX")
    {
        Outlook.ExchangeUser exchUser =
            currentUser.GetExchangeUser();
```

```
            if (exchUser != null)
            {
                Outlook.AddressEntries addrEntries =
                    exchUser.GetMemberOfList();
                if (addrEntries != null)
                {
                    foreach (Outlook.AddressEntry addrEntry
                        in addrEntries)
                    {
                        Debug.WriteLine(addrEntry.Name);
                    }
                }
            }
        }
    }
}
```

Obtaining Proxy Addresses for an *ExchangeUser* Object

The *ExchangeUser* object does not directly expose the proxy addresses for the user. However, you can use the *PropertyAccessor* object to obtain the MAPI property *PR_EMS_AB_PROXY_ADDRESSES*. This property is a multivalued string property that contains all the foreign addresses for a given user. The following *GetSMTPAddress* procedure returns an array of strings containing the proxy addresses for the *ExchangeUser* object passed as a method argument:

```
private string[] GetProxyAddresses(Outlook.ExchangeUser exchUser)
{
    const string PR_EMS_AB_PROXY_ADDRESSES =
        "http://schemas.microsoft.com/mapi/proptag/0x800F101E";
    if (exchUser != null)
    {
        return exchUser.PropertyAccessor.GetProperty(
            PR_EMS_AB_PROXY_ADDRESSES) as string[];
    }
    else
    {
        throw new ArgumentNullException();
    }
}
```

The *ExchangeDistributionList* Object

The *ExchangeDistributionList* object provides detailed information about an *AddressEntry* object that represents an Exchange distribution list. The *ExchangeDistributionList* object is derived from the *AddressEntry* object and is returned instead of an *AddressEntry* object when the caller performs a query interface on the *AddressEntry* object. To perform the cast, just call the *GetExchangeDistributionList* method on the *AddressEntry* object.

Compared to the *ExchangeUser* object, *ExchangeDistributionList* exposes a limited number of properties such as *Alias*, *Comments*, and *PrimarySMTPAddress*. However, this object does allow you to enumerate the members of the list, return an *AddressEntries* collection that contains the owners of the distribution list, and determine distribution list membership.

To obtain an *ExchangeDistributionList* object from an *AddressEntry* object, call the *GetExchangeDistributionList* method on an *AddressEntry* object.

The *GetExchangeDistributionListMembers* Method

The *GetExchangeDistributionListMembers* method returns an *AddressEntries* collection that contains all the members of the list. Because distribution lists can be nested inside of other distribution lists, the *AddressEntries* collection returned by *GetExchangeDistributionListMembers* can represent any type of Exchange *AddressEntry* object. The logged-on user must be online for this method to return an *AddressEntries* collection. If the user is not online, *GetExchangeDistributionListMembers* will return *null* (*Nothing* in Visual Basic). Your code should test for this possibility.

The following code sample displays the All Groups container of the Select Names dialog box. When the user selects a distribution list from the list, the distribution list members are written to the trace listeners of the *Listeners* collection.

> **Important**   Expanding distribution list members programmatically can place a performance burden on an Exchange server. Use the *GetExchangeDistributionListMembers* method cautiously, and understand that your code will be slow when expanding large distribution lists.

```
private void GetDistributionListMembers()
{
    Outlook.SelectNamesDialog snd =
        Application.Session.GetSelectNamesDialog();
    Outlook.AddressLists addrLists =
        Application.Session.AddressLists;
    foreach (Outlook.AddressList addrList in addrLists)
    {
        if (addrList.Name == "All Groups")
        {
            snd.InitialAddressList = addrList;
            break;
        }
    }
    snd.NumberOfRecipientSelectors =
        Outlook.OlRecipientSelectors.olShowTo;
    snd.ToLabel = "D/L";
    snd.ShowOnlyInitialAddressList = true;
    snd.AllowMultipleSelection = false;
    snd.Display();
    if(snd.Recipients.Count > 0)
    {
        Outlook.AddressEntry addrEntry =
```

```
        snd.Recipients[1].AddressEntry;
    if (addrEntry.AddressEntryUserType ==
        Outlook.OlAddressEntryUserType.
        olExchangeDistributionListAddressEntry)
    {
        Outlook.ExchangeDistributionList exchDL =
            addrEntry.GetExchangeDistributionList();
        Outlook.AddressEntries addrEntries =
            exchDL.GetExchangeDistributionListMembers();
        if(addrEntries != null)
            foreach (Outlook.AddressEntry exchDLMember
                in addrEntries)
            {
                Debug.WriteLine(exchDLMember.Name);
            }
    }
}
}
```

The *GetMemberOfList* Method

The *GetMemberOfList* method returns an *AddressEntries* collection that represents the address entries for all distribution lists where the Exchange distribution list is a member. If the distribution list is not a member of any other distribution lists, *GetMemberOfList* returns an *AddressEntries* collection with *Count* equal to zero (0). The logged-on user must be online for this method to return an *AddressEntries* collection. If the user is not online, *GetMemberOfList* will return *null* (*Nothing* in Visual Basic). Your code should test for this possibility.

The *GetOwners* Method

The *GetOwners* method returns an *AddressEntries* collection that represents the address entries for all owners of the Exchange distribution list. If the distribution list has no owners, *GetOwners* returns an *AddressEntries* collection with *Count* equal to zero (0). The logged-on user must be online for this method to return an *AddressEntries* collection. If the user is not online, *GetOwners* will return *null* (*Nothing* in Visual Basic). Your code should test for this possibility.

The *SelectNamesDialog* Object

Finally, the Outlook object model will let you display an Outlook Address Book without having to resort to Collaboration Data Objects 1.21, Extended MAPI, or third-party libraries. The *SelectNamesDialog* object shown in Figure 7-7 displays the Select Names dialog box for the user to select entries from one or more address lists and returns the selected entries in the *Recipients* collection object returned by the read-only property *SelectNamesDialog.Recipients*.

To obtain an instance of the *SelectNamesDialog* instance, you call the *GetSelectNamesDialog* method on the *Namespace* object. Once you have an instance of *SelectNamesDialog*, you set properties or call a method to configure the dialog box in exactly the manner that you desire.

To display the dialog box after configuration, you simply call the *Display* method. After the dialog box has been displayed, you examine the *Recipients* property to determine the selected addresses. If the user clicks Cancel or closes the dialog box without selecting recipients, the *Recipients* property will have a *Count* value of zero (0).

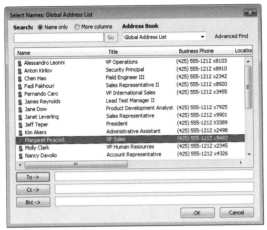

Figure 7-7   The Select Names dialog box displaying the GAL.

Using the *SetDefaultDisplayMode* Method

SelectNamesDialog can be used to present the same dialog box in many different variations to the user. Each of these variations can be configured in a locale-independent manner. For example, the Select Names dialog box can be used to select recipients for a message or attendees for an appointment. The *SetDefaultDisplayMode* method allows you to specify eight different configurations of the dialog box with the *OlDefaultSelectNamesDisplayMode* enumeration. Valid values for *OlDefaultSelectNamesDisplayMode* are shown in Table 7-5.

Table 7-5   *OlDefaultSelectNamesDisplayMode* Values

Name	Description
olDefaultDelegates	Displays one edit box for To recipients, uses localized string representing Add for the To button, and localized string representing Add Users for the caption. *CcLabel* and *BccLabel* are set to an empty string. Sets *AllowMultipleSelection* to *true* and *NumberOfRecipientSelectors* to *olTo*.
olDefaultMail	Displays three edit boxes for To, Cc, and Bcc recipients, uses localized strings representing To, Cc, and Bcc for To, Cc, and Bcc buttons, and localized string representing Select Names for the caption. Sets *AllowMultipleSelection* to *true* and *NumberOfRecipientSelectors* to *olToCcBcc*.

Table 7-5 *OlDefaultSelectNamesDisplayMode* Values

Name	Description
olDefaultMeeting	Displays three edit boxes for Required, Optional, and Resource recipients, uses localized strings representing Required, Optional, and Resources for the To, Cc, and Bcc buttons, and localized string representing Select Attendees and Resources for the caption. Sets *AllowMultipleSelection* to *true* and *NumberOfRecipientSelectors* to *olToCcBcc*.
olDefaultMembers	Displays one edit box for To recipients, uses localized string representing To for the To button, and localized string representing Select Members for caption. *CcLabel* and *BccLabel* are set to an empty string. Sets *AllowMultipleSelection* to *true* and *NumberOfRecipientSelectors* to *olTo*.
olDefaultPickRooms	Displays one edit box for Resource recipients, uses localized string representing Rooms for To button, and localized string representing Select Rooms for caption. *CcLabel* and *BccLabel* are set to an empty string. Sets *AllowMultipleSelection* to *true* and *NumberOfRecipientSelectors* to *olShowTo*. *InitialDisplayList* is set to the GAL.
olDefaultSharingRequest	Displays one edit box for To recipients, uses localized string representing To for To button, and localized string representing Select Names for caption. *CcLabel* and *BccLabel* are set to an empty string. Sets *AllowMultipleSelection* to *true* and *NumberOfRecipientSelectors* to *olTo*.
olDefaultSingleName	Displays no edit boxes for recipients; uses localized string representing Select Name for caption. *ToLabel*, *CcLabel*, and *BccLabel* are set to an empty string. Sets *AllowMultipleSelection* to *false* and *NumberOfRecipientSelectors* to *olNone*.
olDefaultTask	Displays one edit box for To recipients, uses localized string representing To for To button, and localized string representing Select Task Recipient for caption. *CcLabel* and *BccLabel* are set to an empty string. Sets *AllowMultipleSelection* to *true* and *NumberOfRecipientSelectors* to *olTo*.

Dialog Caption and Recipient Selectors

If the *SetDefaultDisplayMode* method doesn't provide the correct configuration for the dialog box, you can set properties that determine the caption for the dialog box, the number of recipient selectors that appear on the dialog box, and the label for each of the recipient selectors. To change the dialog box caption, set the *Caption* property on the *SelectNamesDialog* object. To change the recipient selector labels, set the *ToLabel*, *CcLabel*, or *BccLabel* properties. Each recipient selector corresponds to a different value for the *Type* property of a *Recipient* object that is added to a given recipient selector. For example, if the user adds a recipient to the To recipient selector (its actual label does not change *Recipient.Type*), then *Recipient.Type = olMailRecipientType.olTo* (1). The Cc recipient selector corresponds to a *Recipient.Type = olMailRecipientType.olCC* (2), and the Bcc recipient selector makes the *Recipient.Type = olMailRecipientType.olBcc* (3).

> **Note**   The length of the *Caption* property that is visible in the dialog box depends on screen resolution. The length of the labels for To, Cc, and Bcc recipient selectors is limited to 32 characters. If the recipient selector label contains more than 32 characters, only the first 32 characters will be displayed on the command button. The recipient selector label will always display –> characters after the label text. To provide an accelerator key for the recipient selector edit boxes, include an ampersand (&) character in the label argument string, immediately before the character that serves as the access key. For example, if *ToLabel* is "Local &Attendees," users can press Alt+A to move the focus to the first recipient selector edit box.

Setting the *InitialAddressList* Property

The user can control the initial address list in the Select Names dialog box and address list resolution order. See the section "Determining Resolution Order of Address Lists" earlier in this chapter. You can override the user's preference if you want to show a specific address list first, and you can also show only the initial address list so that other address lists are not available in the Address List drop-down list. To set the initial address list, you set the *InitialAddressList* property of the *SelectNamesDialog* object to an *AddressList* object that represents the initial address list that you want to display.

To show only the initial address list in the dialog box, set the *ShowOnlyInitialAddressList* property to *true*. The default value of this property is *false*, meaning that all address lists are displayed. If you do not set the *InitialAddressList* property and then set *ShowOnlyInitialAddressList* to *true*, the *AddressList* object with *AddressList.IsInitialAddressList* equal to *true* will be the only address list available in the drop-down list box.

The following code sample enumerates the *AddressLists* collection to find the *AddressList* object that represents the default Contacts folder. It then displays a customized Select Names dialog box, as shown in Figure 7-8, that allows the user to select addresses from the Contacts Address Book that represent winners of a contest. Finally, the selections are displayed in a message box.

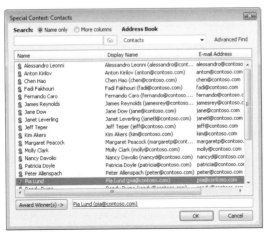

Figure 7-8   Customized Select Names dialog box displaying the Contacts address book.

```csharp
void DemoSetInitialAddressList()
{
    Outlook.AddressList contactsAddrList = null;
    Outlook.SelectNamesDialog snd =
        Application.Session.GetSelectNamesDialog();
    //First obtain the default Contacts folder
    string contactsEntryID =
        Application.Session.GetDefaultFolder(
        Outlook.OlDefaultFolders.olFolderContacts).EntryID;
    //Enumerate AddressLists
    Outlook.AddressLists addrLists =
        Application.Session.AddressLists;
    foreach (Outlook.AddressList addrList in addrLists)
    {
        if (addrList.GetContactsFolder() != null)
        {
            //GetContactsFolder returns Folder object; compare EntryIDs
            if (Application.Session.CompareEntryIDs(
                addrList.GetContactsFolder().EntryID, contactsEntryID))
            {
                contactsAddrList = addrList;
                break;
            }
        }
        else
        {
            MessageBox.Show("Could not find Contacts Address Book.",
                "Lookup Error",
                MessageBoxButtons.OK,
                MessageBoxIcon.Error);
            return;
        }
    }
    //Set additional properties on SelectNamesDialog
    snd.Caption = "Special Contest";
    //Set InitialAddressList to Contacts folder AddressList
    snd.InitialAddressList = contactsAddrList;
    snd.NumberOfRecipientSelectors =
        Outlook.OlRecipientSelectors.olShowTo;
    snd.ToLabel = "Award Winner(s)";
    //Display
    snd.Display();
    //Enumerate names of selected award winners
    Outlook.Recipients recips = snd.Recipients;
    if (recips.Count > 0)
    {
        StringBuilder sb = new StringBuilder();
        foreach (Outlook.Recipient recip in recips)
        {
            sb.AppendLine(recip.Name);
        }
        MessageBox.Show(sb.ToString(),
            "Contest Winners",
            MessageBoxButtons.OK,
            MessageBoxIcon.Information);
    }
}
```

Displaying the Select Names Dialog Box

To display the Select Names dialog box, you call the *Display* method on the *SelectNamesDialog* object. If the user cancels the dialog box, *Recipients.Count* will equal zero (0). The Select Names dialog box is modeless and parented to the Outlook application window. When you call the *Display* method, code execution will halt until the user either clicks OK or dismisses the dialog box.

Using *SelectNamesDialog.Recipients*

The *SelectNamesDialog* object has a *Recipients* property that returns a *Recipients* collection that allows you to set initial addresses in the dialog box or get the addresses selected by the user. The *Recipients* property is read-only, so you cannot set the *Recipients* property to another instance of a *Recipients* collection. However, you can add recipients to the collection by using the *Add* method for *SelectNamesDialog.Recipients*.

If you add a *Recipient* object to the *Recipients* collection for the *SelectNamesDialog* object, be sure to specify the *Type* property of the *Recipient* object. *Recipient.Type* controls the recipient selector in which the *Recipient* object appears. For example, in the next sample, the *Type* property for the *Recipient* object that represents a conference room resource is set to *OlMeetingRecipientType.olResource*, which represents a value of three (3). The conference room consequently appears in the Resources recipient selector. The default *Type* for a *Recipient* object added to the *Recipients* collection is *olTo*, which represents a value of one (1).

After you call the *Display* method, you can enumerate the *Recipients* collection for the *SelectNamesDialog* object and add to the *Recipients* collection for another object such as a *MailItem* or *AppointmentItem*. The following code sample uses the *SetDefaultDisplayMode* method to set the mode to Select Names dialog box for a meeting. It then populates the Resources recipient selector with Conf Room 36/2739. Once the dialog box is displayed to the user, it then enumerates the *Recipients* collection for the instance of *SelectNamesDialog* and adds those recipients to the *Recipients* collection for the meeting request represented by the *appt* variable. Finally, the code displays the meeting request to the user.

```
private void DemoSelectNamesDialogRecipients()
{
    Outlook.AppointmentItem appt = Application.CreateItem(
        Outlook.OlItemType.olAppointmentItem)
        as Outlook.AppointmentItem;
    appt.MeetingStatus = Outlook.OlMeetingStatus.olMeeting;
    appt.Subject = "Team Morale Event";
    appt.Start= DateTime.Parse("5/17/2007 11:00 AM");
    appt.End=DateTime.Parse("5/17/2007 12:00 PM");
    Outlook.SelectNamesDialog snd =
        Application.Session.GetSelectNamesDialog();
    snd.SetDefaultDisplayMode(
        Outlook.OlDefaultSelectNamesDisplayMode.olDefaultMeeting);
    Outlook.Recipient confRoom =
```

```
        snd.Recipients.Add("Conf Room 36/2739");
    //Explicitly specify Recipient.Type
    confRoom.Type = (int)Outlook.OlMeetingRecipientType.olResource;
    snd.Recipients.ResolveAll();
    snd.Display();
    //Add Recipients to meeting request
    Outlook.Recipients recips = snd.Recipients;
    if (recips.Count > 0)
    {
        foreach (Outlook.Recipient recip in recips)
        {
            appt.Recipients.Add(recip.Name);
        }
    }
    appt.Recipients.ResolveAll();
    appt.Display(false);
}
```

Summary

In this chapter, you've learned how to work with Outlook address lists, address entries, and recipients. Unlike previous versions of Outlook, you can now display an Address Book dialog box using the *SelectNamesDialog* object so that you can customize the addressing components of your solution. The *ExchangeUser* and *ExchangeDistibutionList* objects provide richer objects that are easier to program when you are writing code for users connected to an Exchange server. You can determine organizational hierarchy programmatically by using the new *GetExchangeUserManager* and *GetDirectReports* methods. The new and enhanced addressing objects in Outlook 2007 make it possible to write your code without resorting to Collaboration Data Objects 1.21, Extended MAPI, or third-party libraries.

Chapter 8
Responding to Events

Events are the oxygen of add-in development. Using Outlook events, your solution can respond to user actions and enforce business logic. To help you write great add-ins and to satisfy common developer requests, many new events have been added to Microsoft Office Outlook 2007. This chapter introduces you to the multiple classes used to wrap Component Object Model (COM) objects in Microsoft Visual Studio 2005. Some of these classes wrap Outlook events, and you'll learn which event-related class is appropriate to a particular object. Although the sample code in this chapter is predominantly C#, a brief discussion of events in Microsoft Visual Basic .NET will cover two different methods of hooking up events in your add-in. If you are a C# developer, you need to understand how to scope instance variables that are event-aware. After you complete this chapter, you should be ready to hook up event delegates for any of the objects in the Outlook object model. This chapter provides you with a basic understanding of the following topics:

- Learning how COM events are exposed in managed code
- Writing event handlers in Visual Basic
- Writing event handlers in Visual C#
- Learning the new events in Outlook 2007

Writing Event Handlers in Managed Code

Once you get the hang of it, writing event handlers in managed code is straightforward. However, the interop wrapper for the Outlook object model creates many helper objects related to events that can be somewhat intimidating. To give you an idea of how the Outlook Primary Interop Assembly (PIA) adds complexity, take a look at Figure 8-1, which shows the Outlook *Application* interface in the Visual Studio 2005 object browser.

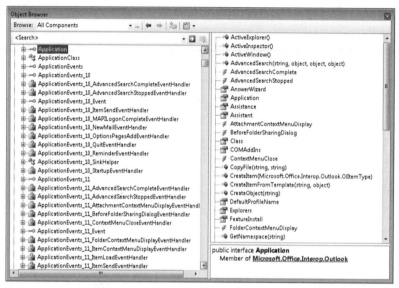

Figure 8-1   Outlook *Application* object in the Visual Studio 2005 object browser.

You'll notice that in addition to the Outlook *Application* object (which the PIA exposes as an interface), there are additional classes such as *ApplicationClass* and *ApplicationEvents_SinkHelper* and event delegates for every event exposed on the Outlook *Application* object. Table 8-1 lists the interfaces, classes, and delegates that pertain to the Outlook *Application* object. Most of these objects created by the PIA are not relevant to writing Outlook code. However, in the case of events, you need to understand the role and function of event delegates.

Table 8-1   Interfaces, Delegates, and Events Associated with the *Application* Object in Outlook

Example	Description
Application	The *Application [Object]* interface is a wrapper for a coclass that is required by managed code for COM interoperability. Use the *Object* interface in your code.
_Application	The *_Application [_Object]* interface is a wrapper for a COM interface implemented by a coclass that is required by managed code for COM interoperability. Do not use the *_Object* interface in your code.
ApplicationClass	The *ApplicationClass [ObjectClass]* class is a wrapper for a coclass or coclass member that is required by managed code for COM interoperability. Do not use *ObjectClass* in your code.
ApplicationEvents_SinkHelper	The *ApplicationEvents_SinkHelper [ObjectEvents_SinkHelper]* class is a wrapper for a coclass or coclass member that is required by managed code for COM interoperability. Do not use *ObjectNameEvents_SinkHelper* in your code.

Table 8-1   Interfaces, Delegates, and Events Associated with the *Application* Object in Outlook

Example	Description
ApplicationEvents	The *ApplicationEvents [ObjectEvents]* interface is a wrapper for a COM interface implemented by a coclass that is required by managed code for COM interoperability.
ApplicationEvents_Event	The *ApplicationEvents_Event [ObjectEvents_Event]* interface is a wrapper for a COM interface implemented by a coclass that is required by managed code for COM interoperability. You can use this interface in your code when a method and event name are identical.
ApplicationEvents_10_Event	The *ApplicationEvents_10_Event [ObjectEvents_10_Event]* interface is a wrapper for a COM interface that has been superseded by a later version. The later version of this interface implements all members of earlier interfaces and additional new members. You can use this interface in your code when a method and event name are identical.
ApplicationEvents_11_Event	The *ApplicationEvents_11_Event [ObjectEvents_11_Event]* interface is a wrapper for a COM interface that has been superseded by a later version. The later version of this interface implements all members of earlier interfaces and additional new members. You can use this interface in your code when a method and event name are identical.

What exactly is an event delegate? An event delegate is represented by one or more delegate classes. *Delegate* is a special type in the Microsoft .NET Framework that provides the functionality of a function pointer. The delegate allows the event sender to communicate with the event receiver. The delegate class can hold a reference to a method. Unlike other classes, a delegate class has a signature, and it can hold references only to methods that match its signature. From a coding perspective, this means that the event handler method for an Outlook event must match the signature defined by the event delegate. With a few exceptions, Visual Studio will automate the process of writing code to hook up an event delegate and its event handler method.

An example of an event delegate would be the *ApplicationEvents_11_ItemContextMenuDisplayEventHandler* delegate. Generally, the event delegates follow the pattern *ApplicationEvents_EventNameEventHandler* where *EventName* is the name of the event such as *ItemSend*. To accommodate events added in later versions, there are also event delegates such as *ApplicationEvents_10_EventNameEventHandler* and *ApplicationEvents_11_EventNameEventHandler*.

Hooking Up Events in Visual Basic .NET

To hook up events in Visual Basic .NET, you should use the *WithEvents* keyword when you declare the instance variable that will expose the events that you want to hook up. Although you can also use the *AddHandler* statement to hook up events, the simplest approach for a Visual Basic developer is to use *WithEvents*.

The Visual Basic Add-in template that accompanies this book provides you with a framework for hooking up events. The Visual Basic Add-in template is especially helpful if you need to handle events for *Explorer* and *Inspector* objects. See the section "Install the Outlook Add-in Templates" in Chapter 3, "Writing Your First Outlook Add-in Using Visual Basic .NET," for step-by-step installation instructions.

Using the *WithEvents* Keyword

Although the *WithEvents* keyword is the most common and easiest way to declare an event-aware instance variable, you should be aware of the following restrictions for *WithEvents*:

- When an instance variable is defined using *WithEvents*, you can declaratively specify that a method handles the variable's events using the *Handles* keyword.

- You can use *WithEvents* only at class or module level. This means the declaration context for a *WithEvents* variable must be a class or module and cannot be a source file, namespace, structure, or procedure.

- You cannot use *WithEvents* for an instance variable that represents an array.

Fortunately, you don't have to focus on unhooking your event procedures when you use the *WithEvents* keyword. Behind the scenes, Visual Basic disconnects the COM connection points when you dereference the event-aware instance variable.

To write an event procedure in Visual Basic, you should follow these steps. This is a generic example and might not apply to every situation in which you need to write an event procedure.

1. Declare an instance variable using the *WithEvents* keyword. Typically, the instance variable will have class- or module-level scope. Assume for this example that the instance variable is named *m_Contact* and is declared in the *OutlookInspector* class.

2. In the *OutlookInspector* class Code Editor, select the *m_Contact* object in the left Class Name drop-down list.

3. Select an event exposed on *m_Contact* in the right Method Name drop-down list. Visual Studio stubs out the event procedure for you. Assuming that *m_Contact* represents a *ContactItem* object, select the *PropertyChange* event.

4. Write code in the *m_Contact_PropertyChange* event procedure. You should see an event procedure similar to the following:

```
'Declare class-level instance variable using WithEvents
Private WithEvents m_Contact As Outlook.ContactItem

Private Sub m_Contact_PropertyChange( _
    ByVal Name As String) Handles m_Contact.PropertyChange
    'Write event code here
End Sub
```

Using *AddHandler* and *RemoveHandler* Statements

For most situations in Visual Basic, you don't need to use the *AddHandler* statement to hook up events. For simplicity and ease of coding, use the *WithEvents* keyword. Whenever you hook up an event using *AddHandler*, you should be sure to unhook the event using the *RemoveHandler* statement. The *AddHandler* and *RemoveHandler* statements allow you to start and stop event handling at any time during program execution. For example, the following code sample hooks up the *ItemLoad* event on the *Application* object using the *AddHandler* and *RemoveHandler* pattern:

```
AddHandler Application.ItemLoad, AddressOf Application_ItemLoad
'Additional statements here...
RemoveHandler Application.ItemLoad, AddressOf Application_ItemLoad

'Event procedure for ItemLoad event
Sub Application_ItemLoad(ByVal Item As Object)
    'ItemLoad code here
End Sub
```

Hooking Up Events in C#

Hooking up events in C# is more complex than hooking up an event in Visual Basic. However, once you understand how to write C# event handler code, the process is fairly straightforward.

Common Errors and Issues for Events

Here are some common errors and issues that developers encounter when writing event handlers in C#. Some of these items also apply to writing an event procedure in Visual Basic.

- The instance variable for the event does not have broad enough scope. Typically, you should declare event-aware instance variables at the class level. If the scope of the instance variable is too narrow, then your instance variable will fall out of scope and be garbage collected. The symptom of this condition is that your event will run once, but on subsequent occasions the event will fail to fire.

- If you do not unhook your C# event delegates using the −= operator, your add-in might not shut down correctly and will cause Outlook to remain in memory.

- Because an event name and method name are identical on a given object, the Intellisense window will only show the method name when you attempt to hook up the event procedure in C#. The event name appears to be missing from the Intellisense window.

- The firing order of events is not always predictable. Although the item-level *Open* event will always follow the item-level *Read* event, in other circumstances the event order might surprise you. For example, the *BeforeAttachmentSave* event fires when the item is saved rather than when the attachment is added to the item.

■ In certain events, you have to be careful not to call additional members on the object during an event procedure. If you do so, Outlook will raise an error or you will experience unpredictable results.

Step-by-Step Event Procedures for C#

To write an event procedure in C#, you should follow these steps. The following procedures assume that you are writing event procedures for the *m_Contact* instance variable in the *OutlookInspector* class.

To write an event procedure in C# when the event name does not collide with a method name, follow these steps:

1. Declare an instance variable with class-level scope. Assume for this example that the instance variable is named *m_Contact* and is declared in the *OutlookInspector* class.

2. In the *OutlookInspector* class Code Editor, click inside the *OutlookInspector* constructor.

3. Type **m_Contact**, and then press the period key (.).

4. In the Intellisense window, use your mouse or the keyboard to scroll to the *PropertyChange* event.

5. Press Enter to select the *PropertyChange* event.

6. Type **+=**. Visual C# offers to hook up the event for you. At this point, press Tab.

7. Press Tab again to insert the event handler.

8. Write code in the *m_Contact_CustomPropertyChange* event handler. You should see code similar to the following:

```
// Class-level instance variable
private Outlook.ContactItem m_Contact;
// Hookup the event delegate
m_Contact.PropertyChange +=
    new Outlook.ItemEvents_10_PropertyChangeEventHandler(
    m_Contact_PropertyChange);
// Event delegate
void m_Contact_PropertyChange(string Name)
{
    // Implement PropertyChange here
}
```

To write an event procedure in C# when the event name collides with a method name, follow these steps:

1. Declare an instance variable with class-level scope. Assume for this example that the instance variable is named *m_Contact* and is declared in the *OutlookInspector* class.

2. In the *OutlookInspector* class Code Editor, click inside the *OutlookInspector* constructor.

3. Type the open parenthesis key twice so that you see ((.

4. Type **Outlook**, and then press the period key. This step assumes that you have created a *using* directive to provide an *Outlook* alias for the *Microsoft.Office.Interop.Outlook* namespace.

5. Find the *<ClassName>Events_Event* interface in the Intellisense window. For most objects such as the *Inspector* or *Explorer* objects, the *<ClassName>* name is the name of the object. For item-level events, always use the *ItemEvents_Event* interface. Because you are writing an event for *m_Contact* that represents a *ContactItem*, select the *ItemEvents_Event*.

6. Type the close parenthesis key once so that you see).

7. In the Intellisense window, use your mouse or keyboard to scroll to the *m_Contact* instance variable, and press the scrollbar.

8. Type the close parenthesis key once so that you see), and then press the period key.

9. In the Intellisense window, use your mouse or the keyboard to scroll to the *Close* event.

10. Press Enter to select the *Close* event.

11. Type **+=**. Visual C# offers to hook up the event for you. At this point, press Tab.

12. Press Tab again to insert the event handler.

13. Write code in the *m_Contact_Close* event handler. You should see code similar to the following:

```
// Class-level instance variable
private Outlook.ContactItem m_Contact;
// Hookup the event delegate
m_Contact.PropertyChange +=
    new Outlook.ItemEvents_10_PropertyChangeEventHandler(
    m_Contact_PropertyChange);
// Event delegate
void m_Contact_Close(ref bool Cancel)
{
    // Implement Close here
}
```

Unhooking Event Handlers

You should always unhook event handlers using the −= operator for events when the class that contains your event-aware instance variable is being destroyed. For example, in the case of the *m_Contact_PropertyChange* and *m_Contact_Close* handlers shown earlier, you should add the following statements to the *OutlookInspectorWindow_Close* procedure:

```
m_Contact.PropertyChange -=
new Outlook.ItemEvents_10_PropertyChangeEventHandler(
m_Contact_PropertyChange);

((Outlook.ItemEvents_10_Event)m_Contact).Close -=
new Outlook.ItemEvents_10_CloseEventHandler(
m_Contact_Close);
```

Outlook 2007 Events

The following sections contain descriptions for all the events in the Outlook 2007 object model with the exception of Outlook control events such as *MouseUp*, *MouseDown*, and *Click*. For detailed information regarding Outlook control events, see the Outlook Developer's Reference.

Application Object Events

The *Application* object supports several new events in Outlook 2007, most notably context menu events that allow you to customize a context menu by adding new commands or repurposing existing commands. The following events are exposed on the *Application* object.

AdvancedSearchComplete

This event occurs when the *AdvancedSearch* method has completed. The *AdvancedSearchComplete* event is used to return the *Search* object that was created by the *AdvancedSearch* method.

```
Application.AdvancedSearchComplete +=
    new Outlook.ApplicationEvents_11_AdvancedSearchCompleteEventHandler(
    Application_AdvancedSearchComplete);
```

AdvancedSearchStopped

This event occurs when a specified *Search* object's *Stop* method has been executed. If you call the *Stop* method on a *Search* object, the *Search.Results* collection might not contain complete results for the search.

> **Note**   Both the *AdvancedSearchComplete* and *AdvancedSearchStopped* events will fire only if the *AdvancedSearch* method is called programmatically. These events do not occur for a search that executes when a user invokes the Advanced Find dialog box in the Outlook user interface or when a user performs an Instant Search query.

AttachmentContextMenuDisplay

This event occurs before a context menu, for one or more selected attachments is to be displayed, allowing the *CommandBar* object representing the context menu to be customized by an add-in. This is a new event for Outlook 2007.

BeforeFolderSharingDialog

This event occurs before the Sharing dialog box is displayed for a selected *Folder* object. This event provides an add-in with the capability of replacing the sharing user interface supplied by Outlook with a custom user interface. This event does not occur if a sharing message is programmatically created and displayed. This event is cancelable, and it is a new event for Outlook 2007.

ContextMenuClose

This is a new event for Outlook 2007 that occurs just after a context menu is closed so that add-ins can dispose of any object references that might have been obtained from one of the following events:

- *AttachmentContextMenuDisplay*
- *FolderContextMenuDisplay*
- *ItemContextMenuDisplay*
- *ShortcutContextMenuDisplay*
- *StoreContextMenuDisplay*
- *ViewContextMenuDisplay*

FolderContextMenuDisplay

This event occurs before a context menu for a folder is to be displayed, allowing the *CommandBar* object representing the context menu to be customized by an add-in. This is a new event for Outlook 2007. The following example hooks up the *Application_FolderContextMenuDisplay* event handler:

```
Application.FolderContextMenuDisplay +=
    new Outlook.ApplicationEvents_11_FolderContextMenuDisplayEventHandler(
    Application_FolderContextMenuDisplay);

void Application_FolderContextMenuDisplay(Office.CommandBar CommandBar,
    Outlook.MAPIFolder Folder)
{
    if((Outlook.Folder)Folder == (Outlook.Folder)
        Application.Session.GetDefaultFolder(
        Outlook.OlDefaultFolders.olFolderInbox))
    {
        //Customize Command Bar object
    }
}
```

ItemContextMenuDisplay

This event occurs before a context menu for either a single highlighted Outlook item or for one or more selected Outlook items is to be displayed, allowing the *CommandBar* object representing the context menu to be customized by an add-in. This is a new event for Outlook 2007. The following example hooks up the *Application_ItemContextMenuDisplay* event handler. In the event handler, the *OutlookItem* class is used to determine if the selected item is a *ContactItem*.

```
Application.ItemContextMenuDisplay +=
    new Outlook.ApplicationEvents_11_ItemContextMenuDisplayEventHandler(
    Application_ItemContextMenuDisplay);

void Application_ItemContextMenuDisplay(Office.CommandBar CommandBar,
    Outlook.Selection Selection)
{
    if (Selection.Count == 1)
    {
        OutlookItem olItem = new OutlookItem(Selection[1]);
        if (olItem.Class = Outlook.OlObjectClass.olContact)
        {
            //Customize CommandBar object
        }
    }
}
```

ItemLoad

This event occurs when an Outlook item loads into memory. This is a new event for Outlook 2007. Other than the values for the *Class* and *MessageClass* properties of the Outlook item, data for the item is not yet available. If you attempt to get or set any property other than *Class* or *MessageClass* on the *Item* object returned in the event, Outlook raises an error. Similarly, an error occurs if you attempt to call any method on the *Item* object, or if you call the *GetObjectReference* method of the *Application* object on the *Item* object returned in the event.

The *ItemLoad* event is a chatty event, which means that the event will fire frequently, and you should exercise caution when hooking up this event so that you don't affect Outlook performance. The *Item* object returned in this event will always be a weak referenced item. This means that Outlook will fire an *Unload* event on the *Item* object when the item reference is about to be destroyed. You cannot prevent the dereferencing of a weak referenced item.

ItemLoad is particularly helpful when you need to enforce business logic for items that can be edited using the in-cell editing feature of a view. Because an Inspector is not displayed during in-cell editing, you cannot rely on the *NewInspector* event to hook up item-level events such as *PropertyChange* or *CustomPropertyChange*. Instead of the *NewInspector* event, you can use the *ItemLoad* event to hook up an event-aware instance variable. If the Reading Pane is not turned on, the *ItemLoad* event will not fire automatically. When the Reading Pane is visible, the *ItemLoad* event will always fire when the user navigates to an item in a view.

The *ItemLoad* event fires before the *NewInspector* event on the *Inspectors* collection (provided that the *Item* is displayed in an Inspector), the item-level *Open* event, or the item-level *Read* event.

ItemLoad fires under the following conditions:

- An item is created through user action or programmatically.

- An item is opened in an Inspector through user action or programmatically.

- A user clicks Previous or Next in an Inspector.

- An item is loaded in the Reading Pane.

- A user uses in-cell editing in a view to modify the item.

- A user displays the context menu for an item in a view and selects the Follow-up or Categories pop-up menus.

- A user displays the context menu for an item in a view, and the item has attachments.

- A meeting request creates an associated item in a user's default calendar folder.

- A task request creates an associated item in a user's default task folder.

- The user displays the context menu for a task.

- The user displays the context menu for a meeting request.

ItemLoad does not fire when the following conditions occur:

- An Outlook item is synchronized with a folder.

- A server-side rule is triggered for an Outlook item.

- A reminder is triggered for an Outlook item.

- A Desktop Alert is displayed for an Outlook item.

ItemSend

This event occurs when an item is sent either because a user clicked Send on the item or because code causes an item to be sent. Typically, the *ItemSend* event occurs after the item-level *Send* event and before the item-level *Write* and *Close* events. You should apply user-interface elements such as alert and dialog boxes with care in the *ItemSend* event. If you use the *Cancel* argument to cancel sending the item, and the item has already been sent from an open Inspector, the Inspector will remain in its previously displayed state. The item's Inspector will not close as it normally would when Send is clicked.

MapiLogonComplete

This event occurs when logon to the Messaging Programming Application Interface (MAPI) session has completed. When *MapiLogonComplete* occurs, it means that a valid *Namespace* object has been created and that you have full access to all the objects, events, and properties in the Outlook object model.

NewMail

This event occurs when one or more new items are received in the Inbox. Generally, you should prefer the *NewMailEx* event over the *NewMail* event. The *NewMail* event tells you that items have been received, but it does not tell which items have received in the Inbox.

NewMailEx

This event occurs when one or more new items are received in the Inbox. This event passes a comma-delimited string containing the entry IDs of all the items received in the Inbox since the last time the event was fired. This event fires for e-mail accounts that provide notifications for received messages, such as Microsoft Exchange Server and Post Office Protocol 3 (POP3) accounts.

For users with an online Exchange Server account (noncached Exchange mode), *NewMailEx* will fire only if Outlook is running. The event will not fire for the items that are received using an online Exchange Server account when Outlook is not running.

For users using cached Exchange mode, the event will fire in all settings: Download Full Items, Download Headers, and Download Headers and then Full Items. In cached Exchange mode, the event will fire before rule processing occurs.

The following code sample uses the *Split* method to return a string array of entry IDs from the *EntryIDsCollection* string passed in the event:

```
Application.NewMailEx +=
    new Outlook.ApplicationEvents_11_NewMailExEventHandler(
    Application_NewMailEx);

void Application_NewMailEx(string EntryIDCollection)
{
    string[] EntryIDs;
    //Create string array from EntryIDCollection delimited by ,
    EntryIDs = EntryIDCollection.Split(',');
    //Remove the leading space
    for (int i = 0; i <= EntryIDs.GetUpperBound(0); i++)
    {
        Debug.WriteLine(EntryIDs[i]);
    }
}
```

OptionsPagesAdd

This event occurs whenever the Options dialog box on the Tools menu is about to be displayed. You can use this event to add custom property pages to the Tools Options dialog box. For additional information on implementing a custom property page, see Chapter 16, "Completing Your User Interface."

Quit

This occurs when Outlook is about to shut down. Because the *Quit* event collides with the *Quit* method, you need to hook up this event as follows:

```
((Outlook.ApplicationEvents_Event)Application).Quit +=
    new Outlook.ApplicationEvents_QuitEventHandler(
    Connect_Quit);
```

Reminder

This event occurs immediately before a reminder is displayed.

ShortcutContextMenuDisplay

This event occurs before a context menu for a shortcut on the Outlook bar (such as the Outlook Today shortcut) is to be displayed, allowing the *CommandBar* object representing the context menu to be customized by an add-in. This is a new event for Outlook 2007.

Startup

This event occurs when Outlook is starting but after all add-in programs have been loaded.

StoreContextMenuDisplay

This event occurs before a context menu for a store, such as an Exchange mailbox or a Personal Folders (.pst) File, is to be displayed, allowing the *CommandBar* object representing the context menu to be customized by an add-in. This is a new event for Outlook 2007.

ViewContextMenuDisplay

This event occurs before a context menu for a view (such as a table view) is to be displayed, allowing the *CommandBar* object representing the context menu to be customized by an add-in. This event is new for Outlook 2007.

Explorers Collection Event

The *Explorers* collection exposes only one event, the *NewExplorer* event.

NewExplorer

The *NewExplorer* event fires after a new Explorer window has been created and before it is displayed. A new Explorer window can be created through a user action or through your code. The *OutlookExplorer* class in the Outlook Add-in Template that accompanies this book demonstrates how you can use the *NewExplorer* event to wrap multiple instances of an *Explorer* object. The Outlook Add-in Template declares a class-level instance variable named *explorers* in the *Connect* class. The *NewExplorer* event is hooked up as follows:

```
// Connect class-level Instance Variables
private Outlook.Explorers explorers;
private List<OutlookExplorer> explorerWindows;

// Hookup NewExplorer event
explorers.NewExplorer +=
    new Outlook.ExplorersEvents_NewExplorerEventHandler(
    explorers_NewExplorer);
// Event handler for NewExplorer
void explorers_NewExplorer(Outlook.Explorer Explorer)
{
    // Check to see if this is a new window we don't already track
    OutlookExplorer existingWindow = FindOutlookExplorer(Explorer);
    if (existingWindow == null)
    {
        AddExplorer(Explorer);
    }
}
// AddExplorer method
private void AddExplorer(Outlook.Explorer explorer)
{
    OutlookExplorer window =
        new OutlookExplorer(explorer);
    window.Close +=
        new EventHandler(WrappedExplorerWindow_Close);
}
// Looks up the window wrapper for a given Explorer window object
private OutlookExplorer FindOutlookExplorer(object window)
{
    foreach (OutlookExplorer explorer in explorerWindows)
    {
        if (explorer.Window == window)
        {
            return explorer;
        }
    }
    return null;
}
```

The code in the *NewExplorer* event calls the *FindOutlookExplorer* method to check if the new Explorer window is already wrapped in the *explorerWindows* list. If *FindOutlookExplorer* does not find the *Explorer* object in *explorerWindows*, then the *AddExplorer* method adds an instance of the *OutlookExplorer* class to *explorerWindows*. You can use the *OutlookExplorer* class to raise events for this particular Explorer window. Remember that multiple Explorer or Inspector windows can be open simultaneously. Typically, you hook up additional events in the constructor of the *OutlookExplorer* class as follows:

```
// OutlookExplorer class-level instance variables
private Outlook.Explorer m_Window;
```

```
// OutlookExplorer constructor
public OutlookExplorer(Outlook.Explorer explorer)
{
    m_Window = explorer;

    // Hookup the close event
    ((Outlook.ExplorerEvents_Event)explorer).Close +=
        new Outlook.ExplorerEvents_CloseEventHandler(
        OutlookExplorerWindow_Close);

    // Hookup explorer-level events as needed.
    m_Window.FolderSwitch +=
        new Outlook.ExplorerEvents_10_FolderSwitchEventHandler(
        m_Window_FolderSwitch);
    m_Window.BeforeViewSwitch +=
        new Outlook.ExplorerEvents_10_BeforeViewSwitchEventHandler(
        m_Window_BeforeViewSwitch);
    m_Window.ViewSwitch +=
        new Outlook.ExplorerEvents_10_ViewSwitchEventHandler(
        m_Window_ViewSwitch);
    m_Window.SelectionChange +=
        new Outlook.ExplorerEvents_10_SelectionChangeEventHandler(
        m_Window_SelectionChange);
}
```

When the Explorer closes, you need to unhook all the events that you've hooked up in the *OutlookExplorer* constructor in the *OutlookExplorerWindow_Close* event handler.

```
private void OutlookExplorerWindow_Close()
{
    // Unhook explorer-level events
    m_Window.BeforeFolderSwitch -=
        Outlook.ExplorerEvents_10_BeforeFolderSwitchEventHandler(
        m_Window_BeforeFolderSwitch);
    m_Window.BeforeViewSwitch -=
        new Outlook.ExplorerEvents_10_BeforeViewSwitchEventHandler(
        m_Window_BeforeViewSwitch);
    m_Window.ViewSwitch -=
        new Outlook.ExplorerEvents_10_ViewSwitchEventHandler(
        m_Window_ViewSwitch);
    m_Window.SelectionChange -=
        new Outlook.ExplorerEvents_10_SelectionChangeEventHandler(
        m_Window_SelectionChange);

    // Unhook events from the window
    ((Outlook.ExplorerEvents_Event)m_Window).Close -=
        new Outlook.ExplorerEvents_CloseEventHandler(
        OutlookExplorerWindow_Close);

    // Raise the OutlookExplorer close event
    if (Close != null)
    {
        Close(this, EventArgs.Empty);
    }
```

```
    // Release instance variables
    m_Window = null;
}
```

Explorer Object Events

Explorer object events provide you with a great deal of control over the Outlook user interface. You can control the size and window state of Explorer windows, respond to selection changes through the *SelectionChange* event and the *Selection* object, and determine when the user has changed his or her view or the current folder. The *BeforeFolderSwitch* and *BeforeViewSwitch* events are cancelable, so you can prevent the user from moving to a folder or activating a view. If you combine the *Explorer* object events with the new events and programmatic control for the *NavigationPane* object and *NavigationGroups* collection, you have considerable programmatic control over the Outlook user interface.

Activate

This event occurs when an Explorer window becomes the active window, either as a result of user action or through program code. Because the *Activate* event collides with the *Activate* method, you need to hook up this event as follows:

```
((Outlook.ExplorerEvents_Event)m_Window).Activate +=
    new Outlook.ExplorerEvents_ActivateEventHandler(
    m_Window_Activate);
```

BeforeFolderSwitch

This event occurs when the Explorer window navigates to a new folder, either as a result of user action or through program code. This event is cancelable, so you can prevent users from navigating to prohibited folders.

BeforeItemCopy

This event occurs when an Outlook item is copied. This event is cancelable.

BeforeItemCut

This event occurs when an Outlook item is cut. This event is cancelable.

BeforeMaximize

This event occurs when an Explorer window is maximized. This event is cancelable.

BeforeMinimize

This event occurs when an Explorer window is minimized. This event is cancelable.

BeforeMove

This event occurs when an Explorer window is moved. This event is cancelable.

BeforeSize

This event occurs when an Explorer window is resized. This event is cancelable.

BeforeViewSwitch

This event occurs before the Explorer window changes to a new view, either as a result of user action or through program code. The *BeforeViewSwitch* event is similar to the *BeforeFolderSwitch* event, except that it occurs before a view is switched to a new view, either through a user action or programmatically. If a user changes from the Contacts folder to the Tasks folder but does not explicitly change the view with the View selector, the *BeforeViewSwitch* event will not fire, even though the default views on the two folders have different names. This event is cancelable.

Close

This event occurs when an Explorer window is being closed. This event is cancelable. If you use the *Close* method to fire this event, it can only be canceled if the *Close* method uses the *olPromptForSave* argument. Because the *Close* event collides with the *Close* method, you need to hook up this event as follows:

```
((Outlook.ExplorerEvents_Event)explorer).Close +=
    new Outlook.ExplorerEvents_CloseEventHandler(
    OutlookExplorerWindow_Close);
```

Deactivate

The *Deactivate* event fires when an Explorer window ceases to be the active window, either as a result of user action or through program code.

> **Warning**   You should not display a message box, dialog box, or any other user interface element during the *Deactivate* event of an *Explorer* or *Inspector* object. Showing a user interface element in the *Deactivate* event might disrupt the activation sequence and make Outlook behave unpredictably.

FolderSwitch

This event occurs when the current folder changes in the Explorer window, either through a user action or a programmatic change.

SelectionChange

This event occurs when the user switches to a different item in a folder, either through a user action or a programmatic change.

ViewSwitch

This event occurs when the view in the Explorer changes, either as a result of user action or through program code.

Folders Collection Events

The *Folders* collection contains all the *Folder* objects belonging to a parent *Folder* object. The *NameSpace* object also contains a *Folders* object containing all the root folders for the current logged-on user. The *Folders* collection events occur when folders are added, changed, or deleted because of user action or program code. The *Folders* collection events give you a powerful means to control folder names, hierarchical structure, and folder contents, in addition to traditional Exchange roles and folder permissions.

FolderAdd

This event occurs when a folder is added to the *Folders* collection, either through a user action or program code.

FolderChange

This event occurs when a folder in a *Folders* collection is changed, either through user action or program code. The *FolderChange* event fires if a user or program code renames a folder or if an item in the folder is added, changed, or removed. To determine which item was added, changed, or removed, use the *ItemAdd*, *ItemChange*, or *ItemRemove* events on the *Items* collection.

FolderRemove

This event occurs when a folder is deleted from its *Folders* collection, either through user action or program code. Unlike the *FolderAdd* and *FolderChange* events, *FolderRemove* does not return a *Folder* object in the event for the folder that has been removed. Instead of the *FolderRemove* event, consider using the *BeforeFolderMove* event on the *Folder* object. This event fires when a folder is deleted or moved.

Folder Object Events

The *Folder* object supports two events, *BeforeFolderMove* and *BeforeItemMove*, to satisfy developer requests for a reliable method of detecting folder or item moves and deletions.

BeforeFolderMove

This event occurs when a folder is about to be moved or deleted, either as a result of user action or through program code. This event fires when the folder is about to be moved to another folder (including the Deleted Items folder) or when the folder is about to be permanently deleted. It does not fire during autoarchiving or synchronizing operations. If the action is a permanent delete, the *MoveTo* folder returned in the event will be *null* (*Nothing* in Visual Basic). This event is cancelable, and it is a new event for Outlook 2007.

BeforeItemMove

This event occurs when an Outlook item is about to be moved or deleted, either as a result of user action or through program code. This event fires when the item is about to be moved to another folder (including the Deleted Items folder) or when the item is about to be permanently deleted. It does not fire during autoarchiving or synchronizing operations. If the action is a permanent delete, the *MoveTo* folder returned in the event will be *null* (*Nothing* in Visual Basic). This event is cancelable, and it is a new event for Outlook 2007.

FormRegion Object

The *FormRegion* object represents a form region in an Outlook form. The *FormRegion* object allows an add-in to add code behind a form region in a custom form to modify the appearance and behavior of the form region.

To obtain an instance of the *FormRegion* object, an add-in must implement the *FormRegionStartup* interface. Outlook allocates storage for the form region, instantiates an instance of the *FormRegion* object, and returns the *FormRegion* object in the *GetFormRegionStorage* method.

The *FormRegion* object supports two events, *Close* and *Expanded*.

Close

This event occurs when the frame is closed for a form region, which occurs just before the *Close* event of the *Inspector* object associated with the Outlook item. This is a new event for Outlook 2007.

Expanded

This event occurs when an adjoining form region expands or collapses. If the *Expand* parameter passed in the event returns *true*, then the form region is expanding. If the *Expand* parameter returns *false*, then the form region is collapsing. It is a new event for Outlook 2007.

Inspectors Collection Event

The *Inspectors* collection exposes only one event, the *NewInspector* event.

NewInspector

The *NewInspector* event fires after a new Inspector window has been created and before it is displayed. A new Inspector window can be created through a user action or through your code. The *OutlookInspector* class in the Outlook Add-in Template that accompanies this book demonstrates how you can use the *NewInspector* event to wrap multiple instances of an *Inspector* object. The Outlook Add-in Template declares a class-level instance variable named *inspectors* in the *Connect* class. The *NewInspector* event is hooked up as follows:

```
// Connect class-level instance variables
private Outlook.Inspectors inspectors;
private List<OutlookInspector> inspectorWindows;

// Hookup NewInspector event
inspectors.NewInspector +=
    new Outlook.InspectorsEvents_NewInspectorEventHandler(
    inspectors_NewInspector);
// Event handler for NewInspector
void inspectors_NewInspector(Outlook.Inspector Inspector)
{
    // Check to see if this is a new window we don't already track
    OutlookInspector existingWindow = FindOutlookInspector(Inspector);
    if (existingWindow == null)
    {
        AddInspector(Inspector);
    }
}
// AddInspector method
private void AddInspector(Outlook.Inspector inspector)
{
    OutlookInspector window =
        new OutlookInspector(inspector);
    window.Close +=
        new EventHandler(WrappedInspectorWindow_Close);
}
// Looks up the window wrapper for a given Inspector window object
private OutlookInspector FindOutlookInspector(object window)
{
    foreach (OutlookInspector inspector in inspectorWindows)
    {
        if (inspector.Window == window)
        {
            return inspector;
        }
    }
    return null;
}
```

The code in the *NewInspector* event calls the *FindOutlookInspector* method to check if the new Inspector window is already wrapped in the *inspectorWindows* list. If *FindOutlookInspector* does not find the *Inspector* object in *inspectorWindows*, then the *AddInspector* method adds an instance of the *OutlookInspector* class to *inspectorWindows*. You can use the *OutlookInspector* class to raise events for this particular Inspector window. Remember that multiple Explorer or Inspector windows can be open simultaneously. If you need to track item-level events such as *Open*, *PropertyChange*, or *CustomPropertyChange*, you hook up these events in the *OutlookInspector* class. Typically, you hook up additional events in the constructor of the *OutlookInspector* class as follows:

```
// OutlookInspector class-level instance variables
private Outlook.Inspector m_Window;
// Use these instance variables to handle item-level events
private Outlook.MailItem m_Mail;
private Outlook.AppointmentItem m_Appointment;
private Outlook.ContactItem m_Contact;
private Outlook.ContactItem m_Task;
// OutlookInspector constructor
public OutlookInspector(Outlook.Inspector inspector)
{
    m_Window = inspector;

    // Hookup the close event
    ((Outlook.InspectorEvents_Event)inspector).Close +=
        new Outlook.InspectorEvents_CloseEventHandler(
        OutlookInspectorWindow_Close);

    // Hookup item-level events as needed
    // For example, the following code hooks up
    // Open, PropertyChange, and CustomPropertyChange, Close
    // events for a ContactItem
    // ---------------------------------------------------------
    OutlookItem olItem = new OutlookItem(inspector.CurrentItem);
    if (olItem.Class == Outlook.OlObjectClass.olContact)
    {
        m_Contact = olItem.InnerObject as Outlook.ContactItem;
        m_Contact.Open +=
            new Outlook.ItemEvents_10_OpenEventHandler(
            m_Contact_Open);
        m_Contact.PropertyChange +=
            new Outlook.ItemEvents_10_PropertyChangeEventHandler(
            m_Contact_PropertyChange);
        m_Contact.CustomPropertyChange +=
            new Outlook.ItemEvents_10_CustomPropertyChangeEventHandler(
            m_Contact_CustomPropertyChange);
        ((Outlook.ItemEvents_Event)m_Contact).Close +=
            new Outlook.ItemEvents_CloseEventHandler(
            m_Contact_Close);
    }
}
```

When the Inspector window closes, you need to unhook all the events that you've hooked up in the *OutlookInspector* constructor in the *OutlookInspectorWindow_Close* event handler.

```
private void OutlookInspectorWindow_Close()
{
    // Unhook events from any item-level instance variables
```

```
      m_Contact.Open -=
          new Outlook.ItemEvents_10_OpenEventHandler(
          m_Contact_Open);
      m_Contact.PropertyChange -=
          new Outlook.ItemEvents_10_PropertyChangeEventHandler(
          m_Contact_PropertyChange);
      m_Contact.CustomPropertyChange -=
          new Outlook.ItemEvents_10_CustomPropertyChangeEventHandler(
          m_Contact_CustomPropertyChange);
      ((Outlook.ItemEvents_Event)m_Contact).Close -=
          new Outlook.ItemEvents_CloseEventHandler(
          m_Contact_Close);

      // Unhook events from the window
      ((Outlook.InspectorEvents_Event)m_Window).Close -=
          new Outlook.InspectorEvents_CloseEventHandler(
          OutlookInspectorWindow_Close);

      // Raise the OutlookInspector close event
      if (Close != null)
      {
          Close(this, EventArgs.Empty);
      }

      // Release instance variables
      m_Mail = null;
      m_Appointment = null;
      m_Contact = null;
      m_Task = null;
      m_Window = null;
  }
```

Inspector Object Events

The *Inspector* object events let you track when an Inspector window is activated, maximized, minimized, moved, sized, or closed. The *Close* event is the most frequently used event, as it lets you tear down an instance of the *OutlookInspector* class when the Inspector is closed.

Activate

This event occurs when an Inspector window becomes the active window, either as a result of user action or through program code. Because the *Activate* event collides with the *Activate* method, you need to hook up this event as follows:

```
((Outlook.InspectorEvents_Event)m_Window).Activate +=
    new Outlook.InspectorEvents_ActivateEventHandler(
    m_Window_Activate);
```

BeforeMaximize

This event occurs when an Inspector window is maximized. This event is cancelable.

BeforeMinimize

This event occurs when an Inspector window is minimized. This event is cancelable.

BeforeMove

This event occurs when an Inspector window is moved. This event is cancelable.

BeforeSize

This event occurs when an Inspector window is resized. This event is cancelable.

Close

This event occurs when an Inspector window is being closed. This event is cancelable. If you use the *Close* method to fire this event, it can only be canceled if the *Close* method uses the *olPromptForSave* argument. Because the *Close* event collides with the *Close* method, you need to hook up this event as follows:

```
((Outlook.InspectorEvents_Event)inspector).Close +=
    new Outlook.InspectorEvents_CloseEventHandler(
    OutlookInspectorWindow_Close);
```

Deactivate

The *Deactivate* event fires when an Inspector window ceases to be the active window, either as a result of user action or through program code.

PageChange

This event occurs when the active form page changes, either programmatically or by user action, on an *Inspector* object. If you call either the *Close* or *SetCurrentFormPage* methods in the event handler for this event, Outlook raises an error. This is a new event for Outlook 2007.

Items Collection Events

Like the *Folders* collection, the *Items* collection gives you a great deal of control over what happens in folders and with the items contained within folders. You can use the *Items* collection events to respond to item created, changed, and deleted events. Because the *Item* object returned in the *ItemAdd* and *ItemChange* events is of type *Object*, consider using the *OutlookItem* class to determine the underlying type of the item and cast it to the correct type such as *MailItem* if necessary.

ItemAdd

This event occurs when one or more items are added to the *Items* collection, either through user action or programmatically.

ItemChange

This event occurs when one or more items are changed in the *Items* collection, either through user action or programmatically.

ItemRemove

This event occurs when one or more items are removed from the *Items* collection, either through user action or programmatically. Unlike the *ItemAdd* and *ItemChange* events, *ItemRemove* does not return an *Item* object in the event for the item that has been removed. Instead of the *ItemRemove* event, consider using the *BeforeItemMove* event on the *Folder* object. This event will fire when an item is deleted or moved.

Item-Level Events

Item-level events provide you with the ability to create event handlers that implement your business logic on the level of an Outlook item. Item-level events are common to all item objects such as *MailItem*, *AppointmentItem*, *ContactItem*, *TaskItem*, and so forth. The only item that does not expose item-level events is the *NoteItem*. For some item types, certain events might never fire. For example, the *Send* event will not fire on a *ContactItem* object.

The entry point for item-level events is generally through the *NewInspector* or *ItemLoad* events. For example, the *NewInspector* event section earlier in the chapter showed you how to hook up item-level events in the constructor for the *OutlookInspector* class. You should always remember that Outlook can display multiple Inspectors, each of which represents an item-level object at the data level. Use the *OutlookInspector* class or a similar class of your own design to wrap each Inspector, and then create event-aware item-level instance variables that can handle item-level events.

AttachmentAdd

This event occurs when an attachment has been added to an instance of the parent object.

AttachmentRead

This event occurs when an attachment in an instance of the parent object has been opened for reading.

AttachmentRemove

This event occurs when an attachment has been removed from an instance of the parent object.

BeforeAttachmentAdd

This event occurs before an attachment is added to an instance of the parent object. This event is cancelable, and it is a new event for Outlook 2007.

BeforeAttachmentPreview

This event occurs before an attachment associated with an instance of the parent object is previewed, either from the attachment strip in the Reading Pane of the active Explorer or from the active Inspector. This event is cancelable, and it is a new event for Outlook 2007.

BeforeAttachmentRead

This event occurs before an attachment associated with an instance of the parent object is read from the file system, an attachment stream, or an *Attachment* object. This event is cancelable. It is also a new event for Outlook 2007.

BeforeAttachmentSave

This event occurs just before an attachment is saved. This event is cancelable. This event corresponds to when attachments are saved to the messaging store. The *BeforeAttachmentSave* event occurs just before an attachment is saved when an item is saved. If a user edits an attachment and then saves those changes, the *BeforeAttachmentSave* event does not occur at that time; instead it occurs when the item itself is later saved. It also does not occur when the attachment is saved on the hard disk using the *SaveAsFile* method.

BeforeAttachmentWriteToTempFile

This event occurs before an attachment associated with an instance of the parent object is written to a temporary file. This event is cancelable. It is also a new event for Outlook 2007.

BeforeAutoSave

This event occurs before the item is automatically saved by Outlook. This event is cancelable, and it is a new event for Outlook 2007. You can use this event to ensure that your business logic is maintained when an item is automatically saved.

BeforeCheckNames

This event occurs just before Outlook starts resolving names in the *Recipients* collection for an item. This event is cancelable. The event does not fire under the following circumstances:

- You customized a Journal Entry form and then resolved a contact in the *Contacts* field.

- You customized a Contact form and then resolved a contact in the *Contacts* field.

- You customized any type of form, and Outlook automatically resolved the name in the background.

- You programmatically created and resolved a recipient.

BeforeDelete

This event occurs before an item is deleted. This event is cancelable. For this event to fire when an item is deleted through a user action, the Inspector for the item must be open. If you need to prevent deletion on an item regardless of whether an Inspector for the item is displayed, use the *BeforeItemMove* event on the *Folder* object.

Close

This event occurs when the Inspector window associated with an item is being closed. This event is cancelable. If you use the *Close* method to fire this event, it can only be canceled if the *Close* method uses the *olPromptForSave* argument. Because the *Close* event collides with the *Close* method, you should hook up this event by casting the item-level interface (in this case, the *ContactItem* interface represented by the *m_Contact* instance variable) to the *ItemEvents_Event* interface.

```
((Outlook.ItemEvents_Event)m_Contact).Close +=
    new Outlook.ItemEvents_CloseEventHandler(
    m_Contact_Close);
```

CustomAction

This event occurs when a custom action executes for an item. This event is cancelable.

CustomPropertyChange

This event occurs when a custom property of an item is changed. The name of the custom property is passed in the event procedure.

> **Note**   The *CustomPropertyChange* event will only fire for custom properties that have been added to the *UserProperties* collection on the object. It will not fire for named properties that have been added to the item through the *PropertyAccessor* object.

Forward

This event occurs when the user selects the Forward action for an item or when the *Forward* method is called for the item. This event is cancelable.

Open

This event occurs when an item is being opened in an Inspector window. This event is cancelable. When this event occurs, the *Inspector* object is initialized but not yet displayed. This event occurs after the *NewInspector* event and allows you to set initial values of custom or built-in properties, for example. The *Open* event differs from the *Read* event in that the *Read* event occurs whenever the user selects the item in a view that supports in-cell editing as well as when the item is being opened in an Inspector window.

PropertyChange

This event occurs when an explicit built-in property (for example, the *Subject* property) for an item is changed.

Read

This event occurs when an item is opened for editing by the user. The *Read* event differs from the *Open* event in that *Read* occurs whenever the user selects the item in a view that supports in-cell editing as well as when the item is being opened in an Inspector window. The *Read* event fires before the *Open* event.

Reply

This event occurs when the user selects the Reply action for an item, or when the *Reply* method is called for the item. This event is cancelable.

ReplyAll

This event occurs when the user selects the Reply to All action for an item or when the *ReplyAll* method is called for the item. This event is cancelable.

Send

This event occurs when the user selects the Send action for an item or when the *Send* method is called for the item. This event is cancelable. When the *Send* event occurs, the item has not yet been persisted to storage, so you can modify the item programmatically during this event. Because the *Send* event collides with the *Send* method, you should hook up this event by casting the item-level interface (in this case, the *MailItem* interface represented by the *m_Mail* instance variable) to the *ItemEvents_Event* interface.

```
((Outlook.ItemEvents_Event)m_Mail).Send +=
    new Outlook.ItemEvents_SendEventHandler(
    m_Mail_Send);
```

Unload

This event occurs before an Outlook item is unloaded from memory, either programmatically or by user action. It is a new event for Outlook 2007. This event occurs after the *Close* event for the Outlook item occurs but before the Outlook item is unloaded from memory, allowing an add-in to release any resources related to the object. Although the event occurs before the Outlook item is unloaded from memory, this event cannot be canceled.

> **Note**   This event is meant only as a notification event so that an add-in can dereference the object. An error occurs if any property or method for this object is called within the *Unload* event.

Write

This event occurs when an item is saved, either programmatically or through user action. This event is cancelable. If an item is automatically saved, the *Write* event occurs after the *BeforeAutoSave* event.

Namespace Object Events

The following events are exposed on the *Namespace* object.

AutoDiscoverComplete

This event occurs after Outlook has finished accessing the autodiscovery service of an Exchange server and has the related information available in the *AutoDiscoverXml* property of the *Namespace* object. The *AutoDiscoverXml* property is an Extensible Markup Language (XML) string that is returned from the autodiscovery service of the Exchange server and contains user, account, and protocol information. The event will not fire unless the logged-on user is configured with an Exchange account, and the Exchange server version supports the autodiscovery service. This is a new event for Outlook 2007.

OptionsPagesAdd

This event occurs whenever the Properties dialog box for the *Folder* object returned in the event is about to be displayed. You can use this event to add custom property pages to the folder's Properties dialog box. For additional information on implementing a custom property page, see Chapter 16, "Completing Your User Interface."

NavigationGroups Collection Events

The *NavigationGroups* collection contains a set of *NavigationGroup* objects that represent the navigation groups displayed by a navigation module in the Navigation Pane. Use the *NavigationGroups* collection events to determine when a navigation folder has been added, removed, or selected.

NavigationFolderAdd

This event occurs after a folder is added to a *NavigationGroups* collection. This is a new event for Outlook 2007.

NavigationFolderRemove

This event occurs after a navigation folder has been removed from the *NavigationGroups* collection. This is a new event for Outlook 2007.

SelectedChange

This event occurs after the selection state is changed for a navigation folder contained in a Calendar navigation module represented by a *CalendarModule* object. This event occurs when the selection state changes for a folder in the Calendar navigation module, either by a user checking or unchecking a folder in the Calendar navigation module of the Navigation Pane or by an add-in changing the value of the *IsSelected* property for a *NavigationFolder* object contained in the *NavigationGroups* collection of a *CalendarModule* object. This is a new event for Outlook 2007.

NavigationPane Object Event

The *NavigationPane* object exposes only the *ModuleSwitch* event.

ModuleSwitch

This event occurs after the selection changes for a navigation module in the *NavigationModules* collection of the *NavigationPane* object. This is a new event for Outlook 2007.

OutlookBarPane Object Events

OutlookBarPane object events let you track changes to the Shortcuts pane in the Navigation Pane. The Shortcuts pane is the area in the Navigation Pane that contains shortcuts and shortcut groups. It can be accessed using the Shortcuts button at the bottom of the Navigation Pane. Although the Shortcuts pane (previously known as the Outlook Bar pane) is customizable through program code, its use was deprecated with the introduction of the Navigation Pane in Microsoft Outlook 2003.

BeforeNavigate

This event occurs when the user clicks a shortcut in the Shortcuts pane to navigate to a different folder. This event is cancelable.

OutlookBarGroup Object Events

These events fire when a Shortcuts pane group is added or removed, either programmatically or through a user action.

GroupAdd

This event occurs after a Shortcuts pane group has been added to the Shortcuts pane, either because of a user action or through program code.

BeforeGroupAdd

This event occurs before a Shortcuts pane group has been added to the Shortcuts pane, either because of a user action or through program code. This event is cancelable.

BeforeGroupRemove

This event occurs before a Shortcuts pane group has been removed from the Shortcuts pane, either because of a user action or through program code. This event is cancelable.

OutlookBarShortcut Object Events

These events occur when a Shortcuts pane shortcut is added or removed, either programmatically or through a user action.

ShortcutAdd

This event occurs after a shortcut has been added to a Shortcuts pane group, either because of user action or through program code.

BeforeShortcutAdd

This event occurs before a shortcut is added to a Shortcuts pane group, either because of user action or through program code. This event is cancelable.

BeforeShortcutRemove

This event occurs before a shortcut is removed from a Shortcuts pane group, either because of user action or through program code. This event is cancelable.

Stores Collection Events

The *Stores* collection is new to Outlook 2007. The *Stores* collection contains a set of *Store* objects that represent each store available in the current profile. Use the *Stores* collection events to determine when a *Store* object is about to be removed or when a store has been added.

BeforeStoreRemove

This event occurs when a store is about to be removed from the current session, either programmatically or through user action. This event is cancelable. This is a new event for Outlook 2007.

Outlook must be running for this event to fire. This event fires when any of the following occurs:

- A store is removed by the user clicking the Close command on the context menu.
- A store is removed programmatically by calling *Session.RemoveStore*.

This event does not fire when any of the following occur:

- Outlook shuts down and closes a primary or delegate store.
- A store is removed through the Mail icon in Microsoft Windows Control Panel and Outlook is not running.
- A delegate store is removed on the Advanced tab of the Microsoft Exchange Server dialog box.
- A store is removed through the Data Files tab of the Account Manager dialog box when Outlook is not running.
- An Internet Message Access Protocol (IMAP) store is removed from the profile.

You can use the *BeforeStoreRemove* event to determine that a store has been removed and take appropriate actions if the store is required for your application. If the store is required, you can use the *AddStore* method on the *Namespace* object to remount the store.

StoreAdd

This event occurs when a store has been added to the current session, either programmatically or through user action. This is a new event for Outlook 2007.

Outlook must be running for this event to fire. This event fires when any of the following occur:

- A store is added through the Open Outlook Data File dialog box by selecting Open and then Outlook Data File on the File menu.

- A store is added through the Data Files tab of the Account Manager dialog box.

- A store is added successfully by calling the *Session.AddStore* method.

This event does not fire when any of the following occurs:

- Outlook starts and opens a primary or delegate store.

- A store is added through the Mail icon in Windows Control Panel and Outlook is not running.

- A delegate store is added through the Advanced tab of the Microsoft Exchange Server dialog box.

SyncObject Object Events

The *SyncObject* object represents a Send/Receive group for a user. Use the *SyncObject* events to monitor the progress of a Send/Receive group.

OnError

This event occurs when Outlook encounters an error while synchronizing a user's folders using the specified Send/Receive group.

Progress

This event occurs periodically while Outlook is synchronizing a user's folders using the specified Send/Receive group.

SyncEnd

This event occurs immediately after Outlook finishes synchronizing a user's folders using the specified Send/Receive group.

SyncStart

This event occurs when Outlook begins synchronizing a user's folders using the specified Send/Receive group.

Reminders Collection Events

The *Reminders* collection represents all the *Reminder* items stored in the hidden Reminders folder of the mailbox of the logged-on user. *Reminder* items include appointment reminders, task reminders, and follow-up reminders. Use the *Reminders* collection events to determine when a reminder is added, changed, removed, snoozed, or displayed in the Reminders dialog box.

BeforeReminderShow

This event occurs before the Reminder dialog box is displayed. This event is cancelable.

ReminderAdd

This event occurs after a reminder is added, either programmatically or through user action.

ReminderChange

This event occurs after a reminder is changed, either programmatically or through user action.

ReminderFire

This event occurs before the reminder is executed. This event is not cancelable.

ReminderRemove

This event occurs when a *Reminder* object has been removed from the collection. Because the *ReminderRemove* event does not pass a *Reminder* object, you cannot determine which reminder has been removed from the *Reminders* collection. A reminder is removed from the *Reminders* collection when any of the following events occur:

- A reminder is dismissed programmatically or by a user action.
- A reminder is turned off programmatically or by a user action in the item containing the reminder.
- The item containing a reminder is deleted.
- A reminder is removed from the *Reminders* collection with the *Remove* method.

Snooze

This event occurs when a reminder is dismissed either programmatically or through user action. Because the *Snooze* event collides with the *Snooze* method, you need to hook up this event as follows:

```
((Outlook.ReminderCollectionEvents_Event)reminders).Snooze +=
    new Outlook.ReminderCollectionEvents_SnoozeEventHandler(
    Connect_Snooze);
```

Views Collection Events

Use the *Views* collection events to determine when a *View* object has been added or removed from the *Views* collection on a *Folder* object. The *Views* collection does not expose an event that lets you know that a view has been modified.

ViewAdd

This event occurs when a view is added to the *Views* collection, either through user action or program code.

ViewRemove

This event occurs when a view is removed from the *Views* collection, either through user action or program code.

Summary

In this chapter, you've learned how writing event handlers in managed code can present some special challenges due to the Outlook PIAs. Visual Basic events are straightforward if you use the *WithEvents* keyword. C# events require that you understand some issues such as scope and method and event name collisions before you start to code event procedures. Once you understand these issues, writing event procedures in C# is not difficult. Finally, this chapter provides an overview of every event in the Outlook 2007 object model. Understanding how and when to use a specific event will get you started on writing events for your own solution. Events bring your add-in to life and allow it to respond to a variety of user actions in a manner that is consistent with the business logic of your application.

Chapter 9
Sharing Information with Other Users

Enabling users to share information is one of the key investment areas in Microsoft Office Outlook 2007. In previous versions of Outlook, the ability to open shared items or work with shared data was restricted to a Microsoft Exchange environment and only enabled accessing shared default folders. For Outlook 2007, this support has been extended to include additional sharing technologies, such as Internet calendars and RSS feeds, and to send and receive sharing invitations and requests.

This chapter describes the different ways of sharing and accessing shared data. Specific topics include:

- **What is sharing?** Learn more about what sharing means and how it applies to solutions.
- **Accessing shared folders** In addition to accessing shared folders via Exchange, you can now access Internet calendars and RSS subscriptions. As an example, you'll see how to subscribe to an online calendar.
- **Sharing items** Learn how to create and use the *SharingItem* object.

Outlook and Shared Data

Outlook 2007 includes several different sharing technologies that enable users to share calendars, mail, and other item types. These technologies are used together through the object model to enable data sharing scenarios to provide access to folders, and send and receive information on shared Web data such as RSS feeds and Internet calendars.

The sharing portions of the object model also enable the sending and receiving of sharing invitations and sharing requests, which can be used to notify users of a new, available shared resource, request that users share the contents of their folder, and set permissions on folders through the object model.

Sharing in iCalendar Format

By sharing calendar items in iCalendar format, you can send items to other Outlook or non-Outlook clients via standard Internet mail formats and protocols. The object model supports folder-level export to the iCalendar format through the *CalendarSharing* object. To create a new instance of this object for a folder, call the *GetCalendarExporter* method on the *Folder* object.

```
Outlook.Folder calendar = Application.Session.GetDefaultFolder(
    Outlook.OlDefaultFolders.olFolderCalendar) as Outlook.Folder;
Outlook.CalendarSharing exporter = calendar.GetCalendarExporter();
```

Once you have obtained an instance of the *CalendarSharing* object, you can then set properties on the object and execute a method to either save the contents to disk or forward the calendar via e-mail.

Sharing a Calendar Through E-Mail

Previously it was necessary to write a complex macro to e-mail a calendar to another user in Outlook. However, Outlook 2007 simplifies the work by providing most of the necessary code through the *CalendarSharing* object. Now this task is straightforward and requires only setting a few properties and executing a method to send the e-mail. The following code sample generates an e-mail that contains the next seven days of calendar information and forwards it to an arbitrary e-mail address. By setting properties on the *CalendarSharing* object, this code shows all appointments in the time range, and includes attachments from those appointments, but will not include details of appointments marked "private."

```
public void SendNextWeekToAddress(string sendToAddresses)
{
    if (string.IsNullOrEmpty(sendToAddresses))
        throw new ArgumentException(
            "sendToAddress",
            "Parameter must contain a value.");

    Outlook.Folder calendar = Application.Session.GetDefaultFolder(
        Outlook.OlDefaultFolders.olFolderCalendar) as Outlook.Folder;
    Outlook.CalendarSharing exporter = calendar.GetCalendarExporter();

    // Set the properties for the export
    exporter.CalendarDetail = Outlook.OlCalendarDetail.olFullDetails;
    exporter.IncludeAttachments = true;
    exporter.IncludePrivateDetails = false;
    exporter.RestrictToWorkingHours = false;
    exporter.StartDate = DateTime.Today.Date;
    exporter.EndDate = exporter.StartDate.AddDays(7);

    // Create a new mail item
    Outlook.MailItem calendarMail = exporter.ForwardAsICal(
        Outlook.OlCalendarMailFormat.olCalendarMailFormatDailySchedule);
    calendarMail.To = sendToAddresses;
    ((Outlook.MailItemClass)calendarMail).Send();
}
```

When calling the *ForwardAsICal* method, the format of the body of the e-mail can be determined by the parameter passed into the method call. Both the daily schedule format and the event list format are supported. Figure 9-1 shows an example of the e-mail message received when using this method.

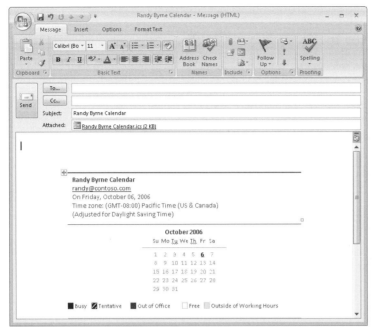

Figure 9-1   An example of a daily schedule format e-mail generated from the object model.

You can customize the information contained in the e-mail by modifying the detail level and other settings. For example, you could only show free/busy information, or just include the subjects of appointments on the calendar instead of the full details.

> **Important**   Calling the *ForwardAsICal* method might take several seconds to complete while Outlook builds the iCalendar information for the calendar. Depending on the size of the calendar and the number of days included, Outlook might become unresponsive to the user for a short period of time. If you anticipate that this will happen when calling the method, you should provide the user with an indication that this is occurring.

Saving a Calendar to Disk

Using the same *CalendarSharing* object you can also save a whole calendar, or a range of appointments from a calendar to disk in an Internet Calendaring and Scheduling (ICS) file. Outlook will automatically optimize the ICS file so that recurring appointments are expressed as recurring appointments in the ICS and not as individual instances, whenever possible.

The process is very much the same as it was for sending a calendar via e-mail. The following code sample obtains an instance of the *CalendarSharing* object from the *Folder* object, sets the appropriate properties for the type of output file, and then calls the *SaveAsICal* method. Instead of exporting just the public details, this time around the code indicates that everything should be saved, including details of items marked as private.

```
public void SaveCalendarToDisk(string calendarFileName)
{
    if (string.IsNullOrEmpty(sendToAddresses))
        throw new ArgumentException(
            "calendarFileName",
            "Parameter must contain a value.");

    Outlook.Folder calendar = Application.Session.GetDefaultFolder(
        Outlook.OlDefaultFolders.olFolderCalendar) as Outlook.Folder;
    Outlook.CalendarSharing exporter = calendar.GetCalendarExporter();

    // Set the properties for the export
    exporter.CalendarDetail = Outlook.OlCalendarDetail.olFullDetails;
    exporter.IncludeAttachments = true;
    exporter.IncludePrivateDetails = true;
    exporter.RestrictToWorkingHours = false;
    exporter.IncludeWholeCalendar = true;

    // Save the calendar to disk
    exporter.SaveAsICal(calendarFileName);
}
```

> **Important**   Saving a calendar to disk can take a noticeable amount of time depending on the size of the calendar being saved. While the command is executing, the Outlook window will appear unresponsive to the user. If the calendar you are saving is large enough, you should warn the user before you execute this command.

Saving an Appointment to Disk

You can also save single-instance appointments and recurring appointments to individual appointment iCalendar files using the *SaveAs* method on the *AppointmentItem* object. This method can be used to serialize the properties of an appointment into a standard format that is readable by other programs.

The following code saves the first appointment in the default Calendar folder to disk as an iCalendar file:

```
public void ExportAppointmentToDisk(string exportFileName))
{
    if (string.IsNullOrEmpty(sendToAddresses))
        throw new ArgumentException(
            "exportFileName",
            "Parameter must contain a value.");

    Outlook.Folder calendar = Application.Session.GetDefaultFolder(
        Outlook.OlDefaultFolders.olFolderCalendar) as Outlook.Folder;

    // Check to see if this is an appointment item; if it's not we do nothing
    OutlookItem item = new OutlookItem(calendar.Items[1]);
    if (item.Class != Outlook.OlObjectClass.olAppointment)
```

```
        return;

    Outlook.AppointmentItem appointment = item.InnerObject as Outlook.AppointmentItem;
    appointment.SaveAs(exportFileName, Outlook.OlSaveAsType.olICal);
}
```

When saving an appointment to disk in the iCalendar format, some properties (including all custom properties) are stripped from the item because they are not supported in the iCalendar format. To save an appointment without losing custom fields and some Outlook-specific information, you should save the item as an Outlook Message (MSG) file by changing the second parameter of the *SaveAs* method to *Outlook.OlSaveAsType.olMSG*.

Opening an iCalendar File

Reading iCalendar format files can be a little trickier than writing those files to disk. Outlook treats iCalendar files that contain a single or recurring appointment or meeting in one way, and a file that contains a group of appointments in another. You need to use two different methods depending on the contents of the file. However, because the contents are not always known before you attempt to load the file, your code for loading an iCalendar file should be robust enough to handle the error case.

The following method opens either type of iCalendar file and displays the resulting item or folder to the user. For iCalendar files that contain multiple appointments, the contents are imported as a new calendar in the default store. For single-appointment iCalendar files, an Inspector window is displayed with the item details, but the item is not copied into the default store. After performing basic validation on the input, this code block attempts to open the file as an item first. If this fails, it then attempts to open the file as a list of items. If either method succeeds, the resulting item or folder is displayed to the user.

```
public void OpenICalendarFile(string fileName)
{
    if (string.IsNullOrEmpty(sendToAddresses))
        throw new ArgumentException(
            "exportFileName",
            "Parameter must contain a value.");
    if (!File.Exists(fileName))
        throw new FileNotFoundException(fileName);

    // First try to open the iCalendar file as an appointment (not a calendar folder).
    object item = null;
    try
    {
        item = Application.Session.OpenSharedItem(fileName);
    }
    catch
    {}

    if (item != null)
    {
        // Display the item
```

```
        OutlookItem olItem = new OutlookItem(item);
        olItem.Display();
        return;
    }

    // If unsuccessful in opening it as an item, try opening it as a folder
    Outlook.Folder importedFolder = null;
    try
    {
        importedFolder = Application.Session.OpenSharedFolder(fileName,
            Type.Missing, Type.Missing, Type.Missing) as Outlook.Folder;
    }
    catch
    { }

    // If successful, open the folder in a new Explorer window
    if (importedFolder != null)
    {
        Outlook.Explorer explorer =
            Application.Explorers.Add(importedFolder,
            Outlook.OlFolderDisplayMode.olFolderDisplayNormal);
        explorer.Display();
    }
}
```

Subscribing to Shared Folders

Outlook 2007 has a new emphasis on providing access to shared data, such as Internet calendars, RSS feeds, and data from Microsoft SharePoint lists and document libraries. The object model includes new functionality to enable connecting to these shared sources of data and setting up the synchronization contexts to continue to poll those shared resources.

The next three sections explain using the *NameSpace.OpenSharedFolder* method to download and synchronize with a particular type of shared folder.

RSS Feeds

Subscribing to a new RSS feed is a straightforward process through the object model. Calling *OpenSharedFolder* on the *NameSpace* object with a Uniform Resource Locator (URL) that refers to a valid RSS feed is all that is necessary. It is also possible to customize properties of the subscription by specifying other properties in the *OpenSharedFolder* method. You can provide a name for the subscription, specify if attachments should be downloaded, and determine if Outlook should use the refresh ratio provided in the RSS feed.

```
public void AddRssFeed()
{
    string feedUrl = "feed://example.org/rssfeed.xml";
    Outlook.Folder subscriptionFolder =
        Application.Session.OpenSharedFolder(feedUrl,
        "Example RSS Feed", true, true) as Outlook.Folder;
```

```
Outlook.Explorer exp =
    Application.Explorers.Add(subscriptionFolder,
    Outlook.OlFolderDisplayMode.olFolderDisplayNormal);
exp.Display();
}
```

In this example, the default title provided by the RSS feed is overridden with "Example RSS Feed," and the feed is configured to download attachments automatically and respect the time-to-live (TTL) of the RSS feed.

Moving an RSS feed folder is as simple as moving the folder returned by the call to *OpenSharedFolder*. Outlook automatically updates the synchronization destination to match the new location of the folder at the next sharing reconciliation opportunity, and items are delivered to the correct location. You cannot, however, move a folder while a send/receive operation on that folder is in progress. Because Outlook immediately starts to download feed items after a call to *OpenSharedFolder*, you might need to wait until that operation is complete to move the folder.

> **Important**   The *OpenSharedFolder* method requires that the correct protocol handler be specified on the folder URL. For instance, you cannot use a URL that begins with *http://* for an RSS feed; you must instead use the *feed://* URL. Outlook cannot open RSS feeds that require authentication unless Windows NT LAN Manager (NTLM) authentication is available, and it cannot load RSS feeds from secure (Secure Sockets Layer [SSL]) locations.

SharePoint Folders

Connecting to a SharePoint folder with the object model is just a straightforward use of the *OpenSharedFolder* method on the *NameSpace* object. To open a SharePoint folder, a special URL is required. This URL uses the *stssync:* protocol to provide details on the SharePoint server, folder path, and other details that Outlook needs in order to create the synchronization relationship.

Outlook supports synchronizing SharePoint folders for calendars, contact lists, task lists, discussion boards, and document libraries. Based on information in the URL provided, Outlook will create a new folder of the same base type as the SharePoint folder. For instance, a SharePoint calendar folder will create a new calendar folder in Outlook when replicated. SharePoint synchronized folders are stored in their own Outlook Personal Folders File (PST) outside of the user's mailbox.

To automate the synchronization of a new SharePoint folder in Outlook, use the *NameSpace.OpenSharedFolder* method and provide the *stssync://* URL. You can provide a custom folder name and specify if Outlook should use the default TTL for the folder. SharePoint folders always download item attachments.

```
public void AddSpsFolder()
{
    string calendarUrl = "stssync://sts/?ver=1.1&type=calendar&cmd=add-folder&" +
        "base-url=http://example.org/calendar&" +
         "list-url=/Lists/Calendar/calendar.aspx&" +
        "guid=&site-name=Example%20Site&list-name=Calendar";
    string folderName = "Example SPS Calendar";
    bool useDefaultTTL = true;

    Outlook.Folder calendarFolder =
        Application.Session.OpenSharedFolder(calendarUrl,
            folderName, Type.Missing, useDefaultTTL) as Outlook.Folder;
    Outlook.Explorer exp =
        Application.Explorers.Add(calendarFolder,
            Outlook.OlFolderDisplayMode.olFolderDisplayNormal);
    exp.Display();
}
```

Locating the SharePoint Sync URL

One of the more difficult parts of connecting to a SharePoint folder programmatically is deter-mining the proper URL to create the sharing relationship. The *stssync://* URL is not provided in the SharePoint user interface for the folder. The format is documented, but constructing the right URL can be painful. One easier way to obtain the right URL for a folder is to manually link the destination folder into Outlook, and then use the following code to display the correct URL:

```
public void DisplaySharePointUrl()
{
    const string PROP_SYNC_URL =
        "http://schemas.microsoft.com/mapi/id/" +
        "{00062040-0000-0000-C000-000000000046}/8A24001E";

    Outlook.Folder folder = Application.ActiveExplorer()
        .CurrentFolder as Outlook.Folder;

    Outlook.Table table = folder.GetTable(Type.Missing,
        Outlook.OlTableContents.olHiddenItems);
    table.Columns.RemoveAll();
    table.Columns.Add("MessageClass");
    table.Columns.Add(PROP_SYNC_URL);

    StringBuilder sb = new StringBuilder();
    while (!table.EndOfTable)
    {
        Outlook.Row row = table.GetNextRow();

        string msgClass, spsUrl;
        msgClass = row["MessageClass"] as string;
        spsUrl = row[PROP_SYNC_URL] as string;

        if (msgClass == "IPM.Sharing.Binding.In")
        {
            sb.Append(spsUrl);
```

```
            sb.Append("\r\n");
        }
    }

    if (sb.Length > 0)
    {
        System.Windows.Forms.MessageBox.Show(
          "The following SharePoint Folder URLs were found:\r\n" +
          sb.ToString());
    }
    else
    {
        System.Windows.Forms.MessageBox.Show(
          "No SharePoint URLs were found in this folder.");
    }
}
```

This example code block uses Outlook's new *Table* object to look for the sharing binding information in the current folder for the active Explorer window. If more than one binding context is found, it will display the URLs for all available sharing contexts.

After running this code against a folder, you can copy and paste the URL and use it in your solution to open that SharePoint folder again later.

Internet Calendars

Subscribing to a new Internet calendar is just a matter of calling the *OpenSharedFolder* method with the correct URL for the Internet calendar. Similar to RSS feeds, when subscribing to an Internet calendar you can provide an alternative title and specify if Outlook should download attachments and respect the TTL of the calendar. The following function adds an example Internet calendar, keeping the default calendar name provided but specifying that attachments are downloaded and the TTL is respected. Once the folder is created, the function displays it to the user in a new Explorer window.

```
public void AddWebCalendar()
{
    string calendarUrl = "webcal://example.org/mycaledar.ics";
    Outlook.Folder calendarFolder =
        Application.Session.OpenSharedFolder(calendarUrl, Type.Missing, true, true)
        as Outlook.Folder;
    Outlook.Explorer exp =
        Application.Explorers.Add(calendarFolder,
        Outlook.OlFolderDisplayMode.olFolderDisplayNormal);
    exp.Display();
}
```

Important   The *OpenSharedFolder* method requires that the correct protocol handler be specified on the folder URL. For instance, you cannot use a URL that begins with *http://* for an Internet calendar; you must instead use the *webcal://* protocol. Outlook cannot open Internet calendars that require authentication unless NTLM authentication is available, and it cannot load calendars from secure (SSL) locations.

Using the *SharingItem* Object

The *SharingItem* object represents both sharing requests and sharing invitations, a new feature of Outlook 2007. These sharing items enable users to easily request access to a shared folder on an Exchange server or to notify other users of shared folder availability. Sharing invitations can be sent for SharePoint folders, Exchange folders, RSS feeds, and Internet calendars. Sharing requests only work to request access to default folders in an Exchange user's mailbox. Figure 9-2 shows an example sharing invitation for an Exchange folder.

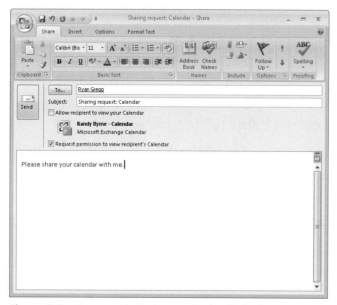

Figure 9-2 An example Exchange sharing invitation.

One benefit of sending a sharing invitation for an Exchange folder is that Outlook will generate the proper permissions for the recipients of the sharing invitation automatically. This feature enables developers to use the object model to add permissions to shared folders, which previously was unavailable using the object model.

SharingItem objects are created differently from other item types in Outlook. To create a *SharingItem* object, you need to use the *NameSpace.CreateSharingItem* method and provide the context for the sharing item and, optionally, a provider to use. The context must be either a *Folder* object or a URL string. If the provider is not specified, Outlook will use the default provider for the context.

Although created differently, the *SharingItem* object inherits most of the behavior of the *MailItem* object. You can work with a *SharingItem* object in much the same way as a *MailItem* object. One exception to this inheritance is that using the *CC* or *BCC* properties or recipient types on *SharingItem* objects using the Exchange provider will cause the item to fail to be sent. Only the *To* property is supported with the Exchange provider.

SharingItem Types

Each *SharingItem* object can represent a sharing invitation, a sharing request, or both. Sharing invitations provide information to the user that a shared resource is available—either an Exchange user's folder, RSS feed, Web calendar subscription, or an iCalendar resource. Sharing requests ask the user to share a default folder with another user, and are only available for mailboxes on an Exchange server.

The *Type* property on the *SharingItem* object allows you to determine the kind of sharing message. A *SharingItem* object can represent a sharing invitation (*olSharingMsgTypeInvite*), a sharing request (*olSharingMsgTypeRequest*), a hybrid invitation and request (*olSharingMsgTypeInviteAndRequest*), or a response from a sharing request (*olSharingMsgTypeResponseAllow* or *olSharingMsgTypeResponseDeny*). When creating a new *SharingItem*, you can set the *Type* property to the invite, request, or invite and request states, but you cannot set the type as a response. To create a response sharing item, use the *Allow* or *Deny* methods on a received *SharingItem* object.

Sharing a Folder with a Sharing Invitation

Sharing a folder on Exchange through the object model is a simple operation with Outlook 2007. To share a folder, you only need to create a new *SharingItem* object, address it to the intended recipient, and then call the item's *Send* method. When the *SharingItem* object is sent, Outlook will assign appropriate permissions to the recipients of the message. Using a *SharingItem* object to set permissions also has the benefit of notifying the recipients that they now have permission to access a shared resource.

This method creates a new sharing invitation for the user's default calendar folder, and sends the item to another user on the same Exchange server:

```
public void SendInvitationForCalendar()
{
    Outlook.Folder myCalendar = Application.Session.GetDefaultFolder(
        Outlook.OlDefaultFolders.olFolderCalendar) as Outlook.Folder;

    Outlook.SharingItem sItem =
        Application.Session.CreateSharingItem(myCalendar,
        Outlook.OlSharingProvider.olProviderExchange);

    sItem.Recipients.Add("user@example.org").Resolve();
    sItem.Type = Outlook.OlSharingMsgType.olSharingMsgTypeInvite;
    sItem.Subject = "I'm sharing my calendar with you";
    sItem.Body = "Here, you now have access to read my calendar!";
    sItem.Send();
}
```

By default, Outlook will grant all the *SharingItem* object's recipients Reviewer permissions (read-only) when the item is sent. If you are sharing a nondefault folder and would like to specify that recipients have both read and write permissions to the folder, you can set the *AllowWriteAccess* property.

```
// Provide write access to the recipients
sItem.AllowWriteAccess = true;
```

If any of the recipients are not Exchange users, the *Send* method will fail and the *SharingItem* object will not be sent to any recipients. For calendar folders, you can use the *CalendarExporter* class to send a copy of the calendar to the user. For more information, see the section "Sharing a Calendar Through E-Mail" earlier in this chapter.

Requesting Folder Access with a Sharing Request

A *SharingItem* object can also be used to request access to a default folder in another user's mailbox on an Exchange server. When a user attempts to open a shared folder and fails because of a lack of permissions, Outlook prompts the user to determine if the user wishes to send a sharing request for that folder. If you are developing a custom solution that connects to shared folders using *NameSpace.GetSharedDefaultFolder*, you don't automatically get this behavior, but it is easy to add to your solution. When the user receives a sharing request, he or she can elect to allow or deny access to the shared folder, and a response can be sent back to the requesting user in the form of a response sharing item.

The process of creating a sharing request works much like a sharing invitation. To create a new *SharingItem* object, you make a call to *NameSpace.CreateSharingItem* and provide the context of the sharing item. For a sharing request, because you do not yet have access to the user's shared folder, you provide a reference to the default folder in your mailbox of the same type you are requesting. For example, if you are trying to access a user's default task folder, you would provide a reference to your default task folder, as shown here:

```
public void RequestTaskFolderAccess()
{
    // Provide your task folder as the context
    Outlook.Folder taskContext = Application.Session.GetDefaultFolder(
        Outlook.OlDefaultFolders.olFolderTasks) as Outlook.Folder;

    Outlook.SharingItem request = Application.Session.CreateSharingItem(
        taskContext, Outlook.OlSharingProvider.olProviderExchange);
    // Set to request access to the user's default task folder
    request.Type = Outlook.OlSharingMsgType.olSharingMsgTypeRequest;

    // Add recipient
    request.Recipients.Add("user@example.org").Resolve();

    // Set the subject and body
    request.Subject = "Please share your tasks with me";
    request.Body = "Would you please allow me to access your task folder";

    request.Send();
}
```

If any of the recipients for the sharing request are not Exchange recipients, the call to *Send* will fail with an error indicating that some of the recipients are invalid. Sharing requests are only supported to Exchange recipients.

Processing a Sharing Item

A single *SharingItem* object in the Inbox can actually represent a number of different possibilities, based on the *Type* property of the *SharingItem* object. It could represent an invitation to access a shared folder, a request to share a folder, or a response from a previous request. Based on the *Type* property, you can determine the correct course of action for the item and which methods and properties are valid for that item. Hybrid sharing items, those that are both a sharing invitation and a sharing request, should be handled in accordance with both sets of guidelines.

Sharing Invitations

SharingItem objects that have a *Type* property equal to either *olSharingMsgTypeInvite* or *olSharingMsgTypeInviteAndRequest* can be used to connect to a shared resource. To determine the type of resource you have been invited to access, examine the properties on the *SharingItem* object in Table 9-1.

Table 9-1   Important Properties on the *SharingItem* Object

Property name	Description	Example
SharingProvider	Indicates the type of resource being shared	The value determines the provider being used; for example, *olProviderExchange* indicates that the resource is a folder from an Exchange mailbox, *olProviderRSS* indicates an RSS feed, and *olProviderWebCal* indicates an Internet calendar subscription.
RemotePath	Provides the path to the remote resource	For an Exchange provider, this will represent a value to the folder, such as \\Mailbox - User\Calendar. For RSS or Internet calendar providers, this is the URL that contains the shared resource.
RemoteName	The name provided to the remote resource, typically the name of the folder	If the sharing message is for the default contacts folder from a user running an English version of Outlook, this would return Contacts.

To open the shared folder, you can call the *OpenSharedFolder* method on the *SharingItem* object. This connects to the shared resource and returns a *Folder* object for the shared folder. The folder is also added to the user's Navigation Pane in the appropriate place.

An example of this in action is provided next. In this example, the code looks for all *SharingItem* objects in the Inbox and enumerates them. For each *SharingItem* object, if it is a sharing invitation or an invitation and request, it checks to see if the provider is RSS. If the provider is RSS, it looks at the feed URL to see if it is on the *blogs.msdn.com* Web site. If these conditions are met, it opens the folder, thereby importing the RSS feed.

```
public void AddMsdnRssFeeds()
{
    Outlook.Folder inbox = Application.Session.GetDefaultFolder(
        Outlook.OlDefaultFolders.olFolderInbox) as Outlook.Folder;

    Outlook.Items sharingItems =
        inbox.Items.Restrict("[MessageClass] = 'IPM.Sharing'");
    foreach (object item in sharingItems)
    {
        Outlook.SharingItem sItem = item as Outlook.SharingItem;
        if (sItem == null) continue;

        if (sItem.Type == Outlook.OlSharingMsgType.olSharingMsgTypeInvite ||
            sItem.Type ==
            Outlook.OlSharingMsgType.olSharingMsgTypeInviteAndRequest)
        {
            // Accept incoming RSS feeds for MSDN blog feeds
            if (sItem.SharingProvider ==
                Outlook.OlSharingProvider.olProviderRSS &&
                sItem.RemotePath.StartsWith("http://blogs.msdn.com/"))
            {
                sItem.OpenSharedFolder();
                sItem.Delete();
            }
        }
    }
}
```

Sharing Requests

If the *SharingItem* object's *Type* property is equal to either *olSharingMsgTypeRequest* or *olSharingMsgTypeInviteAndRequest*, it can be considered a request to share the contents of a folder in the current user's mailbox. Before determining the action to take on the *SharingItem* object, either allowing the request or denying it, you should examine the *RequestedFolder* property to determine to which folder the new permissions will be applied.

The method provided here will look through the Inbox to find all sharing items, and then for each sharing request look to see if the request is for the Tasks folder. If the request is for the user's Tasks folder, it will allow access and then delete the item.

```
public void ProcessSharingItems()
{
    Outlook.Folder inbox = Application.Session.GetDefaultFolder(
        Outlook.OlDefaultFolders.olFolderInbox) as Outlook.Folder;

    Outlook.Items sharingItems
        = inbox.Items.Restrict("[MessageClass] = 'IPM.Sharing'");
    foreach (object item in sharingItems)
    {
        Outlook.SharingItem sItem = item as Outlook.SharingItem;
        if (sItem == null) continue;
```

```
            if (sItem.Type == Outlook.OlSharingMsgType.olSharingMsgTypeRequest ||
                sItem.Type == Outlook.OlSharingMsgType.olSharingMsgTypeInviteAndRequest)
            {
                // Accept requests for the task folder automatically
                if (sItem.RequestedFolder == Outlook.OlDefaultFolders.olFolderTasks)
                {
                    sItem.Allow();
                    sItem.Delete();
                }
            }
        }
    }
}
```

Sharing Responses

Sharing items that represent responses to a request are useful for informational purposes, but cannot be acted on. These types of *SharingItem* objects can be identified by checking the *Type* property to determine if it is equal to *olSharingMsgTypeResponseAllow* or *olSharingMsgTypeResponseDeny*. You can combine this with the *From* property to understand which recipient has responded to a previous request and how the recipient responded.

Summary

In this chapter, you've learned more about Outlook and the new concepts around sharing introduced with Outlook 2007. You've also seen how to connect to RSS feeds, Internet calendars, and SharePoint folders, and how to open and save individual items and calendar folders to a file. For more information on working with the data in these shared folders once they are connected, see Chapter 6, "Accessing Outlook Data."

Chapter 10
Organizing Outlook Data

When you complete this chapter, you should have a good understanding of the following areas:

- Overview of organizing information in Microsoft Office Outlook 2007
- Using categories and task flagging
- Creating rules programmatically
- Writing code to create a search folder
- Customizing views with new View objects

How Outlook 2007 Helps to Organize Information

Outlook 2007 introduces several new features that help to organize the constantly growing number of items that arrive in a user's Inbox. Category colors and task flagging are easy to use and provide a simple tool for getting organized. Organizational schemes for mailbox items are almost as varied as the number of Outlook users. The focus of this chapter is not to prescribe the best method of organizing Outlook data. Rather, you'll learn how to use the Outlook object model to implement organizational schemes programmatically. The good news for developers is that the Outlook object model supports all the new organizational features of Outlook 2007. By writing a few lines of code, you can add color categories to items, mark items for follow-up, create rules, build custom search folders, or add views.

The *Categories* Collection and *Category* Objects

Outlook 2007 provides color categorization functionality in which Outlook items can be categorized and displayed by category. Multiple color categories can be applied to a single Outlook item, and Outlook items can be grouped or sorted by color category. Shortcut keys can be assigned to each color category to allow users to more easily categorize items. Color categories are user defined, and can be created, deleted, and changed either programmatically or by user action within the Outlook user interface.

The *Category* object represents a single user-defined color category in the master category list, the list of color categories presented in the Outlook user interface and represented by the *Categories* collection of the *NameSpace* object. Unlike previous versions of Outlook, Outlook 2007 stores the master category list in the default store so that it will roam by default in most scenarios, as is the case with an Exchange mailbox. *Category* objects are identified with a globally unique identifier (GUID) when created, and this identifier cannot be changed. However, you can change the name, color, and shortcut key associated with a color category by setting the *Name*, *Color*, and *ShortcutKey* properties of the *Category* object. The *CategoryID* property can be used to retrieve the identifier of a *Category* object.

Outlook items are displayed based on the category name stored in the *Categories* property of that Outlook item. The *Categories* property gets or sets a comma-delimited string of category names. It does not return a *Categories* collection object. Because category names are stored as part of the Outlook item, it is possible to add a category to an Outlook item that is not present in the master category list. For example, a category might have been removed. To determine if a category exists in the master category list, use the following *CategoryExists* method:

```
private bool CategoryExists(string categoryName)
{
    try
    {
        Outlook.Category category =
            Application.Session.Categories[categoryName];
        if (category != null)
        {
            return true;
        }
        else
        {
            return false;
        }
    }
    catch { return false; }
}
```

> **Note**   If the *Categories* property of an item contains a category name that does not exist in the *Categories* collection of the *Namespace* object, then the category name associated with that Outlook item is displayed, but without an associated color.

The following code sample enumerates the *Category* objects in the *Categories* collection and writes the *Name* and *CategoryID* properties to the trace listeners in the *Listeners* collection:

```
private void EnumerateCategories()
{
    Outlook.Categories categories =
        Application.Session.Categories;
    foreach (Outlook.Category category in categories)
    {
        Debug.WriteLine(category.Name);
        Debug.WriteLine(category.CategoryID);
    }
}
```

> ## Category Colors
>
> The *Category* object exposes a *Color* property that lets you set or get an *olCategoryColor* constant. If you need to reproduce the color in a custom control, you can use these read-only properties of the *Category* object:
>
> - *CategoryBorderColor*
> - *CategoryGradientBottomColor*
> - *CategoryGradientTopColor*
>
> These properties return an OLE_COLOR value, which is dependent on the *Color* property of the *Category* object. For an advanced example of how to use *CategoryBorderColor*, *CategoryGradientBottomColor*, and *CategoryGradientTopColor*, see *ColorSwatchBuilder.cs* or *ColorSwatchBuilder.vb* in the PrepareMe sample add-in that accompanies this book.

Creating a Category

To create a category programmatically, you call the *Add* method of the *Categories* collection. If the ISV category does not exist, the following code sample adds a category named ISV to the master category list and assigns the dark blue color to this category. It also assigns Ctrl+F11 as the shortcut key for the category.

```
private void AddACategory()
{
    Outlook.Categories categories =
        Application.Session.Categories;
    if(!CategoryExists("ISV"))
    {
        Outlook.Category category = categories.Add("ISV",
            Outlook.OlCategoryColor.olCategoryColorDarkBlue,
            Outlook.OlCategoryShortcutKey.olCategoryShortcutKeyCtrlF11);
    }
}
```

Assigning One or More Categories to an Item

To assign categories to an item, use the *Categories* property on the item. The *Categories* property gets or sets a comma-delimited string that contains all of the categories assigned to the item. This property can contain a maximum of 255 characters, including the commas and spaces, to separate the category values. If you assign a category that is not in the *Categories* collection of the *Namespace* object, that category will not display a color. The following code sample creates a restriction for items that contain "ISV" in the subject. This code sample uses a *for* loop and the *OutlookItem* class to assign the ISV category to any item in the Inbox that contains "ISV" in the subject. Notice that the code sample examines the string returned by *item.Categories* to determine if the *Categories* property is empty or already has been assigned to the ISV category.

```
private void AssignCategories()
{
    string filter = "@SQL=" + "\"" + "urn:schemas:httpmail:subject"
        + "\"" + " ci_phrasematch 'ISV'";
    Outlook.Items items =
        Application.Session.GetDefaultFolder(
        Outlook.OlDefaultFolders.olFolderInbox).Items.Restrict(filter);
    for(int i = 1; i<=items.Count; i++)
    {
        OutlookItem item = new OutlookItem(items[i]);
        string existingCategories = item.Categories;
        if(String.IsNullOrEmpty(existingCategories))
        {
            item.Categories = "ISV";
        }
        else
        {
            if (item.Categories.Contains("ISV") == false)
            {
                item.Categories = existingCategories + ", ISV";
            }
        }
        item.Save();
    }
}
```

Displaying the Categories Dialog Box

The Outlook object model also provides the *ShowCategoriesDialog* method on an item to display the Categories dialog box, shown in Figure 10-1. This dialog box lets the user pick one or more categories that are assigned to the item. The user can also create new categories or clear existing categories with this dialog box. In the following code sample from the sample RulesAddin project that accompanies this book, a dummy mail item is created and the *ShowCategoriesDialog* method is called on the item. In this case, the categories selected by the user are displayed in an edit box and used to create a categories rule.

```
private void cmdCategory_Click(object sender, EventArgs e)
{
    try
    {
        //Create a dummy MailItem and display Categories dialog box
        Outlook.MailItem oMail = (Outlook.MailItem)m_olApp.CreateItem(
            Outlook.OlItemType.olMailItem);
        if (!string.IsNullOrEmpty(txtCategory.Text))
        {
            oMail.Categories = txtCategory.Text;
        }
        oMail.ShowCategoriesDialog();
        Application.DoEvents();
```

```
        if (!string.IsNullOrEmpty(oMail.Categories))
        {
            txtCategory.Text = oMail.Categories;
            chkCategory.Checked = true;
        }
        oMail = null;
    }
    catch(Exception ex)
    {
        LogMessage("cmdCategory_Click: "
            + ex.ToString() , EventLogEntryType.Error);
    }
}
```

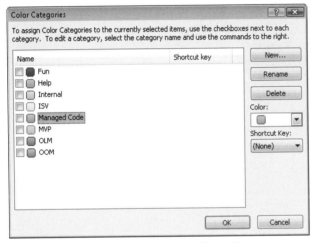

Figure 10-1   Display the Categories dialog box programmatically.

Task Flagging

Outlook 2007 provides a new task flagging system in which certain Outlook items such as mail items or contact items can be flagged for follow-up. Flagging an Outlook item for follow-up displays information about that Outlook item, along with other task-based information, on the To-Do Bar and Calendar navigation module in the Outlook user interface.

Controlling Visibility of the To-Do Bar

The To-Do Bar is displayed as a vertical pane in a typical configuration of the Outlook Explorer window. It contains a date navigator control, upcoming appointments, and items that have been flagged for follow-up. The To-Do Bar itself is not extensible, and configuration options for the To-Do Bar can only be set through the Outlook user interface. You can programmatically change the visibility of the To-Do Bar using the *ShowPane* method of the *Explorer* object.

Creating To-Do Items That Appear in the To-Do Bar

Creating to-do items programmatically is covered in the section "Create a To-Do Item" in Chapter 5, "Built-in Item Types." Any item that is flagged for follow-up will appear in the To-Do Bar. As an organizational technique, item flagging creates a well-defined scheme for prioritizing tasks and to-do items. You should understand how to mark a group of items for a specified follow-up interval. The following code example processes all items in the user's Inbox that are from the user's manager and flags all high-importance items for follow-up today. If the item's importance is normal, then the item is flagged for follow-up this week.

```
private void DemoTaskFlagging()
{
    const string PR_SENT_REPRESENTING_NAME =
        "http://schemas.microsoft.com/mapi/proptag/0x0042001E";
    const string PR_MESSAGE_CLASS =
        "http://schemas.microsoft.com/mapi/proptag/0x001A001E";
    Outlook.AddressEntry currentUser =
        Application.Session.CurrentUser.AddressEntry;
    if (currentUser.Type == "EX")
    {
        Outlook.ExchangeUser manager;
        try
        {
            manager = currentUser.
                GetExchangeUser().GetExchangeUserManager();
        }
        catch
        {
            Debug.WriteLine("Could not obtain user's manager.");
            return;
        }
        if (manager != null)
        {
            string displayName = manager.Name;
            string filter = "@SQL=" + "\""
            + PR_SENT_REPRESENTING_NAME + "\""
            + " = '" + displayName + "'" + " AND " + "\""
            + PR_MESSAGE_CLASS + "\"" + " = 'IPM.NOTE'";
            Outlook.Items items =
                Application.Session.GetDefaultFolder(
                Outlook.OlDefaultFolders.olFolderInbox).
                Items.Restrict(filter);
            foreach(Outlook.MailItem mail in items)
            {
                if (mail.Importance ==
                    Outlook.OlImportance.olImportanceHigh)
                {
                    mail.MarkAsTask(
                        Outlook.OlMarkInterval.olMarkToday);
                    mail.Save();
                }
                if (mail.Importance ==
                    Outlook.OlImportance.olImportanceNormal)
                {
```

```
            mail.MarkAsTask(
                Outlook.OlMarkInterval.olMarkThisWeek);
            mail.Save();
        }
      }
    }
  }
}
```

The *Rules* Collection and *Rule* Objects

Because they can operate either server-side or client-side, depending on the type of account and rule, Outlook rules provide one of the most powerful Outlook features for organizing information in a user's mailbox. Users implement rules to enforce their own organizational schemes. For example, some users like to create a hive of subfolders that contain unread mail and read mail by subject area. Other users might create a subfolder hierarchy that corresponds to the sender of the message. Still others categorize their mail and then use search folders to aggregate the mail by category. As stated at the beginning of this chapter, users follow a multiplicity of schemes when they organize the items in their mailboxes. The new Rules object model in Outlook 2007 allows you as a developer to participate in the power of rules. You can create rules programmatically to enforce a certain organizational scheme, create a specific rule that is unique to your solution, or ensure that certain rules are deployed to a group of users.

The Rules object model supports the programmatic adding, editing, and deleting of rules. The *Rules* collection and *Rule* objects allow you to access, add, and delete rules defined for a session. The *RuleAction* and *RuleCondition* objects, their collection objects, and derived action and condition objects further support editing actions and conditions.

Note   The Rules object model provides partial parity with the Rules and Alerts Wizard in the Outlook user interface. Although it does not support every single rule that you can possibly create using the wizard, it supports the most commonly used rule actions and conditions. Just like any rule created using the Rules and Alerts Wizard, rules created programmatically are applied to messages, which include mail items, meeting requests, task requests, documents, delivery receipts, read receipts, voting responses, and out-of-office notices.

Overview of Rules Programming

Creating one or more rules programmatically is straightforward once you understand the architecture of the Rules object model. Figure 10-2 illustrates the basic architecture of the Rules object model. Note that there is no separate collection that represents rule exception conditions. Rule exception conditions are accessed through the *Exceptions* property of the *Rule* object. The *Exceptions* property returns a *RuleCollections* object.

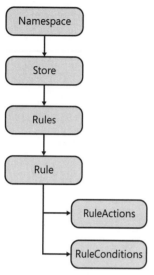

Figure 10-2   Rules object model architecture.

Now that you understand the architecture of the *Rules* objects, it's time to move on to practical coding instructions. From a top-level perspective, follow these steps when you create rules through the Outlook object model:

1. Obtain the *Rules* collection from the *DefaultStore* property of the *Namespace* object. Call the *GetRules* method on *DefaultStore* to obtain the *Rules* collection. You should write this code in a *try...catch* block because Outlook will raise an error if the user is offline or disconnected from the Exchange server.

2. Call the *Create* method on the *Rules* object to create an instance variable for a *Rule* object. When you call the *Create* method, you specify a *Name* and a *RuleType* parameter. *RuleType* determines whether the *Rule* object is a send or receive rule. Send rules operate on outgoing messages and receive rules operate on incoming messages. You cannot change the *RuleType* property after the *Rule* object has been created. If you apply inappropriate conditions to a *Rule* instance (such as a *NewItemAlert* action to a send rule), Outlook raises an error when you call the *Save* method on the *Rules* collection.

3. Use the *RulesActions* and *RuleConditions* collections to enable actions, conditions, and exceptions on the *Rule* object. Note that the *Exceptions* property on a *Rule* object returns a *RuleConditions* collection, and any condition enabled in this collection is treated as a rule exception condition. These collection objects represent static collections, meaning that you cannot add additional built-in or custom actions or conditions to the collection.

4. For any given *Rule* action, condition, or exception to be operational, you must first set its *Enabled* property to *true*. For some actions or conditions, this is all that you have to do. For other actions or conditions, such as the *MoveOrCopyRuleAction.Folder* property, you must set additional properties on the action or condition to save the *Rule* object without an error.

5. Finally, you call the *Save* method on the *Rules* collection to persist the created or modified rules to storage. Again, it is recommended that you enclose the *Save* method in a *try...catch* block to handle exceptions.

Next you'll see a detailed code sample that implements the steps just described. If the *CurrentUser* property represents an *ExchangeUser* object, the *CreateManagerRule* procedure obtains the *ExchangeUser* object for the manager of the *CurrentUser* property of the *Namespace* object. The *Rules* object model is used to create a receive rule that moves received messages to a subfolder of the Inbox if the message is from the user's manager, the recipient is on the To line of the message, and the message is not a meeting request or update. Additionally, the message is marked for follow-up today.

Although this code sample is extensive, it provides you with a great start for understanding how to use the Rules object model. It also illustrates appropriate error handling for conditions that could raise an exception under certain conditions such as the user being offline or disconnected in cached Exchange mode. As you read through the code, notice that each of the steps discussed earlier has been implemented in the code sample.

```csharp
private void CreateManagerRule()
{
    Outlook.ExchangeUser manager;
    Outlook.Folder managerFolder;
    Outlook.AddressEntry currentUser =
        Application.Session.CurrentUser.AddressEntry;
    if (currentUser.Type == "EX")
    {
        try
        {
            manager = currentUser.
                GetExchangeUser().GetExchangeUserManager();
        }
        catch
        {
            Debug.WriteLine("Could not obtain user's manager.");
            return;
        }
        Outlook.Rules rules;
        try
        {
            rules = Application.Session.DefaultStore.GetRules();
        }
        catch
        {
            Debug.WriteLine("Could not obtain rules collection.");
            return;
        }
        if (manager != null)
        {
            string displayName = manager.Name;
            Outlook.Folders folders =
                Application.Session.GetDefaultFolder(
                Outlook.OlDefaultFolders.olFolderInbox).Folders;
```

```
    try
    {
        managerFolder =
            folders[displayName] as Outlook.Folder;
    }
    catch
    {
        managerFolder =
            folders.Add(displayName, Type.Missing)
            as Outlook.Folder;
    }
    Outlook.Rule rule = rules.Create(displayName,
        Outlook.OlRuleType.olRuleReceive);
    //Rule conditions
    //From condition
    rule.Conditions.From.Recipients.Add(
        manager.PrimarySmtpAddress);
    rule.Conditions.From.Recipients.ResolveAll();
    rule.Conditions.From.Enabled = true;
    //Sent only to me
    rule.Conditions.ToMe.Enabled = true;
    //Rule exceptions
    //Meeting invite or update
    rule.Exceptions.MeetingInviteOrUpdate.Enabled = true;
    //Rule actions
    //MarkAsTask action
    rule.Actions.MarkAsTask.MarkInterval =
        Outlook.OlMarkInterval.olMarkToday;
    rule.Actions.MarkAsTask.FlagTo = "Follow-up";
    rule.Actions.MarkAsTask.Enabled = true;
    //MoveToFolder action
    rule.Actions.MoveToFolder.Folder = managerFolder;
    rule.Actions.MoveToFolder.Enabled = true;
    try
    {
        rules.Save(true);
    }
    catch(Exception ex)
    {
        Debug.WriteLine(ex.Message);
    }
        }
    }
}
```

Rules Collection

The *Rules* collection represents a set of *Rule* objects that are the rules available in the current session.

Obtaining the *Rules* Collection

To obtain the *Rules* collection, you call the *GetRules* method on the *DefaultStore* property of the *Namespace* object. For users connected to an Exchange server, calling *GetRules* can be an expensive operation in terms of performance on slow connections.

The order of the *Rule* objects in the collection returned from *GetRules* follows that of *Rule.ExecutionOrder*, with *ExecutionOrder* equal to 1 being the first *Rule* object in the collection and *Rule.ExecutionOrder* equal to *Rules.Count* being the last *Rule* object in the collection.

> **Tip**   You should scope the lifetime of the *Rules* collection to the most constrained possible scope. Outlook enforces "last writer wins" when the *Rules* collection is saved. If another add-in or the Rules and Alerts Wizard modifies rules while your add-in holds onto an instance of the *Rules* collection, you might see unexpected results after you call *Rules.Save.*

Creating a *Rule* Object

To create an instance of a *Rule* object, call the *Create* method on the *Rules* collection. Depending on whether you want to create a send rule or a receive rule, specify an appropriate *OlRuleType* constant to the *Create* method. The *RuleType* parameter of the added rule determines valid rule actions, rule conditions, and rule exception conditions that can be associated with the *Rule* object. Newly created rules are enabled by default. If you want to create the rule and also leave it disabled, you must explicitly set its *Enabled* property to *false.* When a rule is added to the collection, the *Rule.ExecutionOrder* value of the new rule is 1. The *ExecutionOrder* value of other rules in the collection is incremented by 1. The newly created *Rule* object is not persisted until you call the *Save* method on the *Rules* collection. However, you can call the *Execute* method on the *Rule* object before you save the collection.

Enumerating Rules

Use the Indexer to enumerate rules in the *Rules* collection. Once you have obtained a *Rule* object, you can enable or disable the rule by changing its *Enabled* property. You can also modify the existing rule actions, conditions, and exceptions. Finally, you can execute the rule by calling the *Execute* method on the *Rule* object. The following code sample enumerates all the rules in the *Rules* collection and writes the rule's *Name, IsLocalRule,* and *Enabled* properties to the trace listeners in the *Listeners* collection:

```
private void EnumerateRules()
{
    Outlook.Rules rules =
        Application.Session.DefaultStore.GetRules();
    foreach (Outlook.Rule rule in rules)
    {
        StringBuilder sb = new StringBuilder();
        sb.AppendLine("Name: "
```

```
                + rule.Name);
          sb.AppendLine("Local: "
                + rule.IsLocalRule.ToString());
          sb.AppendLine("Enabled: "
                + rule.Enabled.ToString());
          Debug.WriteLine(sb.ToString());
     }
 }
```

Note You can retrieve each rule in a *Rules* collection by indexing the collection using *Rules[Index]*, with *Index* being either the name of the rule (the default property *Rule.Name*), or a value ranging from 1 through the total number of rules in the collection, *Rules.Count.Rule.ExecutionOrder* indicates the order of execution of the rules in the collection and is directly mapped with the numerical value of *Index* in *Rules[Index]*. For example, *Rules[1]* represents a rule with *Rule.ExecutionOrder* being 1, *Rules[2]* represents a rule with *Rule.ExecutionOrder* being 2, and *Rules[Rules.Count]* represents the rule with *Rule.ExecutionOrder* being *Rules.Count*.

RSS Rules Processing

The *Rules* collection exposes an *IsRssRulesProcessingEnabled* property that controls whether RSS rule conditions are evaluated for RSS items. To persist changes to this property, you must call *Rules.Save*. The *IsRssRulesProcessingEnabled* property corresponds to the Enable Rules On All RSS Feeds check box in the Rules And Alerts dialog box, shown in Figure 10-3.

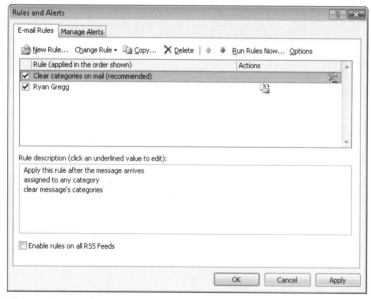

Figure 10-3 Rules And Alerts dialog box.

If you set *IsRssRulesProcessingEnabled* to *true,* you can create RSS rules that operate in a different manner than default RSS rules that move RSS items from a specific feed to a subfolder of the RSS Subscriptions folder. If *IsRssRulesProcessingEnabled* is *false*, then no conditions about RSS feeds will be evaluated during rules processing. To create a rule that operates on RSS items, enable the *FromRssFeed* or *FromAnyRssFeed* rule conditions.

Deleting a Rule

To delete a *Rule*, call the *Remove* method on the *Rules* collection. *Rules.Remove* removes from the *Rules* collection a *Rule* object specified by *Index*, which is either a numerical index into the *Rules* collection or the rule name. You must call *Rules.Save* to persist the deletion.

Saving Rules

You do not save an individual *Rule* object. Instead you must call the *Save* method on the *Rules* collection to save all the *Rule* objects in the collection. After you enable a rule, you must also save the rule by using *Rules.Save* so that the rule and its enabled state will persist beyond the current session. A rule is only enabled after it has been saved successfully.

If you set the *ShowProgress* argument of the *Save* method to *true*, Outlook displays a progress dialog box. If you are saving rules on a slow connection to an Exchange server, *Rules.Save* is an expensive operation in terms of performance. In this circumstance it is advisable to display the progress dialog box; otherwise the user might believe that Outlook has hung.

Handling Errors During a Save Operation

Always place *Rules.Save* in a *try...catch* construct. The connection to the Exchange server can go down, and you must be able to handle this exception. Exchange Server limits the maximum number of rules that can be supported by a store. The rules limit depends on the version of Exchange Server. For Microsoft Exchange Server 2007, an Exchange administrator can also control the rules limit per mailbox. *Rules.Save* returns an error when this limit is reached. The limit is generally not an issue for users running against a Post Office Protocol 3 (POP3) or Internet Message Access Protocol (IMAP) account, because all rules operate locally.

Saving rules that are incompatible or have improperly defined actions or conditions (such as an empty string for *TextRuleCondition.Text* or *MarkAsTaskRuleAction.FlagTo*) will return an error. Some combinations of *RuleActions* and *RuleConditions* are incompatible and will also return an error.

If an error occurs during *Rules.Save,* the entire save operation is rolled back. Modified rules are not saved and newly created or deleted rules are discarded. Unfortunately, the error that bubbles up to your code will not tell you exactly which rules or combination of *RuleActions* and *RuleConditions* caused the error to occur.

The *Rule* Object

The *Rule* object represents an Outlook rule. A *Rule* object has a *RuleType* property that indicates whether the rule is a send or receive rule. *RuleType* is specified when the rule is created. *RuleType* cannot be changed without deleting the rule and re-creating the rule with a different *RuleType* property.

A rule can execute on the Exchange server or on the Outlook client, provided that the current user's mailbox is hosted on an Exchange server. If the rule executes on the server, Outlook does not have to be running for the rule conditions to be evaluated and the rule actions to be completed. If the rule executes on the client, meaning that the *IsLocalRule* property of the *Rule* object returns *true*, then Outlook must be running for the rule to execute.

Executing a Rule

To cause a rule to execute immediately, call the *Execute* method on the *Rule* object. Use *Rule.Execute* to apply a rule as a one-off operation regardless of whether *Rule.Enabled* returns *true*. Use *Rule.Enabled* and then *Rules.Save* if you want to apply the rule consistently and persist the rules beyond the current session. The following code sample executes the rule created in the *CreateManagerRule* procedure shown earlier:

```
private void ExecuteManagerRule()
{
    Outlook.AddressEntry currentUser =
        Application.Session.CurrentUser.AddressEntry;
    if (currentUser.Type == "EX")
    {
        try
        {
            string managerName = currentUser.
                GetExchangeUser().GetExchangeUserManager().Name;
            Outlook.Rule managerRule =
                Application.Session.DefaultStore.GetRules()[managerName];
            if (managerRule != null)
            {
                managerRule.Execute(false, Type.Missing,
                    Type.Missing, Type.Missing);
            }
        }
        catch(Exception ex)
        {
            Debug.WriteLine(ex.Message);
        }
    }
}
```

The parameters to the *Execute* method are optional. If you do not specify any parameters, the rule will be applied to all messages in the Inbox but not to the subfolders of the Inbox. The default values for the optional arguments for the *Execute* method are shown in Table 10-1.

Table 10-1   Parameters for *Rules.Execute*

Parameter	Default value
ShowProgress	False
Folder	Inbox
IncludeSubfolders	False
RuleExecuteOption	OlRuleExecuteOption.olRuleExecuteAllMessages

If *ShowProgress* is *true* and the user cancels the progress dialog box, rule execution is canceled in the same manner as if the user had canceled rule execution through the Rules and Alerts Wizard. *Execute* returns an error when the user cancels the progress dialog box.

If you plan to show a custom progress user interface instead of using the progress dialog box, you should be aware that there are no events that indicate when rule execution starts and stops.

Causing a Rule to Operate Locally

To cause a server-side rule to operate locally, enable the *OnLocalMachine* rule condition. For some rule actions that must run on the client (such as displaying a new mail alert or playing a sound), the *OnLocalMachine* condition will be enabled by default when you set the *Enabled* property to *true* for a client-side only *RuleAction* object. For other rule actions that normally run on the server, you can enable an *OnLocalMachine* condition that will force the rule to run locally on the client. The following code sample illustrates how an *OnLocalMachine* condition forces a server-side rule to run locally. Normally a *Forward* action and *OnlyToMe* condition will operate on the server. In this case they operate as a client-side rule because the *OnLocalMachine* condition has been enabled.

```
private void DemoOnMachineOnly()
{
    Outlook.Rules rules =
        Application.Session.DefaultStore.GetRules();
    Outlook.Rule rule =
        rules.Create("Demo Machine Only Rule",
        Outlook.OlRuleType.olRuleReceive);
    rule.Conditions.OnlyToMe.Enabled = true;
    rule.Actions.Forward.Enabled = true;
    rule.Actions.Forward.Recipients.Add("someone@example.com");
    rule.Actions.Forward.Recipients.ResolveAll();
    //Force the rule to execute locally
    rule.Conditions.OnLocalMachine.Enabled = true;
    rules.Save(true);
}
```

> **Note**   The corollary of enabling the *OnLocalMachine* condition for a rule is that the *OnOtherMachine* condition will be enabled when the same rule is examined from another machine. You cannot programmatically enable or disable a condition of type *olConditionOtherMachine*. This type of rule condition indicates that the rule can run only on a specific computer that is not the current one. This happens when the rule is created on that computer and the *OnLocalMachine* rule condition is enabled, indicating that the rule can run only on that computer. When you run the same rule on another computer, the rule will show that the *OnOtherMachine* rule condition is enabled.

The *RuleActions* Collection

The *RuleActions* collection contains a set of *RuleAction* objects or objects derived from *RuleAction*, representing the actions that are executed on a *Rule* object. The actions exposed on the *RuleActions* collection let you enable or disable the action programmatically by setting the *Enabled* property of a given rule action. The number of rule actions in the *RuleActions* object is fixed.

Although the *RulesActions* collection lets you determine the rule actions that are enabled for a given *Rule* object, not all *RuleAction* objects are supported for programmatic creation of rule actions. For example, you cannot enable a rule action in your code that assigns the *Importance* property to an item. However, your code can recognize a rule action created through the Rules and Alerts Wizard that enables an action that assigns the *Importance* property. In this case, *RuleAction.ActionType* would return *OlRuleActionType.olRuleActionImportance*. You could write code similar to the following to determine that such a rule action exists. Note that you cannot determine the *Importance* value assigned by the rule action.

```
private void ParseImportanceRuleAction()
{
    Outlook.Rules rules =
        Application.Session.DefaultStore.GetRules();
    Outlook.Rule rule =
        rules["Importance Rule"];
    foreach (Outlook.RuleAction ruleAction in rule.Actions)
    {
        if (ruleAction.ActionType ==
            Outlook.OlRuleActionType.olRuleActionImportance)
        {
            Debug.WriteLine(ruleAction.Enabled.ToString());
        }
    }
}
```

Table 10-2 lists all rules actions listed by *OlRuleActionType*. From this table, you can determine which rule actions are supported when creating a rule programmatically by looking at the Valid When Creating New Rules with Code? column. You can also determine which rule actions are valid for receive and send rules.

Table 10-2   Rule Actions by *OlRuleActionType*

Action	Constant in *OlRuleActionType*	Valid when creating new rules with code?	Valid for receive rules?	Valid for send rules?
Assign the message to the categories specified in the *Categories* property.	olRuleActionAssignTo-Category	Yes	Yes	Yes
Cc the message to the recipient list specified in the *Recipients* property.	olRuleActionCcMessage	Yes	No	Yes
Clear all categories for the message.	olRuleActionClear-Categories	Yes	Yes	Yes
Copy the message to the folder specified in the *Folder* property.	olRuleActionCopyToFolder	Yes	Yes	Yes
Run a custom action.	olRuleActionCustomAction	No	Yes	Yes
Defer the delivery by a specified number of minutes.	olRuleActionDefer	No	No	Yes
Delete the message.	olRuleActionDelete	Yes	Yes	No
Permanently delete the message.	olRuleActionDelete-Permanently	Yes	Yes	No
Display a desktop alert.	olRuleActionDesktopAlert	Yes	Yes	No
Clear the message flag.	olRuleActionFlagClear	No	Yes	No
Flag the message with the color specified.	olRuleActionFlagColor	No	Yes	No
Flag the message for action in days specified.	olRuleActionFlagFor-ActionInDays	No	Yes	Yes
Forward the message to the recipient list specified in the *Recipients* property.	olRuleActionForward	Yes	Yes	No
Forward the message as an attachment to the recipient list specified in the *Recipients* property.	olRuleActionForwardAs-Attachment	Yes	Yes	No
Mark the message with the specified *Importance* value.	olRuleActionImportance	No	Yes	Yes
Mark message as a task for follow-up using the *FlagTo* and *MarkInterval* properties of the *MarkAsTask-RuleAction* object.	olRuleActionMarkAsTask	Yes	Yes	No
Mark as read.	olRuleActionMarkRead	No	Yes	No

Table 10-2   Rule Actions by *OlRuleActionType*

Action	Constant in *OlRuleActionType*	Valid when creating new rules with code?	Valid for receive rules?	Valid for send rules?
Move the message to the folder specified in the *Folder* property.	olRuleActionMoveToFolder	Yes	Yes	No
Display the message specified in the *Text* property.	olRuleActionNewItemAlert	Yes	Yes	No
Notify that the message has been delivered.	olRuleActionNotifyDelivery	Yes	No	Yes
Notify that the message has been read.	olRuleActionNotifyRead	Yes	No	Yes
Play the .wav file specified in the *FilePath* property.	olRuleActionPlaysound	Yes	Yes	No
Print the message to the default printer.	olRuleActionPrint	No	Yes	No
Redirect the message to the recipient list specified in the *SendRuleAction-.Recipients* property.	olRuleActionRedirect	Yes	Yes	No
Start a script.	olRuleActionRunScript	No	Yes	No
Mark the message with the specified sensitivity.	olRuleActionSensitivity	No	No	Yes
Have server reply using the specified message.	olRuleActionServerReply	No	Yes	No
Start an .exe file.	olRuleActionStart-Application	No	Yes	No
Stop processing more rules.	olRuleActionStop	Yes	Yes	Yes
Reply using the specified template (.oft) file.	olRuleActionTemplate	No	Yes	No
Unrecognized rule action.	olRuleActionUnknown	No	Yes	No

The *RuleConditions* Collection

The *RuleConditions* collection contains a set of *RuleCondition* objects or objects derived from *RuleCondition*, representing the conditions or exception conditions that must be satisfied for the *Rule* to execute. The conditions exposed on the *RuleConditions* collection let you enable or disable the condition programmatically by setting the *Enabled* property of a given rule condition. The number of rule conditions in the *RuleConditions* collection is fixed.

Although the *RuleConditions* collection lets you determine the rule conditions that are enabled for a given *Rule* object, not all *RuleCondition* objects are supported for programmatic creation of rule conditions. See the earlier discussion of *RuleActions* for a method of determining which conditions are enabled for a given rule.

Table 10-3 lists all rules actions listed by *OlRuleConditionType*. From this table, you can determine which rule conditions are supported when creating a rule programmatically by looking at the Valid When Creating New Rules with Code? column. You can also determine which rule conditions are valid for receive and send rules.

Table 10-3   Rule Actions by *OlRuleConditionType*

Condition	Constant in *OlRuleConditionType*	Valid when creating new rules with code?	Valid for receive rules?	Valid for send rules?
Account is the account specified in the *Account* property.	olConditionAccount	Yes	Yes	Yes
Message is assigned any category.	olConditionAnyCategory	Yes	Yes	Yes
Body contains words specified in *Text* property.	olConditionBody	Yes	Yes	Yes
Body or subject contains words specified in *Text* property.	olConditionBodyOrSubject	Yes	Yes	Yes
Message is assigned the category or categories specified in the *Categories* property.	olConditionCategory	Yes	Yes	Yes
Message has my name in the Cc box.	olConditionCc	Yes	Yes	No
Message was received between x and y, where x and y are *Integer* values.	olConditionDateRange	No	Yes	Yes
Message is flagged for the specified action.	olConditionFlaggedFor-Action	No	Yes	Yes
Message uses the form specified in the *Form-Name* property.	olConditionFormName	Yes	Yes	Yes
Sender is in the recipient list specified in the *Recipients* property.	olConditionFrom	Yes	Yes	No
Message is generated from any RSS subscription.	olConditionFromAnyRss-Feed	Yes	Yes	No
Message is generated from a specified RSS subscription.	olConditionFromRssFeed	Yes	Yes	No

Table 10-3   Rule Actions by *OlRuleConditionType*

Condition	Constant in *OlRuleConditionType*	Valid when creating new rules with code?	Valid for receive rules?	Valid for send rules?
Message has an attachment.	olConditionHasAttachment	Yes	Yes	Yes
Message is marked with the specified level of importance.	olConditionImportance	Yes	Yes	Yes
Rule can run only on this machine.	olConditionLocalMachineOnly	Yes	Yes	Yes
Message is a meeting invitation or update.	olConditionMeetingInviteOrUpdate	Yes	Yes	Yes
Message header contains words specified in the *Text* property.	olConditionMessageHeader	Yes	Yes	No
Message does not have my name in the To box.	olConditionNotTo	Yes	Yes	No
Message is sent only to me.	olConditionOnlyToMe	Yes	Yes	No
Message is an out-of-office message.	olConditionOOF	No	Yes	No
Rule can run only on a specific machine that is not the current one.	olConditionOtherMachine	No	Yes	Yes
Document property is exactly, contains, or does not contain specified properties.	olConditionProperty	No	Yes	Yes
Recipient address contains words specified by the *Text* property.	olConditionRecipientAddress	Yes	Yes	Yes
Sender address contains words specified by the *Text* property.	olConditionSenderAddress	Yes	Yes	No
Sender is in the address list specified in the *Address* property.	olConditionSenderInAddressBook	Yes	Yes	No
Message is marked with the specified level of sensitivity.	olConditionSensitivity	No	Yes	Yes
Sent to recipients (To, Cc) are in the recipient list specified in the *Recipients* property.	olConditionSentTo	Yes	Yes	Yes

Table 10-3   Rule Actions by *OlRuleConditionType*

Condition	Constant in *OlRuleConditionType*	Valid when creating new rules with code?	Valid for receive rules?	Valid for send rules?
Message size is between x and y in units of KB, where x and y are Date values. For example, "10;50" sets the size condition between 10 and 50KB.	olConditionSizeRange	No	Yes	Yes
Subject contains words specified in the *Text* property.	olConditionSubject	Yes	Yes	Yes
My name is in the To box.	olConditionTo	Yes	Yes	No
Message has my name in the To or Cc box.	olConditionToOrCc	Yes	Yes	No
Unrecognized rule condition.	olConditionUnknown	No	Yes	No

Get or Set Action or Condition Properties with an Array

Certain actions or conditions get or set an array that represents the conditions to be evaluated or the actions to be completed. The most notable example is the *Text* property of the *TextRuleCondition*. The *Text* property returns or sets an array of *string* elements that represents the text to be evaluated by the rule condition. For the *Text* property, you must assign an array with one string or multiple strings for evaluation. Multiple text strings assigned in an array are evaluated using the logical *OR* operation. Properties that get or set an array are as follows:

- *AddressRuleCondition.Address*
- *AssignToCategoryRuleAction.Categories*
- *CategoryRuleCondition.Categories*
- *FormNameRuleCondition.FormName*
- *TextRuleCondition.Text*

The following code sample shows you how to use arrays for some of these properties. In this sample, a rule is created that assigns categories based on conditional evaluation of the words "Office," "Outlook," and "2007" in the subject of the item. If the condition is satisfied, then the categories of Office and Outlook are assigned to the item. Note that the code checks for the existence of these categories in the *Categories* collection using the *CategoryExists* method listed earlier in this chapter. If the category does not exist, the category is added to the master category list.

```
private void CreateTextAndCategoryRule()
{
    if(!CategoryExists("Office"))
```

```
    {
        Application.Session.Categories.Add(
            "Office",Type.Missing, Type.Missing);
    }
    if(!CategoryExists("Outlook"))
    {
        Application.Session.Categories.Add(
            "Outlook",Type.Missing, Type.Missing);
    }
    Outlook.Rules rules =
        Application.Session.DefaultStore.GetRules();
    Outlook.Rule textRule =
        rules.Create("Demo Text and Category Rule",
        Outlook.OlRuleType.olRuleReceive);
    Object[] textCondition =
        { "Office", "Outlook", "2007" };
    Object[] categoryAction =
        { "Office", "Outlook" };
    textRule.Conditions.BodyOrSubject.Text =
        textCondition;
    textRule.Conditions.BodyOrSubject.Enabled = true;
    textRule.Actions.AssignToCategory.Categories =
        categoryAction;
    textRule.Actions.AssignToCategory.Enabled = true;
    rules.Save(true);
}
```

Rules Sample Add-In

The Rules Sample add-in is available in a Microsoft Visual Basic .NET version (RulesAddinVB) and in a C# version (RulesAddinCS) in the sample code on this book's companion Web site.

The Rules Sample add-in demonstrates how you can substitute a custom Microsoft Windows Form dialog box for the default Outlook Create Rule dialog box that can be invoked from the context menu for an item. Corporate developers can modify and extend this example to create their own version of the Rules Sample add-in. The custom dialog box could promote the creation of rules that you want to deploy in your organization. Figure 10-4 shows the default Outlook Create Rule dialog box.

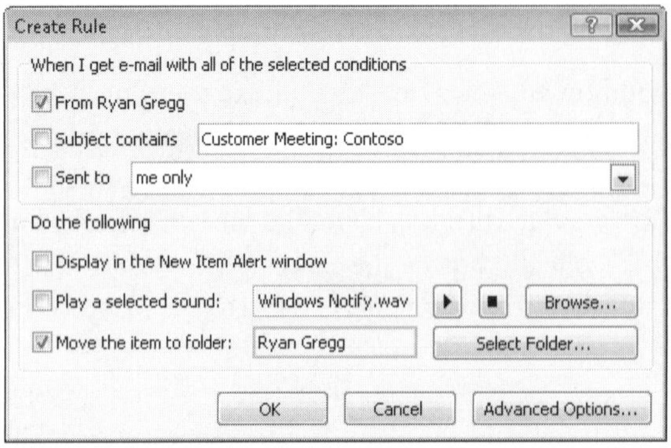

Figure 10-4 Outlook Create Rule dialog box.

When you build and install the Rules Sample add-in following the instructions that accompany the sample, you'll find that the add-in has repurposed the *Create Rule* command on the item context menu so that the custom Windows Form dialog box, shown in Figure 10-5, appears in place of the default Outlook Create Rule dialog box. Due to space limitations, the Rules Sample add-in is not discussed in detail here. Although this sample is relatively simple, it is packed with great code samples for creating rules programmatically and repurposing command bar and *Ribbon* commands.

Figure 10-5   Custom Windows Forms dialog box appears in place of the default Create Rules dialog box.

Search Folders

Search folders provide another way to organize Outlook data. Think of a search folder as a virtual folder that can contain items located across different folders in a given store. This section shows you how to create search folders programmatically. You can create and persist search folders so that they are visible in the Outlook folder hierarchy, or you can create searches dynamically that are not saved. If the search folder is not saved, it will not appear in the folder hierarchy. If a search folder is an integral component of your solution, you should consider adding your solution search folder to the user's favorite folders to promote its visibility. Later in this chapter you'll see how you can create a search folder programmatically and add that search folder to the user's favorite folders.

When to Use a Search Folder

A search folder provides a virtual folder that contains items that meet a set of search criteria. If you want to use a search folder in your solution, you should understand the following guidelines for search folders:

- Search folders are only supported for items in mail folders.

- You can run multiple searches simultaneously by calling the *AdvancedSearch* method in successive lines of code. A maximum of 100 simultaneous searches can be performed using the Microsoft Outlook user interface and the Outlook object model.

- You can only create the criteria for a search folder using a DAV Searching and Locating (DASL) query. For additional information on DASL and Jet query languages, see Chapter 11, "Searching Outlook Data." Note that you cannot use a Microsoft Jet query for the *Filter* parameter of *AdvancedSearch*. If Instant Search is enabled on a store that contains a folder specified in the *Scope* parameter, you can use Instant Search keywords to improve the performance of your search. If you use Instant Search keywords and Instant Search is not enabled, Outlook will return an error and your search will fail.

- Creating search folders on Exchange Server can affect the server's performance. For additional information on search folders and performance, see the section "Performance" in Chapter 11.

- Search folders can search in multiple folders and subfolders within a store. To specify multiple folders for the *Scope* parameter, use a comma character between each folder path and enclose each folder path in single quotes.

- The Outlook object model does not allow you to modify search folder criteria dynamically. If you create a search folder programmatically, the end user cannot modify criteria for the search folder. If you need to modify the criteria for a programmatically created search folder, you must delete the search folder programmatically and then re-create it. The end user can modify the scope for a programmatically created search folder, but it cannot be modified programmatically for an existing search folder.

- Use the *GetTable* method of the *Search* object or the *Search.Results* object to enumerate items returned by the search. When you obtain a *Table* object from the *GetTable* method, you can add or remove table columns. However, you cannot call the *Restrict* method on the *Table* object to modify the original criteria specified by the *Filter* parameter to *AdvancedSearch*.

- Because the results of *AdvancedSearch* can be returned asynchronously, you should use the *AdvancedSearchComplete* event of the *Application* object to obtain the results of the search. Use the *IsSynchronous* property of the *Search* object to determine if the search is synchronous or asynchronous.

- Search folders cannot span stores.

- Outlook 2007 does not support search folders for appointment, contact, task, and other folder types.

Enumerating Search Folders

To enumerate search folders, you call the *GetSearchFolders* method on the *Store* object. *GetSearchFolders* returns all the visible active search folders for the *Store* object. It does not return uninitialized or aged-out search folders. *GetSearchFolders* returns a *Folders* collection object with

Folders.Count equal to zero (0) if no search folders have been defined for the store. Not all store providers (the Exchange public folder store, for example) support search folders. If the store provider does not support search folders, calling *Store.GetSearchFolders* will raise an error.

The following code sample enumerates the search folders on all .pst or .ost stores for the current session and writes the search folder path to the trace listeners in the *Listeners* collection:

```
private void EnumerateAllSearchFolders()
{
    Outlook.Stores stores = Application.Session.Stores;
    foreach (Outlook.Store store in stores)
    {
        if (store.IsDataFileStore)
        {
            Outlook.Folders folders = store.GetSearchFolders();
            foreach (Outlook.Folder folder in folders)
            {
                Debug.WriteLine(folder.FolderPath);
            }
        }
    }
}
```

Note   Although you can enumerate search folders programmatically, you cannot activate a search folder using code. You also cannot determine the built-in or custom criteria for an existing search folder.

Creating a Search Folder Programmatically

To create a search folder programmatically, you call the *AdvancedSearch* method of the *Application* object and pass the *Scope*, *Filter*, *SearchSubFolders*, and *Tag* parameters. The *AdvancedSearch* method returns a *Search* object. Once you have obtained a *Search* object, you can call the *Save* method on the *Search* object to create a search folder that is visible in the Outlook user interface, or you can examine the contents of the search programmatically without saving the search folder. The *GetTable* method of the *Search* object allows you to enumerate items in the *Search* object in a performant manner. Table 10-4 lists the parameters for the *AdvancedSearch* method.

Table 10-4   Parameters for the *AdvancedSearch* Method

Name	Required?	Data type	Description
Scope	Required	String	The scope of the search; for example, the folder path of a folder. It is recommended that the folder path be enclosed within single quotes. Otherwise, the search might not return correct results if the folder path contains special characters, including Unicode characters. To specify multiple folder paths, enclose each folder path in single quotes and separate the single-quoted folder paths with a comma.

Table 10-4   Parameters for the *AdvancedSearch* Method

Name	Required?	Data type	Description
Filter	Optional	String	The DASL search filter that defines the parameters of the search. Do not prefix the DASL filter with the *@SQL*= prefix.
SearchSubFolders	Optional	Boolean	Determines if the search will include any of the folder's subfolders. If *SearchSubFolders* is *true* and multiple folders are specified by *scope*, then the subfolders of all folders specified in *scope* are searched.
Tag	Optional	String	The name given as an identifier for the search.

The following extensive code sample provides an end-to-end illustration of how to create a search folder programmatically. The code creates a search folder that contains all items in the Inbox and RSS Subscriptions folders and their subfolders that contain items with "Office" in the subject. The search folder created by the sample code is shown in Figure 10-6.

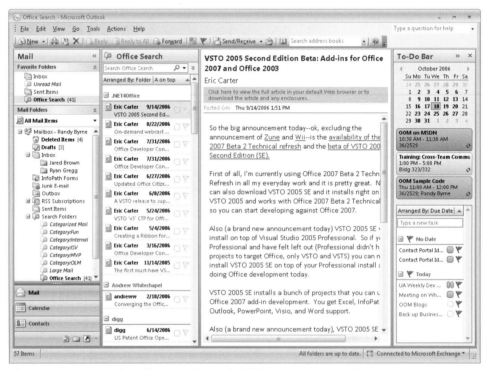

Figure 10-6   Create the Office Search search folder programmatically.

The sample assumes that you are creating a search folder using an Outlook add-in. The *InitializeAddin* procedure is called by the add-in's *OnConnection* procedure.

```
private void InitializeAddin()
{
```

```
        Application.AdvancedSearchComplete += new
            Outlook.ApplicationEvents_11_AdvancedSearchCompleteEventHandler(
            Application_AdvancedSearchComplete);
        CreateOfficeSearch();
}

private void CreateOfficeSearch()
{
    // Construct search filter
    // Only use ci_ keywords if Instant Search is enabled
    string filter;
    if (Application.Session.DefaultStore.IsInstantSearchEnabled)
    {
        filter = "urn:schemas:httpmail:subject"
            + " ci_phrasematch 'Office'";
    }
    else
    {
        filter = "urn:schemas:httpmail:subject"
            + " like '%Office%'";
    }
    // Construct search scope
    StringBuilder sb = new StringBuilder();
    sb.Append("'");
    sb.Append(Application.Session.GetDefaultFolder(
        Outlook.OlDefaultFolders.olFolderInbox).FolderPath);
    sb.Append("'");
    sb.Append(",");
    sb.Append("'");
    sb.Append(Application.Session.GetDefaultFolder(
        Outlook.OlDefaultFolders.olFolderRssFeeds).FolderPath);
    sb.Append("'");
    string scope = sb.ToString();
    // Call AdvancedSearch method
    Outlook.Search search =
        Application.AdvancedSearch(
        scope, filter, true, "My Office Search");
    // To save the search as a search folder,
    // you can call Search.Save()
    search.Save("Office Search");
    // Add the search folder to favorites
    Outlook.Folder folder =
        Application.Session.DefaultStore.GetSearchFolders()
        ["Office Search"] as Outlook.Folder;
    Outlook.NavigationPane pane =
        Application.ActiveExplorer().NavigationPane;
    Outlook.MailModule mailModule =
        pane.Modules.GetNavigationModule(
        Outlook.OlNavigationModuleType.olModuleMail)
        as Outlook.MailModule;
    Outlook.NavigationGroup mailGroup =
        mailModule.NavigationGroups.GetDefaultNavigationGroup(
        Outlook.OlGroupType.olFavoriteFoldersGroup);
    mailGroup.NavigationFolders.Add(folder);
}
```

Each bullet in the following list discusses an important aspect of the sample code just shown:

- The *InitializeAddin* procedure creates an event handler for the *AdvancedSearchComplete* event on the *Outlook.Application* object and calls the *CreateOfficeSearch* procedure. Because *AdvancedSearch* returns results asynchronously, you need to create an event handler to determine when the search has completed.

- *CreateOfficeSearch* creates instance variables named *filter* and *scope*, and then passes those arguments to the *AdvancedSearch* method of the *Application* object. If Instant Search is enabled and *DefaultStore.IsInstantSearchEnabled* is *true*, then *filter* contains the *ci_phrasematch* keyword to create a phrase match search for "Office" in the item subject. If Instant Search is not enabled and *DefaultStore.IsInstantSearchEnabled* is *false*, then *filter* contains the *like* keyword to create a substring match search for "Office" in the item subject. Note that the *filter* does not impose an additional restriction for message class so that all item types (including meeting requests in the Inbox that contain "Office" in the subject) will be returned by the search. If you want to restrict by message class, you should add additional conditions to the criteria. The *scope* string specifies multiple folders for the search, namely the Inbox and RSS Subscriptions folders.

- *CreateOfficeSearch* calls the *AdvancedSearch* method of the *Application* object to return a *Search* object named *search*. The optional *SearchSubfolders* argument is *true* so that subfolders of the target folders will be searched. Also the *Tag* argument is specified so that the *Tag* property of the *Search* object will have the value My Office Search.

- *CreateOfficeSearch* saves the *Search* object named *search* returned by *AdvancedSearch*. The *Save* method is called on the *search* instance variable to persist the search as a search folder. The name of the search folder is Office Search. Although the code does not illustrate this precaution, you might want to check the *Folders* collection returned by *DefaultStore.GetSearchFolders()* to ensure that a search folder with same name does not already exist.

- Once the search folder has been saved, you can find the search folder in the *Folders* collection returned by *DefaultStore.GetSearchFolders()*. In this case, the code returns a *Folder* object that represents the newly created search folder.

- Now that you have an instance variable representing the search folder, you can use *NavigationPane* and related objects to add the newly created search folder to the user's favorite folders.

- Finally, the *AdvancedSearchComplete* method will fire when the search is complete. In the *Application_AdvancedSearchComplete* event procedure, the code checks that the *Search* object passed to the event is the search named My Office Search. You then use the *GetTable* method on the *Search* object and write the subject for every row in the table to the trace listeners in the *Listeners* collection.

Outlook Views

Outlook 2007 allows you to create customizable views that allow you to better sort, group, and ultimately view data of all different types within the View Pane of Explorer. You can also customize built-in views programmatically. There are a variety of different view types that provide the flexibility needed to organize your solution's data. For example, Microsoft Business Contact Manager uses the custom view shown in Figure 10-7 to organize and present solution data in the view named By Campaign Type in the Marketing Campaigns folder.

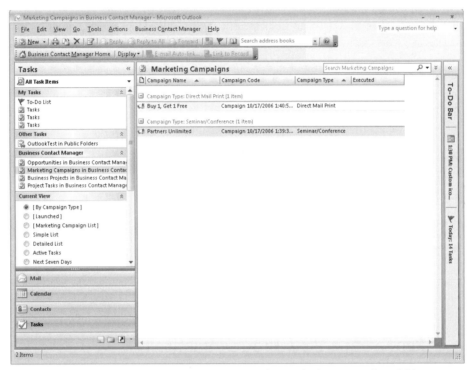

Figure 10-7   Custom By Campaign Type view in the Marketing Campaigns folder.

Objects That Derive from the *View* Object

Outlook 2007 supports the following objects that represent Outlook views. Table 10-5 lists new Outlook 2007 view objects that derive from the *View* object. For a complete listing of all the properties and methods of these view objects, see the Outlook Developer's Reference.

Table 10-5   Outlook 2007 *View* Objects

Object name	Description
BusinessCardView	This object allows you to view data as a series of Electronic Business Card images.
CalendarView	This object allows you to view data in a calendar format.

Table 10-5   Outlook 2007 *View* Objects

Object name	Description
CardView	This object allows you to view data in a series of cards.
IconView	This object allows you to view data as icons, similar to a Windows folder or Explorer.
TableView	This object allows you to view data in a simple, field-based table.
TimelineView	This object allows you to view data in a customizable linear time line.

Although you can use the *View* object to interact with the properties and methods common to all views, you must cast the *View* object to one of the derived view objects, such as the *CardView* object, to access certain properties, such as the *HeadingsFont* property of the *CardView* object. Use the *ViewType* property of the *View* object to determine which type of view is represented by that object. For example, the following code sample obtains the *CurrentView* object for the Inbox. If the *CurrentView* represents a *TableView* object, then the code creates an instance of the *TableView* and sets the *AllowInCellEditing* property to *true*. The code then calls the *Apply* method to reflect the change to the view in the Outlook user interface.

```
private void DemoAllowInCellEditingForView()
{
    Outlook.View view =
        Application.Session.GetDefaultFolder(
        Outlook.OlDefaultFolders.olFolderInbox).CurrentView;
    if (view.ViewType == Outlook.OlViewType.olTableView)
    {
        Outlook.TableView tableView = (Outlook.TableView)view;
        tableView.AllowInCellEditing = true;
        tableView.Apply();
    }
}
```

Adding or Removing a View Programmatically

You can define a new view by using the *Add* method of the *Views* collection for a *Folder* object. Visibility for the view can be set either at the time of creation, by specifying an *OlViewSaveOption* constant in the *SaveOption* parameter of the *Add* method, or any time after the view is created, by specifying an *OlViewSaveOption* constant for the *SaveOption* property of the *View* object. Adding a new view raises the *ViewAdd* event of the *Views* collection. For example, the following code sample adds a new view named Meeting Requests to the user's Inbox. The DASL string supplied for the *Filter* property of the *View* object causes the view to display only items that contain "IPM.Schedule" in the message class for the item.

```
private void CreateMeetingRequestsView()
{
    const string PR_MESSAGE_CLASS =
        "http://schemas.microsoft.com/mapi/proptag/0x001A001E";
    Outlook.Views views =
        Application.Session.GetDefaultFolder(
```

```
        Outlook.OlDefaultFolders.olFolderInbox).Views;
    Outlook.TableView tableView = (Outlook.TableView)
        views.Add("Meeting Requests",
        Outlook.OlViewType.olTableView,
        Outlook.OlViewSaveOption.olViewSaveOptionThisFolderEveryone);
    tableView.Filter = "\"" + PR_MESSAGE_CLASS + "\"" +
        " like 'IPM.Schedule%'";
    tableView.Save();
    tableView.Apply();
}
```

If you need to remove a view from a folder, use the *Remove* method of the *Views* collection to remove an existing custom view. If you attempt to remove a built-in view, Outlook will raise an error. Removing a view raises the *ViewRemove* event of the *Views* collection.

Once a view is defined, you can customize the view programmatically by casting the *View* object to one of the derived view objects and performing whatever changes are needed. Use the *Save* method of the derived view object or the *View* object to save any changes to the view.

You can apply the view, once defined and customized, to the current *Explorer* object by using the *Apply* method of the derived view object or the *View* object. Applying a view raises the *ViewSwitch* event of the *Explorer* object.

Customizing Your View

There are a variety of methods for customizing a built-in or custom view. In previous versions of Outlook, developers used the *XML* property of the *View* object to customize a view. In Outlook 2007, you can use the first-class properties of the derived *View* object to customize the view. Although the *XML* property of the *View* object is still available, you can achieve more consistent and easier results by using new view objects such as *ViewField*, *OrderField*, *ColumnFormat*, and *AutoFormatRule*.

Specifying Fields in a View

You can specify which Outlook item properties are displayed in a view by adding one or more properties to the *ViewFields* collection of any of the following objects:

- *CardView*
- *TableView*

BusinessCardView, *CalendarView*, *IconView*, and *TimelineView* objects use other methods of determining which Outlook item properties are displayed within the view. The fields displayed for the *BusinessCardView* object, for example, are determined by the Electronic Business Card (EBC) layout associated with each displayed Outlook item.

The *ViewFields* collection for those views can be retrieved by accessing the *ViewFields* property of the appropriate *View* object. The *Add* method of the *ViewFields* collection is used to create a *ViewField* object that represents the Outlook item property to be displayed in the view.

> **Note**   To add built-in fields to the *ViewFields* collection, the property must exist in the Outlook field registry; otherwise Outlook will raise an error when you call the *Add* method. Use the Field Chooser to determine if the field exists in the Outlook field registry. To add custom fields to the *ViewFields* collection, the custom property must exist in the *UserDefinedProperties* collection of the parent *Folder* object; otherwise Outlook will raise an error when you call the *Add* method.

A *ViewField* object not only identifies an Outlook item property to display within the view, but also describes how the values for that property should be displayed. You can change how individual column properties are displayed in a view by modifying the *ColumnFormat* property of the *ViewField* object.

The following code sample adds the Start and End fields to the Meeting Requests view. It also changes the label for the From field to *Organized By*.

```
private void ModifyMeetingRequestsView()
{
    Outlook.TableView tableView = null;
    Outlook.ViewField startField = null;
    Outlook.ViewField endField = null;
    Outlook.ViewField fromField = null;
    try
    {
        tableView =
            Application.Session.GetDefaultFolder(
            Outlook.OlDefaultFolders.olFolderInbox)
            .Views["Meeting Requests"] as Outlook.TableView;
    }
    catch { }
    if (tableView != null)
    {
        try
        {
            startField = tableView.ViewFields["Start"];
        }
        catch{}
        if (startField == null)
        {
            startField = tableView.ViewFields.Add("Start");
        }
        try
        {
            endField = tableView.ViewFields["End"];
        }
        catch{}
        if (endField == null)
        {
```

```
            endField = tableView.ViewFields.Add("End");
        }
        try
        {
            fromField = tableView.ViewFields["From"];
        }
        catch{}
        if (fromField != null)
        {
            fromField.ColumnFormat.Label = "Organized By";
        }
        try
        {
            tableView.Save();
        }
        catch (Exception ex)
        {
            Debug.WriteLine(ex.Message);
        }
    }
}
```

Filtering Items in the *View* Object

Outlook items can be filtered in any view derived from the *View* object by specifying a valid DASL filter expression in the *Filter* property of the *View* object. Do not prefix the DASL string for the filter expression with *@SQL=* as you must for the *Restrict* method on the *Table* or *Items* objects. For more information about creating a DASL filter expression to filter Outlook items, see Chapter 11.

> **Warning**   Do not use *ci_phrasematch* and *ci_startswith* keywords in the filter expression for a view. The performance of the view will not be optimized if you use these keywords. For a view filter, use the = or *like* operators to construct your filter expression.

Sorting Items in a View

Items in a view can be sorted by adding one or more Outlook item properties to the *OrderFields* collection of any of the following objects:

- BusinessCardView
- CardView
- IconView
- TableView

Outlook items in a *CalendarView* or *TimelineView* object are displayed in chronological order, depending on the values of the Outlook item properties specified for the *StartField* and *EndField* properties of the view.

The *OrderFields* collection for those views can be accessed with the *SortFields* property of the appropriate view object. The *Add* method of the *OrderFields* collection is used to create an *OrderField* object that represents the Outlook item property to be sorted.

Specifying Properties for Sorting

You can add either built-in or custom Outlook item properties to the *OrderFields* collection. The order in which the properties are included in the *OrderFields* collection determines the order in which the properties are sorted, whereas the *IsDescending* property of the *OrderField* object, which represents an Outlook item property, determines whether the values of that property are sorted in ascending or descending order.

Specifying Built-In Properties for Sorting

The following guidelines should be used when specifying built-in Outlook item properties:

- Built-in properties can be specified either by property name (for example, Subject) or by namespace (for example, *http://schemas.microsoft.com/mapi/proptag/0x0037001E*).

- Property names are not case-sensitive and cannot include spaces.

Namespace identifiers are case-sensitive, must follow URL encoding rules, and cannot be enclosed in square brackets ([]). For more information about property namespace identifiers, see Chapter 17, "Using the *PropertyAccessor* Object."

Specifying Custom Properties for Sorting

The following guidelines should be used when specifying custom properties:

- The custom property must be available in the *UserDefinedProperties* collection for the parent *Folder* object.

- Custom properties should be specified by property name (for example, [Shoe Size]).

- Custom property names are not case-sensitive, can include spaces, and should be enclosed in square brackets ([]) if they contain spaces.

The *AutoFormatRules* Collection

The new *AutoFormatRules* collection lets you add an *AutoFormatRule* object that represents a formatting rule used by a *View* object to determine how to format Outlook items displayed within that view.

Use the *Add* method or the *Insert* method of the *AutoFormatRules* collection to create a new formatting rule for the following objects:

- *CardView*

- *TableView*

For views that support automatic formatting, Outlook provides a set of built-in formatting rules that can be disabled but cannot be removed or reordered. Use the *Standard* property of the *AutoFormatRule* object to determine whether a formatting rule is built-in or custom. You cannot modify a built-in formatting rule. You can add or remove a custom formatting rule subject to the limitation that calling the *Save* or *Apply* methods will not persist *AutoFormatRule.Filter* in the *View* object. If you want to add an *AutoFormatRule* object to your solution, you need to add or remove the formatting rule dynamically.

The following *CreateAutoFormatRule* procedure creates a custom formatting rule named Canceled for the Meeting Requests view discussed earlier in this chapter. If the meeting item is a meeting cancellation, a red font is used to display the item in the view. To remove the formatting rule when the user navigates away from the folder or Outlook shuts down, the *RemoveAutoFormatRule* procedure deletes the Canceled formatting rule. The code sample assumes that you've created a class-level instance variable named *m_Explorer* and lists all the events necessary to make the dynamic formatting rule work correctly. For additional information on handling Outlook events, see Chapter 8, "Responding to Events."

```
private void InitializeAddin()
{
    m_Explorer = Application.ActiveExplorer();
    m_Explorer.BeforeViewSwitch += new
        Outlook.ExplorerEvents_10_BeforeViewSwitchEventHandler(
        m_Explorer_BeforeViewSwitch);
    m_Explorer.ViewSwitch += new
        Outlook.ExplorerEvents_10_ViewSwitchEventHandler(
        m_Explorer_ViewSwitch);
    Outlook.ExplorerEvents_Event explorerEvents =
        (Outlook.ExplorerEvents_Event)m_Explorer;
    explorerEvents.Close += new
        Outlook.ExplorerEvents_CloseEventHandler(m_Explorer_Close);
    m_Explorer.FolderSwitch += new
        Outlook.ExplorerEvents_10_FolderSwitchEventHandler(
        m_Explorer_FolderSwitch);
    if (m_Explorer.CurrentFolder.CurrentView.Name
        == "Meeting Requests")
    {
        CreateAutoFormatRule();
    }
}

void m_Explorer_FolderSwitch()
{
```

```
    if (m_Explorer.CurrentFolder.CurrentView.Name
        == "Meeting Requests")
    {
        CreateAutoFormatRule();
    }
}

void m_Explorer_Close()
{
    RemoveAutoFormatRule();
}

void m_Explorer_ViewSwitch()
{
    if (m_Explorer.CurrentFolder.CurrentView.Name
        == "Meeting Requests")
    {
        CreateAutoFormatRule();
    }
}

void  m_Explorer_BeforeViewSwitch(object NewView, ref bool Cancel)
{
    if (m_Explorer.CurrentFolder.CurrentView.Name
        == "Meeting Requests")
    {
        RemoveAutoFormatRule();
    }
}

private void CreateAutoFormatRule()
{
    Outlook.TableView tableView = null;
    Outlook.AutoFormatRule autoFormat = null;
    const string PR_MESSAGE_CLASS =
        "http://schemas.microsoft.com/mapi/proptag/0x001A001E";
    Outlook.Folder inbox = Application.Session.GetDefaultFolder(
        Outlook.OlDefaultFolders.olFolderInbox) as Outlook.Folder;
    Outlook.Folder currentFolder =
        Application.ActiveExplorer().CurrentFolder
        as Outlook.Folder;
    if (Application.Session.CompareEntryIDs(currentFolder.EntryID,
        inbox.EntryID))
    {
        try
        {
            tableView =
                inbox.Views["Meeting Requests"] as Outlook.TableView;
        }
        catch{ }
        if (tableView != null)
        {
            try
            {
```

```
                    autoFormat =
                        tableView.AutoFormatRules["Canceled"];
                }
                catch{ }
                if (autoFormat == null)
                {
                    autoFormat =
                        tableView.AutoFormatRules.Add("Canceled");
                    autoFormat.Filter = "\"" + PR_MESSAGE_CLASS +
                        "\"" + " like '%Canceled%'";
                    autoFormat.Font.Color = Outlook.OlColor.olColorRed;
                    autoFormat.Enabled = true;
                    // Save the view
                    tableView.Save();
                }
            }
        }
    }
}

private void RemoveAutoFormatRule()
{
    Outlook.TableView tableView = null;
    Outlook.AutoFormatRule autoFormat = null;
    Outlook.Folder inbox = Application.Session.GetDefaultFolder(
        Outlook.OlDefaultFolders.olFolderInbox) as Outlook.Folder;
    Outlook.Folder currentFolder =
        Application.ActiveExplorer().CurrentFolder
        as Outlook.Folder;
    if (Application.Session.CompareEntryIDs(currentFolder.EntryID,
        inbox.EntryID))
    {
        try
        {
            tableView =
                inbox.Views["Meeting Requests"] as Outlook.TableView;
        }
        catch { }
        if (tableView != null)
        {
            try
            {
                autoFormat =
                    tableView.AutoFormatRules["Canceled"];
            }
            catch { }
            if (autoFormat != null)
            {
                tableView.AutoFormatRules.Remove("Canceled");
                tableView.Save();
            }
        }
    }
}
```

Summary

Outlook 2007 provides several features to help organize user or solution data. This chapter shows you how to leverage these features programmatically. You can use category colors, task flagging, rules, search folders, and views to organize or present data to the user. You learned how you can take advantage of these features in your solution and tailor them to your specific scenario.

Chapter 11
Searching Outlook Data

Searching provides relief from information overload. It can also help you build a solution that locates items in folders and stores, and helps end users discover their data and become more productive.

After reading this chapter, you should have a good understanding of the following topics:

- Overview of programmatic search
- Microsoft Office Outlook 2007 query languages
- Entry points for search in the Outlook object model

Overview of Searching Data

Instant Search is one of the premiere features of Outlook 2007. In the past, search was difficult and nonperformant both in the Outlook user interface and programmatically. That story has changed with Outlook 2007. As a developer, you can participate in search in a first-class manner by issuing queries that return results based on the content indexing engine that supports Instant Search. Once your query has been processed, the results can be returned in a variety of objects including the *Table* object, the *Items* collection, and the *Search* object. You can also write code that uses the Advanced Query Syntax (AQS) offered by Microsoft Windows Desktop Search to drive the Instant Search pane, shown in Figure 11-1.

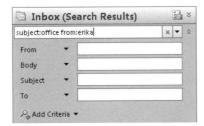

Figure 11-1   Instant Search pane.

Outlook Query Languages

Outlook 2007 supports three different query languages, each of which has appropriate scenarios and entry points. For programmatic search, there are also several different ways of returning results from a search. Before learning how to implement programmatic search, it's important for you to understand the query languages and their appropriate usage. The available query languages in Outlook 2007 are listed in Table 11-1.

Table 11-1   Outlook 2007 Query Languages

Query language	Description
AQS	AQS is used by Windows Desktop Search and is the query language for the Instant Search feature in Outlook 2007.
DASL	DAV Searching and Locating (DASL) query language is based on the Microsoft Exchange implementation of DASL in Outlook. DASL has been used in several versions of Outlook. In Outlook 2007, DASL has new prominence because it can be used to return results in the new *Table* object. DAV is an abbreviated version of Web Distributed Authoring and Versioning (WebDAV).
Jet	Jet query language, based on the Microsoft Jet Expression Service, has been used in several versions of Outlook to provide a simple query language. Note that the Jet query language has the same syntax as that supported by the Microsoft Jet Expression Service, hence the name Jet query language. Jet is used to create filter strings for the *Restrict* method of the *Items* and *Table* objects.

Each query language has one or more entry points in the Outlook object model. Jet is the simplest to use, but it also is less powerful than DASL or AQS. AQS is simple to use but extremely powerful. However, its use is limited to the *Search* method of the *Explorer* object. It cannot be used to provide a restriction for the *Table* or *Items* objects. Results returned by an AQS query can be displayed only in the Outlook user interface. DASL is a difficult query language to write and to master, but it does have significant power for driving both the *Table* object and *Items* collection. For example, the following code sample displays all items that contain the exact phrase "Office 2007" in the subject and that have been received in the last month. The scope of the query is all mail folders in all stores where indexing is enabled. It then displays the results of the search in a separate Explorer window.

```
private void DemoInstantSearch()
{
    if (Application.Session.DefaultStore.IsInstantSearchEnabled)
    {
        Outlook.Explorer explorer = Application.Explorers.Add(
            Application.Session.GetDefaultFolder(
            Outlook.OlDefaultFolders.olFolderInbox)
            as Outlook.Folder,
            Outlook.OlFolderDisplayMode.olFolderDisplayNormal);
        string filter = "subject:" +
            "\"" + "Office 2007" + "\"" +
            " received:(last month)";
        explorer.Search(filter,
            Outlook.OlSearchScope.olSearchScopeAllFolders);
        explorer.Display();
    }
}
```

AQS

AQS is the query language for Windows Desktop Search. For an in-depth discussion of all aspects of Windows Desktop Search, search MSDN at *http://msdn.microsoft.com*. AQS queries cannot be submitted directly to methods such as *Table.Restrict* or *Items.Restrict*. You can supply an AQS query only to the *Search* method of the *Explorer* object. When you call this method, search results are displayed in the Explorer window. You can call the *Search* method on multiple *Explorer* objects, and each will display separate search results. Outlook uses AQS to return search results.

The following discussion concentrates on AQS keywords that you can use to cause the *Search* method of the *Explorer* object to display results in an Explorer window. Some of the keywords are specific to a module such as Mail or Calendar, whereas other keywords are appropriate to all modules.

Case Sensitivity

Keywords and search specifiers for AQS are case-insensitive. When results are returned, they will also be case-insensitive. For example, *subject:office* or *SUBJECT:OFFICE* will both return items that contain "Office," "office," or "OFFICE" in the subject.

Keywords and Locale

Keywords for AQS queries can be submitted based on the locale for the installed Windows operating system. However, to make your life as a developer easier, you can submit the English keywords shown in Tables 11-2 through 11-6 for any operating system locale and still return the correct results. Rather than localize all AQS queries, the recommended best practice is to create your queries using English keywords and then specify the search term in the language of the installed Windows operating system.

Search Scope

If you do not specify a property keyword, the search defaults to all searched fields in a default scope. The default scope is per module, meaning that all contact folders, for example, use the same default scope. Keywords for fields that are searched within a default scope are marked with an asterisk (*) in Tables 11-2 through 11-6. For example, if you specify *contactfirstname:lily*, the search will return all items where the Contact first name starts with "lily." If you do not specify the *contactfirstname* keyword, the search will return all items where any of the searched fields for the Contacts module starts with "lily".

Keywords for All Modules

Table 11-2 lists some of the common keywords that can be used in any module with the exception of the Notes module, which only supports the *subject*, *body*, and *categories* keywords. For additional information about the *<string>*, *<date>*, *<bool>*, and *<systemsize>* specifiers shown in the table, see the relevant specifier topic later. For information on keywords and symbols that are valid for an AQS query, see the section "Keywords and Symbols" later in this chapter.

Table 11-2 Keywords for All Outlook Modules

Search for	Keyword	Example
Attachment contains	attachment:<string>	attachment:office
Body*	contents:<string>	contents:office
Categories*	category:<string>	category:(oom AND isv)
Follow up*	followupflag:<string>	followupflag:completed
Has Attachments*	hasattachments:<bool>	hasattachments:true
Importance	importance: (low, normal, high)	importance:high
In Folder	folderpath:<string>	folderpath:(Sent Items)
Message size	messagesize:<systemsize>	messagesize:(>500kb <700kb)
Modified	modified:<date>	modified:(last week)
Read	read:<bool>	read:yes
Received	received:<date>	received:(last month)
Sensitivity	sensitivity: (normal, personal, private, confidential)	sensitivity:private
Sent	sent:<date>	sent:this week −monday
Subject*	subject:<string>	subject:office

Note The *folderpath* keyword should only be used when you search all items in a module. When you specify folderpath for a query, you should also specify the *OlSearchScope.olSearchScopeAllFolders* value for the *SearchScope* parameter of the *Search* method.

Keywords for Mail Module

Table 11-3 lists additional AQS keywords that can be used in the Mail module. This list is not exhaustive.

Table 11-3 Keywords for Outlook Mail Folders

Search for	Keyword	Example
Bcc*	bcc:<string>	bcc:(fadi fakhouri)
Cc*	cc:<string>	cc:(janet leverling)
Due Date	due:<date>	due:(11/1/06..12/1/06)
From*	from:<string>	from:Mark OR Dan
Received	received:<date>	received:(last month)

Table 11-3   Keywords for Outlook Mail Folders

Search for	Keyword	Example
Sent	sent:<date>	sent:this week–today
Start Date	start:<date>	start:1/1/07
To*	to:<string>	to:(nancy davolio)

Keywords for Calendar Module

Table 11-4 lists additional keywords that can be used in the Calendar module. This list is not exhaustive.

Table 11-4   Keywords for Outlook Calendar Folders

Search for	Keyword	Example
End	end:<date>	end:(<2/1/07)
Location*	meetinglocation:<string>	meetinglocation:36
Optional Attendees*	optionalattendees:<string>	optionalattendees:(ryan gregg)
Organizer*	organizer:<string>	organizer:(nancy davolio)
Recurring	recurring:<bool>	recurring:true
Required Attendees*	requiredattendees:<string>	requiredattendees:(randy byrne)
Resources*	resources:<string>	resources:(conf room 36/2731)
Show Time As	freebusystatus: (free, busy, tentative, out of office)	freebusystatus:tentative
Start	start:<date>	start:tomorrow

Keywords for Contacts Module

Table 11-5 lists additional AQS keywords that can be used in the Contacts module. This list is not exhaustive.

Table 11-5   Keywords for Outlook Contacts Folders

Search for	Keyword	Example
Business Address*	businessaddress:<string>	businessaddress:microsoft
Business Phone*	businessphone:<string>	Businessphone:("425")
City	city:<string>	city:redmond
Company*	company:<string>	company:Microsoft
Department	department:<string>	department:payroll
E-mail*	emailaddress:<string>	emailaddress:microsoft.com
First Name	contactfirstname:<string>	contactfirstname:nancy
Full Name	fullname:<string>	fullname:(peter allenspach)
Home Address*	homeaddress:<string>	homeaddress:17560

Table 11-5   Keywords for Outlook Contacts Folders

Search for	Keyword	Example
Home Phone*	homephone:<string>	homephone:("425")
IM Address	imaddress:<string>	imaddress:lily
Job Title*	jobtitle:<string>	jobtitle:director
Last Name	contactlastname:<string>	contactlastname:"davolio"
Mailing Address	mailingaddress:<string>	mailingaddress:street
Mobile Phone*	mobilephone:<string>	mobilephone:("212")
Other Address*	otheraddress:<string>	otheraddress:way
PO Box	pobox:<string>	pobox:121
Primary Phone	primaryphone:<string>	primaryphone:("518")
State	stateorprovince:<string>	stateorprovince:ca
Street Address	streetaddress:<string>	street:("16255 NE 36th Way")
Title	personaltitle:<string>	personaltitle:ms
Web Page	webpage:<string>	webpage:msdn
Zip/Postal Code	postalcode:<string>	postalcode:98

Keywords for Tasks Module

Table 11-6 lists additional AQS keywords that can be used in the Tasks module. This list is not exhaustive.

Table 11-6   Keywords for Outlook Task Folders

Search for	Keyword	Example
Completed	iscompleted:<bool>	iscompleted:no
Date Completed	datecompleted:<date>	datecompleted:(last week)
Due Date	due:<date>	due:(last week)
Owner*	taskowner:<string>	taskowner:zoe
Priority	priority: (low, normal, high)	priority:high
Reminder Time	remindertime:<date>	remindertime:(next week)
Start Date	start:<date>	start:(next week)
Status	taskstatus: (in progress, completed, not started, waiting on someone else, deferred)	taskstatus:in progress

Keywords and Symbols

You can use various operators and symbols for queries that add power to the simplicity of AQS. Keywords and symbols for queries are listed in Table 11-7.

Table 11-7   Operators and Symbols for Specifiers

Operator/Symbol	Example	Results
–	subject:fast –track	Finds items where subject starts with *fast*, but where any searched field in the default scope does not start with *track*
+	category:"book" +"important"	Finds items categorized with *book* and *important*
>	sent:>11/1/06	Finds items sent after *11/1/06*
<	received:<11/1/06	Finds items received before *11/1/06*
..	sent:11/1/06..11/5/06	Finds items sent after *11/1/06* and before *11/5/06*
AND	category:(book AND dev)	Finds items where category starts with *book* and category starts with *dev*
NOT	subject:(fast NOT track)	Finds items where subject starts with *fast*, but where subject does not start with *track*
OR	subject:(fast OR track)	Finds items where subject starts with *fast* or where subject starts with *track*
Parentheses	subject:(fast track)	Finds items where subject starts with *fast* and subject starts with *track* in any order
Quotation marks	subject:"fast track"	Finds items with subject containing the exact phrase *fast track*

String Specifier *<string>*

You can easily specify a variety of search conditions using a string specifier. Without additional operators such as those described in Table 11-7, a string search performs the equivalent of a DASL *ci_startswith* comparison on the specified string. For example, specifying *subject:off* for the query would find items that start with *"off"* in the subject. Possible results would include off, office, official, and so forth. If you specified *subject:"off"* (the equivalent of a DASL *ci_phrasematch* comparison) in the query, then only items that have the exact phrase *"off"* in the subject would be returned.

Date Specifier *<date>*

To specify a date, use the property name followed by any one of the following:

- A date literal such as *sent:1/1/2007*.

■ A relative date specifier such as *received:(last week)* or *sent:monday* or *due:june*. Note that you can use operators with relative date specifiers such as *received:(last week) NOT received:monday*.

■ A date range specifier such as two consecutive periods (..) or using > and < symbols such as the following: *sent:10/1/06..10/4/06* or *sent:>10/1/06 <10/4/06*.

Boolean Specifier *<bool>*

To specify a Boolean property, follow the property name with a valid Boolean value such as *true, yes, false,* or *no*. For example, both *hasattachments:true* and *iscompleted:no* are valid Boolean specifiers.

Systemsize Specifier *<systemsize>*

A Systemsize specifier lets you query a property such as the size of an item. Typically you specify the size as a range using > and < or double periods. Use the *kb* and *mb* abbreviations (*k* and *m* are also valid shortcuts) to specify kilobytes and megabytes, respectively. For example, *size:10kb..50kb* and *size:>1m* are both valid Systemsize specifiers.

Keywords for Custom Properties

If you need to query custom properties in an AQS query, enclose the name of the custom property in brackets as follows:

[Preferred Gift]:diamonds

The custom property must exist in the *UserDefinedProperties* collection for the *Folder* object where you want to execute the search. You must search for a custom property in the folder where the custom property exists. If you attempt to search for a custom property across all folders by specifying the *OlSearchScope.olSearchScopeAllFolders* value for the *SearchScope* parameter of the *Search* method, the custom property search will not return the correct results. Custom property searches must be scoped to the current folder in the Explorer by specifying *OlSearchScope.olSearchScopeCurrentFolder*.

DASL

DASL excels at retrieving property-based results for item-level searches in folders. Unfortunately, DASL is cumbersome to write, and it would be an understatement to mention that the property formats are opaque. That being said, DASL is the most versatile query language for Outlook, so it's worth the deep dive.

Property Specifiers

DASL uses namespace schema names to represent properties in its query syntax. For a complete discussion of the namespace formats, see Chapter 17, "Using the *PropertyAccessor*

Object." Certain properties such as binary properties are invalid for use in a DASL query. To learn more about invalid properties, see the section "Invalid Properties" later in this chapter. All properties in DASL queries must be enclosed in double quotation marks. You can add a simple routine like the *addQuotes* procedure to do the job for you.

```
/// <summary>
/// Adds double quotation marks to schema name
/// </summary>
/// <param name="schemaName"></param>
/// <returns>string</returns> private string addQuotes(string schemaName)
{
    return ("\"" + schemaName + "\"");
}
```

> **Note**   Namespace property specifiers are always case-sensitive. For example, *urn:schemas:contacts:givenName* is a valid specifier but *urn:schemas:contacts:givenname* is invalid. The only exception to this rule is for the representation of the Hex value in a Messaging Application Programming Interface (MAPI) proptag specification. The following schema names for PR_TRANSPORT_MESSAGE_HEADERS are both valid:
>
> *http://schemas.microsoft.com/mapi/0x007d001e*
>
> *http://schemas.microsoft.com/mapi/0x007D001E*

String Comparisons

The string comparisons that DASL filters support include equivalence, prefix, phrase, and substring matching. Note that when you filter on the *Subject* property, prefixes such as RE: and FW: are ignored.

Equivalence Matching   DASL filters perform string equivalence comparison by using the equal (=) operator. The value of the string property must be equivalent to the comparison string, with the exception of prefixes RE: and FW: as mentioned earlier.

As an example, the following DASL query creates a filter for company name equals 'Microsoft':

```
string filter = "@SQL="
    + "\"" + "urn:schemas-microsoft-com:office:office#Company" + "\""
    + " = 'Microsoft'";
```

As another example, assume that the folder you are searching contains items with the following subjects:

- Question
- Questionable
- Unquestionable

- RE: Question

- The big question

The following = restriction:

```
string filter = "@SQL="
    + "\"" + "urn:schemas:httpmail:subject" + "\""
    + " = 'question'";
```

will return the following results:

- Question

- RE: Question

Prefix, Phrase, and Substring Matching   DASL supports the matching of prefixes, phrases, and substrings in a string property using content indexer keywords *ci_startswith* and *ci_phrasematch*, and the keyword *like*. If a store is indexed, searching with content indexer keywords is more performant than with *like*. If your search scenarios include substring matching (which content indexer keywords do not support), use the *like* keyword in a DASL query.

A DASL query can contain *ci_startswith* or *ci_phrasematch*, and *like*, but all string comparisons will be carried out as substring matching.

ci_startswith   The syntax of *ci_startswith* is as follows:

<PropertySchemaName> ci_startswith <ComparisonString>

where *PropertySchemaName* is a valid name of a property referenced by namespace, and *ComparisonString* is the string used for comparison.

The keyword *ci_startswith* performs a search to match prefixes. It uses tokens (characters, word, or words) in the comparison string to match against the first few characters of any word in the string value of the indexed property. If the comparison string contains multiple tokens, every token in the comparison string must have a prefix match in the indexed property. For example:

- Restricting for "sea" would match "search."

- Restricting for "sea" would not match "research."

- Restricting for "sea" would match "Subject: the deep blue sea."

- Restricting for "law order" would match "law and order" or "law & order."

- Restricting for "law and order" would match "I like the show Law and Order."

- Restricting for "law and order" would not match "above the law."

- Restricting for "sea creatures" would match "Nova special on sea creatures."

- Restricting for "sea creatures" would match "sealife creatures."

- Restricting for "sea creatures" would not match "undersea creatures."

Using the same example in equivalence matching, assume that the folder you are searching contains items with the following subjects:

- Question
- Questionable
- Unquestionable
- RE: Question
- The big question

The following *ci_startswith* restriction:

```
string filter = "@SQL="
    + "\"" + "urn:schemas:httpmail:subject" + "\""
    + " ci_startswith 'question'";
```

will return the following results:

- Question
- Questionable
- RE: Question
- The big question

ci_phrasematch   The syntax of *ci_phrasematch* is as follows:

<PropertySchemaName> ci_phrasematch <ComparisonString>

where *PropertySchemaName* is a valid name of a property referenced by namespace, and *ComparisonString* is the string used for comparison.

The keyword *ci_phrasematch* performs a search to match phrases. It uses tokens (characters, word, a or words) in the comparison string to match entire words in the string value of the indexed property. Tokens are enclosed in double quotes or parentheses. Each token in the comparison string must have an equivalence match, not a substring or prefix match. If the comparison string contains multiple tokens, every token in the comparison string must have an equivalence match. Any word within a multiple word property like *Subject* or *Body* can match; it doesn't have to be the first word. For example:

- Restricting for "cat" would match "cat," "cat box," "black cat."
- Restricting for "cat" would match "re: cat is out."
- Restricting for "cat" would not match "catalog," "kittycat."
- Restricting for "kitty cat" would match "put the kitty cat out."
- Restricting for "kitty cat" would not match "great kitty catalog."

Using the same example in equivalence matching, assume that the folder you are searching contains items with the following subjects:

- Question
- Questionable
- Unquestionable
- RE: Question
- The big question

The following *ci_phrasematch* restriction:

```
string filter = "@SQL="
    + "\"" + "urn:schemas:httpmail:subject" + "\""
    + " ci_startswith 'question'";
```

will return the following results:

- Question
- RE: Question
- The big question

like   The keyword *like* performs prefix, substring, or equivalence matching. Tokens (characters, word, or words) are enclosed with the % character in a specific way depending on the type of matching: *like* '<token>%' provides prefix matching. For example, restricting for *like* 'cat%' would match "cat" and "catalog." *like* '%<token>%' provides substring matching. For example, restricting for *like* '%cat%' would match "cat," "catalog," "kittycat," and "decathlon." *like* '<token>' provides equivalence matching. For example, restricting for *like* 'cat' would match "cat" and "RE: Cat."

Each token can match any part of a word in the string property. If the comparison string contains multiple tokens, every token in the comparison string must have a substring match. Any word within a multiple word property like *Subject* or *Body* can match; it does not have to be the first word.

Using the same example in equivalence matching, assume that the folder you are searching contains items with the following subjects:

- Question
- Questionable
- Unquestionable
- RE: Question
- The big question

The following *like* restriction:

```
string filter = "@SQL="
    + "\"" + "urn:schemas:httpmail:subject" + "\""
    + " like '%question%'";
```

will return the following results:

- Question
- Questionable
- Unquestionable
- RE: Question
- The big question

Searching the Body of an Item

To search for items that contain a specific word in the body, use the *ci_startswith*, *ci_phrasematch*, or *like* operator with the namespace representation of the body property, *urn:schemas:httpmail:textdescription*. When you use a DASL query to search the item body, you cannot determine where in the body the match was found. If you need to determine where the word was found in the body, examine the *Body* property of the found item. The following code sample creates a filter for items using the *ci_phrasematch* keyword, uses the filter for the *Table* object, and writes the *Subject* property to the trace listeners in the *Listeners* collection:

```
private void DemoSearchBody()
{
    string filter;
    if (Application.Session.DefaultStore.IsInstantSearchEnabled)
    {
        filter = "@SQL=" + "\""
            + "urn:schemas:httpmail:textdescription" + "\""
            + " ci_phrasematch 'office'";
    }
    else
    {
        filter = "@SQL=" + "\""
            + "urn:schemas:httpmail:textdescription" + "\""
            + " like '%office%'";
    }
    Outlook.Table table = Application.Session.GetDefaultFolder(
        Outlook.OlDefaultFolders.olFolderInbox).GetTable(
        filter, Outlook.OlTableContents.olUserItems);
    while (!table.EndOfTable)
    {
        Outlook.Row row = table.GetNextRow();
        Debug.WriteLine(row["Subject"]);
    }
}
```

Searching Attachments

To search for items in an indexed store that contain a specific word in an attachment, use the *ci_startswith*, *ci_phrasematch*, or *like* operator with the *PR_SEARCH_ATTACHMENTS* property. This property causes Outlook to evaluate the search criteria against the contents of item attachments. Item attachments are represented by the *Attachments* collection of the parent item. The indexer must be able to parse the contents of the attachment for the query to return reliable results. When you use a DASL query to search item attachments, you cannot determine where in the attachment the match was found or in which attachment the match was found (in the case of an item with multiple attachments). The following code sample creates a filter for items using the *ci_phrasematch* keyword, uses the filter for the *Table* object, and writes the *Subject* property to the trace listeners in the *Listeners* collection:

```
private void DemoSearchAttachments()
{
    string filter;
    const string PR_SEARCH_ATTACHMENTS =
        "http://schemas.microsoft.com/mapi/proptag/0x0EA5001E";
    if (Application.Session.DefaultStore.IsInstantSearchEnabled)
    {
        filter = "@SQL=" + "\""
            + PR_SEARCH_ATTACHMENTS + "\""
            + " ci_phrasematch 'office'";
        Outlook.Table table = Application.Session.GetDefaultFolder(
            Outlook.OlDefaultFolders.olFolderInbox).GetTable(
            filter, Outlook.OlTableContents.olUserItems);
        while (!table.EndOfTable)
        {
            Outlook.Row row = table.GetNextRow();
            Debug.WriteLine(row["Subject"]);
        }
    }
}
```

Boolean Properties in DASL Syntax

In DASL syntax, you must convert *True/False* to an integer value, where 0 represents *False* and 1 represents *True*; likewise for *Yes/No* and *On/Off*. The DASL filter to return unread items is as follows:

```
string filter = "@SQL=" + "\"" + "urn:schemas:httpmail:read" +
    "\"" + "=0";
```

Keywords Properties

The following discussion uses the *Categories* property as an example, but can apply as well to any multivalued string property. The *Categories* property is of Outlook-type keywords, which is designed to hold multiple values. In MAPI, a *Keywords* property corresponds to the type *PT_MV_STRING8*. For additional information on MAPI property types, see Chapter 17.

To overcome the limitations of keyword restrictions using the Jet query syntax discussed later in this chapter, use DASL syntax that allows different restriction types such as phrase matching (*ci_phrasematch* keyword), starts with matching (*ci_startswith* keyword), or substring matching (*like* keyword). The following criteria string will find all items that contain "Business" as a category or as a word in a category, such as an item with the categories "Business" and "Business Intelligence." This filter string will succeed for all items that have "Business" as an exact word in the category field, even if the category has "Business" as one of the words, or the categories field contains more than one category:

```
string filter = "@SQL=" + "\""
    + "urn:schemas-microsoft-com:office:office#Keywords"
    + "\"" + " ci_phrasematch 'Business'";
```

If the multivalued property is added to the *Columns* collection of the *Table* object using a reference by namespace, the format of the values of the property is an array of strings. To access these values, parse the elements in the array. Using the last example, this would also allow you to obtain the items that contain exactly "Business" as a category.

Custom Properties in a DASL Query

In a DASL query, if the name of a custom property contains spaces, you must apply Uniform Resource Locator (URL) encoding to each space character and replace the space with "%20". In general, URL encoding applies the same way to characters in a DASL query as in a URL.

Outlook custom properties can be added in the Outlook user interface through the Field Chooser or added programmatically with the *Add* method of the *UserProperties* collection on an item or the *UserDefinedProperties* collection on a *Folder* object. When you construct a DASL query for an Outlook custom property, you must use the namespace globally unique identifier (GUID) for Outlook custom properties in the following format:

http://schemas.microsoft.com/mapi/string/{GUID}/PropertyName

where *{GUID}* is the following GUID:

{00020329-0000-0000-C000-000000000046}

The following DASL query uses the content indexer keyword *ci_phrasematch* and retrieves all contacts where the custom property named "Preferred Gift" matches "Diamonds":

```
string filter = "@SQL=" + "\""
    + "http://schemas.microsoft.com/mapi/string/"
    + "{00020329-0000-0000-C000-000000000046}/Preferred%20Gift"
    + "\"" + "ci_phrasematch 'Diamonds'";
```

If the custom property you are searching for does not exist in the *UserDefinedProperties* collection for a folder, you must append a type specifier to the namespace representation of the custom property. This requirement only applies to a DASL filter for the *Items* collection, the *Table* object, or the *AdvancedSearch* method. Only properties that use the *String* namespace require appending the type specifier. For additional information about MAPI type specifiers, see "Type Specifiers" in Chapter 17. For example, assume that you want to search for the Unicode string property named *MyProperty*, and this property does not exist in the *UserDefinedProperties* collection for a folder. The following DASL query appends the Unicode string type specifier (/0x0000001f) to the *String* namespace representation of the property:

```
string filter = "@SQL=" + "\""
    + "http://schemas.microsoft.com/mapi/string/"
    + "{00020329-0000-0000-C000-000000000046}/MyProperty"
    + "/0x0000001f" + "\"" + " = '12-74440'";
```

Building DASL Queries

Fortunately, there is a quick way to build DASL queries without too much pain. You can use an undocumented Registry key to display a Query Builder tab on the Filter dialog box associated with the View Summary dialog box (see Figure 11-2). After you use the Query Builder to construct your query, you can then copy the *Filter* syntax displayed on the SQL page and paste it into your code. Do not attempt to add the Query Builder page Registry setting unless you are familiar with the Microsoft Windows Registry Editor.

Figure 11-2   The Query Builder tab of the Filter dialog box.

To display the Query Builder tab of the Filter dialog box, follow these steps:

1. Click Start and point to Run. In the Run dialog box, type **Regedit**, and then click OK to launch the Windows Registry Editor.

2. In the Registry tree, navigate to HKEY_CURRENT_USER\Software \Microsoft\Office\12.0\Outlook.

3. From the Edit menu, select New, and then select Key.

4. In the Key edit box, type **QueryBuilder**. Regedit will suggest New Key #1, but you should replace that key name with QueryBuilder.

To build a filter using the Query Builder tab of the Filter dialog box, follow these steps:

1. In Outlook, from the View menu, select Current View, and then select Customize Current View.

2. In the View Summary dialog box, click Filter.

3. In the Filter dialog box, click the Query Builder tab.

4. Use the Query Builder interface to build your query. When you construct a filter, you actually build a *WHERE* clause without the *WHERE* keyword. Notice that you can use the logical *AND* or logical *OR* operator to develop the query and move clauses up or down.

5. In the Filter dialog box, click the SQL tab shown in Figure 11-3 and clear the Edit These Criteria Directly check box. Once you clear the check box, you can copy the query by selecting it and pressing Ctrl+C to copy it to the Clipboard.

Figure 11-3   Copy a Filter string from the SQL tab of the Filter dialog box to construct a DASL query.

6. Because you don't want to modify the view, click Cancel to close the Filter dialog box. Click Cancel again to close the View Summary dialog box.

Once you have constructed your filter string, the rest of the process is relatively straightforward. Paste the DASL string into the Microsoft Visual Studio code editor. If you are creating a filter for *Table.Restrict* or *Items.Restrict*, you need to concatenate the *@SQL=* prefix for your query to operate correctly. For a filter that is passed to the *AdvanceSearch* method of the *Application* object or used with *View.Filter*, you do not add the *@SQL=* prefix. Using the Query Builder page is certainly easier than typing long DASL strings manually.

The Jet query syntax is the easiest to learn and use in your code, but it does not have the power of DASL. Jet queries can create restrictions for most built-in and custom properties. When you create a Jet query, be aware that there are certain computed and binary properties that are invalid and will cause Outlook to raise an error. Jet query syntax also does not support the new content indexer keywords that leverage the Instant Search feature in Outlook 2007. Consequently, Jet queries will return results slower than DASL queries provided that Instant Search is installed and enabled.

Property Specifiers

Jet property specifiers use the English name of the property enclosed in square brackets to represent built-in properties in Jet queries. The English name of the property is identical with the object model name of the property. Based on this convention, you can use *[Subject]* in your Jet query independent of locale to create a restriction on the *Subject* property of an item. Custom properties use the locale-specific name of the property enclosed in square brackets.

> **Tip**   Don't confuse the object model name of the property with the Field Chooser name of the property, which is localized. For example, if French is the user interface (UI) language, then the Field Chooser will display a field named *Sujet* that represents the *Subject* property of a *MailItem* object. In a Jet equivalence query for "Office 2007" using the *Subject* property, the filter would be *[Subject] = 'Office 2007'* whether the UI language is French or English. Be aware that object model names for built-in properties have no spaces or special characters, whereas the Field Chooser name can contain both spaces and special characters. For example, the object model name for an assistant's phone number is *AssistantTelephoneNumber*. In the Field Chooser, this property is *Assistant's Phone*. Always use the object model name in your Jet queries.

String Comparisons

The string comparison that Jet filters support is limited to equivalence matching as long as the property is not a *Keywords* property. String comparisons for keywords properties use phrase matching. See the section "Keywords Properties in a Jet Query" later in this chapter. You can filter items based on the value of a string property being equivalent to a specific string, for example, the *LastName* property being equal to "Davolio." Note that the comparison is not case-sensitive; in the last example, specifying "Davolio" and "davolio" as the comparison string will return the same results.

When matching string properties, you can use either an apostrophe (') or double quotation marks ("") to delimit the values that are part of the filter. For example, all of the following lines function correctly when the property is a string:

```
string filter = "[CompanyName] = 'Microsoft'";
string filter = "[CompanyName] = " + "\"" + "Microsoft" + "\"";
```

> **Note**   If the search string contains a single quote character, escape the single quote character in the string with another single quote character. Similarly, if the search string contains a double quote character, escape the double quote character in the string with another double quote character.

Boolean Properties in Jet Syntax

In Jet syntax, Boolean operators such as *True/False*, *Yes/No*, *On/Off*, and so on should be used as is and should not be converted to a string. For example, to create a filter to return unread items, create a filter as follows:

```
string filter = "[UnRead] = True";
```

> **Note**   If you convert the Boolean value to a comparison string by enclosing it in quotation marks, then a Jet filter using any nonempty comparison string and filtering on a Boolean property will return items that have the property *True*. A Jet filter comparing an empty string with a Boolean property will return items that have the property *False*.

Custom Properties in a Jet Query

Custom properties are defined as properties that exist in the *UserDefinedProperties* collection for the folder that contains the item, and in the *UserProperties* collection for the item in the folder. Custom properties can contain spaces in the property name. In a Jet query, as in all property name references, simply enclose the custom property name in square brackets. For example, the following Jet query retrieves all contacts where the custom property named *Preferred Gift* is exactly "Diamonds." For the query to succeed, the custom property named *Preferred Gift* must exist in the *UserDefinedProperties* collection in the folder that contains the custom contact items:

```
string filter = "[Preferred Gift] = 'Diamonds'";
```

Keywords Properties in a Jet Query

Keywords properties are defined as Outlook properties that can contain multiple values. Typically keywords properties are multivalued string properties such as the *Categories* property on an item. In a Jet query, you only perform phrase matching on a keywords property. You cannot perform starts with or substring matching with a Jet query. Use a DASL query for starts with or substring restrictions. Consider the following criteria for *Table.Restrict*:

```
string filter  = "[Categories] = 'Partner'";
```

This Jet query will return rows for items where the *Categories* property for the item finds a phrase match for "Partner." It will return rows for items that are categorized as "Partner." It will also return rows for items that are categorized as "Partner" and "Important" and for items that are categorized as "Tier1 Partner." It will not return rows for items where the item category is only "Partnership."

Date-Time Comparisons

The following section covers date-time comparisons and filters for both Jet and DASL queries. The important concept for these restrictions is that Jet filters are evaluated against local time, while DASL filters are evaluated against Coordinated Universal Time (UTC). If you don't understand this distinction, you could return the wrong results from your date-time query because the query is formulated incorrectly. For example, if you want to issue a DASL query against a local date-time value, you must first convert the local time value to its equivalent UTC date-time value for the query to operate correctly.

Filtering Recurring Items in the Calendar Folder

To filter a collection of appointment items that include recurring appointments, you must use the *Items* collection. The *Table* object only returns rows that represent the master series appointment and does not support recurring items in a calendar folder. Use the *Items.IncludeRecurrences* property to specify that *Items.Find* or *Items.Restrict* should include recurring appointments. If *IncludeRecurrences* is *True*, you can filter recurring appointment items only on the *Start* and *End* properties. Use a Jet query to specify the *Start* and *End* properties.

If you need to obtain a subset of filtered recurring appointments, use the *Find* and *FindNext* methods or create a new restriction on an *Items* collection that contains recurrences. For example, the following *SearchRecurringAppointments* procedure creates an *Items* collection that contains recurring appointments between 8/9/2006 and 12/14/2006. It then uses the *Find* and *FindNext* methods to find recurring appointments that contain "Office" in the subject. An alternative, preferred method is to create a new *Items* collection by restricting the original *Items* collection. The filter for the new *Items* collection uses the *ci_startswith* keyword to create a subset of recurring items that start with "Office" in the subject.

```
private void SearchRecurringAppointments()
{
    Outlook.AppointmentItem appt = null;
    Outlook.Folder folder =
        Application.Session.GetDefaultFolder(
        Outlook.OlDefaultFolders.olFolderCalendar)
        as Outlook.Folder;
    //Set start value
    DateTime start =
        new DateTime(2006, 8, 9, 0, 0, 0);
    //Set end value
    DateTime end =
```

```
            new DateTime(2006, 12, 14, 0, 0, 0);
    //Initial restriction is Jet query for date range
    string filter1 = "[Start] >= '" +
        start.ToString("g")
        + "' AND [End] <= '" +
        end.ToString("g") + "'";
    Outlook.Items calendarItems = folder.Items.Restrict(filter1);
    calendarItems.Sort("[Start]", Type.Missing);
    calendarItems.IncludeRecurrences = true;
    //Must use 'like' comparison for Find/FindNext
    string filter2;
        filter2 = "@SQL="
            + "\"" + "urn:schemas:httpmail:subject" + "\""
            + " like '%Office%'";
    //Create DASL query for additional Restrict method
    string filter3;
    if (Application.Session.DefaultStore.IsInstantSearchEnabled)
    {
        filter3 = "@SQL="
            + "\"" + "urn:schemas:httpmail:subject" + "\""
            + " ci_startswith 'Office'";
    }
    else
    {
        filter3 = "@SQL="
            + "\"" + "urn:schemas:httpmail:subject" + "\""
            + " like '%Office%'";
    }
    //Use Find and FindNext methods
    appt = calendarItems.Find(filter2)
        as Outlook.AppointmentItem;
    while (appt != null)
    {
        StringBuilder sb = new StringBuilder();
        sb.AppendLine(appt.Subject);
        sb.AppendLine("Start: " + appt.Start);
        sb.AppendLine("End: " + appt.End);
        Debug.WriteLine(sb.ToString());
        //Find the next appointment
        appt = calendarItems.FindNext()
            as Outlook.AppointmentItem;
    }
    //Restrict calendarItems with DASL query
    Outlook.Items restrictedItems =
        calendarItems.Restrict(filter3);
    foreach (Outlook.AppointmentItem apptItem in restrictedItems)
    {
        StringBuilder sb = new StringBuilder();
        sb.AppendLine(apptItem.Subject);
        sb.AppendLine("Start: " + apptItem.Start);
        sb.AppendLine("End: " + apptItem.End);
        sb.AppendLine();
        Debug.WriteLine(sb.ToString());
    }

}
```

Date-Time Format of Comparison Strings

Date-time values are recognized according to the time format, short date format, and long date format settings in Regional and Language Options in the Windows Control Panel.

Although dates and times are typically stored with a date format, filters using the Jet and DASL syntax require that the date-time value be converted to a string representation. In Jet syntax, the date-time comparison string should be enclosed in either double quotes or single quotes. In DASL syntax, the date-time comparison string should be enclosed in single quotes.

To make sure that the date-time comparison string is formatted as Outlook expects, use the constructor of the *DateTime* structure and the *ToString* method with the "g" format specifier, which converts the *DateTime* value to a string that will be interpreted correctly by Outlook. The following example creates a Jet filter to find all contacts modified before June 12, 2005, at 3:30 p.m. local time:

```
string filter = "[LastModificationTime] < '" +
    new DateTime(2005, 6, 12, 15, 30, 0).ToString("g") + "'";
```

Date-Time Literals for Outlook Date-Time Comparisons

Outlook evaluates date-time strings based on the date and time settings in the Regional and Language Options in Windows Control Panel. Specifically, Outlook evaluates dates according to the short date format and time according to the time format without seconds. If you specify seconds in the date-time string, the query will fail to operate as expected.

The format used by Outlook corresponds to the General (short date and short time) pattern in the *DateTimeFormatInfo* class. If you use the *Parse* method of the *DateTime* structure, you should be certain that the argument to the *Parse* method follows the short date and short time format for the current locale. If you use the constructor for the *DateTime* structure, you need to specify year, month, day, hour, minute, and second arguments and then use the *ToString* method with the "g" format specifier to convert the date-time value to the short date and short time string expected by Outlook. The date specifier argument to the *ToString* method is case-sensitive, so be sure to use "g" as the format specifier. When you use the *DateTime* constructor and the "g" format specifier in the *ToString* method, you create a date-time literal that will be interpreted correctly by Outlook.

Time Zones Used in Comparison

When an explicit built-in property is referenced in a Jet query with its explicit string name, the comparison evaluates the property value and the date-time comparison string as local time values.

When a property is referenced in a DASL query by namespace, the comparison evaluates the property value and the date-time comparison string as UTC values. For example, the following DASL query finds all contacts modified before June 12, 2005, at 3:30 p.m. UTC:

```
string filter = "@SQL=" + "\"" + "DAV:getlastmodified" + "\"" +
    " < '" + new DateTime(2005, 6, 12, 15, 30, 0).ToString("g") + "'";
```

Conversion to UTC for DASL Queries

Because DASL queries always perform date-time comparisons in UTC, if you use a date literal in a comparison string, you must use its UTC value for the comparison. You can use the *Row.LocalTimeToUTC* helper function or Outlook date-time macros to facilitate the conversion.

> **Note**   You should use the local time to UTC conversion functions built into the Outlook object model to perform conversions from local date-time values to UTC date-time values rather than *DateTime* structure conversion functions such as *ToLocalTime* and *ToUniversalTime*.

LocalTimeToUTC

One way to facilitate local time to UTC conversion is to use the helper function, *LocalTimeToUTC*, of the *Row* object. The following line of code uses this helper function to convert the value of the *LastModificationTime* property (which is a default column in all *Table* objects):

```
DateTime modified = nextRow.LocalTimeToUTC("LastModificationTime");
```

Outlook Date-Time Macros

The date macros listed in Table 11-8 return filter strings that compare the value of a given date-time property with a specified relative date or date range in UTC; *SchemaName* is any valid date-time property referenced by namespace.

> **Note**   Outlook date-time macros can be used only in DASL queries.

For example, the *DemoDASLDateMacro* procedure creates a DASL query that filters for items that were modified in the last month, creates a *Table* object with that filter, and then enumerates rows in the restricted *Table* object.

```
private void DemoDASLDateMacro()
{
    string filter = "@SQL=" + "%lastmonth(" + "\"" +
        "DAV:getlastmodified" + "\"" + ")%";
    Outlook.Table table = Application.Session.GetDefaultFolder(
        Outlook.OlDefaultFolders.olFolderInbox).GetTable(
        filter, Outlook.OlTableContents.olUserItems);
    while(!table.EndOfTable)
```

```
    {
        Outlook.Row row = table.GetNextRow();
        Debug.WriteLine(row["Subject"]);
    }
}
```

Table 11-8   Outlook Date Macros for DASL Queries

Macro	Syntax	Description
today	%today("SchemaName")%	Restricts for items with *SchemaName* property value equal to today
tomorrow	%tomorrow("SchemaName")%	Restricts for items with *SchemaName* property value equal to tomorrow
yesterday	%yesterday("SchemaName")%	Restricts for items with *SchemaName* property value equal to yesterday
next7days	%next7days("SchemaName")%	Restricts for items with *SchemaName* property values in range equivalent to next 7 days
last7days	%last7days("SchemaName")%	Restricts for items with *SchemaName* property values in range equivalent to last 7 days
nextweek	%nextweek("SchemaName")%	Restricts for items with *SchemaName* property values in range equivalent to next week
thisweek	%thisweek("SchemaName")%	Restricts for items with *SchemaName* property values in range equivalent to this week
lastweek	%lastweek("SchemaName")%	Restricts for items with *SchemaName* property values in range equivalent to last week
nextmonth	%nextmonth("SchemaName")%	Restricts for items with *SchemaName* property values in range equivalent to next month
thismonth	%thismonth("SchemaName")%	Restricts for items with *SchemaName* property values in range equivalent to this month
lastmonth	%lastmonth("SchemaName")%	Restricts for items with *SchemaName* property values in range equivalent to last month

Integer Comparisons

You can compare an integer property with an integer value in a filter string using Jet or DASL syntax. You can specify the integer value with or without quotation marks as delimiters. The following Jet filter can be used to restrict on the condition that the Importance value is high:

```
string filter = "[Importance] = 2";
```

If you want to use a value from an integer enumeration, convert the value to a string and append it to the filter string. The following filters are equivalent and test for items with Importance set to high:

```
string filter = "[Importance] = " +
    Outlook.OlImportance.olImportanceHigh.ToString();
```

```
string filter = "@SQL=" + "\"" + "urn:schemas:httpmail:importance"
    + "\"" + " = 2";
```

Invalid Properties

Not every property can be used in a filter string for *Items.Restrict* or *Table.Restrict*. For both Jet and DASL queries, you cannot restrict on a binary property such as *EntryID*. You also cannot restrict for computed properties such as *BodyFormat* or *RecurrenceState*. There are some exceptions for DASL properties that are noted later.

Jet

The properties listed in Table 11-9 are invalid in a Jet restriction. Outlook will raise a "Condition is not valid" error if you attempt to use one of the properties listed here in a restriction string.

Table 11-9   Invalid Properties for a Jet Restriction

AutoResolvedWinner	Body	BodyFormat
Class	Companies	CompanyLastFirstNoSpace
CompanyLastFirstSpaceOnly	ContactNames	Contents
ConversationIndex	DLName	DownloadState
Email1EntryID	Email2EntryID	Email3EntryID
EntryID	HtmlBody	InternetCodePage
IsConflict	IsMarkedAsTask	LastFirstAndSuffix
LastFirstNoSpace	LastFirstNoSpaceAndSuffix	LastFirstNoSpaceCompany
LastFirstSpaceOnly	LastFirstSpaceOnlyCompany	MeetingWorkspaceURL
MemberCount	NetMeetingAlias	NetMeetingServer
Permission	PermissionService	ReceivedByEntryID
ReceivedOnBehalfOfEntryID	RecurrenceState	ReplyRecipients
ResponseState	Saved	Sent
Submitted	TaskSubject	VotingOptions

DASL

If a schema name representation of the Jet property exists, using the schema name property in a DASL restriction will also cause Outlook to raise an error. However, there are some exceptions to this rule. For example, you can use the schema name for plain text body to create a restriction as follows:

```
string filter = "@SQL=" +
    "\"" + "urn:schemas:httpmail:textdescription" + "\"" +
    " ci_startswith 'Office'";
```

Another notable exception is the *IsMarkedAsTask* property. You can use the schema name representation of this property to create a filter for items that are marked as a task:

```
string filter = "@SQL=" + "\"" +
    http://schemas.microsoft.com/mapi/proptag/0x0E2B0003
    + "\"" + " = 1";
```

Comparison and Logical Operators

You can write queries that range from the simple Subject equivalence query in Jet to complex DASL queries. The following sections list valid comparison and logical operators for both Jet and DASL queries.

Comparison Operators

Table 11-10 lists valid comparison operators in filter strings using Jet or DASL syntax.

Table 11-10 Comparison Operators

Operator	Description
<	Performs a less-than comparison
>	Performs a greater-than comparison
<=	Performs a less-than-or-equal-to comparison
>=	Performs a greater-than-or-equal-to comparison
<>	Performs a not-equal-to comparison
=	Performs an equal-to comparison

Logical Operators

You can use the logical operators *And*, *Not*, and *Or* in filter strings in Jet or DASL syntax. The order of precedence of these operators, from the highest to the lowest, is *Not*, *And*, *Or*. You can use parentheses to indicate specific precedence in a filter. Logical operators are case-insensitive.

Not

Not performs a logical *NOT* on the condition. The following Jet query retrieves all contacts with a first name of Jane who do not work at Microsoft:

```
string filter = "[FirstName] = 'Jane'" +
    " And Not([CompanyName] = 'Microsoft')";
```

And

And performs a logical *AND* on the condition. The following Jet query retrieves all contacts who work at Microsoft and have a first name of Marina:

```
string filter = "[FirstName] = 'Marina'" +
    " And [CompanyName] = 'Microsoft'";
```

Or

Or performs a logical *OR* on the condition. The following code returns all contact items that have a first name of either Peter or Paul:

```
string filter = "[FirstName] = 'Peter' Or [FirstName] = 'Paul'";
```

Null Comparisons

To perform null comparisons, use the *Is Null* keywords in a DASL query. *Is Null* is invalid in a Jet query. *Is Null* returns *True* if the property is null and *False* if the property is not null.

Is Null operations are useful to determine if a date property has been set or if a string property is empty. If the date is null, the local time value of the date will be equal to 1/1/4501.

The syntax of *Is Null* is as follows:

[PropertyName] IS NULL

where *PropertyName* is the name of a property referenced by namespace.

You can combine the *Is Null* keywords with the *Not* operator to evaluate if a property is not null. The following DASL query retrieves all contacts where the custom property *Order Date* is not null and the *CompanyName* property is exactly Microsoft:

```
string filter = "(NOT(" +
    AddQuotes("http://schemas.microsoft.com/mapi/string/"
    + "{00020329-0000-0000-C000-000000000046}/Order%20Date")
    + " IS NULL) AND "
    + AddQuotes("urn:schemas-microsoft-com:office:office#Company")
    + " = 'Microsoft')";
```

Search Entry Points

The number of object model entry points for search has expanded significantly in Outlook 2007. Table 11-11 lists the entry points for search in the Outlook object model. This table provides a good overview of the search and filtering features of the Outlook 2007 object model. Some of the features, such as the *Search* method of the *Explorer* object or the *Filter* property of the *View* object, only return results in the Outlook UI. Other features, such as the *Restrict* method on the *Items* collection or the *Table* object, return results programmatically. Choose the most appropriate entry point for your specific scenario.

Table 11-11   Search Entry Points

Entry point	Action	Comments
Application.Advanced-Search	Returns a *Search* object using the criteria specified by the *Filter* parameter.	Use the *AdvancedSearchComplete* event on the *Application* object to determine when a given search has completed. *Filter* must be a DASL query without the *@SQL=* prefix.
AutoFormatRule.Filter	Applies a filter to an *AutoFormatRule* object.	The *Filter* property is not persisted when you save the *View* object. You must re-create the filter dynamically. See the code sample for *AutoFormatRule* in Chapter 10, "Organizing Outlook Data." *Filter* must be a DASL query without the *@SQL=* prefix.
Explorer.Search	Based on the *Query* parameter passed to the method, performs a programmatic content indexer search that is analogous to a user executing a search from the Outlook UI.	Use the *IsInstantSearchEnabled* property of the *Store* object to determine if Instant Search is installed and enabled for a given *Store* object. The scope of the search is determined by the *SearchAllItems* parameter. If *SearchAllItems* is *True*, the method will search across all folders that have the same folder type as the current folder and all stores that have been selected for search in the Search Options dialog box. If *SearchAllItems* is *False*, the method will search only the folder represented by *Explorer.CurrentFolder.Query* can be any valid AQS query. You cannot use Jet or DASL syntax for the *Query* parameter.
Folder.GetTable	Returns a *Table* object containing rows determined by the *Filter* parameter.	*Filter* can be a Jet query or a DASL query with the *@SQL=* prefix.

Table 11-11   Search Entry Points

Entry point	Action	Comments
Items.Find	Searches for the first item in the *Items* collection that satisfies the specified *Filter* parameter and returns an *Object* object representing the item.	Use the *FindNext* method to find the next item that meets the criteria established for the *Find* method. You should cast the returned item to the appropriate type. *Filter* can be a Jet query or a DASL query with the *@SQL=* prefix. If you use *ci_phrasematch* or *ci_startswith* in the filter for the *Find* method, Outlook will raise an error.
Items.Restrict	Filters a given set of items based on the *Filter* parameter and returns another *Items* collection.	*Filter* can be a Jet query or a DASL query with the *@SQL=* prefix.
Search.GetTable	Returns a *Table* object containing rows determined by the *Filter* parameter passed to *Application. AdvancedSearch*.	You cannot filter the *Table* object returned by *Search.GetTable* by calling *Table.Restrict*.
Table.FindRow	Searches for the first row in the *Table* object that satisfies the specified filter and returns a *Row* object representing the item.	Use the *FindNextRow* method to find the next row that meets the criteria established for the *FindRow* method. *Filter* can be a Jet query or a DASL query with the *@SQL=* prefix. If you use *ci_phrasematch* or *ci_startswith* in the filter for the *FindRow* method, Outlook will raise an error.
Table.Restrict	Filters rows in the given table based on a specified filter and returns another *Table* object.	*Filter* can be a Jet query or a DASL query with the *@SQL=* prefix.
View.Filter	Sets a view's filter without changing the view's *XML* value. Setting the *Filter* parameter for a *View* object only changes the view in the user interface and does not result in a filtered *Items* collection.	*Filter* must be a DASL query without the *@SQL=* prefix.
View.XML	The *XML* property gets or sets the XML for a view. Modifying the *<Filter>* node changes the view's filter. Setting the XML for a view only changes the view in the UI and does not result in a filtered *Items* collection.	*View.XML* is no longer recommended. Use the *Filter* property of the *View* object instead of modifying the *<Filter>* node in *View.XML*.

Search Considerations

So, you know your solution requires search, but you don't know which type of search will work best for your particular scenario. The following discussion provides some guidelines for programmatic search in Outlook. Not every scenario is covered here, but you should be able to save some time by reading this section with your specific scenario in mind.

Performance

The following guidelines are designed to help you decide how to code your search to achieve the best possible performance. In part, the performance decision you make depends on whether your search operates against Microsoft Exchange Server using online mode, Exchange Server using cached mode, or a Personal Folders File (.pst) without Exchange. Making your search operations perform as fast as possible is important for customer acceptance of your solution and for the performance of Outlook in general. Consider all of the following guidelines when you implement search for your solution.

If you need a persistent and long-lived aggregation of contents from multiple folders in a single store, consider using the *AdvancedSearch* method. The *AdvancedSearch* method requires the store to support search folders, which can degrade store performance, especially as the number of search folders grows. If the *AdvancedSearch* method is called against an Exchange Server store, there are additional performance considerations. If you issue repeated restrictions using the *AdvancedSearch* method of the *Application* object and restrict on different properties in the restriction, the performance of Exchange Server could be affected. When you call the *AdvancedSearch* method (regardless of whether you call *Search.Save*), a hidden search folder is created on Exchange Server. If you find that Exchange Server performance suffers due to the number of restrictions you issue against one or more folders, you should consider using the *Restrict* method for the *Table* object instead of the *AdvancedSearch* method. For additional details on performance degradation on Exchange Server, see the Microsoft Knowledge Base article at *http://support.microsoft.com/kb/216076*.

If you only need contents from a single folder (excluding a folder that contains appointment items), then the *Restrict* method or the *FindRow* method on the *Table* object should be the default choice. The *AdvancedSearch* method introduces unnecessary overhead. The *Restrict* method typically incurs one remote procedure call (RPC) each time the *Restrict* method is called. Another approach is to use the *Find* and *FindNext* methods on the *Items* collection or the *FindRow* and *FindNextRow* methods on the *Table* object. The find methods are appropriate when you have sorted items or rows and then want to seek rows within the *Table* object.

In general, you should prefer the *Table* object over the *Items* collection except for the case when you need to obtain recurring appointments. For cached Exchange mode and Post Office Protocol 3 (POP3) or Internet Message Access Protocol (IMAP) accounts using a Personal Folders File (.pst), using the *Table* object is almost an order of magnitude faster than using the *Items* collection without calling the *SetColumns* method. The improved performance of the

Table object is especially noticeable when you enumerate or filter folders that contain a large number of items (more than 1,000). If your scenario requires that you use the *Items* collection, use the *SetColumns* method to improve performance. For details on the use of the *Items* collection and the *Table* object, see Chapter 6, "Accessing Outlook Data."

If you need recurring appointments for a Calendar folder, use the *Items* collection and set the *IncludeRecurrences* property to *True*. For a Calendar folder, the *Table* object only returns rows that represent the appointment series for recurring appointments. If you need to apply an additional restriction to the returned *Items* collection in this case, use the *Restrict* method of the *Items* collection to return a subset of recurring appointments. For complete details, see the section "Use *IncludeRecurrences* to Expand Recurring Appointments" in Chapter 6.

If the *ExchangeConnectionMode* property indicates that the user is operating in online Exchange mode, the *Restrict* method should generally be considered a relatively expensive operation for the store. Search folders with restrictions can basically be considered a special case of the *Restrict* method, although the longer life of a search folder does cut the performance cost to some degree. In many cases, the *Restrict* method can be changed to the *FindRow* and *FindNextRow* methods, possibly combined with client-side restriction evaluation. The most common case is when you have a restriction that narrows the range of a sortable column (for example, find all mail received in the past seven days). By sorting on the "key" of the restriction, you can use the *FindRow* method to navigate to the first matching row and then query rows until finding a nonmatching row. This approach is less cost-effective, though, if the restricted set of rows are in multiple noncontiguous regions such that each call to the *FindNextRow* method could potentially result in its own RPC, whereas the *Restrict* method ensures that the matching rows are grouped together.

If the store is indexed (the *IsInstantSearchEnabled* property on the *Store* object returns *True*) and the property you are searching is a string property and exists in the index, then use *ci_startswith* or *ci_phrasematch* in a DASL query for the *Restrict* method on the *Table* object.

If you only want to display the search results in an Explorer window, choose an AQS query and use the *Search* method on the *Explorer* object. You cannot programmatically obtain the results from an AQS search.

Read-Only vs. Read/Write

If you need only to read information from a search, the *Table* object is the preferred method of obtaining search results subject to the performance considerations discussed earlier. If you need to span multiple folders, call the *AdvancedSearch* method and use the *GetTable* method on the *Search* object.

If you need to perform write operations on the results of a search, you have a couple options:

- Use the *Table* object for the search, ensure that the *EntryID* value is present in the *Columns* collection, and use the *GetItemFromID* method of the *Namespace* object to obtain a full item. You can then perform read/write operations on the full item. Because the table's *Columns* collection can also return *MessageClass*, you can cast the item to the appropriate type based on *MessageClass*.

■ Use the *Items* collection for the search and enumerate the items using a *foreach* construct. You can perform read/write operations on the item. Remember that the *Items* collection can contain items of different types. Use the *OutlookItem* helper class discussed in Chapter 6 for read/write operations on common properties, or perform a cast to return the correct type. Once you have an item, make appropriate changes and then save the item.

Searching Subfolders

If you need to search in multiple folders, you should consider the *GetTable* method of the *Search* object. The *AdvancedSearch* method of the *Application* object returns a *Search* object. The scope for the search can span multiple folders and their subfolders in a given store. The scope for *AdvancedSearch* cannot span multiple stores. Coding *Search.GetTable* is a little more complicated than writing basic *Table* object code, simply because you must hook up event handlers for the *AdvancedSearchComplete* event on the *Application* object. See Chapter 10 for more information on the *Search* object.

Windows Desktop Search

Another factor that affects performance is whether Windows Desktop Search is installed and enabled for a given *Store* object. For Microsoft Windows Vista, Windows Desktop Search is an integral component of the operating system. For Microsoft Windows XP, Windows Desktop Search must be downloaded and installed as a separate component. Outlook will prompt the user to install Windows Desktop Search if it is not installed. Use the *IsInstantSearchEnabled* property of the *Store* object to determine if Instant Search is installed and enabled.

> **Important**   There is no way to determine programmatically that indexing is complete for a given store. In a first-run scenario when it can take several hours for indexing to complete, this can present a problem for content indexer searches. *IsInstantSearchEnabled* will return *True* even when indexing has not completed for a given folder or store.

Your code should always check the *IsInstantSearchEnabled* property of the *Store* object. This property will return *False* if Windows Desktop Search is not installed on Windows XP. It will also return *False* if the user or group policy has disabled Instant Search on a given *Store*. If *IsInstantSearchEnabled* returns *False,* you typically would create a *like* DASL restriction for string properties. If *IsInstantSearchEnabled* returns *True,* you can create a *ci_startswith* or *ci_phrasematch* DASL restriction for string properties. If you use a content indexer restriction and *IsInstantSearchEnabled* is *False,* Outlook will raise an error.

Summary

This chapter covered all the programmatic query languages for Outlook 2007: Jet, DASL, and AQS. The use of a particular query language depends on your scenario. For most operations, DASL queries are performant and additionally can utilize the Instant Search feature of Outlook 2007. Programmatic search and filtering are greatly improved in this version of Outlook, and you will be able to create some innovative solutions using these new search entry points in the Outlook object model.

Part IV
Providing a User Interface for Your Solution

Chapter 12
Introducing the Outlook User Interface

The majority of Outlook integrations require some customization of the Microsoft Office Outlook 2007 user interface (UI). Because it is composed of different windows, panes, and form regions, the Outlook UI presents a complex UI model to the developer. This chapter provides an introduction to the various components of the Outlook UI and helps you to get acquainted with the terminology used by the object model to describe these various interface components. This chapter also drills down into some of these elements to explain how to work with them programmatically.

Decoding the User Interface

The Outlook UI can be daunting if you aren't used to the terminology used in the object model to reference the components of the UI. Outlook primarily consists of windows, panes, and forms. There are two different window types in Outlook—Explorer windows and Inspector windows—and each of these windows contains panes and forms.

An Explorer window is typically the first window that Outlook displays when launched. The Explorer window contains folder navigation components, the contents of the folder, and other elements in several panes. The standard Explorer window features four panes: the Navigation Pane, a View Pane, the Reading Pane, and the To-Do Bar. Users can also open multiple Explorer windows at the same time to provide simultaneous views of the contents of multiple folders, as when opening their calendar in one window while looking at their Inbox in another.

When a user opens an item from a folder or composes a new item, Outlook displays an Inspector window. Each Inspector window contains a form or forms associated with the item, such as the built-in standard forms, and the form contains controls associated with the item. Custom forms can also contain a custom form or form regions. These forms control which fields are displayed on the form and how they are laid out for the user to work with. With custom task panes, the Inspector window can also include one or more custom panes that display information related to the item open in the window. The Inspector windows also feature a Ribbon element across the top of the window, which provides an easier way to find and use commands.

The Explorer Window (The *Explorer* Object)

The Explorer window is where most Outlook users spend a majority of their time inside Outlook. Figure 12-1 shows the major components of the Explorer window viewed from the platform perspective. This window is represented by the *Explorer* object and the *Explorers* collection in the object model.

Navigation Pane   Folder Contents/View   Reading Pane   To-Do Bar

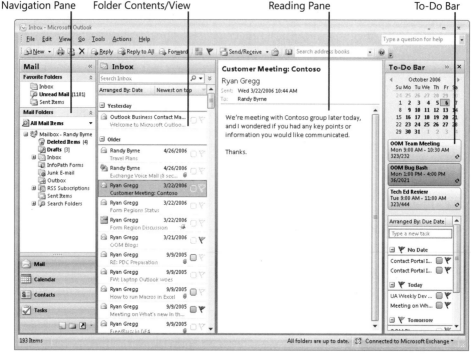

Figure 12-1   Components of the Outlook Explorer window user interface.

Each Explorer window is made up of several components, including the following:

■ **Command bars**   Command bars include the menu bar, standard and advanced toolbars, and any custom toolbars added by add-ins. These toolbars typically are docked at the top of the Explorer window, but can be docked to any edge of the window and can also float above the window. Command bars can be customized by adding new controls to an existing command bar, or creating a custom toolbar for new commands. Command bars support different types of controls, including buttons, drop-down boxes, and text boxes.

■ **The Navigation Pane**   The Navigation Pane allows the user to select different modules in the Outlook interface, such as Mail or Calendar. Additionally, the Navigation Pane displays a list of folders for each module. Depending on the module, folders are displayed either as a tree view (Mail and Folder List modules) or as groups of folders (Contacts, Calendar, Tasks, Journal, and Shortcut modules). The object model includes support for switching modules, controlling which modules are displayed, and modifying the grouping of folders in modules that have folder groups.

- **Folder view**   The folder view displays the contents of the currently selected folder, subject to any applied filter or restriction. Outlook includes several different view types, including Table, Timeline, Card, Business Card, Day/Week/Month, and Icon views. The layout of the folder view can be controlled using the object model to define which view type is used and, for some view types, which fields are displayed. Folder views can also be replaced by folder home pages, which are discussed later.

- **Reading Pane**   The Reading Pane displays a read-only preview of the currently selected item or attachment. Outlook 2007 provides the ability to customize the look of the preview pane for both items and attachments. You can also use a form region to extend or replace the look of the item in the Reading Pane, or a custom preview handler to control the way an attachment is previewed in the Reading Pane.

- **To-Do Bar**   The To-Do Bar provides a quick summary of upcoming appointments and tasks based on the data stored in the mailbox. Although object model support for customizing the look of the To-Do Bar is limited, you can add items to the calendar or task list and have them appear in the To-Do Bar.

- **Custom task panes**   Custom task panes provide you with an opportunity to add a new pane to the Outlook Explorer window. A custom task pane can be docked on any edge of the Explorer or Inspector window or can float above the window. Each custom task pane hosts an ActiveX or WinForm user control, which allows you complete flexibility to design the task pane for your solution.

- **Context menus**   The Explorer window also features a number of context menus that can be customized, including context menus from items, folders, stores, views, and shortcuts. Customizations for context menus are implemented in a way similar to that of command bars, although the changes must be applied to each context menu just before it is displayed to the user.

Programming the *Explorer* Object

Instances of the *Explorer* object cannot be created directly. Instead, you need to use the *Explorers* collection to access existing instances or to create a new instance of the object. The *Explorers* collection is available as a property of the Outlook *Application* object.

The *Explorers* Collection

The *Explorers* collection provides a way to enumerate the active *Explorer* instances and to create a new instance of the *Explorer* object. The collection also provides an event that notifies your add-in or solution when a new *Explorer* instance has been created.

Creating a New Explorer Window

Creating a new Explorer window first requires that you obtain a reference to a *Folder* object that represents the first folder displayed in the Explorer window. You can also customize the appearance of the *Explorer* object by setting the optional second argument on the *Add* method. After creating a new *Explorer* object, you need to call the *Display* method to show the window to the user.

```
private void CreateExplorerWindow()
{
  // Get a folder to display in the Explorer
  Outlook.Folder inbox = Application.Session.GetDefaultFolder(
    Outlook.OlDefaultFolders.olFolderInbox) as Outlook.Folder;

  // Create a new Explorer with this folder
  Outlook.Explorer inboxExplorer = Application.Explorers.Add(inbox,
    Outlook.OlFolderDisplayMode.olFolderDisplayNormal);
  inboxExplorer.Display();
}
```

In this example, the code creates a standard Explorer window. However, you can also use *OlFolderDisplayMode.olFolderNoNavigation* to disable the Navigation Pane for that *Explorer* instance. If you create an Explorer window using this flag, the Navigation Pane cannot be enabled on that Explorer window. This is different than using the *Explorer.ShowPane* method to turn off the Navigation Pane after the Explorer window has been created, which only hides the Navigation Pane.

Accessing the Active Explorer

You can use the *Explorers* collection to enumerate and add Explorer windows, but there is a shortcut to the active Explorer window on the *Application* object. You can use the *ActiveExplorer* function to return an instance of the *Explorer* object for the last used Explorer window. If there are no Explorer windows, this method returns *null* (*Nothing* in Microsoft Visual Basic).

```
public void ShowActiveExplorer()
{
  Outlook.Explorer explorer = Application.ActiveExplorer();
  MessageBox.Show(string.Format("The active explorer window is '{0}'.",
    explorer.Caption));
}
```

Current Folder and Folder Change Events

In many cases you need to determine or change the current folder displayed by the Explorer window. You can use the *CurrentFolder* property of an *Explorer* object to return the active folder in the window. The following example shows the name and path of the currently selected folder in a message box.

```
public void DisplayActiveFolder()
{
  Outlook.Explorer exp = Application.ActiveExplorer();
  Outlook.Folder curFolder = exp.CurrentFolder as Outlook.Folder;

  MessageBox.Show(string.Format("The currently selected folder is '{0}'",
    curFolder.FolderPath));
}
```

In some situations your application might need to update internal state or otherwise respond appropriately if the folder is changed in the *Explorer* object. For example, perhaps you need to disable a button you added to a toolbar when the folder is not a calendar folder. The *Explorer* object provides two events that notify your add-in when the folder is changing: *BeforeFolderSwitch* and *FolderSwitch*.

BeforeFolderSwitch is raised before any folder change has occurred. This event notifies you which folder the window is about to switch to, and allows your code to cancel that switch if necessary through its parameters. *FolderSwitch* occurs after the folder has already changed, providing an indication that the *CurrentFolder* property contains a different value than before the event was raised.

The following example detects when the current folder has changed and displays a message box indicating the new folder path:

```
public Outlook.Explorer explorer;
public void ListenForFolderSwitch()
{
  explorer = Application.ActiveExplorer();
  // Hook up events
  explorer.FolderSwitch +=
    new Outlook.ExplorerEvents_10_FolderSwitchEventHandler(
    explorer_FolderSwitch);
  ((Outlook.ExplorerEvents_10_Event)explorer).Close +=
    new Outlook.ExplorerEvents_10_CloseEventHandler(explorer_Close);
}
void explorer_FolderSwitch()
{
  MessageBox.Show(string.Format("The new folder is '{0}'.",
    explorer.CurrentFolder.FolderPath));
}

void explorer_Close()
{
  // Unhook the event handlers
  explorer.FolderSwitch -=
    new Outlook.ExplorerEvents_10_FolderSwitchEventHandler(
    explorer_FolderSwitch);
  ((Outlook.ExplorerEvents_10_Event)explorer).Close -=
    new Outlook.ExplorerEvents_10_CloseEventHandler(explorer_Close);
}
```

In this example, you cast the *Explorer* object to the *ExplorerEvents_10_Event* interface to hook up the *Close* event. The *Explorer* object has two members named *Close*, an event and a method. Because C# will default to using the method, an explicit cast to the event interface is required to use the *Close* event. It is important to always listen for the *Close* event on the Explorer window and unhook any event handlers from that object. For additional information on Outlook events and event handlers, see Chapter 8, "Responding to Events."

Determining the *Selection* Object in the Explorer Window

The *Selection* object enables you to enumerate the items that are actively selected in the Explorer window. Unlike previous versions of Outlook, the *Selection* object in Outlook 2007 will return the particular instances of a recurring appointment or meeting on the calendar, instead of the master appointment.

The following example retrieves the *Selection* object from the active *Explorer* object and displays a message box window with the count of items and the subject of the selected items:

```
public void ShowSelectedItems()
{
  Outlook.Explorer explorer = Application.ActiveExplorer();
  Outlook.Selection selection = explorer.Selection;

  StringBuilder sb = new StringBuilder();
  sb.AppendFormat("There are {0} items selected:\n", selection.Count);
  for (int i = 1; i <= selection.Count; i++)
  {
    OutlookItem selectedItem = new OutlookItem(selection[i]);
    sb.AppendFormat("\t{0}\n", selectedItem.Subject);
  }
  MessageBox.Show(sb.ToString());
}
```

> **Note**   The *Selection* object only shows items that are actually selected. In some folder views, group headers can be selected. These group headers are not included in the *Selection* object, nor are the items under that group header included.

Working with Panes

You can use the *ShowPane* method on the *Explorer* object to dynamically show and hide some of the panes of the Explorer window. The following example code shows how to turn off the To-Do Bar in the active Explorer window:

```
public void HideToDoBar()
{
  Outlook.Explorer explorer = Application.ActiveExplorer();
  if (explorer != null)
```

```
    {
       explorer.ShowPane(Outlook.OlPane.olToDoBar, false);
    }
}
```

Note   The To-Do Bar visible state is persisted per module. For instance, you can disable the To-Do Bar in the Mail module, but still have it appear in the Contacts module. This is different from the other panes, which are persisted globally across all modules.

The Inspector Window (The *Inspector* Object)

Inspector windows, which are represented by the *Inspector* object and *Inspectors* collection, provide a window to compose new items and read or edit existing items. The term *item window* is sometimes used to denote an Inspector window. For simplicity, in this chapter we use the term *Inspector window* to denote the window that represents item data to the user. Inspector windows include the new 2007 Microsoft Office system user interface and can be customized using custom forms or form regions. Figure 12-2 shows the components of the Inspector window.

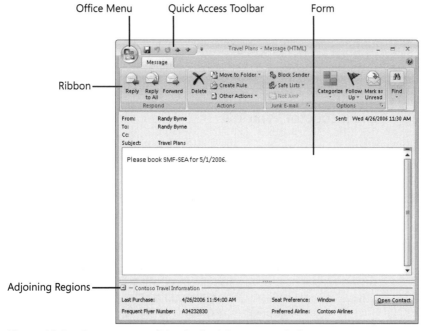

Figure 12-2   Components of the Outlook Inspector window.

- Ribbon. Instead of displaying toolbars and menu bars, Inspector windows in Outlook 2007 use the new Ribbon user interface. For more information on the Ribbon and customizing the appearance of the Ribbon, see Chapter 15, "Extending the Ribbon."

■ Item form. The Inspector window is the primary location for Outlook custom forms and form regions. Using form regions, you can redesign the complete look of the item form, add new fields, and change the layout to match the requirements of your solution. For more information about form regions, see Chapter 13, "Creating Form Regions."

■ Custom task panes. Custom task panes on the Inspector window provide you with an opportunity to add a new pane to the Outlook item window. A custom task pane can be docked on any edge of the Inspector window or can float above the window. Each custom task pane hosts an ActiveX or WinForm user control, which allows you complete flexibility to design the task pane for your solution.

Programming the *Inspectors* Collection and *Inspector* Object

Similar to the *Explorer* object, you cannot directly create a new instance of the *Inspector* object. Instead, you need to use the *Inspectors* collection to either use an existing Inspector window or create a new one. You can also quickly access an Inspector window from any of the Outlook item objects by using the *GetInspector* property. The *Inspectors* collection is available via the *Inspectors* property on the *Application* object.

The *Inspectors* Collection

The *Inspectors* collection provides a way to enumerate the existing instances of *Inspector* objects and to create new instances of the *Inspector* object. The collection also provides an event, *NewInspector,* to notify your add-in when a new Inspector window has been created.

Creating a New Inspector Window

There are a couple of different ways to create a new Inspector window for a particular item. You can use the *Add* method of the *Inspectors* object, or you can access the *GetInspector* property of the item to return an instance of the *Inspector* object. In both cases, if an *Inspector* object already exists for the particular item, a new window will not be created.

This example looks through the Inbox default folder for the first mail item, then displays that item in an Inspector window. If no mail item is found, no window would be displayed.

```
public void ShowInspector()
{
  Outlook.Folder inbox = Application.Session.GetDefaultFolder(
    Outlook.OlDefaultFolders.olFolderInbox) as Outlook.Folder;

  // Find a mail item in the Inbox
  Outlook.MailItem mail = null;
  for (int i = 1; i <= inbox.Items.Count; i++)
  {
    mail = inbox.Items[i] as Outlook.MailItem;
```

```
    if (mail != null) break;
  }
  if (mail != null)
  {
    Outlook.Inspector myInspector = Application.Inspectors.Add(mail);
    myInspector.Display(false);
  }
}
```

The parameter on the *Display* method can be used to show the Inspector window modally. If you call *Display* with the parameter equal to *False*, the Inspector window is displayed non-modally. If you call *Display* with the parameter equal to *True*, the Inspector is displayed modally. When an Inspector is displayed modally, the user must close the Inspector window before he or she can use other parts of Outlook. It is not recommended that you display an Inspector window modally because this might adversely affect certain aspects of the object model or other solutions that integrate with Outlook.

Accessing the Active Inspector

Although you can use the *Inspectors* collection to enumerate all *Inspector* objects and look for a particular window, it is often easier to use the *ActiveInspector* method on the *Application* object when you know the window you are looking for is the active Inspector window. The active Inspector window is the currently focused Inspector window or the last focused Inspector window if no other Inspector window has the focus. Because it is also possible that no Inspector window is displayed, your code should determine if the *Inspector* object returned by the *ActiveInspector* method is *null* (*Nothing* in Visual Basic).

```
public void ShowActiveInspector()
{
  Outlook.Inspector inspector = Application.ActiveInspector();
  if (inspector != null)
  {
    MessageBox.Show(string.Format("The active inspector is '{0}'.",
      inspector.Caption));
  }
}
```

Accessing the *CurrentItem* Property

There are several scenarios where it is useful and necessary to find out which item is currently open in an Inspector window. For instance, when a Ribbon button is pressed, the callback to your add-in will provide the context of the call by providing a window object. If you need to perform an action on the item, it is important to know which item should be used. To this end, the *Inspector* object provides a *CurrentItem* property, which always returns the item currently loaded in the Inspector. This property is read-only in the sense that you cannot assign an item object to this property. However, you can get or set properties on the item returned by the *CurrentItem* property and save changes if required by your scenario. The following code sample retrieves the current item from the active Inspector window and then displays a message box with the subject of the current message. This example uses the *OutlookItem* class so that the code doesn't need to determine what type of item is loaded in the Inspector.

```
public void GetInspectorItem()
{
  Outlook.Inspector inspector = Application.ActiveInspector();
  if (inspector != null)
  {
    OutlookItem item = new OutlookItem(inspector.CurrentItem);
    MessageBox.Show(string.Format(
      "The current item's subject is '{0}'.",
      item.Subject));
  }
}
```

Working with the Navigation Pane

With Outlook 2007, you can now control some aspects of the Navigation Pane from the object model. Although you can't add a new module to the Navigation Pane, you can now customize the way folders are arranged to better organize your solution data. You can also use the events provided by the Navigation Pane objects to better determine the state of the Explorer window and reflect this state in your own custom UI elements.

The main entry point for working with the Navigation Pane is the *NavigationPane* property on the *Explorer* object, which returns a *NavigationPane* object. This object can be used to determine the current module, switch modules, and change which modules are displayed.

Making the Most of Navigation Modules

A lot of the Explorer UI changes depend on the actively selected module. For instance, toolbar buttons are added and removed when a user switches between the Mail and Calendar modules. Using the Navigation Pane, you can use a similar design to display only the UI elements that make sense in the current module. For example, you can determine what module is currently active by looking at the *CurrentModule* property on the *NavigationPane* object.

```
public void ShowTheCurrentModule()
{
  Outlook.Explorer explorer = Application.ActiveExplorer();
  Outlook.NavigationPane navPane = explorer.NavigationPane;
  Outlook.NavigationModule curModule = navPane.CurrentModule;
  Outlook.OlNavigationModuleType currentModule = curModule.NavigationModuleType;

  switch (currentModule)
  {
    case Outlook.OlNavigationModuleType.olModuleCalendar:
      MessageBox.Show("This is the calendar module.");
      break;
    case Outlook.OlNavigationModuleType.olModuleMail:
```

```
      MessageBox.Show("This is the mail module.");
      break;
    default:
      MessageBox.Show(string.Format("This is the '{0}' module.",
        curModule.Name));
      break;
  }
}
```

You can also listen for the *ModuleSwitch* event on the *NavigationPane* object, which will be raised when the current module has changed. This event can then be used to remove UI elements that no longer are valid and add any UI elements that apply to the newly selected module.

```
public Outlook.Explorer explorer;
public Outlook.NavigationPane navigationPane;

public void ListenForChanges()
{
  explorer = Application.ActiveExplorer();
  navigationPane = explorer.NavigationPane;

  ((Outlook.ExplorerEvents_10_Event)explorer).Close +=
    new Outlook.ExplorerEvents_10_CloseEventHandler(explorer_Close);
  navigationPane.ModuleSwitch +=
    new Outlook.NavigationPaneEvents_12_ModuleSwitchEventHandler(
    navigationPane_ModuleSwitch);
}

void navigationPane_ModuleSwitch(Outlook.NavigationModule CurrentModule)
{
  MessageBox.Show(string.Format("Switched to module: {0}", CurrentModule.Name));
}

void explorer_Close()
{
  navigationPane.ModuleSwitch -=
    new Outlook.NavigationPaneEvents_12_ModuleSwitchEventHandler(
    navigationPane_ModuleSwitch);
  ((Outlook.ExplorerEvents_10_Event)explorer).Close -=
    new Outlook.ExplorerEvents_10_CloseEventHandler(explorer_Close);
}
```

Additionally, you can control the display and position of the eight Navigation Pane modules in Outlook. For example, if you wanted to hide the Contact module as part of your solution, the following code would hide the module from the Navigation Pane:

```
public void HideContactsModule()
{
  Outlook.Explorer explorer = Application.ActiveExplorer();
  Outlook.NavigationPane navPane = explorer.NavigationPane;
  navPane.Modules.GetNavigationModule(
    Outlook.OlNavigationModuleType.olModuleContacts).Visible = false;
}
```

> **Note**   Hiding a module does not remove access to that module or otherwise prevent the user from accessing information in folders of that module type. It merely hides the module from the Navigation Pane. A user could later turn the module back on again using the Navigation Pane options.

Adding Structure with Navigation Groups

One of the new features present in the Navigation Pane is the ability to create folder groups for the Calendar, Contacts, Tasks, Notes, and Journal modules. These help to logically organize folders into functional groups. By default, Outlook creates groups for your folders (for example, My Calendars), other people's folders (for example, People's Calendars), and miscellaneous other folders (for example, Other Calendars), as shown in Figure 12-3.

Figure 12-3   An example of the Navigation Pane grouping with the three default group types.

Leveraging this folder grouping mechanism for your solution can help the user logically identify with extra folders that are created by your solution. For example, if you were to connect to a number of shared calendars, it might be useful to group these new calendar folders together under a single group heading.

Creating a Navigation Group and Adding Folders

To organize folders together into a navigation folders group, you need to create a new group on the Navigation module that represents the module in Outlook in which the folder will be located. For instance, if you are creating contact folders, you need to use the *ContactModule* object and the *NavigationGroups* property on that object. After you have created the group, you can add folders to it by calling the *Add* method on the *NavigationGroup* object. When a folder is added to a new group, is it automatically removed from any previous group.

The following example creates a new contact folder as a child folder of the default Contacts folder, and then creates a new group in the Contacts module and adds the newly created folder to that group:

```
public void CreateNewContactGroup()
{
  // Create a folder
  Outlook.Folder contactFolder =
    Application.Session.GetDefaultFolder(
    Outlook.OlDefaultFolders.olFolderContacts)
    as Outlook.Folder;
  Outlook.Folder myContactFolder =
    contactFolder.Folders.Add("Solution Folder 1",
    Outlook.OlDefaultFolders.olFolderContacts)
    as Outlook.Folder;

  Outlook.Explorer explorer = Application.ActiveExplorer();

  // Create a new group
  Outlook.ContactsModule contacts =
    explorer.NavigationPane.Modules.GetNavigationModule(
    Outlook.OlNavigationModuleType.olModuleContacts)
    as Outlook.ContactsModule;
  Outlook.NavigationGroup group =
    contacts.NavigationGroups.Create("Solution Contacts");

  // Add the folder to the group
  group.NavigationFolders.Add(myContactFolder);
}
```

Deleting a Navigation Group

Before you can delete a navigation group, you need to move or delete all of the folders from the group because only empty groups can be deleted.

```
public void RemoveContactGroup()
{
  Outlook.Explorer explorer = Application.ActiveExplorer();

  // Locate a group
  Outlook.ContactsModule contacts =
    explorer.NavigationPane.Modules.GetNavigationModule(
    Outlook.OlNavigationModuleType.olModuleContacts)
    as Outlook.ContactsModule;
  Outlook.NavigationGroup group =
    contacts.NavigationGroups["Solution Contacts"];
  Outlook.NavigationGroup defaultGroup =
    contacts.NavigationGroups.GetDefaultNavigationGroup(
    Outlook.OlGroupType.olOtherFoldersGroup);
```

```
  // Move the folders to a default group
  foreach (Outlook.NavigationFolder navfolder
    in group.NavigationFolders)
  {
    defaultGroup.NavigationFolders.Add(navfolder.Folder);
  }

  // Delete the group
  contacts.NavigationGroups.Delete(group);
}
```

Removing Folders

Due to the way the Navigation Pane works, only certain types of folders are removable. All folders that reside in a connected store and are of the same folder type as the module are displayed in a group, and therefore cannot be removed. You can determine if a folder is removable by checking the *IsRemovable* property on the *NavigationFolder* object. If this property is *True*, the folder can be removed from the Navigation Pane without being deleted (for example, a shared Microsoft Exchange folder). Otherwise the folder cannot be removed from the Navigation Pane except by deleting the folder.

The following example code locates the folder group created in the previous section and then either removes or deletes any folders in that group:

```
public void EmptyContactGroup()
{
  Outlook.Explorer explorer = Application.ActiveExplorer();

  // Create a new group
  Outlook.ContactsModule contacts =
    explorer.NavigationPane.Modules.GetNavigationModule(
    Outlook.OlNavigationModuleType.olModuleContacts)
    as Outlook.ContactsModule;
  Outlook.NavigationGroup group =
    contacts.NavigationGroups["Solution Contacts"];
  Outlook.NavigationGroup defaultGroup =
    contacts.NavigationGroups.GetDefaultNavigationGroup(
    Outlook.OlGroupType.olOtherFoldersGroup);

  // Move the folders to a default group
  foreach (Outlook.NavigationFolder navfolder
    in group.NavigationFolders)
  {
    if (navfolder.IsRemovable)
    {
      group.NavigationFolders.Remove(navfolder);
    }
    else
    {
```

```
        navfolder.Folder.Delete();
    }
  }
}
```

Folder Views

The folder view, which displays the contents of a folder, can be customized using one of the default view types. Outlook 2007 includes six view types: Table, Timeline, Card, Business Card, Day/Week/Month, and Icon. Some of these views can be further customized to control which fields are displayed and the formatting of the text in the view.

For more details about modifying a view programmatically, see Chapter 10, "Organizing Outlook Data."

The Reading Pane

The Reading Pane provides a read-only area in an Explorer window where the contents of an item can be displayed. This pane allows users to get more work done inside the *Explorer* object without opening individual Inspector windows for reading the contents of items (primarily mail items, although the Reading Pane is functional for all item types).

The Reading Pane can be shown or hidden using the *ShowPane* method on the *Explorer* object. For more information about using *ShowPane* in your solution, refer to the "Working with Panes" section earlier in this chapter.

Customizing the Reading Pane

The Reading Pane offers two approaches for customization: one approach for customizing the look of an item and another for customizing the look of a previewed attachment.

To customize the look of an item, you can use a form region to either extend the standard reading pane representation of the item or replace this representation with your own. For more information about form regions and the Reading Pane, see Chapter 13.

When Outlook previews an attachment in the Reading Pane or the Inspector window, it looks for a registered preview handler for the file type of the attachment. If a preview handler is registered, the preview handler will be displayed in the Reading Pane, providing an in-line preview of the attachment. Preview handler extensibility is beyond the scope of this chapter. More information about writing a preview handler is available on MSDN by searching for *IPreviewHandler*.

The To-Do Bar

The new To-Do Bar integrates tasks, e-mails flagged for follow-up, upcoming appointments, and calendar information in one convenient place in the Outlook Explorer window. The To-Do Bar provides users with a consolidated view of their priorities for the day so they do not have to waste time checking multiple locations for this information. The object model provides ways to add new items to the task list or the calendar display by flagging an item as a task or by creating new appointments on the default calendar.

To hide or show the To-Do Bar, see the "Working with Panes" section earlier in this chapter. Information on how to add items to the To-Do Bar and enumerate all the items that appear in the To-Do Bar is available in Chapter 6, "Accessing Outlook Data."

Command Bars

Outlook 2007 continues to use command bars in the Explorer window, whereas the Inspector window now displays the Ribbon instead of toolbars and menus. Both the command bars and Ribbon are customizable through the object model. Detailed descriptions of both command bars and the Ribbon are provided in Chapter 15.

Context Menus

Outlook 2007 also includes a way to customize various context menus displayed in the Explorer and Inspector windows. The mechanism to customize these menus relies on application-level events that fire each time a context menu will be displayed. Because Outlook builds each context menu dynamically when it is about to be displayed, a solution that customizes the menu must add the customizations each time the menu is to be displayed.

Outlook provides individual events on the *Application* object to enable customizing context menus on attachments, folders, items, shortcuts, stores, and views (see Figure 12-4). Each of these menus can be customized by adding new command bar controls to the menu or by hiding existing items. These customizations are not persisted beyond the scope of the event.

When you customize context menus, there are two key events you need to handle. The first is the event for the context menu you are customizing; for instance, if you want to customize the item context menu, you would need to handle the *ItemContextMenuDisplay* event on the *Application* object. The second event is the *ContextMenuClose* event on the *Application* object, which is used to clean up state information persisted previously.

When you customize the context menu, the customizations have a lifetime of only that instance of the context menu. After the menu is closed, you need to clean up any state you have persisted for the menu actions, which is where the *ContextMenuClose* event comes into play. This event is always fired after the user has made a selection in the menu and the menu is closed. This is your opportunity to clean up state that you persisted during the context menu display event.

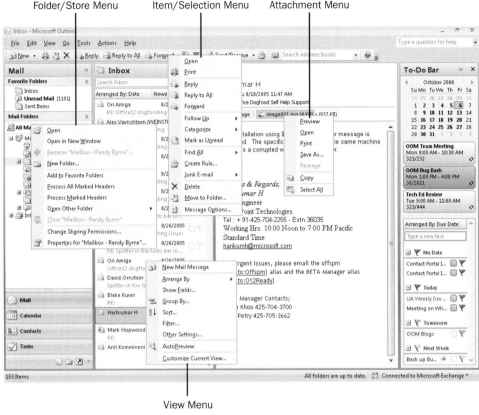

Figure 12-4   A view of the Outlook Explorer window and the context menus that can be customized.

What follows is a simple customization of a context menu. For a more thorough look into how to work with these events and richly customize the context menu, refer to Chapter 8. This sample is split into four parts for simplicity. The first part is used to define the events we want to listen for on the *Application* object. A good place to put this code is in the initialize code for your add-in (either the *InitializeAddin* method, if you are using the add-in template that accompanies this book, or the *ThisAddIn_Startup* method if you are using Visual Studio 2005 Tools for the 2007 Microsoft Office System [VSTO]). In this case, you add event handlers to the *ItemContextMenuDisplay* and *ContextMenuClose* events. Remember to disconnect these event handlers when the add-in is disconnected or shut down; otherwise your customizations might continue to appear, or Outlook could crash.

```
public void HookUpEvents()
{
  Application.ItemContextMenuDisplay +=
    new Outlook.ApplicationEvents_11_ItemContextMenuDisplayEventHandler(
```

```
      Application_ItemContextMenuDisplay);
    Application.ContextMenuClose += new
      Outlook.ApplicationEvents_11_ContextMenuCloseEventHandler(
      Application_ContextMenuClose);
}
```

Next, you write the code for these two event handlers. You start with the *ItemContextMenuDisplay* event handler. In this block of code, there are three instance variables defined: *lastSelection*, *lastItem*, and *button*. These maintain the state information about what item is selected and provide the reference to the *CommandBarButton* object you add to the context menu. The actual event handler checks to see if only one item is selected, and to make sure the item selected is a *MailItem*. If these conditions are met, the code adds a new *CommandBarButton* object to the context menu, sets the caption and visibility, and then adds a new event handler for the *Click* event on the *button* object.

```
private Outlook.Selection lastSelection;
private OutlookItem lastItem;
private Office.CommandBarButton button;
void Application_ItemContextMenuDisplay(
  Office.CommandBar CommandBar, Outlook.Selection Selection)
{
  lastSelection = Selection;
  if (Selection.Count == 1)
  {
    lastItem = new OutlookItem(Selection[1]);
    if (lastItem.Class == Microsoft.Office.Interop.Outlook.OlObjectClass.olMail)
    {
      button = (Office.CommandBarButton)CommandBar.Controls.Add(
        Office.MsoControlType.msoControlButton,
        Type.Missing, Type.Missing, Type.Missing, Type.Missing);
      button.Caption = "Display Message Class";
      button.Visible = true;
      button.Click +=
      new Microsoft.Office.Core._CommandBarButtonEvents_ClickEventHandler(
      button_Click);
    }
  }
}
```

The second event you listen for on the *Application* object is the *ContextMenuClose* event. You can use this event to clean up the variables that are maintaining the state information for this context menu. In this example, the code sets *lastSelection* and *lastItem* to *null*, and then removes the event handler on the *button* object before setting it to *null*.

```
void Application_ContextMenuClose(Outlook.OlContextMenu ContextMenu)
{
  lastSelection = null;
  lastItem = null;

  if (button != null)
    button.Click -=
      new Microsoft.Office.Core._CommandBarButtonEvents_ClickEventHandler(
```

```
      button_Click);
   button = null;
}
```

The fourth part of this example is the code that executes when the user clicks the button we added to the context menu. In this case, the code displays a message box that displays the message class of the item selected.

```
void button_Click(Office.CommandBarButton Ctrl, ref bool CancelDefault)
{
  if (lastItem != null)
  {
    MessageBox.Show("The item's message class is " + lastItem.MessageClass);
  }
}
```

Because the *ContextMenuClose* event fires after the *Click* event on the *CommandBarButton* object, you do not need to clean up any of the state variables that were created during the *ItemContextMenuDisplay* event. These variables will be cleaned up immediately afterward when the *ContextMenuClose* event fires.

Performance Considerations

Being able to customize context menus is a very powerful addition to the object model in Outlook 2007. However, with this ability you need to be careful that you are not using too many cycles during the context menu display events. Remember that the code in these events is executed every time the user right-clicks in a location that causes the menu to appear. You should avoid expensive operations, such as creating large objects, initializing forms, or pinging remote data connections, as this will cause Outlook to hang until the operation finishes, and frustrate the user who doesn't know why Outlook takes so long to display the context menu.

As a general rule, your add-in should not take more than a few milliseconds of time to perform the tasks in the display event. With several add-ins customizing the same context menu, even 50 milliseconds per add-in could add up to a noticeable delay in the context menu appearing for the user.

Folder Home Pages

Folder home pages provide a means to extend views for application folders. Folder home pages let you set a default view on a folder based on a home page Uniform Resource Locator (URL) that points to a page on your Web server or locally on the disk. This page can contain custom script to render a view in the Outlook view pane. Think of a folder home page as a customizable Outlook Today page for a given folder or a hierarchy of subfolders. Another example of where folder home pages are used is the RSS Feeds folder, which displays information about RSS feeds and provides a mechanism to subscribe to new feeds.

Changes for Outlook 2007

Outlook 2007 has made a change to the way folder home pages work to improve the security of folder home pages. Folder home pages are available only in the default mailbox of the running profile. If you attempt to create a folder home page in a store that is not the default mailbox, the user will still see the standard folder view when selecting the folder.

This change in behavior can be overridden via policy in an organization. For more information on applying this policy, refer to the Office Resource Kit on Office Online.

Additionally, if you have written a custom Messaging Application Programming Interface (MAPI) store provider and you would like to use folder home pages in your store, you can set a flag on the provider that indicates it supports secure folder home pages. More information about this flag is available in the Outlook 2007 Integration APIs.

Here are several important factors to consider when you are considering using a folder home page in your solution:

- Folder home page designs should look and behave like Outlook to avoid user confusion. Using the Outlook View Control can help provide a view of data similar to the view Outlook provides.

- A folder owner or application designer might elect to display a folder home page, but an individual user can override this setting and turn off the folder home page.

- Using an add-in can help you ensure that a folder home page will always appear when a user navigates to a folder.

- Folder home page settings are established on a per-mailbox basis, independent of the Exchange profile on a given machine.

- Folder home pages can be made available offline as long as the folder home page resides on a Web server.

Summary

This chapter provides an introduction to some of the UI components of Outlook, but there is much more detail available in other chapters of the book. Here you learned how to work with the *Explorer* and *Inspector* objects and some of the capabilities of the Outlook platform in customizing the user experience. In the chapters to come you will learn more about how to customize the folder view, how to create form regions that customize the Inspector and Reading Pane layout, and how to work with custom task panes and other UI elements.

Chapter 13
Creating Form Regions

In this chapter, you'll find a high-level introduction to the form region design experience and then a deep dive into creating a custom form solution using form regions in Microsoft Office Outlook 2007. Form regions provide a custom user interface mechanism that allows you to extend built-in forms in multiple ways or completely replace a built-in form with your own custom interface. Through this deep dive, we'll cover the following:

- Form region scenarios
- Designing a form region with Outlook
- Programming a form region from an add-in

To facilitate our discussion, most of the scenarios and concepts explained in this chapter revolve around the travel agency sample code available on the book's companion Web site. However, the detail level will be sufficient that you will not need the sample code to understand the concepts explained in this chapter.

Introduction to Form Regions

This section provides a high-level overview of Outlook form region components and the differences between form regions and custom forms using form pages. For the purposes of this chapter, we use the following terminology:

- **Custom forms with form pages**   This refers to custom forms and their associated user interface (UI) pages designed in the Outlook Forms Designer in Microsoft Outlook 97 through Outlook 2007 that can be published to a forms library such as the Organizational or Personal Forms Library, a Folder Forms Library, or embedded as a one-off form.

- **Custom forms with form regions**   This refers to custom or built-in forms and their associated UI regions designed in the Outlook 2007 Forms Designer and saved as .ofs files. A custom form with form regions is made up of individual form regions registered on the same message class.

- **Custom forms**   This refers to a collection of form pages or form regions that make up one whole form. Each item in Outlook has either a standard or custom form associated with it that Outlook will use to render the display of that item in the Inspector, the Reading Pane, or both.

Form Pages Compared with Form Regions

Outlook 2007 provides two different technologies for developing form solutions with Outlook. Both of these customization techniques use the same Outlook Forms Designer, but form regions provide many options and abilities that are lacking with form pages. Custom forms with form pages that are designed for previous versions of Outlook will continue to work; however, the new Ribbon command UI might change the way custom command bars and controls appear on these custom forms. For new solutions that support Outlook 2007 and future versions, custom forms with form regions are the preferred way to customize Outlook forms. Table 13-1 provides a summary of the top features provided by custom forms and form regions.

Table 13-1   Comparing Custom Forms and Form Regions

Feature/Area	Custom forms with form pages	Custom forms with form regions
Supported Outlook versions	Outlook 97 through Outlook 2007	Outlook 2007
Visual appearance	No support for Windows theming; forms look like Microsoft Windows 95	Full support for Windows themes; forms match Outlook visuals
Form layout	Designed using Outlook Forms Designer	Designed using Outlook Forms Designer
Supported controls	Standard form controls, ActiveX controls	Enhanced form controls, Outlook controls, ActiveX controls
Reading Pane	Standard form is always displayed; if there is script behind the form, Reading Pane display is disabled	Adjoining and replacement form regions can be displayed
Business logic	Written in Microsoft Visual Basic Scripting Edition (VBScript) using Outlook script editor	Written as Component Object Model (COM) add-in in any language
Deployment	Published to a forms library	Distributed with an add-in
Localization	Separate form version required for each localized language; difficult to maintain and deploy	Integrated solution for localizing form text and optional layout changes

Form Region Types

Form regions can be displayed in four different styles, based on the needs of a solution. Each type of form region is designed using the same experience and the same process with the Outlook Forms Designer. The manifest file that defines a form region determines the way Outlook displays the form region.

Adjoining Form Regions

Adjoining form regions are an additive option for an existing standard form or custom form. Adjoining form regions, as shown in Figure 13-1, are displayed in a special region at the bottom of the Inspector, the Reading Pane, or both, and are shown with a header that enables the region to be expanded and collapsed. Adjoining form regions enable developers to add additional fields or related information to the first form page without customizing the entire form body.

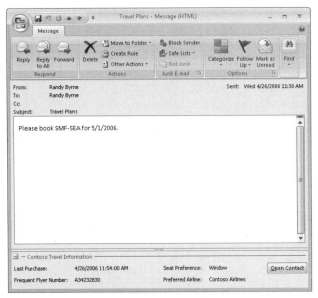

Figure 13-1   An example of an adjoining form region on a mail item.

Separate Form Regions

Separate form regions are another additive option for standard forms or custom forms. Separate form regions are displayed as a new form page on a pre-existing form (either custom or standard), as shown in Figure 13-2. The additional form page appears to be part of the form and can be selected using an additional button in the Show group on the Ribbon. Several separate form region pages can be added to a replacement or replace-all form region to build a multipage form.

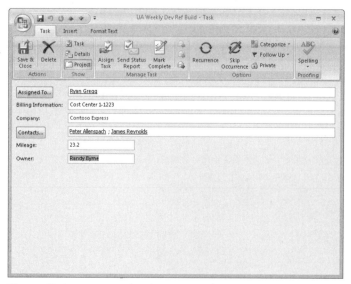

Figure 13-2   An example of a separate form region on a task item.

Replacement and Replace-All Form Regions

Replacement and replace-all form regions are a special type of separate form region that causes default form pages to be removed from an item. A replacement form region will delete the first page of the form pages and replace it with the form region (see Figure 13-3). A replace-all form region will delete all the form pages and display only the replace-all form region and other form regions registered with the item's message class. To build up a multi-page custom form with form regions, you combine a replace-all form region with several separate form regions.

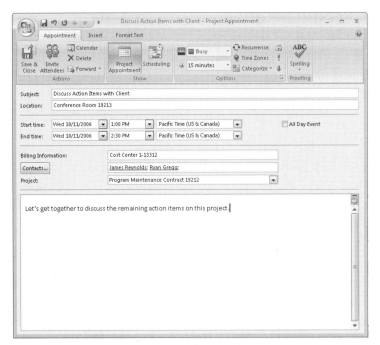

Figure 13-3   An example of a replacement form region on an appointment item.

Standard Form Types

In addition to the types of form regions, there are also several types of forms in Outlook. Each built-in form type describes one of the standard item types in Outlook. The built-in forms include Message, Post, Task, Appointment, Journal, and Contacts. Using form regions, any part of these built-in forms can be replaced and customized, so you should use the base form type that most closely matches the type of item your form region solution provides. When creating a new form region, the designer does not provide a base template for that particular item type.

Selecting the right base form can make it easier for you to design your form because the Field Chooser will display a list of the most commonly used fields for that item type. However, just because you started to design a form on a contact item, for example, does not mean that form will not function on other item types. As long as the fields used on the form are defined on the item, your form region can be displayed on any item type.

Anatomy of a Form Region Solution

A solution built around form regions includes the following elements:

- **Form region manifest**   This file is an Extensible Markup Language (XML) file that provides details that define the form region, including how the form region is loaded, what type of form region, and the display text for the form region and the controls. See the section "Authoring a Form Region Manifest" later in this chapter for details on this manifest format.

- **Form storage file**   The storage file is a binary file that describes the layout of the form. This file can be created and edited using the Outlook Forms Designer.

- **Registry entries**   Each form region needs one or more registry entries that point to the form region manifest. Each registry entry defines one message class that will use the form region. See the section "Registering a Form Region" later in this chapter for more details.

- **COM add-in (optional)**   If a form region needs business logic or other custom code running with the form region, that logic is implemented in a COM add-in. The form region manifest file indicates the *ProgID* or name of the add-in that will be called when the form region is loaded. An add-in can also be used to supply Ribbon customizations for form region items.

Becoming Familiar with Form Region Design

This section covers the components of forms in Design mode and discusses the parts of an Outlook form region.

How Is a Form Opened?

Because of security work that went into Microsoft Office Outlook 2003 and Outlook 2007, Outlook no longer supports, by default, loading a form definition from an item. This question then arises: If the form definition doesn't travel with the item, how is the form opened? The answer is that the form is launched by looking for a form that matches the message class on the item in a few different locations. Each item includes a property that indicates the message class of the form that was used to compose the item, such as *IPM.Contact*. This message class provides an identifier that Outlook compares against the identifier on a form or form region to determine if the form should be displayed.

When Outlook starts to look for a form with the matching message class, it first checks to see if any form regions are registered for the message class of the item. If a form region is registered and is a replacement or replace-all form region, Outlook stops the search and loads the form regions. If no form region is registered or the form regions are adjoining or separate form regions, Outlook continues to look for a form to load.

If no form region is loaded, Outlook then looks to see if a custom form is published in the same folder as the item. If no form is found in the folder, Outlook then looks to the Personal Forms Library and then the Organizational Forms Library to see if a form is available in that library.

If no form is located using the exact message class on the item, Outlook repeats the check for the next class in common. For example, if *IPM.Note.Myform.ThisForm* does not exist, Outlook tries to open *IPM.Note.Myform*. If that form definition does not exist, *IPM.Note* loads and the user sees a standard message form. A form region can override this behavior using a special value in the manifest file that tells Outlook that only items that match the message class exactly should show the form region.

Designing a Form Region

Designing a new form region is very similar to working with a custom form. You can use the same designer interface that Outlook provides for developing custom forms, although the behavior of form regions is more advanced than custom forms. This section describes how to access the Outlook Forms Designer, describes the implications of Design mode, and walks you through creating a new form region.

Outlook Form Design Mode

The following elements (shown in Figure 13-4) are available when an Outlook form is in Design mode:

- **Forms Designer window**   This shows the various pages of the form and the form properties and actions.
- **Toolbox**   This allows you to add new controls (such as buttons) to the form.
- **Field Chooser**   This allows you to select fields for the form.
- **Properties dialog box**   This allows you to modify a control or field.
- **Advanced Properties**   This is used to modify an advanced property of the form or control.

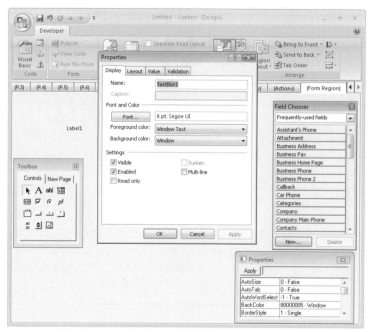

Figure 13-4   These elements are available when Outlook forms are in Design mode.

Entering Design Mode

To design a form region, you must start with a custom form. To enter Design mode for a custom form, follow these steps:

1. In the Outlook Explorer window, select the Tools menu, point to Forms, and click Design A Form.

2. Select the base form type that matches the type of form region you will be designing, and click Open. For this example, select Contact.

Outlook then opens a Contact custom form in Design mode. This form is a custom form that contains form pages but does not yet contain a form region. To add a new form region to the Outlook Forms Designer, on the Developer tab, in the Design group, click Form Region, and then click New Form Region. A new tab with the name "(Form Region)" will appear with an empty design surface. This is where you can design the layout of your new form region. Once a form region is open in Design mode, you can adjust the layout of controls, add or remove controls, and adjust the properties of controls on the form.

> **Important**   Form regions should only be designed using the standard DPI resolution in Windows (96 dpi). Form regions include a feature to automatically scale a form region to the appropriate resolution, but this feature only works one way. Designing your form at a high DPI setting will cause unexpected behavior when the form is displayed or opened again in the designer.

Renaming a Form Region Tab

To make it easier to keep track of multiple open form regions, you can rename the text that is displayed in the tab strip in the Outlook Forms Designer. To rename the form region page, click the Developer tab. In the Design group, click Page, and then select Rename Page.

The value entered for the page name is only used in the Forms Designer. To rename the text used to represent a separate, replacement, or replace-all form region in the Show group of the Ribbon when the form is running, you need to specify the *<formRegionName>* element in the form region manifest, which is described later in this chapter.

Saving a Form Region

To save a form region as an Outlook Form Storage (OFS) file, click the Developer tab. In the Design group, click Form Region, and then click Save Form Region As. This displays a Save File dialog box that will let you select the path to save the form region. Form regions can only be saved as .ofs files.

> **Important**   Do not use the Microsoft Office menu's Save command to save a form region. This will save the form as an item in an Outlook folder. Also, do not use the Microsoft Office menu's Save As command to save a form as an .msg or .oft file. Neither of these methods persist the form region information. The form region must always be saved separately.

Adding Controls

Controls can be added to a form region in two different ways: using the Control Toolbox or using the Field Chooser. These two methods for adding controls are explained in the following sections.

The Control Toolbox

The Control Toolbox window displays the available controls that can be added to the form. To access the Control Toolbox, on the Developer tab, in the Tools group, click Control Toolbox. By default, this toolbox displays only the Microsoft Forms 2.0 controls that are available for use on custom forms and form regions. For more information on adding the new controls discussed in Chapter 14, "Form Region Controls," see the next section, "Adding Additional Controls to the Control Toolbox." Custom ActiveX controls can also be added to the Control Toolbox and dropped onto a custom form or form region.

To add a control from the Control Toolbox to the form, click that control's icon in the Control Toolbox, and then click the location where the control should be created. If you click the control and then drag it to the form, the control will use a nondefault size. The recommended practice for adding controls to a form region is to use the click and click method rather than click and drag.

Adding Additional Controls to the Control Toolbox

To add additional ActiveX controls, such as the Outlook 2007 form controls, to the Control Toolbox, follow these steps:

1. Right-click the Controls tab of the Control Toolbox, and select Custom Controls. The Additional Controls window opens, showing all the available controls.

2. Select the check box next to the ActiveX controls you want to display on the Control Toolbox. Display names for Outlook 2007 form controls begin with "Microsoft Office Outlook."

3. Click OK to return to the Forms Designer.

Figure 13-5 shows an example of the Control Toolbox and Additional Controls dialog box with the Outlook 2007 form controls selected.

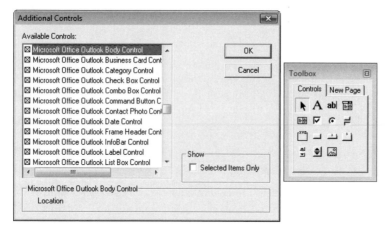

Figure 13-5   Control Toolbox and Additional Controls dialog box with the Outlook 2007 form controls selected.

Creating a Control Template

To increase your productivity during the form design phase, you can create a control template by using the selection tool to select a group of controls and then dragging the selection back to the Control Toolbox. Follow these steps to create a control template:

1. Select the controls you wish to use in the template with the selection tool.

2. Drag the selection to the Control Toolbox.

3. Outlook uses the default label New Group for the control template. If you want to rename the control template, right-click the template in the Control Toolbox, and then select Customize New Group.

4. Enter the correct template name in the Customize Control dialog box in the ToolTip Text edit box. For example, you might create a label and edit box template (see Figure 13-6) and use Label/Edit Controls for the ToolTip text.

5. Click OK to accept the new ToolTip text for the control template.

When you use a control template, you can either click the control template and drag it from the Control Toolbox to your form or you can select the control template in the Control Toolbox and then click on the form design surface to insert a copy of the control template.

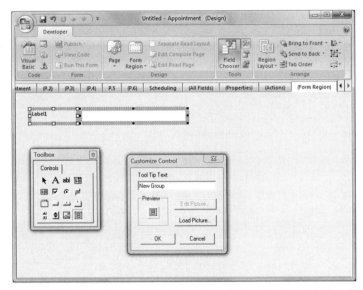

Figure 13-6   Creating a control template that contains a label and edit box.

Accessing Control Properties

After a control has been added to the custom form or form region, you can set the properties of the control. Control properties determine what the control looks like and how it behaves when the control is running on the form.

Each control added to a form region has the same set of basic properties, which can be set using the Properties window (see Figure 13-7). To open the Properties window, select a control on the form. On the Ribbon Developer tab, in the Tools group, click Property Sheet. If no control is selected, this button will be disabled.

Figure 13-7 Properties window with the Display tab selected.

The Properties window has three or four tabs, depending on the type of control selected. If the control supports Outlook data binding, you will see four tabs: Display, Layout, Value, and Validation. If the control does not support Outlook data binding, you will see only three tabs: Display, Layout, and Validation.

The Display tab of the Properties window displays basic properties that adjust the look of the control. On this tab, you can set the name of the control, caption, font, foreground and background color, and whether the control is visible, enabled, read-only, sunken, or multiline. Note that not all of these options are available on every control.

The Layout tab of the Properties window displays properties that adjust how the control is positioned on the form. On this tab, you can adjust the top value, left value, height, and width of the control, and set properties on how the control is automatically positioned on the form. For more information on the automatic layout functionality of form regions, see the section "Understanding Automatic Layout" later in this chapter.

The Value tab of the Properties window displays properties that enable data binding between Outlook properties and the control. On this tab, you select a field from the Outlook item that will be data bound to a property of the control. If you use the Field Chooser to create new controls (see the section "Using the Field Chooser" later in this chapter), this information is automatically populated according to the field you selected.

The Validation tab of the Properties window provides options for basic data validation on some controls. Validation is only available if the control supports data validation, and the control is bound to an Outlook field on the Value tab. If the control does not support data binding or is not bound to a field, the controls on this tab are disabled.

Control Advanced Properties

Beyond the properties exposed through the Properties window, you can access more properties of a control, including properties that are specific to the selected control, by using the Advanced Properties dialog box.

To display the Advanced Properties dialog box, on the Ribbon, on the Developer tab, in the Tools group, click Advanced Properties. This displays the Advanced Properties dialog box for the current control, as shown in Figure 13-8. Unlike the Properties window, the Advanced Properties dialog box can stay open and automatically adjusts the list of properties for the currently selected control. If no control is selected, the properties for the form container are displayed.

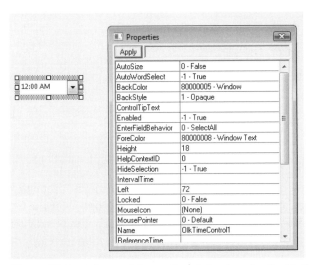

Figure 13-8   Advanced Properties dialog box for the Outlook Time Control.

Working with Fields

Nearly every form region solution will want to display some information that is stored on the item the form region represents. The best way to accomplish this result is to use Outlook's data binding mechanism to bind the field (also known as an item property or user property) to the control. You can accomplish this data binding by using the Field Chooser, by using the Value tab of the Properties window, or via business logic (code). When a control is data bound, the value of the field is automatically loaded into the control when the form region is opened. The value is also automatically saved back into the field if the control is changed while the form region is open.

Using the Field Chooser

The Field Chooser is the easiest way to add a bound field to a form region. To open the Field Chooser window, on the Ribbon, on the Developer tab, in the Tools group, click Field Chooser. This displays the Field Chooser window shown in Figure 13-9. The Field Chooser window has two components: a drop-down control that shows the field groups, and a list of fields. There are also two buttons at the bottom of the window used to create or remove custom fields.

Figure 13-9   The default Field Chooser appearance for a Contact form.

To create a new control on the form data bound to a field, drag the name of the field to the form design surface. This action automatically creates a label and control for the field. Depending on the field type, the control will either be a text box, combo box, or other standard control. Dragging a control from the Field Chooser window will not create any of the new Outlook-specific controls, like the Outlook Category Control or the Outlook Business Card Control. To use these controls on your form, you must explicitly add them to the form using the Control Toolbox as explained earlier in this chapter.

Binding Data with a Control

Instead of dragging a field from the Field Chooser to the form and allowing Outlook to automatically configure the data binding properties, you can data bind a control already on the form. If you are using a custom ActiveX control, you need to use this approach because the Field Chooser will not create a new custom ActiveX control for a field.

To adjust the data binding properties, click a control and then on the Ribbon, on the Developer tab, in the Tools group, click the Property Sheet button. After the Properties window opens, click the Value tab to view the data binding properties. Figure 13-10 illustrates what these settings look like.

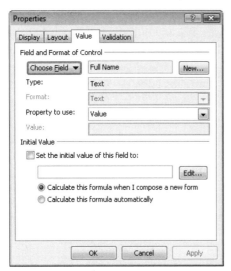

Figure 13-10   Data binding properties for a control in the Properties window.

To select the field with which the control will data bind, click Choose Field, and select a new field using the menu that appears. The Type and Format values will automatically be updated to the default for the type of field selected. For some field types, the Format property can be changed to adjust the formatting used when displaying the contents of the property.

You can also use the Property To Use drop-down list to determine which property will be set with the value of the field. If you are using a custom ActiveX control, you can assign the value to a different property than the default Value property. For example, if you want the field data to go into the Text property of the control, you can set Property To Use to be Text.

Creating Custom Fields

In addition to using the standard fields on the item, you can create custom fields known as user properties. There are two ways to create custom fields, and the method of creating the field determines how the field will roam with the form.

If you create a new user property using the Field Chooser, the field will be created in the default folder for the type of form being designed. Fields that have the field definition stored in the folder must be re-created in each folder when an item is copied into that folder for the field to work properly and be available in the Folder Contents view. You will need to use an add-in to make sure the field is properly created before opening an instance of the form in a folder for the first time. See *UserDefinedProperties* in Chapter 6, "Accessing Outlook Data," for more information on creating a user property in a folder.

If you create a new user property using the Value tab of the Properties window, the field definition will be stored in the form region file and will automatically be available on any item after the form region has been loaded. In this case, you do not need to write an add-in to create the user property in a folder each time an item is opened from a new folder. However, user properties that are defined in the form region cannot be added to the view or used in a search filter for the *Restrict* method of the *Items* collection or the *Table* object. Table 13-2 illustrates how custom property creation for a form region determines the availability of the custom property in a folder.

Table 13-2 Creating a User Property in a Form Region

Description	Custom property available in folder	Custom property available in View	Custom property available for *Table.Restrict* or *Items.Restrict*
Created on Value tab of Control Properties window by clicking New	Always	Not available	Not available
Created in Field Chooser by clicking New	Must use add-in code to create *UserDefinedProperty* in any folder that contains the item	Available	Available

Polishing Your Form Region

Once you have completed the initial design of a form region, you should take some time to polish the design of the form region to make sure that it fits with the standard Outlook look and feel. Form regions support an advanced automatic layout system that will allow your form to grow and shrink as the user resizes the window. Taking advantage of this system requires understanding how it works and ensuring that your form is designed within the guidelines of the system. If you choose not to use the automatic layout, you can control the layout of the form manually by writing your own resizing code or using a third-party control.

Understanding Automatic Layout

Form regions provide a layout ability that works different from the Resize With Form option that is available on custom form pages. The system used by form regions works similar to what Outlook's built-in forms use to automatically adjust the size of the form to fit the window as it is resized.

The form layout is calculated by fitting a table over the form design, where there is one control per table cell. Each row and column of this layout table will pick up certain margins that keep the controls spaced out as they were initially designed. When the user resizes the window displaying a form region, this table is stretched to fit the new window, and the controls in each cell of the table are adjusted as appropriate. This method is designed to help keep controls aligned in their individual columns on the form so that a control's label and the control itself maintain alignment relative to other controls on the form.

However, there are some limitations to this method, including these:

- Controls cannot overlap or intersect. Controls that do overlap or intersect will be ignored when the layout is calculated.

- Some controls might "snap" into their place and not stay exactly where they were positioned on the form.

To adjust the way controls are positioned on the form, there are several options on the Layout tab of the Properties window for any control placed on a form region. Figure 13-11 shows an example of these settings. There are five settings that pertain to the layout of the control on the form:

- **Enable Automatic Layout For This Control**   This check box determines whether this control is included in the automatic layout scheme or not. If this check box is cleared, the control will not be automatically positioned on the form.

- **Horizontal**   The value chosen in this drop-down list box determines how the control is aligned in the layout cell horizontally. If the value is Grow/Shrink With Form, then the control will automatically grow or shrink to fit the available space. Otherwise the control will align according to the selected value.

- **Minimum Width**   The value in this text box sets the smallest width to which the control will automatically resize. This allows you to keep a control at a particular minimum size, even as the form shrinks further.

- **Vertical**   The setting in this drop-down list box determines how the control is aligned in the layout cell vertically. If the value is set to Grow/Shrink With Form, then the control will automatically expand or collapse vertically to fit the available space. Other values will keep the control aligned vertically without causing the control to resize.

- **Minimum Height**   The value in this text box sets the smallest height to which the control will automatically resize. This allows you to keep a control at a particular minimum height, even as the form shrinks smaller.

Figure 13-11   Options on the Layout tab of the Properties window for a control.

Layout Guidelines

Designing your form region solution to work in a way similar to Outlook's built-in features will make it easier for your users to understand your solution because it will work in a manner with which they are already familiar. As part of designing a form region, you should attempt to follow some of the form design guidelines used by the standard Outlook forms, including the following:

- Keep four pixels of padding between the edge of the form and any control.

- Remember to add the *Infobar* and *Category* controls to a replacement or replace-all form region. These controls show important information that might not be displayed in any other way to the user. These controls should be arranged at the top of the form, with the *Infobar* control above the *Category* control.

- Use a one- or two-column layout to keep the controls organized.

- Allow fields that might contain a large amount of text to resize with the form. Fields that contain a small amount of text or a fixed length should not resize.

- Configure the body/notes field to resize both vertically and horizontally.

- Use additional form pages for less prominent controls.

- Use the Ribbon instead of a command button for actions that are not associated with any particular control on the form.

Fixing Layout Errors

Sometimes when a form region uses automatic layout, it might not appear as the designer expected. This is usually due to a problem with the way the form was designed, violating a limitation of the automatic layout logic. A special command exists to detect any controls that might be in a conflict state so that the form developer can adjust the controls as necessary.

To find controls that are in an error state and will not be properly adjusted by the automatic layout logic, on the Ribbon, on the Developer tab, in the Arrange group, click the Region Layout button, and then click Select Controls With Layout Errors. This command selects any controls that are in conflict. Figure 13-12 shows the Region Layout menu expanded. If no controls are selected after clicking this command, everything should lay out properly. This same menu also includes two other options, Recalculate Layout and Resize Layout With Form Designer. These commands can be used to test how the layout will work when the form is run by enabling automatic layout to be used in the designer. However, as a general rule, designing a form with automatic layout enabled might not work as expected and should be avoided.

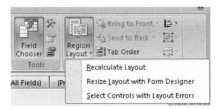

Figure 13-12   Commands in the Arrange group of the Developer tab that can help diagnose layout problems with a form region.

Form Region Theme Support

To make it easier for a form region solution to look like it is a part of Outlook, form regions automatically support the Outlook visual theme. All of the new Outlook form controls support the Windows themed appearance by default. There are also new Outlook form controls that provide UI elements unique to Outlook 2007, such as the Business Card preview, new colored category strip, and the Contact Photo Control. These controls can be used to ensure a visual similarity between a form region and Outlook built-in forms.

Additionally, special values for some properties of the controls will be automatically adjusted to display using the Outlook colors selected by the user. Table 13-3 explains which properties and values can be used in this way.

Table 13-3   Theme Supporting Properties and Values

Control	Property	Values/Description
All Olk* controls, form region	BackColor	Button face is automatically adjusted to be the appropriate background color for the form (usually white in the Reading Pane, blue in the Inspector, and black in high-contrast mode).
All Olk* controls, form region	ForeColor	Button Text is used to represent the standard text color on the form (usually black in the Reading Pane and Inspector and white in high-contrast mode).
OlkLabel	UseHeaderColor	True: The label will use the font color that represents header values (usually blue in the Reading Pane and black in the Inspector window).

Making a Form Region Sendable

In some cases, you might want to make a custom form with form regions that can be sent via e-mail to other recipients. In particular, if you wanted to customize the message or appointment forms in a particular way for a custom form type, you would still want to make sure someone could send one of these messages in a way with which he or she is familiar.

With Outlook 2007, the Send button has moved onto the form page itself instead of being in a toolbar or the Ribbon. To re-create this functionality in a form region, you need to add a command button that provides the same capability. To add a Send button to your form region, follow these steps:

1. Open the Field Chooser window.

2. From the drop-down list of field collections, select All Mail Fields.

3. Find the *Submit* field in the list, and drag it to your form region. A new button will be created with the label *Submit*.

You can also add a picture to the Send button by setting the *Picture* and *PictureAlignment* properties on the button. The large Send button on e-mail messages and appointment forms shows an envelope icon centered and aligned above the text.

You should also add the Accounts button for users who have more than one account and need to select which account should be used to send the message. To add the Accounts button, follow these steps:

1. Open the Field Chooser.

2. From the drop-down list of field collections, select All Mail Fields.

3. Find the *Accounts* field in the list, and drag it to the form region.

4. Click the newly created Accounts button, and open the Advanced Properties dialog box for the control.

5. Set the *DisplayDropArrow* property to *True*.

If your solution is running with an add-in behind the form that contains business logic, you might want to hide the Accounts button if only one account is defined in the Outlook profile. To determine the number of accounts available, you can use the *NameSpace.Accounts.Count* property and adjust the visibility of the button accordingly.

Differences Between Custom Forms with Form Regions and Custom Forms with Form Pages

For Outlook custom forms with form pages, Outlook automatically adds Send and Accounts buttons to the default built-in Ribbon tab for the item type to allow legacy forms that relied on Microsoft Outlook 2003 behavior to continue to work. These buttons will always be enabled and visible, even if VBScript for the custom form disables the Send button on the legacy command bars. Form designers who want to disable the Send button on custom forms in Outlook 2007 need to use Ribbon extensibility or convert the forms to form regions to maintain this behavior.

Form Region End to End

Now that you've read more about the concepts around form regions and the form region designer, you can move into creating a form region solution. In this example, you will see how to build all the important pieces of an end-to-end form region solution, including creating a form region, hooking that form region up to an add-in, registering the form region, and deploying the solution.

All of the code mentioned in this section is available in the Travel Agency sample on this book's companion Web site. The scenario covered here is an extension to the standard Contact form in Outlook that will provide a new form page with specific client fields, like frequent flyer number, and a list of purchased itineraries.

Step 1: Creating a Form Region

Before you get started writing an add-in behind the form or otherwise working on business logic and deployment, you need to have a form region design. To complete this step, use the Outlook Forms Designer, and create the .ofs file that contains the layout information. Figure 13-13 shows the form region you are creating.

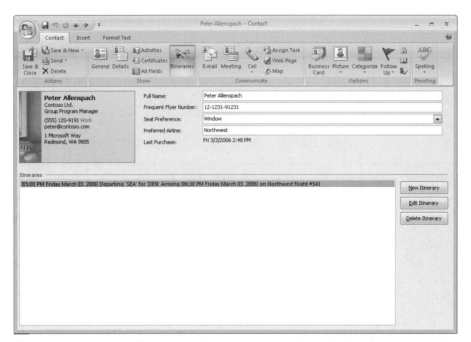

Figure 13-13   Separate form region for a Contact item from the Travel Agency sample.

To design this form, follow these steps:

1. Start Outlook 2007.

2. On the main menu, point to Tools, click Forms, and then click Design A Form.

3. Select Contact, and then click Open, as shown in Figure 13-14.

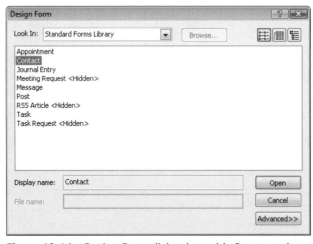

Figure 13-14   Design Form dialog box with Contact selected.

4. In the Design group, click Form Region, and then click New Form Region. Figure 13-15 shows the form designer with a new empty form region.

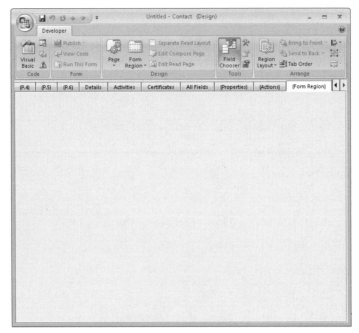

Figure 13-15   Designing a new form region.

Outlook creates a tab in the Forms Designer titled (Form Region). This tab is now a new form region design surface that you use to design the form region, saving it as an Outlook Form Storage (.ofs) file. For this solution, you need three text boxes, three buttons, one Outlook Business Card Control, one Outlook ComboBox Control, six labels, one Outlook Frame Header Control, and one list box.

To add these controls to the form, follow these steps:

1. Display the Control Toolbox by going to the Design group of the Ribbon and clicking the Control Toolbox button.

2. Right-click the Control Toolbox, and select Custom Controls.

3. Scroll through the list of controls, select the following controls, and click OK.

   ❑ Microsoft Office Outlook Command Button Control

   ❑ Microsoft Office Outlook List Control

   ❑ Microsoft Office Outlook TextBox Control

   ❑ Microsoft Office Outlook Frame Header Control

   ❑ Microsoft Office Outlook Business Card Control

❑   Microsoft Office Outlook Label Control

❑   Microsoft Office Outlook ComboBox Control

4. Drag these controls to the form, and arrange them to look like Figure 13-13.

5. To adjust the properties of each control, including the control name and caption, right-click each control, and select Properties. For each control, keep the default settings and adjust the properties accordingly:

❑   Full Name text box

●   Layout: Horizontal: Grow/shrink with form

●   Value: bound to Full Name field

❑   Frequent Flyer text box

●   Name: TextBoxFFN

●   Layout: Horizontal: Grow/shrink with form

●   Value: bound to FrequentFlyerNumber (new Text field)

❑   Seat Preference combo box

●   Name: ComboBoxSeatPref

●   Layout: Horizontal: Grow/shrink with form

●   Value: bound to SeatPreference

●   Value: List Type: Droplist

●   Value: Possible values: Window;Aisle;Middle

❑   Preferred Airline text box

●   Name: TextBoxPreferredAirline

●   Layout: Horizontal: Grow/shrink with form

●   Value: bound to PreferredAirline (new Text field)

❑   Last Purchased text box

●   Name: TextBoxLastPurchase

●   Layout: Horizontal: Grow/shrink with form

●   Value: bound to LastPurchaseDate (new Date/Time field)

❑   Frame Header Control

●   Name: FrameHeaderItineraries

●   Caption: Itineraries

●   Layout: Horizontal: Grow/shrink with form

- ❑ Itineraries list box
  - ● Name: listItineraries
  - ● Layout: Horizontal: Grow/shrink with form
  - ● Layout: Minimum width: 100
  - ● Layout: Vertical: Grow/shrink with form
- ❑ New Itinerary command button
  - ● Name: ButtonNewItinerary
  - ● Caption: &New Itinerary
- ❑ Edit Itinerary command button
  - ● Name: ButtonEditItinerary
  - ● Caption: &Edit Itinerary
- ❑ Delete Itinerary command button
  - ● Name: ButtonDeleteItinerary
  - ● Caption: &Delete Itinerary

6. To save the form region, on the Developer tab in the Design group, click Form Region, and then click Save Form Region As.

7. Save the new form region in a folder as TravelAgencyRegion.ofs, and close the window. When Outlook prompts you to save the changes to the item underlying the designer, click No. We'll import this file later into our add-in project.

Step 2: Writing Business Logic

Now that the design of the form region is complete, you need to craft the add-in that will run in Outlook and provide the business logic for the form. First, you write the basic form region hookup code, which involves implementing and handling an interface defined by Outlook. To encapsulate the business logic for a form region, you will create a form region wrapper class that maintains state for an instance of a form region.

Hooking Up a Form Region and an Add-In

To get started, you need to create a new add-in in Microsoft Visual Studio using either the Shared Add-in template or the Outlook 2007 Add-in template provided on this book's companion Web site. For the purposes of this example, name the project *TravelAgencyAddinCS*. After the project has been created, you should have a Connect.cs file that contains the *Connect* class of your add-in.

Before you continue, you must add a few references to the project. If you are using the template that comes with this book, you should already have references for the Outlook and

Office type libraries. If you are using the Shared Add-in template, you must add these references. You will also need to add a reference to the Microsoft Forms 2.0 type library (Fm20.dll) in either case.

Inside the *Connect* class, you implement the *FormRegionStartup* interface, which is the interface Outlook will use to communicate with the add-in about any form regions tied to the add-in. This interface includes two methods: *GetFormRegionStorage* and *BeforeFormRegionShow*, which are called when Outlook is requesting the OFS file for the form region and just before the form region is displayed to the user, respectively. To implement this interface, change the definition of the *Connect* class to look like this:

```
public partial class Connect : Outlook.FormRegionStartup
```

If you are using the Shared Add-in template, you need to create an alias for the Outlook namespace to refer to the interface in this way by adding this line to the top of the file:

```
using Outlook = Microsoft.Office.Interop.Outlook;
```

Next, you should have Visual Studio generate the method prototypes for the interface. Right-click the FormRegionStartup text, and select Implement Interface from the context menu. Visual Studio then creates the prototypes for the two methods, and you can start writing the code to handle these methods.

Implementing *GetFormRegionStorage* Because *GetFormRegionStorage* is called first, you will start with this method. Outlook will accept a number of return values from this method, depending on how your solution works. Outlook is looking for one of the following resources to supply the form region storage:

- An absolute file path (in the form of a string) to the OFS file
- A byte array containing the contents of the OFS file
- An *IStorage* instance that contains the contents of the OFS file

From managed code, the best mechanism to use is the byte array, because Visual Studio will natively generate the appropriate code when the OFS file is added as a resource for the project.

To add the form region storage to the project as a resource, in the Project Explorer, right-click the Project node, and select Properties to open the Properties window for the project. Click the Resources tab, and create a new default resource file by selecting the hyperlink. Press Ctrl+5 to switch to the File resources display, which should be empty at this point. Click Add Resource on the toolbar, and then find and open the OFS file for the form region you designed and saved in Step 1. Visual Studio automatically copies the OFS file into a Resources folder in the project and creates a new resource variable for the file. Figure 13-16 shows what the resource editor should look like after the file is added.

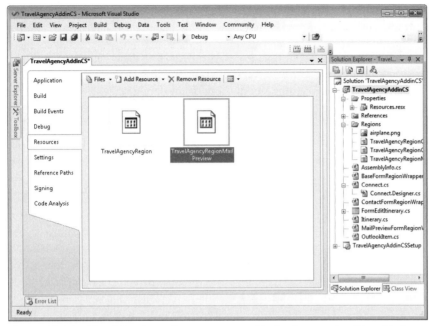

Figure 13-16   Visual Studio project resources with the form region file added as a resource.

Close the Properties window to return back to the source code for the *Connect* class, where you can now return the resource during the *GetFormRegionStorage* method. To ensure that you return the right resource for the right form region (or to handle multiple form regions), use a *switch* statement to switch based on the *FormRegionName* property.

```
public object GetFormRegionStorage(string FormRegionName, object Item,
    int LCID, Outlook.OlFormRegionMode FormRegionMode,
    Outlook.OlFormRegionSize FormRegionSize)
{
    switch (FormRegionName)
    {
        case "TravelAgencyRegion":
            return Properties.Resources.TravelAgencyRegion;

        default:
            return null;
    }
}
```

Because Visual Studio automatically creates a new property for each resource added to the project's resources, and assumes that binary files should be returned as a byte array, no additional code is required in the *GetFormRegionStorage* method of the interface. To handle other form regions, just add additional *case* statements to the *switch* block for each form region name.

Implementing a Form Region Wrapper   Because Outlook can have multiple windows open at a time, and each window could show an instance of the same form region type, you need a wrapper class that will track the state of a particular instance.

Because several elements of the form region wrapper will be the same across different form regions, you use a base class to implement these details, and then you can create another class that derives from the base class to manage the business logic and variables for a specific type of form region. To get started, create the base class, *BaseFormRegionWrapper*. Add a new class file to the project, and type **BaseFormRegionWrapper** for the name of the class. To the top of the class file, add *using* directives for the Outlook object model and the Microsoft Forms 2.0 object model.

```
using Outlook = Microsoft.Office.Interop.Outlook;
using Forms = Microsoft.Vbe.Interop.Forms;
```

Next, edit the class file to contain the following code. This code will create instance variables to hold on to the *FormRegion* instance, hold on to the *UserForm* instance, and provide a *Close* event that will be raised when the form region is closed. The class also implements *IDisposable* to clean up the native code references for *FormRegion* and *UserForm* when the object is disposed.

```
abstract class BaseFormRegionWrapper : IDisposable
{
    #region Instance Variables
    private bool disposed = false;
    protected object Item;
    protected Outlook.FormRegion FormRegion;
    protected Forms.UserForm UserForm;
    #endregion
    #region Constructor
    public BaseFormRegionWrapper(Outlook.FormRegion region)
    {
        this.Item = region.Item;
        this.FormRegion = region;
        this.UserForm = FormRegion.Form as Forms.UserForm;
        this.FormRegion.Close +=
        new Outlook.FormRegionEvents_CloseEventHandler(
        FormRegion_Close);
    }
    #endregion
    #region Events/Handlers
    /// <summary>
    /// Event is raised when the wrapped form region raises its close event
    /// </summary>
    public event EventHandler Close;

    /// <summary>
    /// Raises the close event on this class
    /// </summary>
    protected virtual void OnFormRegionClose()
    {
```

```
        if (Close != null)
        {
            Close(this, EventArgs.Empty);
        }
    }

    private void FormRegion_Close()
    {
        OnFormRegionClose();
    }

    #endregion
    #region IDisposable Members

    ~BaseFormRegionWrapper()
    {
        // call Dispose with false. Because we're in the
        // destructor call, the managed resources will be
        // disposed of anyway.
        Dispose(false);
    }

    public void Dispose()
    {
        // dipose of managed & unmanaged resources
        Dispose(true);

        // tell the GC that the Finalize process no longer needs
        // to be run for this object.
        GC.SuppressFinalize(this);
    }

    protected void Dispose(bool disposeManagedResources)
    {
        // process only if managed and unmanaged resources have
        // not been disposed of.
        if (!this.disposed)
        {
            if (disposeManagedResources)
            {
                // dispose managed resources
                Item = null;
            }

            if (FormRegion != null)
            {

System.Runtime.InteropServices.Marshal.ReleaseComObject(FormRegion);
                FormRegion = null;
            }
            if (UserForm != null)
            {

System.Runtime.InteropServices.Marshal.ReleaseComObject(UserForm);
                UserForm = null;
```

```
        }

            disposed = true;
        }
    }

    #endregion
}
```

Now that you have the base class defined for the form region wrapper, you need to create a class for your specific form region. In this case, you want to handle the form region state while the form region is open and implement your business logic. To do this, add a new class file named *ContactFormRegionWrapper*, which will contain the business logic implementation for this form region.

Inside the *ContactFormRegionWrapper* class, you will create instance variables for every control on the form and hook up those variables during the constructor for the class. You will then implement some business logic around those controls and provide data for the list of itineraries from a data source.

To get started, you need to define variables for all the form controls on the form. To start with, you should add namespace aliases, so insert the following lines at the top of the new class file:

```
using Outlook = Microsoft.Office.Interop.Outlook;
using Office = Microsoft.Office.Core;
using Forms = Microsoft.Vbe.Interop.Forms;
```

You also want to make sure that the new *ContactFormRegionWrapper* class derives from the *BaseFormRegionWrapper* class that you wrote previously. This provides the basic functionality around handling the closing of the form region. To derive from this class, change the class definition to look like this:

```
class ContactFormRegionWrapper : BaseFormRegionWrapper
```

You will continue to define the rest of the methods in the *ContactFormRegionWrapper* class in a bit, but first, to keep track of the itinerary state, you need to have a data class. In this case, you create a new class named *Itinerary* and define properties for the fields that you want to keep track of. In this case, you should create a simple data class with the following fields: *string DepartingAirport*, *string ArrivingAirport*, *DateTime DepartureDate*, *DateTime ArrivalDate*, *string Airline*, and *string FlightNumber*. You should consider overriding the *ToString()* method of the class to provide a representative view of the data, as this is the way the item will be displayed to the user.

Now that you have a data class, you should switch back to working on the *ContactFormRegionWrapper* class. To provide an easy reference to the form controls, define a variable for each control on the form (or at least the controls that are important in the business logic you will write). In this case, you'll add variables for all the controls to the class. You'll also add another variable to maintain a list of available itinerary information.

```
private Outlook.OlkLabel LabelFFN;
private Outlook.OlkTextBox TextBoxFFN;
private Outlook.OlkLabel LabelPreferredAirline;
private Outlook.OlkTextBox TextBoxPreferredAirline;
private Outlook.OlkLabel LabelSeatPref;
private Outlook.OlkComboBox ComboBoxSeatPref;
private Outlook.OlkLabel LabelLastPurchase;
private Outlook.OlkTextBox TextBoxLastPurchase;
private Outlook.OlkCommandButton ButtonNewItinerary;
private Outlook.OlkCommandButton ButtonEditItinerary;
private Outlook.OlkCommandButton ButtonDeleteItinerary;
private Outlook.OlkListBox ListItineraries;
private List<Itinerary> Itineraries;
```

Next up is the constructor for this helper class, which will extend the base constructor provided in *BaseFormRegionWrapper* to actually initialize the member variables for this particular form region. In the constructor you call two helper methods, one to initialize the control variables just defined and another to load itinerary information from the data source. The code should look something like this:

```
public ContactFormRegionWrapper(Outlook.FormRegion region) : base(region)
{
    Itineraries = new List<Itinerary>();
    // Initialize controls
    InitializeControls();
    // Load data from persistence
    LoadItineraries();
}
```

Next, you need to write the helper function *InitializeControls* that will take the instances available on the user form and map them down to the instance variables and cast them to the appropriate type. At the same time, you will wire up some event handlers that will handle the events that you must listen for on these controls.

```
void InitalizeControls()
{
    try
    {
        // Locate control references
        LabelFFN =
            UserForm.Controls.Item("LabelFFN") as Outlook.OlkLabel;
        TextBoxFFN =
            UserForm.Controls.Item("TextBoxFFN") as Outlook.OlkTextBox;
        LabelPreferredAirline =
            UserForm.Controls.Item("LabelPreferredAirline") as Outlook.OlkLabel;
        TextBoxPreferredAirline =
            UserForm.Controls.Item("TextBoxPreferredAirline")
            as Outlook.OlkTextBox;
        LabelSeatPref =
            UserForm.Controls.Item("LabelSeatPref")
            as Outlook.OlkLabel;
        ComboBoxSeatPref =
            UserForm.Controls.Item("ComboBoxSeatPref")
            as Outlook.OlkComboBox;
```

```
            LabelLastPurchase =
                UserForm.Controls.Item("LabelLastPurchase")
                as Outlook.OlkLabel;
            TextBoxLastPurchase =
                UserForm.Controls.Item("TextBoxLastPurchase")
                as Outlook.OlkTextBox;
            ButtonNewItinerary =
                UserForm.Controls.Item("ButtonNewItinerary")
                as Outlook.OlkCommandButton;
            ButtonEditItinerary =
                UserForm.Controls.Item("ButtonEditItinerary")
                as Outlook.OlkCommandButton;
            ButtonDeleteItinerary =
                UserForm.Controls.Item("ButtonDeleteItinerary")
                as Outlook.OlkCommandButton;
            ListItineraries =
                UserForm.Controls.Item("listItineraries")
                as Outlook.OlkListBox;
            Forms.Frame Frame2 =
                UserForm.Controls.Item("Frame2") as Forms.Frame;
            Frame2.BorderStyle =
                Microsoft.Vbe.Interop.Forms.fmBorderStyle.fmBorderStyleNone;
            Frame2.ScrollBars =
                Microsoft.Vbe.Interop.Forms.fmScrollBars.fmScrollBarsNone;
            // Hook up events
            ButtonNewItinerary.Click +=
                new Outlook.OlkCommandButtonEvents_ClickEventHandler(
                ButtonNewItinerary_Click);
            ButtonEditItinerary.Click +=
                new Outlook.OlkCommandButtonEvents_ClickEventHandler(
                ButtonEditItinerary_Click);
            ButtonDeleteItinerary.Click +=
                new Outlook.OlkCommandButtonEvents_ClickEventHandler(
                ButtonDeleteItinerary_Click);
            ListItineraries.DoubleClick +=
                new Outlook.OlkListBoxEvents_DoubleClickEventHandler(
                ListItineraries_DoubleClick);
        }
        catch (Exception ex)
        {
            Debug.WriteLine ("An error occured while hooking up Form Region controls: " +
ex.Message);
        }
    }
}
```

Now that you have all that glue out of the way, you can actually start writing the business logic. In this case, you'll be using a file named Itineraries.xml to maintain information about a given contact's itineraries. This file will live as a hidden attachment on the contact. In a real-world solution, you might use a database connection or Web service to retrieve this data from a server, but the basic form region code would look similar.

The *LoadItineraries* method called in the constructor looks for an attachment on the Contact with a particular filename (in this case Itineraries.xml) and then deserializes the contents of that file back into an instance of a *List* class containing the itineraries. If the attachment does not exist, an empty list will be created and the file will be created when the contact is saved if any itineraries are added while the form region is open. This method can be downloaded as part of the sample code available for the book and is not printed here.

Now that the form initialization code is finished, you can write the event handlers that you wired up in the *InitializeControls* method previously. These events handle adding a new itinerary, editing an existing itinerary, and deleting an itinerary. When the event fires, you display a WinForm dialog box that allows the user to create or edit an itinerary object, which is added back to the *Itineraries List* object after the user clicks OK. Because this code does not directly affect the operation of the form region, it is not included here but can be downloaded from this book's companion Web site.

Each of these event handlers also saves the changes back to the attached XML file after making the change to the list so that the file is always in sync with the displayed list of itineraries. Because the file attachment is not saved if the user cancels making changes to the item, this behavior is still consistent with the way Outlook behaves. If you are using a database or other back-end store, you might want to wait for the *Save* event to occur on the item before persisting the changes to the back-end store so that if a user cancels saving the item, the item remains in a consistent state.

Step 3: Registering the Form Region

Once you have the business logic written and the form design complete, you can write the manifest file and register the form region. The manifest file describes the form region to Outlook and includes details about where to load the form region layout file, which icons to display, and any custom actions that should be added to the item. After the manifest is created, it is registered in the Windows registry under registry keys for each message class that should load the form region.

Authoring a Form Region Manifest

The form region manifest file is a simple XML file described as the Form Region Manifest XML Schema, which is available as part of the Office 2007 XML Reference on MSDN. The following sections provide a quick overview of the important schema elements.

Manifest Basics   Each form region manifest is composed of one document element, the *<FormRegion>* element, which has several child elements that are mostly optional. Default values are assumed for any element that is not included in the manifest file, and these default values are defined in the XML schema for the manifest. If no *<name>* element is provided, the name of the registry value for the form region will be used instead. The following is a relatively simple manifest example, which provides a name, type, page name, accelerator key, add-in, and an icon for the form region that appears in the Show group in the Ribbon:

```
<?xml version="1.0" encoding="utf-8"?>
<FormRegion xmlns="http://schemas.microsoft.com/office/outlook/12/formregion.xsd">
```

```
<name>TravelAgencyRegion</name>
<formRegionType>separate</formRegionType>
<formRegionName>Itineraries</formRegionName>
<ribbonAccelerator>I</ribbonAccelerator>
<showInspectorCompose>true</showInspectorCompose>
<showInspectorRead>true</showInspectorRead>
<showReadingPane>false</showReadingPane>
<addin>TravelAgencyAddinCS.Connect</addin>
<icons>
    <page>plane.png</page>
</icons>
<stringOverride file="TravelAgencyRegionCS.%langid%.xml" language="all" />
</FormRegion>
```

Optional Elements   Each of the following elements is optional and will have the default value assumed if it is not specified in the manifest XML. Each of these elements should be a child of the *<FormRegion>* element if included, and should only appear once.

- **<name>**   The internal name of the add-in. This value is passed to the *GetFormRegionStorage* and *BeforeFormRegionStartup* methods to identify this form region. It can also be used in other form region *<displayAfter>* elements.

- **<title>**   The title of the form region, which is displayed in the Choose Form dialog box and the Actions menu for replacement and replace-all forms. This title is also displayed for adjoining form regions as the header name above the form region. *<name>* will be used if this value is not included.

- **<formRegionName>**   The text displayed on the Show group on the Ribbon for this form region (only valid for separate, replacement, and replace-all form regions). *<title>* will be used if this value is not included.

- **<description>**   Text that describes the use of the form region, displayed in the Choose Form dialog box.

- **<formRegionType>**   Specifies the type of form region. Must be *separate, adjoining, replace,* or *replaceAll.*

- **<showInspectorCompose>**   Controls if this form region is displayed in the Inspector window in compose mode for this item type. Default value is *True.*

- **<showInspectorRead>**   Controls if this form region is displayed in the Inspector window in read mode for this item type. Not all item types have a read mode. Default value is *True.*

- **<showReadingPane>**   Controls if this form region is displayed in the Reading Pane for this item type. Only affects adjoining, replacement, and replace-all form regions.

- **<hidden>**   Controls if the form region title is displayed in the Choose Form dialog box and Actions menu. The default value is *False.* Only works for replacement and replace-all form regions.

- **<exactMessageClass>**   Controls how the form region behaves on derived message classes. Default value is *False.* When *True,* the form region will only be displayed on message classes that match exactly how it was registered; otherwise, message classes that are derived from the original registration will also display this form region.

■ ***<layoutFile>***   Specifies the OFS file that Outlook should load to display this form region. This value is only used if *<addin>* is not specified.

■ ***<addin>***   Specifies the *ProgID* or identifier for the add-in that should be called for this form region. The add-in must implement the *FormRegionStartup* interface to be called.

■ ***<displayAfter>***   Specifies the name of another form region that this form region should be positioned after. This does not guarantee that the form region directly preceding this one will be the one specified, based on load order and other form regions that might have the same *<displayAfter>* value.

■ ***<contact>***   Specifies a contact name for the form region. This information can be used for supportability of a form region.

■ ***<version>***   Specifies a version of the form region. This information can be used for supportability of a form region.

■ ***<loadLegacyForm>***   This option determines if Outlook looks for a custom form with form pages with the same message class if it finds a form region first. This value defaults to *False* and, for performance reasons, should remain *False* unless you need to load form pages and form regions at the same time.

■ ***<ribbonAccelerator>***   Specifies one to three characters that should be used as the hot key for the form region's Ribbon button. This value is ignored for adjoining form regions.

■ ***<icons>***   Specifies custom icons for the item type. For more information, see the section "Custom Icons" later in this chapter.

■ ***<customActions>***   Specifies custom actions for the item type. For more information, see the section "Describing Custom Actions" later in this chapter.

■ ***<stringOverride>***   Specifies localized strings that can be used for a particular language. For more information on localizing form regions, see the section "Localizing a Form Region" later in this chapter.

Custom Icons

Replacement and replace-all form regions can specify a range of custom icons that are shown when items of the form region message class are displayed in the view. Additionally, separate form regions can specify an icon that shows up in the Ribbon on the button to activate that form region page. All of these icons are specified in the *<icons>* element of the *<FormRegion>* element in the manifest. Table 13-4 lists custom icon elements.

If you include the *<icons>* element in your form region manifest, you should include at least one child element. Each child element represents a particular icon visible to the user somewhere in Outlook. Each child element should contain either (a) a path to the icon file or (b) a path to a dynamic link library (DLL) and a resource number to load from the file. Relative paths are resolved against the location of the manifest XML file. For example:

```
<FormRegion xmlns="http://schemas.microsoft.com/office/outlook/12/formregion.xsd">
    <icons>
        <!-- relative path -->
        <default>icons\default.ico</default>
        <!-- embedded resource -->
        <window>%SystemRoot%\system32\SHELL32.dll,102</window>
        <!-- relative path to bitmap -->
        <page>icons\plane.png</page>
    </icons>
</FormRegion>
```

Table 13-4 Custom Icon Elements

Element name	Description	Supported format	Applies to
<default>	An icon that will be used by default when no other icon is provided, except for the *<page>* icon	ICO only	Replacement and replace-all form regions only
<unread>	An icon displayed in the Folder view for unread items	ICO only	Replacement and replace-all form regions only
<read>	An icon displayed in the Folder view for read items	ICO only	Replacement and replace-all form regions only
<replied>	An icon displayed in the Folder view for items that have been replied to	ICO only	Replacement and replace-all form regions only
<forwarded>	An icon displayed in the Folder view for items that have been forwarded	ICO only	Replacement and replace-all form regions only
<unsent>	An icon displayed in the Folder view for items that are unsent, which are typically found in the Drafts folder	ICO only	Replacement and replace-all form regions only
<submitted>	An icon displayed in the Folder view for items that have been submitted for sending, but are not yet sent; these are typically found in the Outbox	ICO only	Replacement and replace-all form regions only
<signed>	An icon displayed in the Folder view for items that have been digitally signed	ICO only	Replacement and replace-all form regions only
<encrypted>	An icon displayed in the Folder view for items that have been encrypted	ICO only	Replacement and replace-all form regions only
<window>	An icon displayed for the item Inspector window when the form is open, displayed in the Windows Taskbar and Alt+Tab dialog box	ICO only	Replacement and replace-all form regions only

Table 13-4   Custom Icon Elements

Element name	Description	Supported format	Applies to
`<recurring>`	An icon displayed in the Folder view for items that are recurring items, such as recurring tasks or appointments	ICO only	Replacement and replace-all form regions only
`<page>`	An icon or bitmap displayed in the Ribbon on the button to switch to the form region	ICO or PNG	Separate, replacement, and replace-all form regions

Describing Custom Actions

Each form region can have custom actions included as part of the form as well. These custom actions work in a manner similar to the built-in actions provided by the standard Outlook forms (for example, Reply, Reply All, Forward). You can also use custom actions to disable the built-in actions if they are not applicable to your custom form.

Custom actions are defined using the *<customActions>* element, which is always a child of the *<FormRegion>* element. Under the *<customActions>* element, you can define individual actions for the form or disable built-in actions. For example, if you wanted to create a new action titled "Post Reply" that would create a new post item in the form of a reply to the current item, the XML in your form region manifest would look like this:

```
<FormRegion xmlns="http://schemas.microsoft.com/office/outlook/12/formregion.xsd">
    <!-- Other elements would go here -->
    <customActions>
        <action name="postReply">
            <title>Post Reply</title>
            <targetForm>IPM.Post</targetForm>
            <addressLike>reply</addressLike>
            <body>user</body>
            <showOnRibbon>true</showOnRibbon>
            <method>open</method>
            <subjectPrefix>RE</subjectPrefix>
        </action>
    </customActions>
</FormRegion>
```

This action would then be available via the *Actions* collection in the object model and on the Ribbon under the Custom Actions menu to allow the user to execute the action.

Each *<action>* element must have a name attribute that specifies an internal name for the action. This value must be unique across the actions defined for a form region. This value can be used to provide localized strings using the *<stringOverride>* element. Additionally, the following elements are defined as child elements for the *<action>* element:

- **<title>**   The display text for the custom action. This value will be shown in the Ribbon and other locations where the action is displayed.

- **<targetForm>** Specifies the message class of the target form for the action. When the action is executed, a new item will be created with this message class.

- **<addressLike>** Specifies how the target form will be addressed. Possible values are *reply, replyAll, forward, replyToFolder,* and *response*. For more information about the meaning of these values, see the XML schema for form regions.

- **<body>** Specifies how the body of the target form should be set. Possible values are *omit, attach, include, indent, prefix, link,* and *user*. For more information about the meaning of these values, see the XML schema for form regions.

- **<showOnRibbon>** Boolean value that determines if the custom action is displayed on the Ribbon in the Custom Actions menu.

- **<method>** Specifies the method Outlook will use when creating the target form. The value of this element should be either *open, prompt,* or *send*. For more information about the meaning of these values, see the XML schema for form regions.

- **<subjectPrefix>** Specifies the characters that will be prepended to the subject when creating the target form. For a reply, this might be "RE."

You can also disable any of the built-in actions by defining an action named with a particular keyword. The keywords shown in Table 13-5 are the same regardless of the language in which Outlook is running.

Table 13-5 Custom Action Name Keywords for Built-in Actions

Name keyword	Action name
Reply	Reply
replyAll	Reply All
forward	Forward
replyToFolder	Reply to Folder

To disable the Reply All action for a form region, you could use the following XML in your manifest file:

```
<FormRegion xmlns="http://schemas.microsoft.com/office/outlook/12/formregion.xsd">
    <!-- Other elements would go here -->
    <customActions>
        <action name="replyAll" disable="true"></action>
    </customActions>
</FormRegion>
```

Localizing a Form Region

Form regions include a built-in mechanism to enable localization of form region data (title, description, and so on), as well as the strings displayed on a form region's controls. All of this information can be defined in the manifest file, or you can reference an external localization manifest from the form region manifest where these values can be loaded.

Using String Overrides   To localize a form region, you can use the *<stringOverride>* element in the form region manifest file. This element contains child elements that redefine the displayed strings defined in the manifest file for a particular language. Each *<stringOverride>* element has one required attribute, language, which contains a list of the Locale IDs (LCIDs) of each language that should use the strings defined inside the element.

For example, to provide localized string information for U.S. English, you could add this XML snippet to your form region manifest:

```
<FormRegion>
    <!-- other elements here -->
    <stringOverride language="1033">
        <title>US English Title</title>
        <formRegionName>US English Page Name</formRegionName>
        <description>US English Description</description>

        <control name="OlkLabel1">
            <caption>English Display Text</caption>
        </control>

        <action name="postReply">
            <title>English Post Reply</title>
            <subjectPrefix>US-FW</subjectPrefix>
        </action>
    </stringOverride>
</FormRegion>
```

The following elements are defined in the schema for use inside the *<stringOverride>* element:

- **<title>**   The title of the form region, which is displayed in the Choose Form dialog box and the Actions menu for replacement and replace-all form regions. This title is also displayed for adjoining form regions as the header name above the form region. *<name>* will be used if this value is not included.

- **<formRegionName>**   The text displayed on the Ribbon in the Show group for this form region (only valid for separate, replacement, and replace-all form regions). *<title>* will be used if this value is not included.

- **<description>**   Text that describes the use of the form region, displayed in the Choose Form dialog box.

- **<control>**   Represents strings that will be used for a given control on the form region. The *name* attribute is required on this element and should provide the value of the *Name* property of the control referenced from the form region.

- **<caption>**   A child element of *control*, this element contains the text that will be set as the *Caption* property of the control referenced by the *name* attribute.

- **<action>**   Represents strings that will be used for a given custom action on the form region. The *name* attribute is required on this element and should be the value of the *name* attribute on the custom action.

■ **<title>**   A child element of *action*, this element contains the text that will be used for the localized title of the custom action.

■ **<subjectPrefix>**   A child element of *action*, this element contains the text that will be used for the localized subject preview of the custom action.

Additionally, instead of including all the localized resources in one file, you can use an optional attribute on the *<stringOverride>* element to point Outlook to another file that contains the resources. In the next example, the *<stringOverride>* element redirects all languages to look for a file in a directory based on the LCID of the language.

```
<FormRegion>
    <!-- other elements here -->
    <stringOverride language="all"
        file="%LCID%\resources.xml"></stringOverride>
</FormRegion>
```

Outlook will replace the *%LCID%* value in the file attribute with the actual LCID for the language being loaded. Outlook will look up relative paths based on the location of the manifest XML file. In this case, to provide resources for U.S. English, you can create a subdirectory in the same location as the manifest XML file named 1033. Inside this folder, you should have a Resources.xml file that contains this XML:

```
<FormRegionStrings xmlns="http://schemas.microsoft.com/office/outlook/12/
formregionstrings.xsd">
    <title>US English Title</title>
    <formRegionName>US English Page Name</formRegionName>
    <description>US English Description</description>

    <control name="OlkLabel1">
        <caption>English Display Text</caption>
    </control>

    <action name="postReply">
        <title>English Post Reply</title>
        <subjectPrefix>US-FW</subjectPrefix>
    </action>
</FormRegionStrings>
```

> **Note**   The resource files use a document element named *FormRegionStrings* instead of *FormRegion*. The child elements for *<FormRegionStrings>* are identical to the contents of the *<stringOverride>* element in the form region manifest.

Registering a Form Region

Each form region has to be registered in the Windows registry before Outlook will load and display the form region. The registration process is a simple matter of writing the correct registry key for the form region message class and specifying the location of the manifest file.

Form regions are registered under the key HKEY_CURRENT_USER\Software\Microsoft \Office\Outlook\FormRegions, or HKEY_LOCAL_MACHINE\Software\Microsoft \Office\Outlook\FormRegions. Most solutions should use the user-based key so that administrative privileges are not required to install the solution. Under the FormRegions key in the registry, you will need to create a key for each message class with which your form region will be used. For example, to register a form region on *IPM.Contact*, you would create HKEY_CURRENT_USER\Software\Microsoft\Office\Outlook\FormRegions \IPM.Contact, and then create a new value under that key. To register a form region on a custom message class, create a new key under the FormRegions key with the name of the message class (see Figure 13-17).

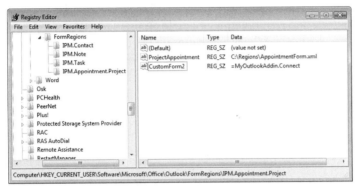

Figure 13-17   Registry editor showing a form region registered on a custom message class.

The value for your form region should be the name of the form region (as defined in the <*name*> element of the manifest) and the full path to the XML manifest file. The path name can also use environment variables that will be expanded when the value is read; for example, to specify a manifest file from the program files folder, you could use %*ProgramFiles*%\Solution \MyManifest.xml as the value.

Replacing the Default Form for a Folder

For replacement or replace-all form regions, you can make a form region become the default form for a folder. If the form region is the default form for a folder, the form region is displayed to the user when he or she performs any of the following actions in the folder:

- Clicks the New button on the Standard toolbar in the Explorer window.

- Selects the New <*Item*> command on the New menu on the Standard toolbar in the Explorer window, where <*Item*> represents the built-in item type for a folder. If the built-in item type is Contact, then selecting New Contact on the New menu in the Explorer window will display the form region.

- Selects the New <*Item*> command on the View context menu in the Explorer window, where <*Item*> represents the built-in item type for a folder.

- Presses Ctrl+N to create a new default item for the folder.

■ Clicks the "new item row" in a Folder view. To show the "new item row" in a view, set the *ShowNewItemRow* property of the *TableView* object to *True*.

> **Note**   Changing the default form for a folder does not change the default form when the user selects New *<Item>* from the Office menu in an Inspector window. If you want to ensure that your replacement or replace-all form region appears when the user selects the New *<Item>* command in an Inspector window, monitor the *NewInspector* and *Item_Open* events. In the *Item_Open* event, you cancel the display of the built-in form and then create an instance of the replacement or replace-all form region by calling the *Add* method of the *Items* collection. For additional details on creating a custom item, see the section "Creating an Item" in Chapter 5, "Built-in Item Types."

Although the *Folder* object does not implement a method that lets you set the default form for a folder directly, you can use the *PropertyAccessor* object to set the correct folder properties. The following code sample shows you how to set the default form for a folder. The *DemoSetDefaultFormForFolder* method sets the default form for the current folder to "Shoe Store" by calling the *SetDefaultFormForFolder* method. The message class for the "Shoe Store" replacement form region is "IPM.Contact.Shoe Store."

```
private void DemoCustomDefaultFormForFolder()
{
    Outlook.Folder folder =
        Application.ActiveExplorer().CurrentFolder as Outlook.Folder;
    SetDefaultFormForFolder(
        "IPM.Contact.Shoe Store", "Shoe Store", folder);
}

private void SetDefaultFormForFolder(string defaultMessageClass,
    string defaultDisplayName, Outlook.Folder folder)
{
    const string PR_DEF_POST_MSGCLASS =
        "http://schemas.microsoft.com/mapi/proptag/0x36E5001E";
    const string PR_DEF_POST_DISPLAYNAME =
        "http://schemas.microsoft.com/mapi/proptag/0x36E6001E";
    if (folder == null)
    {
        throw new ArgumentNullException(
            "folder", "Parameter must contain a value.");
    }
    if(string.IsNullOrEmpty(defaultMessageClass))
    {
        throw new ArgumentNullException(
            "defaultMessageClass",
            "Parameter must contain a value.");
    }
    if (string.IsNullOrEmpty(defaultDisplayName))
    {
        throw new ArgumentNullException(
            "defaultDisplayName",
            "Parameter must contain a value.");
    }
```

```
    try
    {
        // Calling SetProperty sets the property without saving
        folder.PropertyAccessor.SetProperty(
            PR_DEF_POST_DISPLAYNAME, defaultDisplayName);
        folder.PropertyAccessor.SetProperty(
            PR_DEF_POST_MSGCLASS, defaultMessageClass);
    }
    catch (Exception ex)
    {
        Debug.WriteLine(ex.Message);
    }
}
```

To reset the default form for a folder, you call the *SetDefaultFormForFolder* method and pass the *DefaultMessageClass* property for the *Folder* object as the *defaultMessageClass* argument. The *DefaultMessageClass* property always returns the built-in default message class for a folder rather than a custom message class such as "IPM.Contact.Shoe Store." The following code sample resets the default message class for the current folder:

```
private void DemoResetDefaultFormForFolder()
{
    Outlook.Folder folder =
        Application.ActiveExplorer().CurrentFolder as Outlook.Folder;
    SetDefaultFormForFolder(
        folder.DefaultMessageClass, " ", folder);
}
```

Advanced Form Region Methods

In addition to the methods described earlier in the *FormRegionStartup* interface, there are two other methods provided on this interface: *GetFormRegionManifest* and *GetFormRegionIcon*. Advanced form region developers can use these methods to let the add-in provide all of the content Outlook needs for the form region: the manifest file, the icons, and the form storage. This allows add-ins that cannot reliably know where files are installed to the disk to provide form region solutions, and it also improves the reliability of the solution because all the associated files can be stored as resources inside the compiled assembly.

Outlook will only call these advanced functions if the form region is registered in a special way in the Windows registry. Instead of registering the form region with XML or a path to the XML file as the setting value, add-ins must register their *ProgID* with an equal sign appended to the front, such as *=MyAddingProgID.Class*. This indicates to Outlook that it needs to look for this add-in and call the *GetFormRegionManifest* method on the *FormRegionStartup* interface to find out more about the registered form region.

When manifest information is provided through *GetFormRegionManifest*, a few of the elements defined in the form region XML schema are treated differently. For example, the

<name> element is ignored from the XML schema because Outlook is already using the registry setting name as the form region name. Additionally, both the *<layoutFile>* and *<addin>* attributes are ignored because Outlook already knows which add-in should be contacted for the form region. Finally, the children of the *<icons>* element cannot be used to refer to a location on disk for the icons. If the child element exists and contains no value or the string *addin*, then Outlook automatically calls *GetFormRegionIcon* for that icon. Icons that are completely omitted from the manifest XML will inherit the default icon and will not be requested from *GetFormRegionIcon*.

Summary

In this chapter, you learned the basics of using the Outlook Forms Designer to create a new form region solution. You've looked at how to design a form, how to hook up the business logic for a form using an add-in in managed code, and how to write a form region manifest file and register it with Outlook. You should now be able to use Outlook form regions to create deeply integrated, rich solutions that really extend the power and usefulness of Outlook while still feeling like an integrated part of the Outlook experience.

Chapter 14
Form Region Controls

One of the developer trouble spots for custom forms in previous versions of Outlook was that it was difficult to establish parity with Outlook's built-in forms in terms of visual appearance and control behavior. With form regions in Microsoft Office Outlook 2007, the story is significantly improved. In addition to form regions supporting the Office and Windows themes, Outlook includes a collection of controls that provide parity with the control used on built-in Outlook forms.

In this chapter, you learn about standard controls for form regions and Outlook controls for form regions. You get step-by-step instructions for adding controls in design mode. You also learn how to add controls at run time. This chapter highlights all of the new controls included with Outlook 2007 and discusses how to add these controls to your form and how to work with the controls programmatically.

Standard Controls

Outlook provides replacements for the standard form controls that were previously provided by the Microsoft Forms 2.0 library. These controls support the visual appearance of Windows and Office themes and Outlook data binding support. Each of these controls should function nearly identically to the Microsoft Forms 2.0 version of the control with a few exceptions, which are detailed for those controls. Although the control should behave similar to the Forms 2.0 version of the control, the interface might not match exactly in all cases.

The Outlook Check Box

The Microsoft Office Outlook Check Box Control provides a standard user interface concept for a Boolean option, which is one that can be either selected or not selected. The control provides a label that appears next to a check box that indicates the selection status of the control.

The Outlook Combo Box

The Microsoft Office Outlook Combo Box Control provides a standard user interface control that works like a combination of a text box and a list box control. Depending on the value of the control's *Style* property, the combo box allows users to type values or select values from a drop-down list.

If the control is data bound to an Outlook built-in or custom field, you specify values for the drop-down list at design time by using the Properties dialog box for the control. If the bound property for the control is a keywords field, you specify the possible values for the field on the

Values tab of the Properties dialog box in the Initial Values text box in the Outlook Forms Designer. Separate each possible value in the Initial Values text box with a semicolon. For example, for the bound custom keywords field named "Primary Color," you type **Blue; Green; Red** in the Initial Values text box.

If the control is not data bound, you add possible values at run time by calling the *AddItem* method on an instance of the class. Unlike the Forms 2.0 version of the combo box control, this control does not support setting the possible values using an array for the *List* or *Column* properties. If you need to persist the selected item in the combo box and the control is not data bound, write code to assign the *ListIndex* or *Text* property to a built-in or custom property for the item. When the item is opened, read the value of the built-in or custom property, and set the *ListIndex* property of the control to select the desired value in the control.

The Outlook Command Button

In addition to the standard interface members expected for a Microsoft Forms Command Button, the Outlook version of this control has two additional features: support for displaying images and displaying a drop-down arrow (see Figure 14-1). These additional properties are available in the Advanced Properties dialog box for the *OlkCommandButton* control.

Figure 14-1   Use the Microsoft Office Outlook Command Button Control with pictures or drop-down arrows.

The drop-down arrow is typically displayed when a menu will appear after the button is clicked. This type of interface is used in several places throughout Outlook, most notably the Contact form. When creating this type of button for your custom form, you should set the *DisplayDropArrow* property equal to *true*.

Images are used on several buttons across the product, including the new Send button that is displayed prominently on the default mail form in Outlook 2007. To re-create this button, use the *Picture* and *PictureAlignment* properties to specify a bitmap image that should be displayed on the button and how the picture should be aligned. Outlook will use the color of the top-left pixel in the bitmap as the transparent color when rendering the image on the button.

The Outlook Label Control

The Microsoft Office Outlook Label Control has one additional property that allows the control to take on the themed color for header elements as displayed on a form in the preview pane and read Inspector windows.

When the *UseHeaderColor* property is set to *true*, the color used to display the label's text will be automatically set to the color specified by the Office theme used in the rest of Outlook. When the *UseHeaderColor* property is set to *false*, Outlook will use the value of the *ForeColor* property to determine what color will be used to draw the label's text (see Figure 14-2).

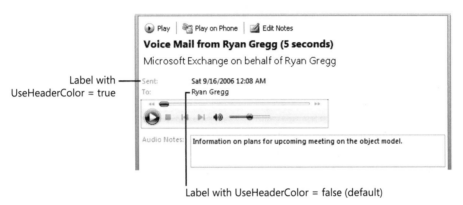

Figure 14-2 Use the *UseHeaderColor* property to set label color.

The Outlook List Box

The Microsoft Office Outlook List Box Control provides a standard Windows list box, which is displayed as a list of items that can be selected by the user. If the *MultiSelect* property is set to 1, the user can select more than one item in the list using the Ctrl and Shift keys on the keyboard. When multiple selections are enabled, you use the *GetSelected* method to determine which items in the list are selected and which are not.

Unlike the Forms 2.0 version of the List Box Control, this control does not support setting the list values using an array for the *List* or *Column* properties or showing multiple columns of data.

The Outlook Option Button

The Microsoft Office Outlook Option Button Control provides a standard user interface concept for a value that is mutually exclusive in a group of option buttons. Each group of option button controls can only have one option button control with a selected state. Selecting a different control automatically unselects other controls in the group. Grouping is determined based on the parent container of the option button or by the *GroupName* property of the control.

This control is provided for use on Outlook forms with form regions and is designed to pick up the Windows theme for this style of control. The control can also be data bound to Outlook data using the Properties dialog box in the Outlook Forms Designer. This control implements the most common set of properties, methods, and events provided by the Forms 2.0 Option Button control but does not implement the full interface provided by Forms 2.0.

The Outlook Text Box

The Microsoft Office Outlook Text Box Control provides a standard Microsoft Windows text box, which provides functionality for editing or inputting string data. The Outlook Text Box Control can display a single line or multiple lines by setting the *MultiLine* property to *false* or *true,* respectively. The value of the control can be retrieved or set by using the *Text* property on the control.

Outlook-Specific Controls

Outlook 2007 also includes a number of specific controls that are displayed on built-in item forms. These controls provide the same functionality the user experiences on the Outlook forms without the need to re-create the logic embedded in those controls. These controls are only supported on form region style forms and should not be used on classic custom forms because these controls will not work with previous versions of Outlook.

The Outlook Body Control

The Microsoft Office Outlook Body Control provides a rich editing and composing surface that is used as the item body. This control is always automatically bound to the *Body* property of the item and cannot be altered or changed. The control includes two properties: *ReadOnly* and *SuppressAttachments*. The *ReadOnly* property enables the body control to appear read-only, as it does when displayed in the preview pane or on a read-only item. *SuppressAttachments* can be used to disable the attachment well that is also displayed inside the control for Hypertext Markup Language (HTML) or plain-text formatted messages. Messages or items that use Rich Text Format (RTF) formatting will display attachments inline regardless of the value of *SuppressAttachments*.

The Outlook Business Card Control

The Microsoft Office Outlook Business Card Control shows a contact's business card preview and provides an entry point to editing a contact's business card (see Figure 14-3). This control can only be used on Contact items and automatically data binds to the underlying item. This control also automatically sizes accordingly to fit the business card preview size and should not be resized.

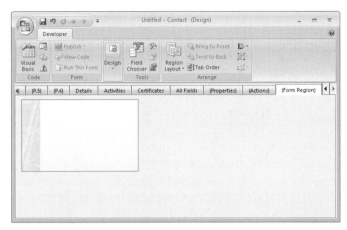

Figure 14-3   The Outlook Business Card Control on a custom contact form.

The Outlook Category Control

The Microsoft Office Outlook Category Control displays the categories assigned to a particular item on the form in a visual representation that shows the category name and color for each category assigned to the item (see Figure 14-4). This control is used at the top of all built-in forms to visually represent the assigned categories for an item. The Outlook Category Control automatically data binds to the underlying item and does not have any data binding properties.

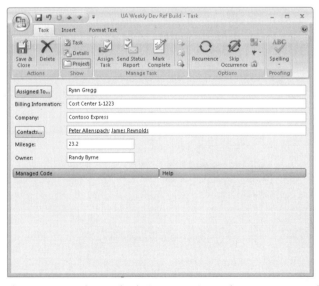

Figure 14-4   The Outlook Category Control on a custom task form.

Note The Outlook Category Control should usually be positioned as the second topmost control on the form, directly below the Microsoft Office Outlook InfoBar Control, which should be the topmost control. This placement is consistent with the location of the Outlook Category Control on all Outlook built-in forms.

The *AutoSize* property of the Outlook Category Control has special behavior that is different from the standard *AutoSize* property behavior. When *AutoSize* is set to *true*, Outlook automatically expands and collapses the control based on the number of categories assigned to the item. If there are no categories assigned, the control will be hidden, and the space it uses on the form can be used by other controls. If a category is added, the control expands and becomes visible again. With *AutoSize* set to *false*, the control does not automatically resize and displays "(none)" if no categories are selected on the item.

Note Setting the *ForeColor* property on this control has no effect. The color used for the name of each category is determined by the category color and cannot be changed.

The Outlook Contact Photo Control

Previously, one of the biggest problems with creating a custom contact form in Outlook 2003 was that there was no way to replicate the functionality for viewing or assigning a contact photo to the contact. For Outlook 2007, a control is provided that enables a form designer to replicate this functionality without writing code. The Microsoft Office Outlook Contact Photo Control has no properties to customize the appearance or behavior of the control and automatically data binds to the contact picture of the contact represented by the form region (see Figure 14-5).

Figure 14-5 Using the Outlook Contact Photo Control to display a contact photo on a custom contact form.

The Outlook Date Control

Outlook makes use of a custom date picker control on several built-in forms in Outlook, such as the Task and Appointment forms. This Microsoft Office Outlook Date Control has a lot of built-in parsing logic that can be difficult to replicate. For example, if the user types **today** or **two days from tomorrow**, the control parses the language and sets the appropriate date. Previously, this type of behavior was difficult or impossible to replicate on a custom form.

For Outlook 2007, this control is wrapped as a custom control that can be used on any form region. The Outlook Date Control can be bound using Outlook data binding to built-in date/time fields or to a user-defined date/time field using the Value tab of the Properties dialog box for the control. Figure 14-6 shows an example of this control in use on a form region.

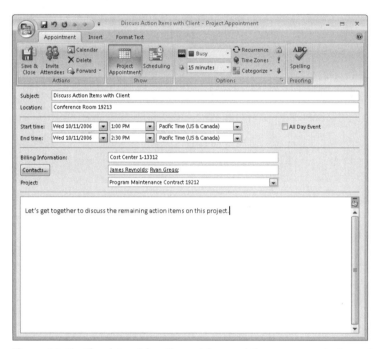

Figure 14-6   The date picker, time picker, and time zone controls used on a custom form region.

The Outlook Date Control can also work in conjunction with the Microsoft Office Outlook Time Control to set both the date and time for a particular field. Just bind both controls to the same field, and each control will adjust the correct part of the value (date or time).

The Outlook Frame Header Control

Many of the built-in Outlook forms include a division between groups of controls. This division is typically represented by a name for the group of controls and a themed horizontal line separating the controls. Although this effect was previously accomplished using a Frame control from the Microsoft Forms 2.0 library, that effect did not support themes properly.

For Outlook 2007, the Microsoft Office Outlook Frame Header Control wraps the functionality displayed by the built-in forms into an easy-to-use control (see Figure 14-7). You can set the *Caption*, *Alignment*, and *ForeColor* properties to customize the appearance of this control.

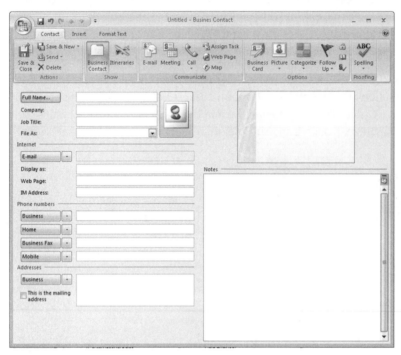

Figure 14-7   An example custom form region using the Outlook Frame Header Control to separate form regions of controls into logical groups.

The Outlook InfoBar Control

The Microsoft Office Outlook InfoBar Control wraps the functionality of the Outlook InfoBar as a control that you can use on your form region pages. The InfoBar displays additional information about the item, such as when the user replied, or if the item is flagged for follow-up (see Figure 14-8). Previously, this functionality was not possible for a custom form solution.

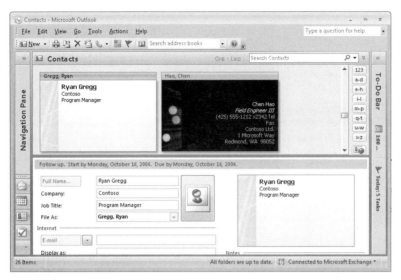

Figure 14-8   The Outlook InfoBar Control used on a form region displayed in the Reading Pane.

The Outlook InfoBar Control should only be added to the default page of a form region, as Outlook does not typically show this information on other pages of a built-in form. The Outlook InfoBar Control should be the topmost control on the form and should span the width of the form. On most forms, the Outlook Category Control should be immediately below the InfoBar if any categories are assigned to the item.

The Outlook InfoBar Control does not have any properties that enable customization of the appearance of the InfoBar. The color and other properties of the InfoBar text will be determined by Outlook based on the type of messages displayed. Because it only displays existing messages on the item, you cannot set the text of the InfoBar using the Outlook InfoBar Control.

The Outlook Page Control

The Microsoft Office Outlook Page Control wraps functionality of built-in tabs provided on Outlook forms into a control that allows these pages to be reused on form regions. For example, if you were to create a custom meeting request form but wanted to provide the functionality of the Scheduling page, you could use the Outlook Page Control and a separate form region to display this page with your custom form region. Figure 14-9 shows an example of using this control to provide the scheduling grid on a custom Appointment form.

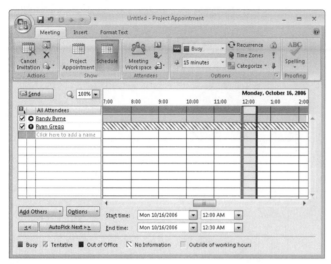

Figure 14-9 An example of the Outlook Page Control used on a custom Appointment form.

The Outlook Page Control can be set to display two different form pages: the Scheduling page and the Tracking page. Both of these pages are used on the Appointment form and can only be used on Appointment items. You can use the *Page* property of the control to set which page is displayed.

The Outlook Page Control is designed to take over the whole form region on which it is placed. It should be designed so that it spans the entire width and height of the form region and is set to grow automatically with the form in both height and width. The Outlook Page Control also automatically provides an InfoBar if one is required on the page selected.

The Outlook Recipient Control

The Microsoft Office Outlook Recipient Control provides an equivalent control to the addressing text box used in built-in Outlook forms. When a recipient address is entered in the control, the control provides autocompletion for previously entered names, distribution list highlighting and expansion, automatic name resolution, and presence information.

The Outlook Sender Photo Control

The Microsoft Office Outlook Sender Photo Control allows custom mail forms to duplicate the Sender Photo feature of Outlook, which displays a contact's photo in the headers of received mail messages from that contact (see Figure 14-10).

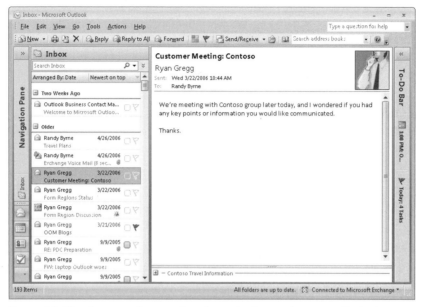

Figure 14-10   A custom form region shown in the preview pane displaying a sender contact photo using the Outlook Sender Photo Control.

The Outlook Sender Photo Control does not automatically resize to fit the contact photo because the control cannot understand the best way to resize for your form layout. If you are writing a form region implemented by an add-in, you can use the *PreferredHeight* and *PreferredWidth* properties of the control to determine the preferred size of the control and adjust the layout of the control accordingly. If you are using the automatic layout for form regions, after your program adjusts the size of the control, other controls should be moved to accommodate the resized photo control. If *PreferredHeight* or *PreferredWidth* are equal to 0, the contact photo could not be found or does not exist, and the control should not be displayed.

This control automatically data binds to a contact that represents the From address on the mail item. This behavior cannot be altered when using this control.

The Outlook Time Zone Control

Outlook 2007 includes the new ability to control the time zone for the start and end time of appointments and meetings through new time zone selector controls that are displayed when the Time Zones button on the Ribbon is selected. The Microsoft Office Outlook Time Zone Control enables a form region to use a similar control to provide a way to set the time zone (see Figure 14-11) for times without implementing the behavior in the form logic.

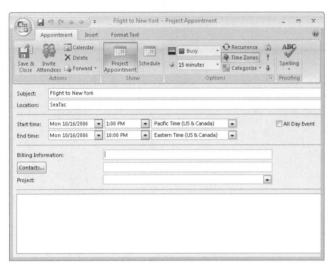

Figure 14-11   Custom Appointment form uses the Outlook Time Zone Control to enable setting the start and end time zones for the appointment.

The Outlook Time Zone Control does not support the standard Outlook data binding model but can be used in conjunction with the built-in *Start* and *End* properties of an appointment item by setting a property on the item. Setting the control's *AppointmentTimeField* property to either *olAppointmentTimeFieldStart* or *olAppointmentTimeFieldEnd* will bind the control to the time zone used for the *Start* or *End* field's date and time. You can also use the *olAppointmentTimeFieldNone* value and then the *SelectedTimeZoneIndex* property to return the selected *TimeZone* object from the *Appointment.TimeZones* collection. You can then use the *TimeZones.ConvertTime* method to convert the displayed time to the appropriate local or Coordinated Universal Time to set on a custom field.

The Outlook Time Control

Outlook makes use of a custom time control on built-in forms in Outlook like the Appointment form. This custom time picker control has a lot of built-in parsing logic that can be difficult to replicate. For example, if the user types **three thirty** or **midnight**, the control parses the language and sets the appropriate time. Previously, this type of behavior was difficult or impossible to replicate on a custom form.

For Outlook 2007, the Microsoft Office Outlook Time Control is available as a custom control that can be used on any form region. The Outlook Time Control can be bound using Outlook data binding to built-in date/time fields or to a user-defined date/time field using the Value tab of the Properties dialog box for the control. Figure 14-6 shows an example of this control in use on a form region along with the date control.

The Outlook Time Control can also work in conjunction with an Outlook Date Control to set both the date and time for a particular field. Just bind both controls to the same field, and each control will adjust the correct part of the value (date or time).

The Outlook View Control

The Microsoft Office Outlook View Control can be used to display items from a folder on a form. The control has properties that allow you to select which folder is displayed in the control and which view is applied to the items in the folder. You can also set a filter for the view. This control can be used to re-create functionality similar to the Activities page of the Contact form.

The Outlook View Control can be used on folder home pages and in custom forms with form pages and custom forms with form regions.

Using Form Region Controls

By default, the new Outlook form region controls are not displayed in the Control Toolbox or used when you drag a field from the Field Chooser. To use these controls, you need to add them to the Control Toolbox or add them programmatically to a form region. Unless your scenario requires controls to be dynamically added to the form, you should always add these controls at design time using the Control Toolbox.

Adding Controls to the Control Toolbox

To access the new Outlook form region controls using the Control Toolbox, follow these steps:

1. When you have a custom form or form region open in Design mode, on the Ribbon's Developer tab, in the Tools group, click the Control Toolbox button.

2. Right-click any of the icons for existing controls, and select Custom Controls from the context menu.

3. Scroll down the list of custom controls to find controls that begin with "Microsoft Office Outlook," select the check box next to each of the controls, and then click OK.

After you have added the Outlook controls, your Control Toolbox should look like Figure 14-12. These controls can now be added to the form region you are designing.

Figure 14-12 The form designer Control Toolbox with the Microsoft Forms 2.0 controls and Outlook controls selected.

Automatic Control Replacement

For compatibility reasons, Outlook does not include the new form region controls in the toolbox by default. However, if you use one of the old Microsoft Forms 2.0 controls on a form region, the Outlook Forms Designer automatically substitutes the equivalent Outlook control when it is placed on the form.

For example, if you drag and drop the default Text Box control from the Control Toolbox to a form region, the control actually added to the form is the new Outlook Text Box Control. This allows form regions to use the new themed controls by default, even if you do not add the new controls to the Control Toolbox.

Adding Controls Programmatically

Each of the controls can also be programmatically added to the form region during run time.

> **Note** Controls should be added to a form region during the *BeforeFormRegionShow* event if they are going to use the automatic layout engine provided by Outlook. Controls added after this event has completed will not be included in the layout.

To add controls to your form region at run time, you could use code similar to the following code sample, which adds a new Text Box control named *textbox1* to the form and then repositions it on the form:

```
public void BeforeFormRegionShow(Outlook.FormRegion FormRegion)
{
    if (FormRegion.InternalName == "MyFormRegion")
    {
        Forms.UserForm form = FormRegion.Form as Forms.UserForm;
        Outlook.OlkTextBox textbox1 =
            (Outlook.OlkTextBox)form.Controls.Add(
            "Outlook.OlkTextBox", "TextBox1", true);
        Forms.Control ctrl_textbox1 = (Forms.Control)textbox1;
        ctrl_textbox1.Move(150, 150, 100, 20, Type.Missing);
```

```
        textbox1.Text = "This is the default";
        Outlook.OlkControl layout_textbox1 = (Outlook.OlkControl)textbox1;
        layout_textbox1.EnableAutoLayout = true;
        layout_textbox1.HorizontalLayout =
            Outlook.OlHorizontalLayout.olHorizontalLayoutGrow;
        layout_textbox1.VerticalLayout =
            Outlook.OlVerticalLayout.olVerticalLayoutAlignTop;
    }
}
```

If you have a solution that uses some controls that are prepositioned on the form region at design time and other controls that will be dynamically added to the form at run time, you should use a Frame control to contain the area where controls will be added at run time. This type of scenario occurs most often when your solution enables some level of customization of the available fields for your item types. Following this practice ensures that the automatic layout preserves space for the controls and that your controls will position properly without affecting the layout of the rest of the form.

To access all available properties for a given control on a form region, you might need to cast the control to three different interfaces: the *Olk** interface matching the *ProgID* of the control you have created, the *MSForms.Control* interface to access common properties among all controls (like *Top*, *Left*, *Width*, *Height*, and *Move*), and the *Outlook.OlkControl* interface that provides Outlook-specific common properties, like layout details and data binding information. More details on these specific interfaces are provided in the following section, "Programmatic Access to Controls."

Table 14-1 lists the *ProgID* values for all the Outlook form region controls and on which item types these controls are supported. Adding a control to an unsupported item type can result in unexpected behavior of the control.

Table 14-1   Control Names and Program IDs for Outlook Controls

Control name	Program ID (*ProgID*)	Supported items
Business Card Preview Control	Outlook.OlkBusinessCard	Contact
Category Control	Outlook.OlkCategory	All items
Check Box Control	Outlook.OlkCheckBox	All items
Combo Box Control	Outlook.OlkComboBox	All items
Command Button Control	Outlook.OlkCommandButton	All items
Contact Photo Control	Outlook.OlkContactPhoto	Contact
Date Control	Outlook.OlkDateControl	All items
Frame Header Control	Outlook.OlkFrameHeader	All items
InfoBar Control	Outlook.OlkInfoBar	All items
Label Control	Outlook.OlkLabel	All items
List Box Control	Outlook.OlkListBox	All items
Option Button Control	Outlook.OlkOptionButton	All items
Page Control	Outlook.OlkPage	Appointment

Table 14-1   Control Names and Program IDs for Outlook Controls

Control name	Program ID (*ProgID*)	Supported items
Sender Photo Control	Outlook.OlkSenderPhoto	Mail
Text Box Control	Outlook.OlkTextBox	All items
Time Zone Control	Outlook.OlkTimeZone	All items
Time Control	Outlook.OlkTimeControl	All items

Programmatic Access to Controls

To access the controls from an add-in running a form region, you need to access the *Controls* collection on the *UserForm* object returned from the *FormRegion.Form* property. *UserForm* is included in the Microsoft Forms 2.0 type library, which you will need to add to your add-in project when working with form regions.

The *Controls* collection provides an enumeration and also direct access to the controls using either the control ID or the index of the control on the form. For instance, to obtain a reference to a control named *Label1*, you might write the following code in your form region initialization method:

```
Forms.UserForm form = FormRegion.Form as Forms.UserForm;
Outlook.OlkLabel label1 =
    (Outlook.OlkLabel)form.Controls.Item("label1");
```

All controls on the form are required to have a unique ID value, which you can use as the parameter to the *Item* method on the *Controls* collection. If the control you are attempting to access does not exist, an exception will be raised.

Using the Control Interface

All the Outlook controls (controls that begin with *Olk* in their class names) indirectly implement the *MSForms.Control* interface. However, because the Outlook type library does not have a dependency on the Forms 2.0 type library, this interface is not visible using the Primary Interop Assemblies or looking at the type library. To access members on this interface, you need to explicitly cast the control to the *Control* interface or use reflection to query the type for these members and invoke them.

The *Control* interface implements a number of common properties and methods that will be necessary to set or use when working with controls. For instance, *Control* includes properties for *Top*, *Left*, *Width*, *Height*, *TabIndex*, *TabStop*, *Visible*, and *ControlTipText* and methods like *Move*, *SetFocus*, and *ZOrder*. For example, to set the width of the label from the previous example, you would need to write code that looks like this:

```
Forms.UserForm form = FormRegion.Form as Forms.UserForm;
Outlook.OlkLabel label1 =
```

```
    (Outlook.OlkLabel)form.Controls.Item("label1");
((Forms.Control)label1).Width = 160;
```

If you will be performing multiple operations on the *Control* interface, it is more efficient to store the object casted to the *Forms.Control* interface in another member variable. Just make sure to release the reference as soon as you are finished using it.

Using the *OlkControl* Interface

All controls hosted on a form region surface are provided with an implementation of the *Outlook.OlkControl* interface. Members in this interface are actually implemented by Outlook and are transparently applied to any ActiveX control hosted on a form region so that callers using the *Controls* collection can cast each object to this interface without error. The *OlkControl* interface includes properties for configuring data binding information and layout details for a control on a form region.

If you are adding a control at run time during *BeforeFormRegionShow* and you want to have the control grow horizontally with the form, you could write the following code in your form region initialization code:

```
Forms.UserForm form = FormRegion.Form as Forms.UserForm;
Outlook.OlkTextBox textbox1 = (Outlook.OlkTextBox)form.Controls.Add(
    "Outlook.OlkTextBox", "TextBox1", true);
((Outlook.OlkControl)textbox1).HorizontalLayout =
    Outlook.OlHorizontalLayout.olHorizontalLayoutGrow;
```

This code would set the control to automatically resize as the form grows and collapses horizontally.

You can also use the *OlkControl* interface to configure data binding for Outlook controls. In particular, if the control supports Outlook data binding, you can use *ControlProperty*, *ItemProperty*, *Format*, and *PossibleValues* to determine how data binding functions. For more information about these properties, refer to the Outlook Developer's Reference.

Hooking Up Control Events

Events for controls are wired up in a way similar to that of other events in the Outlook object model. If you need to listen to an event from a control on a form region, you should hook up the event handler in the *BeforeFormRegionShow* method of *FormRegionStartup*. For each control where you will listen for events, make sure you hold onto a reference to the control such that it will not go out of scope until the form is closed; otherwise, the event handler might not be called. For an example of how to hook up events for controls on a form region, see the Travel Agency sample provided on this book's companion Web site.

Summary

Previously, Outlook custom forms were restricted in a number of ways from appearing to be part of the Outlook application. One of the largest problems in re-creating built-in forms was a lack of controls that implemented similar functionality to the controls that appear on the built-in forms. Outlook 2007 has added a number of controls that replicate the behavior of the built-in Outlook controls, providing rich user interface elements that form designers and developers can take advantage of to match the behavior of built-in forms from Outlook.

Chapter 15
Extending the Ribbon

The Microsoft Office Fluent user interface is the term used to describe the new user interface (UI) for the 2007 Microsoft Office system. The Ribbon is a component of the Microsoft Office Fluent user interface and the term used throughout this chapter to refer to the Ribbon component. The Ribbon is unquestionably the premiere UI feature in the 2007 Microsoft Office system. Microsoft Office Outlook 2007 uses the Ribbon in Inspector windows. This chapter covers how you can customize the Ribbon for your Outlook solution. If your solution customizes one or more Inspector windows using form regions, you might need to customize the Ribbon as well. In this chapter, you learn how Ribbon extensibility works within the context of Outlook. The chapter covers the following topics:

- Introduction to Ribbon extensibility in Outlook 2007
- What happens with existing code that customizes Inspector command bars
- Installing and running the Outlook RibbonX sample add-in
- Understanding how to write RibbonX code in an Outlook add-in

Introducing Ribbon Extensibility

This chapter focuses on how you can customize the Ribbon in Outlook 2007. The Ribbon UI (hereafter known as the Ribbon) provides a new and enhanced UI model for the 2007 Microsoft Office system. In comparison to other Office applications such as Microsoft Office Word, Excel, and PowerPoint that rely exclusively on the Ribbon, Outlook 2007 uses both the Ribbon and menus and toolbars.

In the main application window, Outlook displays the menu and toolbar UI that is familiar to users of previous versions of Office. Programmatically, these elements are contained in the *CommandBars* collection. In Inspector windows such as a mail message, where authoring is the central user experience, Outlook uses the new Ribbon. To provide the best authoring experience for end users, an Outlook Inspector window displays a Ribbon that is optimized for a particular item type. From an object model perspective, an Outlook item window is an *Inspector* object. If you have existing code that uses *Inspector.CommandBars* to customize command bars for built-in or custom items, you will learn what happens to your existing customizations of command bars for an Outlook Inspector.

The main application window, represented by the *Explorer* object, still uses command bars introduced in earlier versions of Office. For an Outlook Explorer window, developers will continue to use *Explorer.CommandBars* to customize the Outlook application window. This chapter makes the assumption that you know how to write code for the Office command bars object model and does not focus on the *CommandBars* object and related objects. If you don't know how to write code for Office command bars, there are numerous resources on the Web that provide assistance.

The Ribbon has its own extensibility model known as RibbonX. This chapter discusses RibbonX, but the main focus is on elements of Ribbon extensibility that pertain exclusively to Outlook. There are extensive RibbonX blogs and technical resources on MSDN that cover all aspects of RibbonX, including the schema for RibbonX markup, writing Ribbon Extensible Markup Language (XML) for your custom Ribbon UI, supported controls for the Ribbon and callback signatures, and a detailed discussion of Ribbon extensibility issues and best practices. Rather than duplicate this material, this chapter concentrates on Outlook-specific concerns for RibbonX.

What Happens with Existing Code

If you've already written code to customize Inspector command bars in an Outlook add-in or Outlook custom forms with form pages, you need to know what that code does in Outlook 2007 (see Table 15-1). Don't be alarmed; your existing code will still work. However, your Inspector command bars code will place your command bar customizations in the Add-Ins tab on the Ribbon. This might be acceptable to you, or you might decide that the Add-Ins tab experience is less than optimal for your command UI. In this case, you should consider updating your code to use Ribbon extensibility.

Table 15-1   Entry Points for *CommandBar* Customization in Outlook 2007

Entry point	Outlook 2007 behavior
Explorer.CommandBars	Existing code continues to work because Outlook 2007 uses command bars in the Explorer window.
Inspector.CommandBars to add custom *CommandBarControls* on a built-in menu	Existing code continues to work, but customizations appear in the Menu Commands group on the Add-Ins tab. Menu customizations for all add-ins that customize built-in menus appear together in the Menu Commands group.
Inspector.CommandBars to add custom *CommandBarControls* on a built-in toolbar	Existing code continues to work, but customizations appear in the Toolbar Commands group on the Add-Ins tab. Toolbar customizations for all add-ins that customize built-in toolbars appear together in the Toolbar Commands group.
Inspector.CommandBars to add a custom toolbar	Existing code continues to work, but customizations appear in the Custom Toolbars group on the Add-Ins tab. Custom toolbars for all add-ins appear together in the Custom Toolbars group.

Table 15-1 **Entry Points for *CommandBar* Customization in Outlook 2007**

Entry point	Outlook 2007 behavior
Word.CommandBars to add custom toolbars and controls for WordMail in Outlook 2000–2003	Existing code will not work. Word macros stored in Normal.dot or Email.dot will no longer run, as WordMail in Outlook 2007 runs in the Outlook process instead of the Word process. Prior to 2007, Word macros that added custom toolbars and controls executed from Word. Existing code must be updated for Outlook 2007. If you have an extensive library of WordMail macros, consider moving that code into an Outlook add-in. Use the *Inspector.WordEditor* object to return a Word *Document* object displayed in the current *Inspector* object. Because WordMail is integrated into Outlook, all item types including Appointments, Contacts, and Tasks support Word's rich editing environment.

Inspector Command Bars

Let's take a look at an example of Inspector command bar customization in the Outlook RibbonX Sample add-in. The RibbonX Sample add-in adds a Color Widgets custom command bar to an Outlook contact item, but only if the contact has a mailing address. Figure 15-1 shows the Color Widgets custom command bar on the Add-Ins tab of the Outlook Contact Inspector. Notice that the name of the Color Widgets command bar does not appear in the Custom Toolbars group.

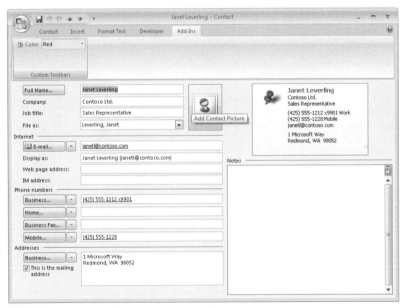

Figure 15-1   Color Widgets custom toolbar appears in the Custom Toolbars group on the Add-Ins tab.

Due to space limitations, the sample code that creates the custom Color Widgets toolbar has been omitted. In the sample Outlook RibbonX add-in, take a look at the *CreateColorWidgets* and *RemoveColorWidgets* methods in the *OutlookInspector* class. The custom Color Widgets toolbar is built using the events listed in Table 15-2.

Table 15-2   Events Used for Color Widgets Toolbar

Event	Description
Inspectors_NewInspector in *Connect* class	If the *Inspector* object is not found in *m_Windows*, creates a new instance of *OutlookInspector* and adds the instance to *m_Windows*.
ContactItem_Open in *OutlookInspector* class	Adds the custom toolbar using the *CreateColorWidgets* method. If the *ContactItem* has a nonempty *BusinessAddress*, *HomeAddress*, or *OtherAddress* property, makes the custom toolbar visible.
ContactItem_Close in *OutlookInspector* class	Removes the custom toolbar using the *RemoveColorWidgets* method.

Voting Options

Outlook 2007 continues to support voting options on messages. Voting options are used to present a list of choices to message recipients and track their responses. If you create voting options programmatically by setting a semicolon-delimited list of values for the *VotingOptions* property of a *MailItem*, those voting options will appear in the Vote menu on the Respond group of the Ribbon of a read note. A read note is the e-mail message that is received by the recipient. For example, the following code creates voting options on a compose note:

```
private void OrderPizza()
{
    Outlook.MailItem mail =
        (Outlook.MailItem)Application.CreateItem(
        Outlook.OlItemType.olMailItem);
    mail.VotingOptions = "Cheese; Mushroom; Sausage; Combo; Veg Combo";
    mail.Subject="Pizza Order";
    mail.Display(false);
}
```

When the user sends the "Pizza Order" message to team members, the voting options appear to recipients as shown in Figure 15-2. When the sender of the original message receives the responses, recipient choices are tallied on the Tracking page of the message in the sender's Sent Items folder.

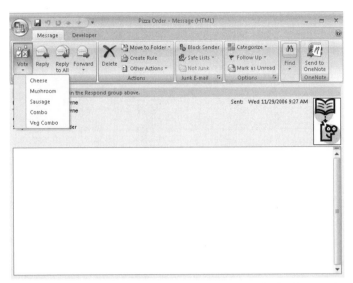

Figure 15-2   The Voting Options menu appears in the Respond group of a received message.

Custom Actions

Custom actions can also be created programmatically and appear on the Ribbon in the Actions group on the Message tab. Custom actions can be added at design time using the Outlook Forms Designer, specified in form region markup, or created programmatically by calling the *Add* method on the *Actions* collection. The following code adds a custom action named "Reply with Voice Mail" to the Inspector shown in Figure 15-3:

```
private void ReplyWithVoiceMail()
{
    Outlook.MailItem mail =
        (Outlook.MailItem)Application.ActiveInspector().CurrentItem;
    Outlook.Action action = mail.Actions.Add();
    action.Name = "Reply with Voice Mail";
    action.ReplyStyle = Outlook.OlActionReplyStyle.olUserPreference;
    action.ResponseStyle = Outlook.OlActionResponseStyle.olOpen;
    action.CopyLike = Outlook.OlActionCopyLike.olReply;
    action.MessageClass = "IPM.Post.Voice Message";
    mail.Save();
}
```

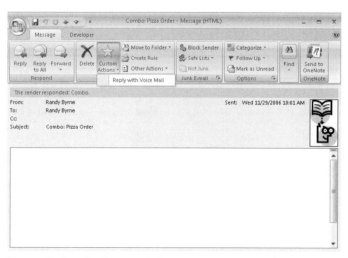

Figure 15-3   The Custom Actions menu appears in the Custom Actions group.

Outlook RibbonX Sample Add-In

The Outlook RibbonX Sample add-in is a learning tool that will help you to understand how to customize an item-level Outlook Ribbon using an add-in. The Outlook RibbonX Sample add-in provides coverage of the following important new areas:

- Provides Ribbon XML for an item based on the *RibbonID* passed in the *IRibbonExtensibility.GetCustomUI* method.

- Provides an understanding of how to use the *IRibbonControl.Context* object passed in Ribbon callbacks. *IRibbonControl.Context* represents the *Inspector* object that is about to be displayed in Outlook.

- Uses the *OutlookInspector* class to track the state of multiple Inspector windows and to track property change events on a given item displayed in its Inspector window.

- After a state change in an item, calls *IRibbonUI.InvalidateControl* to invalidate the Ribbon and cause callbacks to fire again.

The sample code included in this chapter uses C#. The code examples require any edition of Microsoft Visual Studio 2005 and Outlook 2007. The sample code for this article is available in the Outlook RibbonX Add-in, available in both a Visual Basic and C# version on the Web site that accompanies this book. The inline code snippets provided here will help you to understand how to customize the Ribbon in Outlook 2007.

Installation Instructions

1. Before you can run the Outlook RibbonX sample add-ins, you must download the sample code installation package. Once you have downloaded the sample code installation

package to your hard disk, double-click the downloaded file to begin the setup process. Follow the steps in the setup wizard to complete the installation.

2.   The sample code installation package will install *OutlookRibbonXCS*, *OutlookRibbonXVB*, *OutlookRibbonXCS_VSTO*, and *OutlookRibbonXVB_VSTO* to the following folder:

   My Documents\Visual Studio 2005\Projects

> **Note**   The name of your personal documents folder depends on the operating system installed on your computer. On Microsoft Windows Vista, your personal documents folder is named Documents. On Microsoft Windows XP, your personal documents folder is named My Documents. You should adjust path specifications for your personal documents folder according to your installed operating system.

> **Note**   If you are using Visual C# Express Edition or Visual Basic Express Edition to open the sample add-ins, you will not be able to build the setup/deployment project and install the sample add-ins.

Running the Sample Add-In

To run the sample add-in, follow these instructions:

1.   Shut down Outlook 2007.

2.   In the Visual Studio 2005\Projects\OutlookRibbonXCS folder under your Documents folder, open the OutlookRibbonXCS solution.

3.   In the Solution Explorer, select OutlookRibbonXAddinCSSetup.

4.   From the Build menu, select Build OutlookRibbonXAddinCSSetup.

5.   Once the build process has completed, from the Project menu, select Install to install the solution.

6.   Start Outlook to start the add-in in Run mode or press F5 to start the add-in in Debug mode.

7.   To launch the add-in in Debug mode, in the Solution Explorer, select OutlookRibbonX-AddinCS. From the Project menu, select OutlookRibbonXAddinCS Properties, click the Debug tab, and under Start Action, select the Start External Program check box. Click . . . and select Outlook.exe in the following folder: *[Drive:]*\Program Files\Microsoft Office \Office12.

Modifying Your Code to Use RibbonX

This section assumes that you have an existing add-in that you want to update for Outlook 2007. If you are writing an add-in that exclusively targets Outlook 2007, you should definitely use the Ribbon user experience for your solution.

Ribbon customization in Outlook 2007 uses the add-in model for Ribbon extensibility, also known as RibbonX. Outlook does not offer document-level customization of the Ribbon similar to Word, Excel, or PowerPoint. The first question you should ask yourself is whether your existing code requires modification to use RibbonX. If your existing code adds custom commands to Inspector command bars, you should consider reworking your code for RibbonX. If you do not modify your code and you modify Inspector command bars, your customizations will appear in the global groupings of the Add-Ins tab in an Inspector window.

Because these groups do not identify the source of the command, user confusion will occur. Aside from the user impact, the Ribbon offers a much wider range of controls in comparison to the Office command bars object model. You can implement button, toggle button, check box, combo box, drop-down, or gallery controls by writing Ribbon markup. I urge you to take a close look at updating your existing code to utilize the control palette of the Ribbon. If you're designing a solution that runs only on Outlook 2007, your decision is a simple one: implement the Ribbon and take advantage of the rich programming model for RibbonX.

Next you'll learn how the sample Outlook RibbonX add-in provides Ribbon customization for an Outlook contact item. Figure 15-4 illustrates the Color Widgets toolbar transformed into a Ribbon group. Unlike the behavior of command bar customizations on the Add-Ins tab, a pop-up window identifies the add-in that has added the control to the Ribbon when you hover your mouse over the control. In this case, the Color Widgets commands participate as first-class citizens of the Ribbon.

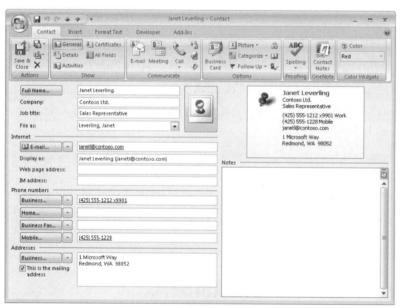

Figure 15-4   The Color Widgets group on the Contact Inspector Ribbon.

Authoring Ribbon XML

The first step in customizing the Ribbon is writing declarative XML markup that specifies the tabs, groups, and controls for your customization. For a detailed list of all of the elements, types, and groups included in the Ribbon for the 2007 Microsoft Office system, see the 2007 Office System XML Schema Reference on MSDN. In the case of the sample Outlook RibbonX add-in, the Ribbon XML is contained in a resource in the Add-in project. Because Color Widgets is a very simple example, the markup is simple as well. Here is the customUI.xml resource from the sample:

```
onLoad="Ribbon_OnLoad">`
 <ribbon>
   <tabs>
     <tab idMso="TabContact">
       <group id="ColorWidgetsGroup"
         getVisible="ColorWidgetsGroup_GetVisible"
         getLabel="ColorWidgetsGroup_GetLabel">
           <button
               id="ColorButton"
               getLabel = "ColorButton_GetLabel"
               getSupertip="ColorButton_GetSupertip"
               onAction ="ColorButton_Action"
               imageMso="ShadingColorsMoreColorsDialog"
               />
           <comboBox
               id="ColorCombo"
               onChange ="ColorCombo_OnChange"
               getText="ColorCombo_GetText"
               getItemCount ="ColorCombo_GetItemCount"
               getItemLabel ="ColorCombo_GetItemLabel"
               />
       </group>
     </tab>
   </tabs>
 </ribbon>
</customUI>
```

This Ribbon markup specifies two controls, a button and combo box, for the Color Widgets group. The Color Widgets group appears on the Contact tab, which is specified by its *idMso* attribute of *TabContact*. The markup specifies several callbacks that will run when a contact item is opened. These callbacks are used to execute an action, supply text for controls, specify an image, or control visibility of the Color Widgets group. To keep things simple in the sample code, this markup uses built-in images specified by *imageMso* rather than dynamically loading an image using the *GetImage* callback for the Color button.

Because the RibbonX resources cited previously discuss the schema for Ribbon XML, details on authoring Ribbon XML are not included here. If you need information on control IDs for built-in controls for all Outlook Ribbons, please see the downloads area on the Web site that accompanies this book or visit the Outlook 2007 Developer Portal at *http:// msdn.microsoft.com/office/program/outlook/2007/*.

The important aspect of authoring Ribbon XML for Outlook is that different item types can require a separate XML markup. If you need to customize an appointment and a contact item, for example, you should consider adding two markup documents to your add-in resources. You'll understand this point better when the discussion focuses on the loading of Ribbon markup in the *IRibbonExtensibility.GetCustomUI* procedure.

IRibbonExtensibility Interface

An Outlook add-in that customizes the Ribbon must implement this interface:

- *Office.IRibbonExtensibility*

In the Outlook RibbonX sample add-in, this interface is implemented in the *Connect* class. Once you have implemented the *IRibbonExtensibility* interface, you write code to return your Ribbon markup in the *IRibbonExtensibility.GetCustomUI* method. Before you look at the sample code for *GetCustomUI*, you must understand exactly how *GetCustomUI* is called in Outlook 2007.

- *GetCustomUI* does not get called until an Outlook Inspector is opened by a user or programmatic action.

- Selecting an item in the Reading Pane does not call *GetCustomUI*. The item must be opened in an Outlook Inspector.

- *GetCustomUI* is called only once when the Ribbon is first loaded for a given *RibbonID*.

- *RibbonID* is a unique string that identifies the type of Inspector. *RibbonID* correlates to the item's message class. However, different *RibbonID* values can be associated with the same message class.

- In some cases, such as a *MailItem* or *PostItem* object, *GetCustomUI* will be called once when the first compose note is displayed where *RibbonID* is Microsoft.Outlook.Mail.Compose and once when the first read note is displayed where *RibbonID* is Microsoft.Outlook.Mail.Read.

The unique *RibbonID* values used by Outlook are listed in Table 15-3.

Table 15-3 *RibbonID* Values Returned in the *GetCustomUI* Method

RibbonID	MessageClass
Microsoft.Outlook.Mail.Read	IPM.Note.*
Microsoft.Outlook.Mail.Compose	IPM.Note.*
Microsoft.Outlook.MeetingRequest.Read	IPM.Schedule.Meeting.Request or IPM.Schedule.Meeting.Canceled
Microsoft.Outlook.MeetingRequest.Send	IPM.Schedule.Meeting.Request
Microsoft.Outlook.Appointment	IPM.Appointment.*
Microsoft.Outlook.Contact	IPM.Contact.*
Microsoft.Outlook.Journal	IPM.Activity.*

Table 15-3   *RibbonID* Values Returned in the *GetCustomUI* Method

RibbonID	MessageClass
Microsoft.Outlook.Task	IPM.Task.* and IPM.TaskRequest.*
Microsoft.Outlook.DistributionList	IPM.DistList.*
Microsoft.Outlook.Report	IPM.Report.*
Microsoft.Outlook.Resend	IPM.Resend.*
Microsoft.Outlook.Response.Read	IPM.Schedule.Meeting.Resp.*
Microsoft.Outlook.Response.Compose	IPM.Schedule.Meeting.Resp.*
Microsoft.Outlook.Response.CounterPropose	IPM.Schedule.Meeting.Resp.*
Microsoft.Outlook.RSS	IPM.Post.Rss.*
Microsoft.Outlook.Post.Read	IPM.Post.*
Microsoft.Outlook.Post.Compose	IPM.Post.*
Microsoft.Outlook.Sharing.Read	IPM.Sharing.*
Microsoft.Outlook.Sharing.Compose	IPM.Sharing.*

Note   Sticky notes do not implement the Ribbon, so *IPM.StickyNote* is not listed in the table of RibbonIDs and message classes.

You'll notice that message class is represented as *IPM.Type.** in most cases in the table. This notation means that either the first instance of the base message class (for example, *IPM.Contact*) or a custom message class (*IPM.Contact.Foo*) that appears in an Inspector will cause *GetCustomUI* to be called. What does this mean to you if you are only interested in customizing the Ribbon on Inspectors for your custom message class?

■ You should return Ribbon XML in *GetCustomUI* for the *RibbonID* that represents the Inspector type for your custom message class such as *IPM.Contact.Shoe Store*.

■ If you are only controlling the visibility of your custom Ribbon tabs, groups, and controls on your custom message class, call the *InvalidateControl* method on the *IRibbonUI* object in the *NewInspector* event. In the *NewInspector* event, evaluate whether *Inspector.CurrentItem.MessageClass* represents your custom message class. To improve performance, only call the *InvalidateControl* method on appropriate tabs, groups, and controls for your custom message class. Calling the *InvalidateControl* method in the *NewInspector* event will cause *GetVisible* and other callbacks to be called each time an Inspector displays for your custom message class. For example, the following code in the *NewInspector* event illustrates this technique for the custom message class *IPM.Contact.Shoe Store*:

```
private void Inspectors_NewInspector(Outlook.Inspector Inspector)
{
    try
    {
        OutlookItem olItem = new OutlookItem(Inspector.CurrentItem);
        // Make sure this is an "IPM.Contact.Shoe Store" item
```

```
                    if (olItem.MessageClass == "IPM.Contact.Shoe Store")
                    {
                        m_Ribbon.InvalidateControl("ShoeSizeGroup");
                        m_Ribbon.InvalidateControl("ShoeColorGroup");
                    }
                }
                catch (Exception ex)
                {
                    Debug.WriteLine(ex.Message);
                }
            }
```

- If you are controlling the visibility of built-in Ribbon tabs, groups, and controls in addition to your custom Ribbon tabs, groups, and controls, call the *Invalidate* method on the *IRibbonUI* object in the *NewInspector* event. In the *NewInspector* event, evaluate whether *Inspector.CurrentItem.MessageClass* represents your custom message class before you call the *Invalidate* method. Calling the *Invalidate* method is expensive in terms of performance, so you should only call this method for the appropriate message class. Calling the *Invalidate* method in the *NewInspector* event will cause *GetVisible* and other callbacks to be called each time an Inspector displays for your custom message class.

- Use *GetVisible* callbacks to control the visibility of your custom Ribbon tabs, groups, and controls. The *IRibbonControl.Context* object passed in the callback represents an Outlook *Inspector* object. Once you have an *Inspector* object in the callback, use *Inspector.CurrentItem.MessageClass* to determine whether to return *true* or *false* in the *GetVisible* callback.

If you need to customize the Ribbon on all or multiple Outlook message classes, a different set of recommendations apply.

- If you want to customize the first built-in tab on all Outlook Inspectors, you will have to supply separate Ribbon XML for different *RibbonID* values because built-in first tabs do not have the same name across all *RibbonID* values.

- If you want to customize the Ribbon on multiple Outlook Inspectors, you might have to supply separate Ribbon XML for different *RibbonID* values depending on the tab name.

Let's take a look at *GetCustomUI* in the sample add-in that accompanies this chapter. You'll notice that *customUI* is stored as a resource in the Add-in project. If you need to supply Ribbon markup for more than one *RibbonID*, you should name your resources appropriately and return the correct resource in the *GetCustomUI* procedure. The following example returns the Ribbon markup for Color Widgets:

```
public string GetCustomUI(string ribbonID)
{
    switch (ribbonID)
    {
        case "Microsoft.Outlook.Contact":
            //Return the RibbonX markup stored as a resource
            string xmlMarkup = Properties.Resources.customUI;
            return xmlMarkup;
```

```
        default
           return String.Empty;
       }
   }
```

Detecting Errors

The Ribbon markup that you return in the *GetCustomUI* call will usually contain callbacks
that run when an Inspector is about to be displayed. For each callback in your Ribbon
markup, you must add the callback to the add-in class that implements *IRibbonExtensibility*.
These callbacks must be declared as public procedures. If for some reason you omit a callback
or use an incorrect callback signature, your Ribbon customization will fail silently unless you
turn on error detection when you debug your solution.

To turn on error detection when your Ribbon markup is loaded, you should follow these steps
to display the Advanced Options dialog box shown in Figure 15-5.

Figure 15-5 The Advanced Options dialog box allows reporting of Ribbon markup errors.

To display custom user interface errors, follow these steps:

1. From the Tools menu in an Outlook Explorer window, select Options, and then click the
   Other tab.

2. Click Advanced Options; then in the In All Office Applications frame, select the Show
   Add-In User Interface Errors check box.

3. Click OK to save the changes.

Note If you select the Show Add-In User Interface Errors check box, you have turned on
error reporting for all Office applications.

NewInspector Event

Once *GetCustomUI* is called and Ribbon markup is returned, your add-in should hook up the *NewInspector* event so that your code can track the state of the Inspector window. The sample add-in has a trivial example of state tracking. The Color Widget group has a combo box control where the user can select Red, Green, or Blue as a color. If the user clicks the Color button control, a message box displays the currently selected color. Although this example is very simple, it demonstrates a problem that is common to implementing Ribbon controls on Outlook Inspectors. Outlook can display multiple Inspectors, and the user can switch context between these windows. For example, let's assume that for Inspector 1 the selected color is green and for Inspector 2 the selected color is red. How can the sample code determine the selected color for a given Inspector? The solution is provided by the *NewInspector* event in combination with a wrapper class named *OutlookInspector*.

In the Visual Basic sample add-in, the *InitializeAddin* procedure instantiates the *m_Inspectors* object dimensioned using the *WithEvents* keyword. In the C# sample add-in, you hook up the *NewInspector* event on the *m_Inspectors* object. Here is the *InitializeAddin* method that is called from the *IDTExtensibility2_OnConnection* method:

```
private void InitializeAddin()
{
    // Initialize variables
    m_Inspectors =  this.Application.Inspectors;
    m_Windows = new List<OutlookInspector>();

    // Wire up event handlers
    m_Inspectors.NewInspector +=
        new Outlook.InspectorsEvents_NewInspectorEventHandler(
        Inspectors_NewInspector);
}
```

Besides hooking up the *NewInspector* event handler in *InitializeAddin*, an instance variable named *m_Windows* is created that acts as a generic *List* class for instances of the *OutlookInspector* class. A *List* class represents a strongly typed list of objects that can be accessed by index and provides methods to search, sort, and manipulate lists.

Next let's look at the *NewInspector* event procedure. Because the only relevant inspectors are for contact items, the code first evaluates if *Inspector.CurrentItem.Class* equals *olContact*. If the *Inspector* object represents a contact item, the *FindOutlookInspector* method attempts to find a given Inspector window in the *m_Windows* List. If the *existingWindow* value is *null*, a new instance of *OutlookInspector* is created for the *Inspector* object and that class instance is added to *m_Windows*.

```
private void Inspectors_NewInspector(Outlook.Inspector Inspector)
{
    try
    {
        OutlookItem olItem = new OutlookItem(Inspector.CurrentItem);
```

```
    // Make sure this is a contact item
    if (olItem.Class == Outlook.OlObjectClass.olContact)
    {
        // Check to see if this is a new window
        // we don't already track
        OutlookInspector existingWindow =
            FindOutlookInspector(Inspector);
        // If the m_Windows collection does not
        // have a window for this Inspector,
        // we should add it to m_Windows
        if (existingWindow == null)
        {
            OutlookInspector window = new OutlookInspector(Inspector);
            window.Close += new EventHandler(WrappedWindow_Close);
            window.InvalidateControl += new EventHandler<
                OutlookInspector.InvalidateEventArgs>(
                WrappedWindow_InvalidateControl);
            m_Windows.Add(window);
        }
    }
}
catch (Exception ex)
{
    Debug.WriteLine(ex.Message);
}
}
```

OutlookInspector Class

The *OutlookInspector* class wraps an *Inspector* object. Each instance of this class allows you to track the state of a given Inspector window. The following functions are provided by the *OutlookInspector* class:

■ Wraps each instance of an *Inspector* object

■ Provides *Open*, *Close*, and *PropertyChange* events for the wrapped Inspector's *CurrentItem*, which in this case is a *ContactItem*

■ Exposes *Properties* so that callbacks in the *Connect* class can set or get properties such as *RibbonColor*

Let's look at a bit more of the business logic of the sample Outlook RibbonX add-in. The visibility of the Color Widgets group is dependent on the existence of a mailing address in the *ContactItem* item represented by the *Inspector* object. If a given contact has a business, home, or other address, the Color Widgets group will appear on the Ribbon. If the contact has no business, home, or other address, the Color Widgets group will not appear on the Ribbon. If the state of the contact changes (for example, the user adds a business address to a new contact), the *PropertyChange* event will detect that change and cause controls on the Ribbon to be invalidated. Once the Ribbon control is invalidated, the callbacks for that control will be called again.

IRibbonUI Object

The *IRibbonUI* object represents all the Ribbon controls that are defined by your add-in. You specify a callback in your Ribbon markup (see *Ribbon_OnLoad* in *CustomUI* earlier). This callback provides an *IRibbonUI* object that you can use to invalidate all controls defined by your add-in or a single control specified by name. *IRibbonUI* is scoped to your add-in. The methods of *IRibbonUI* are shown in Table 15-4. If you call the methods of *IRibbonUI*, they only apply to your add-in rather than all connected add-ins in Outlook. Here is the *Ribbon_OnLoad* callback in the sample add-in:

```
public void Ribbon_OnLoad(Office.IRibbonUI ribbon)
{
    m_Ribbon = ribbon;
}
```

Table 15-4 *IRibbonUI* Methods

Method	Action	Description
Invalidate()	callback	Marks all of the custom controls in your add-in for update
InvalidateControl(string controlID)	callback	Marks a specific control defined by *controlID* in your add-in for update

For performance reasons, a best practice when using the *IRibbonUI* object is to call *InvalidateControl* rather than *Invalidate*. If you call *Invalidate*, all Ribbon controls defined by your add-in are invalidated and callbacks will occur on open Inspectors. Note that the instance variable that represents *IRibbonUI* is *m_Ribbon*. This instance variable is defined in the *Connect* class. To call *m_Ribbon.InvalidateControl* from the *OutlookInspector* class when the *PropertyChange* event detects that the Color Widgets group requires invalidation due to an address change, the *RaiseInvalidateControl* method is called in the *OutlookInspector* class. This method fires the *InvalidateControl* event in the *OutlookInspector* class, which is handled by the *WrappedWindow_InvalidateControl* event procedure in the *Connect* class.

```
private void RaiseInvalidateControl(string controlID)
{
    if (InvalidateControl != null)
        InvalidateControl(this, new InvalidateEventArgs(controlID));
}
```

IRibbonControl Object

The *IRibbonControl* object is passed in most of the callbacks available for Ribbon controls. This object is especially useful for Outlook developers because it provides a *Context* object that represents the Outlook Inspector that is about to be displayed. Table 15-5 lists the properties of the *IRibbonControl* object.

Table 15-5   *IRibbonControl* Properties

Property	Type	Description
Context	Object	Read-only. Returns an object that represents the window where the Ribbon is about to be displayed.
Id	String	Read-only. Returns a string that represents the ID attribute for the control.
Tag	String	Read-only. Returns a string that represents the tag attribute for the control.

To understand how to use the *Context* object and cast it to an Outlook *Inspector* object, code examples are in order. First let's look at the *ColorWidgetsGroup_GetVisible* callback in the *Connect* class. This callback fires whenever a Contact Inspector window is created or an existing Inspector window is activated. *Control.Context* is passed to the *FindOutlookWindow* procedure and ensures that the code examines the state of the correct *ContactItem*. Using our simple business logic, the callback returns *true* if the item has an address or *false* if the item does not have an address. Returning *true* makes the *ColorWidgetsGroup* control visible, and returning *False* hides the control.

```
public bool ColorWidgetsGroup_GetVisible(Office.IRibbonControl control)
{
    Debug.WriteLine("ColorWidgetsGroup_GetVisible");
    OutlookInspector window = FindOutlookInspector(control.Context);
    if (window != null)
    {
        Outlook.ContactItem contact = window.CurrentItem;
        //Make the group visible only if an address exists
        if (String.IsNullOrEmpty(contact.BusinessAddress) &
                String.IsNullOrEmpty(contact.HomeAddress) &
                String.IsNullOrEmpty(contact.OtherAddress))
        {
            return false;
        }
        else
        {
            return true;
        }
    }
    return false;
}
```

When the Color button is clicked in the Color Widgets group, the *ColorButton_Action* callback defined for the *ColorButton* control is called. It's also helpful to take a look at how the *IRibbonControl.Context* object is used in this callback. In this callback, the *FindOutlookWindow* procedure returns the *Inspector* object where the color button has been clicked. In the *ColorButton_Action* method, *window.RibbonColor* returns the currently selected color for that Inspector window and the currently selected color is displayed in a message box. How does the *RibbonColor* property of the *OutlookInspector* class know the correct selected color in

Color Widgets? When the *ColorCombo_OnChange* callback is called, *window.RibbonColor* is set for a specific instance of the *OutlookInspector* class. *ColorButton_Action* and *ColorCombo_OnChange* are in the following listing:

```
public void ColorButton_Action(Office.IRibbonControl control)
{
    try
    {
        Debug.WriteLine("ColorButton_Action");
        OutlookInspector window = FindOutlookInspector(control.Context);
        if (window != null)
        {
            MessageBox.Show(Properties.Resources.AlertMessage +
                window.RibbonColor,
                Properties.Resources.Ribbon_ColorWidgetsGroup,
                MessageBoxButtons.OK, MessageBoxIcon.Information);
        }
    }
    catch (Exception ex)
    {
        Debug.WriteLine(ex.Message);
    }
}

public void ColorCombo_OnChange(Office.IRibbonControl control, string text)
{
    try
    {
        Debug.WriteLine("ColorCombo_OnChange");
        OutlookInspector window = FindOutlookInspector(control.Context);
        if (window != null)
        {
            window.RibbonColor = text;
        }
    }
    catch (Exception ex)
    {
        Debug.WriteLine(ex.Message);
    }
}
```

Summary

The Ribbon offers a compelling new UI for Outlook 2007 Inspector windows. If your existing Outlook solution uses command bar customizations in an Inspector, you should consider modifying your code to support the enhanced controls of the Ribbon. RibbonX in Outlook differs somewhat from other Office applications that extend the Ribbon by using an add-in. Using the techniques demonstrated in the sample Outlook RibbonX add-in, you can implement the Ribbon so that state changes in an Outlook item are reflected in Ribbon controls.

Chapter 16
Completing Your User Interface

In this chapter, you learn about the final pieces of Outlook's user interface customization story. Microsoft Office Outlook 2007 provides two more user interface customization pieces: custom task panes and custom property pages. Custom task panes can be added to both Inspector and Explorer windows, providing a canvas for additional related information. Custom property pages allow you to extend the Tools Options or Folder Properties dialog boxes with a custom property page. Typically, a custom property page exposes application- or folder-level settings for your solution.

In this chapter, you learn how to create a custom task pane and display the task pane in an Outlook window. You also learn how to design and display a custom property page with theme support.

Custom Task Panes

Microsoft Office 2003 introduced the concept of Document Action task panes in Microsoft Word and Excel. A task pane is a dockable window that provides additional contextual assistance to users. For Microsoft Office 2007, the task panes model was extended to create application-level task panes, and the supported applications were broadened to include Outlook 2007.

Outlook's custom task pane support provides an opportunity to add contextual information to Inspector or Explorer windows in Outlook. Task panes can be docked to any edge of the window or can be displayed floating above the parent window. Multiple task panes are displayed simultaneously at up to half the width of the window in which they are docked. For an example, see Figure 16-1.

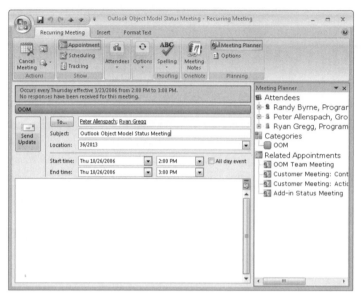

Figure 16-1   The Prepare Me add-in task pane on an Outlook appointment item.

When to Use a Custom Task Pane

Custom task panes and form regions can be used in similar ways to add additional information to be displayed to the user while working in Outlook. Before deciding on an implementation approach, it is important to consider the guidelines for using custom task panes and form regions.

Form regions are best for displaying additional information that is specific to an item when that information lives in the Outlook data store. For example, if you add custom properties to a Contact to maintain details about shoe size or hair color, the recommended way to display this to the user is through a form region on the Contact.

Custom task panes are best for displaying additional information that is specific to an item that lives outside the Outlook data store. For example, you might display a custom task pane that has information retrieved from a research Web service about the currently open Contact. Custom task panes can also be used in scenarios where information about multiple items will be displayed to the user. For instance, the To-Do Bar in Outlook 2007 is a good example of task pane style functionality provided in Outlook. The included Prepare Me sample add-in is also a good example of how information from multiple items in Outlook can be displayed in a custom task pane.

Implementing a Custom Task Pane

Implementing a custom task pane solution is a two-step process. The first step is to build the functionality that will be contained in the task pane as a Windows Forms *UserControl*. The second step involves hooking up the control as a task pane and attaching it to an Outlook window. Both of these steps will be covered using the Prepare Me example add-in available on this book's companion Web site. This sample shows information related to an open appointment or meeting such as previous e-mail messages from the attendees of the meeting, related appointments from a user's calendar, and an ability to access other data categorized with the same categories as the appointment.

To build this task pane solution, you should create two projects inside a single Microsoft Visual Studio solution. The first project will be used to implement the task pane control, and the second project will be an Outlook add-in that will hook up the control as a task pane and manage state.

Building a User Control Task Pane Implementation

The first step in building a task pane solution is to create the *UserControl* object that will be hosted inside the custom task pane. This class should implement all of the logic necessary to drive the task pane and should expect input from the Outlook add-in in the form of an Outlook item or *Inspector* instance if the task pane is added to the Inspector window or an *Explorer* instance if the task pane is added to an Explorer window. Because your add-in is ultimately responsible for providing the input, you could choose to use any object as input for your task pane, but using the window object or item is, in general, the best practice.

To begin, create a new Class Library project in Visual Studio, and add a new User Control class named *TaskPaneControl* to the project. This User Control class will provide the implementation and user interface for the custom task pane. In the Prepare Me sample, the *UserControl* hosts a single *TreeView* control, which will be used to display a hierarchy of information related to the selected meeting. You can, however, use any Microsoft .NET Framework control that can be hosted on *UserControl* and expect it to work.

Because the custom task pane will be created by Outlook and then handed back to your add-in, you need to ensure the *UserControl* object only has a parameterless constructor. Otherwise, when Outlook attempts to create the Component Object Model (COM) object representing the *UserControl*, it will fail. If you want to pass objects or parameters into the custom task pane, you can create your own initialize method on the *UserControl* object that your add-in will call before displaying the task pane. For example, the Prepare Me add-in has the following method, which is used to initialize the task pane and provide it with a reference to the meeting with which it is displayed:

```
public void LoadAppointment(Outlook.AppointmentItem appointment)
{
    if (appointment == null)
        throw new ArgumentNullException("appointment");

    m_Appointment = appointment;
    m_Application = appointment.Application;
```

```
m_Appointment.PropertyChange +=
    new Outlook.ItemEvents_10_PropertyChangeEventHandler(
    m_Appointment_PropertyChange);

LoadRecipients();
LoadCategories();
LoadMeetings();
}
```

The *LoadAppointment* method is then called by the add-in before it sets the task pane to be visible and passes in a reference to the *AppointmentItem* that is displayed in the Inspector window. The task pane control then uses this appointment item to listen for property changes and to load information on the recipients, categories, and related meetings. The remainder of the source code for the Prepare Me sample task pane control is not discussed here, as it is primarily accessing data from the item and using search and other object model members to retrieve and display that data.

Providing a Program ID

To make the *UserControl* object you just created available to be consumed in a custom task pane, you need to make it COM visible and provide a Program ID and globally unique identifier (GUID) for the class. Without these attributes, Outlook will be unable to create the task pane.

Inside the source code file for the *UserControl* object you've created as a task pane, you need to include three attributes on the class definition. These attributes are *GuidAttribute*, *ProgIdAttribute*, and *ComVisibleAttribute*, which are part of the *System.Runtime.InteropServices* namespace. First, you should include this namespace in your code by adding a *using* statement to the top of the file.

```
using System.Runtime.InteropServices;
Next, define these attributes on the class:
[
Guid("DCC2C95E-4F16-42e7-A7CF-B76983144E14"),
ProgId("PrepareMeControlCS.TaskPaneControl"),
ComVisible(true)
]
public partial class TaskPaneControl : UserControl
{
    // Other code would be contained here
}
```

You should ensure that the value in *GuidAttribute* is a unique GUID. You can use the Immediate window in Visual Studio to programmatically generate a new GUID:

1. Press Ctrl+Alt+I to display the Immediate window.

2. Type **System.Guid.NewGuid()**, and then press Enter. A new GUID value will be printed to the window. This value can be copied into *GuidAttribute*.

Note   If you are using Visual Basic, run guidgen.exe in a Visual Studio 2005 command prompt window to generate a new Guid. Search for "Create Guid" in the Visual Basic documentation.

The value of *ProgIdAttribute* should be a unique program ID for this control. You should use the format *<ProjectName>.<ClassName>* to configure the *ProgID*.

Adding *ComVisibleAttribute* with a value of *true* makes this class visible as a COM object. This is necessary for it to be used as a custom task pane. Running RegAsm.exe on the compiled assembly adds the necessary information to the registry to make this component available to COM clients.

Adding a Custom Task Pane in an Add-In

Now that you have implemented the custom task pane control, you need to have an add-in that will tell Outlook about the custom task pane and display it. To accomplish this, you just need to create a standard Outlook add-in, implement an additional interface for consuming custom task panes, and hook up your custom task pane when the time is right.

To get started, create a new Outlook add-in project using the Outlook add-in template provided online, and add it to the existing solution. You should now have both the task pane control and the Outlook add-in project in the same solution.

Implementing Interfaces

To hook up a task pane to an Outlook window, you'll need to implement the *ICustomTaskPaneConsumer* interface on your add-in. This interface has one method, *CTPFactoryAvailable*, which will be called to provide a factory object for creating new custom task panes.

Implementing this interface on your add-in is simple. Open the *Connect* class of the add-in project, and find the class definition. Extend the class to support the interface by editing the class definition to look like this:

```
public partial class Connect : Office.ICustomTaskPaneConsumer
{
    // Other code should already be here
}
```

Next, you need to add the function defined by this interface to this class. Add the instance variable and the *CTPFactoryAvailable* definition from the following code to your class. This method will be called by Outlook sometime after the add-in is connected when a custom task pane factory is available for your add-in to use.

```
private Office.ICTPFactory m_CtpFactory;

public void CTPFactoryAvailable(Microsoft.Office.Core.ICTPFactory CTPFactoryInst)
{
    m_CtpFactory = CTPFactoryInst;
}
```

Once the custom task pane factory is available, your add-in can use it to create new custom task panes on the Inspector or Explorer windows in Outlook.

Adding a Custom Task Pane to a Window

Once you have an instance of the custom task pane factory, adding a new custom task pane to an Outlook window is as simple as calling a method on the factory object. However, depending on your solution, you might need to keep track of which windows have task panes added and be able to show or hide those task panes based on property changes, clicking a button on the Ribbon, or other user actions.

To add a custom task pane to a window, you can use the following code. Replace the parameters on the *CreateCTP* method with the *ProgID*, title, and window object on which you want to display the task pane.

```
Office.CustomTaskPane taskPane;
try
{
    taskPane = m_CtpFactory.CreateCTP("TaskPaneProject.TaskPaneClass",
        "My Task Pane", window);
}
catch (COMException ex)
{
    taskPane = null;
}

if (taskPane != null)
{
    taskPane.DockPositionRestrict = Microsoft.Office.Core
        .MsoCTPDockPositionRestrict.msoCTPDockPositionRestrictNoHorizontal;
    taskPane.DockPosition = Microsoft.Office.Core
        .MsoCTPDockPosition.msoCTPDockPositionRight;
    taskPane.Visible = m_ShowTaskPane;
}
```

Using the properties on the *CustomTaskPane* object, you can adjust how the task pane behaves. The properties *DockPosition* and *DockPositionRestrict* can be used to determine where the custom task pane is docked and where it can and cannot be docked by the user. Use the *Visible* property control if the task pane is visible to the user.

In most scenarios, you will need to do something more than just let the *CustomTaskPane* object created by the factory go out of scope. If you need to hide or show the task pane based on changes in the item or the result of user action, you will need to hold onto the *CustomTaskPane* object in a collection of some sort so that you can set the *Visible* property. You can also listen for events on the object to determine if the user has changed where the task pane is docked or if you want to remember the last position of the task pane so that it can be shown in the same place next time. The Prepare Me add-in shows an example of how to use a Ribbon button to show or hide a custom task pane on an Inspector window.

Important You should use caution when adding task panes to Inspector windows in Outlook. Sometimes Outlook recycles a window (in particular, MailItem windows), and any custom task panes that were previously attached to that window will still be attached and potentially displayed to the user. To ensure that a custom task pane is never duplicated, you should call *CustomTaskPane.Delete()* when the *Close* event fires on the attached window.

Windows Theme Support in Custom Task Panes

Custom task panes, like other user interface elements provided by an add-in, are themed according to the theme setup of the add-in that provides the user interface. By default, Outlook does not display add-in user interface elements using the current Windows theme and will instead use the default nonthemed controls (see Figure 16-2).

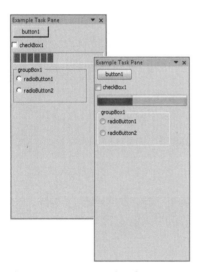

Figure 16-2 Example of a custom task pane with and without Windows theme support enabled.

To enable support for Windows themes for controls on a task pane, you need to enable visual styles in the add-in initialization logic before any custom task pane or other form controls are created. The best place to do this is at the top of the *InitializeAddin()* method in the provided templates. To enable visual styles, you need to execute the *EnableVisualStyles* method on the *Application* object in the *System.Windows.Forms* namespace. For example:

```
private void InitializeAddin()
{
    System.Windows.Forms.Application.EnableVisualStyles();
    // other initialize logic here
}
```

You will need to make sure a reference to the *System.Windows.Forms* namespace is added to the project. To add a reference to this namespace, follow these steps:

1. Select the project in the Solution Explorer pane of Visual Studio.

2. From the Project menu, select Add Reference.

3. Scroll down the list of .NET assemblies, select System.Windows.Forms, and then click OK.

Custom Property Pages

Another method for extending the Outlook user interface is by adding a custom property page to the Folder Properties or Tools Options dialog boxes. Figure 16-3 shows a sample custom property page for the Tools Options dialog box. This section walks you through creating this sample property page, and you learn how to use a custom property page to persist user settings for your add-in.

Figure 16-3   A sample property page in the Tools Options dialog box.

When deciding whether a custom property page is the right choice for your solution, you should consider the scope and discoverability of the Options dialog box. For custom property pages that are displayed in the Tools Options dialog box, the settings should be scoped to the whole add-in solution. If your property page will display in the Folder Properties dialog box, you should make sure those settings are scoped to the selected folder. You should also decide if using the screen space in the Tools Options or Folder Properties dialog box is the most appropriate way to display your settings, as these locations are often filled with many other property pages and commands that display additional dialog boxes. If your settings are too complex for a single property page, consider displaying your custom dialog box from your custom property page. Be aware that both the Folder Properties and Tool Options dialog boxes are application modal.

Designing a Custom Property Page

To get started building a custom property page, you need to start with an Outlook add-in project. In this project, you create a new *UserControl* object that will contain the design of the custom property page. To fully support the Windows theme in the dialog box, we need to add a few more classes to provide the themed appearance for a property page in this user control.

To get started, create a new Outlook 2007 add-in, and open the class that contains the add-in initialization method (for the template provided with this book, open the *Connect* class). In the initialize method, you need to hook up an event handler for the appropriate event. If you want to add a property page to the Tools Options dialog box, you want to listen on the *Application.OptionsPagesAdd* event. For the Folder Properties dialog box, you want to listen on the *NameSpace.OptionsPagesAdd* event. In either case, make sure the reference to the object that contains the event is held in an instance variable so that the event handler isn't garbage collected unintentionally.

```
private void InitializeAddin()
{
    System.Windows.Forms.Application.EnableVisualStyles();
    Application.OptionsPagesAdd += new
        Outlook.ApplicationEvents_11_OptionsPagesAddEventHandler(
        Application_OptionsPagesAdd);
}
```

If you are using the Shared Add-in template or the Outlook 2007 Add-in Template from this book, you need to make sure you call *EnableVisualStyles* in the initialize method as well; otherwise, the visual appearance of controls on the user control will not take on the Windows theme. Figure 16-4 illustrates the proper appearance of controls in the designer.

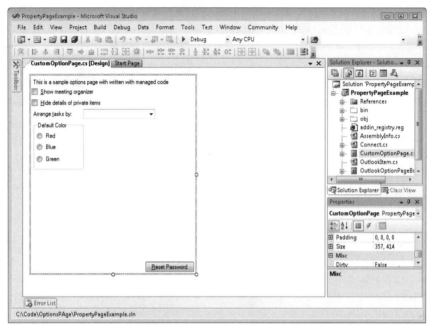

Figure 16-4   Custom property page user control in the Visual Studio designer.

To add the property page to the *Pages* collection, inside the event handler for *OptionsPagesAdd*, add a new instance of the *UserControl* object to the *Pages* collection. To add your custom property page, your event handler method should look like this:

```
void Application_OptionsPagesAdd(
    Microsoft.Office.Interop.Outlook.PropertyPages Pages)
{
    OutlookOptionPageBase myPage = new CustomOptionPage();
    myPage.Title = "Backup";
    Pages.Add(myPage, string.Empty);
}
```

Additionally, you need to add two more class files to the project. These files provide some "glue" around creating a themed property page in managed code. The first of these classes is *OutlookOptionPageBase*, which implements the basic functionality of an Outlook property page, including the ability for the page to tell Outlook a setting has changed, and a virtual method that is called when Outlook asks each page to save changes. The class also defines properties for the title of the page and what help file and context should be invoked if the user requests help.

To create this file in your project, add a new *UserControl* in Visual Studio, and then add the code listed here to the generated file. This way the Visual Studio Forms Designer will see the class as a designable *UserControl* and allow visual design to take place.

```
// OutlookOptionPageBase.cs
using System;
```

```csharp
using System.Windows.Forms;
using System.Runtime.InteropServices;
using Outlook = Microsoft.Office.Interop.Outlook;
public partial class OutlookOptionPageBase
    : UserControl, Outlook.PropertyPage
{
    #region Instance Variables
    private bool m_Dirty;                             // dirty/clean state
    private Outlook.PropertyPageSite m_PropPageSite;   // site information
    private string m_PageTitle;            // Caption for the option page tab
    private string m_PageHelpFile;
    private int m_PageHelpContext;
    private bool m_isLoading = false;
    public event EventHandler Save;
    #endregion

    #region Constructors
    public OutlookOptionPageBase()
        : this(string.Empty, string.Empty, 0)
    {
    }

    public OutlookOptionPageBase(string title, string helpFile,
        int helpFileContext)
    {

        InitializeComponent();

        m_PageTitle = title;
        m_PageHelpFile = helpFile;
        m_PageHelpContext = helpFileContext;
        m_Dirty = false;
    }
    #endregion

    #region Virtual Methods
    /// <summary>
    /// This method is invoked when the user clicks the OK or Apply buttons
    /// in the Options dialog box. An add-in should use this method to persist
    /// settings displayed on the form. After this method finishes executing
    /// the Dirty state of the form is reset.
    /// </summary>
    protected virtual void OnSaveSettings()
    {
        if (null != Save)
        {
            Save(this, EventArgs.Empty);
        }
    }
    #endregion

    #region Outlook Property Page Helper Code
    /// <summary>
    /// Look up the property page site information so that we can inform Outlook
    /// when we become dirty.
```

```csharp
        /// </summary>
        private void GetPropertyPageSite()
        {
            try
            {
                System.Reflection.Assembly swf =
                System.Reflection.Assembly.GetAssembly(
                    typeof(System.Windows.Forms.UserControl));
                Type unsafeMethods =
                    swf.GetType(
                    "System.Windows.Forms.UnsafeNativeMethods");
                Type oleObj = unsafeMethods.GetNestedType("IOleObject");
                System.Reflection.MethodInfo getClientSite =
                    oleObj.GetMethod("GetClientSite");
                object objPropPageSite = getClientSite.Invoke(this, null);
                m_PropPageSite = (Outlook.PropertyPageSite)objPropPageSite;
            }
            catch (Exception ex)
            {
                System.Diagnostics.Debug.WriteLine(ex.ToString());
            }
        }


        /// <summary>
        /// Sets the local dirty flag to be true and informs the
        /// parent container that our status has changed
        /// </summary>
        private void PageDirty()
        {
            if (m_isLoading)
                return;
            if (m_PropPageSite == null)
            {
                GetPropertyPageSite();
            }

            if (m_PropPageSite != null)
            {
                m_PropPageSite.OnStatusChange();
            }
        }

        protected bool IsLoading
        {
            get { return m_isLoading; }
            set { m_isLoading = value; }
        }

        /// <summary>
        /// Return the display caption for the tab page
        /// </summary>
        [DispId(-518)]
        public string Title
        {
            get { return m_PageTitle; }
```

```
        set { m_PageTitle = value; }
    }
    #endregion

    #region PropertyPage Members Called by Outlook

    public void Apply()
    {
        OnSaveSettings();
        m_Dirty = false;
    }

    public bool Dirty
    {
        get { return m_Dirty; }
        set
        {
            m_Dirty = value;
            if (m_Dirty)
                PageDirty();
        }
    }

    public void GetPageInfo(ref string HelpFile, ref int HelpContext)
    {
        HelpFile = m_PageHelpFile;
        HelpContext = m_PageHelpContext;
    }

    #endregion
}
```

The other new class you should create is *PropertyPageBackgroundPanel*. This file extends the *Panel* control provided by the .NET Framework and paints the appropriate background gradient for the Windows theme for the background color. Although it might seem more reasonable to paint this as part of the user control instead of a panel on the user control, you can't use a transparent background color on certain controls unless those controls are hosted on a child control, like the *Panel* control. Without a transparent background, controls will have a standard gray background behind text that will stick out from the page.

```
// PropertyPageBackgroundPanel.cs
using System;
using System.Windows.Forms;
using System.Windows.Forms.VisualStyles;
using System.Drawing;

class PropertyPageBackgroundPanel : Panel
{
    protected override void OnPaintBackground(PaintEventArgs e)
    {
        base.OnPaintBackground(e);

        // Draw the visual style in the background if necessary
```

```
        if (VisualStyleRenderer.IsSupported)
        {
            VisualStyleRenderer render =
                new VisualStyleRenderer(VisualStyleElement.Tab.Body.Normal);
            render.DrawBackground(e.Graphics, this.ClientRectangle));
        }
    }
}
```

Both of these files will be used shortly when you create the custom user control that will actually be displayed to the user.

Creating a Windows Form User Control

Now that you have the basic framework for building a custom property page, you can get started extending the base user control and designing the look of your custom property page. However, before you can create the new inherited user control, you need to build the assembly that contains the base user control. You might need to comment out the contents for the *OptionsPagesAdd* event handler temporarily to get the assembly to build. Once the assembly has built successfully, you should uncomment those lines again.

To create the inherited user control that will be used as your custom options page, follow these steps:

1. Right-click the project node in Solution Explorer, select Add, and then select New Item.

2. Select Inherited User Control, type **CustomOptionPage.cs** for the name, and then click OK.

3. When the Inheritance Picker dialog box appears, select OutlookOptionBasePage as the component from which to inherit, and then click OK.

This new user control class will be displayed by Outlook in the Options dialog box of your choice. To get started designing the page, first you need to add *PropertyPageBackgroundPanel* to the user form. Open the Toolbox window in Visual Studio, and scroll to the top of the list where controls defined in current projects are displayed. Drag the *PropertyPageBackgroundPanel* control to the user control designer. You should also set the new panel control's *Dock* property to *Fill* so that the control will fill the entire user control. All of the controls you add to the user control should be added on this panel.

Some controls—in particular *CheckBox*, *GroupBox*, *Label*, *LinkLabel*, and *RadioButton*—will need to have their *BackColor* property set to *Color.Transparent* for them to show the gradient behind text on the control.

Dirtying the Page and Saving Changes

For your custom property page to behave like other pages, you need to tell Outlook when the dirty state of the settings on your custom page has changed, and respond properly to requests to save changes from Outlook. Fortunately, this behavior is implemented for you by the *OutlookOptionPageBase* class, which your custom property page has inherited.

When using an inherited user control from *OutlookOptionPageBase*, you can use the *Dirty* property and the *Save* event on the control to notify Outlook about changes to the data and to save those changes when the user clicks the Apply or OK button on the Options or Folder Properties dialog boxes. For example, if you have a *CheckBox* control on the form, you should wire up an event handler for the *CheckedChanged* event on the control and set the *Dirty* property to *true*, indicating a change in the dirty state of your custom property page.

```
private void checkBox1_CheckedChanged(object sender, EventArgs e)
{
    this.Dirty = true;
}
```

Additionally, you should handle the *Save* event on the user control class and persist the settings to where your add-in stores settings (using a *StorageItem* so that your settings roam is a great solution for add-in settings). To handle the *Save* event, wire up an event handler for the event, and write out your settings in this event handler.

```
public CustomOptionPage()
{
    InitializeComponent();
    this.Save += new EventHandler(CustomOptionPage_Save);
}

void CustomOptionPage_Save(object sender, EventArgs e)
{
    // Save the changes to my options here
}
```

You could choose to store your solution's settings in the Windows registry, a configuration file, or a *StorageItem* object. A *StorageItem* object is a hidden message in a folder that cannot be accessed by a user. During the *Save* event you would just write the new settings to the appropriate configuration file and have the add-in reload the settings. The Prepare Me sample, referenced in other places in this book, uses *StorageItem* to maintain settings and provides a good example for saving settings in this manner. For additional details on the *StorageItem* object, see Chapter 5, "Built-in Item Types."

Loading Settings

When your Folder Properties or Options dialog box is loading the settings, it might change the values of the controls on the *UserControl* object, which could end up setting the dirtiness of the custom property page incorrectly. The base class provided here includes a protected property, *IsLoading,* which can be used to avoid this. By setting the *IsLoading* property to *true* while you are loading values into the controls, and then setting it to *false* again after the loading is complete, you can avoid an incorrect dirty state. The base class will ignore any attempts to set the *Dirty* property to *true* while *IsLoading* is *true*.

For example, the code used to load settings should look something like this:

```
private void LoadSettings()
{
    this.IsLoading = true;

    checkBox1.Checked = true;
    textBox1.Text = "Persisted Setting";

    this.IsLoading = false;
}
```

Just remember to set *IsLoading* back to *False* after the settings have been loaded from persisted storage; otherwise, the custom property page will never report that the settings have been dirtied, and the Apply button in the Options dialog box or the Folder Properties dialog box will not be enabled.

Summary

In this chapter, you have learned a couple of additional ways that you can use to extend the Outlook user interface to provide a rich and deeply integrated solution. Using custom task panes to show related or associated information in the Inspector and Explorer windows can be a powerful way to bring external information into the Outlook user experience. Likewise, using custom property pages can really make your solution feel like part of Outlook because the settings for your solution live alongside similar settings for the Outlook application.

However, you should take care in using both of these methods so that the user interface doesn't feel cluttered or overwhelming to the user. This is particularly true for both custom task panes and custom property pages, because in some scenarios there are already several panes or property pages displayed by Outlook, and adding additional panes or property pages might make the user interface difficult for some users to operate.

Part V
Advanced Topics

Chapter 17
Using the *PropertyAccessor* (

The *PropertyAccessor* object has been added to the Microsoft Office Outlook 200/ _ _
model to provide parity with the Collaboration Data Objects (CDO) 1.21 *Fields* and *Field*
objects. Unlike the *Field* object in CDO, the *PropertyAccessor* object uses string representations of Messaging Application Programming Interface (MAPI) and named properties. To
enhance performance, the *PropertyAccessor* object also supports batch operations using the
GetProperties and *SetProperties* methods. Unlike CDO, the *PropertyAccessor* object is fully
supported for both native and managed code development.

In this chapter, scenarios for use of the *PropertyAccessor* object are discussed. You learn
about namespaces for the *PropertyAccessor* object and about *PropertyAccessor* methods and
helper functions. You also discover how error conditions are reported by method calls on
the *PropertyAccessor* object.

Scenarios for *PropertyAccessor*

For most property access on Outlook items, the *PropertyAccessor* object is not required.
Built-in properties in the Outlook object model allow you read-write access to both common and uncommon properties on Outlook objects. However, there are cases when the
Outlook object model does not expose the property you need to access. The canonical case
is *PR_TRANSPORT_MESSAGE_HEADERS*, which contains the message transport header.
You can use the *PropertyAccessor* object to access this property for use in your solution. In fact,
you can use the *PropertyAccessor* object to tunnel down to the "raw" properties on the underlying MAPI objects that contain Outlook data. A property is an attribute of a MAPI object.
Properties describe something about the object, such as the subject line of a message or the
address type of a messaging user. MAPI defines many properties, some to describe many
objects and some that are appropriate only for an object of a particular type. Consequently,
PropertyAccessor is a very powerful object that you should use with care. Outlook built-in properties encapsulate Outlook's business logic and are the preferred means of implementing that
business logic programmatically. If you change a built-in property using the *PropertyAccessor*
object, you risk breaking Outlook's business logic, and your solution might not act as
expected. The most risk-prone area is in the area of Appointment items, where use of the built-
in object model properties is always recommended to set recurrence patterns and appointment start and end times.

More Info   For more information regarding Microsoft's support policy for scenarios using *PropertyAccessor* and various other application programming interfaces (APIs) to access MAPI-based data, please see *http://support.microsoft.com/kb/266353*.

Another scenario for use of *PropertyAccessor* is when you want to decorate an item with custom properties that cannot be used in a view or are not visible in the Outlook Field Chooser. Essentially, these are hidden custom properties on the item. Typically, custom properties are added to items in form region Design mode or through the *UserProperties* collection. Custom properties added through the *UserProperties* collection on an item (such as *AppointmentItem* or *ContactItem*) or the *UserDefinedProperties* collection on a *Folder* object are visible in the Outlook Field Chooser and can be added to a view. Custom properties added through the *SetProperty* method of the *PropertyAccessor* object are named properties on the item that are hidden from the Outlook user interface.

Objects That Implement *PropertyAccessor*

Objects that implement the *PropertyAccessor* property typically represent Outlook data, such as a *MailItem* or *AppointmentItem* object. Table 17-1 lists the objects that implement *PropertyAccessor* in Outlook 2007.

Table 17-1   Objects That Implement *PropertyAccessor*

AddressEntry	AddressList
AppointmentItem	Attachment
ContactItem	DistListItem
DocumentItem	ExchangeDistributionList
ExchangeUser	Folder
JournalItem	MailItem
MeetingItem	NoteItem
PostItem	Recipient
RemoteItem	ReportItem
SharingItem	Store
TaskItem	TaskRequestAcceptItem
TaskRequestDeclineItem	TaskRequestItem
TaskRequestUpdateItem	

PropertyAccessor Namespaces

PropertyAccessor supports several different namespace formats. You use a representation of a specific property in a namespace to provide a *SchemaName* string for a method of *PropertyAccessor*. Whether a format is supported depends on the parent object of the *PropertyAccessor* object. Table 17-2 indicates which objects support a given namespace format.

Table 17-2   Namespaces by Object

Namespaces	Supported Outlook objects
http://schemas.microsoft.com/mapi /proptag	Outlook item objects, *AddressEntry*, *AddressList*, *Attachment*, *ExchangeDistributionList*, *ExchangeUser*, *Folder*, *Recipient*, and *Store* objects
http://schemas.microsoft.com/mapi/id	Outlook item objects; other objects depend on store provider
http://schemas.microsoft.com/mapi /string	Outlook item objects; other objects depend on store provider
http://schemas.microsoft.com /exchange	Outlook item objects
urn:schemas-microsoft-com:office: office	Outlook item objects
urn:schemas-microsoft-com:office: outlook	Outlook item objects
DAV:	Outlook item objects
urn:schemas:calendar	Outlook item objects
urn:schemas:contacts	Outlook item objects
urn:schemas:httpmail	Outlook item objects
urn:schemas:mailheader	Outlook item objects

Obtaining a Specific *SchemaName* String

Microsoft does not publish schemas for all objects that implement the *PropertyAccessor* object. However, there are tools available that can help you determine the correct *SchemaName* string to use for the *SchemaName* argument of various *PropertyAccessor* methods. The following tools provide representations of the low-level MAPI properties that are available for use with *PropertyAccessor*:

- **Microsoft Exchange Server MAPI Editor (formally known as MFCMapi)**   MAPI Editor provides access to a wealth of MAPI information.

> **More Info**   See *http://www.microsoft.com/downloads/details.aspx?familyid=55FDFFD7-1878-4637-9808-1E21ABB3AE37&displaylang=en.*

- **Outlook Spy**   Outlook Spy is a third-party utility that displays MAPI properties for an object in a separate window. Outlook Spy also provides windows for Outlook objects and lets you quickly write scripts to test object model properties and methods.

> **More Info**   See *http://www.dimastr.com/outspy.*

Type Specifiers

Certain namespaces, such as the *Proptag* namespace, require that you provide the type of the returned property in the lower order 16 bits of the property tag. If you need more information about single-valued and multivalued MAPI property types, see the section entitled "About Property Types" in the MAPI Software Development Kit on MSDN. Table 17-3 lists the common type specifiers used in the *Proptag* and *ID* formats.

Table 17-3   MAPI Type Specifiers

MAPI property type	Hex value	OLE variant type	Description
PT_BINARY	0102	VT_BLOB	Binary (unknown format)
PT_BOOLEAN	000B	VT_BOOL	Boolean
PT_CLSID	0102	VT_CLSID	OLE GUID
PT_CURRENCY	0006	VT_CY	8-byte integer (scaled by 10,000)
PT_OBJECT	000D	VT_UNKNOWN	Data object
PT_SYSTIME	0040	VT_DATE	8-byte real (date in integer, time in fraction)
PT_DOUBLE	0005	VT_R8	8-byte real (floating point)
PT_ERROR	000A	VT_ERROR	SCODE value; 32-bit unsigned integer
PT_SHORT	0002	VT_I2	2-byte integer
PT_LONG	0003	VT_I4	4-byte integer
PT_NULL	0001	VT_NULL	Null (no valid data)
PT_FLOAT	0004	VT_R4	4-byte real (floating point)
PT_STRING8	001E or 001F	VT_BSTR	String

The *Proptag* Namespace

The *Proptag* namespace is used to access properties in the MAPI namespace using the property tag of a property. It supports only properties in the MAPI property range (that is, properties with a property identifier below 0x8000). If you use a property identifier above 0x8000, Outlook raises an error. The following is the format to reference a property in this namespace:

http://schemas.microsoft.com/mapi/proptag/0xHHHHHHHH

HHHHHHHH represents a hexadecimal property tag value, with a unique property identifier in the higher order 16 bits, and a property type in the lower order 16 bits. Every MAPI property must have a property tag, regardless of whether the property is defined by MAPI, Outlook, or a service provider. The hexadecimal value must follow the prefix 0x.

> **Note**   Schema names are case-sensitive. The only exception to this rule is that the hexa-decimal characters that appear after 0x or in a globally unique identifier (GUID) are not case-sensitive. 0x for *Proptag* format is case-sensitive.

For example, the following code sample obtains the MAPI property *PR_TRANSPORT_MESSAGE_HEADERS* for the first item in the Inbox. *PR_TRANSPORT_MESSAGE_HEADERS* uses the *Proptag* format and is not exposed in the Outlook object model.

```
private void DemoProptagNamespace()
{
    Outlook.Items items =
        Application.Session.GetDefaultFolder(
        Outlook.OlDefaultFolders.olFolderInbox).Items;
    //Sort by last modification time
    items.Sort("LastModificationTime",
        Outlook.OlSortOrder.olAscending);
    //Get first item in Inbox
    Outlook.MailItem oMail =
        items.Find("[MessageClass]='IPM.Note'")
        as Outlook.MailItem;
    //PR_TRANSPORT_MESSAGE_HEADERS
    string PR_TRANSPORT_MESSAGE_HEADERS =
        "http://schemas.microsoft.com/mapi/proptag/0x007D001E";
    //Obtain an instance of PropertyAccessor class
    Outlook.PropertyAccessor oPA = oMail.PropertyAccessor;
    //Call GetProperty using Try Catch block
    try
    {
        string Transport = (string)oPA.GetProperty(
            PR_TRANSPORT_MESSAGE_HEADERS);
        MessageBox.Show(this, Transport,
            "Transport Header: " + oMail.Subject);
    }
    catch (Exception ex)
    {
        Debug.WriteLine(ex.Message);
    }
}
```

Named Property *ID* Namespace

The *ID* namespace is used to access ID-named properties in a namespace identified by the GUID of the namespace, using the identifier of the property. The following is the format to reference a property in this namespace:

http://schemas.microsoft.com/mapi/id/{HHHHHHHH-HHHH-HHHH-HHHH-HHHHHHHHH-HHH}/HHHHHHHH

{HHHHHHHH-HHHH-HHHH-HHHH-HHHHHHHHHHHH} represents the namespace GUID, and *HHHHHHHH* represents the property tag.

For example, the following code sample obtains the named property *Use_TNEF* for the first item in the Inbox. *Use_TNEF* uses the ID format and is not exposed in the Outlook object model.

```
private void DemoIDNamespace()
{
    Outlook.Items items =
        Application.Session.GetDefaultFolder(
        Outlook.OlDefaultFolders.olFolderInbox).Items;
    //Sort by last modification time
    items.Sort("LastModificationTime",
        Outlook.OlSortOrder.olAscending);
    //Get first item in Inbox
    Outlook.MailItem oMail =
        items.Find("[MessageClass]='IPM.Note'")
        as Outlook.MailItem;
    //Named property referenced by ID
    string UseTNEF =
        "http://schemas.microsoft.com/mapi/id/"
        + "{00062008-0000-0000-C000-000000000046}/8582000B";
    Outlook.PropertyAccessor oPA = oMail.PropertyAccessor;
    try
    {
        bool isTNEF = (bool)oPA.GetProperty(UseTNEF);
        if (isTNEF)
        {
            Debug.WriteLine("Uses TNEF");
        }
        else
        {
            Debug.WriteLine("Does not use TNEF");
        }
    }
    catch(Exception ex)
    {
        Debug.WriteLine(ex.Message);
    }
}
```

Named Property *String* Namespace

The *String* namespace is used to access string-named properties in an identified namespace. The following is the format to reference a property in this namespace:

http://schemas.microsoft.com/mapi/string/{HHHHHHHH-HHHH-HHHH-HHHH-HHHHHHH-HHHHH}/name

{HHHHHHHH-HHHH-HHHH-HHHH-HHHHHHHHHHHH} represents the namespace GUID, and *name* is the local property name defined as a string.

For example, the following code sample obtains the named property *x-scanned-by* for the first item in the Inbox. *x-scanned-by* uses the *String* format and is not exposed in the Outlook object model.

```
private void DemoStringNamespace()
{
    Outlook.Items items =
        Application.Session.GetDefaultFolder(
        Outlook.OlDefaultFolders.olFolderInbox).Items;
    //Sort by last modification time
    items.Sort("LastModificationTime",
        Outlook.OlSortOrder.olAscending);
    //Get first item in Inbox
    Outlook.MailItem oMail =
        items.Find("[MessageClass]='IPM.Note'")
        as Outlook.MailItem;
    //Named property referenced by String
    string xScannedBy =
        "http://schemas.microsoft.com/mapi/string/"
        + "{00062008-0000-0000-C000-000000000046}/x-scanned-by";
    Outlook.PropertyAccessor oPA = oMail.PropertyAccessor;
    try
    {
        string scannedBy = (string)oPA.GetProperty(xScannedBy);
        if (!string.IsNullOrEmpty(ScannedBy))
        {
            Debug.WriteLine(scannedBy);
        }
    }
    catch (Exception ex)
    {
        Debug.WriteLine(ex.Message);
    }
}
```

Office Namespaces

The *PropertyAccessor* object supports two *Office* subnamespaces:

The *Office* Namespace

The *Office* namespace is used to access properties of the *DocumentItem* object. The following is the format to reference a property in this namespace:

urn:schemas-microsoft-com:office:office#name

where *name* is the local property name defined as a string.

The following are some examples that reference *DocumentItem* properties using the *Office* namespace:

- *urn:schemas-microsoft-com:office:office#Author*
- *urn:schemas-microsoft-com:office:office#Title*

The following property uses the *Office* namespace and references the *Categories* property that appears on almost all item types:

- *urn:schemas-microsoft-com:office:office#Keywords*

The *Outlook* Namespace

This namespace is used to access Outlook item-level properties. Similar to other namespaces that support property referencing, use this namespace to access Outlook properties that are not explicitly exposed in the object model. The following is the format to reference a property in this namespace:

urn:schemas-microsoft-com:office:outlook#name

where *name* is the local property name defined as a string.

The following example shows how to reference an Outlook item-level property using the *Outlook* namespace:

urn:schemas-microsoft-com:office:outlook#remotemessagesize

DAV Namespaces

Distributed Authoring and Versioning (DAV) namespaces are used to access Outlook item-level properties. A property in a DAV namespace is scoped using a Uniform Resource Identifier (URI) namespace reference. The format is a concatenation of the namespace URI prefix and the local property name expressed in a string, with the namespace URI being either a Uniform Resource Name (URN) or Uniform Resource Locator (URL).

The following are the DAV namespaces that the *PropertyAccessor* object supports:

- DAV
- urn:schemas:calendar
- urn:schemas:contacts
- urn:schemas:httpmail
- urn:schemas:mailheader

The following examples demonstrate properties being referenced by different DAV namespaces:

- DAV:getlastmodified
- urn:schemas:httpmail:subject
- urn:schemas:contacts:givenName
- urn:schemas:contacts:organization

The *PropertyAccessor* Object

The *PropertyAccessor* object provides the ability to create, get, set, and delete properties on objects. *Set* and *Delete* operations are dependent on the property type, the parent object, and the store provider. The *PropertyAccessor* object only exposes methods such as *GetProperty* and *SetProperty*. It does not expose properties or events. To enhance performance and reduce network traffic in a Microsoft Exchange environment, *PropertyAccessor* provides methods such as *GetProperties* and *SetProperties* that allow you to access multiple properties in a single call.

> **Note**   If untrusted code attempts to access the *PropertyAccessor* object, the Outlook object model guard warning dialog box will appear. For more information regarding the Outlook object model guard, see Chapter 19, "Trust and Security."

The *GetProperty* Method

The *GetProperty* method returns an *object* that represents the value of the property specified by *SchemaName*. Note that you must cast the returned *object* to a type that is appropriate to the underlying MAPI property. To determine the type of the underlying MAPI property, see the section "Type Specifiers" earlier in this chapter. Certain raw property types such as *PT_OBJECT* are unsupported and will raise an error. If you require conversion of the raw property type, for example, from *PT_BINARY* to a string, or from *PT_SYSTIME* to a local time, use the helper methods *BinaryToString* and *UTCToLocalTime*. The following code sample returns the normalized subject for *MailItem* passed to the method. The normalized subject is the subject of the item without the subject prefix such as RE: or FW:.

```
private string GetNormalizedSubject(Outlook.MailItem mail)
{
    const string PR_NORMALIZED_SUBJECT =
        "http://schemas.microsoft.com/mapi/proptag/0x0E1D001E";
    try
    {
        return(mail.PropertyAccessor.GetProperty(
            PR_NORMALIZED_SUBJECT) as string);
    }
    catch{return null;}
}
```

The *SetProperty* Method

The *SetProperty* method sets the property specified by *SchemaName* to the value specified by *Value*. If the property does not exist and the *SchemaName* contains a valid property specifier, then *SetProperty* creates the property and assigns the value specified by *Value*. If the property does exist and *SchemaName* is valid, then *SetProperty* assigns the property with the value specified by *Value*.

> **Important**   If the parent object of *PropertyAccessor* supports an explicit *Save* operation, you must persist *PropertyAccessor* modifications with an explicit *Save* method call. For example, you must call *Item.Save* to persist changes made with *SetProperty* or *SetProperties*. If the object does not support an explicit *Save* operation, then the properties are saved to the object when *SetProperty* is called.

The following code sample finds the first item in the Inbox, creates a custom property using the *String* namespace, sets the value of the property to DW043733, and then calls the *Save* method on the item:

```
private void DemoPropertyAccessorSetProperty()
{
    string myProp = "http://schemas.microsoft.com/mapi/string/"
        + "{FFF40745-D92F-4C11-9E14-92701F001EB3}/myCustomer";
    string myValue = "DW043733";
    Outlook.Items items =
        Application.Session.GetDefaultFolder(
        Outlook.OlDefaultFolders.olFolderInbox).Items;
    //Sort by last modification time
    items.Sort("LastModificationTime",
        Outlook.OlSortOrder.olAscending);
    //Get first item in Inbox
    Outlook.MailItem oMail =
        items.Find("[MessageClass]='IPM.Note'")
        as Outlook.MailItem;
    //Obtain an instance of PropertyAccessor class
    Outlook.PropertyAccessor oPA = oMail.PropertyAccessor;
    //Set value with SetProperty call
    //If the property does not exist, then SetProperty
    //adds the property to the object when saved.
    //The type of the property is the type of the element
    //passed in myValue.
    try
    {
        oPA.SetProperty(myProp, myValue);
        oMail.Save();
    }
    catch (Exception ex)
    {
        Debug.WriteLine(ex.Message);
    }
}
```

The *GetProperties* Method

The *GetProperties* method obtains the values of the properties specified by the one-dimensional *SchemaNames* array. *GetProperties* returns an array of values, with each element corresponding to the property specified in the *SchemaNames* array. The type of the array element returned by *GetProperties* will be the same as the type of the underlying property. Certain raw property types such as *PT_OBJECT* are unsupported and will raise an error. If you require conversion of the raw property type, for example, from *PT_BINARY* to a string, or from *PT_SYSTIME* to a local time, use the *BinaryToString* or *UTCToLocalTime* helper methods. If the property cannot be found or an error occurs, then an error is returned in the element that corresponds to the element specified in the *SchemaNames* array.

The following code sample uses a single *GetProperties* call to return the values for the properties *PR_ATTR_HIDDEN*, *PR_ATTR_READONLY*, and *PR_ATTR_SYSTEM*:

```
private void DemoPropertyAccessorGetProperties()
{
    Outlook.Items items =
        Application.Session.GetDefaultFolder(
        Outlook.OlDefaultFolders.olFolderInbox).Items;
    //Sort by last modification time
    items.Sort("LastModificationTime",
        Outlook.OlSortOrder.olAscending);
    //Get first item in Inbox
    Outlook.MailItem oMail =
        items.Find("[MessageClass]='IPM.Note'")
        as Outlook.MailItem;
    const string PR_ATTR_HIDDEN =
        "http://schemas.microsoft.com/mapi/proptag/0x10F4000B";
    const string PR_ATTR_READONLY =
        "http://schemas.microsoft.com/mapi/proptag/0x10F6000B";
    const string PR_ATTR_SYSTEM =
        "http://schemas.microsoft.com/mapi/proptag/0x10F5000B";
    Object[] propNames =
        new Object[] { PR_ATTR_HIDDEN, PR_ATTR_READONLY, PR_ATTR_SYSTEM };
    Outlook.PropertyAccessor oPA = oMail.PropertyAccessor;
    try
    {
        //Call Get Properties
        Object[] propValues = (Object[])oPA.GetProperties(
            propNames);
        //Examine propValues
        for (int i = 0; i < propValues.Length; i++)
        {
            Debug.WriteLine(propValues[i].ToString());
        }
    }
    catch (Exception ex)
    {
        Debug.WriteLine(ex.Message);
    }
}
```

The *SetProperties* Method

The *SetProperties* method sets the properties specified by the one-dimensional *SchemaNames* array to the values specified by the one-dimensional *Values* array. If the property specified by the element in the *SchemaNames* array does not exist and contains a valid property specifier, then *SetProperties* creates the property specified by the element in *SchemaNames* and assigns the value of the corresponding element in the *Values* array. The type of the property will be the type of the element passed in *Values*. The length of the *SchemaNames* array must be equal to the length of the *Values* array. If the property does exist and the element in *SchemaNames* is valid, then *SetProperties* assigns the property to the value of the corresponding element in the *Values* array.

If no error occurs when the property represented by each element in *SchemaNames* is set or created, an empty array is returned from the *SetProperties* call. If an error occurs for any of the properties specified in *SchemaNames*, *SetProperties* returns an array with the same number of elements as the *SchemaNames* array. Elements that did not generate an error return *null*. Elements that did generate an error return a MAPI extended error code. For additional information on errors returned by the *SetProperties*, *GetProperties*, or *DeleteProperties* methods, see the section "Detecting and Reporting Error Conditions" later in this chapter.

The following code sample finds the first item in the Inbox, creates a set of custom properties using the *SetProperties* method, and then calls the *Save* method on the item:

```
private void DemoPropertyAccessorSetProperties()
{
    Outlook.Items items =
        Application.Session.GetDefaultFolder(
        Outlook.OlDefaultFolders.olFolderInbox).Items;
    //Sort by last modification time
    items.Sort("LastModificationTime",
        Outlook.OlSortOrder.olAscending);
    //Get first item in Inbox
    Outlook.MailItem oMail =
        items.Find("[MessageClass]='IPM.Note'")
        as Outlook.MailItem;
    //Names for properties using the MAPI string namespace
    string prop1 = "http://schemas.microsoft.com/mapi/string/" +
        "{FFF40745-D92F-4C11-9E14-92701F001EB3}/mylongprop";
    string prop2 = "http://schemas.microsoft.com/mapi/string/" +
        "{FFF40745-D92F-4C11-9E14-92701F001EB3}/mystringprop";
    string prop3 = "http://schemas.microsoft.com/mapi/string/" +
        "{FFF40745-D92F-4C11-9E14-92701F001EB3}/mydateprop";
    string prop4 = "http://schemas.microsoft.com/mapi/string/" +
        "{FFF40745-D92F-4C11-9E14-92701F001EB3}/myboolprop";
    Object[] propNames =
        new Object[] {prop1, prop2, prop3, prop4};
    Object[] propValues =
        new Object[] { 1020, "111-222-Kudo",
        DateTime.Now.ToUniversalTime(), false };
    //Set values with SetProperties call
```

```
//If the properties do not exist, then SetProperties
//adds the properties to the object when saved.
//The type of the property is the type of the element
//passed in propValues array.
Outlook.PropertyAccessor oPA = oMail.PropertyAccessor;
try
{
    //Call Set Properties
    Object[] arrErrors = (Object[])oPA.SetProperties(
        propNames, propValues);
    //Examine arrErrors to determine errors
    for(int i = 0; i < arrErrors.Length; i++)
    {
        if (arrErrors[i] != null)
        {
            GetMAPIError((int)arrErrors[i], propNames[i].ToString());
        }
    }
    oMail.Save();
}
catch (Exception ex)
{
    Debug.WriteLine(ex.Message);
}
}
```

The *DeleteProperty* Method

The *DeleteProperty* method deletes the property specified by *SchemaName*. The caller must have the permission to delete properties. The *DeleteProperty* method deletes only custom properties; it does not delete any Outlook built-in property or any MAPI property. It also does not delete custom properties of the *DocumentItem* object.

The *DeleteProperties* Method

The *DeleteProperties* method deletes the properties specified in the array *SchemaNames*. The caller must have the permission to delete properties. The *DeleteProperties* method deletes only custom properties; it does not delete any Outlook built-in property or any MAPI property. It also does not delete custom properties of the *DocumentItem* object.

If no error occurs when the property represented by each element in *SchemaNames* is deleted, then an empty array is returned from the *DeleteProperties* call. If an error occurs for any of the properties specified in *SchemaNames*, then *DeleteProperties* returns an array with the same number of elements as the *SchemaNames* array. Elements that did not generate an error return *null*. Elements that did generate an error return a MAPI extended error code. For additional information on errors returned by *SetProperties*, *GetProperties*, or *DeleteProperties* methods, see the section "Detecting and Reporting Error Conditions" later in this chapter.

Date-Time Properties

Although most Outlook date-time values are stored in Coordinated Universal Time (UTC) format, there is no guarantee that all properties of the MAPI type *PT_SYSTIME* will always return UTC. Getting a *PT_SYSTIME* property will return a *VT_DATE* value. When setting a *PT_SYSTIME* property, ensure that you are setting the property as a UTC value rather than a local date-time value. The *GetProperty*, *SetProperty*, *GetProperties*, and *SetProperties* methods do not perform time zone conversion. Use the helper methods *PropertyAccessor.LocalTimeToUTC* and *PropertyAccessor.UTCToLocalTime* to perform explicit time zone conversion.

> **Warning**   [Due to the way that Outlook stores dates internally, date-time values returned by *PropertyAccessor* methods such as *GetProperty*, *LocalTimeToUTC*, or *UTCToLocalTime* will always be rounded to the nearest minute.

Multivalued Properties

A multivalued property (such as a *PT_MV_STRING8* property) is stored as a one-dimensional array that contains the same number of elements as there are values in the property. Multivalued properties are also known as keywords properties. Getting a multivalued property returns a *VT_ARRAY* value. When setting a multivalued property, pass a one-dimensional array (*VT_ARRAY*) with one element for each value that you want to set for the property. The following code sample uses *PropertyAccessor* to obtain the categories for the *ActiveInspector.CurrentItem* object:

```
private void DemoMultiValuedProperty()
{
    const string categoriesSchema =
        "http://schemas.microsoft.com/mapi/string/" +
        "{00020329-0000-0000-C000-000000000046}/Keywords";
    if (Application.ActiveInspector() != null)
    {
        //Create an instance of OutlookItem
        OutlookItem myItem = new OutlookItem(
            Application.ActiveInspector().CurrentItem);
        Outlook.PropertyAccessor oPA = myItem.PropertyAccessor;
        try
        {
            Object[] categories =
                (Object[])oPA.GetProperty(categoriesSchema);
            for (int i = 0; i < categories.Length; i++)
            {
                Debug.WriteLine(categories[i].ToString());
            }
        }
```

```
            catch (Exception ex)
            {
                Debug.WriteLine(ex.Message);
            }
        }
    }
}
```

Helper Methods

PropertyAccessor implements several helper methods that make your life easier. For example, Outlook stores certain properties such as an *EntryID* property as an array of bytes. To turn the array of bytes into a string that is expected by *Namespace* methods such as *GetItemFromID* or *GetAddressEntryFromID*, you use a helper method instead of developing your own conversion routines.

The *BinaryToString* Method

The *BinaryToString* method converts an array of bytes to a string. Because Outlook stores "raw" binary properties as an array of bytes, binary properties are returned from the *GetProperty* method as an array of bytes. The following code snippet returns an *AddressEntry* object and uses the *BinaryToString* method to convert an array of bytes to a string. The string that represents the *AddressEntry* object is then passed to the *GetAddressEntryID* method of the *Namespace* object to return an *AddressEntry* object that represents the sender of the *MailItem* object passed to the procedure. Note that you must first call the *GetProperty* method of *PropertyAccessor* to return the array of bytes that *BinaryToString* converts to a string.

```
private Outlook.AddressEntry GetSenderAddressEntry(Outlook.MailItem mail)
{
    const string PR_SENT_REPRESENTING_ENTRYID =
        "http://schemas.microsoft.com/mapi/proptag/0x00410102";
    try
    {
        Outlook.PropertyAccessor pa = mail.PropertyAccessor;
        string entryID = pa.BinaryToString(pa.GetProperty(
            PR_SENT_REPRESENTING_ENTRYID));
        return Application.Session.GetAddressEntryFromID(entryID);
    }
    catch { return null; }
}
```

The *LocalTimeToUTC* Method

The *LocalTimeToUTC* method converts a date-time value from the local time format to UTC format. The local time format is determined by the local time zone established in the Date and Time item in Windows Control Panel and the Time and Date settings on the Regional Options page of the Regional and Language Options item in Windows Control Panel. Use this method if you need to convert a local date-time value to a UTC date-time value and store the value using the *SetProperty* method of the *PropertyAccessor* object. All date-time values on the underlying item storage are saved in UTC format. If you attempt to write a date-time value using the *SetProperty* method and don't convert from local time to UTC time, Outlook displays an incorrect date-time value.

The *StringToBinary* Method

The *StringToBinary* method converts a string to an array of bytes. Use this method if you need to convert a string representation of a binary property to an array of bytes and store the value using the *SetProperty* method of *PropertyAccessor*. All binary values on the underlying item storage are saved as an array of bytes. If you attempt to write a string to a binary property using the *SetProperty* method and don't convert from a string to an array of bytes, Outlook raises an error.

The *UTCToLocalTime* Method

The *UTCToLocalTime* method converts a date-time value in UTC format to the local time format. The local time format is determined by the local time zone established in the Date and Time item in Windows Control Panel and the Time and Date settings on the Regional Options page of the Regional and Language Options item in Windows Control Panel. Use this method if you need to convert a UTC date-time value obtained by calling the *GetProperty* method to a local date-time value. All date-time values on the underlying item storage are saved in UTC format. If you attempt to access a date-time value using the *GetProperty* method and don't convert from UTC time to local time, Outlook will display an incorrect date-time value. The following code sample displays the local time for the date-time value property *PR_CLIENT_SUBMIT_TIME*:

```
private void DemoUTCToLocalTime()
{
    const string PR_CLIENT_SUBMIT_TIME =
        "http://schemas.microsoft.com/mapi/proptag/0x00390040";
    Outlook.Items items =
        Application.Session.GetDefaultFolder(
        Outlook.OlDefaultFolders.olFolderInbox).Items;
    //Sort by last modification time
    items.Sort("LastModificationTime",
        Outlook.OlSortOrder.olAscending);
    //Get first item in Inbox
    Outlook.MailItem oMail =
        items.Find("[MessageClass]='IPM.Note'")
        as Outlook.MailItem;
    //Obtain an instance of PropertyAccessor class
    Outlook.PropertyAccessor oPA = oMail.PropertyAccessor;
    //Call GetProperty within Try Catch block
    try
    {
```

```
            DateTime submitTime = oPA.UTCToLocalTime(
                (DateTime) oPA.GetProperty(
                PR_CLIENT_SUBMIT_TIME));
            MessageBox.Show(this, submitTime.ToString("g"),
                "Client Submit Time: " + oMail.Subject);
        }
        catch (Exception ex)
        {
            Debug.WriteLine(ex.Message);
        }
    }
}
```

Detecting and Reporting Error Conditions

You should write *try...catch* blocks around all *PropertyAccessor* methods to handle error conditions. There is no guarantee that a given property exists on an item when you perform read
operations. For set operations, Outlook raises an error if you attempt to call *SetProperty* on a
folder object or set a read-only property such as *EntryID*. The run-time error message for a
failed set operation is as follows:

The property 'SchemaName' does not support this operation

where *'SchemaName'* is the actual namespace representation of the property.

Additional conditions that can cause a *PropertyAccessor* operation to fail are as follows:

- The property is read-only, as some Outlook and MAPI properties are read-only.

- The property referenced by the specified namespace is not found.

- The property is specified in an invalid format and cannot be parsed.

- The property does not exist and cannot be created.

- The property exists but is passed a value of an incorrect type.

- The property cannot be opened because the client is offline.

- The size of the property is too large for a *Set* or *Get* operation.

Delete operations can also raise errors. For the most part, you should attempt to delete only
custom properties that you have created. Otherwise, you risk corrupting Outlook data or creating unexpected results due to problems with the custom properties and business logic of
another add-in.

When you call the *SetProperties* or *DeleteProperties* methods, the returned array can contain
a MAPI extended error code. If no error occurs during the method call, the returned array
is empty, meaning that it contains zero elements. If an error occurs for any of the elements
specified by *SchemaNames,* then the returned array has the same number of elements as the
SchemaNames array. If an error occurs when an element of the *SchemaNames* array attempts
to set or delete a property, then the corresponding element in the returned array contains a

MAPI extended error code. The following *GetMAPIError* procedure will write the MAPI error and the property that caused the error to the trace listeners in the *Listeners* collection:

```
private void GetMAPIError(int errorCode, string property)
{
    if (property == null)
    {
        property = "property is null";
    }
    switch (errorCode)
    {
        case -2147221233:
            Debug.WriteLine("MAPI_NOT_FOUND - " + property);
            break;
        case -2147221222:
            Debug.WriteLine("MAPI_E_COMPUTED - " + property);
            break;
        case -2147221246:
            Debug.WriteLine("MAPI_E_NO_SUPPORT - " + property);
            break;
        case -2147024891:
            Debug.WriteLine("MAPI_E_NO_SUPPORT - " + property);
            break;
        case -2147352571:
            Debug.WriteLine("DISP_E_TYPEMISMATCH - " + property);
            break;
        default:
            Debug.WriteLine("Unknown error - " + property);
            break;
    }
}
```

Table 17-4 lists the most common MAPI extended error codes that could be returned in an element of the array returned by *GetProperties*, *SetProperties*, or *DeleteProperties*.

Table 17-4   MAPI Extended Error Codes

Error	Hex value	Integer value
MAPI_E_NOT_FOUND	0x8004010F	-2147221233
MAPI_E_COMPUTED	0x8004011A	-2147221222
MAPI_E_NO_SUPPORT	0x80040102	-2147221246
E_ACCESSDENIED	0x80070005	-2147024891
DISP_E_TYPEMISMATCH	0x80020005	-2147352571

Property Size Limitations

The size of the property that can be accessed by the *PropertyAccessor* object is dependent on the store that obtains the parent object. If you attempt to set or get a property that is larger than the limitation imposed by a given store, Outlook raises an error. At the MAPI level, the error is MAPI_E_NOT_ENOUGH_MEMORY. Unfortunately, when the error bubbles up to

Outlook, the reported error is misleading: "Out of memory or system resources. Close some windows or programs and try again."

Closing windows or programs and trying again will not solve the problem because you have run into the size limitation imposed by the store. Table 17-5 lists the size limitation in bytes for common store types. The size limitation depends on whether you are attempting to access a *PT_STRING8* or *PT_BINARY* property. If you need to set properties that are larger than the size allowed by the store, consider adding an attachment to the item rather than using the *PropertyAccessor* object.

Table 17-5   Property Size Limitations for the *PropertyAccessor* Object

Store	Maximum property size in bytes for *GetProperty* or *SetProperty* calls when property is *PT_STRING8*	Maximum property size in bytes for *GetProperty* or *SetProperty* calls when property is *PT_BINARY*
Personal Folders File (.pst)	4088	4088
Offline Folders File (.ost)	4088	4088
Exchange Mailbox store (online mode)	16372	4088
Exchange Public Folder store	16372	4088

Summary

In this chapter, you learned how to use the *PropertyAccessor* object. You should also understand appropriate scenarios for use of *PropertyAccessor*; it is not a replacement for the built-in properties exposed in the Outlook object model. You should now understand how to write code that uses *PropertyAccessor* and how to provide error handling for this powerful object. Use *PropertyAccessor* with care!

Chapter 18
Add-in Setup and Deployment

Once you have worked through the steps of creating and testing your solution, you need to deploy it to customers. Typically, you create a setup package to install your solution. You can use Microsoft Visual Studio 2005 to create and build a setup package, or you can use a third-party tool. Depending on how you create your add-in project, Visual Studio might add a setup project to your solution. This chapter focuses on the registry keys required for a Microsoft Office Outlook 2007 add-in. Depending on the features of your solution, you will have to create certain registry keys for your add-in (and form regions, if applicable) to load successfully. You also must ensure that certain prerequisites, such as the Microsoft .NET Framework version 2.0, have been installed before the user attempts to run your setup project. Finally, you must install required assemblies and other components into the application folder on a target computer. Although most of the setup requirements are handled for you by Visual Studio, there are numerous small details that you must attend to for your setup to complete successfully. This chapter covers the basic requirements for add-in setup and deployment. Once you have read this chapter, you should have an understanding of the following topics:

- An overview of setup and deployment
- Creating a setup project using Visual Studio 2005
- Writing required keys to the Windows registry
- Determining required components for your setup package

Creating a Setup Project

Depending on how you create your add-in, the setup project might be created for you. The following types of add-in projects create a setup project automatically:

- Shared Add-ins
- Microsoft Visual Studio 2005 Tools for the 2007 Microsoft Office System (VSTO) add-ins

The following type of add-in project does not create a setup project automatically:

- Add-ins created with the Outlook add-in template supplied with this book

If you use either the Shared Add-in template or VSTO to create your add-in project, all the details of registering your add-in will be handled by Visual Studio. In general, you should avoid using the Shared Add-in template for your add-in unless you plan to shim the add-in with the Component Object Model (COM) Shim Wizard.

If you use the Outlook Add-in Templates that accompany this book to create your add-in, you will have to create a separate Visual Studio setup project and add that setup project to your solution. Assuming that you also add a COM shim to your add-in project to provide application domain isolation, the COM Shim Wizard handles the COM registration of the shim. You can download the COM Shim Wizard from MSDN or use the link provided on the Web site that accompanies this book. For additional details on creating a setup project for an add-in created with the Outlook Add-in Template and the language of your choice, see the section "Creating a Setup Project" in Chapter 3, "Writing Your First Outlook Add-in Using Visual Basic .NET," or in Chapter 4, "Writing Your First Outlook Add-in Using C#."

Writing Required Keys to the Windows Registry

Certain keys and entry and value pairs must be written to the Windows registry for your add-in to function correctly. The following sections discuss the location of registry entries and the required entry and value pairs.

Installing to HKEY_CURRENT_USER

Installing to HKEY_CURRENT_USER (HKCU) is the preferred method of writing registry keys for an Outlook add-in. Add-ins installed to HKCU are visible in the COM Add-Ins dialog box, which is accessed through the Outlook Trust Center dialog box on the Add-Ins tab. To display the Trust Center dialog box, on the Tools menu in an Outlook Explorer window, select Trust Center.

Installing to HKEY_LOCAL_MACHINE

For the Microsoft 2007 Office system, installation to HKEY_LOCAL_MACHINE (HKLM) is not recommended. Unlike previous versions of Office, an add-in installed to HKLM is visible in the COM Add-Ins dialog box. Because the add-in is visible in the COM Add-Ins dialog box, the user can disconnect the add-in if the COM Add-Ins dialog box has not been disabled through policy and the user has administrative privileges on the machine. Finally, the 2007 Office system will not load a VSTO add-in that has been registered under HKLM. VSTO add-ins can only be loaded from HKCU.

Registry Keys Required for an Add-In

The registry keys required for an add-in depend on whether you use VSTO, the Shared Add-in template, or the Outlook Add-in Templates that accompany this book to create the add-in.

Add-ins that are created using VSTO require a set of registry entries on each computer that runs the add-in. These registry entries point to the location of the application manifest and provide additional information about the add-in. Add-ins that are not created with VSTO do not require a manifest entry, for example, for the add-in to load. In either case, there is a certain minimum set of registry entries that are required for an Outlook add-in.

Table 18-1 lists the required and optional registry entries and values for an Outlook add-in. All registry keys must be created under the following registry key:

HKEY_CURRENT_USER\Software\Microsoft\Office\Outlook\Addins\<ProgID>

The text *<ProgID>* represents a unique programmatic identifier (*ProgID*) for your add-in. Typically, *ProgID* represents the assembly name of the add-in or the *ProgID* attribute of your COM-visible assembly. Note that there are additional registry keys and entries required to register your add-in assembly for COM. These keys, typically listed under HKEY_CLASSES_ROOT or HKEY_CURRENT_USER\Software\Classes, are not represented in this table.

Table 18-1   Required Registry Keys for an Outlook Add-In

Entry	Type	Value
CommandLineSafe	REG_DWORD	Optional. Indicates whether the add-in is safe for operations that do not support a user interface. A value of 1 indicates the add-in is command-line safe, whereas a value of 0 (the default) indicates that it is not command-line safe.
Description	REG_SZ	Required. A brief description of the add-in. In add-ins for the 2007 Microsoft Office system, this description is displayed when the user selects the add-in on the Add-Ins tab of the Trust Center dialog box in Outlook.
FriendlyName	REG_SZ	Required. The friendly name of the add-in that is displayed in the COM Add-Ins dialog box. The friendly name is also displayed when the user selects the add-in on the Add-Ins tab of the Trust Center dialog box.
LoadBehavior	REG_DWORD	Required. A value that determines when the add-in is loaded. This value should be set to 3, which specifies that the add-in is loaded at startup. For additional supported values of *LoadBehavior*, see Table 18-2.
Manifest	REG_SZ	Optional. The full path of the application manifest for the add-in. This must be a local path on the client computer. The *Manifest* key is only required for add-ins created with VSTO.

The DWORD value in the *LoadBehavior* entry controls how Outlook loads the add-in. The typical setting is to load the add-in at startup, which corresponds to a DWORD value of 0x03. Table 18-2 lists valid *LoadBehavior* settings.

Table 18-2   Valid *LoadBehavior* Settings

Initial *Load-Behavior* setting	*LoadBehavior* DWORD	Behavior description
None	0x00 (Disconnected) or 0x01 (Connected)	The COM add-in is not loaded when Outlook boots. It can be loaded in the COM Add-Ins dialog box or by setting the *Connect* property of the corresponding *COMAddin* object.

Table 18-2   Valid *LoadBehavior* Settings

Initial *Load-Behavior* setting	*LoadBehavior* DWORD	Behavior description
Startup	0x02 (Disconnected) or 0x03 (Connected)	The add-in is loaded when Outlook boots. Once the add-in is loaded, it remains loaded until it is explicitly unloaded.
Load On Demand	0x08 (Disconnected) or 0x09 (Connected)	The add-in is not loaded until the user clicks the button or menu item that loads the add-in, or until a procedure sets its *Connect* property to *True*. In most cases, you won't set the initial load behavior to Load On Demand directly; you'll set it to Load At Next Startup Only, and it will automatically be set to Load On Demand on subsequent boots of Outlook.
Load At Next Startup Only	0x10 (Reverts to 0x09 on next boot)	After the COM add-in has been registered, it loads as soon as the user runs Outlook for the first time, and it creates a button or menu item for itself. The next time the user boots Outlook, the add-in is loaded on demand; that is, it doesn't load until the user clicks the button or menu item associated with the add-in.

Registry Keys Required for a Form Region

If your add-in implements a form region, you must ensure that your setup project writes the correct keys to the registry. Form region registry keys can be written to HKCU or HKLM. Writing form region registry keys to HKCU is recommended. Writing registry keys for a form region is covered in the section "Registering a Form Region" in Chapter 13, "Creating Form Regions."

Required Installation Components

The following section discusses required installation components for an Outlook add-in built with Visual Studio 2005. Additional components are required if you build your add-in with VSTO.

.NET Framework Version 2.0

If you have created a managed add-in using Visual Studio 2005, target computers must have the Microsoft .NET Framework version 2.0 installed before your add-in setup package runs. If the .NET Framework is not installed, the installer for your setup will fail.

To obtain the .NET Framework 2.0 redistributable package, follow these steps:

1. Download the most recent version of Dotnetfx.exe from the MSDN Download Center or the Microsoft Windows Update Web site.

2. If you need to direct users to the Internet to install the .NET Framework, do not post Dotnetfx.exe. Instead, direct users to the Microsoft Windows Update Web site.

3. If you download the Microsoft .NET Redistributable Package from MSDN, you receive a file named Dotnetredist.exe. This file contains Dotnetfx.exe. To extract Dotnetfx.exe, double-click Dotnetredist.exe. You will be prompted to save the extracted file on your computer. The extracted file is Dotnetfx.exe. Use Dotnetfx.exe for deployment purposes.

There are several options to install the .NET Framework 2.0 on a target computer. You should understand that .NET Framework 2.0 must specifically be installed.

The following options are available for installation of Dotnetfx.exe:

■ Distribute Dotnetfx.exe using an electronic software distribution tool such as Microsoft Systems Management Server or Microsoft Active Directory. See the topic "Distributing Dotnetfx.exe Using an Electronic Software Distribution Tool" in the Visual Studio 2005 documentation.

■ Install Dotnetfx.exe from a network share or an intranet site. See the topic "Manually Installing Dotnetfx.exe from a Share or Web Site" in the Visual Studio 2005 documentation.

■ Create a single setup project to install Dotnetfx.exe and your managed add-in. This approach installs Dotnetfx.exe if required and then installs the assemblies and other required files for your add-in. See the topic "Creating a Single Setup Project to Install a .NET Framework Application and Dotnetfx.exe" in the Visual Studio 2005 documentation.

If you use Visual Studio 2005 to create your setup project, you can have the installation project automatically check for the .NET Framework 2.0 and download it from Microsoft automatically if the component is not already installed. To enable the setup project to check for and download the .NET Framework 2.0, follow these steps:

1. Right-click the setup project in your project solution, and then select Properties.

2. In the Property Pages dialog box, select the Build page, and then click Prerequisites.

3. Select the Create Setup Program To Install Prerequisite Components check box.

4. In the Prerequisites To Install list, select .NET Framework 2.0.

5. Select Download Prerequisites From The Component Vendor's Web Site.

6. Click OK twice to return to the project.

Visual Studio Tools for Office Runtime

You are required to install the Visual Studio Tools for Office runtime only if you have created a VSTO add-in. The VSTO runtime is available for download from the MSDN Download Center. You must install the .NET Framework version 2.0 before you install the VSTO runtime.

> **Note**   The user must be an Administrator on the target computer to install the .NET Framework version 2.0 or the VSTO runtime.

Primary Interop Assemblies

For the 2007 Office system, Primary Interop Assemblies (PIAs) are redistributable. You can download the redistributable package (PrimaryInteropAssembly.exe) for the 2007 Office system PIAs from the MSDN Download Center. Once you have extracted the package to your hard disk, the redistributable installer (O2007pia.msi) is placed in a local folder. You can then wrap the O2007pia.msi in another setup package through Visual Studio or another Windows Installer-aware setup editor. By using the PIA redistributable, you ensure that all the required PIAs are available on the target machine. You do not have to depend on whether the .NET Programmability Support feature is configured to run from My Computer in the 2007 Office system setup.

The following assemblies are installed by the PIA redistributable:

- ADODB
- DAO
- extensibility
- ipdmctrl
- Microsoft.mshtml
- Microsoft.Office.InfoPath.Permission
- Microsoft.Office.Interop.Access
- Microsoft.Office.interop.access.dao
- Microsoft.Office.Interop.Excel
- Microsoft.Office.Interop.Graph
- Microsoft.Office.Interop.InfoPath
- Microsoft.Office.Interop.InfoPath.SemiTrust
- Microsoft.Office.Interop.InfoPath.Xml
- Microsoft.Office.Interop.MSProject
- Microsoft.Office.Interop.OneNote
- Microsoft.Office.Interop.Outlook
- Microsoft.Office.Interop.OutlookViewCtl
- Microsoft.Office.Interop.PowerPoint
- Microsoft.Office.Interop.Publisher
- Microsoft.Office.Interop.SharePointDesigner
- Microsoft.Office.Interop.SharePointDesignerPage

- Microsoft.Office.Interop.SmartTag

- Microsoft.Office.Interop.Visio

- Microsoft.Office.Interop.Visio.SaveAsWeb

- Microsoft.Office.Interop.VisOcx

- Microsoft.Office.Interop.Word

- Microsoft.stdformat

- Microsoft.Vbe.Interop

- Microsoft.Vbe.Interop.Forms

- MSCOMCTL

- msdatasrc

- OFFICE

- stdole

- Policy.11.0.Microsoft.Office.Interop.Access

- Policy.11.0.Microsoft.Office.Interop.Excel

- Policy.11.0.Microsoft.Office.Interop.Graph

- Policy.11.0.Microsoft.Office.Interop.InfoPath

- Policy.11.0.Microsoft.Office.Interop.InfoPath.Xml

- Policy.11.0.Microsoft.Office.Interop.MSProject

- Policy.11.0.Microsoft.Office.Interop.Outlook

- Policy.11.0.Microsoft.Office.Interop.OutlookViewCtl

- Policy.11.0.Microsoft.Office.Interop.PowerPoint

- Policy.11.0.Microsoft.Office.Interop.Publisher

- Policy.11.0.Microsoft.Office.Interop.SmartTag

- Policy.11.0.Microsoft.Office.Interop.Visio

- Policy.11.0.Microsoft.Office.Interop.Visio.SaveAsWeb

- Policy.11.0.Microsoft.Office.Interop.VisOcx

- Policy.11.0.Microsoft.Office.Interop.Word

- Policy.11.0.Microsoft.Vbe.Interop

- Policy.11.0.Office

Add-in Assembly and Other Required Components

You also need to ensure that the assembly for your add-in and any other required components are installed to the application folder for your solution. Typically, you install the assembly and other required components to the [*ProductName*] folder under the [*Manufacturer*] folder in the Program Files folder. You control the location of your application folder in the File System Editor window for your setup project.

If you have developed your add-in using VSTO, the manifest for your assembly will also be installed to the application folder. VSTO handles this requirement for you by adding the manifest and the add-in assembly as components of the primary output for the add-in project. A VSTO setup project installs both the add-in assembly and the add-in manifest to the application folder.

Using a COM Shim

If you are using the COM Shim Wizard to add a COM shim to your project, you must ensure that the output of the COM shim has been added to your setup project. The COM shim should reside in the same application folder as your managed add-in assembly. See Chapter 3 or Chapter 4 (depending on whether you use Visual Basic or C# to create your add-in) for additional instructions on creating the COM shim and adding it to your setup project.

When you run the COM Shim Wizard, you are prompted for the FriendlyName and Description of your add-in. The COM Shim Wizard creates the necessary registry entries in ConnectProxy.rgs to ensure that Outlook loads your add-in. If you need to modify the registry entries created by the COM Shim Wizard, you can edit the registry entries in ConnectProxy.rgs, which is located in your COM Shim project.

If you have added the output for the COM shim dynamic link library (DLL) to your setup project, you should make the COM shim self-registering. To ensure that the COM shim self-registers, click the *Register* property in the Properties window for the COM shim output, and select vsdrpCOMSelfReg in the drop-down list box.

Writing Custom Actions

If you are writing a VSTO add-in, you must grant full trust to the assemblies in the application folder. If you are writing an add-in that implements form regions and your setup creates subfolders of the application folder, you must also grant full trust to the subfolders of the application folder in the security policy of each user or computer. By default, your VSTO add-in will not load unless full trust has been granted explicitly. Only explicit changes made to the .NET security policy enable managed code extensions to execute. Typically, you write a custom action for your setup package to grant full trust to the appropriate folders.

> **More Info**   For a complete discussion of security for VSTO add-ins, including a sample custom action, see the article "Deploying Visual Studio 2005 Tools for Office Solutions Using Windows Installer" (a two-part article) on MSDN.

Deploying to Users Who Are Not Administrators

In the Microsoft Windows environments that support the 2007 Microsoft Office system, default users have limited access to system areas of the computer. Limited access is especially a concern on Microsoft Windows Vista, where a user can be an administrator on a computer but still does not run with elevated privileges. Because your setup program writes to system areas of the operating system and the Windows registry, a user must have administrative rights on the local computer to install your solution.

To install your add-in on computers where users lack administrative rights, you must run Setup in a context that provides it with administrative rights.

In organizations where users are not the administrators of their computers, there are three methods of providing your solution setup with the appropriate rights:

- Log on to the computer as an administrator, and install the solution.
- Assign your solution to the computer using Group Policy Software Deployment.
- Use a software management tool such as Systems Management Server in an administrative context.
- On Vista, log on to the computer as an administrator when prompted for credentials after launching the installation package.

Summary

Setup and deployment help to deliver your solution to a customer's computer. Although most of the details of setup are handled for you by VSTO or the Shared Add-in Wizard, using the COM shim requires that you follow extra steps to ensure that your setup package installs the correct components on a target computer. If you follow the guidelines set forth in this chapter, your add-in will be deployed successfully to your customers.

Chapter 19
Trust and Security

This chapter covers how Microsoft Office Outlook 2007 handles security for the object model and other application programming interfaces (APIs) provided by Outlook. If you are not familiar with the Outlook object model guard, you learn how Outlook enforces code and attachment security. This chapter helps you understand which methods and properties are protected by the guard and how you can write a trusted add-in that does not display security prompts to the user. You also learn how administrator policy can trust add-ins in a locked-down environment and how to control code security settings via policy. Specifically, this chapter discusses the following:

- What is the Outlook object model guard?

- More about code security in Outlook

- Code security changes made in Outlook 2007

- Protected object model methods and properties and what happens when you access those members in your code

- Implications of the Component Object Model (COM) add-in trust model for managed add-in developers

- How to write a trusted add-in

- How to administratively control the object model guard

Code Security for Outlook 2007

To prevent malicious programs and viruses from propagating through e-mail messages, later versions of Outlook have included the object model guard to help protect against malicious use of the Outlook object model. Outlook solutions that access these protected properties and methods in the object model might invoke security warnings that the user must respond to before the solution can continue. Outlook 2007 introduces several changes to the behavior of the object model guard to improve the developer and user experience while helping to keep Outlook secure.

The preferred method for extending and automating Outlook is through a trusted Outlook add-in. Out of the box, Outlook considers all add-ins trusted and does not display security prompts if the add-in is properly written. This behavior can be overridden by an administrator using Group Policy to adjust the security settings and provide a list of explicitly trusted add-ins.

The object model guard in Outlook 2007 takes advantage of the status of antivirus software installed on a computer to avoid burdening the user with unnecessary prompts. This change represents a departure from the way the object model guard worked in previous versions. If Outlook is able to detect that antivirus software is running on the computer with an acceptable status, Outlook disables security warnings for the user. This allows external applications that previously needed to use Extended Messaging Application Programming Interface (MAPI) or third-party libraries to avoid security prompts to use the object model directly if the user is known to be running antivirus software. This new behavior helps keep Outlook secure without overwhelming the user with excessive warning messages. Solutions that use simple MAPI to automate Outlook will continue to show security prompts according to the security policy applied to the machine, regardless of the state of antivirus software.

All out-of-process COM callers and add-ins run without security prompts if all of the following conditions are true:

■ The client computer is running Microsoft Windows XP Service Pack 2 (SP2) or Microsoft Windows Vista.

■ The antivirus software installed on the client computer is designed for Windows XP SP2 or Windows Vista.

■ The Windows Security Center (WSC) indicates that antivirus software on the computer is in a "Good" health status. If the computer is joined to a domain, the health-status indicator might not be visible, but it is still maintained.

■ Outlook 2007 is configured on the client computer in one of the following ways:

  ❑ Uses the default security settings

  ❑ Uses security settings defined by Group Policy and set to warn when antivirus software is inactive or out of date

  ❑ Uses security settings defined by Group Policy but does not have a programmatic access policy applied

Additionally, Outlook 2007 suppresses security warnings when it is configured to Never Warn Me About Suspicious Activity (Not Recommended) through the Outlook Trust Center or via Group Policy. Using this setting in Outlook effectively disables the object model guard for COM add-ins and out-of-process callers, but it can be a security risk if other protection measures are not in place.

Administrators can use the Trust Center in Outlook 2007 to manually adjust the policy applied to Outlook's object model guard as well, using the Programmatic Access tab of the Trust Center. The selected value is used for all users of the computer, not just the currently logged-in user. You must be running as an Administrator to change these settings; otherwise, they appear to be disabled. Figure 19-1 shows an example of this page.

The Programmatic Access tab also displays the current antivirus status as detected by Outlook. If the status is displayed as Valid, Outlook does not show security prompts if the Warn Me About Suspicious Activity When My Antivirus Software Is Inactive Or Out-Of-Date (Recommended) option is selected.

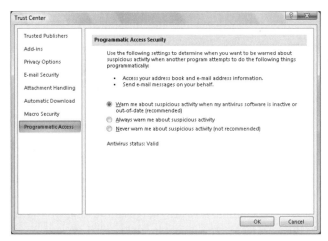

Figure 19-1   Programmatic Access settings in the Outlook 2007 Trust Center.

To detect the status of the antivirus software on client computers, Outlook 2007 depends on the Windows Security Center (WSC). Currently, antivirus products that are compatible with Windows XP SP2 and Windows Vista register status information with the WSC to indicate if they are running and up to date. Outlook first checks for the current status of antivirus software by querying the WSC. Microsoft Windows Server 2003 does not provide a WSC; therefore, Outlook is unable to detect the status of antivirus software and does not disable security prompts except under policy settings.

For Outlook 2007 to disable security prompts, the antivirus software must report the following three conditions to the WSC:

■   Software is installed and registered with the WSC.

■   Software is up to date.

■   On access (or real-time) virus scanning is enabled.

Outlook 2007 examines all of the antivirus products that are installed and registered with the WSC. If at least one of those products meets the previous three conditions, Outlook turns off the object model security prompts. Over each session of Outlook, the status of antivirus software is continually monitored. At any point, if no antivirus product on the computer meets all three conditions, Outlook enables the security prompts again. Later, if an installed antivirus product returns to meeting all three conditions, Outlook disables the prompts again.

This new behavior applies to all programs that access Outlook 2007 through the Outlook object model. These include add-ins and external COM callers. Programs that access Outlook data through other APIs (for example, Collaboration Data Objects, Exchange Client Extensions, or simple MAPI) are not affected by this change. Solutions using Extended MAPI are not restricted by the object model guard.

Guard Principles

The object model guard originated through a security update known as the Outlook E-Mail Security Update for Outlook 98 and Outlook 2000. Since then, all shipping versions of Outlook have included the object model guard. The guard was introduced in response to damage wrought by e-mail viruses like Melissa and ILoveYou. Since the original introduction, Windows and Office have become more secure, and the guard now acts as a defense-in-depth measure to protect against viruses instead of a front-line defense.

Although Outlook 2007 defines new circumstances for untrusted callers to invoke security warnings, it inherits the set of protected objects and members from the Outlook 2003 object model guard. In addition, Outlook 2007 displays warnings for code that attempts to access several new members added to the object model. Outlook raises warnings in five major scenarios, when untrusted code attempts to use the object model to retrieve data or execute certain methods:

- Properties or methods that return address objects, including properties and members of these objects:
  - *AddressEntry* and *AddressEntries*
  - *Recipient* and *Recipients*
  - *ExchangeDistributionList* and *ExchangeUser*
  - *SelectNamesDialog*
  - *PropertyAccessor*

- Properties of various objects that might contain addresses or address information, such as:
  - *Alias*
  - *Address*
  - *Body* and *HTMLBody*
  - *ID*
  - *WordEditor*

- Methods that allow writing items to a storage location outside of Outlook, such as:
  - *Item.SaveAs*
  - *CalendarSharing.SaveAsICal*

- Entry points that provide access to properties using explicit, built-in property names or references to namespaces, such as:
  - *UserProperties.Find*
  - *ItemProperties.Item("IMAddress")* and other protected properties
  - *Table.Columns.Add*

  ❏ *PropertyAccessor.GetProperties*

  ❏ *PropertyAccessor.GetProperty*

■ Programmatic sending of an item:

  ❏ *Item.Allow* and *Item.Send*

  ❏ *Action.Execute*

Security Warning Types

The object model guard in all versions of Outlook consists of three different prompt messages. These messages are displayed based on the action the untrusted code is attempting to execute. For Outlook 2007, the prompt dialog boxes were updated to make them easier to understand and to show a consistent security user interface (UI) with Windows XP and Windows Vista.

Address Book Warning

The address book warning is the most common prompt a user sees when an untrusted program is accessing Outlook data. This prompt appears for members whose prompt type is Address Book in the Protected Members List discussed later in this chapter. Generally, however, this prompt appears for any programmatic access of recipient data in Outlook.

This warning, shown in Figure 19-2, enables the user to allow or deny the action the untrusted program is attempting. The user can also choose to allow access to this call and subsequent calls for all solutions for a period of time indicated by the Allow Access For drop-down list box. The time values in the dialog box cannot be changed via policy or other means.

Figure 19-2   Outlook 2007 address book access warning dialog box.

If the user clicks Deny, Outlook immediately blocks the call that invoked the warning and returns *MAPI_E_NOT_SUPPORTED* as an error code for the call. Outlook does not return any data for the call. If the program making the call does not handle the error properly, it can crash or cause Outlook to crash. As a developer, you should expect that any call to a member in the Protected Members List might throw an exception, and you should handle these exceptions accordingly.

If the user clicks Allow without selecting the Allow Access For check box, only the call that generated the warning will be allowed. Because of the way the object model protects all levels of the object model and not just entry points to protected data, a single line of code can generate multiple warning prompts. Take this code snippet, for example, which attempts to print the name of the first address entry in the first address list in the current Outlook session:

```
Application.Session.AddressLists[1].AddressEntries[1].Name
```

This statement actually generated three separate security prompt dialog boxes: one prompt for accessing a specific address list from the *AddressLists* collection, one for accessing the *AddressEntries* collection on the *AddressList* object, and another for accessing a specific *AddressEntry* object from the collection. If you were accessing multiple properties from the *AddressEntry* object, it would be better to hold a reference to the specific object so that the user wouldn't potentially see three prompts for each member you accessed, and would only see those prompts once.

If the user clicks Allow after selecting the Allow Access For check box, the call that generated the prompt, as well as future calls, will be allowed for the duration that the user has selected. During this time period, all callers to the object model—not just the program that originally invoked the security warning—are approved for address book access. After this time period expires, the security warnings will reappear when a program attempts to access a blocked property.

Send Message Warning

The send message warning is invoked when an untrusted solution attempts to send an item programmatically. This prompt appears for members whose prompt type is Sending Mail in the Protected Members List discussed later in this chapter. This dialog box, shown in Figure 19-3, has a built-in timer that prevents untrusted add-ins from sending messages rapidly and automatically. The user must wait 5 seconds before clicking Allow.

Figure 19-3   Outlook 2007 e-mail send message warning dialog box.

If the user clicks Deny, Outlook blocks the call that invoked the warning and returns the *MAPI_E_NOT_SUPPORTED* error. Subsequent calls to send messages programmatically will invoke the dialog box again. Your program should be written to handle this error code and respond accordingly.

If the user clicks Allow, the call that invoked the warning, and only that call, is allowed to proceed. Subsequent calls from the same solution or other untrusted solutions to send messages programmatically will continue to generate warnings.

Execute Actions Warning

The execute actions warning is invoked when an untrusted solution executes a custom action from the *Actions* collection on an item. This prompt, shown in Figure 19-4, appears for members whose prompt type is Custom Action in the Protected Members List discussed later in this chapter. Outlook displays a message similar to the send message warning, indicating that an action is being executed that might result in an e-mail being sent. The user must wait five seconds before he or she can click Allow to execute the action.

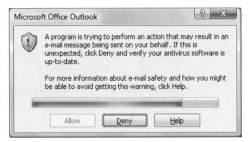

Figure 19-4   Outlook 2007 execute actions warning dialog box.

If the user clicks Deny, Outlook blocks the call to the method that generated the prompt and returns the *MAPI_E_NOT_SUPPORTED* error. Your code should handle this error code and respond accordingly.

If the user clicks Allow, the call that invoked the warning, and only that call, is allowed. Subsequent calls from the same solution or other untrusted solutions will invoke the warning dialog box again.

Detecting Trusted State

In Outlook 2007, a new member has been added to the *Application* object that enables an add-in to determine if Outlook considers the *Application* instance to be trusted. Add-ins can query the value of this property and evaluate whether or not the application will generate security dialog boxes when it attempts to access a trusted member of the object model. The following sample code illustrates how this works:

```
private void IsApplicationTrusted()
{
    bool isTrusted = Application.IsTrusted;
    if (isTrusted)
    {
        MessageBox.Show("Object is trusted and will not prompt.");
    }
    else
    {
        MessageBox.Show("Object is not trusted and may prompt.");
    }
}
```

Although this method can be beneficial for an add-in to determine if it will not display prompts, there are other mitigating factors that determine if object model guard prompts will be displayed or not. For example, only trusted add-ins will ever have the *IsTrusted* property return *True*. Out-of-process callers and untrusted add-ins will always see *False* for the property value. However, if the object model guard has been disabled or administrator policy has disabled certain prompts, the prompts will not appear, even though *IsTrusted* will return *False*.

Trapping Errors

If you make a call to a restricted object model property or method and the object model guard is active, Outlook displays the appropriate warning prompt. If the user cancels the restricted object model call by clicking Deny in the dialog box, your code will raise an exception that you should catch. In managed code, the exception will be thrown as a *System.Runtime.InteropServices.COMException* with an error code of -2147467260. It is worth noting that this is a generic exception that does not map directly to the error you would see in a native code add-in.

To trap the error, you need to wrap code that can generate the error in a *try-catch* block and handle the error appropriately. In this example, a message box is displayed if the user clicks Deny on the prompt that indicates the operation was not successful:

```
private void TrapGuardError()
{
    Outlook.AddressList firstList;
    try
    {
        // Do something that generates a prompt
        firstList = Application.Session.AddressLists[1];
    }
    catch (COMException ex)
    {
        if (ex.ErrorCode == -2147467260)
        {
            MessageBox.Show("Could not access data from Outlook.  " +
                "You may have canceled the operation in Outlook.");
        }
    }
}
```

Restricted Properties and Methods

Table 19-1 lists the properties and methods that cause the object model guard warning to display in Outlook 2007, subject to the conditions outlined in the section "Guard Principles" earlier in this chapter. Rows in the table where the member value is Everything indicate that all properties specific to that object are protected. Everything does not include properties available on all objects, like *Application*, *Class*, *Parent*, and *Session*.

Table 19-1   Listing of Properties and Methods Protected by the Object Model Guard

Object/Interface	Member	Prompt type
Account	SmtpAddress	Address Book
Action	Execute()	Custom Action
AddressEntries	GetFirst()	Address Book
AddressEntries	GetLast()	Address Book
AddressEntries	GetNext()	Address Book
AddressEntries	GetPrevious()	Address Book
AddressEntries	Add()	Address Book
AddressEntries	Item()	Address Book
AddressEntry	Address	Address Book
AddressEntry	ID	Address Book
AddressEntry	Manager	Address Book
AddressEntry	Members	Address Book
AddressEntry	Parent	Address Book
AddressEntry	GetExchangeDistributionList()	Address Book
AddressEntry	GetExchangeUser()	Address Book
AddressEntry	Update()	Address Book
AddressEntry	PropertyAccessor	Address Book
AddressLists	Item()	Address Book
AddressList	PropertyAccessor	Address Book
AddressList	AddressEntries	Address Book
AddressList	ID	Address Book
AppointmentItem	Body	Address Book
AppointmentItem	NetMeetingOrganizerAlias	Address Book
AppointmentItem	OptionalAttendees	Address Book
AppointmentItem	Organizer	Address Book
AppointmentItem	PropertyAccessor	Address Book
AppointmentItem	RequiredAttendees	Address Book
AppointmentItem	Resources	Address Book
AppointmentItem	Respond()	Sending Mail
AppointmentItem	SaveAs()	Address Book
Attachment	PropertyAccessor	Address Book
CalendarSharing	SaveAsICal()	Address Book
Columns	Add()	Address Book
ContactItem	Body	Address Book
ContactItem	Email1Address	Address Book
ContactItem	Email1AddressType	Address Book
ContactItem	Email1DisplayName	Address Book
ContactItem	Email1EntryID	Address Book

Table 19-1 Listing of Properties and Methods Protected by the Object Model Guard

Object/Interface	Member	Prompt type
ContactItem	Email2Address	Address Book
ContactItem	Email2AddressType	Address Book
ContactItem	Email2DisplayName	Address Book
ContactItem	Email2EntryID	Address Book
ContactItem	Email3Address	Address Book
ContactItem	Email3AddressType	Address Book
ContactItem	Email3DisplayName	Address Book
ContactItem	Email3EntryID	Address Book
ContactItem	IMAddress	Address Book
ContactItem	NetMeetingAlias	Address Book
ContactItem	PropertyAccessor	Address Book
ContactItem	ReferredBy	Address Book
ContactItem	SaveAs()	Address Book
DistListItem	Body	Address Book
DistListItem	GetMember()	Address Book
DistListItem	PropertyAccessor	Address Book
DistListItem	SaveAs()	Address Book
DocumentItem	Body	Address Book
DocumentItem	PropertyAccessor	Address Book
ExchangeDistributionList	Address	Address Book
ExchangeDistributionList	Alias	Address Book
ExchangeDistributionList	GetExchangeDistributionList()	Address Book
ExchangeDistributionList	GetExchangeUser()	Address Book
ExchangeDistributionList	GetMemberOfList()	Address Book
ExchangeDistributionList	GetExchangeDistributionListMembers()	Address Book
ExchangeDistributionList	GetOwners()	Address Book
ExchangeDistributionList	ID	Address Book
ExchangeDistributionList	Parent	Address Book
ExchangeDistributionList	PrimarySmtpAddress	Address Book
ExchangeDistributionList	PropertyAccessor	Address Book
ExchangeDistributionList	Update()	Address Book
ExchangeUser	Address	Address Book
ExchangeUser	Alias	Address Book
ExchangeUser	GetDirectReports()	Address Book
ExchangeUser	GetExchangeDistributionList()	Address Book
ExchangeUser	GetExchangeUser()	Address Book
ExchangeUser	GetExchangeUserManager()	Address Book
ExchangeUser	GetMemberOfList()	Address Book

Table 19-1   Listing of Properties and Methods Protected by the Object Model Guard

Object/Interface	Member	Prompt type
ExchangeUser	ID	Address Book
ExchangeUser	Parent	Address Book
ExchangeUser	PrimarySmtpAddress	Address Book
ExchangeUser	PropertyAccessor	Address Book
ExchangeUser	Update()	Address Book
Folder	GetCalendarExporter()	Address Book
Folder	PropertyAccessor	Address Book
Inspector	HTMLEditor	Address Book
Inspector	WordEditor	Address Book
ItemProperties	Any protected property for an item	Address Book
JournalItem	Body	Address Book
JournalItem	ContactNames	Address Book
JournalItem	PropertyAccessor	Address Book
JournalItem	SaveAs()	Address Book
MailItem	Bcc	Address Book
MailItem	Body	Address Book
MailItem	Cc	Address Book
MailItem	HTMLBody	Address Book
MailItem	PropertyAccessor	Address Book
MailItem	ReceivedByName	Address Book
MailItem	ReceivedOnBehalfOfName	Address Book
MailItem	Recipients	Address Book
MailItem	ReplyRecipientNames	Address Book
MailItem	SaveAs()	Address Book
MailItem	Send()	Sending Mail
MailItem	SenderEmailAddress	Address Book
MailItem	SenderEmailType	Address Book
MailItem	SenderName	Address Book
MailItem	SendOnBehalfOfName	Address Book
MailItem	To	Address Book
MeetingItem	Body	Address Book
MeetingItem	PropertyAccessor	Address Book
MeetingItem	SaveAs()	Address Book
MeetingItem	SenderName	Address Book
MeetingItem	Recipients	Address Book
NameSpace	CurrentUser	Address Book
NameSpace	GetAddressEntryFromID()	Address Book
NameSpace	GetRecipientFromID()	Address Book

Table 19-1   Listing of Properties and Methods Protected by the Object Model Guard

Object/Interface	Member	Prompt type
NameSpace	SelectNamesDialog	Address Book
NoteItem	Body	Address Book
NoteItem	PropertyAccessor	Address Book
PostItem	Body	Address Book
PostItem	HTMLBody	Address Book
PostItem	PropertyAccessor	Address Book
PostItem	SaveAs()	Address Book
PostItem	SenderName	Address Book
Recipient	Everything	Address Book
Recipient	PropertyAccessor	Address Book
Recipients	Everything	Address Book
RemoteItem	Body	Address Book
RemoteItem	PropertyAccessor	Address Book
ReportItem	Body	Address Book
ReportItem	PropertyAccessor	Address Book
SelectNamesDialog	Recipients	Address Book
SharingItem	Allow()	Sending Mail
SharingItem	Bcc	Address Book
SharingItem	Body	Address Book
SharingItem	Cc	Address Book
SharingItem	HTMLBody	Address Book
SharingItem	PropertyAccessor	Address Book
SharingItem	ReceivedByName	Address Book
SharingItem	ReceivedOnBehalfOfName	Address Book
SharingItem	ReplyRecipientNames	Address Book
SharingItem	SaveAs()	Address Book
SharingItem	Send()	Sending Mail
SharingItem	SenderEmailAddress	Address Book
SharingItem	SenderEmailType	Address Book
SharingItem	SenderName	Address Book
SharingItem	SendOnBehalfOfName	Address Book
SharingItem	To	Address Book
StorageItem	Body	Address Book
StorageItem	PropertyAccessor	Address Book
Store	PropertyAccessor	Address Book
TaskItem	Body	Address Book
TaskItem	ContactNames	Address Book
TaskItem	Contacts	Address Book

Table 19-1   Listing of Properties and Methods Protected by the Object Model Guard

Object/Interface	Member	Prompt type
TaskItem	Delegator	Address Book
TaskItem	Owner	Address Book
TaskItem	SaveAs()	Address Book
TaskItem	Send()	Sending Mail
TaskItem	StatusOnCompletionRecipients	Address Book
TaskItem	StatusUpdateRecipients	Address Book
TaskItem	PropertyAccessor	Address Book
TaskRequestItem	Body	Address Book
TaskRequestItem	PropertyAccessor	Address Book
TaskRequestAcceptItem	Body	Address Book
TaskRequestAcceptItem	PropertyAccessor	Address Book
TaskRequestDeclineItem	Body	Address Book
TaskRequestDeclineItem	PropertyAccessor	Address Book
TaskRequestUpdateItem	Body	Address Book
TaskRequestUpdateItem	PropertyAccessor	Address Book
UserProperties	Find()	Address Book
UserProperty	Formula	Address Book

Trusting Managed Code

As a writer of a managed code add-in, there are a few additional hurdles you need to deal with to make sure your add-in can be trusted by an administrator in a controlled environment. This is because the object model guard and ability to trust an add-in dates to before managed code add-ins were possible. However, with a little extra work by the add-in developer, you can ensure that your add-in is trustable and administrator-friendly.

The steps required to make sure that your add-in can be trusted by the object model guard vary depending on the type of managed code add-in project you are using. If you are using a Microsoft Visual Studio 2005 Tools for the 2007 Microsoft Office System (VSTO) add-in, you do not need to do any additional work. The administrator just needs to add the add-in manifest to the trusted add-ins list, and the add-in will be trusted. If you are using the Shared Add-in templates from Microsoft Visual Studio or the templates provided on the Web site that accompanies this book, the steps are a little more elaborate.

Trustable Shared Add-Ins

The ability to trust an add-in and avoid receiving object model guard prompts is tied closely to a unique hash code generated for the add-in assembly or dynamic link library (DLL) that Outlook references when it loads an add-in. When writing a COM add-in, this is not a problem because Outlook directly references the COM add-in DLL and can properly validate that the add-in about to be loaded is the add-in that was authorized by an administrator.

However, due to the way managed code handles COM interop, Outlook only sees the Microsoft .NET Framework's shim, Mscoree.dll, when it looks for which DLL will be loaded for the add-in. If the administrator has added the managed code assembly to the trusted list, Outlook will be unable to match the file loaded to the add-in that was authorized, and the add-in will run untrusted. If instead the administrator chooses to trust Mscoree.dll, then all managed code add-ins registered on the system will be allowed to run trusted, which is likely an undesired mode of operation by the administrator.

To rectify this situation and ensure that an administrator can trust your managed code add-in without trusting every other managed code add-in, you need to develop a COM shim for your add-in project. This shim will effectively do the same thing that the .NET Framework file Mscoree.dll does, except that it will be specifically created for your add-in. Outlook will find the COM shim DLL, which can be trusted without trusting other managed code add-ins installed, and allow your add-in to run trusted without requiring other add-ins to be trusted as well.

Writing a COM shim is usually an exercise in C++ development and managed code interop, which isn't something most managed code developers want to deal with. However, Microsoft has provided a utility that plugs into Visual Studio and automatically generates a COM shim for managed code add-ins. The download for the COM Shim Wizard is also available on the book's companion Web site. With this utility, any managed code developer can produce a trustable managed code add-in while using the Shared Add-in template in Visual Studio. The sample add-ins that accompany this book use a COM shim to provide application domain (AppDomain) isolation. An application domain is an isolated environment where code within a process runs. In this case, the add-in is running in process with Outlook.exe. More information about the COM Shim Wizard and other benefits of using a shim are available on MSDN at *http://msdn.microsoft.com/library/en-us/dno2k3ta/html /ODC_Office_COM_Shim_Wizards.asp*.

Trust Center

The 2007 Microsoft Office system introduced a new user paradigm for Office trust settings—the Office Trust Center. The Trust Center provides a common location for users to find and manage all trust, privacy, and security settings. In Outlook 2007, the Trust Center is used to manage most of the available user settings for application add-ins and extensions and combines these settings in one location instead of scattered in Options dialog boxes across the product. To open the Trust Center, in an Explorer window, select Tools and then select Trust Center.

Managing Add-Ins

One of the features of the new Trust Center is that all applications and extensions can be managed from the Add-ins tab. On the Add-ins tab, a list of installed add-ins is provided along with information about the state of the add-in. This tab also provides the entry point to enable or disable a COM add-in or Exchange Client Extension and the ability to reenable a disabled extension.

Exchange Client Extensions are not displayed in the list of add-ins shown in the Trust Center. To see a list of installed Exchange Client Extensions, in the Manage list, select Exchange Client Extensions and then click Go. Extensions can be loaded or unloaded by toggling the check box next to the extension's name and then clicking OK.

To manage the connected state of a COM add-in, use the Manage drop-down list box to select COM Add-ins and then click Go. Outlook displays the COM Add-ins dialog box, which allows COM add-ins to be connected or disconnected. If the check box for the add-in is selected, the add-in is connected and running. An add-in without a selected check box is disconnected.

Add-ins can also be added to or removed from the list of COM add-ins from this dialog box. However, using the Remove feature in this dialog box does not automatically uninstall the add-in. Users should use an add-in's uninstall feature instead of removing the add-in using this dialog box. Figure 19-5 shows the add-in management interface in the Trust Center.

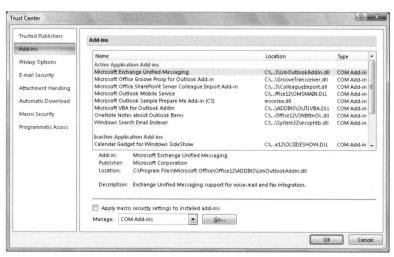

Figure 19-5   The Add-in tab of the Trust Center dialog box.

Macro Security

Outlook 2007 continues to use the same macro security levels that were used in previous versions of Outlook. Macro security operates independently of the object model guard and by default does not affect COM add-ins (although this can be changed by selecting the Apply Macro Security Settings To Installed Add-Ins check box on the Add-ins tab in the Trust Center). Figure 19-6 illustrates the Macro Security tab of the Trust Center.

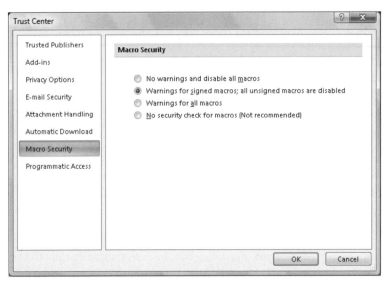

Figure 19-6   Macro Security tab of the Trust Center dialog box.

Macro security settings determine what verification is performed by Outlook on the VBA project file or the COM add-in when Outlook is loading the component. There are four security level options that can be selected by the user:

- **No Warnings And Disable All Macros**   When this option is selected, the user will not be able to use any macros from a VBA project file and will not see any warning indicating that macros are available.

- **Warnings For Signed Macros; All Unsigned Macros Are Disabled**   When this option is selected, Outlook displays a prompt indicating that a macro will be loaded and providing the user with the ability to disable the macro. If the macro is signed by an author who is not listed in the trusted publishers list, the user must add the publisher to the trusted list before the macro is allowed to run. The user must decide if the macro can run before Outlook starts.

- **Warnings For All Macros**   When running with this option selected, Outlook displays a prompt for all macros even if the macro does not contain a digital signature. The user must choose to enable or disable the macro before Outlook starts.

- **No Security Check For Macros (Not Recommended)**   When Outlook is configured with this option selected, all macros are allowed to run and the user is not prompted about the existence of the macros. This setting is not recommended because all macro code will be allowed to run without warning.

Programmatic Access

Outlook 2007 includes a new set of options that provide an administrator with the ability to alter the behavior of the object model guard directly. The Programmatic Access tab in the

Trust Center allows an administrator or user to select which mode the object model guard should use to operate Outlook. This tab also shows an indication of the antivirus status that Outlook uses by default to determine when to show object model guard prompts.

The three options that can be used for the object model guard are as follows:

- Warn Me About Suspicious Activity When My Antivirus Software Is Inactive Or Out-Of-Date (Recommended)

- Always Warn Me About Suspicious Activity

- Never Warn Me About Suspicious Activity (Not Recommended)

By default, Outlook 2007 is configured to use the first setting, which uses the information from antivirus software installed on the computer to determine when and if security prompts are necessary. To revert to the behavior used by previous versions of Outlook, a user with administrator permission can select the middle setting, Always Warn Me About Suspicious Activity. A third option allows the administrator to disable the object model guard altogether, and Outlook will never show object model guard prompts. Use of this last setting is not recommended.

These settings apply to all users on the computer, not just the currently logged-in user. These settings can only be changed when Outlook is running with the credentials of an Administrator on the computer. On Windows Vista, you might need to run Outlook with elevated privileges to be able to change these settings.

Administrative Options

In addition to the settings that are provided by default, administrators can use two methods in Outlook 2007 to lock down the object model guard settings and alter the default behavior.

One big change from previous versions of Outlook is the policy key that Outlook uses to determine the source of security configuration information. Previously Outlook would use the CheckAdminSettings policy key that was version-independent and not directly associated with the Outlook application. For Outlook 2007, this policy key has been changed to be more consistent with other Outlook security policies. Administrators will need to redeploy this new value when upgrading to the 2007 Microsoft Office system to ensure that Outlook 2007 clients continue to use any defined security policies.

Group Policy Security for COM Add-Ins

Outlook 2007 supports using Windows Group Policy settings to manage code security settings in Outlook. When Outlook is configured to load security settings from Group Policy, it might include a list of trusted add-ins. If this list is present, if Group Policy has been configured to enable this list, and if a COM add-in matches the hash information provided in the trusted list, Outlook provides a trusted *Application* object to the COM add-in. If an add-in is not in the list or has been updated since it was added to the list, Outlook does not trust the add-in.

Additionally, administrators can set how Outlook handles the security warnings generated by the object model guard. Four options are available: Automatically Accept, Automatically Deny, Prompt User, and Prompt User Based On Computer Security. These settings apply to all add-ins not included in the list of trusted add-ins, and to external COM callers to the object model.

For more information about Group Policy and code security settings, see the topic "Manage trusted add-ins for Outlook 2007" in the 2007 Office Resource Kit, available at *http:// technet2.microsoft.com/Office/*.

Exchange-Brokered Security for COM Add-Ins

Overall, there has been no change in the way Outlook 2007 trusts COM add-ins in a Microsoft Exchange environment where security settings are obtained from the Exchange server. By using the new AdminSecurityMode registry key discussed later in this chapter, you can still configure Outlook 2007 to locate the Outlook security form in a public folder. When Outlook is configured to load settings from this form, Outlook trusts, by default, only those add-ins that are listed in the security form. Administrators can use Group Policy settings to override this behavior and continue to trust all installed add-ins as necessary.

If Outlook 2007 is configured to use security settings from the security form, it does not leverage the status of antivirus software. In this scenario, there are only three prompt behaviors: prompt user, never prompt and automatically allow, and never prompt and automatically deny. To take advantage of the new code security behavior based on the status of antivirus software, Outlook must be configured to use Windows Group Policy or the Outlook 2007 default security settings.

Configuring a Security Policy

Outlook 2007 ships with a strong set of security features enabled out of the box. However, system administrators can choose to alter these security settings to match requirements for the deployed environment. Part of writing a solution that works with Outlook involves understanding how Outlook works differently and how to make sure your solution continues to work in different environments.

Outlook has two methods for setting security-related policies. Some policies are stored only in policy registry keys that can be deployed as Group Policy objects. Another set of policies can be deployed either via publishing an Outlook security form to an Exchange public folder, or via Group Policy objects. Because the code security settings are maintained in the latter group, this section focuses mainly on how to deploy these settings. For more information about deploying all settings for Outlook, refer to the Office Resource Kit online.

Setting *AdminSecurityMode*

In a change from previous versions of Outlook, Outlook 2007 uses a new registry key to determine which security mode should be used across Outlook. This new key, *AdminSecurityMode*,

is located under HKEY_CURRENT_USER\Software\Policies\Microsoft\Office\12.0
\Outlook\Security. The value is a DWORD that can be set to one of four values, listed in
Table 19-2.

Table 19-2   Values for the *AdminSecurityMode* Policy Key

Value	Description
0x0, Any value not defined here	Use the default Outlook security policy.
0x1	Load the security policy from the Outlook Security Settings public folder.
0x2	Load the security policy from the Outlook 10 Security Settings public folder.
0x3	Load security policy from the registry.

Outlook checks the value of this key each time the application starts and loads the appropriate security policy. The value of the key is not checked once Outlook has started running, so changes in policy types only occur when Outlook is shut down and restarted.

You can determine the mode in which Outlook is running by opening the About dialog box from the Help menu of the Explorer window. The Security Mode string in the About dialog box varies based on the type of security settings loaded. If *AdminSecurityMode* is set to load a security form but no form is available, the default policy will be used and the dialog box indicates the default policy.

Trusting an Add-In

By default, Outlook trusts all add-ins and provides a trusted *Application* object during the *OnConnection* method of *IDTExtensibility2*. However, if the administrator has modified the security policy and created a list of trusted add-ins, then only add-ins that are matched against entries in the list are provided a trusted *Application* object. Add-ins that are not on the trusted list receive an untrusted object and might generate security prompts when accessing guarded methods.

To add an add-in to the list of trusted add-ins for the Group Policy settings, you need to compute the unique hash code for the particular add-in assembly. Depending on the type of add-in, you might need to generate the hash for a file other than the main add-in assembly.

COM and Shared Add-ins with COM Shims

For native code COM add-ins and shared add-ins with a COM shim, you need to generate a hash code for the native code COM component that will be loaded by Outlook first. If you are unsure which file Outlook is using, you can use the Outlook Trust Center to determine which file needs to be added to the trusted list.

Open the Trust Center in Outlook from an Explorer window by selecting Tools, Trust Center. In the Trust Center, click the Add-ins tab, and then select the add-in you would like to have trusted. The details of the selected add-in are displayed under the list of add-ins, and the Location field contains the name of the file that Outlook will validate against the trusted list. Once you know the file you need to add to the list, proceed to the section "Creating a Hash for a Trusted Add-In." Figure 19-7 shows an example of an installed add-in location as viewed in the Trust Center.

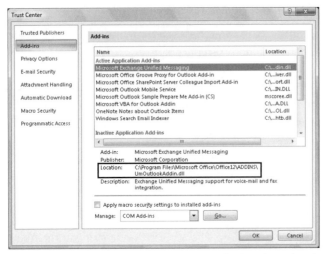

Figure 19-7   The Trust Center displaying the location of an installed add-in.

Note   For shared add-ins or managed code add-ins that are not written using VSTO, you should always use a COM shim if the add-in needs to be trusted. Shared add-ins that do not provide a COM shim will be listed in the Trust Center with Mscoree.dll in the Location field. Trusting this file will result in all unshimmed managed code add-ins becoming trusted, which is likely undesired behavior.

VSTO Add-Ins

Managed code add-ins written with VSTO are loaded in a different manner than shared add-ins or native COM add-ins. These add-ins provide a manifest file that provides both the necessary information on which assembly should be loaded and the context for loading the add-in. Because the manifest controls which add-in is ultimately loaded, instead of adding the assembly file to the trusted list you need to add the manifest file to the trusted list.

The Outlook Trust Center also enables you to find the location of the manifest file for an installed add-in in the same manner used for shared add-ins. The Location field displayed when a VSTO add-in is selected shows which manifest file is being used to load the add-in.

Creating a Hash for a Trusted Add-In

Previously, when using the Outlook security form to generate a trusted list of applications, an administrator was able to use the Browse button to select an add-in file and automatically add the file to the trusted list of add-ins. However, because these settings are now deployed using

Group Policy tools, the process is a little more complicated. To add an add-in to the Group Policy–based trusted list, you need to first generate the appropriate hash code for the add-in. To compute the hash value for a trusted add-in, follow these steps:

1. Download the hash calculation program—the Outlook 2007 Security Hash Generator Tool—from the Microsoft Office Download Center.

2. Run the downloaded program and extract the contents to a known location (such as C:\Hashtool\).

3. Run the command prompt (click Start, All Programs, Accessories, Command Prompt) and change to the directory where the hash tool was extracted. In Windows Vista, you should run the command prompt program as Administrator.

4. Type the command **createhash.bat /register** and press Enter to register the necessary components (you need to do this only the first time).

5. Type the command **createhash.bat <*filename*>** replacing <*filename*> with the full path and file name of the add-in file for which you are creating a hash.

6. Copy the hash value displayed on the screen to the Clipboard. This is the value you need to add to the Group Policy Editor.

Specify a Trusted Add-in in Group Policy

After you have created the hash value for an add-in, you need to add this to the Group Policy configuration. The easiest way to work with Group Policy settings is by using the Group Policy tool and the Office Outlook 2007 template (Outlk12.adm) provided in the Office Resource Kit.

1. To launch the Group Policy Object Editor, click Start, click Run, type **gpedit.msc**, and then click OK.

2. In the Group Policy Object Editor, load the Outlook 2007 template and go to User Configuration\Administrative Templates\Microsoft Office Outlook 2007\Security\Security Form Settings\Programmatic Security\Trusted Add-ins.

3. Double-click Configure Trusted Add-Ins, and then click Enabled.

4. Click Show.

5. In the Show Contents dialog box, click Add.

6. In the Add Item dialog box, in the Enter The Name Of The Item To Be Added field, type a descriptive name for the add-in. This can be the file name or any other way you want to refer to the add-in you are adding to the list.

7. In the Enter The Value To Be Added field, paste the hash value of the add-in that you copied when you ran the hash generator tool. Then click OK three times.

Now that the add-in has been added to the trusted list, if Outlook is configured to read security settings from Group Policy, the add-in will be allowed to run without prompts for users who use this security setting.

Form Region Policy

Outlook form regions have a set of policy registry keys associated with them that allow administrators to control the behavior of form regions for users. Using these policies, form regions can be disabled completely, or only certain types of form regions can be allowed to run.

Disabling Form Regions

Custom forms with form regions can be be controlled with three different states. By default, all form region customizations are enabled and allowed to work. However, an administrator can deploy policy to disable form region customizations registered as user-specific, or all form regions can be disabled.

To prevent all form regions from loading, create a DWORD value under the registry key HKEY_CURRENT_USER\Software\Policies\Microsoft\Office\12.0\Outlook\Addins named *DisableFormRegions*. The value of this DWORD can be one of the values in Table 19-3.

Table 19-3 Possible Values for *DisableFormRegions* Policy

Value	Behavior
0x0	All form regions are enabled.
0x1	Only form regions registered in the local machine key are enabled.
0x2	All form regions are disabled.

Disabling Extensions on a Particular Message Type

It is also possible to adjust what types of solutions are allowed on a per-message class basis. Administrators can use this policy to prevent or allow specific types of form region customizations on a message class. For example, if an organization has a custom form deployed and does not want adjoining form regions to appear on that form, policy could be used to disable all adjoining form regions on the form's message class.

To determine if form regions should be disabled for a particular message class, Outlook looks for a registry value under HKEY_CURRENT_USER\Software\Policies\Microsoft\Office\12.0\Outlook\Addins\ExclusiveFormRegions for a DWORD type value with the value name matching the message class value for the form, and one of the possible values (listed in Table 19-4).

Table 19-4 Possible Values for *ExclusiveFormRegions* Policy

Value	Behavior
0x0 (default)	Allow all form region customizations.
0x1	Disable adjoining form regions.
0x2	Disable replacement, replace-all, and separate form regions.
0x3	Allow only separate, replacement, or replace-all form regions.

Table 19-4   Possible Values for *ExclusiveFormRegions* Policy

Value	Behavior
0x4	Allow only adjoining regions.
0x5	Don't allow any form regions.

Values defined on a message class in the *ExclusiveFormRegions* key apply only to the listed message class and do not inherit to derived message classes. For example, if a policy is deployed to block all form regions on *IPM.Note.CompanyName*, form regions would still be allowed on *IPM.Note.CompanyName.FormName*.

Locking an Adjoining Form Region

An adjoining form region can be locked so that it is always visible and the user cannot collapse the form region. This can be useful to ensure that the user always sees the content of the adjoining form region, such as when the form region contains security information or other important details.

To lock an adjoining form region, create a DWORD value under the registry key HKEY_CURRENT_USER\Software\Policies\Microsoft\Office\12.0\Outlook\Addins \LockedFormRegions. The name of the DWORD value should match the internal name of the adjoining form region that should be locked. For example, if the manifest Extensible Markup Language (XML) for the form region shows *<name>AccountDetails</name>*, then the value should be named *AccountDetails*. Set the value of the key to 0x1 to indicate that the form region should always be expanded. Any other value will allow the user to expand or collapse the form region.

Folder Home Page Policy

New for Outlook 2007, folder home pages are blocked for all stores except the default store. This behavior was implemented to increase the security of Outlook and make sure that unexpected script was not executed by default. This policy can be overridden by the administrator using Group Policy to reenable folder home pages for all stores in Outlook.

To reenable folder home pages for all stores, administrators should create a registry key entry under HEY_CURRENT_USER\Software\Policies\Microsoft\Office\12.0\Outlook\Security named *NonDefaultStoreScript* as a DWORD type, with a value of 0x1. Administrators can also use the policy templates provided as part of the Office Resource Kit to set this value and deploy it to different organization units.

It is also possible for a solution that implements a custom MAPI store provider to enable folder home pages for that particular store. For example, Microsoft Business Contact Manager for Office Outlook 2007 enables folder home pages in the Business Contact Manager data store to provide rich dashboard views on Business Contact Manager data types. For more information on how to enable folder home pages for custom MAPI stores, see the Outlook 2007 Integration API reference on MSDN.

Summary

Now that you've read this chapter, you should have a good idea of what it takes to write a trusted add-in that works with Outlook without generating the dreaded security prompt that has been the scorn of Outlook developers in the past. You've also learned more about the changes made to Outlook 2007 that reduce the likelihood of the security prompt appearing even if you aren't using a trusted add-in to integrate with Outlook.

This chapter also covered the available administrator options for locking down the security model in Outlook and other policies that affect the way Outlook solutions work. These are provided here both as a reference for administrators and as a reference for developers who will need to understand the ways administrators can make Outlook behave so that your solution will continue to work in a well-behaved manner when Outlook isn't using the default settings.

Index

Symbols

A